ANNE OF GREEN GABLES COLLECTION VOLUME II

Anne's House of Dreams, Rainbow Valley, Rilla of Ingleside, Further Chronicles of Avonlea

LUCY MAUD MONTGOMERY

CONTENTS

ANNE'S HOUSE OF DREAMS

ANNE'S HOUSE OF DREAMS

I. IN THE GARRET OF GREEN GABLES

"THANKS BE, I'm done with geometry, learning or teaching it," said Anne Shirley, a trifle vindictively, as she thumped a somewhat battered volume of Euclid into a big chest of books, banged the lid in triumph, and sat down upon it, looking at Diana Wright across the Green Gables garret, with gray eyes that were like a morning sky.

The garret was a shadowy, suggestive, delightful place, as all garrets should be. Through the open window, by which Anne sat, blew the sweet, scented, sun-warm air of the August afternoon; outside, poplar boughs rustled and tossed in the wind; beyond them were the woods, where Lover's Lane wound its enchanted path, and the old apple orchard which still bore its rosy harvests munificently. And, over all, was a great mountain range of snowy clouds in the blue southern sky. Through the other window was glimpsed a distant, white-capped, blue sea—the beautiful St. Lawrence Gulf, on which floats, like a jewel, Abegweit, whose softer, sweeter Indian name has long been forsaken for the more prosaic one of Prince Edward Island.

Diana Wright, three years older than when we last saw her, had grown somewhat matronly in the intervening time. But her eyes were as black and brilliant, her cheeks as rosy, and her dimples as enchanting, as in the long-ago days when she and Anne Shirley had vowed eternal friendship in the garden at Orchard Slope. In her arms she held a small, sleeping, black-curled creature, who for two happy years had been known to the world of Avonlea as "Small Anne Cordelia." Avonlea folks knew why Diana had called her Anne, of course, but Avonlea folks were puzzled by the Cordelia. There had never been a Cordelia in the Wright or Barry connections. Mrs. Harmon Andrews said she supposed Diana had found the name in some trashy novel, and wondered that Fred hadn't more sense than to allow it. But Diana and Anne smiled at each other. They knew how Small Anne Cordelia had come by her name.

"You always hated geometry," said Diana with a retrospective smile. "I should think you'd be real glad to be through with teaching, anyhow."

"Oh, I've always liked teaching, apart from geometry. These past three years in Summerside have been very pleasant ones. Mrs. Harmon Andrews told me when I came home that I wouldn't likely find married life as much better than teaching as I expected. Evidently Mrs. Harmon is of Hamlet's opinion that it may be better to bear the ills that we have than fly to others that we know not of."

Anne's laugh, as blithe and irresistible as of yore, with an added note of sweetness and maturity, rang through the garret. Marilla in the kitchen below, compounding blue plum preserve, heard it and smiled; then sighed to think how seldom that dear laugh would echo through Green Gables in the years to come. Nothing in her life had ever given Marilla so much happiness as the knowledge that Anne was going to marry Gilbert Blythe; but every joy must bring with it its little shadow of sorrow. During the three Summerside years Anne had been home often for vacations and weekends; but, after this, a bi-annual visit would be as much as could be hoped for.

"You needn't let what Mrs. Harmon says worry you," said Diana, with the calm assurance of the four-years matron. "Married life has its ups and downs, of course. You mustn't expect that everything will always go smoothly. But I can assure you, Anne, that it's a happy life, when you're married to the right man."

Anne smothered a smile. Diana's airs of vast experience always amused her a little.

"I daresay I'll be putting them on too, when I've been married four years," she thought. "Surely my sense of humor will preserve me from it, though."

"Is it settled yet where you are going to live?" asked Diana, cuddling Small Anne Cordelia with the inimitable gesture of motherhood which always sent through Anne's heart, filled with sweet, unuttered dreams and hopes, a thrill that was half pure pleasure and half a strange, ethereal pain.

"Yes. That was what I wanted to tell you when I 'phoned to you to come down today. By the way, I can't realize that we really have telephones in Avonlea now. It sounds so preposterously up-to-date and modernish for this darling, leisurely old place."

"We can thank the A. V. I. S. for them," said Diana. "We should never have got the line if they hadn't taken the matter up and carried it through. There was enough cold water thrown to discourage any society. But they stuck to it, nevertheless. You did a splendid thing for Avonlea when you founded that society, Anne. What fun we did have at our meetings! Will you ever forget the blue hall and Judson Parker's scheme for painting medicine advertisements on his fence?"

"I don't know that I'm wholly grateful to the A. V. I. S. in the matter of the telephone," said Anne. "Oh, I know it's most convenient—even more so than our old device of signalling to each other by flashes of candlelight! And, as Mrs. Rachel says, 'Avonlea must keep up with the procession, that's what.' But somehow I feel as if I didn't want Avonlea spoiled by what Mr. Harrison, when he wants to be witty, calls 'modern inconveniences.' I should like to have it kept always just as it was in the dear old years. That's foolish—and sentimental—and impossible. So I shall immediately become wise and practical and possible. The telephone, as Mr. Harrison concedes, is 'a buster of a good thing'—even if you do know that probably half a dozen interested people are listening along the line."

"That's the worst of it," sighed Diana. "It's so annoying to hear the receivers going down whenever you ring anyone up. They say Mrs. Harmon Andrews insisted that their 'phone should be put in their kitchen just so that she could listen whenever it rang and keep an eye on the dinner at the same time. Today, when you called me, I distinctly heard that queer clock of the Pyes' striking. So no doubt Josie or Gertie was listening."

"Oh, so that is why you said, 'You've got a new clock at Green Gables, haven't you?' I couldn't imagine what you meant. I heard a vicious click as soon as you had spoken. I suppose it was the Pye receiver being hung up with profane energy. Well, never mind the Pyes. As Mrs.

Rachel says, 'Pyes they always were and Pyes they always will be, world without end, amen.' I want to talk of pleasanter things. It's all settled as to where my new home shall be."

"Oh, Anne, where? I do hope it's near here."

"No-o-o, that's the drawback. Gilbert is going to settle at Four Winds Harbor—sixty miles from here."

"Sixty! It might as well be six hundred," sighed Diana. "I never can get further from home now than Charlottetown."

"You'll have to come to Four Winds. It's the most beautiful harbor on the Island. There's a little village called Glen St. Mary at its head, and Dr. David Blythe has been practicing there for fifty years. He is Gilbert's great-uncle, you know. He is going to retire, and Gilbert is to take over his practice. Dr. Blythe is going to keep his house, though, so we shall have to find a habitation for ourselves. I don't know yet what it is, or where it will be in reality, but I have a little house o'dreams all furnished in my imagination—a tiny, delightful castle in Spain."

"Where are you going for your wedding tour?" asked Diana.

"Nowhere. Don't look horrified, Diana dearest. You suggest Mrs. Harmon Andrews. She, no doubt, will remark condescendingly that people who can't afford wedding 'towers' are real sensible not to take them; and then she'll remind me that Jane went to Europe for hers. I want to spend MY honeymoon at Four Winds in my own dear house of dreams."

"And you've decided not to have any bridesmaid?"

"There isn't any one to have. You and Phil and Priscilla and Jane all stole a march on me in the matter of marriage; and Stella is teaching in Vancouver. I have no other 'kindred soul' and I won't have a bridesmaid who isn't."

"But you are going to wear a veil, aren't you?" asked Diana, anxiously.

"Yes, indeedy. I shouldn't feel like a bride without one. I remember telling Matthew, that evening when he brought me to Green Gables, that I never expected to be a bride because I was so homely no one would ever want to marry me—unless some foreign missionary did. I had an idea then that foreign missionaries couldn't afford to be finicky in the matter of looks if they wanted a girl to risk her life among cannibals. You should have seen the foreign missionary Priscilla married. He was as handsome and inscrutable as those daydreams we once planned to marry ourselves, Diana; he was the best dressed man I ever met, and he raved over Priscilla's 'ethereal, golden beauty.' But of course there are no cannibals in Japan."

"Your wedding dress is a dream, anyhow," sighed Diana rapturously. "You'll look like a perfect queen in it—you're so tall and slender. How DO you keep so slim, Anne? I'm fatter than ever—I'll soon have no waist at all."

"Stoutness and slimness seem to be matters of predestination," said Anne. "At all events, Mrs. Harmon Andrews can't say to you what she said to me when I came home from Summerside, 'Well, Anne, you're just about as skinny as ever.' It sounds quite romantic to be 'slender,' but 'skinny' has a very different tang."

"Mrs. Harmon has been talking about your trousseau. She admits it's as nice as Jane's, although she says Jane married a millionaire and you are only marrying a 'poor young doctor without a cent to his name.'"

Anne laughed.

"My dresses ARE nice. I love pretty things. I remember the first pretty dress I ever had—the brown gloria Matthew gave me for our school concert. Before that everything I had was so ugly. It seemed to me that I stepped into a new world that night."

"That was the night Gilbert recited 'Bingen on the Rhine,' and looked at you when he said, 'There's another, NOT a sister.' And you were so furious because he put your pink tissue rose in his breast pocket! You didn't much imagine then that you would ever marry him."

"Oh, well, that's another instance of predestination," laughed Anne, as they went down the garret stairs.

2. THE HOUSE OF DREAMS

There was more excitement in the air of Green Gables than there had ever been before in all its history. Even Marilla was so excited that she couldn't help showing it—which was little short of being phenomenal.

"There's never been a wedding in this house," she said, half apologetically, to Mrs. Rachel Lynde. "When I was a child I heard an old minister say that a house was not a real home until it had been consecrated by a birth, a wedding and a death. We've had deaths here—my father and mother died here as well as Matthew; and we've even had a birth here. Long ago, just after we moved into this house, we had a married hired man for a little while, and his wife had a baby here. But there's never been a wedding before. It does seem so strange to think of Anne being married. In a way she just seems to me the little girl Matthew brought home here fourteen years ago. I can't realize that she's grown up. I shall never forget what I felt when I saw Matthew bringing in a GIRL. I wonder what became of the boy we would have got if there hadn't been a mistake. I wonder what HIS fate was."

"Well, it was a fortunate mistake," said Mrs. Rachel Lynde, "though, mind you, there was a time I didn't think so—that evening I came up to see Anne and she treated us to such a scene. Many things have changed since then, that's what."

Mrs. Rachel sighed, and then brisked up again. When weddings were in order Mrs. Rachel was ready to let the dead past bury its dead.

"I'm going to give Anne two of my cotton warp spreads," she resumed. "A tobacco-stripe one and an apple-leaf one. She tells me they're getting to be real fashionable again. Well, fashion or no fashion, I don't believe there's anything prettier for a spare-room bed than a nice apple-leaf spread, that's what. I must see about getting them bleached. I've had them sewed up in cotton bags ever since Thomas died, and no doubt they're an awful color. But there's a month yet, and dew-bleaching will work wonders."

Only a month! Marilla sighed and then said proudly:

"I'm giving Anne that half dozen braided rugs I have in the garret. I never supposed she'd want them—they're so old-fashioned, and nobody seems to want anything but hooked mats now. But she asked me for them—said she'd rather have them than anything else for her floors. They ARE pretty. I made them of the nicest rags, and braided them in stripes. It was such company these last few winters. And I'll make her enough blue plum preserve to stock her jam closet for a year. It seems real strange. Those blue plum trees hadn't even a blossom for three years, and I thought they might as well be cut down. And this last spring they were white, and such a crop of plums I never remember at Green Gables."

"Well, thank goodness that Anne and Gilbert really are going to be married after all. It's what I've always prayed for," said Mrs. Rachel, in the tone of one who is comfortably sure that her prayers have availed much. "It was a great relief to find out that she really didn't mean to take the Kingsport man. He was rich, to be sure, and Gilbert is poor—at least, to begin with; but then he's an Island boy."

"He's Gilbert Blythe," said Marilla contentedly. Marilla would have died the death before she would have put into words the thought that was always in the background of her mind whenever she had looked at Gilbert from his childhood up—the thought that, had it not been for her own wilful pride long, long ago, he might have been HER son. Marilla felt that, in some strange way, his marriage with Anne would put right that old mistake. Good had come out of the evil of the ancient bitterness.

As for Anne herself, she was so happy that she almost felt frightened. The gods, so says the old superstition, do not like to behold too happy mortals. It is certain, at least, that some human beings do not. Two of that ilk descended upon Anne one violet dusk and proceeded to do what in them lay to prick the rainbow bubble of her satisfaction. If she thought she was getting any particular prize in young Dr. Blythe, or if she imagined that he was still as infatuated with her as he might have been in his salad days, it was surely their duty to put the matter before her in another light. Yet these two worthy ladies were not enemies of Anne; on the contrary, they were really quite fond of her, and would have defended her as their own young had anyone else attacked her. Human nature is not obliged to be consistent.

Mrs. Inglis—nee Jane Andrews, to quote from the Daily Enterprise—came with her mother and Mrs. Jasper Bell. But in Jane the milk of human kindness had not been curdled by years of matrimonial bickerings. Her lines had fallen in pleasant places. In spite of the fact—as Mrs. Rachel Lynde would say—that she had married a millionaire, her marriage had been happy. Wealth had not spoiled her. She was still the placid, amiable, pink-cheeked Jane of the old quartette, sympathising with her old chum's happiness and as keenly interested in all the dainty details of Anne's trousseau as if it could rival her own silken and bejewelled splendors. Jane was not brilliant, and had probably never made a remark worth listening to in her life; but she never said anything that would hurt anyone's feelings—which may be a negative talent but is likewise a rare and enviable one.

"So Gilbert didn't go back on you after all," said Mrs. Harmon Andrews, contriving to convey an expression of surprise in her tone. "Well, the Blythes generally keep their word when they've once passed it, no matter what happens. Let me see—you're twenty-five, aren't you, Anne? When I was a girl twenty-five was the first corner. But you look quite young. Red-headed people always do."

"Red hair is very fashionable now," said Anne, trying to smile, but speaking rather coldly. Life had developed in her a sense of humor which helped her over many difficulties; but as yet nothing had availed to steel her against a reference to her hair.

"So it is—so it is," conceded Mrs. Harmon. "There's no telling what queer freaks fashion will take. Well, Anne, your things are very pretty, and very suitable to your position in life, aren't they, Jane? I hope you'll be very happy. You have my best wishes, I'm sure. A long engagement doesn't often turn out well. But, of course, in your case it couldn't be helped."

"Gilbert looks very young for a doctor. I'm afraid people won't have much confidence in him," said Mrs. Jasper Bell gloomily. Then she shut her mouth tightly, as if she had said what she considered it her duty to say and held her conscience clear. She belonged to the type which always has a stringy black feather in its hat and straggling locks of hair on its neck.

Anne's surface pleasure in her pretty bridal things was temporarily shadowed; but the deeps of happiness below could not thus be disturbed; and the little stings of Mesdames Bell and Andrews were forgotten when Gilbert came later, and they wandered down to the birches of the brook, which had been saplings when Anne had come to Green Gables, but were now tall, ivory columns in a fairy palace of twilight and stars. In their shadows Anne and Gilbert talked in lover-fashion of their new home and their new life together.

"I've found a nest for us, Anne."

"Oh, where? Not right in the village, I hope. I wouldn't like that altogether."

"No. There was no house to be had in the village. This is a little white house on the harbor shore, half way between Glen St. Mary and Four Winds Point. It's a little out of the way, but when we get a 'phone in that won't matter so much. The situation is beautiful. It looks to the sunset and has the great blue harbor before it. The sand-dunes aren't very far away—the sea winds blow over them and the sea spray drenches them."

"But the house itself, Gilbert,—OUR first home? What is it like?"

"Not very large, but large enough for us. There's a splendid living room with a fireplace in it downstairs, and a dining room that looks out on the harbor, and a little room that will do for my office. It is about sixty years old—the oldest house in Four Winds. But it has been kept in pretty good repair, and was all done over about fifteen years ago—shingled, plastered and re-floored. It was well built to begin with. I understand that there was some romantic story connected with its building, but the man I rented it from didn't know it."

"He said Captain Jim was the only one who could spin that old yarn now."

"Who is Captain Jim?"

"The keeper of the lighthouse on Four Winds Point. You'll love that Four Winds light, Anne. It's a revolving one, and it flashes like a magnificent star through the twilights. We can see it from our living room windows and our front door."

"Who owns the house?"

"Well, it's the property of the Glen St. Mary Presbyterian Church now, and I rented it from the trustees. But it belonged until lately to a very old lady, Miss Elizabeth Russell. She died last spring, and as she had no near relatives she left her property to the Glen St. Mary Church. Her furniture is still in the house, and I bought most of it—for a mere song you might say, because it was all so old-fashioned that the trustees despaired of selling it. Glen St. Mary folks prefer plush brocade and sideboards with mirrors and ornamentations, I fancy. But Miss Russell's furniture is very good and I feel sure you'll like it, Anne."

"So far, good," said Anne, nodding cautious approval. "But, Gilbert, people cannot live by furniture alone. You haven't yet mentioned one very important thing. Are there TREES about this house?"

"Heaps of them, oh, dryad! There is a big grove of fir trees behind it, two rows of Lombardy poplars down the lane, and a ring of white birches around a very delightful garden. Our front door opens right into the garden, but there is another entrance—a little gate hung between two firs. The hinges are on one trunk and the catch on the other. Their boughs form an arch overhead."

"Oh, I'm so glad! I couldn't live where there were no trees—something vital in me would starve. Well, after that, there's no use asking you if there's a brook anywhere near. THAT would be expecting too much."

"But there IS a brook—and it actually cuts across one corner of the garden."

"Then," said Anne, with a long sigh of supreme satisfaction, "this house you have found IS my house of dreams and none other."

3. THE LAND OF DREAMS AMONG

"Have you made up your mind who you're going to have to the wedding, Anne?" asked Mrs. Rachel Lynde, as she hemstitched table napkins industriously. "It's time your invitations were sent, even if they are to be only informal ones."

"I don't mean to have very many," said Anne. "We just want those we love best to see us married. Gilbert's people, and Mr. and Mrs. Allan, and Mr. and Mrs. Harrison."

"There was a time when you'd hardly have numbered Mr. Harrison among your dearest friends," said Marilla drily.

"Well, I wasn't VERY strongly attracted to him at our first meeting," acknowledged Anne, with a laugh over the recollection. "But Mr. Harrison has improved on acquaintance, and Mrs. Harrison is really a dear. Then, of course, there are Miss Lavendar and Paul."

"Have they decided to come to the Island this summer? I thought they were going to Europe."

"They changed their minds when I wrote them I was going to be married. I had a letter from Paul today. He says he MUST come to my wedding, no matter what happens to Europe."

"That child always idolised you," remarked Mrs. Rachel.

"That 'child' is a young man of nineteen now, Mrs. Lynde."

"How time does fly!" was Mrs. Lynde's brilliant and original response.

"Charlotta the Fourth may come with them. She sent word by Paul that she would come if her husband would let her. I wonder if she still wears those enormous blue bows, and whether her husband calls her Charlotta or Leonora. I should love to have Charlotta at my wedding. Charlotta and I were at a wedding long syne. They expect to be at Echo Lodge next week. Then there are Phil and the Reverend Jo——"

"It sounds awful to hear you speaking of a minister like that, Anne," said Mrs. Rachel severely.

"His wife calls him that."

"She should have more respect for his holy office, then," retorted Mrs. Rachel.

"I've heard you criticise ministers pretty sharply yourself," teased Anne.

"Yes, but I do it reverently," protested Mrs. Lynde. "You never heard me NICKNAME a minister."

Anne smothered a smile.

"Well, there are Diana and Fred and little Fred and Small Anne Cordelia—and Jane Andrews. I wish I could have Miss Stacey and Aunt Jamesina and Priscilla and Stella. But Stella is in Vancouver, and Pris is in Japan, and Miss Stacey is married in California, and Aunt Jamesina has gone to India to explore her daughter's mission field, in spite of her horror of snakes. It's really dreadful—the way people get scattered over the globe."

"The Lord never intended it, that's what," said Mrs. Rachel authoritatively. "In my young days people grew up and married and settled down where they were born, or pretty near it. Thank goodness you've stuck to the Island, Anne. I was afraid Gilbert would insist on rushing off to the ends of the earth when he got through college, and dragging you with him."

"If everybody stayed where he was born places would soon be filled up, Mrs. Lynde."

"Oh, I'm not going to argue with you, Anne. *I* am not a B.A. What time of the day is the ceremony to be?"

"We have decided on noon—high noon, as the society reporters say. That will give us time to catch the evening train to Glen St. Mary."

"And you'll be married in the parlor?"

"No—not unless it rains. We mean to be married in the orchard—with the blue sky over us and the sunshine around us. Do you know when and where I'd like to be married, if I could? It would be at dawn—a June dawn, with a glorious sunrise, and roses blooming in the gardens; and I would slip down and meet Gilbert and we would go together to the heart of the beech woods,—and there, under the green arches that would be like a splendid cathedral, we would be married."

Marilla sniffed scornfully and Mrs. Lynde looked shocked.

"But that would be terrible queer, Anne. Why, it wouldn't really seem legal. And what would Mrs. Harmon Andrews say?"

"Ah, there's the rub," sighed Anne. "There are so many things in life we cannot do because of the fear of what Mrs. Harmon Andrews would say. "Tis true, 'tis pity, and pity 'tis, 'tis true.' What delightful things we might do were it not for Mrs. Harmon Andrews!"

"By times, Anne, I don't feel quite sure that I understand you altogether," complained Mrs. Lynde.

"Anne was always romantic, you know," said Marilla apologetically.

"Well, married life will most likely cure her of that," Mrs. Rachel responded comfortingly.

Anne laughed and slipped away to Lover's Lane, where Gilbert found her; and neither of them seemed to entertain much fear, or hope, that their married life would cure them of romance.

The Echo Lodge people came over the next week, and Green Gables buzzed with the delight of them. Miss Lavendar had changed so little that the three years since her last Island visit might have been a watch in the night; but Anne gasped with amazement over Paul. Could this splendid six feet of manhood be the little Paul of Avonlea schooldays?

"You really make me feel old, Paul," said Anne. "Why, I have to look up to you!"

"You'll never grow old, Teacher," said Paul. "You are one of the fortunate mortals who have found and drunk from the Fountain of Youth,—you and Mother Lavendar. See here! When you're married I WON'T call you Mrs. Blythe. To me you'll always be 'Teacher'—the teacher of the best lessons I ever learned. I want to show you something."

The "something" was a pocketbook full of poems. Paul had put some of his beautiful fancies into verse, and magazine editors had not been as unappreciative as they are sometimes supposed to be. Anne read Paul's poems with real delight. They were full of charm and promise.

"You'll be famous yet, Paul. I always dreamed of having one famous pupil. He was to be a college president—but a great poet would be even better. Some day I'll be able to boast that I whipped the distinguished Paul Irving. But then I never did whip you, did I, Paul? What an opportunity lost! I think I kept you in at recess, however."

"You may be famous yourself, Teacher. I've seen a good deal of your work these last three years."

"No. I know what I can do. I can write pretty, fanciful little sketches that children love and editors send welcome cheques for. But I can do nothing big. My only chance for earthly immortality is a corner in your Memoirs."

Charlotta the Fourth had discarded the blue bows but her freckles were not noticeably less.

"I never did think I'd come down to marrying a Yankee, Miss Shirley, ma'am," she said. "But you never know what's before you, and it isn't his fault. He was born that way."

"You're a Yankee yourself, Charlotta, since you've married one."

"Miss Shirley, ma'am, I'm NOT! And I wouldn't be if I was to marry a dozen Yankees! Tom's kind of nice. And besides, I thought I'd better not be too hard to please, for I mightn't get another chance. Tom don't drink and he don't growl because he has to work between meals, and when all's said and done I'm satisfied, Miss Shirley, ma'am."

"Does he call you Leonora?" asked Anne.

"Goodness, no, Miss Shirley, ma'am. I wouldn't know who he meant if he did. Of course, when we got married he had to say, 'I take thee, Leonora,' and I declare to you, Miss Shirley, ma'am, I've had the most dreadful feeling ever since that it wasn't me he was talking to and I haven't been rightly married at all. And so you're going to be married yourself, Miss Shirley, ma'am? I always thought I'd like to marry a doctor. It would be so handy when the children had measles and croup. Tom is only a bricklayer, but he's real good-tempered. When I said to him, says I, 'Tom, can I go to Miss Shirley's wedding? I mean to go anyhow, but I'd like to have your consent,' he just says, 'Suit yourself, Charlotta, and you'll suit me.' That's a real pleasant kind of husband to have, Miss Shirley, ma'am."

Philippa and her Reverend Jo arrived at Green Gables the day before the wedding. Anne and Phil had a rapturous meeting which presently simmered down to a cosy, confidential chat over all that had been and was about to be.

"Queen Anne, you're as queenly as ever. I've got fearfully thin since the babies came. I'm not half so good-looking; but I think Jo likes it. There's not such a contrast between us, you see. And oh, it's perfectly magnificent that you're going to marry Gilbert. Roy Gardner wouldn't have done at all, at all. I can see that now, though I was horribly disappointed at the time. You know, Anne, you did treat Roy very badly."

"He has recovered, I understand," smiled Anne.

"Oh, yes. He is married and his wife is a sweet little thing and they're perfectly happy. Everything works together for good. Jo and the Bible say that, and they are pretty good authorities."

"Are Alec and Alonzo married yet?"

"Alec is, but Alonzo isn't. How those dear old days at Patty's Place come back when I'm talking to you, Anne! What fun we had!"

"Have you been to Patty's Place lately?"

"Oh, yes, I go often. Miss Patty and Miss Maria still sit by the fireplace and knit. And that reminds me—we've brought you a wedding gift from them, Anne. Guess what it is."

"I never could. How did they know I was going to be married?"

"Oh, I told them. I was there last week. And they were so interested. Two days ago Miss Patty wrote me a note asking me to call; and then she asked if I would take her gift to you. What would you wish most from Patty's Place, Anne?"

"You can't mean that Miss Patty has sent me her china dogs?"

"Go up head. They're in my trunk this very moment. And I've a letter for you. Wait a moment and I'll get it."

"Dear Miss Shirley," Miss Patty had written, "Maria and I were very much interested in hearing of your approaching nuptials. We send you our best wishes. Maria and I have never married, but we have no objection to other people doing so. We are sending you the china dogs. I intended to leave them to you in my will, because you seemed to have sincere affection for them. But Maria and I expect to live a good while yet (D.V.), so I have decided to give you the dogs while you are young. You will not have forgotten that Gog looks to the right and Magog to the left."

"Just fancy those lovely old dogs sitting by the fireplace in my house of dreams," said Anne rapturously. "I never expected anything so delightful."

That evening Green Gables hummed with preparations for the following day; but in the twilight Anne slipped away. She had a little pilgrimage to make on this last day of her girlhood and she must make it alone. She went to Matthew's grave, in the little poplar-shaded Avonlea graveyard, and there kept a silent tryst with old memories and immortal loves.

"How glad Matthew would be tomorrow if he were here," she whispered. "But I believe he does know and is glad of it—somewhere else. I've read somewhere that 'our dead are never dead until we have forgotten them.' Matthew will never be dead to me, for I can never forget him."

She left on his grave the flowers she had brought and walked slowly down the long hill. It was a gracious evening, full of delectable lights and shadows. In the west was a sky of mackerel clouds—crimson and amber-tinted, with long strips of apple-green sky between. Beyond was the glimmering radiance of a sunset sea, and the ceaseless voice of many waters came up from the tawny shore. All around her, lying in the fine, beautiful country silence, were the hills and fields and woods she had known and loved so long.

"History repeats itself," said Gilbert, joining her as she passed the Blythe gate. "Do you remember our first walk down this hill, Anne—our first walk together anywhere, for that matter?"

"I was coming home in the twilight from Matthew's grave—and you came out of the gate; and I swallowed the pride of years and spoke to you."

"And all heaven opened before me," supplemented Gilbert. "From that moment I looked forward to tomorrow. When I left you at your gate that night and walked home I was the happiest boy in the world. Anne had forgiven me."

"I think you had the most to forgive. I was an ungrateful little wretch—and after you had really saved my life that day on the pond, too. How I loathed that load of obligation at first! I don't deserve the happiness that has come to me."

Gilbert laughed and clasped tighter the girlish hand that wore his ring. Anne's engagement ring was a circlet of pearls. She had refused to wear a diamond.

"I've never really liked diamonds since I found out they weren't the lovely purple I had dreamed. They will always suggest my old disappointment."

"But pearls are for tears, the old legend says," Gilbert had objected.

"I'm not afraid of that. And tears can be happy as well as sad. My very happiest moments have been when I had tears in my eyes—when Marilla told me I might stay at Green Gables—when Matthew gave me the first pretty dress I ever had—when I heard that you were going to recover from the fever. So give me pearls for our troth ring, Gilbert, and I'll willingly accept the sorrow of life with its joy."

But tonight our lovers thought only of joy and never of sorrow. For the morrow was their wedding day, and their house of dreams awaited them on the misty, purple shore of Four Winds Harbor.

4. THE FIRST BRIDE OF GREEN GABLES

Anne wakened on the morning of her wedding day to find the sunshine winking in at the window of the little porch gable and a September breeze frolicking with her curtains.

"I'm so glad the sun will shine on me," she thought happily.

She recalled the first morning she had wakened in that little porch room, when the sunshine had crept in on her through the blossom-drift of the old Snow Queen. That had not been a happy wakening, for it brought with it the bitter disappointment of the preceding night. But since then the little room had been endeared and consecrated by years of happy childhood dreams and maiden visions. To it she had come back joyfully after all her absences; at its window she had knelt through that night of bitter agony when she believed Gilbert dying, and by it she had sat in speechless happiness the night of her betrothal. Many vigils of joy and some of sorrow had been kept there; and today she must leave it forever. Henceforth it would be hers no more; fifteen-year-old Dora was to inherit it when she had gone. Nor did Anne wish it otherwise; the little room was sacred to youth and girlhood—to the past that was to close today before the chapter of wifehood opened.

Green Gables was a busy and joyous house that forenoon. Diana arrived early, with little Fred and Small Anne Cordelia, to lend a hand. Davy and Dora, the Green Gables twins, whisked the babies off to the garden.

"Don't let Small Anne Cordelia spoil her clothes," warned Diana anxiously.

"You needn't be afraid to trust her with Dora," said Marilla. "That child is more sensible and careful than most of the mothers I've known. She's really a wonder in some ways. Not much like that other harum-scarum I brought up."

Marilla smiled across her chicken salad at Anne. It might even be suspected that she liked the harum-scarum best after all.

"Those twins are real nice children," said Mrs. Rachel, when she was sure they were out of earshot. "Dora is so womanly and helpful, and Davy is developing into a very smart boy. He isn't the holy terror for mischief he used to be."

"I never was so distracted in my life as I was the first six months he was here," acknowledged Marilla. "After that I suppose I got used to him. He's taken a great notion to farming lately, and wants me to let him try running the farm next year. I may, for Mr. Barry doesn't think he'll want to rent it much longer, and some new arrangement will have to be made."

"Well, you certainly have a lovely day for your wedding, Anne," said Diana, as she slipped a voluminous apron over her silken array. "You couldn't have had a finer one if you'd ordered it from Eaton's."

"Indeed, there's too much money going out of this Island to that same Eaton's," said Mrs. Lynde indignantly. She had strong views on the subject of octopus-like department stores, and never lost an opportunity of airing them. "And as for those catalogues of theirs, they're the Avonlea girls' Bible now, that's what. They pore over them on Sundays instead of studying the Holy Scriptures."

"Well, they're splendid to amuse children with," said Diana. "Fred and Small Anne look at the pictures by the hour."

"*I* amused ten children without the aid of Eaton's catalogue," said Mrs. Rachel severely.

"Come, you two, don't quarrel over Eaton's catalogue," said Anne gaily. "This is my day of days, you know. I'm so happy I want every one else to be happy, too."

"I'm sure I hope your happiness will last, child," sighed Mrs. Rachel. She did hope it truly, and believed it, but she was afraid it was in the nature of a challenge to Providence to flaunt your happiness too openly. Anne, for her own good, must be toned down a trifle.

But it was a happy and beautiful bride who came down the old, homespun-carpeted stairs that September noon—the first bride of Green Gables, slender and shining-eyed, in the mist of her maiden veil, with her arms full of roses. Gilbert, waiting for her in the hall below, looked up at her with adoring eyes. She was his at last, this evasive, long-sought Anne, won after years of patient waiting. It was to him she was coming in the sweet surrender of the bride. Was he worthy of her? Could he make her as happy as he hoped? If he failed her—if he could not measure up to her standard of manhood—then, as she held out her hand, their eyes met and all doubt was swept away in a glad certainty. They belonged to each other; and, no matter what life might hold for them, it could never alter that. Their happiness was in each other's keeping and both were unafraid.

They were married in the sunshine of the old orchard, circled by the loving and kindly faces of long-familiar friends. Mr. Allan married them, and the Reverend Jo made what Mrs. Rachel Lynde afterwards pronounced to be the "most beautiful wedding prayer" she had ever heard. Birds do not often sing in September, but one sang sweetly from some hidden bough while Gilbert and Anne repeated their deathless vows. Anne heard it and thrilled to it; Gilbert heard it, and wondered only that all the birds in the world had not burst into jubilant song; Paul heard it and later wrote a lyric about it which was one of the most admired in his first volume of verse; Charlotta the Fourth heard it and was blissfully sure it meant good luck for her adored Miss Shirley. The bird sang until the ceremony was ended and then it wound up with one mad little, glad little trill. Never had the old gray-green house among its enfolding orchards known a blither, merrier afternoon. All the old jests and quips that must have done duty at weddings since Eden were served up, and seemed as new and brilliant and mirth-provoking as if they had never been uttered before. Laughter and joy had their way; and when Anne and Gilbert left to catch the Carmody train, with Paul as driver, the twins were ready with rice and old shoes, in the throwing of which Charlotta the Fourth and Mr. Harrison bore a valiant part. Marilla stood at the gate and watched the carriage out of sight down the long lane with its banks of goldenrod. Anne turned at its end to wave her last good-bye. She was gone—Green Gables was her home no more; Marilla's face looked very gray and old as she turned to the house which Anne had filled for fourteen years, and even in her absence, with light and life.

But Diana and her small fry, the Echo Lodge people and the Allans, had stayed to help the two old ladies over the loneliness of the first evening; and they contrived to have a quietly pleasant little supper time, sitting long around the table and chatting over all the details of the day. While they were sitting there Anne and Gilbert were alighting from the train at Glen St. Mary.

5. THE HOME COMING

Dr. David Blythe had sent his horse and buggy to meet them, and the urchin who had brought it slipped away with a sympathetic grin, leaving them to the delight of driving alone to their new home through the radiant evening.

Anne never forgot the loveliness of the view that broke upon them when they had driven over the hill behind the village. Her new home could not yet be seen; but before her lay Four Winds Harbor like a great, shining mirror of rose and silver. Far down, she saw its entrance between the bar of sand dunes on one side and a steep, high, grim, red sandstone cliff on the other. Beyond the bar the sea, calm and austere, dreamed in the afterlight. The little fishing village, nestled in the cove where the sand-dunes met the harbor shore, looked like a great opal in the haze. The sky over them was like a jewelled cup from which the dusk was pouring; the air was crisp with the compelling tang of the sea, and the whole landscape was infused with the subtleties of a sea evening. A few dim sails drifted along the darkening, fir-clad harbor shores. A bell was ringing from the tower of a little white church on the far side; mellowly and dreamily sweet, the chime floated across the water blent with the moan of the sea. The great revolving light on the cliff at the channel flashed warm and golden against the clear northern sky, a trembling, quivering star of good hope. Far out along the horizon was the crinkled gray ribbon of a passing steamer's smoke.

"Oh, beautiful, beautiful," murmured Anne. "I shall love Four Winds, Gilbert. Where is our house?"

"We can't see it yet—the belt of birch running up from that little cove hides it. It's about two miles from Glen St. Mary, and there's another mile between it and the light-house. We won't have many neighbors, Anne. There's only one house near us and I don't know who lives in it. Shall you be lonely when I'm away?"

"Not with that light and that loveliness for company. Who lives in that house, Gilbert?"

"I don't know. It doesn't look—exactly—as if the occupants would be kindred spirits, Anne, does it?"

The house was a large, substantial affair, painted such a vivid green that the landscape seemed quite faded by contrast. There was an orchard behind it, and a nicely kept lawn before it, but, somehow, there was a certain bareness about it. Perhaps its neatness was responsible for this; the whole establishment, house, barns, orchard, garden, lawn and lane, was so starkly neat.

"It doesn't seem probable that anyone with that taste in paint could be VERY kindred," acknowledged Anne, "unless it were an accident—like our blue hall. I feel certain there are no children there, at least. It's even neater than the old Copp place on the Tory road, and I never expected to see anything neater than that."

They had not met anybody on the moist, red road that wound along the harbor shore. But just before they came to the belt of birch which hid their home, Anne saw a girl who was driving a flock of snow-white geese along the crest of a velvety green hill on the right. Great, scattered firs grew along it. Between their trunks one saw glimpses of yellow harvest fields, gleams of golden sand-hills, and bits of blue sea. The girl was tall and wore a dress of pale blue print. She walked with a certain springiness of step and erectness of bearing. She and her geese came out of the gate at the foot of the hill as Anne and Gilbert passed. She stood with her hand on the fastening of the gate, and looked steadily at them, with an expression that hardly attained to interest, but did not descend to curiosity. It seemed to Anne, for a fleeting moment, that there was even a veiled hint of hostility in it. But it was the girl's beauty which made Anne give a little gasp—a beauty so marked that it must have attracted attention anywhere. She was hatless, but heavy braids of burnished hair, the hue of ripe wheat, were twisted about her head like a coronet; her eyes were blue and star-like; her figure, in its plain print gown, was magnificent; and her lips were as crimson as the bunch of blood-red poppies she wore at her belt.

"Gilbert, who is the girl we have just passed?" asked Anne, in a low voice.

"I didn't notice any girl," said Gilbert, who had eyes only for his bride.

"She was standing by that gate—no, don't look back. She is still watching us. I never saw such a beautiful face."

"I don't remember seeing any very handsome girls while I was here. There are some pretty girls up at the Glen, but I hardly think they could be called beautiful."

"This girl is. You can't have seen her, or you would remember her. Nobody could forget her. I never saw such a face except in pictures. And her hair! It made me think of Browning's 'cord of gold' and 'gorgeous snake'!"

"Probably she's some visitor in Four Winds—likely some one from that big summer hotel over the harbor."

"She wore a white apron and she was driving geese."

"She might do that for amusement. Look, Anne—there's our house."

Anne looked and forgot for a time the girl with the splendid, resentful eyes. The first glimpse of her new home was a delight to eye and spirit—it looked so like a big, creamy seashell stranded on the harbor shore. The rows of tall Lombardy poplars down its lane stood out in stately, purple silhouette against the sky. Behind it, sheltering its garden from the too keen breath of sea winds, was a cloudy fir wood, in which the winds might make all kinds of weird and haunting music. Like all woods, it seemed to be holding and enfolding secrets in its recesses,—secrets whose charm is only to be won by entering in and patiently seeking. Outwardly, dark green arms keep them inviolate from curious or indifferent eyes.

The night winds were beginning their wild dances beyond the bar and the fishing hamlet across the harbor was gemmed with lights as Anne and Gilbert drove up the poplar lane. The door of the little house opened, and a warm glow of firelight flickered out into the dusk. Gilbert lifted Anne from the buggy and led her into the garden, through the little gate between the ruddy-tipped firs, up the trim, red path to the sandstone step.

"Welcome home," he whispered, and hand in hand they stepped over the threshold of their house of dreams.

6. CAPTAIN JIM

"Old Doctor Dave" and "Mrs. Doctor Dave" had come down to the little house to greet the bride and groom. Doctor Dave was a big, jolly, white-whiskered old fellow, and Mrs. Doctor was a trim rosy-cheeked, silver-haired little lady who took Anne at once to her heart, literally and figuratively.

"I'm so glad to see you, dear. You must be real tired. We've got a bite of supper ready, and Captain Jim brought up some trout for you. Captain Jim—where are you? Oh, he's slipped out to see to the horse, I suppose. Come upstairs and take your things off."

Anne looked about her with bright, appreciative eyes as she followed Mrs. Doctor Dave upstairs. She liked the appearance of her new home very much. It seemed to have the atmosphere of Green Gables and the flavor of her old traditions.

"I think I would have found Miss Elizabeth Russell a 'kindred spirit,'" she murmured when she was alone in her room. There were two windows in it; the dormer one looked out on the lower harbor and the sand-bar and the Four Winds light.

"A magic casement opening on the foam
Of perilous seas in fairy lands forlorn,"

quoted Anne softly. The gable window gave a view of a little harvest-hued valley through which a brook ran. Half a mile up the brook was the only house in sight—an old, rambling, gray one surrounded by huge willows through which its windows peered, like shy, seeking eyes, into the dusk. Anne wondered who lived there; they would be her nearest neighbors and she hoped they would be nice. She suddenly found herself thinking of the beautiful girl with the white geese.

"Gilbert thought she didn't belong here," mused Anne, "but I feel sure she does. There was something about her that made her part of the sea and the sky and the harbor. Four Winds is in her blood."

When Anne went downstairs Gilbert was standing before the fireplace talking to a stranger. Both turned as Anne entered.

"Anne, this is Captain Boyd. Captain Boyd, my wife."

It was the first time Gilbert had said "my wife" to anybody but Anne, and he narrowly escaped bursting with the pride of it. The old captain held out a sinewy hand to Anne; they smiled at each other and were friends from that moment. Kindred spirit flashed recognition to kindred spirit.

"I'm right down pleased to meet you, Mistress Blythe; and I hope you'll be as happy as the first bride was who came here. I can't wish you no better than THAT. But your husband doesn't introduce me jest exactly right. 'Captain Jim' is my week-a-day name and you might as well begin as you're sartain to end up—calling me that. You sartainly are a nice little bride, Mistress Blythe. Looking at you sorter makes me feel that I've jest been married myself."

Amid the laughter that followed Mrs. Doctor Dave urged Captain Jim to stay and have supper with them.

"Thank you kindly. 'Twill be a real treat, Mistress Doctor. I mostly has to eat my meals alone, with the reflection of my ugly old phiz in a looking-glass opposite for company. 'Tisn't often I have a chance to sit down with two such sweet, purty ladies."

Captain Jim's compliments may look very bald on paper, but he paid them with such a gracious, gentle deference of tone and look that the woman upon whom they were bestowed felt that she was being offered a queen's tribute in a kingly fashion.

Captain Jim was a high-souled, simple-minded old man, with eternal youth in his eyes and heart. He had a tall, rather ungainly figure, somewhat stooped, yet suggestive of great strength and endurance; a clean-shaven face deeply lined and bronzed; a thick mane of iron-gray hair falling quite to his shoulders, and a pair of remarkably blue, deep-set eyes, which sometimes twinkled and sometimes dreamed, and sometimes looked out seaward with a wistful quest in them, as of one seeking something precious and lost. Anne was to learn one day what it was for which Captain Jim looked.

It could not be denied that Captain Jim was a homely man. His spare jaws, rugged mouth, and square brow were not fashioned on the lines of beauty; and he had passed through many hardships and sorrows which had marked his body as well as his soul; but though at first sight Anne thought him plain she never thought anything more about it—the spirit shining through that rugged tenement beautified it so wholly.

They gathered gaily around the supper table. The hearth fire banished the chill of the September evening, but the window of the dining room was open and sea breezes entered at their own sweet will. The view was magnificent, taking in the harbor and the sweep of low, purple hills beyond. The table was heaped with Mrs. Doctor's delicacies but the piece de resistance was undoubtedly the big platter of sea trout.

"Thought they'd be sorter tasty after travelling," said Captain Jim. "They're fresh as trout can be, Mistress Blythe. Two hours ago they were swimming in the Glen Pond."

"Who is attending to the light tonight, Captain Jim?" asked Doctor Dave.

"Nephew Alec. He understands it as well as I do. Well, now, I'm real glad you asked me to stay to supper. I'm proper hungry—didn't have much of a dinner today."

"I believe you half starve yourself most of the time down at that light," said Mrs. Doctor Dave severely. "You won't take the trouble to get up a decent meal."

"Oh, I do, Mistress Doctor, I do," protested Captain Jim. "Why, I live like a king gen'rally. Last night I was up to the Glen and took home two pounds of steak. I meant to have a spanking good dinner today."

"And what happened to the steak?" asked Mrs. Doctor Dave. "Did you lose it on the way home?"

"No." Captain Jim looked sheepish. "Just at bedtime a poor, ornery sort of dog came along and asked for a night's lodging. Guess he belonged to some of the fishermen 'long shore. I couldn't turn the poor cur out—he had a sore foot. So I shut him in the porch, with an old bag to lie on, and went to bed. But somehow I couldn't sleep. Come to think it over, I sorter remembered that the dog looked hungry."

"And you got up and gave him that steak—ALL that steak," said Mrs. Doctor Dave, with a kind of triumphant reproof.

"Well, there wasn't anything else TO give him," said Captain Jim deprecatingly. "Nothing a dog'd care for, that is. I reckon he WAS hungry, for he made about two bites of it. I had a fine sleep the rest of the night but my dinner had to be sorter scanty—potatoes and point, as you might say. The dog, he lit out for home this morning. I reckon HE weren't a vegetarian."

"The idea of starving yourself for a worthless dog!" sniffed Mrs. Doctor.

"You don't know but he may be worth a lot to somebody," protested Captain Jim. "He didn't LOOK of much account, but you can't go by looks in jedging a dog. Like meself, he might be a real beauty inside. The First Mate didn't approve of him, I'll allow. His language was right down forcible. But the First Mate is prejudiced. No use in taking a cat's opinion of a dog. 'Tennyrate, I lost my dinner, so this nice spread in this dee-lightful company is real pleasant. It's a great thing to have good neighbors."

"Who lives in the house among the willows up the brook?" asked Anne.

"Mrs. Dick Moore," said Captain Jim—"and her husband," he added, as if by way of an afterthought.

Anne smiled, and deduced a mental picture of Mrs. Dick Moore from Captain Jim's way of putting it; evidently a second Mrs. Rachel Lynde.

"You haven't many neighbors, Mistress Blythe," Captain Jim went on. "This side of the harbor is mighty thinly settled. Most of the land belongs to Mr. Howard up yander past the Glen, and he rents it out for pasture. The other side of the harbor, now, is thick with folks—'specially MacAllisters. There's a whole colony of MacAllisters you can't throw a stone but you hit one. I was talking to old Leon Blacquiere the other day. He's been working on the harbor all summer. 'Dey're nearly all MacAllisters over thar,' he told me. 'Dare's Neil MacAllister and Sandy MacAllister and William MacAllister and Alec MacAllister and Angus MacAllister—and I believe dare's de Devil MacAllister.'"

"There are nearly as many Elliotts and Crawfords," said Doctor Dave, after the laughter had subsided. "You know, Gilbert, we folk on this side of Four Winds have an old saying—'From the conceit of the Elliotts, the pride of the MacAllisters, and the vainglory of the Crawfords, good Lord deliver us.'"

"There's a plenty of fine people among them, though," said Captain Jim. "I sailed with William Crawford for many a year, and for courage and endurance and truth that man hadn't an equal. They've got brains over on that side of Four Winds. Mebbe that's why this side is sorter inclined to pick on 'em. Strange, ain't it, how folks seem to resent anyone being born a mite cleverer than they be."

Doctor Dave, who had a forty years' feud with the over-harbor people, laughed and subsided.

"Who lives in that brilliant emerald house about half a mile up the road?" asked Gilbert.

Captain Jim smiled delightedly.

"Miss Cornelia Bryant. She'll likely be over to see you soon, seeing you're Presbyterians. If you were Methodists she wouldn't come at all. Cornelia has a holy horror of Methodists."

"She's quite a character," chuckled Doctor Dave. "A most inveterate man-hater!"

"Sour grapes?" queried Gilbert, laughing.

"No, 'tisn't sour grapes," answered Captain Jim seriously. "Cornelia could have had her pick when she was young. Even yet she's only to say the word to see the old widowers jump. She jest seems to have been born with a sort of chronic spite agin men and Methodists. She's got the bitterest tongue and the kindest heart in Four Winds. Wherever there's any trouble, that woman is there, doing everything to help in the tenderest way. She never says a harsh word about another woman, and if she likes to card us poor scalawags of men down I reckon our tough old hides can stand it."

"She always speaks well of you, Captain Jim," said Mrs. Doctor.

"Yes, I'm afraid so. I don't half like it. It makes me feel as if there must be something sorter unnateral about me."

7. THE SCHOOLMASTER'S BRIDE

"Who was the first bride who came to this house, Captain Jim?" Anne asked, as they sat around the fireplace after supper.

"Was she a part of the story I've heard was connected with this house?" asked Gilbert. "Somebody told me you could tell it, Captain Jim."

"Well, yes, I know it. I reckon I'm the only person living in Four Winds now that can remember the schoolmaster's bride as she was when she come to the Island. She's been dead this thirty year, but she was one of them women you never forget."

"Tell us the story," pleaded Anne. "I want to find out all about the women who have lived in this house before me."

"Well, there's jest been three—Elizabeth Russell, and Mrs. Ned Russell, and the schoolmaster's bride. Elizabeth Russell was a nice, clever little critter, and Mrs. Ned was a nice woman, too. But they weren't ever like the schoolmaster's bride.

"The schoolmaster's name was John Selwyn. He came out from the Old Country to teach school at the Glen when I was a boy of sixteen. He wasn't much like the usual run of derelicts who used to come out to P.E.I. to teach school in them days. Most of them were clever, drunken critters who taught the children the three R's when they were sober, and lambasted them when they wasn't. But John Selwyn was a fine, handsome young fellow. He boarded at my father's, and he and me were cronies, though he was ten years older'n me. We read and walked and talked a heap together. He knew about all the poetry that was ever written, I reckon, and he used to quote it to me along shore in the evenings. Dad thought it an awful waste of time, but he sorter endured it, hoping it'd put me off the notion of going to sea. Well, nothing could do THAT—mother come of a race of sea-going folk and it was born in me. But I loved to hear John read and recite. It's almost sixty years ago, but I could repeat yards of poetry I learned from him. Nearly sixty years!"

Captain Jim was silent for a space, gazing into the glowing fire in a quest of the bygones. Then, with a sigh, he resumed his story.

"I remember one spring evening I met him on the sand-hills. He looked sorter uplifted—jest like you did, Dr. Blythe, when you brought Mistress Blythe in tonight. I thought of him the minute I seen you. And he told me that he had a sweetheart back home and that she was coming out to him. I wasn't more'n half pleased, ornery young lump of selfishness that I was; I thought he wouldn't be as much my friend after she came. But I'd enough decency not to let him see it. He told me all about her. Her name was Persis Leigh, and she would have come out with him if it hadn't been for her old uncle. He was sick, and he'd looked after her when her parents died and she wouldn't leave him. And now he was dead and she was coming out to marry John Selwyn. 'Twasn't no easy journey for a woman in them days. There weren't no steamers, you must ricollect.

"'When do you expect her?' says I.

"'She sails on the Royal William, the 20th of June,' says he, 'and so she should be here by mid-July. I must set Carpenter Johnson to building me a home for her. Her letter come today. I know before I opened it that it had good news for me. I saw her a few nights ago.'

"I didn't understand him, and then he explained—though I didn't understand THAT much better. He said he had a gift—or a curse. Them was his words, Mistress Blythe—a gift or a curse. He didn't know which it was. He said a great-great-grandmother of his had had it, and they burned her for a witch on account of it. He said queer spells—trances, I think was the name he give 'em—come over him now and again. Are there such things, Doctor?"

"There are people who are certainly subject to trances," answered Gilbert. "The matter is more in the line of psychical research than medical. What were the trances of this John Selwyn like?"

"Like dreams," said the old Doctor skeptically.

"He said he could see things in them," said Captain Jim slowly.

"Mind you, I'm telling you jest what HE said—things that were happening—things that were GOING to happen. He said they were sometimes a comfort to him and sometimes a horror. Four nights before this he'd been in one—went into it while he was sitting looking at the fire. And he saw an old room he knew well in England, and Persis Leigh in it, holding out her hands to him and looking glad and happy. So he knew he was going to hear good news of her."

"A dream—a dream," scoffed the old Doctor.

"Likely—likely," conceded Captain Jim. "That's what *I* said to him at the time. It was a vast more comfortable to think so. I didn't like the idea of him seeing things like that—it was real uncanny.

"'No,' says he, 'I didn't dream it. But we won't talk of this again. You won't be so much my friend if you think much about it.'

"I told him nothing could make me any less his friend. But he jest shook his head and says, says he:

"'Lad, I know. I've lost friends before because of this. I don't blame them. There are times when I feel hardly friendly to myself because of it. Such a power has a bit of divinity in it—whether of a good or an evil divinity who shall say? And we mortals all shrink from too close contact with God or devil.'

"Them was his words. I remember them as if 'twas yesterday, though I didn't know jest what he meant. What do you s'pose he DID mean, doctor?"

"I doubt if he knew what he meant himself," said Doctor Dave testily.

"I think I understand," whispered Anne. She was listening in her old attitude of clasped lips and shining eyes. Captain Jim treated himself to an admiring smile before he went on with his story.

"Well, purty soon all the Glen and Four Winds people knew the schoolmaster's bride was coming, and they were all glad because they thought so much of him. And everybody took an interest in his new house—THIS house. He picked this site for it, because you could see the harbor and hear the sea from it. He made the garden out there for his bride, but he didn't plant the Lombardies. Mrs. Ned Russell planted THEM. But there's a double row of rose-bushes in the garden that the little girls who went to the Glen school set out there for the schoolmaster's bride. He said they were pink for her cheeks and white for her brow and red for her lips. He'd quoted poetry so much that he sorter got into the habit of talking it, too, I reckon.

"Almost everybody sent him some little present to help out the furnishing of the house. When the Russells came into it they were well-to-do and furnished it real handsome, as you can see; but the first furniture that went into it was plain enough. This little house was rich in love, though. The women sent in quilts and tablecloths and towels, and one man made a chest for her, and another a table and so on. Even blind old Aunt Margaret Boyd wove a little basket for her out of the sweet-scented sand-hill grass. The schoolmaster's wife used it for years to keep her handkerchiefs in.

"Well, at last everything was ready—even to the logs in the big fireplace ready for lighting. 'Twasn't exactly THIS fireplace, though 'twas in the same place. Miss Elizabeth had this put in when she made the house over fifteen years ago. It was a big, old-fashioned fireplace where you could have roasted an ox. Many's the time I've sat here and spun yarns, same's I'm doing tonight."

Again there was a silence, while Captain Jim kept a passing tryst with visitants Anne and Gilbert could not see—the folks who had sat with him around that fireplace in the vanished years, with mirth and bridal joy shining in eyes long since closed forever under churchyard sod or heaving leagues of sea. Here on olden nights children had tossed laughter lightly to and fro. Here on winter evenings friends had gathered. Dance and music and jest had been here. Here youths and maidens had dreamed. For Captain Jim the little house was tenanted with shapes entreating remembrance.

"It was the first of July when the house was finished. The schoolmaster began to count the days then. We used to see him walking along the shore, and we'd say to each other, 'She'll soon be with him now.'

"She was expected the middle of July, but she didn't come then. Nobody felt anxious. Vessels were often delayed for days and mebbe weeks. The Royal William was a week overdue —and then two—and then three. And at last we began to be frightened, and it got worse and worse. Fin'lly I couldn't bear to look into John Selwyn's eyes. D'ye know, Mistress Blythe"—Captain Jim lowered his voice—"I used to think that they looked just like what his old great-great-grandmother's must have been when they were burning her to death. He never said much but he taught school like a man in a dream and then hurried to the shore. Many a night he walked there from dark to dawn. People said he was losing his mind. Everybody had given up hope—the Royal William was eight weeks overdue. It was the middle of September and the schoolmaster's bride hadn't come—never would come, we thought.

"There was a big storm then that lasted three days, and on the evening after it died away I went to the shore. I found the schoolmaster there, leaning with his arms folded against a big rock, gazing out to sea.

"I spoke to him but he didn't answer. His eyes seemed to be looking at something I couldn't see. His face was set, like a dead man's.

"'John—John,' I called out—jest like that—jest like a frightened child, 'wake up—wake up.'

"That strange, awful look seemed to sorter fade out of his eyes.

"He turned his head and looked at me. I've never forgot his face—never will forget it till I ships for my last voyage.

"'All is well, lad,' he says. 'I've seen the Royal William coming around East Point. She will be here by dawn. Tomorrow night I shall sit with my bride by my own hearth-fire.'

"Do you think he did see it?" demanded Captain Jim abruptly.

"God knows," said Gilbert softly. "Great love and great pain might compass we know not what marvels."

"I am sure he did see it," said Anne earnestly.

"Fol-de-rol," said Doctor Dave, but he spoke with less conviction than usual.

"Because, you know," said Captain Jim solemnly, "the Royal William came into Four Winds Harbor at daylight the next morning.

"Every soul in the Glen and along the shore was at the old wharf to meet her. The schoolmaster had been watching there all night. How we cheered as she sailed up the channel."

Captain Jim's eyes were shining. They were looking at the Four Winds Harbor of sixty years agone, with a battered old ship sailing through the sunrise splendor.

"And Persis Leigh was on board?" asked Anne.

"Yes—her and the captain's wife. They'd had an awful passage—storm after storm—and their provisions give out, too. But there they were at last. When Persis Leigh stepped onto the old wharf John Selwyn took her in his arms—and folks stopped cheering and begun to cry. I cried myself, though 'twas years, mind you, afore I'd admit it. Ain't it funny how ashamed boys are of tears?"

"Was Persis Leigh beautiful?" asked Anne.

"Well, I don't know that you'd call her beautiful exactly—I—don't—know," said Captain Jim slowly. "Somehow, you never got so far along as to wonder if she was handsome or not. It jest didn't matter. There was something so sweet and winsome about her that you had to love her, that was all. But she was pleasant to look at—big, clear, hazel eyes and heaps of glossy brown hair, and an English skin. John and her were married at our house that night at early candle-lighting; everybody from far and near was there to see it and we all brought them down here afterwards. Mistress Selwyn lighted the fire, and we went away and left them sitting here, jest as John had seen in that vision of his. A strange thing—a strange thing! But I've seen a turrible lot of strange things in my time."

Captain Jim shook his head sagely.

"It's a dear story," said Anne, feeling that for once she had got enough romance to satisfy her. "How long did they live here?"

"Fifteen years. I ran off to sea soon after they were married, like the young scalawag I was. But every time I come back from a voyage I'd head for here, even before I went home, and tell Mistress Selwyn all about it. Fifteen happy years! They had a sort of talent for happiness, them two. Some folks are like that, if you've noticed. They COULDN'T be unhappy for long, no matter what happened. They quarrelled once or twice, for they was both high-sperrited. But Mistress Selwyn says to me once, says she, laughing in that pretty way of hers, 'I felt dreadful when John and I quarrelled, but underneath it all I was very happy because I had such a nice husband to quarrel with and make it up with.' Then they moved to Charlottetown, and Ned Russell bought this house and brought his bride here. They were a gay young pair, as I remember them. Miss Elizabeth Russell was Alec's sister. She came to live with them a year or so later, and she was a creature of mirth, too. The walls of this house must be sorter SOAKED with laughing and good times. You're the third bride I've seen come here, Mistress Blythe—and the handsomest."

Captain Jim contrived to give his sunflower compliment the delicacy of a violet, and Anne wore it proudly. She was looking her best that night, with the bridal rose on her cheeks and the love-light in her eyes; even gruff old Doctor Dave gave her an approving glance, and told his wife, as they drove home together, that that red-headed wife of the boy's was something of a beauty.

"I must be getting back to the light," announced Captain Jim. "I've enj'yed this evening something tremenjus."

"You must come often to see us," said Anne.

"I wonder if you'd give that invitation if you knew how likely I'll be to accept it," Captain Jim remarked whimsically.

"Which is another way of saying you wonder if I mean it," smiled Anne. "I do, 'cross my heart,' as we used to say at school."

"Then I'll come. You're likely to be pestered with me at any hour. And I'll be proud to have you drop down and visit me now and then, too. Gin'rally I haven't anyone to talk to but the First Mate, bless his sociable heart. He's a mighty good listener, and has forgot more'n any MacAllister of them all ever knew, but he isn't much of a conversationalist. You're young and I'm old, but our souls are about the same age, I reckon. We both belong to the race that knows Joseph, as Cornelia Bryant would say."

"The race that knows Joseph?" puzzled Anne.

"Yes. Cornelia divides all the folks in the world into two kinds—the race that knows Joseph and the race that don't. If a person sorter sees eye to eye with you, and has pretty much the same ideas about things, and the same taste in jokes—why, then he belongs to the race that knows Joseph."

"Oh, I understand," exclaimed Anne, light breaking in upon her.

"It's what I used to call—and still call in quotation marks 'kindred spirits.'"

"Jest so—jest so," agreed Captain Jim. "We're it, whatever IT is. When you come in tonight, Mistress Blythe, I says to myself, says I, 'Yes, she's of the race that knows Joseph.' And mighty glad I was, for if it wasn't so we couldn't have had any real satisfaction in each other's company. The race that knows Joseph is the salt of the airth, I reckon."

The moon had just risen when Anne and Gilbert went to the door with their guests. Four

Winds Harbor was beginning to be a thing of dream and glamour and enchantment—a spellbound haven where no tempest might ever ravin. The Lombardies down the lane, tall and sombre as the priestly forms of some mystic band, were tipped with silver.

"Always liked Lombardies," said Captain Jim, waving a long arm at them. "They're the trees of princesses. They're out of fashion now. Folks complain that they die at the top and get ragged-looking. So they do—so they do, if you don't risk your neck every spring climbing up a light ladder to trim them out. I always did it for Miss Elizabeth, so her Lombardies never got out-at-elbows. She was especially fond of them. She liked their dignity and stand-offishness. THEY don't hobnob with every Tom, Dick and Harry. If it's maples for company, Mistress Blythe, it's Lombardies for society."

"What a beautiful night," said Mrs. Doctor Dave, as she climbed into the Doctor's buggy.

"Most nights are beautiful," said Captain Jim. "But I 'low that moonlight over Four Winds makes me sorter wonder what's left for heaven. The moon's a great friend of mine, Mistress Blythe. I've loved her ever since I can remember. When I was a little chap of eight I fell asleep in the garden one evening and wasn't missed. I woke up along in the night and I was most scared to death. What shadows and queer noises there was! I dursn't move. Jest crouched there quaking, poor small mite. Seemed 's if there weren't anyone in the world but meself and it was mighty big. Then all at once I saw the moon looking down at me through the apple boughs, jest like an old friend. I was comforted right off. Got up and walked to the house as brave as a lion, looking at her. Many's the night I've watched her from the deck of my vessel, on seas far away from here. Why don't you folks tell me to take in the slack of my jaw and go home?"

The laughter of the goodnights died away. Anne and Gilbert walked hand in hand around their garden. The brook that ran across the corner dimpled pellucidly in the shadows of the birches. The poppies along its banks were like shallow cups of moonlight. Flowers that had been planted by the hands of the schoolmaster's bride flung their sweetness on the shadowy air, like the beauty and blessing of sacred yesterdays. Anne paused in the gloom to gather a spray.

"I love to smell flowers in the dark," she said. "You get hold of their soul then. Oh, Gilbert, this little house is all I've dreamed it. And I'm so glad that we are not the first who have kept bridal tryst here!"

8. MISS CORNELIA BRYANT COMES TO CALL

That September was a month of golden mists and purple hazes at Four Winds Harbor—a month of sun-steeped days and of nights that were swimming in moonlight, or pulsating with stars. No storm marred it, no rough wind blew. Anne and Gilbert put their nest in order, rambled on the shores, sailed on the harbor, drove about Four Winds and the Glen, or through the ferny, sequestered roads of the woods around the harbor head; in short, had such a honeymoon as any lovers in the world might have envied them.

"If life were to stop short just now it would still have been richly worth while, just for the sake of these past four weeks, wouldn't it?" said Anne. "I don't suppose we will ever have four such perfect weeks again—but we've HAD them. Everything—wind, weather, folks, house of dreams—has conspired to make our honeymoon delightful. There hasn't even been a rainy day since we came here."

"And we haven't quarrelled once," teased Gilbert.

"Well, 'that's a pleasure all the greater for being deferred,'" quoted Anne. "I'm so glad we decided to spend our honeymoon here. Our memories of it will always belong here, in our house of dreams, instead of being scattered about in strange places."

There was a certain tang of romance and adventure in the atmosphere of their new home which Anne had never found in Avonlea. There, although she had lived in sight of the sea, it had not entered intimately into her life. In Four Winds it surrounded her and called to her constantly. From every window of her new home she saw some varying aspect of it. Its haunting murmur was ever in her ears. Vessels sailed up the harbor every day to the wharf at the Glen, or sailed out again through the sunset, bound for ports that might be half way round the globe. Fishing boats went white-winged down the channel in the mornings, and returned laden in the evenings. Sailors and fisher-folk travelled the red, winding harbor roads, light-hearted and content. There was always a certain sense of things going to happen—of adventures and farings-forth. The ways of Four Winds were less staid and settled and grooved than those of Avonlea; winds of change blew over them; the sea called ever to the dwellers on shore, and even those who might not answer its call felt the thrill and unrest and mystery and possibilities of it.

"I understand now why some men must go to sea," said Anne. "That desire which comes to us all at times—'to sail beyond the bourne of sunset'—must be very imperious when it is born in you. I don't wonder Captain Jim ran away because of it. I never see a ship sailing out of the channel, or a gull soaring over the sand-bar, without wishing I were on board the ship or had wings, not like a dove 'to fly away and be at rest,' but like a gull, to sweep out into the very heart of a storm."

"You'll stay right here with me, Anne-girl," said Gilbert lazily. "I won't have you flying away from me into the hearts of storms."

They were sitting on their red sand-stone doorstep in the late afternoon. Great tranquillities were all about them in land and sea and sky. Silvery gulls were soaring over them. The horizons were laced with long trails of frail, pinkish clouds. The hushed air was threaded with a murmurous refrain of minstrel winds and waves. Pale asters were blowing in the sere and misty meadows between them and the harbor.

"Doctors who have to be up all night waiting on sick folk don't feel very adventurous, I suppose," Anne said indulgently. "If you had had a good sleep last night, Gilbert, you'd be as ready as I am for a flight of imagination."

"I did good work last night, Anne," said Gilbert quietly. "Under God, I saved a life. This is the first time I could ever really claim that. In other cases I may have helped; but, Anne, if I had not stayed at Allonby's last night and fought death hand to hand, that woman would have died before morning. I tried an experiment that was certainly never tried in Four Winds before. I doubt if it was ever tried anywhere before outside of a hospital. It was a new thing in Kingsport hospital last winter. I could never have dared try it here if I had not been absolutely certain that there was no other chance. I risked it—and it succeeded. As a result, a good wife and mother is saved for long years of happiness and usefulness. As I drove home this morning, while the sun was rising over the harbor, I thanked God that I had chosen the profession I did. I had fought a good fight and won—think of it, Anne, WON, against the Great Destroyer. It's what I dreamed of doing long ago when we talked together of what we wanted to do in life. That dream of mine came true this morning."

"Was that the only one of your dreams that has come true?" asked Anne, who knew perfectly well what the substance of his answer would be, but wanted to hear it again.

"YOU know, Anne-girl," said Gilbert, smiling into her eyes. At that moment there were certainly two perfectly happy people sitting on the doorstep of a little white house on the Four Winds Harbor shore.

Presently Gilbert said, with a change of tone, "Do I or do I not see a full-rigged ship sailing up our lane?"

Anne looked and sprang up.

"That must be either Miss Cornelia Bryant or Mrs. Moore coming to call," she said.

"I'm going into the office, and if it is Miss Cornelia I warn you that I'll eavesdrop," said Gilbert. "From all I've heard regarding Miss Cornelia I conclude that her conversation will not be dull, to say the least."

"It may be Mrs. Moore."

"I don't think Mrs. Moore is built on those lines. I saw her working in her garden the other day, and, though I was too far away to see clearly, I thought she was rather slender. She doesn't seem very socially inclined when she has never called on you yet, although she's your nearest neighbor."

"She can't be like Mrs. Lynde, after all, or curiosity would have brought her," said Anne. "This caller is, I think, Miss Cornelia."

Miss Cornelia it was; moreover, Miss Cornelia had not come to make any brief and fashionable wedding call. She had her work under her arm in a substantial parcel, and when Anne asked her to stay she promptly took off her capacious sun-hat, which had been held on her head, despite irreverent September breezes, by a tight elastic band under her hard little knob of fair hair. No hat pins for Miss Cornelia, an it please ye! Elastic bands had been good enough for her mother and they were good enough for HER. She had a fresh, round, pink-and-white face, and jolly brown eyes. She did not look in the least like the traditional old maid, and there was something in her expression which won Anne instantly. With her old instinctive quickness to discern kindred spirits she knew she was going to like Miss Cornelia, in spite of uncertain oddities of opinion, and certain oddities of attire.

Nobody but Miss Cornelia would have come to make a call arrayed in a striped blue-and-white apron and a wrapper of chocolate print, with a design of huge, pink roses scattered over it. And nobody but Miss Cornelia could have looked dignified and suitably garbed in it. Had Miss Cornelia been entering a palace to call on a prince's bride, she would have been just as dignified and just as wholly mistress of the situation. She would have trailed her rose-spattered flounce over the marble floors just as unconcernedly, and she would have proceeded just as calmly to disabuse the mind of the princess of any idea that the possession of a mere man, be he prince or peasant, was anything to brag of.

"I've brought my work, Mrs. Blythe, dearie," she remarked, unrolling some dainty material. "I'm in a hurry to get this done, and there isn't any time to lose."

Anne looked in some surprise at the white garment spread over Miss Cornelia's ample lap. It was certainly a baby's dress, and it was most beautifully made, with tiny frills and tucks. Miss Cornelia adjusted her glasses and fell to embroidering with exquisite stitches.

"This is for Mrs. Fred Proctor up at the Glen," she announced. "She's expecting her eighth baby any day now, and not a stitch has she ready for it. The other seven have wore out all she made for the first, and she's never had time or strength or spirit to make any more. That woman is a martyr, Mrs. Blythe, believe ME. When she married Fred Proctor *I* knew how it would turn out. He was one of your wicked, fascinating men. After he got married he left off being fascinating and just kept on being wicked. He drinks and he neglects his family. Isn't that like a man? I don't know how Mrs. Proctor would ever keep her children decently clothed if her neighbors didn't help her out."

As Anne was afterwards to learn, Miss Cornelia was the only neighbor who troubled herself much about the decency of the young Proctors.

"When I heard this eighth baby was coming I decided to make some things for it," Miss Cornelia went on. "This is the last and I want to finish it today."

"It's certainly very pretty," said Anne. "I'll get my sewing and we'll have a little thimble party of two. You are a beautiful sewer, Miss Bryant."

"Yes, I'm the best sewer in these parts," said Miss Cornelia in a matter-of-fact tone. "I ought to be! Lord, I've done more of it than if I'd had a hundred children of my own, believe ME! I s'pose I'm a fool, to be putting hand embroidery on this dress for an eighth baby. But, Lord, Mrs. Blythe, dearie, it isn't to blame for being the eighth, and I kind of wished it to have one real pretty dress, just as if it WAS wanted. Nobody's wanting the poor mite—so I put some extra fuss on its little things just on that account."

"Any baby might be proud of that dress," said Anne, feeling still more strongly that she was going to like Miss Cornelia.

"I s'pose you've been thinking I was never coming to call on you," resumed Miss Cornelia. "But this is harvest month, you know, and I've been busy—and a lot of extra hands hanging round, eating more'n they work, just like the men. I'd have come yesterday, but I went to Mrs. Roderick MacAllister's funeral. At first I thought my head was aching so badly I couldn't enjoy myself if I did go. But she was a hundred years old, and I'd always promised myself that I'd go to her funeral."

"Was it a successful function?" asked Anne, noticing that the office door was ajar.

"What's that? Oh, yes, it was a tremendous funeral. She had a very large connection. There was over one hundred and twenty carriages in the procession. There was one or two funny things happened. I thought that die I would to see old Joe Bradshaw, who is an infidel and never darkens the door of a church, singing 'Safe in the Arms of Jesus' with great gusto and fervor. He glories in singing—that's why he never misses a funeral. Poor Mrs. Bradshaw didn't look much like singing—all wore out slaving. Old Joe starts out once in a while to buy her a present and brings home some new kind of farm machinery. Isn't that like a man? But what else would you expect of a man who never goes to church, even a Methodist one? I was real thankful to see you and the young Doctor in the Presbyterian church your first Sunday. No doctor for me who isn't a Presbyterian."

"We were in the Methodist church last Sunday evening," said Anne wickedly.

"Oh, I s'pose Dr. Blythe has to go to the Methodist church once in a while or he wouldn't get the Methodist practice."

"We liked the sermon very much," declared Anne boldly. "And I thought the Methodist minster's prayer was one of the most beautiful I ever heard."

"Oh, I've no doubt he can pray. I never heard anyone make more beautiful prayers than old Simon Bentley, who was always drunk, or hoping to be, and the drunker he was the better he prayed."

"The Methodist minister is very fine looking," said Anne, for the benefit of the office door.

"Yes, he's quite ornamental," agreed Miss Cornelia. "Oh, and VERY ladylike. And he thinks that every girl who looks at him falls in love with him—as if a Methodist minister, wandering about like any Jew, was such a prize! If you and the young doctor take MY advice, you won't have much to do with the Methodists. My motto is—if you ARE a Presbyterian, BE a Presbyterian."

"Don't you think that Methodists go to heaven as well as Presbyterians?" asked Anne smilelessly.

"That isn't for US to decide. It's in higher hands than ours," said Miss Cornelia solemnly. "But I ain't going to associate with them on earth whatever I may have to do in heaven. THIS Methodist minister isn't married. The last one they had was, and his wife was the silliest, flightiest little thing I ever saw. I told her husband once that he should have waited till she was grown up before he married her. He said he wanted to have the training of her. Wasn't that like a man?"

"It's rather hard to decide just when people ARE grown up," laughed Anne.

"That's a true word, dearie. Some are grown up when they're born, and others ain't grown up when they're eighty, believe ME. That same Mrs. Roderick I was speaking of never grew up. She was as foolish when she was a hundred as when she was ten."

"Perhaps that was why she lived so long," suggested Anne.

"Maybe 'twas. *I'd* rather live fifty sensible years than a hundred foolish ones."

"But just think what a dull world it would be if everyone was sensible," pleaded Anne.

Miss Cornelia disdained any skirmish of flippant epigram.

"Mrs. Roderick was a Milgrave, and the Milgraves never had much sense. Her nephew, Ebenezer Milgrave, used to be insane for years. He believed he was dead and used to rage at his wife because she wouldn't bury him. *I'd* a-done it."

Miss Cornelia looked so grimly determined that Anne could almost see her with a spade in her hand.

"Don't you know ANY good husbands, Miss Bryant?"

"Oh, yes, lots of them—over yonder," said Miss Cornelia, waving her hand through the open window towards the little graveyard of the church across the harbor.

"But living—going about in the flesh?" persisted Anne.

"Oh, there's a few, just to show that with God all things are possible," acknowledged Miss Cornelia reluctantly. "I don't deny that an odd man here and there, if he's caught young and trained up proper, and if his mother has spanked him well beforehand, may turn out a decent being. YOUR husband, now, isn't so bad, as men go, from all I hear. I s'pose"—Miss Cornelia looked sharply at Anne over her glasses—"you think there's nobody like him in the world."

"There isn't," said Anne promptly.

"Ah, well, I heard another bride say that once," sighed Miss Cornelia. "Jennie Dean thought when she married that there wasn't anybody like HER husband in the world. And she was right—there wasn't! And a good thing, too, believe ME! He led her an awful life—and he was courting his second wife while Jennie was dying.

"Wasn't that like a man? However, I hope YOUR confidence will be better justified, dearie. The young doctor is taking real well. I was afraid at first he mightn't, for folks hereabouts have always thought old Doctor Dave the only doctor in the world. Doctor Dave hadn't much tact, to be sure—he was always talking of ropes in houses where someone had hanged himself. But folks forgot their hurt feelings when they had a pain in their stomachs. If he'd been a minister instead of a doctor they'd never have forgiven him. Soul-ache doesn't worry folks near as much as stomach-ache. Seeing as we're both Presbyterians and no Methodists around, will you tell me your candid opinion of OUR minister?"

"Why—really—I—well," hesitated Anne.

Miss Cornelia nodded.

"Exactly. I agree with you, dearie. We made a mistake when we called HIM. His face just looks like one of those long, narrow stones in the graveyard, doesn't it? 'Sacred to the memory' ought to be written on his forehead. I shall never forget the first sermon he preached after he came. It was on the subject of everyone doing what they were best fitted for—a very good subject, of course; but such illustrations as he used! He said, 'If you had a cow and an apple tree, and if you tied the apple tree in your stable and planted the cow in your orchard, with her legs up, how much milk would you get from the apple tree, or how many apples from the cow?' Did you ever hear the like in your born days, dearie? I was so thankful there were no Methodists there that day—they'd never have been done hooting over it. But what I dislike most in him is his habit of agreeing with everybody, no matter what is said. If you said to him, 'You're a scoundrel,' he'd say, with that smooth smile of his, 'Yes, that's so.' A minister should have more backbone. The long and the short of it is, I consider him a reverend jackass. But, of course, this is just between you and me. When there are Methodists in hearing I praise him to the skies. Some folks think his wife dresses too gay, but *I* say when she has to live with a face like that she needs something to cheer her up. You'll never hear ME condemning a woman for her dress. I'm only too thankful when her husband isn't too mean and miserly to allow it. Not that I bother much with dress myself. Women just dress to please the men, and I'd never stoop to THAT. I have had a real placid, comfortable life, dearie, and it's just because I never cared a cent what the men thought."

"Why do you hate the men so, Miss Bryant?"

"Lord, dearie, I don't hate them. They aren't worth it. I just sort of despise them. I think I'll like YOUR husband if he keeps on as he has begun. But apart from him about the only men in the world I've much use for are the old doctor and Captain Jim."

"Captain Jim is certainly splendid," agreed Anne cordially.

"Captain Jim is a good man, but he's kind of vexing in one way. You CAN'T make him mad. I've tried for twenty years and he just keeps on being placid. It does sort of rile me. And I s'pose the woman he should have married got a man who went into tantrums twice a day."

"Who was she?"

"Oh, I don't know, dearie. I never remember of Captain Jim making up to anybody. He was edging on old as far as my memory goes. He's seventy-six, you know. I never heard any reason for his staying a bachelor, but there must be one, believe ME. He sailed all his life till five years ago, and there's no corner of the earth he hasn't poked his nose into. He and Elizabeth Russell were great cronies, all their lives, but they never had any notion of sweet-hearting. Elizabeth never married, though she had plenty of chances. She was a great beauty when she was young. The year the Prince of Wales came to the Island she was visiting her uncle in Charlottetown and he was a Government official, and so she got invited to the great ball. She was the prettiest girl there, and the Prince danced with her, and all the other women he didn't dance with were furious about it, because their social standing was higher than hers and they said he shouldn't have passed them over. Elizabeth was always very proud of that dance. Mean folks said that was why she never married—she couldn't put up with an ordinary man after dancing with a prince. But that wasn't so. She told me the reason once—it was because she had such a temper that she was afraid she couldn't live peaceably with any man. She HAD an awful temper—she used to have to go upstairs and bite pieces out of her bureau to keep it down by times. But I told her that wasn't any reason for not marrying if she wanted to. There's no reason why we should let the men have a monopoly of temper, is there, Mrs. Blythe, dearie?"

"I've a bit of temper myself," sighed Anne.

"It's well you have, dearie. You won't be half so likely to be trodden on, believe ME! My, how that golden glow of yours is blooming! Your garden looks fine. Poor Elizabeth always took such care of it."

"I love it," said Anne. "I'm glad it's so full of old-fashioned flowers. Speaking of gardening, we want to get a man to dig up that little lot beyond the fir grove and set it out with strawberry plants for us. Gilbert is so busy he will never get time for it this fall. Do you know anyone we can get?"

"Well, Henry Hammond up at the Glen goes out doing jobs like that. He'll do, maybe. He's always a heap more interested in his wages than in his work, just like a man, and he's so slow in the uptake that he stands still for five minutes before it dawns on him that he's stopped. His father threw a stump at him when he was small.

"Nice gentle missile, wasn't it? So like a man! Course, the boy never got over it. But he's the only one I can recommend at all. He painted my house for me last spring. It looks real nice now, don't you think?"

Anne was saved by the clock striking five.

"Lord, is it that late?" exclaimed Miss Cornelia. "How time does slip by when you're enjoying yourself! Well, I must betake myself home."

"No, indeed! You are going to stay and have tea with us," said Anne eagerly.

"Are you asking me because you think you ought to, or because you really want to?" demanded Miss Cornelia.

"Because I really want to."

"Then I'll stay. YOU belong to the race that knows Joseph."

"I know we are going to be friends," said Anne, with the smile that only they of the household of faith ever saw.

"Yes, we are, dearie. Thank goodness, we can choose our friends. We have to take our relatives as they are, and be thankful if there are no penitentiary birds among them. Not that I've many—none nearer than second cousins. I'm a kind of lonely soul, Mrs. Blythe."

There was a wistful note in Miss Cornelia's voice.

"I wish you would call me Anne," exclaimed Anne impulsively. "It would seem more HOMEY. Everyone in Four Winds, except my husband, calls me Mrs. Blythe, and it makes me feel like a stranger. Do you know that your name is very near being the one I yearned after when I was a child. I hated 'Anne' and I called myself 'Cordelia' in imagination."

"I like Anne. It was my mother's name. Old-fashioned names are the best and sweetest in my opinion. If you're going to get tea you might send the young doctor to talk to me. He's been lying on the sofa in that office ever since I came, laughing fit to kill over what I've been saying."

"How did you know?" cried Anne, too aghast at this instance of Miss Cornelia's uncanny prescience to make a polite denial.

"I saw him sitting beside you when I came up the lane, and I know men's tricks," retorted Miss Cornelia. "There, I've finished my little dress, dearie, and the eighth baby can come as soon as it pleases."

9. AN EVENING AT FOUR WINDS POINT

It was late September when Anne and Gilbert were able to pay Four Winds light their promised visit. They had often planned to go, but something always occurred to prevent them. Captain Jim had "dropped in" several times at the little house.

"I don't stand on ceremony, Mistress Blythe," he told Anne. "It's a real pleasure to me to come here, and I'm not going to deny myself jest because you haven't got down to see me. There oughtn't to be no bargaining like that among the race that knows Joseph. I'll come when I can, and you come when you can, and so long's we have our pleasant little chat it don't matter a mite what roof's over us."

Captain Jim took a great fancy to Gog and Magog, who were presiding over the destinies of the hearth in the little house with as much dignity and aplomb as they had done at Patty's Place.

"Aren't they the cutest little cusses?" he would say delightedly; and he bade them greeting and farewell as gravely and invariably as he did his host and hostess. Captain Jim was not going to offend household deities by any lack of reverence and ceremony.

"You've made this little house just about perfect," he told Anne. "It never was so nice before. Mistress Selwyn had your taste and she did wonders; but folks in those days didn't have the pretty little curtains and pictures and nicknacks you have. As for Elizabeth, she lived in the past. You've kinder brought the future into it, so to speak. I'd be real happy even if we couldn't talk at all, when I come here—jest to sit and look at you and your pictures and your flowers would be enough of a treat. It's beautiful—beautiful."

Captain Jim was a passionate worshipper of beauty. Every lovely thing heard or seen gave him a deep, subtle, inner joy that irradiated his life. He was quite keenly aware of his own lack of outward comeliness and lamented it.

"Folks say I'm good," he remarked whimsically upon one occasion, "but I sometimes wish the Lord had made me only half as good and put the rest of it into looks. But there, I reckon He knew what He was about, as a good Captain should. Some of us have to be homely, or the purty ones—like Mistress Blythe here—wouldn't show up so well."

One evening Anne and Gilbert finally walked down to the Four Winds light. The day had begun sombrely in gray cloud and mist, but it had ended in a pomp of scarlet and gold. Over the western hills beyond the harbor were amber deeps and crystalline shallows, with the fire of sunset below. The north was a mackerel sky of little, fiery golden clouds. The red light flamed on the white sails of a vessel gliding down the channel, bound to a southern port in a land of palms. Beyond her, it smote upon and incarnadined the shining, white, grassless faces of the sand dunes. To the right, it fell on the old house among the willows up the brook, and gave it for a fleeting space casements more splendid than those of an old cathedral. They glowed out of its quiet and grayness like the throbbing, blood-red thoughts of a vivid soul imprisoned in a dull husk of environment.

"That old house up the brook always seems so lonely," said Anne. "I never see visitors there. Of course, its lane opens on the upper road—but I don't think there's much coming and going. It seems odd we've never met the Moores yet, when they live within fifteen minutes' walk of us. I may have seen them in church, of course, but if so I didn't know them. I'm sorry they are so unsociable, when they are our only near neighbors."

"Evidently they don't belong to the race that knows Joseph," laughed Gilbert. "Have you ever found out who that girl was whom you thought so beautiful?"

"No. Somehow I have never remembered to ask about her. But I've never seen her anywhere, so I suppose she must have been a stranger. Oh, the sun has just vanished—and there's the light."

As the dusk deepened, the great beacon cut swathes of light through it, sweeping in a circle over the fields and the harbor, the sandbar and the gulf.

"I feel as if it might catch me and whisk me leagues out to sea," said Anne, as one drenched them with radiance; and she felt rather relieved when they got so near the Point that they were inside the range of those dazzling, recurrent flashes.

As they turned into the little lane that led across the fields to the Point they met a man coming out of it—a man of such extraordinary appearance that for a moment they both frankly stared. He was a decidedly fine-looking person-tall, broad-shouldered, well-featured, with a Roman nose and frank gray eyes; he was dressed in a prosperous farmer's Sunday best; in so far he might have been any inhabitant of Four Winds or the Glen. But, flowing over his breast nearly to his knees, was a river of crinkly brown beard; and adown his back, beneath his commonplace felt hat, was a corresponding cascade of thick, wavy, brown hair.

"Anne," murmured Gilbert, when they were out of earshot, "you didn't put what Uncle Dave calls 'a little of the Scott Act' in that lemonade you gave me just before we left home, did you?"

"No, I didn't," said Anne, stifling her laughter, lest the retreating enigma should hear here. "Who in the world can he be?"

"I don't know; but if Captain Jim keeps apparitions like that down at this Point I'm going to carry cold iron in my pocket when I come here. He wasn't a sailor, or one might pardon his eccentricity of appearance; he must belong to the over-harbor clans. Uncle Dave says they have several freaks over there."

"Uncle Dave is a little prejudiced, I think. You know all the over-harbor people who come to the Glen Church seem very nice. Oh, Gilbert, isn't this beautiful?"

The Four Winds light was built on a spur of red sand-stone cliff jutting out into the gulf. On one side, across the channel, stretched the silvery sand shore of the bar; on the other, extended a long, curving beach of red cliffs, rising steeply from the pebbled coves. It was a shore that knew the magic and mystery of storm and star. There is a great solitude about such a shore. The woods are never solitary—they are full of whispering, beckoning, friendly life. But the sea is a mighty soul, forever moaning of some great, unshareable sorrow, which shuts it up into itself for all eternity. We can never pierce its infinite mystery—we may only wander, awed and spellbound, on the outer fringe of it. The woods call to us with a hundred voices, but the sea has one only—a mighty voice that drowns our souls in its majestic music. The woods are human, but the sea is of the company of the archangels.

Anne and Gilbert found Uncle Jim sitting on a bench outside the lighthouse, putting the finishing touches to a wonderful, full-rigged, toy schooner. He rose and welcomed them to his abode with the gentle, unconscious courtesy that became him so well.

"This has been a purty nice day all through, Mistress Blythe, and now, right at the last, it's brought its best. Would you like to sit down here outside a bit, while the light lasts? I've just finished this bit of a plaything for my little grand nephew, Joe, up at the Glen. After I promised to make it for him I was kinder sorry, for his mother was vexed. She's afraid he'll be wanting to go to sea later on and she doesn't want the notion encouraged in him. But what could I do, Mistress Blythe? I'd PROMISED him, and I think it's sorter real dastardly to break a promise you make to a child. Come, sit down. It won't take long to stay an hour."

The wind was off shore, and only broke the sea's surface into long, silvery ripples, and sent sheeny shadows flying out across it, from every point and headland, like transparent wings. The dusk was hanging a curtain of violet gloom over the sand dunes and the headlands where gulls were huddling. The sky was faintly filmed over with scarfs of silken vapor. Cloud fleets rode at anchor along the horizons. An evening star was watching over the bar.

"Isn't that a view worth looking at?" said Captain Jim, with a loving, proprietary pride. "Nice and far from the market-place, ain't it? No buying and selling and getting gain. You don't have to pay anything—all that sea and sky free—'without money and without price.' There's going to be a moonrise purty soon, too—I'm never tired of finding out what a moonrise can be over them rocks and sea and harbor. There's a surprise in it every time."

They had their moonrise, and watched its marvel and magic in a silence that asked nothing of the world or each other. Then they went up into the tower, and Captain Jim showed and explained the mechanism of the great light. Finally they found themselves in the dining room, where a fire of driftwood was weaving flames of wavering, elusive, sea-born hues in the open fireplace.

"I put this fireplace in myself," remarked Captain Jim. "The Government don't give lighthouse keepers such luxuries. Look at the colors that wood makes. If you'd like some driftwood for your fire, Mistress Blythe, I'll bring you up a load some day. Sit down. I'm going to make you a cup of tea."

Captain Jim placed a chair for Anne, having first removed therefrom a huge, orange-colored cat and a newspaper.

"Get down, Matey. The sofa is your place. I must put this paper away safe till I can find time to finish the story in it. It's called A Mad Love. 'Tisn't my favorite brand of fiction, but I'm reading it jest to see how long she can spin it out. It's at the sixty-second chapter now, and the wedding ain't any nearer than when it begun, far's I can see. When little Joe comes I have to read him pirate yarns. Ain't it strange how innocent little creatures like children like the bloodthirstiest stories?"

"Like my lad Davy at home," said Anne. "He wants tales that reek with gore."

Captain Jim's tea proved to be nectar. He was pleased as a child with Anne's compliments, but he affected a fine indifference.

"The secret is I don't skimp the cream," he remarked airily. Captain Jim had never heard of Oliver Wendell Holmes, but he evidently agreed with that writer's dictum that "big heart never liked little cream pot."

"We met an odd-looking personage coming out of your lane," said Gilbert as they sipped. "Who was he?"

Captain Jim grinned.

"That's Marshall Elliott—a mighty fine man with jest one streak of foolishness in him. I s'pose you wondered what his object was in turning himself into a sort of dime museum freak."

"Is he a modern Nazarite or a Hebrew prophet left over from olden times?" asked Anne.

"Neither of them. It's politics that's at the bottom of his freak. All those Elliotts and Crawfords and MacAllisters are dyed-in-the-wool politicians. They're born Grit or Tory, as the case may be, and they live Grit or Tory, and they die Grit or Tory; and what they're going to do in heaven, where there's probably no politics, is more than I can fathom. This Marshall Elliott was born a Grit. I'm a Grit myself in moderation, but there's no moderation about Marshall. Fifteen years ago there was a specially bitter general election. Marshall fought for his party tooth and nail. He was dead sure the Liberals would win—so sure that he got up at a public meeting and vowed that he wouldn't shave his face or cut his hair until the Grits were in power. Well, they didn't go in—and they've never got in yet—and you saw the result today for yourselves. Marshall stuck to his word."

"What does his wife think of it?" asked Anne.

"He's a bachelor. But if he had a wife I reckon she couldn't make him break that vow. That family of Elliotts has always been more stubborn than natteral. Marshall's brother Alexander had a dog he set great store by, and when it died the man actilly wanted to have it buried in the graveyard, 'along with the other Christians,' he said. Course, he wasn't allowed to; so he buried it just outside the graveyard fence, and never darkened the church door again. But Sundays he'd drive his family to church and sit by that dog's grave and read his Bible all the time service was going on. They say when he was dying he asked his wife to bury him beside the dog; she was a meek little soul but she fired up at THAT. She said SHE wasn't going to be buried beside no dog, and if he'd rather have his last resting place beside the dog than beside her, jest to say so. Alexander Elliott was a stubborn mule, but he was fond of his wife, so he give in and said, 'Well, durn it, bury me where you please. But when Gabriel's trump blows I expect my dog to rise with the rest of us, for he had as much soul as any durned Elliott or Crawford or MacAllister that ever strutted.' Them was HIS parting words. As for Marshall, we're all used to him, but he must strike strangers as right down peculiar-looking. I've known him ever since he was ten—he's about fifty now—and I like him. Him and me was out cod-fishing today. That's about all I'm good for now—catching trout and cod occasional. But 'tweren't always so—not by no manner of means. I used to do other things, as you'd admit if you saw my life-book."

Anne was just going to ask what his life-book was when the First Mate created a diversion by springing upon Captain Jim's knee. He was a gorgeous beastie, with a face as round as a full moon, vivid green eyes, and immense, white, double paws. Captain Jim stroked his velvet back gently.

"I never fancied cats much till I found the First Mate," he remarked, to the accompaniment of the Mate's tremendous purrs. "I saved his life, and when you've saved a creature's life you're bound to love it. It's next thing to giving life. There's some turrible thoughtless people in the world, Mistress Blythe. Some of them city folks who have summer homes over the harbor are so thoughtless that they're cruel. It's the worst kind of cruelty—the thoughtless kind. You can't cope with it. They keep cats there in the summer, and feed and pet 'em, and doll 'em up with ribbons and collars. And then in the fall they go off and leave 'em to starve or freeze. It makes my blood boil, Mistress Blythe. One day last winter I found a poor old mother cat dead on the shore, lying against the skin-and-bone bodies of her three little kittens. She'd died trying to shelter 'em. She had her poor stiff paws around 'em. Master, I cried. Then I swore. Then I carried them poor little kittens home and fed 'em up and found good homes for 'em. I knew the woman who left the cat and when she come back this summer I jest went over the harbor and told her my opinion of her. It was rank meddling, but I do love meddling in a good cause."

"How did she take it?" asked Gilbert.

"Cried and said she 'didn't think.' I says to her, says I, 'Do you s'pose that'll be held for a good excuse in the day of Jedgment, when you'll have to account for that poor old mother's life? The Lord'll ask you what He give you your brains for if it wasn't to think, I reckon.' I don't fancy she'll leave cats to starve another time."

"Was the First Mate one of the forsaken?" asked Anne, making advances to him which were responded to graciously, if condescendingly.

"Yes. I found HIM one bitter cold day in winter, caught in the branches of a tree by his durn-fool ribbon collar. He was almost starving. If you could have seen his eyes, Mistress Blythe! He was nothing but a kitten, and he'd got his living somehow since he'd been left until he got hung up. When I loosed him he gave my hand a pitiful swipe with his little red tongue. He wasn't the able seaman you see now. He was meek as Moses. That was nine years ago. His life has been long in the land for a cat. He's a good old pal, the First Mate is."

"I should have expected you to have a dog," said Gilbert.

Captain Jim shook his head.

"I had a dog once. I thought so much of him that when he died I couldn't bear the thought of getting another in his place. He was a FRIEND—you understand, Mistress Blythe? Matey's only a pal. I'm fond of Matey—all the fonder on account of the spice of devilment that's in him—like there is in all cats. But I LOVED my dog. I always had a sneaking sympathy for Alexander Elliott about HIS dog. There isn't any devil in a good dog. That's why they're more lovable than cats, I reckon. But I'm darned if they're as interesting. Here I am, talking too much. Why don't you check me? When I do get a chance to talk to anyone I run on turrible. If you've done your tea I've a few little things you might like to look at—picked 'em up in the queer corners I used to be poking my nose into."

Captain Jim's "few little things" turned out to be a most interesting collection of curios, hideous, quaint and beautiful. And almost every one had some striking story attached to it.

Anne never forgot the delight with which she listened to those old tales that moonlit evening by that enchanted driftwood fire, while the silver sea called to them through the open window and sobbed against the rocks below them.

Captain Jim never said a boastful word, but it was impossible to help seeing what a hero the man had been—brave, true, resourceful, unselfish. He sat there in his little room and made those things live again for his hearers. By a lift of the eyebrow, a twist of the lip, a gesture, a word, he painted a whole scene or character so that they saw it as it was.

Some of Captain Jim's adventures had such a marvellous edge that Anne and Gilbert secretly wondered if he were not drawing a rather long bow at their credulous expense. But in this, as they found later, they did him injustice. His tales were all literally true. Captain Jim had the gift of the born storyteller, whereby "unhappy, far-off things" can be brought vividly before the hearer in all their pristine poignancy.

Anne and Gilbert laughed and shivered over his tales, and once Anne found herself crying. Captain Jim surveyed her tears with pleasure shining from his face.

"I like to see folks cry that way," he remarked. "It's a compliment. But I can't do justice to the things I've seen or helped to do. I've 'em all jotted down in my life-book, but I haven't got the knack of writing them out properly. If I could hit on jest the right words and string 'em together proper on paper I could make a great book. It would beat A Mad Love holler, and I believe Joe'd like it as well as the pirate yarns. Yes, I've had some adventures in my time; and, do you know, Mistress Blythe, I still lust after 'em. Yes, old and useless as I be, there's an awful longing sweeps over me at times to sail out—out—out there—forever and ever."

"Like Ulysses, you would

'sail beyond the sunset and the baths
of all the western stars until you die,'"

said Anne dreamily.

"Ulysses? I've read of him. Yes, that's just how I feel—jest how all us old sailors feel, I reckon. I'll die on land after all, I s'pose. Well, what is to be will be. There was old William Ford at the Glen who never went on the water in his life, 'cause he was afraid of being drowned. A fortune-teller had predicted he would be. And one day he fainted and fell with his face in the barn trough and was drowned. Must you go? Well, come soon and come often. The doctor is to do the talking next time. He knows a heap of things I want to find out. I'm sorter lonesome here by times. It's been worse since Elizabeth Russell died. Her and me was such cronies."

Captain Jim spoke with the pathos of the aged, who see their old friends slipping from them one by one—friends whose place can never be quite filled by those of a younger generation, even of the race that knows Joseph. Anne and Gilbert promised to come soon and often.

"He's a rare old fellow, isn't he?" said Gilbert, as they walked home.

"Somehow, I can't reconcile his simple, kindly personality with the wild, adventurous life he has lived," mused Anne.

"You wouldn't find it so hard if you had seen him the other day down at the fishing village. One of the men of Peter Gautier's boat made a nasty remark about some girl along the shore. Captain Jim fairly scorched the wretched fellow with the lightning of his eyes. He seemed a man transformed. He didn't say much—but the way he said it! You'd have thought it would strip the flesh from the fellow's bones. I understand that Captain Jim will never allow a word against any woman to be said in his presence."

"I wonder why he never married," said Anne. "He should have sons with their ships at sea now, and grandchildren climbing over him to hear his stories—he's that kind of a man. Instead, he has nothing but a magnificent cat."

But Anne was mistaken. Captain Jim had more than that. He had a memory.

10. LESLIE MOORE

"I'm going for a walk to the outside shore tonight," Anne told Gog and Magog one October evening. There was no one else to tell, for Gilbert had gone over the harbor. Anne had her little domain in the speckless order one would expect of anyone brought up by Marilla Cuthbert, and felt that she could gad shoreward with a clear conscience. Many and delightful had been her shore rambles, sometimes with Gilbert, sometimes with Captain Jim, sometimes alone with her own thoughts and new, poignantly-sweet dreams that were beginning to span life with their rainbows. She loved the gentle, misty harbor shore and the silvery, wind-haunted sand shore, but best of all she loved the rock shore, with its cliffs and caves and piles of surf-worn boulders, and its coves where the pebbles glittered under the pools; and it was to this shore she hied herself tonight.

There had been an autumn storm of wind and rain, lasting for three days. Thunderous had been the crash of billows on the rocks, wild the white spray and spume that blew over the bar, troubled and misty and tempest-torn the erstwhile blue peace of Four Winds Harbor. Now it was over, and the shore lay clean-washed after the storm; not a wind stirred, but there was still a fine surf on, dashing on sand and rock in a splendid white turmoil—the only restless thing in the great, pervading stillness and peace.

"Oh, this is a moment worth living through weeks of storm and stress for," Anne exclaimed, delightedly sending her far gaze across the tossing waters from the top of the cliff where she stood. Presently she scrambled down the steep path to the little cove below, where she seemed shut in with rocks and sea and sky.

"I'm going to dance and sing," she said. "There's no one here to see me—the seagulls won't carry tales of the matter. I may be as crazy as I like."

She caught up her skirt and pirouetted along the hard strip of sand just out of reach of the waves that almost lapped her feet with their spent foam. Whirling round and round, laughing like a child, she reached the little headland that ran out to the east of the cove; then she stopped suddenly, blushing crimson; she was not alone; there had been a witness to her dance and laughter.

The girl of the golden hair and sea-blue eyes was sitting on a boulder of the headland, half-hidden by a jutting rock. She was looking straight at Anne with a strange expression—part wonder, part sympathy, part—could it be?—envy. She was bare-headed, and her splendid hair, more than ever like Browning's "gorgeous snake," was bound about her head with a crimson ribbon. She wore a dress of some dark material, very plainly made; but swathed about her waist, outlining its fine curves, was a vivid girdle of red silk. Her hands, clasped over her knee, were brown and somewhat work-hardened; but the skin of her throat and cheeks was as white as cream. A flying gleam of sunset broke through a low-lying western cloud and fell across her hair. For a moment she seemed the spirit of the sea personified—all its mystery, all its passion, all its elusive charm.

"You—you must think me crazy," stammered Anne, trying to recover her self-possession. To be seen by this stately girl in such an abandon of childishness—she, Mrs. Dr. Blythe, with all the dignity of the matron to keep up—it was too bad!

"No," said the girl, "I don't."

She said nothing more; her voice was expressionless; her manner slightly repellent; but there was something in her eyes—eager yet shy, defiant yet pleading—which turned Anne from her purpose of walking away. Instead, she sat down on the boulder beside the girl.

"Let's introduce ourselves," she said, with the smile that had never yet failed to win confidence and friendliness. "I am Mrs. Blythe—and I live in that little white house up the harbor shore."

"Yes, I know," said the girl. "I am Leslie Moore—Mrs. Dick Moore," she added stiffly.

Anne was silent for a moment from sheer amazement. It had not occurred to her that this girl was married—there seemed nothing of the wife about her. And that she should be the neighbor whom Anne had pictured as a commonplace Four Winds housewife! Anne could not quickly adjust her mental focus to this astonishing change.

"Then—then you live in that gray house up the brook," she stammered.

"Yes. I should have gone over to call on you long ago," said the other. She did not offer any explanation or excuse for not having gone.

"I wish you WOULD come," said Anne, recovering herself somewhat. "We're such near neighbors we ought to be friends. That is the sole fault of Four Winds—there aren't quite enough neighbors. Otherwise it is perfection."

"You like it?"

"LIKE it! I love it. It is the most beautiful place I ever saw."

"I've never seen many places," said Leslie Moore, slowly, "but I've always thought it was very lovely here. I—I love it, too."

She spoke, as she looked, shyly, yet eagerly. Anne had an odd impression that this strange girl—the word "girl" would persist—could say a good deal if she chose.

"I often come to the shore," she added.

"So do I," said Anne. "It's a wonder we haven't met here before."

"Probably you come earlier in the evening than I do. It is generally late—almost dark—when I come. And I love to come just after a storm—like this. I don't like the sea so well when it's calm and quiet. I like the struggle—and the crash—and the noise."

"I love it in all its moods," declared Anne. "The sea at Four Winds is to me what Lover's Lane was at home. Tonight it seemed so free—so untamed—something broke loose in me, too, out of sympathy. That was why I danced along the shore in that wild way. I didn't suppose anybody was looking, of course. If Miss Cornelia Bryant had seen me she would have forboded a gloomy prospect for poor young Dr. Blythe."

"You know Miss Cornelia?" said Leslie, laughing. She had an exquisite laugh; it bubbled up suddenly and unexpectedly with something of the delicious quality of a baby's. Anne laughed, too.

"Oh, yes. She has been down to my house of dreams several times."

"Your house of dreams?"

"Oh, that's a dear, foolish little name Gilbert and I have for our home. We just call it that between ourselves. It slipped out before I thought."

"So Miss Russell's little white house is YOUR house of dreams," said Leslie wonderingly. "*I* had a house of dreams once—but it was a palace," she added, with a laugh, the sweetness of which was marred by a little note of derision.

"Oh, I once dreamed of a palace, too," said Anne. "I suppose all girls do. And then we settle down contentedly in eight-room houses that seem to fulfill all the desires of our hearts—because our prince is there. YOU should have had your palace really, though—you are so beautiful. You MUST let me say it—it has to be said—I'm nearly bursting with admiration. You are the loveliest thing I ever saw, Mrs. Moore."

"If we are to be friends you must call me Leslie," said the other with an odd passion.

"Of course I will. And MY friends call me Anne."

"I suppose I am beautiful," Leslie went on, looking stormily out to sea. "I hate my beauty. I wish I had always been as brown and plain as the brownest and plainest girl at the fishing village over there. Well, what do you think of Miss Cornelia?"

The abrupt change of subject shut the door on any further confidences.

"Miss Cornelia is a darling, isn't she?" said Anne. "Gilbert and I were invited to her house to a state tea last week. You've heard of groaning tables."

"I seem to recall seeing the expression in the newspaper reports of weddings," said Leslie, smiling.

"Well, Miss Cornelia's groaned—at least, it creaked—positively. You couldn't have believed she would have cooked so much for two ordinary people. She had every kind of pie you could name, I think—except lemon pie. She said she had taken the prize for lemon pies at the Charlottetown Exhibition ten years ago and had never made any since for fear of losing her reputation for them."

"Were you able to eat enough pie to please her?"

"*I* wasn't. Gilbert won her heart by eating—I won't tell you how much. She said she never knew a man who didn't like pie better than his Bible. Do you know, I love Miss Cornelia."

"So do I," said Leslie. "She is the best friend I have in the world."

Anne wondered secretly why, if this were so, Miss Cornelia had never mentioned Mrs. Dick Moore to her. Miss Cornelia had certainly talked freely about every other individual in or near Four Winds.

"Isn't that beautiful?" said Leslie, after a brief silence, pointing to the exquisite effect of a shaft of light falling through a cleft in the rock behind them, across a dark green pool at its base. "If I had come here—and seen nothing but just that—I would go home satisfied."

"The effects of light and shadow all along these shores are wonderful," agreed Anne. "My little sewing room looks out on the harbor, and I sit at its window and feast my eyes. The colors and shadows are never the same two minutes together."

"And you are never lonely?" asked Leslie abruptly. "Never—when you are alone?"

"No. I don't think I've ever been really lonely in my life," answered Anne. "Even when I'm alone I have real good company—dreams and imaginations and pretendings. I LIKE to be alone now and then, just to think over things and TASTE them. But I love friendship—and nice, jolly little times with people. Oh, WON'T you come to see me—often? Please do. I believe," Anne added, laughing, "that you'd like me if you knew me."

"I wonder if YOU would like ME," said Leslie seriously. She was not fishing for a compliment. She looked out across the waves that were beginning to be garlanded with blossoms of moonlit foam, and her eyes filled with shadows.

"I'm sure I would," said Anne. "And please don't think I'm utterly irresponsible because you saw me dancing on the shore at sunset. No doubt I shall be dignified after a time. You see, I haven't been married very long. I feel like a girl, and sometimes like a child, yet."

"I have been married twelve years," said Leslie.

Here was another unbelievable thing.

"Why, you can't be as old as I am!" exclaimed Anne. "You must have been a child when you were married."

"I was sixteen," said Leslie, rising, and picking up the cap and jacket lying beside her. "I am twenty-eight now. Well, I must go back."

"So must I. Gilbert will probably be home. But I'm so glad we both came to the shore tonight and met each other."

Leslie said nothing, and Anne was a little chilled. She had offered friendship frankly but it had not been accepted very graciously, if it had not been absolutely repelled. In silence they climbed the cliffs and walked across a pasture-field of which the feathery, bleached, wild grasses were like a carpet of creamy velvet in the moonlight. When they reached the shore lane Leslie turned.

"I go this way, Mrs. Blythe. You will come over and see me some time, won't you?"

Anne felt as if the invitation had been thrown at her. She got the impression that Leslie Moore gave it reluctantly.

"I will come if you really want me to," she said a little coldly.

"Oh, I do—I do," exclaimed Leslie, with an eagerness which seemed to burst forth and beat down some restraint that had been imposed on it.

"Then I'll come. Good-night—Leslie."

"Good-night, Mrs. Blythe."

Anne walked home in a brown study and poured out her tale to Gilbert.

"So Mrs. Dick Moore isn't one of the race that knows Joseph?" said Gilbert teasingly.

"No—o—o, not exactly. And yet—I think she WAS one of them once, but has gone or got into exile," said Anne musingly. "She is certainly very different from the other women about here. You can't talk about eggs and butter to HER. To think I've been imagining her a second Mrs. Rachel Lynde! Have you ever seen Dick Moore, Gilbert?"

"No. I've seen several men working about the fields of the farm, but I don't know which was Moore."

"She never mentioned him. I KNOW she isn't happy."

"From what you tell me I suppose she was married before she was old enough to know her own mind or heart, and found out too late that she had made a mistake. It's a common tragedy enough, Anne.

"A fine woman would have made the best of it. Mrs. Moore has evidently let it make her bitter and resentful."

"Don't let us judge her till we know," pleaded Anne. "I don't believe her case is so ordinary. You will understand her fascination when you meet her, Gilbert. It is a thing quite apart from her beauty. I feel that she possesses a rich nature, into which a friend might enter as into a kingdom; but for some reason she bars every one out and shuts all her possibilities up in herself, so that they cannot develop and blossom. There, I've been struggling to define her to myself ever since I left her, and that is the nearest I can get to it. I'm going to ask Miss Cornelia about her."

11. THE STORY OF LESLIE MOORE

"Yes, the eighth baby arrived a fortnight ago," said Miss Cornelia, from a rocker before the fire of the little house one chilly October afternoon. "It's a girl. Fred was ranting mad—said he wanted a boy—when the truth is he didn't want it at all. If it had been a boy he'd have ranted because it wasn't a girl. They had four girls and three boys before, so I can't see that it made much difference what this one was, but of course he'd have to be cantankerous, just like a man. The baby is real pretty, dressed up in its nice little clothes. It has black eyes and the dearest, tiny hands."

"I must go and see it. I just love babies," said Anne, smiling to herself over a thought too dear and sacred to be put into words.

"I don't say but what they're nice," admitted Miss Cornelia. "But some folks seem to have more than they really need, believe ME. My poor cousin Flora up at the Glen had eleven, and such a slave as she is! Her husband suicided three years ago. Just like a man!"

"What made him do that?" asked Anne, rather shocked.

"Couldn't get his way over something, so he jumped into the well. A good riddance! He was a born tyrant. But of course it spoiled the well. Flora could never abide the thought of using it again, poor thing! So she had another dug and a frightful expense it was, and the water as hard as nails. If he HAD to drown himself there was plenty of water in the harbor, wasn't there? I've no patience with a man like that. We've only had two suicides in Four Winds in my recollection. The other was Frank West—Leslie Moore's father. By the way, has Leslie ever been over to call on you yet?"

"No, but I met her on the shore a few nights ago and we scraped an acquaintance," said Anne, pricking up her ears.

Miss Cornelia nodded.

"I'm glad, dearie. I was hoping you'd foregather with her. What do you think of her?"

"I thought her very beautiful."

"Oh, of course. There was never anybody about Four Winds could touch her for looks. Did you ever see her hair? It reaches to her feet when she lets it down. But I meant how did you like her?"

"I think I could like her very much if she'd let me," said Anne slowly.

"But she wouldn't let you—she pushed you off and kept you at arm's length. Poor Leslie! You wouldn't be much surprised if you knew what her life has been. It's been a tragedy—a tragedy!" repeated Miss Cornelia emphatically.

"I wish you would tell me all about her—that is, if you can do so without betraying any confidence."

"Lord, dearie, everybody in Four Winds knows poor Leslie's story. It's no secret—the OUTSIDE, that is. Nobody knows the INSIDE but Leslie herself, and she doesn't take folks into her confidence. I'm about the best friend she has on earth, I reckon, and she's never uttered a word of complaint to me. Have you ever seen Dick Moore?"

"No."

"Well, I may as well begin at the beginning and tell you everything straight through, so you'll understand it. As I said, Leslie's father was Frank West. He was clever and shiftless—just like a man. Oh, he had heaps of brains—and much good they did him! He started to go to college, and he went for two years, and then his health broke down. The Wests were all inclined to be consumptive. So Frank came home and started farming. He married Rose Elliott from over harbor. Rose was reckoned the beauty of Four Winds—Leslie takes her looks from her mother, but she has ten times the spirit and go that Rose had, and a far better figure. Now you know, Anne, I always take the ground that us women ought to stand by each other. We've got enough to endure at the hands of the men, the Lord knows, so I hold we hadn't ought to clapper-claw one another, and it isn't often you'll find me running down another woman. But I never had much use for Rose Elliott. She was spoiled to begin with, believe ME, and she was nothing but a lazy, selfish, whining creature. Frank was no hand to work, so they were poor as Job's turkey. Poor! They lived on potatoes and point, believe ME. They had two children—Leslie and Kenneth. Leslie had her mother's looks and her father's brains, and something she didn't get from either of them. She took after her Grandmother West—a splendid old lady. She was the brightest, friendliest, merriest thing when she was a child, Anne. Everybody liked her. She was her father's favorite and she was awful fond of him. They were 'chums,' as she used to say. She couldn't see any of his faults—and he WAS a taking sort of man in some ways.

"Well, when Leslie was twelve years old, the first dreadful thing happened. She worshipped little Kenneth—he was four years younger than her, and he WAS a dear little chap. And he was killed one day—fell off a big load of hay just as it was going into the barn, and the wheel went right over his little body and crushed the life out of it. And mind you, Anne, Leslie saw it. She was looking down from the loft. She gave one screech—the hired man said he never heard such a sound in all his life—he said it would ring in his ears till Gabriel's trump drove it out. But she never screeched or cried again about it. She jumped from the loft onto the load and from the load to the floor, and caught up the little bleeding, warm, dead body, Anne—they had to tear it from her before she would let it go. They sent for me—I can't talk of it."

Miss Cornelia wiped the tears from her kindly brown eyes and sewed in bitter silence for a few minutes.

"Well," she resumed, "it was all over—they buried little Kenneth in that graveyard over the harbor, and after a while Leslie went back to her school and her studies. She never mentioned Kenneth's name—I've never heard it cross her lips from that day to this. I reckon that old hurt still aches and burns at times; but she was only a child and time is real kind to children, Anne, dearie. After a while she began to laugh again—she had the prettiest laugh. You don't often hear it now."

"I heard it once the other night," said Anne. "It IS a beautiful laugh."

"Frank West began to go down after Kenneth's death. He wasn't strong and it was a shock to him, because he was real fond of the child, though, as I've said, Leslie was his favorite. He got mopy and melancholy, and couldn't or wouldn't work. And one day, when Leslie was fourteen years of age, he hanged himself—and in the parlor, too, mind you, Anne, right in the middle of the parlor from the lamp hook in the ceiling. Wasn't that like a man? It was the anniversary of his wedding day, too. Nice, tasty time to pick for it, wasn't it? And, of course, that poor Leslie had to be the one to find him. She went into the parlor that morning, singing, with some fresh flowers for the vases, and there she saw her father hanging from the ceiling, his face as black as a coal. It was something awful, believe ME!"

"Oh, how horrible!" said Anne, shuddering. "The poor, poor child!"

"Leslie didn't cry at her father's funeral any more then she had cried at Kenneth's. Rose whooped and howled for two, however, and Leslie had all she could do trying to calm and comfort her mother. I was disgusted with Rose and so was everyone else, but Leslie never got out of patience. She loved her mother. Leslie is clannish—her own could never do wrong in her eyes. Well, they buried Frank West beside Kenneth, and Rose put up a great big monument to him. It was bigger than his character, believe ME! Anyhow, it was bigger than Rose could afford, for the farm was mortgaged for more than its value. But not long after Leslie's old grandmother West died and she left Leslie a little money—enough to give her a year at Queen's Academy. Leslie had made up her mind to pass for a teacher if she could, and then earn enough to put herself through Redmond College. That had been her father's pet scheme—he wanted her to have what he had lost. Leslie was full of ambition and her head was chock full of brains. She went to Queen's, and she took two years' work in one year and got her First; and when she came home she got the Glen school. She was so happy and hopeful and full of life and eagerness. When I think of what she was then and what she is now, I say—drat the men!"

Miss Cornelia snipped her thread off as viciously as if, Nero-like, she was severing the neck of mankind by the stroke.

"Dick Moore came into her life that summer. His father, Abner Moore, kept store at the Glen, but Dick had a sea-going streak in him from his mother; he used to sail in summer and clerk in his father's store in winter. He was a big, handsome fellow, with a little ugly soul. He was always wanting something till he got it, and then he stopped wanting it—just like a man. Oh, he didn't growl at the weather when it was fine, and he was mostly real pleasant and agreeable when everything went right. But he drank a good deal, and there were some nasty stories told of him and a girl down at the fishing village. He wasn't fit for Leslie to wipe her feet on, that's the long and short of it. And he was a Methodist! But he was clean mad about her—because of her good looks in the first place, and because she wouldn't have anything to say to him in the second. He vowed he'd have her—and he got her!"

"How did he bring it about?"

"Oh, it was an iniquitous thing! I'll never forgive Rose West. You see, dearie, Abner Moore held the mortgage on the West farm, and the interest was overdue some years, and Dick just went and told Mrs. West that if Leslie wouldn't marry him he'd get his father to foreclose the mortgage. Rose carried on terrible—fainted and wept, and pleaded with Leslie not to let her be turned out of her home. She said it would break her heart to leave the home she'd come to as a bride. I wouldn't have blamed her for feeling dreadful bad over it—but you wouldn't have thought she'd be so selfish as to sacrifice her own flesh and blood because of it, would you? Well, she was.

"And Leslie gave in—she loved her mother so much she would have done anything to save her pain. She married Dick Moore. None of us knew why at the time. It wasn't till long afterward that I found out how her mother had worried her into it. I was sure there was something wrong, though, because I knew how she had snubbed him time and again, and it wasn't like Leslie to turn face—about like that. Besides, I knew that Dick Moore wasn't the kind of man Leslie could ever fancy, in spite of his good looks and dashing ways. Of course, there was no wedding, but Rose asked me to go and see them married. I went, but I was sorry I did. I'd seen Leslie's face at her brother's funeral and at her father's funeral—and now it seemed to me I was seeing it at her own funeral. But Rose was smiling as a basket of chips, believe ME!

"Leslie and Dick settled down on the West place—Rose couldn't bear to part with her dear daughter!—and lived there for the winter. In the spring Rose took pneumonia and died—a year too late! Leslie was heart-broken enough over it. Isn't it terrible the way some unworthy folks are loved, while others that deserve it far more, you'd think, never get much affection? As for Dick, he'd had enough of quiet married life—just like a man. He was for up and off. He went over to Nova Scotia to visit his relations—his father had come from Nova Scotia—and he wrote back to Leslie that his cousin, George Moore, was going on a voyage to Havana and he was going too. The name of the vessel was the Four Sisters and they were to be gone about nine weeks.

"It must have been a relief to Leslie. But she never said anything. From the day of her marriage she was just what she is now—cold and proud, and keeping everyone but me at a distance. I won't BE kept at a distance, believe ME! I've just stuck to Leslie as close as I knew how in spite of everything."

"She told me you were the best friend she had," said Anne.

"Did she?" exclaimed Miss Cornelia delightedly. "Well, I'm real thankful to hear it. Sometimes I've wondered if she really did want me around at all—she never let me think so. You must have thawed her out more than you think, or she wouldn't have said that much itself to you. Oh, that poor, heart-broken girl! I never see Dick Moore but I want to run a knife clean through him."

Miss Cornelia wiped her eyes again and having relieved her feelings by her blood-thirsty wish, took up her tale.

"Well, Leslie was left over there alone. Dick had put in the crop before he went, and old Abner looked after it. The summer went by and the Four Sisters didn't come back. The Nova Scotia Moores investigated, and found she had got to Havana and discharged her cargo and took on another and left for home; and that was all they ever found out about her. By degrees people began to talk of Dick Moore as one that was dead. Almost everyone believed that he was, though no one felt certain, for men have turned up here at the harbor after they'd been gone for years. Leslie never thought he was dead—and she was right. A thousand pities too! The next summer Captain Jim was in Havana—that was before he gave up the sea, of course. He thought he'd poke round a bit—Captain Jim was always meddlesome, just like a man—and he went to inquiring round among the sailors' boarding houses and places like that, to see if he could find out anything about the crew of the Four Sisters. He'd better have let sleeping dogs lie, in my opinion! Well, he went to one out-of-the-way place, and there he found a man he knew at first sight it was Dick Moore, though he had a big beard. Captain Jim got it shaved off and then there was no doubt—Dick Moore it was—his body at least. His mind wasn't there—as for his soul, in my opinion he never had one!"

"What had happened to him?"

"Nobody knows the rights of it. All the folks who kept the boarding house could tell was that about a year before they had found him lying on their doorstep one morning in an awful condition—his head battered to a jelly almost. They supposed he'd got hurt in some drunken row, and likely that's the truth of it. They took him in, never thinking he could live. But he did—and he was just like a child when he got well. He hadn't memory or intellect or reason. They tried to find out who he was but they never could. He couldn't even tell them his name—he could only say a few simple words. He had a letter on him beginning 'Dear Dick' and signed 'Leslie,' but there was no address on it and the envelope was gone. They let him stay on—he learned to do a few odd jobs about the place—and there Captain Jim found him. He brought him home—I've always said it was a bad day's work, though I s'pose there was nothing else he could do. He thought maybe when Dick got home and saw his old surroundings and familiar faces his memory would wake up. But it hadn't any effect. There he's been at the house up the brook ever since. He's just like a child, no more nor less. Takes fractious spells occasionally, but mostly he's just vacant and good humored and harmless. He's apt to run away if he isn't watched. That's the burden Leslie has had to carry for eleven years—and all alone. Old Abner Moore died soon after Dick was brought home and it was found he was almost bankrupt. When things were settled up there was nothing for Leslie and Dick but the old West farm. Leslie rented it to John Ward, and the rent is all she has to live on. Sometimes in summer she takes a boarder to help out. But most visitors prefer the other side of the harbor where the hotels and summer cottages are. Leslie's house is too far from the bathing shore. She's taken care of Dick and she's never been away from him for eleven years—she's tied to that imbecile for life. And after all the dreams and hopes she once had! You can imagine what it has been like for her, Anne, dearie—with her beauty and spirit and pride and cleverness. It's just been a living death."

"Poor, poor girl!" said Anne again. Her own happiness seemed to reproach her. What right had she to be so happy when another human soul must be so miserable?

"Will you tell me just what Leslie said and how she acted the night you met her on the shore?" asked Miss Cornelia.

She listened intently and nodded her satisfaction.

"YOU thought she was stiff and cold, Anne, dearie, but I can tell you she thawed out wonderful for her. She must have taken to you real strong. I'm so glad. You may be able to help her a good deal. I was thankful when I heard that a young couple was coming to this house, for I hoped it would mean some friends for Leslie; especially if you belonged to the race that knows Joseph. You WILL be her friend, won't you, Anne, dearie?"

"Indeed I will, if she'll let me," said Anne, with all her own sweet, impulsive earnestness.

"No, you must be her friend, whether she'll let you or not," said Miss Cornelia resolutely. "Don't you mind if she's stiff by times—don't notice it. Remember what her life has been—and is—and must always be, I suppose, for creatures like Dick Moore live forever, I understand. You should see how fat he's got since he came home. He used to be lean enough. Just MAKE her be friends—you can do it—you're one of those who have the knack. Only you mustn't be sensitive. And don't mind if she doesn't seem to want you to go over there much. She knows that some women don't like to be where Dick is—they complain he gives them the creeps. Just get her to come over here as often as she can. She can't get away so very much—she can't leave Dick long, for the Lord knows what he'd do—burn the house down most likely. At nights, after he's in bed and asleep, is about the only time she's free. He always goes to bed early and sleeps like the dead till next morning. That is how you came to meet her at the shore likely. She wanders there considerable."

"I will do everything I can for her," said Anne. Her interest in Leslie Moore, which had been vivid ever since she had seen her driving her geese down the hill, was intensified a thousand fold by Miss Cornelia's narration. The girl's beauty and sorrow and loneliness drew her with an irresistible fascination. She had never known anyone like her; her friends had hitherto been wholesome, normal, merry girls like herself, with only the average trials of human care and bereavement to shadow their girlish dreams. Leslie Moore stood apart, a tragic, appealing figure of thwarted womanhood. Anne resolved that she would win entrance into the kingdom of that lonely soul and find there the comradeship it could so richly give, were it not for the cruel fetters that held it in a prison not of its own making.

"And mind you this, Anne, dearie," said Miss Cornelia, who had not yet wholly relieved her mind, "You mustn't think Leslie is an infidel because she hardly ever goes to church—or even that she's a Methodist. She can't take Dick to church, of course—not that he ever troubled church much in his best days. But you just remember that she's a real strong Presbyterian at heart, Anne, dearie."

12. LESLIE COMES OVER

Leslie came over to the house of dreams one frosty October night, when moonlit mists were hanging over the harbor and curling like silver ribbons along the seaward glens. She looked as if she repented coming when Gilbert answered her knock; but Anne flew past him, pounced on her, and drew her in.

"I'm so glad you picked tonight for a call," she said gaily. "I made up a lot of extra good fudge this afternoon and we want someone to help us eat it—before the fire—while we tell stories. Perhaps Captain Jim will drop in, too. This is his night."

"No. Captain Jim is over home," said Leslie. "He—he made me come here," she added, half defiantly.

"I'll say a thank-you to him for that when I see him," said Anne, pulling easy chairs before the fire.

"Oh, I don't mean that I didn't want to come," protested Leslie, flushing a little. "I—I've been thinking of coming—but it isn't always easy for me to get away."

"Of course it must be hard for you to leave Mr. Moore," said Anne, in a matter-of-fact tone. She had decided that it would be best to mention Dick Moore occasionally as an accepted fact, and not give undue morbidness to the subject by avoiding it. She was right, for Leslie's air of constraint suddenly vanished. Evidently she had been wondering how much Anne knew of the conditions of her life and was relieved that no explanations were needed. She allowed her cap and jacket to be taken, and sat down with a girlish snuggle in the big armchair by Magog. She was dressed prettily and carefully, with the customary touch of color in the scarlet geranium at her white throat. Her beautiful hair gleamed like molten gold in the warm firelight. Her sea-blue eyes were full of soft laughter and allurement. For the moment, under the influence of the little house of dreams, she was a girl again—a girl forgetful of the past and its bitterness. The atmosphere of the many loves that had sanctified the little house was all about her; the companionship of two healthy, happy, young folks of her own generation encircled her; she felt and yielded to the magic of her surroundings—Miss Cornelia and Captain Jim would scarcely have recognized her; Anne found it hard to believe that this was the cold, unresponsive woman she had met on the shore—this animated girl who talked and listened with the eagerness of a starved soul. And how hungrily Leslie's eyes looked at the bookcases between the windows!

"Our library isn't very extensive," said Anne, "but every book in it is a FRIEND. We've picked our books up through the years, here and there, never buying one until we had first read it and knew that it belonged to the race of Joseph."

Leslie laughed—beautiful laughter that seemed akin to all the mirth that had echoed through the little house in the vanished years.

"I have a few books of father's—not many," she said. "I've read them until I know them almost by heart. I don't get many books. There's a circulating library at the Glen store—but I don't think the committee who pick the books for Mr. Parker know what books are of Joseph's race—or perhaps they don't care. It was so seldom I got one I really liked that I gave up getting any."

"I hope you'll look on our bookshelves as your own," said Anne.

"You are entirely and wholeheartedly welcome to the loan of any book on them."

"You are setting a feast of fat things before me," said Leslie, joyously. Then, as the clock struck ten, she rose, half unwillingly.

"I must go. I didn't realise it was so late. Captain Jim is always saying it doesn't take long to stay an hour. But I've stayed two—and oh, but I've enjoyed them," she added frankly.

"Come often," said Anne and Gilbert. They had risen and stood together in the firelight's glow. Leslie looked at them—youthful, hopeful, happy, typifying all she had missed and must forever miss. The light went out of her face and eyes; the girl vanished; it was the sorrowful, cheated woman who answered the invitation almost coldly and got herself away with a pitiful haste.

Anne watched her until she was lost in the shadows of the chill and misty night. Then she turned slowly back to the glow of her own radiant hearthstone.

"Isn't she lovely, Gilbert? Her hair fascinates me. Miss Cornelia says it reaches to her feet. Ruby Gillis had beautiful hair—but Leslie's is ALIVE—every thread of it is living gold."

"She is very beautiful," agreed Gilbert, so heartily that Anne almost wished he were a LITTLE less enthusiastic.

"Gilbert, would you like my hair better if it were like Leslie's?" she asked wistfully.

"I wouldn't have your hair any color but just what it is for the world," said Gilbert, with one or two convincing accompaniments.

You wouldn't be ANNE if you had golden hair—or hair of any color but"—

"Red," said Anne, with gloomy satisfaction.

"Yes, red—to give warmth to that milk-white skin and those shining gray-green eyes of yours. Golden hair wouldn't suit you at all Queen Anne—MY Queen Anne—queen of my heart and life and home."

"Then you may admire Leslie's all you like," said Anne magnanimously.

13. A GHOSTLY EVENING

One evening, a week later, Anne decided to run over the fields to the house up the brook for an informal call. It was an evening of gray fog that had crept in from the gulf, swathed the harbor, filled the glens and valleys, and clung heavily to the autumnal meadows. Through it the sea sobbed and shuddered. Anne saw Four Winds in a new aspect, and found it weird and mysterious and fascinating; but it also gave her a little feeling of loneliness. Gilbert was away and would be away until the morrow, attending a medical pow-wow in Charlottetown. Anne longed for an hour of fellowship with some girl friend. Captain Jim and Miss Cornelia were "good fellows" each, in their own way; but youth yearned to youth.

"If only Diana or Phil or Pris or Stella could drop in for a chat," she said to herself, "how delightful it would be! This is such a GHOSTLY night. I'm sure all the ships that ever sailed out of Four Winds to their doom could be seen tonight sailing up the harbor with their drowned crews on their decks, if that shrouding fog could suddenly be drawn aside. I feel as if it concealed innumerable mysteries—as if I were surrounded by the wraiths of old generations of Four Winds people peering at me through that gray veil. If ever the dear dead ladies of this little house came back to revisit it they would come on just such a night as this. If I sit here any longer I'll see one of them there opposite me in Gilbert's chair. This place isn't exactly canny tonight. Even Gog and Magog have an air of pricking up their ears to hear the footsteps of unseen guests. I'll run over to see Leslie before I frighten myself with my own fancies, as I did long ago in the matter of the Haunted Wood. I'll leave my house of dreams to welcome back its old inhabitants. My fire will give them my good-will and greeting—they will be gone before I come back, and my house will be mine once more. Tonight I am sure it is keeping a tryst with the past."

Laughing a little over her fancy, yet with something of a creepy sensation in the region of her spine, Anne kissed her hand to Gog and Magog and slipped out into the fog, with some of the new magazines under her arm for Leslie.

"Leslie's wild for books and magazines," Miss Cornelia had told her, "and she hardly ever sees one. She can't afford to buy them or subscribe for them. She's really pitifully poor, Anne. I don't see how she makes out to live at all on the little rent the farm brings in. She never even hints a complaint on the score of poverty, but I know what it must be. She's been handicapped by it all her life. She didn't mind it when she was free and ambitious, but it must gall now, believe ME. I'm glad she seemed so bright and merry the evening she spent with you. Captain Jim told me he had fairly to put her cap and coat on and push her out of the door. Don't be too long going to see her either. If you are she'll think it's because you don't like the sight of Dick, and she'll crawl into her shell again. Dick's a great, big, harmless baby, but that silly grin and chuckle of his do get on some people's nerves. Thank goodness, I've no nerves myself. I like Dick Moore better now than I ever did when he was in his right senses—though the Lord knows that isn't saying much. I was down there one day in housecleaning time helping Leslie a bit, and I was frying doughnuts. Dick was hanging round to get one, as usual, and all at once he picked up a scalding hot one I'd just fished out and dropped it on the back of my neck when I was bending over. Then he laughed and laughed. Believe ME, Anne, it took all the grace of God in my heart to keep me from just whisking up that stew-pan of boiling fat and pouring it over his head."

Anne laughed over Miss Cornelia's wrath as she sped through the darkness. But laughter accorded ill with that night. She was sober enough when she reached the house among the willows. Everything was very silent. The front part of the house seemed dark and deserted, so Anne slipped round to the side door, which opened from the veranda into a little sitting room. There she halted noiselessly.

The door was open. Beyond, in the dimly lighted room, sat Leslie Moore, with her arms flung out on the table and her head bent upon them. She was weeping horribly—with low, fierce, choking sobs, as if some agony in her soul were trying to tear itself out. An old black dog was sitting by her, his nose resting on his lap, his big doggish eyes full of mute, imploring sympathy and devotion. Anne drew back in dismay. She felt that she could not intermeddle with this bitterness. Her heart ached with a sympathy she might not utter. To go in now would be to shut the door forever on any possible help or friendship. Some instinct warned Anne that the proud, bitter girl would never forgive the one who thus surprised her in her abandonment of despair.

Anne slipped noiselessly from the veranda and found her way across the yard. Beyond, she heard voices in the gloom and saw the dim glow of a light. At the gate she met two men—Captain Jim with a lantern, and another who she knew must be Dick Moore—a big man, badly gone to fat, with a broad, round, red face, and vacant eyes. Even in the dull light Anne got the impression that there was something unusual about his eyes.

"Is this you, Mistress Blythe?" said Captain Jim. "Now, now, you hadn't oughter be roaming about alone on a night like this. You could get lost in this fog easier than not. Jest you wait till I see Dick safe inside the door and I'll come back and light you over the fields. I ain't going to have Dr. Blythe coming home and finding that you walked clean over Cape Leforce in the fog. A woman did that once, forty years ago.

"So you've been over to see Leslie," he said, when he rejoined her.

"I didn't go in," said Anne, and told what she had seen. Captain Jim sighed.

"Poor, poor, little girl! She don't cry often, Mistress Blythe—she's too brave for that. She must feel terrible when she does cry. A night like this is hard on poor women who have sorrows. There's something about it that kinder brings up all we've suffered—or feared."

"It's full of ghosts," said Anne, with a shiver. "That was why I came over—I wanted to clasp a human hand and hear a human voice.

"There seem to be so many INHUMAN presences about tonight. Even my own dear house was full of them. They fairly elbowed me out. So I fled over here for companionship of my kind."

"You were right not to go in, though, Mistress Blythe. Leslie wouldn't have liked it. She wouldn't have liked me going in with Dick, as I'd have done if I hadn't met you. I had Dick down with me all day. I keep him with me as much as I can to help Leslie a bit."

"Isn't there something odd about his eyes?" asked Anne.

"You noticed that? Yes, one is blue and t'other is hazel—his father had the same. It's a Moore peculiarity. That was what told me he was Dick Moore when I saw him first down in Cuby. If it hadn't a-bin for his eyes I mightn't a-known him, with his beard and fat. You know, I reckon, that it was me found him and brought him home. Miss Cornelia always says I shouldn't have done it, but I can't agree with her. It was the RIGHT thing to do—and so 'twas the only thing. There ain't no question in my mind about THAT. But my old heart aches for Leslie. She's only twenty-eight and she's eaten more bread with sorrow than most women do in eighty years."

They walked on in silence for a little while. Presently Anne said, "Do you know, Captain Jim, I never like walking with a lantern. I have always the strangest feeling that just outside the circle of light, just over its edge in the darkness, I am surrounded by a ring of furtive, sinister things, watching me from the shadows with hostile eyes. I've had that feeling from childhood. What is the reason? I never feel like that when I'm really in the darkness—when it is close all around me—I'm not the least frightened."

"I've something of that feeling myself," admitted Captain Jim. "I reckon when the darkness is close to us it is a friend. But when we sorter push it away from us—divorce ourselves from it, so to speak, with lantern light—it becomes an enemy. But the fog is lifting.

"There's a smart west wind rising, if you notice. The stars will be out when you get home."

They were out; and when Anne re-entered her house of dreams the red embers were still glowing on the hearth, and all the haunting presences were gone.

14. NOVEMBER DAYS

The splendor of color which had glowed for weeks along the shores of Four Winds Harbor had faded out into the soft gray-blue of late autumnal hills. There came many days when fields and shores were dim with misty rain, or shivering before the breath of a melancholy sea-wind—nights, too, of storm and tempest, when Anne sometimes wakened to pray that no ship might be beating up the grim north shore, for if it were so not even the great, faithful light whirling through the darkness unafraid, could avail to guide it into safe haven.

"In November I sometimes feel as if spring could never come again," she sighed, grieving over the hopeless unsightliness of her frosted and bedraggled flower-plots. The gay little garden of the schoolmaster's bride was rather a forlorn place now, and the Lombardies and birches were under bare poles, as Captain Jim said. But the fir-wood behind the little house was forever green and staunch; and even in November and December there came gracious days of sunshine and purple hazes, when the harbor danced and sparkled as blithely as in midsummer, and the gulf was so softly blue and tender that the storm and the wild wind seemed only things of a long-past dream.

Anne and Gilbert spent many an autumn evening at the lighthouse. It was always a cheery place. Even when the east wind sang in minor and the sea was dead and gray, hints of sunshine seemed to be lurking all about it. Perhaps this was because the First Mate always paraded it in panoply of gold. He was so large and effulgent that one hardly missed the sun, and his resounding purrs formed a pleasant accompaniment to the laughter and conversation which went on around Captain Jim's fireplace. Captain Jim and Gilbert had many long discussions and high converse on matters beyond the ken of cat or king.

"I like to ponder on all kinds of problems, though I can't solve 'em," said Captain Jim. "My father held that we should never talk of things we couldn't understand, but if we didn't, doctor, the subjects for conversation would be mighty few. I reckon the gods laugh many a time to hear us, but what matters so long as we remember that we're only men and don't take to fancying that we're gods ourselves, really, knowing good and evil. I reckon our pow-wows won't do us or anyone much harm, so let's have another whack at the whence, why and whither this evening, doctor."

While they "whacked," Anne listened or dreamed. Sometimes Leslie went to the lighthouse with them, and she and Anne wandered along the shore in the eerie twilight, or sat on the rocks below the lighthouse until the darkness drove them back to the cheer of the driftwood fire. Then Captain Jim would brew them tea and tell them

"tales of land and sea
and whatsoever might betide
the great forgotten world outside."

Leslie seemed always to enjoy those lighthouse carousals very much, and bloomed out for the time being into ready wit and beautiful laughter, or glowing-eyed silence. There was a certain tang and savor in the conversation when Leslie was present which they missed when she was absent. Even when she did not talk she seemed to inspire others to brilliancy. Captain Jim told his stories better, Gilbert was quicker in argument and repartee, Anne felt little gushes and trickles of fancy and imagination bubbling to her lips under the influence of Leslie's personality.

"That girl was born to be a leader in social and intellectual circles, far away from Four Winds," she said to Gilbert as they walked home one night. "She's just wasted here—wasted."

"Weren't you listening to Captain Jim and yours truly the other night when we discussed that subject generally? We came to the comforting conclusion that the Creator probably knew how to run His universe quite as well as we do, and that, after all, there are no such things as 'wasted' lives, saving and except when an individual wilfully squanders and wastes his own life—which Leslie Moore certainly hasn't done. And some people might think that a Redmond B.A., whom editors were beginning to honor, was 'wasted' as the wife of a struggling country doctor in the rural community of Four Winds."

"Gilbert!"

"If you had married Roy Gardner, now," continued Gilbert mercilessly, "YOU could have been 'a leader in social and intellectual circles far away from Four Winds.'"

"Gilbert BLYTHE!"

"You KNOW you were in love with him at one time, Anne."

"Gilbert, that's mean—'pisen mean, just like all the men,' as Miss Cornelia says. I NEVER was in love with him. I only imagined I was. YOU know that. You KNOW I'd rather be your wife in our house of dreams and fulfillment than a queen in a palace."

Gilbert's answer was not in words; but I am afraid that both of them forgot poor Leslie speeding her lonely way across the fields to a house that was neither a palace nor the fulfillment of a dream.

The moon was rising over the sad, dark sea behind them and transfiguring it. Her light had not yet reached the harbor, the further side of which was shadowy and suggestive, with dim coves and rich glooms and jewelling lights.

"How the home lights shine out tonight through the dark!" said Anne. "That string of them over the harbor looks like a necklace. And what a coruscation there is up at the Glen! Oh, look, Gilbert; there is ours. I'm so glad we left it burning. I hate to come home to a dark house. OUR homelight, Gilbert! Isn't it lovely to see?"

"Just one of earth's many millions of homes, Anne—girl—but ours—OURS—our beacon in 'a naughty world.' When a fellow has a home and a dear, little, red-haired wife in it what more need he ask of life?"

"Well, he might ask ONE thing more," whispered Anne happily. "Oh, Gilbert, it seems as if I just COULDN'T wait for the spring."

15. CHRISTMAS AT FOUR WINDS

At first Anne and Gilbert talked of going home to Avonlea for Christmas; but eventually they decided to stay in Four Winds. "I want to spend the first Christmas of our life together in our own home," decreed Anne.

So it fell out that Marilla and Mrs. Rachel Lynde and the twins came to Four Winds for Christmas. Marilla had the face of a woman who had circumnavigated the globe. She had never been sixty miles away from home before; and she had never eaten a Christmas dinner anywhere save at Green Gables.

Mrs. Rachel had made and brought with her an enormous plum pudding. Nothing could have convinced Mrs. Rachel that a college graduate of the younger generation could make a Christmas plum pudding properly; but she bestowed approval on Anne's house.

"Anne's a good housekeeper," she said to Marilla in the spare room the night of their arrival. "I've looked into her bread box and her scrap pail. I always judge a housekeeper by those, that's what. There's nothing in the pail that shouldn't have been thrown away, and no stale pieces in the bread box. Of course, she was trained up with you—but, then, she went to college afterwards. I notice she's got my tobacco stripe quilt on the bed here, and that big round braided mat of yours before her living-room fire. It makes me feel right at home."

Anne's first Christmas in her own house was as delightful as she could have wished. The day was fine and bright; the first skim of snow had fallen on Christmas Eve and made the world beautiful; the harbor was still open and glittering.

Captain Jim and Miss Cornelia came to dinner. Leslie and Dick had been invited, but Leslie made excuse; they always went to her Uncle Isaac West's for Christmas, she said.

"She'd rather have it so," Miss Cornelia told Anne. "She can't bear taking Dick where there are strangers. Christmas is always a hard time for Leslie. She and her father used to make a lot of it."

Miss Cornelia and Mrs. Rachel did not take a very violent fancy to each other. "Two suns hold not their courses in one sphere." But they did not clash at all, for Mrs. Rachel was in the kitchen helping Anne and Marilla with the dinner, and it fell to Gilbert to entertain Captain Jim and Miss Cornelia,—or rather to be entertained by them, for a dialogue between those two old friends and antagonists was assuredly never dull.

"It's many a year since there was a Christmas dinner here, Mistress Blythe," said Captain Jim. "Miss Russell always went to her friends in town for Christmas. But I was here to the first Christmas dinner that was ever eaten in this house—and the schoolmaster's bride cooked it. That was sixty years ago today, Mistress Blythe—and a day very like this—just enough snow to make the hills white, and the harbor as blue as June. I was only a lad, and I'd never been invited out to dinner before, and I was too shy to eat enough. I've got all over THAT."

"Most men do," said Miss Cornelia, sewing furiously. Miss Cornelia was not going to sit with idle hands, even on Christmas.

Babies come without any consideration for holidays, and there was one expected in a poverty-stricken household at Glen St. Mary. Miss Cornelia had sent that household a substantial dinner for its little swarm, and so meant to eat her own with a comfortable conscience.

"Well, you know, the way to a man's heart is through his stomach, Cornelia," explained Captain Jim.

"I believe you—when he HAS a heart," retorted Miss Cornelia. "I suppose that's why so many women kill themselves cooking—just as poor Amelia Baxter did. She died last Christmas morning, and she said it was the first Christmas since she was married that she didn't have to cook a big, twenty-plate dinner. It must have been a real pleasant change for her. Well, she's been dead a year, so you'll soon hear of Horace Baxter taking notice."

"I heard he was taking notice already," said Captain Jim, winking at Gilbert. "Wasn't he up to your place one Sunday lately, with his funeral blacks on, and a boiled collar?"

"No, he wasn't. And he needn't come neither. I could have had him long ago when he was fresh. I don't want any second-hand goods, believe ME. As for Horace Baxter, he was in financial difficulties a year ago last summer, and he prayed to the Lord for help; and when his wife died and he got her life insurance he said he believed it was the answer to his prayer. Wasn't that like a man?"

"Have you really proof that he said that, Cornelia?"

"I have the Methodist minister's word for it—if you call THAT proof. Robert Baxter told me the same thing too, but I admit THAT isn't evidence. Robert Baxter isn't often known to tell the truth."

"Come, come, Cornelia, I think he generally tells the truth, but he changes his opinion so often it sometimes sounds as if he didn't."

"It sounds like it mighty often, believe ME. But trust one man to excuse another. I have no use for Robert Baxter. He turned Methodist just because the Presbyterian choir happened to be singing 'Behold the bridegroom cometh' for a collection piece when him and Margaret walked up the aisle the Sunday after they were married. Served him right for being late! He always insisted the choir did it on purpose to insult him, as if he was of that much importance. But that family always thought they were much bigger potatoes than they really were. His brother Eliphalet imagined the devil was always at his elbow—but *I* never believed the devil wasted that much time on him."

"I—don't—know," said Captain Jim thoughtfully. "Eliphalet Baxter lived too much alone—hadn't even a cat or dog to keep him human. When a man is alone he's mighty apt to be with the devil—if he ain't with God. He has to choose which company he'll keep, I reckon. If the devil always was at Life Baxter's elbow it must have been because Life liked to have him there."

"Man-like," said Miss Cornelia, and subsided into silence over a complicated arrangement of tucks until Captain Jim deliberately stirred her up again by remarking in a casual way:

"I was up to the Methodist church last Sunday morning."

"You'd better have been home reading your Bible," was Miss Cornelia's retort.

"Come, now, Cornelia, *I* can't see any harm in going to the Methodist church when there's no preaching in your own. I've been a Presbyterian for seventy-six years, and it isn't likely my theology will hoist anchor at this late day."

"It's setting a bad example," said Miss Cornelia grimly.

"Besides," continued wicked Captain Jim, "I wanted to hear some good singing. The Methodists have a good choir; and you can't deny, Cornelia, that the singing in our church is awful since the split in the choir."

"What if the singing isn't good? They're doing their best, and God sees no difference between the voice of a crow and the voice of a nightingale."

"Come, come, Cornelia," said Captain Jim mildly, "I've a better opinion of the Almighty's ear for music than THAT."

"What caused the trouble in our choir?" asked Gilbert, who was suffering from suppressed laughter.

"It dates back to the new church, three years ago," answered Captain Jim. "We had a fearful time over the building of that church—fell out over the question of a new site. The two sites wasn't more'n two hundred yards apart, but you'd have thought they was a thousand by the bitterness of that fight. We was split up into three factions—one wanted the east site and one the south, and one held to the old. It was fought out in bed and at board, and in church and at market. All the old scandals of three generations were dragged out of their graves and aired. Three matches was broken up by it. And the meetings we had to try to settle the question! Cornelia, will you ever forget the one when old Luther Burns got up and made a speech? HE stated his opinions forcibly."

"Call a spade a spade, Captain. You mean he got red-mad and raked them all, fore and aft. They deserved it too—a pack of incapables. But what would you expect of a committee of men? That building committee held twenty-seven meetings, and at the end of the twenty-seventh weren't no nearer having a church than when they begun—not so near, for a fact, for in one fit of hurrying things along they'd gone to work and tore the old church down, so there we were, without a church, and no place but the hall to worship in."

"The Methodists offered us their church, Cornelia."

"The Glen St. Mary church wouldn't have been built to this day," went on Miss Cornelia, ignoring Captain Jim, "if we women hadn't just started in and took charge. We said WE meant to have a church, if the men meant to quarrel till doomsday, and we were tired of being a laughing-stock for the Methodists. We held ONE meeting and elected a committee and canvassed for subscriptions. We got them, too. When any of the men tried to sass us we told them they'd tried for two years to build a church and it was our turn now. We shut them up close, believe ME, and in six months we had our church. Of course, when the men saw we were determined they stopped fighting and went to work, man-like, as soon as they saw they had to, or quit bossing. Oh, women can't preach or be elders; but they can build churches and scare up the money for them."

"The Methodists allow women to preach," said Captain Jim.

Miss Cornelia glared at him.

"I never said the Methodists hadn't common sense, Captain. What I say is, I doubt if they have much religion."

"I suppose you are in favor of votes for women, Miss Cornelia," said Gilbert.

"I'm not hankering after the vote, believe ME," said Miss Cornelia scornfully. "*I* know what it is to clean up after the men. But some of these days, when the men realize they've got the world into a mess they can't get it out of, they'll be glad to give us the vote, and shoulder their troubles over on us. That's THEIR scheme. Oh, it's well that women are patient, believe ME!"

"What about Job?" suggested Captain Jim.

"Job! It was such a rare thing to find a patient man that when one was really discovered they were determined he shouldn't be forgotten," retorted Miss Cornelia triumphantly. "Anyhow, the virtue doesn't go with the name. There never was such an impatient man born as old Job Taylor over harbor."

"Well, you know, he had a good deal to try him, Cornelia. Even you can't defend his wife. I always remember what old William MacAllister said of her at her funeral, 'There's nae doot she was a Chreestian wumman, but she had the de'il's own temper.'"

"I suppose she WAS trying," admitted Miss Cornelia reluctantly, "but that didn't justify what Job said when she died. He rode home from the graveyard the day of the funeral with my father. He never said a word till they got near home. Then he heaved a big sigh and said, 'You may not believe it, Stephen, but this is the happiest day of my life!' Wasn't that like a man?"

"I s'pose poor old Mrs. Job did make life kinder uneasy for him," reflected Captain Jim.

"Well, there's such a thing as decency, isn't there? Even if a man is rejoicing in his heart over his wife being dead, he needn't proclaim it to the four winds of heaven. And happy day or not, Job Taylor wasn't long in marrying again, you might notice. His second wife could manage him. She made him walk Spanish, believe me! The first thing she did was to make him hustle round and put up a tombstone to the first Mrs. Job—and she had a place left on it for her own name. She said there'd be nobody to make Job put up a monument to HER."

"Speaking of Taylors, how is Mrs. Lewis Taylor up at the Glen, doctor?" asked Captain Jim.

"She's getting better slowly—but she has to work too hard," replied Gilbert.

"Her husband works hard too—raising prize pigs," said Miss Cornelia. "He's noted for his beautiful pigs. He's a heap prouder of his pigs than of his children. But then, to be sure, his pigs are the best pigs possible, while his children don't amount to much. He picked a poor mother for them, and starved her while she was bearing and rearing them. His pigs got the cream and his children got the skim milk.

"There are times, Cornelia, when I have to agree with you, though it hurts me," said Captain Jim. "That's just exactly the truth about Lewis Taylor. When I see those poor, miserable children of his, robbed of all children ought to have, it p'isens my own bite and sup for days afterwards."

Gilbert went out to the kitchen in response to Anne's beckoning. Anne shut the door and gave him a connubial lecture.

"Gilbert, you and Captain Jim must stop baiting Miss Cornelia. Oh, I've been listening to you—and I just won't allow it."

'Anne, Miss Cornelia is enjoying herself hugely. You know she is.'

"Well, never mind. You two needn't egg her on like that. Dinner is ready now, and, Gilbert, DON'T let Mrs. Rachel carve the geese. I know she means to offer to do it because she doesn't think you can do it properly. Show her you can."

"I ought to be able to. I've been studying A-B-C-D diagrams of carving for the past month," said Gilbert. "Only don't talk to me while I'm doing it, Anne, for if you drive the letters out of my head I'll be in a worse predicament than you were in old geometry days when the teacher changed them."

Gilbert carved the geese beautifully. Even Mrs. Rachel had to admit that. And everybody ate of them and enjoyed them. Anne's first Christmas dinner was a great success and she beamed with housewifely pride. Merry was the feast and long; and when it was over they gathered around the cheer of the red hearth flame and Captain Jim told them stories until the red sun swung low over Four Winds Harbor, and the long blue shadows of the Lombardies fell across the snow in the lane.

"I must be getting back to the light," he said finally. "I'll jest have time to walk home before sundown. Thank you for a beautiful Christmas, Mistress Blythe. Bring Master Davy down to the light some night before he goes home.

"I want to see those stone gods," said Davy with a relish.

16. NEW YEAR'S EVE AT THE LIGHT

The Green Gables folk went home after Christmas, Marilla under solemn covenant to return for a month in the spring. More snow came before New Year's, and the harbor froze over, but the gulf still was free, beyond the white, imprisoned fields. The last day of the old year was one of those bright, cold, dazzling winter days, which bombard us with their brilliancy, and command our admiration but never our love. The sky was sharp and blue; the snow diamonds sparkled insistently; the stark trees were bare and shameless, with a kind of brazen beauty; the hills shot assaulting lances of crystal. Even the shadows were sharp and stiff and clear-cut, as no proper shadows should be. Everything that was handsome seemed ten times handsomer and less attractive in the glaring splendor; and everything that was ugly seemed ten times uglier, and everything was either handsome or ugly. There was no soft blending, or kind obscurity, or elusive mistiness in that searching glitter. The only things that held their own individuality were the firs—for the fir is the tree of mystery and shadow, and yields never to the encroachments of crude radiance.

But finally the day began to realise that she was growing old. Then a certain pensiveness fell over her beauty which dimmed yet intensified it; sharp angles, glittering points, melted away into curves and enticing gleams. The white harbor put on soft grays and pinks; the far-away hills turned amethyst.

"The old year is going away beautifully," said Anne.

She and Leslie and Gilbert were on their way to the Four Winds Point, having plotted with Captain Jim to watch the New Year in at the light. The sun had set and in the southwestern sky hung Venus, glorious and golden, having drawn as near to her earth-sister as is possible for her. For the first time Anne and Gilbert saw the shadow cast by that brilliant star of evening, that faint, mysterious shadow, never seen save when there is white snow to reveal it, and then only with averted vision, vanishing when you gaze at it directly.

"It's like the spirit of a shadow, isn't it?" whispered Anne. "You can see it so plainly haunting your side when you look ahead; but when you turn and look at it—it's gone."

"I have heard that you can see the shadow of Venus only once in a lifetime, and that within a year of seeing it your life's most wonderful gift will come to you," said Leslie. But she spoke rather hardly; perhaps she thought that even the shadow of Venus could bring her no gift of life. Anne smiled in the soft twilight; she felt quite sure what the mystic shadow promised her.

They found Marshall Elliott at the lighthouse. At first Anne felt inclined to resent the intrusion of this long-haired, long-bearded eccentric into the familiar little circle. But Marshall Elliott soon proved his legitimate claim to membership in the household of Joseph. He was a witty, intelligent, well-read man, rivalling Captain Jim himself in the knack of telling a good story. They were all glad when he agreed to watch the old year out with them.

Captain Jim's small nephew Joe had come down to spend New Year's with his great-uncle, and had fallen asleep on the sofa with the First Mate curled up in a huge golden ball at his feet.

"Ain't he a dear little man?" said Captain Jim gloatingly. "I do love to watch a little child asleep, Mistress Blythe. It's the most beautiful sight in the world, I reckon. Joe does love to get down here for a night, because I have him sleep with me. At home he has to sleep with the other two boys, and he doesn't like it. Why can't I sleep with father, Uncle Jim?" says he. 'Everybody in the Bible slept with their fathers.' As for the questions he asks, the minister himself couldn't answer them. They fair swamp me. 'Uncle Jim, if I wasn't ME who'd I be?' and, 'Uncle Jim, what would happen if God died?' He fired them two off at me tonight, afore he went to sleep. As for his imagination, it sails away from everything. He makes up the most remarkable yarns—and then his mother shuts him up in the closet for telling stories. And he sits down and makes up another one, and has it ready to relate to her when she lets him out. He had one for me when he come down tonight. 'Uncle Jim,' says he, solemn as a tombstone, 'I had a 'venture in the Glen today.' 'Yes, what was it?' says I, expecting something quite startling, but nowise prepared for what I really got. 'I met a wolf in the street,' says he, 'a 'normous wolf with a big, red mouf and AWFUL long teeth, Uncle Jim.' 'I didn't know there was any wolves up at the Glen,' says I. 'Oh, he comed there from far, far away,' says Joe, 'and I fought he was going to eat me up, Uncle Jim.' 'Were you scared?' says I. 'No, 'cause I had a big gun,' says Joe, 'and I shot the wolf dead, Uncle Jim,—solid dead—and then he went up to heaven and bit God,' says he. Well, I was fair staggered, Mistress Blythe."

The hours bloomed into mirth around the driftwood fire. Captain Jim told tales, and Marshall Elliott sang old Scotch ballads in a fine tenor voice; finally Captain Jim took down his old brown fiddle from the wall and began to play. He had a tolerable knack of fiddling, which all appreciated save the First Mate, who sprang from the sofa as if he had been shot, emitted a shriek of protest, and fled wildly up the stairs.

"Can't cultivate an ear for music in that cat nohow," said Captain Jim. "He won't stay long enough to learn to like it. When we got the organ up at the Glen church old Elder Richards bounced up from his seat the minute the organist began to play and scuttled down the aisle and out of the church at the rate of no-man's-business. It reminded me so strong of the First Mate tearing loose as soon as I begin to fiddle that I come nearer to laughing out loud in church than I ever did before or since."

There was something so infectious in the rollicking tunes which Captain Jim played that very soon Marshall Elliott's feet began to twitch. He had been a noted dancer in his youth. Presently he started up and held out his hands to Leslie. Instantly she responded. Round and round the firelit room they circled with a rhythmic grace that was wonderful. Leslie danced like one inspired; the wild, sweet abandon of the music seemed to have entered into and possessed her. Anne watched her in fascinated admiration. She had never seen her like this. All the innate richness and color and charm of her nature seemed to have broken loose and overflowed in crimson cheek and glowing eye and grace of motion. Even the aspect of Marshall Elliott, with his long beard and hair, could not spoil the picture. On the contrary, it seemed to enhance it. Marshall Elliott looked like a Viking of elder days, dancing with one of the blue-eyed, golden-haired daughters of the Northland.

"The purtiest dancing I ever saw, and I've seen some in my time," declared Captain Jim, when at last the bow fell from his tired hand. Leslie dropped into her chair, laughing, breathless.

"I love dancing," she said apart to Anne. "I haven't danced since I was sixteen—but I love it. The music seems to run through my veins like quicksilver and I forget everything—everything—except the delight of keeping time to it. There isn't any floor beneath me, or walls about me, or roof over me—I'm floating amid the stars."

Captain Jim hung his fiddle up in its place, beside a large frame enclosing several banknotes.

"Is there anybody else of your acquaintance who can afford to hang his walls with banknotes for pictures?" he asked. "There's twenty ten-dollar notes there, not worth the glass over them. They're old Bank of P. E. Island notes. Had them by me when the bank failed, and I had 'em framed and hung up, partly as a reminder not to put your trust in banks, and partly to give me a real luxurious, millionairy feeling. Hullo, Matey, don't be scared. You can come back now. The music and revelry is over for tonight. The old year has just another hour to stay with us. I've seen seventy-six New Years come in over that gulf yonder, Mistress Blythe."

"You'll see a hundred," said Marshall Elliott.

Captain Jim shook his head.

"No; and I don't want to—at least, I think I don't. Death grows friendlier as we grow older. Not that one of us really wants to die though, Marshall. Tennyson spoke truth when he said that. There's old Mrs. Wallace up at the Glen. She's had heaps of trouble all her life, poor soul, and she's lost almost everyone she cared about. She's always saying that she'll be glad when her time comes, and she doesn't want to sojourn any longer in this vale of tears. But when she takes a sick spell there's a fuss! Doctors from town, and a trained nurse, and enough medicine to kill a dog. Life may be a vale of tears, all right, but there are some folks who enjoy weeping, I reckon."

They spent the old year's last hour quietly around the fire. A few minutes before twelve Captain Jim rose and opened the door.

"We must let the New Year in," he said.

Outside was a fine blue night. A sparkling ribbon of moonlight garlanded the gulf. Inside the bar the harbor shone like a pavement of pearl. They stood before the door and waited—Captain Jim with his ripe, full experience, Marshall Elliott in his vigorous but empty middle life, Gilbert and Anne with their precious memories and exquisite hopes, Leslie with her record of starved years and her hopeless future. The clock on the little shelf above the fireplace struck twelve.

"Welcome, New Year," said Captain Jim, bowing low as the last stroke died away. "I wish you all the best year of your lives, mates. I reckon that whatever the New Year brings us will be the best the Great Captain has for us—and somehow or other we'll all make port in a good harbor."

17. A FOUR WINDS WINTER

Winter set in vigorously after New Year's. Big, white drifts heaped themselves about the little house, and palms of frost covered its windows. The harbor ice grew harder and thicker, until the Four Winds people began their usual winter travelling over it. The safe ways were "bushed" by a benevolent Government, and night and day the gay tinkle of the sleigh-bells sounded on it. On moonlit nights Anne heard them in her house of dreams like fairy chimes. The gulf froze over, and the Four Winds light flashed no more. During the months when navigation was closed Captain Jim's office was a sinecure.

"The First Mate and I will have nothing to do till spring except keep warm and amuse ourselves. The last lighthouse keeper used always to move up to the Glen in winter; but I'd rather stay at the Point. The First Mate might get poisoned or chewed up by dogs at the Glen. It's a mite lonely, to be sure, with neither the light nor the water for company, but if our friends come to see us often we'll weather it through."

Captain Jim had an ice boat, and many a wild, glorious spin Gilbert and Anne and Leslie had over the glib harbor ice with him. Anne and Leslie took long snowshoe tramps together, too, over the fields, or across the harbor after storms, or through the woods beyond the Glen. They were very good comrades in their rambles and their fireside communings. Each had something to give the other—each felt life the richer for friendly exchange of thought and friendly silence; each looked across the white fields between their homes with a pleasant consciousness of a friend beyond. But, in spite of all this, Anne felt that there was always a barrier between Leslie and herself—a constraint that never wholly vanished.

"I don't know why I can't get closer to her," Anne said one evening to Captain Jim. "I like her so much—I admire her so much—I WANT to take her right into my heart and creep right into hers. But I can never cross the barrier."

"You've been too happy all your life, Mistress Blythe," said Captain Jim thoughtfully. "I reckon that's why you and Leslie can't get real close together in your souls. The barrier between you is her experience of sorrow and trouble. She ain't responsible for it and you ain't; but it's there and neither of you can cross it."

"My childhood wasn't very happy before I came to Green Gables," said Anne, gazing soberly out of the window at the still, sad, dead beauty of the leafless tree-shadows on the moonlit snow.

"Mebbe not—but it was just the usual unhappiness of a child who hasn't anyone to look after it properly. There hasn't been any TRAGEDY in your life, Mistress Blythe. And poor Leslie's has been almost ALL tragedy. She feels, I reckon, though mebbe she hardly knows she feels it, that there's a vast deal in her life you can't enter nor understand—and so she has to keep you back from it—hold you off, so to speak, from hurting her. You know if we've got anything about us that hurts we shrink from anyone's touch on or near it. It holds good with our souls as well as our bodies, I reckon. Leslie's soul must be near raw—it's no wonder she hides it away."

"If that were really all, I wouldn't mind, Captain Jim. I would understand. But there are times—not always, but now and again—when I almost have to believe that Leslie doesn't—doesn't like me. Sometimes I surprise a look in her eyes that seems to show resentment and dislike—it goes so quickly—but I've seen it, I'm sure of that. And it hurts me, Captain Jim. I'm not used to being disliked—and I've tried so hard to win Leslie's friendship."

"You have won it, Mistress Blythe. Don't you go cherishing any foolish notion that Leslie don't like you. If she didn't she wouldn't have anything to do with you, much less chumming with you as she does. I know Leslie Moore too well not to be sure of that."

"The first time I ever saw her, driving her geese down the hill on the day I came to Four Winds, she looked at me with the same expression," persisted Anne. "I felt it, even in the midst of my admiration of her beauty. She looked at me resentfully—she did, indeed, Captain Jim."

"The resentment must have been about something else, Mistress Blythe, and you jest come in for a share of it because you happened past. Leslie DOES take sullen spells now and again, poor girl. I can't blame her, when I know what she has to put up with. I don't know why it's permitted. The doctor and I have talked a lot abut the origin of evil, but we haven't quite found out all about it yet. There's a vast of onunderstandable things in life, ain't there, Mistress Blythe? Sometimes things seem to work out real proper-like, same as with you and the doctor. And then again they all seem to go catawampus. There's Leslie, so clever and beautiful you'd think she was meant for a queen, and instead she's cooped up over there, robbed of almost everything a woman'd value, with no prospect except waiting on Dick Moore all her life. Though, mind you, Mistress Blythe, I daresay she'd choose her life now, such as it is, rather than the life she lived with Dick before he went away. THAT'S something a clumsy old sailor's tongue mustn't meddle with. But you've helped Leslie a lot—she's a different creature since you come to Four Winds. Us old friends see the difference in her, as you can't. Miss Cornelia and me was talking it over the other day, and it's one of the mighty few p'ints that we see eye to eye on. So jest you throw overboard any idea of her not liking you."

Anne could hardly discard it completely, for there were undoubtedly times when she felt, with an instinct that was not to be combated by reason, that Leslie harbored a queer, indefinable resentment towards her. At times, this secret consciousness marred the delight of their comradeship; at others it was almost forgotten; but Anne always felt the hidden thorn was there, and might prick her at any moment. She felt a cruel sting from it on the day when she told Leslie of what she hoped the spring would bring to the little house of dreams. Leslie looked at her with hard, bitter, unfriendly eyes.

"So you are to have THAT, too," she said in a choked voice. And without another word she had turned and gone across the fields homeward. Anne was deeply hurt; for the moment she felt as if she could never like Leslie again. But when Leslie came over a few evenings later she was so pleasant, so friendly, so frank, and witty, and winsome, that Anne was charmed into forgiveness and forgetfulness. Only, she never mentioned her darling hope to Leslie again; nor did Leslie ever refer to it. But one evening, when late winter was listening for the word of spring, she came over to the little house for a twilight chat; and when she went away she left a small, white box on the table. Anne found it after she was gone and opened it wonderingly. In it was a tiny white dress of exquisite workmanship—delicate embroidery, wonderful tucking, sheer loveliness. Every stitch in it was handwork; and the little frills of lace at neck and sleeves were of real Valenciennes. Lying on it was a card—"with Leslie's love."

"What hours of work she must have put on it," said Anne. "And the material must have cost more than she could really afford. It is very sweet of her."

But Leslie was brusque and curt when Anne thanked her, and again the latter felt thrown back upon herself.

Leslie's gift was not alone in the little house. Miss Cornelia had, for the time being, given up sewing for unwanted, unwelcome eighth babies, and fallen to sewing for a very much wanted first one, whose welcome would leave nothing to be desired. Philippa Blake and Diana Wright each sent a marvellous garment; and Mrs. Rachel Lynde sent several, in which good material and honest stitches took the place of embroidery and frills. Anne herself made many, desecrated by no touch of machinery, spending over them the happiest hours of the happy winter.

Captain Jim was the most frequent guest of the little house, and none was more welcome.

Every day Anne loved the simple-souled, true-hearted old sailor more and more. He was as refreshing as a sea breeze, as interesting as some ancient chronicle. She was never tired of listening to his stories, and his quaint remarks and comments were a continual delight to her. Captain Jim was one of those rare and interesting people who "never speak but they say something." The milk of human kindness and the wisdom of the serpent were mingled in his composition in delightful proportions.

Nothing ever seemed to put Captain Jim out or depress him in any way.

"I've kind of contracted a habit of enj'ying things," he remarked once, when Anne had commented on his invariable cheerfulness. "It's got so chronic that I believe I even enj'y the disagreeable things. It's great fun thinking they can't last. 'Old rheumatiz,' says I, when it grips me hard, 'you've GOT to stop aching sometime. The worse you are the sooner you'll stop, mebbe. I'm bound to get the better of you in the long run, whether in the body or out of the body.'"

One night, by the fireside at the light Anne saw Captain Jim's "life-book." He needed no coaxing to show it and proudly gave it to her to read.

"I writ it to leave to little Joe," he said. "I don't like the idea of everything I've done and seen being clean forgot after I've shipped for my last v'yage. Joe, he'll remember it, and tell the yarns to his children."

It was an old leather-bound book filled with the record of his voyages and adventures. Anne thought what a treasure trove it would be to a writer. Every sentence was a nugget. In itself the book had no literary merit; Captain Jim's charm of storytelling failed him when he came to pen and ink; he could only jot roughly down the outline of his famous tales, and both spelling and grammar were sadly askew. But Anne felt that if anyone possessed of the gift could take that simple record of a brave, adventurous life, reading between the bald lines the tales of dangers staunchly faced and duty manfully done, a wonderful story might be made from it. Rich comedy and thrilling tragedy were both lying hidden in Captain Jim's "life-book," waiting for the touch of the master hand to waken the laughter and grief and horror of thousands.

Anne said something of this to Gilbert as they walked home.

"Why don't you try your hand at it yourself, Anne?"

Anne shook her head.

"No. I only wish I could. But it's not in the power of my gift. You know what my forte is, Gilbert—the fanciful, the fairylike, the pretty. To write Captain Jim's life-book as it should be written one should be a master of vigorous yet subtle style, a keen psychologist, a born humorist and a born tragedian. A rare combination of gifts is needed. Paul might do it if he were older. Anyhow, I'm going to ask him to come down next summer and meet Captain Jim."

"Come to this shore," wrote Anne to Paul. "I am afraid you cannot find here Nora or the Golden Lady or the Twin Sailors; but you will find one old sailor who can tell you wonderful stories."

Paul, however wrote back, saying regretfully that he could not come that year. He was going abroad for two year's study.

"When I return I'll come to Four Winds, dear Teacher," he wrote.

"But meanwhile, Captain Jim is growing old," said Anne, sorrowfully, "and there is nobody to write his life-book."

18. SPRING DAYS

The ice in the harbor grew black and rotten in the March suns; in April there were blue waters and a windy, white-capped gulf again; and again the Four Winds light begemmed the twilights.

"I'm so glad to see it once more," said Anne, on the first evening of its reappearance. "I've missed it so all winter. The northwestern sky has seemed blank and lonely without it."

The land was tender with brand-new, golden-green, baby leaves. There was an emerald mist on the woods beyond the Glen. The seaward valleys were full of fairy mists at dawn.

Vibrant winds came and went with salt foam in their breath. The sea laughed and flashed and preened and allured, like a beautiful, coquettish woman. The herring schooled and the fishing village woke to life. The harbor was alive with white sails making for the channel. The ships began to sail outward and inward again.

"On a spring day like this," said Anne, "I know exactly what my soul will feel like on the resurrection morning."

"There are times in spring when I sorter feel that I might have been a poet if I'd been caught young," remarked Captain Jim. "I catch myself conning over old lines and verses I heard the schoolmaster reciting sixty years ago. They don't trouble me at other times. Now I feel as if I had to get out on the rocks or the fields or the water and spout them."

Captain Jim had come up that afternoon to bring Anne a load of shells for her garden, and a little bunch of sweet-grass which he had found in a ramble over the sand dunes.

"It's getting real scarce along this shore now," he said. "When I was a boy there was a-plenty of it. But now it's only once in a while you'll find a plot—and never when you're looking for it. You jest have to stumble on it—you're walking along on the sand hills, never thinking of sweet-grass—and all at once the air is full of sweetness—and there's the grass under your feet. I favor the smell of sweet-grass. It always makes me think of my mother."

"She was fond of it?" asked Anne.

"Not that I knows on. Dunno's she ever saw any sweet-grass. No, it's because it has a kind of motherly perfume—not too young, you understand—something kind of seasoned and wholesome and dependable—jest like a mother. The schoolmaster's bride always kept it among her handkerchiefs. You might put that little bunch among yours, Mistress Blythe. I don't like these boughten scents—but a whiff of sweet-grass belongs anywhere a lady does."

Anne had not been especially enthusiastic over the idea of surrounding her flower beds with quahog shells; as a decoration they did not appeal to her on first thought. But she would not have hurt Captain Jim's feelings for anything; so she assumed a virtue she did not at first feel, and thanked him heartily. And when Captain Jim had proudly encircled every bed with a rim of the big, milk-white shells, Anne found to her surprise that she liked the effect. On a town lawn, or even up at the Glen, they would not have been in keeping, but here, in the old-fashioned, sea-bound garden of the little house of dreams, they BELONGED.

"They DO look nice," she said sincerely.

"The schoolmaster's bride always had cowhawks round her beds," said Captain Jim. "She was a master hand with flowers. She LOOKED at 'em—and touched 'em—SO—and they grew like mad. Some folks have that knack—I reckon you have it, too, Mistress Blythe."

"Oh, I don't know—but I love my garden, and I love working in it. To potter with green, growing things, watching each day to see the dear, new sprouts come up, is like taking a hand in creation, I think. Just now my garden is like faith—the substance of things hoped for. But bide a wee."

"It always amazes me to look at the little, wrinkled brown seeds and think of the rainbows in 'em," said Captain Jim. "When I ponder on them seeds I don't find it nowise hard to believe that we've got souls that'll live in other worlds. You couldn't hardly believe there was life in them tiny things, some no bigger than grains of dust, let alone color and scent, if you hadn't seen the miracle, could you?"

Anne, who was counting her days like silver beads on a rosary, could not now take the long walk to the lighthouse or up the Glen road. But Miss Cornelia and Captain Jim came very often to the little house. Miss Cornelia was the joy of Anne's and Gilbert's existence. They laughed side-splittingly over her speeches after every visit. When Captain Jim and she happened to visit the little house at the same time there was much sport for the listening. They waged wordy warfare, she attacking, he defending. Anne once reproached the Captain for his baiting of Miss Cornelia.

"Oh, I do love to set her going, Mistress Blythe," chuckled the unrepentant sinner. "It's the greatest amusement I have in life. That tongue of hers would blister a stone. And you and that young dog of a doctor enj'y listening to her as much as I do."

Captain Jim came along another evening to bring Anne some mayflowers. The garden was full of the moist, scented air of a maritime spring evening. There was a milk-white mist on the edge of the sea, with a young moon kissing it, and a silver gladness of stars over the Glen. The bell of the church across the harbor was ringing dreamily sweet. The mellow chime drifted through the dusk to mingle with the soft spring-moan of the sea. Captain Jim's mayflowers added the last completing touch to the charm of the night.

"I haven't seen any this spring, and I've missed them," said Anne, burying her face in them.

"They ain't to be found around Four Winds, only in the barrens away behind the Glen up yander. I took a little trip today to the Land-of-nothing-to-do, and hunted these up for you. I reckon they're the last you'll see this spring, for they're nearly done."

"How kind and thoughtful you are, Captain Jim. Nobody else—not even Gilbert"—with a shake of her head at him—"remembered that I always long for mayflowers in spring."

"Well, I had another errand, too—I wanted to take Mr. Howard back yander a mess of trout. He likes one occasional, and it's all I can do for a kindness he did me once. I stayed all the afternoon and talked to him. He likes to talk to me, though he's a highly eddicated man and I'm only an ignorant old sailor, because he's one of the folks that's GOT to talk or they're miserable, and he finds listeners scarce around here. The Glen folks fight shy of him because they think he's an infidel. He ain't that far gone exactly—few men is, I reckon—but he's what you might call a heretic. Heretics are wicked, but they're mighty int'resting. It's jest that they've got sorter lost looking for God, being under the impression that He's hard to find—which He ain't never. Most of 'em blunder to Him after awhile, I guess. I don't think listening to Mr. Howard's arguments is likely to do me much harm. Mind you, I believe what I was brought up to believe. It saves a vast of bother—and back of it all, God is good. The trouble with Mr. Howard is that he's a leetle TOO clever. He thinks that he's bound to live up to his cleverness, and that it's smarter to thrash out some new way of getting to heaven than to go by the old track the common, ignorant folks is travelling. But he'll get there sometime all right, and then he'll laugh at himself."

"Mr. Howard was a Methodist to begin with," said Miss Cornelia, as if she thought he had not far to go from that to heresy.

"Do you know, Cornelia," said Captain Jim gravely, "I've often thought that if I wasn't a Presbyterian I'd be a Methodist."

"Oh, well," conceded Miss Cornelia, "if you weren't a Presbyterian it wouldn't matter much what you were. Speaking of heresy, reminds me, doctor—I've brought back that book you lent me—that Natural Law in the Spiritual World—I didn't read more'n a third of it. I can read sense, and I can read nonsense, but that book is neither the one nor the other."

"It IS considered rather heretical in some quarters," admitted Gilbert, "but I told you that before you took it, Miss Cornelia."

"Oh, I wouldn't have minded its being heretical. I can stand wickedness, but I can't stand foolishness," said Miss Cornelia calmly, and with the air of having said the last thing there was to say about Natural Law.

"Speaking of books, A Mad Love come to an end at last two weeks ago," remarked Captain Jim musingly. "It run to one hundred and three chapters. When they got married the book stopped right off, so I reckon their troubles were all over. It's real nice that that's the way in books anyhow, isn't it, even if 'tistn't so anywhere else?"

"I never read novels," said Miss Cornelia. "Did you hear how Geordie Russell was today, Captain Jim?"

"Yes, I called in on my way home to see him. He's getting round all right—but stewing in a broth of trouble, as usual, poor man.

"'Course he brews up most of it for himself, but I reckon that don't make it any easier to bear."

"He's an awful pessimist," said Miss Cornelia.

"Well, no, he ain't a pessimist exactly, Cornelia. He only jest never finds anything that suits him."

"And isn't that a pessimist?"

"No, no. A pessimist is one who never expects to find anything to suit him. Geordie hain't got THAT far yet."

"You'd find something good to say of the devil himself, Jim Boyd."

"Well, you've heard the story of the old lady who said he was persevering. But no, Cornelia, I've nothing good to say of the devil."

"Do you believe in him at all?" asked Miss Cornelia seriously.

"How can you ask that when you know what a good Presbyterian I am, Cornelia? How could a Presbyterian get along without a devil?"

"DO you?" persisted Miss Cornelia.

Captain Jim suddenly became grave.

"I believe in what I heard a minister once call 'a mighty and malignant and INTELLIGENT power of evil working in the universe,'" he said solemnly. "I do THAT, Cornelia. You can call it the devil, or the 'principle of evil,' or the Old Scratch, or any name you like. It's THERE, and all the infidels and heretics in the world can't argue it away, any more'n they can argue God away. It's there, and it's working. But, mind you, Cornelia, I believe it's going to get the worst of it in the long run."

"I am sure I hope so," said Miss Cornelia, none too hopefully. "But speaking of the devil, I am positive that Billy Booth is possessed by him now. Have you heard of Billy's latest performance?"

"No, what was that?"

"He's gone and burned up his wife's new, brown broadcloth suit, that she paid twenty-five dollars for in Charlottetown, because he declares the men looked too admiring at her when she wore it to church the first time. Wasn't that like a man?"

"Mistress Booth IS mighty pretty, and brown's her color," said Captain Jim reflectively.

"Is that any good reason why he should poke her new suit into the kitchen stove? Billy Booth is a jealous fool, and he makes his wife's life miserable. She's cried all the week about her suit. Oh, Anne, I wish I could write like you, believe ME. Wouldn't I score some of the men round here!"

"Those Booths are all a mite queer," said Captain Jim. "Billy seemed the sanest of the lot till he got married and then this queer jealous streak cropped out in him. His brother Daniel, now, was always odd."

"Took tantrums every few days or so and wouldn't get out of bed," said Miss Cornelia with a relish. "His wife would have to do all the barn work till he got over his spell. When he died people wrote her letters of condolence; if I'd written anything it would have been one of congratulation. Their father, old Abram Booth, was a disgusting old sot. He was drunk at his wife's funeral, and kept reeling round and hiccuping 'I didn't dri—i—i—nk much but I feel a—a—awfully que—e—e—r.' I gave him a good jab in the back with my umbrella when he came near me, and it sobered him up until they got the casket out of the house. Young Johnny Booth was to have been married yesterday, but he couldn't be because he's gone and got the mumps. Wasn't that like a man?"

"How could he help getting the mumps, poor fellow?"

"I'd poor fellow him, believe ME, if I was Kate Sterns. I don't know how he could help getting the mumps, but I DO know the wedding supper was all prepared and everything will be spoiled before he's well again. Such a waste! He should have had the mumps when he was a boy."

"Come, come, Cornelia, don't you think you're a mite unreasonable?"

Miss Cornelia disdained to reply and turned instead to Susan Baker, a grim-faced, kind-hearted elderly spinster of the Glen, who had been installed as maid-of-all-work at the little house for some weeks. Susan had been up to the Glen to make a sick call, and had just returned.

"How is poor old Aunt Mandy tonight?" asked Miss Cornelia.

Susan sighed.

"Very poorly—very poorly, Cornelia. I am afraid she will soon be in heaven, poor thing!"

"Oh, surely, it's not so bad as that!" exclaimed Miss Cornelia, sympathetically.

Captain Jim and Gilbert looked at each other. Then they suddenly rose and went out.

"There are times," said Captain Jim, between spasms, "when it would be a sin NOT to laugh. Them two excellent women!"

19. DAWN AND DUSK

In early June, when the sand hills were a great glory of pink wild roses, and the Glen was smothered in apple blossoms, Marilla arrived at the little house, accompanied by a black horsehair trunk, patterned with brass nails, which had reposed undisturbed in the Green Gables garret for half a century. Susan Baker, who, during her few weeks' sojourn in the little house, had come to worship "young Mrs. Doctor," as she called Anne, with blind fervor, looked rather jealously askance at Marilla at first. But as Marilla did not try to interfere in kitchen matters, and showed no desire to interrupt Susan's ministrations to young Mrs. Doctor, the good handmaiden became reconciled to her presence, and told her cronies at the Glen that Miss Cuthbert was a fine old lady and knew her place.

One evening, when the sky's limpid bowl was filled with a red glory, and the robins were thrilling the golden twilight with jubilant hymns to the stars of evening, there was a sudden commotion in the little house of dreams. Telephone messages were sent up to the Glen, Doctor Dave and a white-capped nurse came hastily down, Marilla paced the garden walks between the quahog shells, murmuring prayers between her set lips, and Susan sat in the kitchen with cotton wool in her ears and her apron over her head.

Leslie, looking out from the house up the brook, saw that every window of the little house was alight, and did not sleep that night.

The June night was short; but it seemed an eternity to those who waited and watched.

"Oh, will it NEVER end?" said Marilla; then she saw how grave the nurse and Doctor Dave looked, and she dared ask no more questions. Suppose Anne—but Marilla could not suppose it.

"Do not tell me," said Susan fiercely, answering the anguish in Marilla's eyes, "that God could be so cruel as to take that darling lamb from us when we all love her so much."

"He has taken others as well beloved," said Marilla hoarsely.

But at dawn, when the rising sun rent apart the mists hanging over the sandbar, and made rainbows of them, joy came to the little house. Anne was safe, and a wee, white lady, with her mother's big eyes, was lying beside her. Gilbert, his face gray and haggard from his night's agony, came down to tell Marilla and Susan.

"Thank God," shuddered Marilla.

Susan got up and took the cotton wool out of her ears.

"Now for breakfast," she said briskly. "I am of the opinion that we will all be glad of a bite and sup. You tell young Mrs. Doctor not to worry about a single thing—Susan is at the helm. You tell her just to think of her baby."

Gilbert smiled rather sadly as he went away. Anne, her pale face blanched with its baptism of pain, her eyes aglow with the holy passion of motherhood, did not need to be told to think of her baby. She thought of nothing else. For a few hours she tasted of happiness so rare and exquisite that she wondered if the angels in heaven did not envy her.

"Little Joyce," she murmured, when Marilla came in to see the baby. "We planned to call her that if she were a girlie. There were so many we would have liked to name her for; we couldn't choose between them, so we decided on Joyce—we can call her Joy for short—Joy—it suits so well. Oh, Marilla, I thought I was happy before. Now I know that I just dreamed a pleasant dream of happiness. THIS is the reality."

"You mustn't talk, Anne—wait till you're stronger," said Marilla warningly.

"You know how hard it is for me NOT to talk," smiled Anne.

At first she was too weak and too happy to notice that Gilbert and the nurse looked grave and Marilla sorrowful. Then, as subtly, and coldly, and remorselessly as a sea-fog stealing landward, fear crept into her heart. Why was not Gilbert gladder? Why would he not talk about the baby? Why would they not let her have it with her after that first heavenly—happy hour? Was—was there anything wrong?

"Gilbert," whispered Anne imploringly, "the baby—is all right—isn't she? Tell me —tell me."

Gilbert was a long while in turning round; then he bent over Anne and looked in her eyes. Marilla, listening fearfully outside the door, heard a pitiful, heartbroken moan, and fled to the kitchen where Susan was weeping.

"Oh, the poor lamb—the poor lamb! How can she bear it, Miss Cuthbert? I am afraid it will kill her. She has been that built up and happy, longing for that baby, and planning for it. Cannot anything be done nohow, Miss Cuthbert?"

"I'm afraid not, Susan. Gilbert says there is no hope. He knew from the first the little thing couldn't live."

"And it is such a sweet baby," sobbed Susan. "I never saw one so white—they are mostly red or yallow. And it opened its big eyes as if it was months old. The little, little thing! Oh, the poor, young Mrs. Doctor!"

At sunset the little soul that had come with the dawning went away, leaving heartbreak behind it. Miss Cornelia took the wee, white lady from the kindly but stranger hands of the nurse, and dressed the tiny waxen form in the beautiful dress Leslie had made for it. Leslie had asked her to do that. Then she took it back and laid it beside the poor, broken, tear-blinded little mother.

"The Lord has given and the Lord has taken away, dearie," she said through her own tears. "Blessed be the name of the Lord."

Then she went away, leaving Anne and Gilbert alone together with their dead.

The next day, the small white Joy was laid in a velvet casket which Leslie had lined with apple-blossoms, and taken to the graveyard of the church across the harbor. Miss Cornelia and Marilla put all the little love-made garments away, together with the ruffled basket which had been befrilled and belaced for dimpled limbs and downy head. Little Joy was never to sleep there; she had found a colder, narrower bed.

"This has been an awful disappointment to me," sighed Miss Cornelia. "I've looked forward to this baby—and I did want it to be a girl, too."

"I can only be thankful that Anne's life was spared," said Marilla, with a shiver, recalling those hours of darkness when the girl she loved was passing through the valley of the shadow.

"Poor, poor lamb! Her heart is broken," said Susan.

"I ENVY Anne," said Leslie suddenly and fiercely, "and I'd envy her even if she had died! She was a mother for one beautiful day. I'd gladly give my life for THAT!"

"I wouldn't talk like that, Leslie, dearie," said Miss Cornelia deprecatingly. She was afraid that the dignified Miss Cuthbert would think Leslie quite terrible.

Anne's convalescence was long, and made bitter for her by many things. The bloom and sunshine of the Four Winds world grated harshly on her; and yet, when the rain fell heavily, she pictured it beating so mercilessly down on that little grave across the harbor; and when the wind blew around the eaves she heard sad voices in it she had never heard before.

Kindly callers hurt her, too, with the well-meant platitudes with which they strove to cover the nakedness of bereavement. A letter from Phil Blake was an added sting. Phil had heard of the baby's birth, but not of its death, and she wrote Anne a congratulatory letter of sweet mirth which hurt her horribly.

"I would have laughed over it so happily if I had my baby," she sobbed to Marilla. "But when I haven't it just seems like wanton cruelty—though I know Phil wouldn't hurt me for the world. Oh, Marilla, I don't see how I can EVER be happy again—EVERYTHING will hurt me all the rest of my life."

"Time will help you," said Marilla, who was racked with sympathy but could never learn to express it in other than age-worn formulas.

"It doesn't seem FAIR," said Anne rebelliously. "Babies are born and live where they are not wanted—where they will be neglected—where they will have no chance. I would have loved my baby so—and cared for it so tenderly—and tried to give her every chance for good. And yet I wasn't allowed to keep her."

"It was God's will, Anne," said Marilla, helpless before the riddle of the universe—the WHY of undeserved pain. "And little Joy is better off."

"I can't believe THAT," cried Anne bitterly. Then, seeing that Marilla looked shocked, she added passionately, "Why should she be born at all—why should any one be born at all—if she's better off dead? I DON'T believe it is better for a child to die at birth than to live its life out—and love and be loved—and enjoy and suffer—and do its work—and develop a character that would give it a personality in eternity. And how do you know it was God's will? Perhaps it was just a thwarting of His purpose by the Power of Evil. We can't be expected to be resigned to THAT."

"Oh, Anne, don't talk so," said Marilla, genuinely alarmed lest Anne were drifting into deep and dangerous waters. "We can't understand—but we must have faith—we MUST believe that all is for the best. I know you find it hard to think so, just now. But try to be brave—for Gilbert's sake. He's so worried about you. You aren't getting strong as fast as you should."

"Oh, I know I've been very selfish," sighed Anne. "I love Gilbert more than ever—and I want to live for his sake. But it seems as if part of me was buried over there in that little harbor graveyard—and it hurts so much that I'm afraid of life."

"It won't hurt so much always, Anne."

"The thought that it may stop hurting sometimes hurts me worse than all else, Marilla."

"Yes, I know, I've felt that too, about other things. But we all love you, Anne. Captain Jim has been up every day to ask for you—and Mrs. Moore haunts the place—and Miss Bryant spends most of her time, I think, cooking up nice things for you. Susan doesn't like it very well. She thinks she can cook as well as Miss Bryant."

"Dear Susan! Oh, everybody has been so dear and good and lovely to me, Marilla. I'm not ungrateful—and perhaps—when this horrible ache grows a little less—I'll find that I can go on living."

20. LOST MARGARET

Anne found that she could go on living; the day came when she even smiled again over one of Miss Cornelia's speeches. But there was something in the smile that had never been in Anne's smile before and would never be absent from it again.

On the first day she was able to go for a drive Gilbert took her down to Four Winds Point, and left her there while he rowed over the channel to see a patient at the fishing village. A rollicking wind was scudding across the harbor and the dunes, whipping the water into white-caps and washing the sandshore with long lines of silvery breakers.

"I'm real proud to see you here again, Mistress Blythe," said Captain Jim. "Sit down—sit down. I'm afeared it's mighty dusty here today—but there's no need of looking at dust when you can look at such scenery, is there?"

"I don't mind the dust," said Anne, "but Gilbert says I must keep in the open air. I think I'll go and sit on the rocks down there."

"Would you like company or would you rather be alone?"

"If by company you mean yours I'd much rather have it than be alone," said Anne, smiling. Then she sighed. She had never before minded being alone. Now she dreaded it. When she was alone now she felt so dreadfully alone.

"Here's a nice little spot where the wind can't get at you," said Captain Jim, when they reached the rocks. "I often sit here. It's a great place jest to sit and dream."

"Oh—dreams," sighed Anne. "I can't dream now, Captain Jim—I'm done with dreams."

"Oh, no, you're not, Mistress Blythe—oh, no, you're not," said Captain Jim meditatively. "I know how you feel jest now—but if you keep on living you'll get glad again, and the first thing you know you'll be dreaming again—thank the good Lord for it! If it wasn't for our dreams they might as well bury us. How'd we stand living if it wasn't for our dream of immortality? And that's a dream that's BOUND to come true, Mistress Blythe. You'll see your little Joyce again some day."

"But she won't be my baby," said Anne, with trembling lips. "Oh, she may be, as Longfellow says, 'a fair maiden clothed with celestial grace'—but she'll be a stranger to me."

"God will manage better'n THAT, I believe," said Captain Jim.

They were both silent for a little time. Then Captain Jim said very softly:

"Mistress Blythe, may I tell you about lost Margaret?"

"Of course," said Anne gently. She did not know who "lost Margaret" was, but she felt that she was going to hear the romance of Captain Jim's life.

"I've often wanted to tell you about her," Captain Jim went on.

"Do you know why, Mistress Blythe? It's because I want somebody to remember and think of her sometime after I'm gone. I can't bear that her name should be forgotten by all living souls. And now nobody remembers lost Margaret but me."

Then Captain Jim told the story—an old, old forgotten story, for it was over fifty years since Margaret had fallen asleep one day in her father's dory and drifted—or so it was supposed, for nothing was ever certainly known as to her fate—out of the channel, beyond the bar, to perish in the black thundersquall which had come up so suddenly that long-ago summer afternoon. But to Captain Jim those fifty years were but as yesterday when it is past.

"I walked the shore for months after that," he said sadly, "looking to find her dear, sweet little body; but the sea never give her back to me. But I'll find her sometime, Mistress Blythe—I'll find her sometime. She's waiting for me. I wish I could tell you jest how she looked, but I can't. I've seen a fine, silvery mist hanging over the bar at sunrise that seemed like her—and then again I've seen a white birch in the woods back yander that made me think of her. She had pale, brown hair and a little white, sweet face, and long slender fingers like yours, Mistress Blythe, only browner, for she was a shore girl. Sometimes I wake up in the night and hear the sea calling to me in the old way, and it seems as if lost Margaret called in it. And when there's a storm and the waves are sobbing and moaning I hear her lamenting among them. And when they laugh on a gay day it's HER laugh—lost Margaret's sweet, roguish, little laugh. The sea took her from me, but some day I'll find her. Mistress Blythe. It can't keep us apart forever."

"I am glad you have told me about her," said Anne. "I have often wondered why you had lived all your life alone."

"I couldn't ever care for anyone else. Lost Margaret took my heart with her—out there," said the old lover, who had been faithful for fifty years to his drowned sweetheart. "You won't mind if I talk a good deal about her, will you, Mistress Blythe? It's a pleasure to me—for all the pain went out of her memory years ago and jest left its blessing. I know you'll never forget her, Mistress Blythe. And if the years, as I hope, bring other little folks to your home, I want you to promise me that you'll tell THEM the story of lost Margaret, so that her name won't be forgotten among humankind."

21. BARRIERS SWEPT AWAY

"Anne," said Leslie, breaking abruptly a short

silence, "you don't know how GOOD it is to be sitting here with you again—working—and talking—and being silent together."

They were sitting among the blue-eyed grasses on the bank of the brook in Anne's garden. The water sparkled and crooned past them; the birches threw dappled shadows over them; roses bloomed along the walks. The sun was beginning to be low, and the air was full of woven music. There was one music of the wind in the firs behind the house, and another of the waves on the bar, and still another from the distant bell of the church near which the wee, white lady slept. Anne loved that bell, though it brought sorrowful thoughts now.

She looked curiously at Leslie, who had thrown down her sewing and spoken with a lack of restraint that was very unusual with her.

"On that horrible night when you were so ill," Leslie went on, "I kept thinking that perhaps we'd have no more talks and walks and WORKS together. And I realised just what your friendship had come to mean to me—just what YOU meant—and just what a hateful little beast I had been."

"Leslie! Leslie! I never allow anyone to call my friends names."

"It's true. That's exactly what I am—a hateful little beast. There's something I've GOT to tell you, Anne. I suppose it will make you despise me, but I MUST confess it. Anne, there have been times this past winter and spring when I have HATED you."

"I KNEW it," said Anne calmly.

"You KNEW it?"

"Yes, I saw it in your eyes."

"And yet you went on liking me and being my friend."

"Well, it was only now and then you hated me, Leslie. Between times you loved me, I think."

"I certainly did. But that other horrid feeling was always there, spoiling it, back in my heart. I kept it down—sometimes I forgot it—but sometimes it would surge up and take possession of me. I hated you because I ENVIED you—oh, I was sick with envy of you at times. You had a dear little home—and love—and happiness—and glad dreams—everything I wanted—and never had—and never could have. Oh, never could have! THAT was what stung. I wouldn't have envied you, if I had had any HOPE that life would ever be different for me. But I hadn't—I hadn't—and it didn't seem FAIR. It made me rebellious—and it hurt me—and so I hated you at times. Oh, I was so ashamed of it—I'm dying of shame now—but I couldn't conquer it.

"That night, when I was afraid you mightn't live—I thought I was going to be punished for my wickedness—and I loved you so then. Anne, Anne, I never had anything to love since my mother died, except Dick's old dog—and it's so dreadful to have nothing to love—life is so EMPTY—and there's NOTHING worse than emptiness—and I might have loved you so much —and that horrible thing had spoiled it—"

Leslie was trembling and growing almost incoherent with the violence of her emotion.

"Don't, Leslie," implored Anne, "oh, don't. I understand—don't talk of it any more."

"I must—I must. When I knew you were going to live I vowed that I would tell you as soon as you were well—that I wouldn't go on accepting your friendship and companionship without telling you how unworthy I was of it. And I've been so afraid—it would turn you against me."

"You needn't fear that, Leslie."

"Oh, I'm so glad—so glad, Anne." Leslie clasped her brown, work-hardened hands tightly together to still their shaking. "But I want to tell you everything, now I've begun. You don't remember the first time I saw you, I suppose—it wasn't that night on the shore—"

"No, it was the night Gilbert and I came home. You were driving your geese down the hill. I should think I DO remember it! I thought you were so beautiful—I longed for weeks after to find out who you were."

"I knew who YOU were, although I had never seen either of you before. I had heard of the new doctor and his bride who were coming to live in Miss Russell's little house. I—I hated you that very moment, Anne."

"I felt the resentment in your eyes—then I doubted—I thought I must be mistaken—because WHY should it be?"

"It was because you looked so happy. Oh, you'll agree with me now that I AM a hateful beast—to hate another woman just because she was happy,—and when her happiness didn't take anything from me! That was why I never went to see you. I knew quite well I ought to go —even our simple Four Winds customs demanded that. But I couldn't. I used to watch you from my window—I could see you and your husband strolling about your garden in the evening—or you running down the poplar lane to meet him. And it hurt me. And yet in another way I wanted to go over. I felt that, if I were not so miserable, I could have liked you and found in you what I've never had in my life—an intimate, REAL friend of my own age. And then you remember that night at the shore? You were afraid I would think you crazy. You must have thought *I* was."

"No, but I couldn't understand you, Leslie. One moment you drew me to you—the next you pushed me back."

"I was very unhappy that evening. I had had a hard day. Dick had been very—very hard to manage that day. Generally he is quite good-natured and easily controlled, you know, Anne. But some days he is very different. I was so heartsick—I ran away to the shore as soon as he went to sleep. It was my only refuge. I sat there thinking of how my poor father had ended his life, and wondering if I wouldn't be driven to it some day. Oh, my heart was full of black thoughts! And then you came dancing along the cove like a glad, light-hearted child. I—I hated you more then than I've ever done since. And yet I craved your friendship. The one feeling swayed me one moment; the other feeling the next. When I got home that night I cried for shame of what you must think of me. But it's always been just the same when I came over here. Sometimes I'd be happy and enjoy my visit. And at other times that hideous feeling would mar it all. There were times when everything about you and your house hurt me. You had so many dear little things I couldn't have. Do you know—it's ridiculous—but I had an especial spite at those china dogs of yours. There were times when I wanted to catch up Gog and Magog and bang their pert black noses together! Oh, you smile, Anne—but it was never funny to me. I would come here and see you and Gilbert with your books and your flowers, and your household gods, and your little family jokes—and your love for each other showing in every look and word, even when you didn't know it—and I would go home to—you know what I went home to! Oh, Anne, I don't believe I'm jealous and envious by nature. When I was a girl I lacked many things my schoolmates had, but I never cared—I never disliked them for it. But I seem to have grown so hateful—"

"Leslie, dearest, stop blaming yourself. You are NOT hateful or jealous or envious. The life you have to live has warped you a little, perhaps-but it would have ruined a nature less fine and noble than yours. I'm letting you tell me all this because I believe it's better for you to talk it out and rid your soul of it. But don't blame yourself any more."

"Well, I won't. I just wanted you to know me as I am. That time you told me of your darling hope for the spring was the worst of all, Anne. I shall never forgive myself for the way I behaved then. I repented it with tears. And I DID put many a tender and loving thought of you into the little dress I made. But I might have known that anything I made could only be a shroud in the end."

"Now, Leslie, that IS bitter and morbid—put such thoughts away.

"I was so glad when you brought the little dress; and since I had to lose little Joyce I like to think that the dress she wore was the one you made for her when you let yourself love me."

"Anne, do you know, I believe I shall always love you after this. I don't think I'll ever feel that dreadful way about you again. Talking it all out seems to have done away with it, somehow. It's very strange—and I thought it so real and bitter. It's like opening the door of a dark room to show some hideous creature you've believed to be there—and when the light streams in your monster turns out to have been just a shadow, vanishing when the light comes. It will never come between us again."

"No, we are real friends now, Leslie, and I am very glad."

"I hope you won't misunderstand me if I say something else. Anne, I was grieved to the core of my heart when you lost your baby; and if I could have saved her for you by cutting off one of my hands I would have done it. But your sorrow has brought us closer together. Your perfect happiness isn't a barrier any longer. Oh, don't misunderstand, dearest—I'm NOT glad that your happiness isn't perfect any longer—I can say that sincerely; but since it isn't, there isn't such a gulf between us."

"I DO understand that, too, Leslie. Now, we'll just shut up the past and forget what was unpleasant in it. It's all going to be different. We're both of the race of Joseph now. I think you've been wonderful—wonderful. And, Leslie, I can't help believing that life has something good and beautiful for you yet."

Leslie shook her head.

"No," she said dully. "There isn't any hope. Dick will never be better—and even if his memory were to come back—oh, Anne, it would be worse, even worse, than it is now. This is something you can't understand, you happy bride. Anne, did Miss Cornelia ever tell you how I came to marry Dick?"

"Yes."

"I'm glad—I wanted you to know—but I couldn't bring myself to talk of it if you hadn't known. Anne, it seems to me that ever since I was twelve years old life has been bitter. Before that I had a happy childhood. We were very poor—but we didn't mind. Father was so splendid—so clever and loving and sympathetic. We were chums as far back as I can remember. And mother was so sweet. She was very, very beautiful. I look like her, but I am not so beautiful as she was."

"Miss Cornelia says you are far more beautiful."

"She is mistaken—or prejudiced. I think my figure IS better—mother was slight and bent by hard work—but she had the face of an angel. I used just to look up at her in worship. We all worshipped her,—father and Kenneth and I."

Anne remembered that Miss Cornelia had given her a very different impression of Leslie's mother. But had not love the truer vision? Still, it WAS selfish of Rose West to make her daughter marry Dick Moore.

"Kenneth was my brother," went on Leslie. "Oh, I can't tell you how I loved him. And he was cruelly killed. Do you know how?"

"Yes."

"Anne, I saw his little face as the wheel went over him. He fell on his back. Anne—Anne—I can see it now. I shall always see it. Anne, all I ask of heaven is that that recollection shall be blotted out of my memory. O my God!"

"Leslie, don't speak of it. I know the story—don't go into details that only harrow your soul up unavailingly. It WILL be blotted out."

After a moment's struggle, Leslie regained a measure of self-control.

"Then father's health got worse and he grew despondent—his mind became unbalanced—you've heard all that, too?"

"Yes."

"After that I had just mother to live for. But I was very ambitious. I meant to teach and earn my way through college. I meant to climb to the very top—oh, I won't talk of that either. It's no use. You know what happened. I couldn't see my dear little heart-broken mother, who had been such a slave all her life, turned out of her home. Of course, I could have earned enough for us to live on. But mother COULDN'T leave her home. She had come there as a bride—and she had loved father so—and all her memories were there. Even yet, Anne, when I think that I made her last year happy I'm not sorry for what I did. As for Dick—I didn't hate him when I married him—I just felt for him the indifferent, friendly feeling I had for most of my schoolmates. I knew he drank some—but I had never heard the story of the girl down at the fishing cove. If I had, I COULDN'T have married him, even for mother's sake. Afterwards—I DID hate him—but mother never knew. She died—and then I was alone. I was only seventeen and I was alone. Dick had gone off in the Four Sisters. I hoped he wouldn't be home very much more. The sea had always been in his blood. I had no other hope. Well, Captain Jim brought him home, as you know—and that's all there is to say. You know me now, Anne—the worst of me—the barriers are all down. And you still want to be my friend?"

Anne looked up through the birches, at the white paper-lantern of a half moon drifting downwards to the gulf of sunset. Her face was very sweet.

"I am your friend and you are mine, for always," she said. "Such a friend as I never had before. I have had many dear and beloved friends—but there is a something in you, Leslie, that I never found in anyone else. You have more to offer me in that rich nature of yours, and I have more to give you than I had in my careless girlhood. We are both women—and friends forever."

They clasped hands and smiled at each other through the tears that filled the gray eyes and the blue.

22. MISS CORNELIA ARRANGES MATTERS

Gilbert insisted that Susan should be kept on at the little house for the summer. Anne protested at first.

"Life here with just the two of us is so sweet, Gilbert. It spoils it a little to have anyone else. Susan is a dear soul, but she is an outsider. It won't hurt me to do the work here."

"You must take your doctor's advice," said Gilbert. "There's an old proverb to the effect that shoemakers' wives go barefoot and doctors' wives die young. I don't mean that it shall be true in my household. You will keep Susan until the old spring comes back into your step, and those little hollows on your cheeks fill out."

"You just take it easy, Mrs. Doctor, dear," said Susan, coming abruptly in. "Have a good time and do not worry about the pantry. Susan is at the helm. There is no use in keeping a dog and doing your own barking. I am going to take your breakfast up to you every morning."

"Indeed you are not," laughed Anne. "I agree with Miss Cornelia that it's a scandal for a woman who isn't sick to eat her breakfast in bed, and almost justifies the men in any enormities."

"Oh, Cornelia!" said Susan, with ineffable contempt. "I think you have better sense, Mrs. Doctor, dear, than to heed what Cornelia Bryant says. I cannot see why she must be always running down the men, even if she is an old maid. *I* am an old maid, but you never hear ME abusing the men. I like 'em. I would have married one if I could. Is it not funny nobody ever asked me to marry him, Mrs. Doctor, dear? I am no beauty, but I am as good-looking as most of the married women you see. But I never had a beau. What do you suppose is the reason?"

"It may be predestination," suggested Anne, with unearthly solemnity.

Susan nodded.

"That is what I have often thought, Mrs. Doctor, dear, and a great comfort it is. I do not mind nobody wanting me if the Almighty decreed it so for His own wise purposes. But sometimes doubt creeps in, Mrs. Doctor, dear, and I wonder if maybe the Old Scratch has not more to do with it than anyone else. I cannot feel resigned THEN. But maybe," added Susan, brightening up, "I will have a chance to get married yet. I often and often think of the old verse my aunt used to repeat:

There never was a goose so gray but sometime soon or late
Some honest gander came her way and took her for his mate!

A woman cannot ever be sure of not being married till she is buried, Mrs. Doctor, dear, and meanwhile I will make a batch of cherry pies. I notice the doctor favors 'em, and I DO like cooking for a man who appreciates his victuals."

Miss Cornelia dropped in that afternoon, puffing a little.

"I don't mind the world or the devil much, but the flesh DOES rather bother me," she admitted. "You always look as cool as a cucumber, Anne, dearie. Do I smell cherry pie? If I do, ask me to stay to tea. Haven't tasted a cherry pie this summer. My cherries have all been stolen by those scamps of Gilman boys from the Glen."

"Now, now, Cornelia," remonstrated Captain Jim, who had been reading a sea novel in a corner of the living room, "you shouldn't say that about those two poor, motherless Gilman boys, unless you've got certain proof. Jest because their father ain't none too honest isn't any reason for calling them thieves. It's more likely it's been the robins took your cherries. They're turrible thick this year."

"Robins!" said Miss Cornelia disdainfully. "Humph! Two-legged robins, believe ME!"

"Well, most of the Four Winds robins ARE constructed on that principle," said Captain Jim gravely.

Miss Cornelia stared at him for a moment. Then she leaned back in her rocker and laughed long and ungrudgingly.

"Well, you HAVE got one on me at last, Jim Boyd, I'll admit. Just look how pleased he is, Anne, dearie, grinning like a Chessy-cat. As for the robins' legs if robins have great, big, bare, sunburned legs, with ragged trousers hanging on 'em, such as I saw up in my cherry tree one morning at sunrise last week, I'll beg the Gilman boys' pardon. By the time I got down they were gone. I couldn't understand how they had disappeared so quick, but Captain Jim has enlightened me. They flew away, of course."

Captain Jim laughed and went away, regretfully declining an invitation to stay to supper and partake of cherry pie.

"I'm on my way to see Leslie and ask her if she'll take a boarder," Miss Cornelia resumed. "I'd a letter yesterday from a Mrs. Daly in Toronto, who boarded a spell with me two years ago. She wanted me to take a friend of hers for the summer. His name is Owen Ford, and he's a newspaper man, and it seems he's a grandson of the schoolmaster who built this house. John Selwyn's oldest daughter married an Ontario man named Ford, and this is her son. He wants to see the old place his grandparents lived in. He had a bad spell of typhoid in the spring and hasn't got rightly over it, so his doctor has ordered him to the sea. He doesn't want to go to the hotel—he just wants a quiet home place. I can't take him, for I have to be away in August. I've been appointed a delegate to the W.F.M.S. convention in Kingsport and I'm going. I don't know whether Leslie'll want to be bothered with him, either, but there's no one else. If she can't take him he'll have to go over the harbor."

"When you've seen her come back and help us eat our cherry pies," said Anne. "Bring Leslie and Dick, too, if they can come. And so you're going to Kingsport? What a nice time you will have. I must give you a letter to a friend of mine there—Mrs. Jonas Blake."

"I've prevailed on Mrs. Thomas Holt to go with me," said Miss Cornelia complacently. "It's time she had a little holiday, believe ME. She has just about worked herself to death. Tom Holt can crochet beautifully, but he can't make a living for his family. He never seems to be able to get up early enough to do any work, but I notice he can always get up early to go fishing. Isn't that like a man?"

Anne smiled. She had learned to discount largely Miss Cornelia's opinions of the Four Winds men. Otherwise she must have believed them the most hopeless assortment of reprobates and ne'er-do-wells in the world, with veritable slaves and martyrs for wives. This particular Tom Holt, for example, she knew to be a kind husband, a much loved father, and an excellent neighbor. If he were rather inclined to be lazy, liking better the fishing he had been born for than the farming he had not, and if he had a harmless eccentricity for doing fancy work, nobody save Miss Cornelia seemed to hold it against him. His wife was a "hustler," who gloried in hustling; his family got a comfortable living off the farm; and his strapping sons and daughters, inheriting their mother's energy, were all in a fair way to do well in the world. There was not a happier household in Glen St. Mary than the Holts'.

Miss Cornelia returned satisfied from the house up the brook.

"Leslie's going to take him," she announced. "She jumped at the chance. She wants to make a little money to shingle the roof of her house this fall, and she didn't know how she was going to manage it. I expect Captain Jim'll be more than interested when he hears that a grandson of the Selwyns' is coming here. Leslie said to tell you she hankered after cherry pie, but she couldn't come to tea because she has to go and hunt up her turkeys. They've strayed away. But she said, if there was a piece left, for you to put it in the pantry and she'd run over in the cat's light, when prowling's in order, to get it. You don't know, Anne, dearie, what good it did my heart to hear Leslie send you a message like that, laughing like she used to long ago.

"There's a great change come over her lately. She laughs and jokes like a girl, and from her talk I gather she's here real often."

"Every day—or else I'm over there," said Anne. "I don't know what I'd do without Leslie, especially just now when Gilbert is so busy. He's hardly ever home except for a few hours in the wee sma's. He's really working himself to death. So many of the over-harbor people send for him now."

"They might better be content with their own doctor," said Miss Cornelia. "Though to be sure I can't blame them, for he's a Methodist. Ever since Dr. Blythe brought Mrs. Allonby round folks think he can raise the dead. I believe Dr. Dave is a mite jealous—just like a man. He thinks Dr. Blythe has too many new-fangled notions! 'Well,' I says to him, 'it was a new-fangled notion saved Rhoda Allonby. If YOU'D been attending her she'd have died, and had a tombstone saying it had pleased God to take her away.' Oh, I DO like to speak my mind to Dr. Dave! He's bossed the Glen for years, and he thinks he's forgotten more than other people ever knew. Speaking of doctors, I wish Dr. Blythe'd run over and see to that boil on Dick Moore's neck. It's getting past Leslie's skill. I'm sure I don't know what Dick Moore wants to start in having boils for—as if he wasn't enough trouble without that!"

"Do you know, Dick has taken quite a fancy to me," said Anne. "He follows me round like a dog, and smiles like a pleased child when I notice him."

"Does it make you creepy?"

"Not at all. I rather like poor Dick Moore. He seems so pitiful and appealing, somehow."

"You wouldn't think him very appealing if you'd see him on his cantankerous days, believe ME. But I'm glad you don't mind him—it's all the nicer for Leslie. She'll have more to do when her boarder comes. I hope he'll be a decent creature. You'll probably like him—he's a writer."

"I wonder why people so commonly suppose that if two individuals are both writers they must therefore be hugely congenial," said Anne, rather scornfully. "Nobody would expect two blacksmiths to be violently attracted toward each other merely because they were both blacksmiths."

Nevertheless, she looked forward to the advent of Owen Ford with a pleasant sense of expectation. If he were young and likeable he might prove a very pleasant addition to society in Four Winds. The latch-string of the little house was always out for the race of Joseph.

23. OWEN FORD COMES

One evening Miss Cornelia telephoned down to Anne.

"The writer man has just arrived here. I'm going to drive him down to your place, and you can show him the way over to Leslie's. It's shorter than driving round by the other road, and I'm in a mortal hurry. The Reese baby has gone and fallen into a pail of hot water at the Glen, and got nearly scalded to death and they want me right off—to put a new skin on the child, I presume. Mrs. Reese is always so careless, and then expects other people to mend her mistakes. You won't mind, will you, dearie? His trunk can go down tomorrow."

"Very well," said Anne. "What is he like, Miss Cornelia?"

"You'll see what he's like outside when I take him down. As for what he's like inside only the Lord who made him knows THAT. I'm not going to say another word, for every receiver in the Glen is down."

"Miss Cornelia evidently can't find much fault with Mr. Ford's looks, or she would find it in spite of the receivers," said Anne. "I conclude therefore, Susan, that Mr. Ford is rather handsome than otherwise."

"Well, Mrs. Doctor, dear, I DO enjoy seeing a well-looking man," said Susan candidly. "Had I not better get up a snack for him? There is a strawberry pie that would melt in your mouth."

"No, Leslie is expecting him and has his supper ready. Besides, I want that strawberry pie for my own poor man. He won't be home till late, so leave the pie and a glass of milk out for him, Susan."

"That I will, Mrs. Doctor, dear. Susan is at the helm. After all, it is better to give pie to your own men than to strangers, who may be only seeking to devour, and the doctor himself is as well-looking a man as you often come across."

When Owen Ford came Anne secretly admitted, as Miss Cornelia towed him in, that he was very "well-looking" indeed. He was tall and broad-shouldered, with thick, brown hair, finely-cut nose and chin, large and brilliant dark-gray eyes.

"And did you notice his ears and his teeth, Mrs. Doctor, dear?" queried Susan later on. "He has got the nicest-shaped ears I ever saw on a man's head. I am choice about ears. When I was young I was scared that I might have to marry a man with ears like flaps. But I need not have worried, for never a chance did I have with any kind of ears."

Anne had not noticed Owen Ford's ears, but she did see his teeth, as his lips parted over them in a frank and friendly smile. Unsmiling, his face was rather sad and absent in expression, not unlike the melancholy, inscrutable hero of Anne's own early dreams; but mirth and humor and charm lighted it up when he smiled. Certainly, on the outside, as Miss Cornelia said, Owen Ford was a very presentable fellow.

"You cannot realise how delighted I am to be here, Mrs. Blythe," he said, looking around him with eager, interested eyes. "I have an odd feeling of coming home. My mother was born and spent her childhood here, you know. She used to talk a great deal to me of her old home. I know the geography of it as well as of the one I lived in, and, of course, she told me the story of the building of the house, and of my grandfather's agonised watch for the Royal William. I had thought that so old a house must have vanished years ago, or I should have come to see it before this."

"Old houses don't vanish easily on this enchanted coast," smiled Anne. "This is a 'land where all things always seem the same'—nearly always, at least. John Selwyn's house hasn't even been much changed, and outside the rose-bushes your grandfather planted for his bride are blooming this very minute."

"How the thought links me with them! With your leave I must explore the whole place soon."

"Our latch-string will always be out for you," promised Anne. "And do you know that the old sea captain who keeps the Four Winds light knew John Selwyn and his bride well in his boyhood? He told me their story the night I came here—the third bride of the old house."

"Can it be possible? This IS a discovery. I must hunt him up."

"It won't be difficult; we are all cronies of Captain Jim. He will be as eager to see you as you could be to see him. Your grandmother shines like a star in his memory. But I think Mrs. Moore is expecting you. I'll show you our 'cross-lots' road."

Anne walked with him to the house up the brook, over a field that was as white as snow with daisies. A boat-load of people were singing far across the harbor. The sound drifted over the water like faint, unearthly music wind-blown across a starlit sea. The big light flashed and beaconed. Owen Ford looked around him with satisfaction.

"And so this is Four Winds," he said. "I wasn't prepared to find it quite so beautiful, in spite of all mother's praises. What colors—what scenery—what charm! I shall get as strong as a horse in no time. And if inspiration comes from beauty, I should certainly be able to begin my great Canadian novel here."

"You haven't begun it yet?" asked Anne.

"Alack-a-day, no. I've never been able to get the right central idea for it. It lurks beyond me—it allures—and beckons—and recedes—I almost grasp it and it is gone. Perhaps amid this peace and loveliness, I shall be able to capture it. Miss Bryant tells me that you write."

"Oh, I do little things for children. I haven't done much since I was married. And—I have no designs on a great Canadian novel," laughed Anne. "That is quite beyond me."

Owen Ford laughed too.

"I dare say it is beyond me as well. All the same I mean to have a try at it some day, if I can ever get time. A newspaper man doesn't have much chance for that sort of thing. I've done a good deal of short story writing for the magazines, but I've never had the leisure that seems to be necessary for the writing of a book. With three months of liberty I ought to make a start, though—if I could only get the necessary motif for it—the SOUL of the book."

An idea whisked through Anne's brain with a suddenness that made her jump. But she did not utter it, for they had reached the Moore house. As they entered the yard Leslie came out on the veranda from the side door, peering through the gloom for some sign of her expected guest. She stood just where the warm yellow light flooded her from the open door. She wore a plain dress of cheap, cream-tinted cotton voile, with the usual girdle of crimson. Leslie was never without her touch of crimson. She had told Anne that she never felt satisfied without a gleam of red somewhere about her, if it were only a flower. To Anne, it always seemed to symbolise Leslie's glowing, pent-up personality, denied all expression save in that flaming glint. Leslie's dress was cut a little away at the neck and had short sleeves. Her arms gleamed like ivory-tinted marble. Every exquisite curve of her form was outlined in soft darkness against the light. Her hair shone in it like flame. Beyond her was a purple sky, flowering with stars over the harbor.

Anne heard her companion give a gasp. Even in the dusk she could see the amazement and admiration on his face.

"Who is that beautiful creature?" he asked.

"That is Mrs. Moore," said Anne. "She is very lovely, isn't she?"

"I—I never saw anything like her," he answered, rather dazedly. "I wasn't prepared—I didn't expect—good heavens, one DOESN'T expect a goddess for a landlady! Why, if she were clothed in a gown of sea-purple, with a rope of amethysts in her hair, she would be a veritable sea-queen. And she takes in boarders!"

"Even goddesses must live," said Anne. "And Leslie isn't a goddess. She's just a very beautiful woman, as human as the rest of us. Did Miss Bryant tell you about Mr. Moore?"

"Yes,—he's mentally deficient, or something of the sort, isn't he? But she said nothing about Mrs. Moore, and I supposed she'd be the usual hustling country housewife who takes in boarders to earn an honest penny."

"Well, that's just what Leslie is doing," said Anne crisply. "And it isn't altogether pleasant for her, either. I hope you won't mind Dick. If you do, please don't let Leslie see it. It would hurt her horribly. He's just a big baby, and sometimes a rather annoying one."

"Oh, I won't mind him. I don't suppose I'll be much in the house anyhow, except for meals. But what a shame it all is! Her life must be a hard one."

"It is. But she doesn't like to be pitied."

Leslie had gone back into the house and now met them at the front door. She greeted Owen Ford with cold civility, and told him in a business-like tone that his room and his supper were ready for him. Dick, with a pleased grin, shambled upstairs with the valise, and Owen Ford was installed as an inmate of the old house among the willows.

24. THE LIFE-BOOK OF CAPTAIN JIM

"I have a little brown cocoon of an idea that may possibly expand into a magnificent moth of fulfilment," Anne told Gilbert when she reached home. He had returned earlier than she had expected, and was enjoying Susan's cherry pie. Susan herself hovered in the background, like a rather grim but beneficent guardian spirit, and found as much pleasure in watching Gilbert eat pie as he did in eating it.

"What is your idea?" he asked.

"I sha'n't tell you just yet—not till I see if I can bring the thing about."

"What sort of a chap is Ford?"

"Oh, very nice, and quite good-looking."

"Such beautiful ears, doctor, dear," interjected Susan with a relish.

"He is about thirty or thirty-five, I think, and he meditates writing a novel. His voice is pleasant and his smile delightful, and he knows how to dress. He looks as if life hadn't been altogether easy for him, somehow."

Owen Ford came over the next evening with a note to Anne from Leslie; they spent the sunset time in the garden and then went for a moonlit sail on the harbor, in the little boat Gilbert had set up for summer outings. They liked Owen immensely and had that feeling of having known him for many years which distinguishes the freemasonry of the house of Joseph. "He is as nice as his ears, Mrs. Doctor, dear," said Susan, when he had gone. He had told Susan that he had never tasted anything like her strawberry shortcake and Susan's susceptible heart was his forever.

"He has got a way with him," she reflected, as she cleared up the relics of the supper. "It is real queer he is not married, for a man like that could have anybody for the asking. Well, maybe he is like me, and has not met the right one yet."

Susan really grew quite romantic in her musings as she washed the supper dishes.

Two nights later Anne took Owen Ford down to Four Winds Point to introduce him to Captain Jim. The clover fields along the harbor shore were whitening in the western wind, and Captain Jim had one of his finest sunsets on exhibition. He himself had just returned from a trip over the harbor.

"I had to go over and tell Henry Pollack he was dying. Everybody else was afraid to tell him. They expected he'd take on turrible, for he's been dreadful determined to live, and been making no end of plans for the fall. His wife thought he oughter be told and that I'd be the best one to break it to him that he couldn't get better. Henry and me are old cronies—we sailed in the Gray Gull for years together. Well, I went over and sat down by Henry's bed and I says to him, says I, jest right out plain and simple, for if a thing's got to be told it may as well be told first as last, says I, 'Mate, I reckon you've got your sailing orders this time,' I was sorter quaking inside, for it's an awful thing to have to tell a man who hain't any idea he's dying that he is. But lo and behold, Mistress Blythe, Henry looks up at me, with those bright old black eyes of his in his wizened face and says, says he, 'Tell me something I don't know, Jim Boyd, if you want to give me information. I've known THAT for a week.' I was too astonished to speak, and Henry, he chuckled. 'To see you coming in here,' says he, 'with your face as solemn as a tombstone and sitting down there with your hands clasped over your stomach, and passing me out a blue-mouldy old item of news like that! It'd make a cat laugh, Jim Boyd,' says he. 'Who told you?' says I, stupid like. 'Nobody,' says he. 'A week ago Tuesday night I was lying here awake—and I jest knew. I'd suspicioned it before, but then I KNEW. I've been keeping up for the wife's sake. And I'd LIKE to have got that barn built, for Eben'll never get it right. But anyhow, now that you've eased your mind, Jim, put on a smile and tell me something interesting,' Well, there it was. They'd been so scared to tell him and he knew it all the time. Strange how nature looks out for us, ain't it, and lets us know what we should know when the time comes? Did I never tell you the yarn about Henry getting the fish hook in his nose, Mistress Blythe?"

"No."

"Well, him and me had a laugh over it today. It happened nigh unto thirty years ago. Him and me and several more was out mackerel fishing one day. It was a great day—never saw such a school of mackerel in the gulf—and in the general excitement Henry got quite wild and contrived to stick a fish hook clean through one side of his nose. Well, there he was; there was barb on one end and a big piece of lead on the other, so it couldn't be pulled out. We wanted to take him ashore at once, but Henry was game; he said he'd be jiggered if he'd leave a school like that for anything short of lockjaw; then he kept fishing away, hauling in hand over fist and groaning between times. Fin'lly the school passed and we come in with a load; I got a file and begun to try to file through that hook. I tried to be as easy as I could, but you should have heard Henry—no, you shouldn't either. It was well no ladies were around. Henry wasn't a swearing man, but he'd heard some few matters of that sort along shore in his time, and he fished 'em all out of his recollection and hurled 'em at me. Fin'lly he declared he couldn't stand it and I had no bowels of compassion. So we hitched up and I drove him to a doctor in Charlottetown, thirty-five miles—there weren't none nearer in them days—with that blessed hook still hanging from his nose. When we got there old Dr. Crabb jest took a file and filed that hook jest the same as I'd tried to do, only he weren't a mite particular about doing it easy!"

Captain Jim's visit to his old friend had revived many recollections and he was now in the full tide of reminiscences.

"Henry was asking me today if I remembered the time old Father Chiniquy blessed Alexander MacAllister's boat. Another odd yarn—and true as gospel. I was in the boat myself. We went out, him and me, in Alexander MacAllister's boat one morning at sunrise. Besides, there was a French boy in the boat—Catholic of course. You know old Father Chiniquy had turned Protestant, so the Catholics hadn't much use for him. Well, we sat out in the gulf in the broiling sun till noon, and not a bite did we get. When we went ashore old Father Chiniquy had to go, so he said in that polite way of his, 'I'm very sorry I cannot go out with you dis afternoon, Mr. MacAllister, but I leave you my blessing. You will catch a t'ousand dis afternoon.

'Well, we did not catch a thousand, but we caught exactly nine hundred and ninety-nine—the biggest catch for a small boat on the whole north shore that summer. Curious, wasn't it? Alexander MacAllister, he says to Andrew Peters, 'Well, and what do you think of Father Chiniquy now?' 'Vell,' growled Andrew, 'I t'ink de old devil has got a blessing left yet.' Laws, how Henry did laugh over that today!"

"Do you know who Mr. Ford is, Captain Jim?" asked Anne, seeing that Captain Jim's fountain of reminiscence had run out for the present. "I want you to guess."

Captain Jim shook his head.

"I never was any hand at guessing, Mistress Blythe, and yet somehow when I come in I thought, 'Where have I seen them eyes before?'—for I HAVE seen 'em."

"Think of a September morning many years ago," said Anne, softly. "Think of a ship sailing up the harbor—a ship long waited for and despaired of. Think of the day the Royal William came in and the first look you had at the schoolmaster's bride."

Captain Jim sprang up.

"They're Persis Selwyn's eyes," he almost shouted. "You can't be her son—you must be her—"

"Grandson; yes, I am Alice Selwyn's son."

Captain Jim swooped down on Owen Ford and shook his hand over again.

"Alice Selwyn's son! Lord, but you're welcome! Many's the time I've wondered where the descendants of the schoolmaster were living. I knew there was none on the Island. Alice—Alice—the first baby ever born in that little house. No baby ever brought more joy! I've dandled her a hundred times. It was from my knee she took her first steps alone. Can't I see her mother's face watching her—and it was near sixty years ago. Is she living yet?"

"No, she died when I was only a boy."

"Oh, it doesn't seem right that I should be living to hear that," sighed Captain Jim. "But I'm heart-glad to see you. It's brought back my youth for a little while. You don't know yet what a boon THAT is. Mistress Blythe here has the trick—she does it quite often for me."

Captain Jim was still more excited when he discovered that Owen Ford was what he called a "real writing man." He gazed at him as at a superior being. Captain Jim knew that Anne wrote, but he had never taken that fact very seriously. Captain Jim thought women were delightful creatures, who ought to have the vote, and everything else they wanted, bless their hearts; but he did not believe they could write.

"Jest look at A Mad Love," he would protest. "A woman wrote that and jest look at it—one hundred and three chapters when it could all have been told in ten. A writing woman never knows when to stop; that's the trouble. The p'int of good writing is to know when to stop."

"Mr. Ford wants to hear some of your stories, Captain Jim" said Anne. "Tell him the one about the captain who went crazy and imagined he was the Flying Dutchman."

This was Captain Jim's best story. It was a compound of horror and humor, and though Anne had heard it several times she laughed as heartily and shivered as fearsomely over it as Mr. Ford did. Other tales followed, for Captain Jim had an audience after his own heart. He told how his vessel had been run down by a steamer; how he had been boarded by Malay pirates; how his ship had caught fire; how he helped a political prisoner escape from a South African republic; how he had been wrecked one fall on the Magdalens and stranded there for the winter; how a tiger had broken loose on board ship; how his crew had mutinied and marooned him on a barren island—these and many other tales, tragic or humorous or grotesque, did Captain Jim relate. The mystery of the sea, the fascination of far lands, the lure of adventure, the laughter of the world—his hearers felt and realised them all. Owen Ford listened, with his head on his hand, and the First Mate purring on his knee, his brilliant eyes fastened on Captain Jim's rugged, eloquent face.

"Won't you let Mr. Ford see your life-book, Captain Jim?" asked Anne, when Captain Jim finally declared that yarn-spinning must end for the time.

"Oh, he don't want to be bothered with THAT," protested Captain Jim, who was secretly dying to show it.

"I should like nothing better than to see it, Captain Boyd," said Owen. "If it is half as wonderful as your tales it will be worth seeing."

With pretended reluctance Captain Jim dug his life-book out of his old chest and handed it to Owen.

"I reckon you won't care to wrastle long with my old hand o' write. I never had much schooling," he observed carelessly. "Just wrote that there to amuse my nephew Joe. He's always wanting stories. Comes here yesterday and says to me, reproachful-like, as I was lifting a twenty-pound codfish out of my boat, 'Uncle Jim, ain't a codfish a dumb animal?' I'd been a-telling him, you see, that he must be real kind to dumb animals, and never hurt 'em in any way. I got out of the scrape by saying a codfish was dumb enough but it wasn't an animal, but Joe didn't look satisfied, and I wasn't satisfied myself. You've got to be mighty careful what you tell them little critters. THEY can see through you."

While talking, Captain Jim watched Owen Ford from the corner of his eye as the latter examined the life-book; and presently observing that his guest was lost in its pages, he turned smilingly to his cupboard and proceeded to make a pot of tea. Owen Ford separated himself from the life-book, with as much reluctance as a miser wrenches himself from his gold, long enough to drink his tea, and then returned to it hungrily.

"Oh, you can take that thing home with you if you want to," said Captain Jim, as if the "thing" were not his most treasured possession. "I must go down and pull my boat up a bit on the skids. There's a wind coming. Did you notice the sky tonight?

Mackerel skies and mares' tails
Make tall ships carry short sails."

Owen Ford accepted the offer of the life-book gladly. On their way home Anne told him the story of lost Margaret.

"That old captain is a wonderful old fellow," he said. "What a life he has led! Why, the man had more adventures in one week of his life than most of us have in a lifetime. Do you really think his tales are all true?"

"I certainly do. I am sure Captain Jim could not tell a lie; and besides, all the people about here say that everything happened as he relates it. There used to be plenty of his old shipmates alive to corroborate him. He's one of the last of the old type of P.E. Island sea-captains. They are almost extinct now."

25. THE WRITING OF THE BOOK

Owen Ford came over to the little house the next morning in a state of great excitement. "Mrs. Blythe, this is a wonderful book—absolutely wonderful. If I could take it and use the material for a book I feel certain I could make the novel of the year out of it. Do you suppose Captain Jim would let me do it?"

"Let you! I'm sure he would be delighted," cried Anne. "I admit that it was what was in my head when I took you down last night. Captain Jim has always been wishing he could get somebody to write his life-book properly for him."

"Will you go down to the Point with me this evening, Mrs. Blythe? I'll ask him about that life-book myself, but I want you to tell him that you told me the story of lost Margaret and ask him if he will let me use it as a thread of romance with which to weave the stories of the life-book into a harmonious whole."

Captain Jim was more excited than ever when Owen Ford told him of his plan. At last his cherished dream was to be realized and his "life-book" given to the world. He was also pleased that the story of lost Margaret should be woven into it.

"It will keep her name from being forgotten," he said wistfully.

"That's why I want it put in."

"We'll collaborate," cried Owen delightedly. "You will give the soul and I the body. Oh, we'll write a famous book between us, Captain Jim. And we'll get right to work."

"And to think my book is to be writ by the schoolmaster's grandson!" exclaimed Captain Jim. "Lad, your grandfather was my dearest friend. I thought there was nobody like him. I see now why I had to wait so long. It couldn't be writ till the right man come. You BELONG here—you've got the soul of this old north shore in you—you're the only one who COULD write it."

It was arranged that the tiny room off the living room at the lighthouse should be given over to Owen for a workshop. It was necessary that Captain Jim should be near him as he wrote, for consultation upon many matters of sea-faring and gulf lore of which Owen was quite ignorant.

He began work on the book the very next morning, and flung himself into it heart and soul. As for Captain Jim, he was a happy man that summer. He looked upon the little room where Owen worked as a sacred shrine. Owen talked everything over with Captain Jim, but he would not let him see the manuscript.

"You must wait until it is published," he said. "Then you'll get it all at once in its best shape."

He delved into the treasures of the life-book and used them freely. He dreamed and brooded over lost Margaret until she became a vivid reality to him and lived in his pages. As the book progressed it took possession of him and he worked at it with feverish eagerness. He let Anne and Leslie read the manuscript and criticise it; and the concluding chapter of the book, which the critics, later on, were pleased to call idyllic, was modelled upon a suggestion of Leslie's.

Anne fairly hugged herself with delight over the success of her idea.

"I knew when I looked at Owen Ford that he was the very man for it," she told Gilbert. "Both humor and passion were in his face, and that, together with the art of expression, was just what was necessary for the writing of such a book. As Mrs. Rachel would say, he was predestined for the part."

Owen Ford wrote in the mornings. The afternoons were generally spent in some merry outing with the Blythes. Leslie often went, too, for Captain Jim took charge of Dick frequently, in order to set her free. They went boating on the harbor and up the three pretty rivers that flowed into it; they had clambakes on the bar and mussel-bakes on the rocks; they picked strawberries on the sand-dunes; they went out cod-fishing with Captain Jim; they shot plover in the shore fields and wild ducks in the cove—at least, the men did. In the evenings they rambled in the low-lying, daisied, shore fields under a golden moon, or they sat in the living room at the little house where often the coolness of the sea breeze justified a driftwood fire, and talked of the thousand and one things which happy, eager, clever young people can find to talk about.

Ever since the day on which she had made her confession to Anne Leslie had been a changed creature. There was no trace of her old coldness and reserve, no shadow of her old bitterness. The girlhood of which she had been cheated seemed to come back to her with the ripeness of womanhood; she expanded like a flower of flame and perfume; no laugh was readier than hers, no wit quicker, in the twilight circles of that enchanted summer. When she could not be with them all felt that some exquisite savor was lacking in their intercourse. Her beauty was illumined by the awakened soul within, as some rosy lamp might shine through a flawless vase of alabaster. There were hours when Anne's eyes seemed to ache with the splendor of her. As for Owen Ford, the "Margaret" of his book, although she had the soft brown hair and elfin face of the real girl who had vanished so long ago, "pillowed where lost Atlantis sleeps," had the personality of Leslie Moore, as it was revealed to him in those halcyon days at Four Winds Harbor.

All in all, it was a never-to-be-forgotten summer—one of those summers which come seldom into any life, but leave a rich heritage of beautiful memories in their going—one of those summers which, in a fortunate combination of delightful weather, delightful friends and delightful doings, come as near to perfection as anything can come in this world.

"Too good to last," Anne told herself with a little sigh, on the September day when a certain nip in the wind and a certain shade of intense blue on the gulf water said that autumn was hard by.

That evening Owen Ford told them that he had finished his book and that his vacation must come to an end.

"I have a good deal to do to it yet—revising and pruning and so forth," he said, "but in the main it's done. I wrote the last sentence this morning. If I can find a publisher for it it will probably be out next summer or fall."

Owen had not much doubt that he would find a publisher. He knew that he had written a great book—a book that would score a wonderful success—a book that would LIVE. He knew that it would bring him both fame and fortune; but when he had written the last line of it he had bowed his head on the manuscript and so sat for a long time. And his thoughts were not of the good work he had done.

26. OWEN FORD'S CONFESSION

"I'm so sorry Gilbert is away," said Anne. "He had to go—Allan Lyons at the Glen has met with a serious accident. He will not likely be home till very late. But he told me to tell you he'd be up and over early enough in the morning to see you before you left. It's too provoking. Susan and I had planned such a nice little jamboree for your last night here."

She was sitting beside the garden brook on the little rustic seat Gilbert had built. Owen Ford stood before her, leaning against the bronze column of a yellow birch. He was very pale and his face bore the marks of the preceding sleepless night. Anne, glancing up at him, wondered if, after all, his summer had brought him the strength it should. Had he worked too hard over his book? She remembered that for a week he had not been looking well.

"I'm rather glad the doctor is away," said Owen slowly. "I wanted to see you alone, Mrs. Blythe. There is something I must tell somebody, or I think it will drive me mad. I've been trying for a week to look it in the face—and I can't. I know I can trust you—and, besides, you will understand. A woman with eyes like yours always understands. You are one of the folks people instinctively tell things to. Mrs. Blythe, I love Leslie. LOVE her! That seems too weak a word!"

His voice suddenly broke with the suppressed passion of his utterance. He turned his head away and hid his face on his arm. His whole form shook. Anne sat looking at him, pale and aghast. She had never thought of this! And yet—how was it she had never thought of it? It now seemed a natural and inevitable thing. She wondered at her own blindness. But—but—things like this did not happen in Four Winds. Elsewhere in the world human passions might set at defiance human conventions and laws—but not HERE, surely. Leslie had kept summer boarders off and on for ten years, and nothing like this had happened. But perhaps they had not been like Owen Ford; and the vivid, LIVING Leslie of this summer was not the cold, sullen girl of other years. Oh, SOMEBODY should have thought of this! Why hadn't Miss Cornelia thought of it? Miss Cornelia was always ready enough to sound the alarm where men were concerned. Anne felt an unreasonable resentment against Miss Cornelia. Then she gave a little inward groan. No matter who was to blame the mischief was done. And Leslie—what of Leslie? It was for Leslie Anne felt most concerned.

"Does Leslie know this, Mr. Ford?" she asked quietly.

"No—no,—unless she has guessed it. You surely don't think I'd be cad and scoundrel enough to tell her, Mrs. Blythe. I couldn't help loving her—that's all—and my misery is greater than I can bear."

"Does SHE care?" asked Anne. The moment the question crossed her lips she felt that she should not have asked it. Owen Ford answered it with overeager protest.

"No—no, of course not. But I could make her care if she were free—I know I could."

"She does care—and he knows it," thought Anne. Aloud she said, sympathetically but decidedly:

"But she is not free, Mr. Ford. And the only thing you can do is to go away in silence and leave her to her own life."

"I know—I know," groaned Owen. He sat down on the grassy bank and stared moodily into the amber water beneath him. "I know there's nothing to do—nothing but to say conventionally, 'Good-bye, Mrs. Moore. Thank you for all your kindness to me this summer,' just as I would have said it to the sonsy, bustling, keen-eyed housewife I expected her to be when I came. Then I'll pay my board money like any honest boarder and go! Oh, it's very simple. No doubt—no perplexity—a straight road to the end of the world!

"And I'll walk it—you needn't fear that I won't, Mrs. Blythe. But it would be easier to walk over red-hot ploughshares."

Anne flinched with the pain of his voice. And there was so little she could say that would be adequate to the situation. Blame was out of the question—advice was not needed—sympathy was mocked by the man's stark agony. She could only feel with him in a maze of compassion and regret. Her heart ached for Leslie! Had not that poor girl suffered enough without this?

"It wouldn't be so hard to go and leave her if she were only happy," resumed Owen passionately. "But to think of her living death—to realise what it is to which I do leave her! THAT is the worst of all. I would give my life to make her happy—and I can do nothing even to help her—nothing. She is bound forever to that poor wretch—with nothing to look forward to but growing old in a succession of empty, meaningless, barren years. It drives me mad to think of it. But I must go through my life, never seeing her, but always knowing what she is enduring. It's hideous—hideous!"

"It is very hard," said Anne sorrowfully. "We—her friends here—all know how hard it is for her."

"And she is so richly fitted for life," said Owen rebelliously.

"Her beauty is the least of her dower—and she is the most beautiful woman I've ever known. That laugh of hers! I've angled all summer to evoke that laugh, just for the delight of hearing it. And her eyes—they are as deep and blue as the gulf out there. I never saw such blueness—and gold! Did you ever see her hair down, Mrs. Blythe?"

"No."

"I did—once. I had gone down to the Point to go fishing with Captain Jim but it was too rough to go out, so I came back. She had taken the opportunity of what she expected to be an afternoon alone to wash her hair, and she was standing on the veranda in the sunshine to dry it. It fell all about her to her feet in a fountain of living gold. When she saw me she hurried in, and the wind caught her hair and swirled it all around her—Danae in her cloud. Somehow, just then the knowledge that I loved her came home to me—and realised that I had loved her from the moment I first saw her standing against the darkness in that glow of light. And she must live on here—petting and soothing Dick, pinching and saving for a mere existence, while I spend my life longing vainly for her, and debarred, by that very fact, from even giving her the little help a friend might. I walked the shore last night, almost till dawn, and thrashed it all out over and over again. And yet, in spite of everything, I can't find it in my heart to be sorry that I came to Four Winds. It seems to me that, bad as everything is, it would be still worse never to have known Leslie. It's burning, searing pain to love her and leave her—but not to have loved her is unthinkable. I suppose all this sounds very crazy—all these terrible emotions always do sound foolish when we put them into our inadequate words. They are not meant to be spoken—only felt and endured. I shouldn't have spoken—but it has helped—some. At least, it has given me strength to go away respectably tomorrow morning, without making a scene. You'll write me now and then, won't you, Mrs. Blythe, and give me what news there is to give of her?"

"Yes," said Anne. "Oh, I'm so sorry you are going—we'll miss you so—we've all been such friends! If it were not for this you could come back other summers. Perhaps, even yet—by-and-by—when you've forgotten, perhaps—"

"I shall never forget—and I shall never come back to Four Winds," said Owen briefly.

Silence and twilight fell over the garden. Far away the sea was lapping gently and monotonously on the bar. The wind of evening in the poplars sounded like some sad, weird, old rune—some broken dream of old memories. A slender shapely young aspen rose up before them against the fine maize and emerald and paling rose of the western sky, which brought out every leaf and twig in dark, tremulous, elfin loveliness.

"Isn't that beautiful?" said Owen, pointing to it with the air of a man who puts a certain conversation behind him.

"It's so beautiful that it hurts me," said Anne softly. "Perfect things like that always did hurt me—I remember I called it 'the queer ache' when I was a child. What is the reason that pain like this seems inseparable from perfection? Is it the pain of finality—when we realise that there can be nothing beyond but retrogression?"

"Perhaps," said Owen dreamily, "it is the prisoned infinite in us calling out to its kindred infinite as expressed in that visible perfection."

"You seem to have a cold in the head. Better rub some tallow on your nose when you go to bed," said Miss Cornelia, who had come in through the little gate between the firs in time to catch Owen's last remark. Miss Cornelia liked Owen; but it was a matter of principle with her to visit any "high-falutin" language from a man with a snub.

Miss Cornelia personated the comedy that ever peeps around the corner at the tragedy of life. Anne, whose nerves had been rather strained, laughed hysterically, and even Owen smiled. Certainly, sentiment and passion had a way of shrinking out of sight in Miss Cornelia's presence. And yet to Anne nothing seemed quite as hopeless and dark and painful as it had seemed a few moments before. But sleep was far from her eyes that night.

27. ON THE SAND BAR

Owen Ford left Four Winds the next morning. In the evening Anne went over to see Leslie, but found nobody. The house was locked and there was no light in any window. It looked like a home left soulless. Leslie did not run over on the following day—which Anne thought a bad sign.

Gilbert having occasion to go in the evening to the fishing cove, Anne drove with him to the Point, intending to stay awhile with Captain Jim. But the great light, cutting its swathes through the fog of the autumn evening, was in care of Alec Boyd and Captain Jim was away.

"What will you do?" asked Gilbert. "Come with me?"

"I don't want to go to the cove—but I'll go over the channel with you, and roam about on the sand shore till you come back. The rock shore is too slippery and grim tonight."

Alone on the sands of the bar Anne gave herself up to the eerie charm of the night. It was warm for September, and the late afternoon had been very foggy; but a full moon had in part lessened the fog and transformed the harbor and the gulf and the surrounding shores into a strange, fantastic, unreal world of pale silver mist, through which everything loomed phantom-like. Captain Josiah Crawford's black schooner sailing down the channel, laden with potatoes for Bluenose ports, was a spectral ship bound for a far uncharted land, ever receding, never to be reached. The calls of unseen gulls overhead were the cries of the souls of doomed seamen. The little curls of foam that blew across the sand were elfin things stealing up from the sea-caves. The big, round-shouldered sand-dunes were the sleeping giants of some old northern tale. The lights that glimmered palely across the harbor were the delusive beacons on some coast of fairyland. Anne pleased herself with a hundred fancies as she wandered through the mist. It was delightful—romantic—mysterious to be roaming here alone on this enchanted shore.

But was she alone? Something loomed in the mist before her—took shape and form—suddenly moved towards her across the wave-rippled sand.

"Leslie!" exclaimed Anne in amazement. "Whatever are you doing—HERE—tonight?"

"If it comes to that, whatever are YOU doing here?" said Leslie, trying to laugh. The effort was a failure. She looked very pale and tired; but the love locks under her scarlet cap were curling about her face and eyes like little sparkling rings of gold.

"I'm waiting for Gilbert—he's over at the Cove. I intended to stay at the light, but Captain Jim is away."

"Well, *I* came here because I wanted to walk—and walk—and WALK," said Leslie restlessly. "I couldn't on the rock shore—the tide was too high and the rocks prisoned me. I had to come here—or I should have gone mad, I think. I rowed myself over the channel in Captain Jim's flat. I've been here for an hour. Come—come—let us walk. I can't stand still. Oh, Anne!"

"Leslie, dearest, what is the trouble?" asked Anne, though she knew too well already.

"I can't tell you—don't ask me. I wouldn't mind your knowing—I wish you did know—but I can't tell you—I can't tell anyone. I've been such a fool, Anne—and oh, it hurts so terribly to be a fool. There's nothing so painful in the world."

She laughed bitterly. Anne slipped her arm around her.

"Leslie, is it that you have learned to care for Mr. Ford?"

Leslie turned herself about passionately.

"How did you know?" she cried. "Anne, how did you know? Oh, is it written in my face for everyone to see? Is it as plain as that?"

"No, no. I—I can't tell you how I knew. It just came into my mind, somehow. Leslie, don't look at me like that!"

"Do you despise me?" demanded Leslie in a fierce, low tone. "Do you think I'm wicked—unwomanly? Or do you think I'm just plain fool?"

"I don't think you any of those things. Come, dear, let's just talk it over sensibly, as we might talk over any other of the great crises of life. You've been brooding over it and let yourself drift into a morbid view of it. You know you have a little tendency to do that about everything that goes wrong, and you promised me that you would fight against it."

"But—oh, it's so—so shameful," murmured Leslie. "To love him—unsought—and when I'm not free to love anybody."

"There's nothing shameful about it. But I'm very sorry that you have learned to care for Owen, because, as things are, it will only make you more unhappy."

"I didn't LEARN to care," said Leslie, walking on and speaking passionately. "If it had been like that I could have prevented it. I never dreamed of such a thing until that day, a week ago, when he told me he had finished his book and must soon go away. Then—then I knew. I felt as if someone had struck me a terrible blow. I didn't say anything—I couldn't speak—but I don't know what I looked like. I'm so afraid my face betrayed me. Oh, I would die of shame if I thought he knew—or suspected."

Anne was miserably silent, hampered by her deductions from her conversation with Owen. Leslie went on feverishly, as if she found relief in speech.

"I was so happy all this summer, Anne—happier than I ever was in my life. I thought it was because everything had been made clear between you and me, and that it was our friendship which made life seem so beautiful and full once more. And it WAS, in part—but not all—oh, not nearly all. I know now why everything was so different. And now it's all over—and he has gone. How can I live, Anne? When I turned back into the house this morning after he had gone the solitude struck me like a blow in the face."

"It won't seem so hard by and by, dear," said Anne, who always felt the pain of her friends so keenly that she could not speak easy, fluent words of comforting. Besides, she remembered how well-meant speeches had hurt her in her own sorrow and was afraid.

"Oh, it seems to me it will grow harder all the time," said Leslie miserably. "I've nothing to look forward to. Morning will come after morning—and he will not come back—he will never come back. Oh, when I think that I will never see him again I feel as if a great brutal hand had twisted itself among my heartstrings, and was wrenching them. Once, long ago, I dreamed of love—and I thought it must be beautiful—and NOW—its like THIS. When he went away yesterday morning he was so cold and indifferent. He said 'Good-bye, Mrs. Moore' in the coldest tone in the world—as if we had not even been friends—as if I meant absolutely nothing to him. I know I don't—I didn't want him to care—but he MIGHT have been a little kinder."

"Oh, I wish Gilbert would come," thought Anne. She was racked between her sympathy for Leslie and the necessity of avoiding anything that would betray Owen's confidence. She knew why his good-bye had been so cold—why it could not have the cordiality that their good-comradeship demanded—but she could not tell Leslie.

"I couldn't help it, Anne—I couldn't help it," said poor Leslie.

"I know that."

"Do you blame me so very much?"

"I don't blame you at all."

"And you won't—you won't tell Gilbert?"

"Leslie! Do you think I would do such a thing?"

"Oh, I don't know—you and Gilbert are such CHUMS. I don't see how you could help telling him everything."

"Everything about my own concerns—yes. But not my friends' secrets."

"I couldn't have HIM know. But I'm glad YOU know. I would feel guilty if there were anything I was ashamed to tell you. I hope Miss Cornelia won't find out. Sometimes I feel as if those terrible, kind brown eyes of hers read my very soul. Oh, I wish this mist would never lift —I wish I could just stay in it forever, hidden away from every living being. I don't see how I can go on with life. This summer has been so full. I never was lonely for a moment. Before Owen came there used to be horrible moments—when I had been with you and Gilbert—and then had to leave you. You two would walk away together and I would walk away ALONE. After Owen came he was always there to walk home with me—we would laugh and talk as you and Gilbert were doing—there were no more lonely, envious moments for me. And NOW! Oh, yes, I've been a fool. Let's have done talking about my folly. I'll never bore you with it again."

"Here is Gilbert, and you are coming back with us," said Anne, who had no intention of leaving Leslie to wander alone on the sand-bar on such a night and in such a mood. "There's plenty of room in our boat for three, and we'll tie the flat on behind."

"Oh, I suppose I must reconcile myself to being the odd one again," said poor Leslie with another bitter laugh. "Forgive me, Anne—that was hateful. I ought to be thankful—and I AM—that I have two good friends who are glad to count me in as a third. Don't mind my hateful speeches. I just seem to be one great pain all over and everything hurts me."

"Leslie seemed very quiet tonight, didn't she?" said Gilbert, when he and Anne reached home. "What in the world was she doing over there on the bar alone?"

"Oh, she was tired—and you know she likes to go to the shore after one of Dick's bad days."

"What a pity she hadn't met and married a fellow like Ford long ago," ruminated Gilbert. "They'd have made an ideal couple, wouldn't they?"

"For pity's sake, Gilbert, don't develop into a match-maker. It's an abominable profession for a man," cried Anne rather sharply, afraid that Gilbert might blunder on the truth if he kept on in this strain.

"Bless us, Anne-girl, I'm not matchmaking," protested Gilbert, rather surprised at her tone. "I was only thinking of one of the might-have-beens."

"Well, don't. It's a waste of time," said Anne. Then she added suddenly:

"Oh, Gilbert, I wish everybody could be as happy as we are."

28. ODDS AND ENDS

"I've been reading obituary notices," said Miss Cornelia, laying down the Daily Enterprise and taking up her sewing.

The harbor was lying black and sullen under a dour November sky; the wet, dead leaves clung drenched and sodden to the window sills; but the little house was gay with firelight and spring-like with Anne's ferns and geraniums.

"It's always summer here, Anne," Leslie had said one day; and all who were the guests of that house of dreams felt the same.

"The Enterprise seems to run to obituaries these days," quoth Miss Cornelia. "It always has a couple of columns of them, and I read every line. It's one of my forms of recreation, especially when there's some original poetry attached to them. Here's a choice sample for you:

She's gone to be with her Maker,
Never more to roam.
She used to play and sing with joy
The song of Home, Sweet Home.

Who says we haven't any poetical talent on the Island! Have you ever noticed what heaps of good people die, Anne, dearie? It's kind of pitiful. Here's ten obituaries, and every one of them saints and models, even the men. Here's old Peter Stimson, who has 'left a large circle of friends to mourn his untimely loss.' Lord, Anne, dearie, that man was eighty, and everybody who knew him had been wishing him dead these thirty years. Read obituaries when you're blue, Anne, dearie—especially the ones of folks you know. If you've any sense of humor at all they'll cheer you up, believe ME. I just wish *I* had the writing of the obituaries of some people. Isn't 'obituary' an awful ugly word? This very Peter I've been speaking of had a face exactly like one. I never saw it but I thought of the word OBITUARY then and there. There's only one uglier word that I know of, and that's RELICT. Lord, Anne, dearie, I may be an old maid, but there's this comfort in it—I'll never be any man's 'relict.'"

"It IS an ugly word," said Anne, laughing. "Avonlea graveyard was full of old tombstones 'sacred to the memory of So-and-So, RELICT of the late So-and-So.' It always made me think of something worn out and moth eaten. Why is it that so many of the words connected with death are so disagreeable? I do wish that the custom of calling a dead body 'the remains' could be abolished. I positively shiver when I hear the undertaker say at a funeral, 'All who wish to see the remains please step this way.' It always gives me the horrible impression that I am about to view the scene of a cannibal feast."

"Well, all I hope," said Miss Cornelia calmly, "is that when I'm dead nobody will call me 'our departed sister.' I took a scunner at this sister-and-brothering business five years ago when there was a travelling evangelist holding meetings at the Glen. I hadn't any use for him from the start. I felt in my bones that there was something wrong with him. And there was. Mind you, he was pretending to be a Presbyterian—PresbyTARian, HE called it—and all the time he was a Methodist. He brothered and sistered everybody. He had a large circle of relations, that man had. He clutched my hand fervently one night, and said imploringly, 'My DEAR sister Bryant, are you a Christian?' I just looked him over a bit, and then I said calmly, 'The only brother I ever had, MR. Fiske, was buried fifteen years ago, and I haven't adopted any since. As for being a Christian, I was that, I hope and believe, when you were crawling about the floor in petticoats.' THAT squelched him, believe ME. Mind you, Anne dearie, I'm not down on all evangelists. We've had some real fine, earnest men, who did a lot of good and made the old sinners squirm. But this Fiske-man wasn't one of them. I had a good laugh all to myself one evening. Fiske had asked all who were Christians to stand up. *I* didn't, believe me! I never had any use for that sort of thing. But most of them did, and then he asked all who wanted to be Christians to stand up. Nobody stirred for a spell, so Fiske started up a hymn at the top of his voice. Just in front of me poor little Ikey Baker was sitting in the Millison pew. He was a home boy, ten years old, and Millison just about worked him to death. The poor little creature was always so tired he fell asleep right off whenever he went to church or anywhere he could sit still for a few minutes. He'd been sleeping all through the meeting, and I was thankful to see the poor child getting a rest, believe ME. Well, when Fiske's voice went soaring skyward and the rest joined in, poor Ikey wakened with a start. He thought it was just an ordinary singing and that everybody ought to stand up, so he scrambled to his feet mighty quick, knowing he'd get a combing down from Maria Millison for sleeping in meeting. Fiske saw him, stopped and shouted, 'Another soul saved! Glory Hallelujah!' And there was poor, frightened Ikey, only half awake and yawning, never thinking about his soul at all. Poor child, he never had time to think of anything but his tired, overworked little body.

"Leslie went one night and the Fiske-man got right after her—oh, he was especially anxious about the souls of the nice-looking girls, believe me!—and he hurt her feelings so she never went again. And then he prayed every night after that, right in public, that the Lord would soften her hard heart. Finally I went to Mr. Leavitt, our minister then, and told him if he didn't make Fiske stop that I'd just rise up the next night and throw my hymn book at him when he mentioned that 'beautiful but unrepentant young woman.' I'd have done it too, believe ME. Mr. Leavitt did put a stop to it, but Fiske kept on with his meetings until Charley Douglas put an end to his career in the Glen. Mrs. Charley had been out in California all winter. She'd been real melancholy in the fall—religious melancholy—it ran in her family. Her father worried so much over believing that he had committed the unpardonable sin that he died in the asylum. So when Rose Douglas got that way Charley packed her off to visit her sister in Los Angeles. She got perfectly well and came home just when the Fiske revival was in full swing. She stepped off the train at the Glen, real smiling and chipper, and the first thing she saw staring her in the face on the black, gable-end of the freight shed, was the question, in big white letters, two feet high, 'Whither goest thou—to heaven or hell?' That had been one of Fiske's ideas, and he had got Henry Hammond to paint it. Rose just gave a shriek and fainted; and when they got her home she was worse than ever. Charley Douglas went to Mr. Leavitt and told him that every Douglas would leave the church if Fiske was kept there any longer. Mr. Leavitt had to give in, for the Douglases paid half his salary, so Fiske departed, and we had to depend on our Bibles once more for instructions on how to get to heaven. After he was gone Mr. Leavitt found out he was just a masquerading Methodist, and he felt pretty sick, believe ME. Mr. Leavitt fell short in some ways, but he was a good, sound Presbyterian."

"By the way, I had a letter from Mr. Ford yesterday," said Anne. "He asked me to remember him kindly to you."

"I don't want his remembrances," said Miss Cornelia, curtly.

"Why?" said Anne, in astonishment. "I thought you liked him."

"Well, so I did, in a kind of way. But I'll never forgive him for what he done to Leslie. There's that poor child eating her heart out about him—as if she hadn't had trouble enough—and him ranting round Toronto, I've no doubt, enjoying himself same as ever. Just like a man."

"Oh, Miss Cornelia, how did you find out?"

"Lord, Anne, dearie, I've got eyes, haven't I? And I've known Leslie since she was a baby. There's been a new kind of heartbreak in her eyes all the fall, and I know that writer-man was behind it somehow. I'll never forgive myself for being the means of bringing him here. But I never expected he'd be like he was. I thought he'd just be like the other men Leslie had boarded—conceited young asses, every one of them, that she never had any use for. One of them did try to flirt with her once and she froze him out—so bad, I feel sure he's never got himself thawed since. So I never thought of any danger."

"Don't let Leslie suspect you know her secret," said Anne hurriedly. "I think it would hurt her."

"Trust me, Anne, dearie. *I* wasn't born yesterday. Oh, a plague on all the men! One of them ruined Leslie's life to begin with, and now another of the tribe comes and makes her still more wretched. Anne, this world is an awful place, believe me."

"There's something in the world amiss
Will be unriddled by and by,"

quoted Anne dreamily.

"If it is, it'll be in a world where there aren't any men," said Miss Cornelia gloomily.

"What have the men been doing now?" asked Gilbert, entering.

"Mischief—mischief! What else did they ever do?"

"It was Eve ate the apple, Miss Cornelia."

"'Twas a he-creature tempted her," retorted Miss Cornelia triumphantly.

Leslie, after her first anguish was over, found it possible to go on with life after all, as most of us do, no matter what our particular form of torment has been. It is even possible that she enjoyed moments of it, when she was one of the gay circle in the little house of dreams. But if Anne ever hoped that she was forgetting Owen Ford she would have been undeceived by the furtive hunger in Leslie's eyes whenever his name was mentioned. Pitiful to that hunger, Anne always contrived to tell Captain Jim or Gilbert bits of news from Owen's letters when Leslie was with them. The girl's flush and pallor at such moments spoke all too eloquently of the emotion that filled her being. But she never spoke of him to Anne, or mentioned that night on the sand-bar.

One day her old dog died and she grieved bitterly over him.

"He's been my friend so long," she said sorrowfully to Anne. "He was Dick's old dog, you know—Dick had him for a year or so before we were married. He left him with me when he sailed on the Four Sisters. Carlo got very fond of me—and his dog-love helped me through that first dreadful year after mother died, when I was alone. When I heard that Dick was coming back I was afraid Carlo wouldn't be so much mine. But he never seemed to care for Dick, though he had been so fond of him once. He would snap and growl at him as if he were a stranger. I was glad. It was nice to have one thing whose love was all mine. That old dog has been such a comfort to me, Anne. He got so feeble in the fall that I was afraid he couldn't live long—but I hoped I could nurse him through the winter. He seemed pretty well this morning. He was lying on the rug before the fire; then, all at once, he got up and crept over to me; he put his head on my lap and gave me one loving look out of his big, soft, dog eyes—and then he just shivered and died. I shall miss him so."

"Let me give you another dog, Leslie," said Anne. "I'm getting a lovely Gordon setter for a Christmas present for Gilbert. Let me give you one too."

Leslie shook her head.

"Not just now, thank you, Anne. I don't feel like having another dog yet. I don't seem to have any affection left for another. Perhaps—in time—I'll let you give me one. I really need one as a kind of protection. But there was something almost human about Carlo—it wouldn't be DECENT to fill his place too hurriedly, dear old fellow."

Anne went to Avonlea a week before Christmas and stayed until after the holidays. Gilbert came up for her, and there was a glad New Year celebration at Green Gables, when Barrys and Blythes and Wrights assembled to devour a dinner which had cost Mrs. Rachel and Marilla much careful thought and preparation. When they went back to Four Winds the little house was almost drifted over, for the third storm of a winter that was to prove phenomenally stormy had whirled up the harbor and heaped huge snow mountains about everything it encountered. But Captain Jim had shovelled out doors and paths, and Miss Cornelia had come down and kindled the hearth-fire.

"It's good to see you back, Anne, dearie! But did you ever see such drifts? You can't see the Moore place at all unless you go upstairs. Leslie'll be so glad you're back. She's almost buried alive over there. Fortunately Dick can shovel snow, and thinks it's great fun. Susan sent me word to tell you she would be on hand tomorrow. Where are you off to now, Captain?"

"I reckon I'll plough up to the Glen and sit a bit with old Martin Strong. He's not far from his end and he's lonesome. He hasn't many friends—been too busy all his life to make any. He's made heaps of money, though."

"Well, he thought that since he couldn't serve God and Mammon he'd better stick to Mammon," said Miss Cornelia crisply. "So he shouldn't complain if he doesn't find Mammon very good company now."

Captain Jim went out, but remembered something in the yard and turned back for a moment.

"I'd a letter from Mr. Ford, Mistress Blythe, and he says the life-book is accepted and is going to be published next fall. I felt fair uplifted when I got the news. To think that I'm to see it in print at last."

"That man is clean crazy on the subject of his life-book," said Miss Cornelia compassionately. "For my part, I think there's far too many books in the world now."

29. GILBERT AND ANNE DISAGREE

Gilbert laid down the ponderous medical tome over which he had been poring until the increasing dusk of the March evening made him desist. He leaned back in his chair and gazed meditatively out of the window. It was early spring—probably the ugliest time of the year. Not even the sunset could redeem the dead, sodden landscape and rotten black harbor ice upon which he looked. No sign of life was visible, save a big black crow winging his solitary way across a leaden field. Gilbert speculated idly concerning that crow. Was he a family crow, with a black but comely crow wife awaiting him in the woods beyond the Glen? Or was he a glossy young buck of a crow on courting thoughts intent? Or was he a cynical bachelor crow, believing that he travels the fastest who travels alone? Whatever he was, he soon disappeared in congenial gloom and Gilbert turned to the cheerier view indoors.

The firelight flickered from point to point, gleaming on the white and green coats of Gog and Magog, on the sleek, brown head of the beautiful setter basking on the rug, on the picture frames on the walls, on the vaseful of daffodils from the window garden, on Anne herself, sitting by her little table, with her sewing beside her and her hands clasped over her knee while she traced out pictures in the fire—Castles in Spain whose airy turrets pierced moonlit cloud and sunset bar-ships sailing from the Haven of Good Hopes straight to Four Winds Harbor with precious burthen. For Anne was again a dreamer of dreams, albeit a grim shape of fear went with her night and day to shadow and darken her visions.

Gilbert was accustomed to refer to himself as "an old married man." But he still looked upon Anne with the incredulous eyes of a lover. He couldn't wholly believe yet that she was really his. It MIGHT be only a dream after all, part and parcel of this magic house of dreams. His soul still went on tip-toe before her, lest the charm be shattered and the dream dispelled.

"Anne," he said slowly, "lend me your ears. I want to talk with you about something."

Anne looked across at him through the fire-lit gloom.

"What is it?" she asked gaily. "You look fearfully solemn, Gilbert. I really haven't done anything naughty today. Ask Susan."

"It's not of you—or ourselves—I want to talk. It's about Dick Moore."

"Dick Moore?" echoed Anne, sitting up alertly. "Why, what in the world have you to say about Dick Moore?"

"I've been thinking a great deal about him lately. Do you remember that time last summer I treated him for those carbuncles on his neck?"

"Yes—yes."

"I took the opportunity to examine the scars on his head thoroughly. I've always thought Dick was a very interesting case from a medical point of view. Lately I've been studying the history of trephining and the cases where it has been employed. Anne, I have come to the conclusion that if Dick Moore were taken to a good hospital and the operation of trephining performed on several places in his skull, his memory and faculties might be restored."

"Gilbert!" Anne's voice was full of protest. "Surely you don't mean it!"

"I do, indeed. And I have decided that it is my duty to broach the subject to Leslie."

"Gilbert Blythe, you shall NOT do any such thing," cried Anne vehemently. "Oh, Gilbert, you won't—you won't. You couldn't be so cruel. Promise me you won't."

"Why, Anne-girl, I didn't suppose you would take it like this. Be reasonable—"

"I won't be reasonable—I can't be reasonable—I AM reasonable. It is you who are unreasonable. Gilbert, have you ever once thought what it would mean for Leslie if Dick Moore were to be restored to his right senses? Just stop and think! She's unhappy enough now; but life as Dick's nurse and attendant is a thousand times easier for her than life as Dick's wife. I know—I KNOW! It's unthinkable. Don't you meddle with the matter. Leave well enough alone."

"I HAVE thought over that aspect of the case thoroughly, Anne. But I believe that a doctor is bound to set the sanctity of a patient's mind and body above all other considerations, no matter what the consequences may be. I believe it his duty to endeavor to restore health and sanity, if there is any hope whatever of it."

"But Dick isn't your patient in that respect," cried Anne, taking another tack. "If Leslie had asked you if anything could be done for him, THEN it might be your duty to tell her what you really thought. But you've no right to meddle."

"I don't call it meddling. Uncle Dave told Leslie twelve years ago that nothing could be done for Dick. She believes that, of course."

"And why did Uncle Dave tell her that, if it wasn't true?" cried Anne, triumphantly. "Doesn't he know as much about it as you?"

"I think not—though it may sound conceited and presumptuous to say it. And you know as well as I that he is rather prejudiced against what he calls 'these new-fangled notions of cutting and carving.' He's even opposed to operating for appendicitis."

"He's right," exclaimed Anne, with a complete change of front. 'I believe myself that you modern doctors are entirely too fond of making experiments with human flesh and blood."

"Rhoda Allonby would not be a living woman today if I had been afraid of making a certain experiment," argued Gilbert. "I took the risk—and saved her life."

"I'm sick and tired of hearing about Rhoda Allonby," cried Anne—most unjustly, for Gilbert had never mentioned Mrs. Allonby's name since the day he had told Anne of his success in regard to her. And he could not be blamed for other people's discussion of it.

Gilbert felt rather hurt.

"I had not expected you to look at the matter as you do, Anne," he said a little stiffly, getting up and moving towards the office door. It was their first approach to a quarrel.

But Anne flew after him and dragged him back.

"Now, Gilbert, you are not 'going off mad.' Sit down here and I'll apologise bee-YEW-tifully, I shouldn't have said that. But—oh, if you knew—"

Anne checked herself just in time. She had been on the very verge of betraying Leslie's secret.

"Knew what a woman feels about it," she concluded lamely.

"I think I do know. I've looked at the matter from every point of view—and I've been driven to the conclusion that it is my duty to tell Leslie that I believe it is possible that Dick can be restored to himself; there my responsibility ends. It will be for her to decide what she will do."

"I don't think you've any right to put such a responsibility on her. She has enough to bear. She is poor—how could she afford such an operation?"

"That is for her to decide," persisted Gilbert stubbornly.

"You say you think that Dick can be cured. But are you SURE of it?"

"Certainly not. Nobody could be sure of such a thing. There may have been lesions of the brain itself, the effect of which can never be removed. But if, as I believe, his loss of memory and other faculties is due merely to the pressure on the brain centers of certain depressed areas of bone, then he can be cured."

"But it's only a possibility!" insisted Anne. "Now, suppose you tell Leslie and she decides to have the operation. It will cost a great deal. She will have to borrow the money, or sell her little property. And suppose the operation is a failure and Dick remains the same.

"How will she be able to pay back the money she borrows, or make a living for herself and that big helpless creature if she sells the farm?"

"Oh, I know—I know. But it is my duty to tell her. I can't get away from that conviction."

"Oh, I know the Blythe stubbornness," groaned Anne. "But don't do this solely on your own responsibility. Consult Doctor Dave."

"I HAVE done so," said Gilbert reluctantly.

"And what did he say?"

"In brief—as you say—leave well enough alone. Apart from his prejudice against new-fangled surgery, I'm afraid he looks at the case from your point of view—don't do it, for Leslie's sake."

"There now," cried Anne triumphantly. "I do think, Gilbert, that you ought to abide by the judgment of a man nearly eighty, who has seen a great deal and saved scores of lives himself—surely his opinion ought to weigh more than a mere boy's."

"Thank you."

"Don't laugh. It's too serious."

"That's just my point. It IS serious. Here is a man who is a helpless burden. He may be restored to reason and usefulness—"

"He was so very useful before," interjected Anne witheringly.

"He may be given a chance to make good and redeem the past. His wife doesn't know this. I do. It is therefore my duty to tell her that there is such a possibility. That, boiled down, is my decision."

"Don't say 'decision' yet, Gilbert. Consult somebody else. Ask Captain Jim what he thinks about it."

"Very well. But I'll not promise to abide by his opinion, Anne.

"This is something a man must decide for himself. My conscience would never be easy if I kept silent on the subject."

"Oh, your conscience!" moaned Anne. "I suppose that Uncle Dave has a conscience too, hasn't he?"

"Yes. But I am not the keeper of his conscience. Come, Anne, if this affair did not concern Leslie—if it were a purely abstract case, you would agree with me,—you know you would."

"I wouldn't," vowed Anne, trying to believe it herself. "Oh, you can argue all night, Gilbert, but you won't convince me. Just you ask Miss Cornelia what she thinks of it."

"You're driven to the last ditch, Anne, when you bring up Miss Cornelia as a reinforcement. She will say, 'Just like a man,' and rage furiously. No matter. This is no affair for Miss Cornelia to settle. Leslie alone must decide it."

"You know very well how she will decide it," said Anne, almost in tears. "She has ideals of duty, too. I don't see how you can take such a responsibility on your shoulders. *I* couldn't."

"'Because right is right to follow right
Were wisdom in the scorn of consequence,'"

quoted Gilbert.

"Oh, you think a couplet of poetry a convincing argument!" scoffed Anne. "That is so like a man."

And then she laughed in spite of herself. It sounded so like an echo of Miss Cornelia.

"Well, if you won't accept Tennyson as an authority, perhaps you will believe the words of a Greater than he," said Gilbert seriously. "'Ye shall know the truth and the truth shall make you free.' I believe that, Anne, with all my heart. It's the greatest and grandest verse in the Bible—or in any literature—and the TRUEST, if there are comparative degrees of trueness. And it's the first duty of a man to tell the truth, as he sees it and believes it."

"In this case the truth won't make poor Leslie free," sighed Anne. "It will probably end in still more bitter bondage for her. Oh, Gilbert, I CAN'T think you are right."

30. LESLIE DECIDES

A sudden outbreak of a virulent type of influenza at the Glen and down at the fishing village kept Gilbert so busy for the next fortnight that he had no time to pay the promised visit to Captain Jim. Anne hoped against hope that he had abandoned the idea about Dick Moore, and, resolving to let sleeping dogs lie, she said no more about the subject. But she thought of it incessantly.

"I wonder if it would be right for me to tell him that Leslie cares for Owen," she thought. "He would never let her suspect that he knew, so her pride would not suffer, and it MIGHT convince him that he should let Dick Moore alone. Shall I—shall I? No, after all, I cannot. A promise is sacred, and I've no right to betray Leslie's secret. But oh, I never felt so worried over anything in my life as I do over this. It's spoiling the spring—it's spoiling everything."

One evening Gilbert abruptly proposed that they go down and see Captain Jim. With a sinking heart Anne agreed, and they set forth. Two weeks of kind sunshine had wrought a miracle in the bleak landscape over which Gilbert's crow had flown. The hills and fields were dry and brown and warm, ready to break into bud and blossom; the harbor was laughter-shaken again; the long harbor road was like a gleaming red ribbon; down on the dunes a crowd of boys, who were out smelt fishing, were burning the thick, dry sandhill grass of the preceding summer. The flames swept over the dunes rosily, flinging their cardinal banners against the dark gulf beyond, and illuminating the channel and the fishing village. It was a picturesque scene which would at other times have delighted Anne's eyes; but she was not enjoying this walk. Neither was Gilbert. Their usual good-comradeship and Josephian community of taste and viewpoint were sadly lacking. Anne's disapproval of the whole project showed itself in the haughty uplift of her head and the studied politeness of her remarks. Gilbert's mouth was set in all the Blythe obstinacy, but his eyes were troubled. He meant to do what he believed to be his duty; but to be at outs with Anne was a high price to pay. Altogether, both were glad when they reached the light—and remorseful that they should be glad.

Captain Jim put away the fishing net upon which he was working, and welcomed them joyfully. In the searching light of the spring evening he looked older than Anne had ever seen him. His hair had grown much grayer, and the strong old hand shook a little. But his blue eyes were clear and steady, and the staunch soul looked out through them gallant and unafraid.

Captain Jim listened in amazed silence while Gilbert said what he had come to say. Anne, who knew how the old man worshipped Leslie, felt quite sure that he would side with her, although she had not much hope that this would influence Gilbert. She was therefore surprised beyond measure when Captain Jim, slowly and sorrowfully, but unhesitatingly, gave it as his opinion that Leslie should be told.

"Oh, Captain Jim, I didn't think you'd say that," she exclaimed reproachfully. "I thought you wouldn't want to make more trouble for her."

Captain Jim shook his head.

"I don't want to. I know how you feel about it, Mistress Blythe—just as I feel meself. But it ain't our feelings we have to steer by through life—no, no, we'd make shipwreck mighty often if we did that. There's only the one safe compass and we've got to set our course by that—what it's right to do. I agree with the doctor. If there's a chance for Dick, Leslie should be told of it. There's no two sides to that, in my opinion."

"Well," said Anne, giving up in despair, "wait until Miss Cornelia gets after you two men."

"Cornelia'll rake us fore and aft, no doubt," assented Captain Jim. "You women are lovely critters, Mistress Blythe, but you're just a mite illogical. You're a highly eddicated lady and Cornelia isn't, but you're like as two peas when it comes to that. I dunno's you're any the worse for it. Logic is a sort of hard, merciless thing, I reckon. Now, I'll brew a cup of tea and we'll drink it and talk of pleasant things, jest to calm our minds a bit."

At least, Captain Jim's tea and conversation calmed Anne's mind to such an extent that she did not make Gilbert suffer so acutely on the way home as she had deliberately intended to do. She did not refer to the burning question at all, but she chatted amiably of other matters, and Gilbert understood that he was forgiven under protest.

"Captain Jim seems very frail and bent this spring. The winter has aged him," said Anne sadly. "I am afraid that he will soon be going to seek lost Margaret. I can't bear to think of it."

"Four Winds won't be the same place when Captain Jim 'sets out to sea,'" agreed Gilbert.

The following evening he went to the house up the brook. Anne wandered dismally around until his return.

"Well, what did Leslie say?" she demanded when he came in.

"Very little. I think she felt rather dazed."

"And is she going to have the operation?"

"She is going to think it over and decide very soon."

Gilbert flung himself wearily into the easy chair before the fire. He looked tired. It had not been an easy thing for him to tell Leslie. And the terror that had sprung into her eyes when the meaning of what he told her came home to her was not a pleasant thing to remember. Now, when the die was cast, he was beset with doubts of his own wisdom.

Anne looked at him remorsefully; then she slipped down on the rug beside him and laid her glossy red head on his arm.

"Gilbert, I've been rather hateful over this. I won't be any more. Please just call me red-headed and forgive me."

By which Gilbert understood that, no matter what came of it, there would be no I-told-you-so's. But he was not wholly comforted. Duty in the abstract is one thing; duty in the concrete is quite another, especially when the doer is confronted by a woman's stricken eyes.

Some instinct made Anne keep away from Leslie for the next three days. On the third evening Leslie came down to the little house and told Gilbert that she had made up her mind; she would take Dick to Montreal and have the operation.

She was very pale and seemed to have wrapped herself in her old mantle of aloofness. But her eyes had lost the look which had haunted Gilbert; they were cold and bright; and she proceeded to discuss details with him in a crisp, business-like way. There were plans to be made and many things to be thought over. When Leslie had got the information she wanted she went home. Anne wanted to walk part of the way with her.

"Better not," said Leslie curtly. "Today's rain has made the ground damp. Good-night."

"Have I lost my friend?" said Anne with a sigh. "If the operation is successful and Dick

Moore finds himself again Leslie will retreat into some remote fastness of her soul where none of us can ever find her."

"Perhaps she will leave him," said Gilbert.

"Leslie would never do that, Gilbert. Her sense of duty is very strong. She told me once that her Grandmother West always impressed upon her the fact that when she assumed any responsibility she must never shirk it, no matter what the consequences might be. That is one of her cardinal rules. I suppose it's very old-fashioned."

"Don't be bitter, Anne-girl. You know you don't think it old-fashioned—you know you have the very same idea of sacredness of assumed responsibilities yourself. And you are right. Shirking responsibilities is the curse of our modern life—the secret of all the unrest and discontent that is seething in the world."

"Thus saith the preacher," mocked Anne. But under the mockery she felt that he was right; and she was very sick at heart for Leslie.

A week later Miss Cornelia descended like an avalanche upon the little house. Gilbert was away and Anne was compelled to bear the shock of the impact alone.

Miss Cornelia hardly waited to get her hat off before she began.

"Anne, do you mean to tell me it's true what I've heard—that Dr. Blythe has told Leslie Dick can be cured, and that she is going to take him to Montreal to have him operated on?"

"Yes, it is quite true, Miss Cornelia," said Anne bravely.

"Well, it's inhuman cruelty, that's what it is," said Miss Cornelia, violently agitated. "I did think Dr. Blythe was a decent man. I didn't think he could have been guilty of this."

"Dr. Blythe thought it was his duty to tell Leslie that there was a chance for Dick," said Anne with spirit, "and," she added, loyalty to Gilbert getting the better of her, "I agree with him."

"Oh, no, you don't, dearie," said Miss Cornelia. "No person with any bowels of compassion could."

"Captain Jim does."

"Don't quote that old ninny to me," cried Miss Cornelia. "And I don't care who agrees with him. Think—THINK what it means to that poor hunted, harried girl."

"We DO think of it. But Gilbert believes that a doctor should put the welfare of a patient's mind and body before all other considerations."

"That's just like a man. But I expected better things of you, Anne," said Miss Cornelia, more in sorrow than in wrath; then she proceeded to bombard Anne with precisely the same arguments with which the latter had attacked Gilbert; and Anne valiantly defended her husband with the weapons he had used for his own protection. Long was the fray, but Miss Cornelia made an end at last.

"It's an iniquitous shame," she declared, almost in tears. "That's just what it is—an iniquitous shame. Poor, poor Leslie!"

"Don't you think Dick should be considered a little too?" pleaded Anne.

"Dick! Dick Moore! HE'S happy enough. He's a better behaved and more reputable member of society now than he ever was before.

"Why, he was a drunkard and perhaps worse. Are you going to set him loose again to roar and to devour?"

"He may reform," said poor Anne, beset by foe without and traitor within.

"Reform your grandmother!" retorted Miss Cornelia. "Dick Moore got the injuries that left him as he is in a drunken brawl. He DESERVES his fate. It was sent on him for a punishment. I don't believe the doctor has any business to tamper with the visitations of God."

"Nobody knows how Dick was hurt, Miss Cornelia. It may not have been in a drunken brawl at all. He may have been waylaid and robbed."

"Pigs MAY whistle, but they've poor mouths for it," said Miss Cornelia. "Well, the gist of what you tell me is that the thing is settled and there's no use in talking. If that's so I'll hold my tongue. I don't propose to wear MY teeth out gnawing files. When a thing has to be I give in to it. But I like to make mighty sure first that it HAS to be. Now, I'll devote MY energies to comforting and sustaining Leslie. And after all," added Miss Cornelia, brightening up hopefully, "perhaps nothing can be done for Dick."

31. THE TRUTH MAKES FREE

Leslie, having once made up her mind what to do, proceeded to do it with characteristic resolution and speed. House-cleaning must be finished with first, whatever issues of life and death might await beyond. The gray house up the brook was put into flawless order and cleanliness, with Miss Cornelia's ready assistance. Miss Cornelia, having said her say to Anne, and later on to Gilbert and Captain Jim—sparing neither of them, let it be assured—never spoke of the matter to Leslie. She accepted the fact of Dick's operation, referred to it when necessary in a business-like way, and ignored it when it was not. Leslie never attempted to discuss it. She was very cold and quiet during these beautiful spring days. She seldom visited Anne, and though she was invariably courteous and friendly, that very courtesy was as an icy barrier between her and the people of the little house. The old jokes and laughter and chumminess of common things could not reach her over it. Anne refused to feel hurt. She knew that Leslie was in the grip of a hideous dread—a dread that wrapped her away from all little glimpses of happiness and hours of pleasure. When one great passion seizes possession of the soul all other feelings are crowded aside. Never in all her life had Leslie Moore shuddered away from the future with more intolerable terror. But she went forward as unswervingly in the path she had elected as the martyrs of old walked their chosen way, knowing the end of it to be the fiery agony of the stake.

The financial question was settled with greater ease than Anne had feared. Leslie borrowed the necessary money from Captain Jim, and, at her insistence, he took a mortgage on the little farm.

"So that is one thing off the poor girl's mind," Miss Cornelia told Anne, "and off mine too. Now, if Dick gets well enough to work again he'll be able to earn enough to pay the interest on it; and if he doesn't I know Captain Jim'll manage someway that Leslie won't have to. He said as much to me. 'I'm getting old, Cornelia,' he said, 'and I've no chick or child of my own. Leslie won't take a gift from a living man, but mebbe she will from a dead one.' So it will be all right as far as THAT goes. I wish everything else might be settled as satisfactorily. As for that wretch of a Dick, he's been awful these last few days. The devil was in him, believe ME! Leslie and I couldn't get on with our work for the tricks he'd play. He chased all her ducks one day around the yard till most of them died. And not one thing would he do for us. Sometimes, you know, he'll make himself quite handy, bringing in pails of water and wood. But this week if we sent him to the well he'd try to climb down into it. I thought once, 'If you'd only shoot down there head-first everything would be nicely settled.'"

"Oh, Miss Cornelia!"

"Now, you needn't Miss Cornelia me, Anne, dearie. ANYBODY would have thought the same. If the Montreal doctors can make a rational creature out of Dick Moore they're wonders."

Leslie took Dick to Montreal early in May. Gilbert went with her, to help her, and make the necessary arrangements for her. He came home with the report that the Montreal surgeon whom they had consulted agreed with him that there was a good chance of Dick's restoration.

"Very comforting," was Miss Cornelia's sarcastic comment.

Anne only sighed. Leslie had been very distant at their parting.

But she had promised to write. Ten days after Gilbert's return the letter came. Leslie wrote that the operation had been successfully performed and that Dick was making a good recovery.

"What does she mean by 'successfully?'" asked Anne. "Does she mean that Dick's memory is really restored?"

"Not likely—since she says nothing of it," said Gilbert. "She uses the word 'successfully' from the surgeon's point of view. The operation has been performed and followed by normal results. But it is too soon to know whether Dick's faculties will be eventually restored, wholly or in part. His memory would not be likely to return to him all at once. The process will be gradual, if it occurs at all. Is that all she says?"

"Yes—there's her letter. It's very short. Poor girl, she must be under a terrible strain. Gilbert Blythe, there are heaps of things I long to say to you, only it would be mean."

"Miss Cornelia says them for you," said Gilbert with a rueful smile. "She combs me down every time I encounter her. She makes it plain to me that she regards me as little better than a murderer, and that she thinks it a great pity that Dr. Dave ever let me step into his shoes. She even told me that the Methodist doctor over the harbor was to be preferred before me. With Miss Cornelia the force of condemnation can no further go."

"If Cornelia Bryant was sick, it would not be Doctor Dave or the Methodist doctor she would send for," sniffed Susan. "She would have you out of your hard-earned bed in the middle of the night, doctor, dear, if she took a spell of misery, that she would. And then she would likely say your bill was past all reason. But do not mind her, doctor, dear. It takes all kinds of people to make a world."

No further word came from Leslie for some time. The May days crept away in a sweet succession and the shores of Four Winds Harbor greened and bloomed and purpled. One day in late May Gilbert came home to be met by Susan in the stable yard.

"I am afraid something has upset Mrs. Doctor, doctor, dear," she said mysteriously. "She got a letter this afternoon and since then she has just been walking round the garden and talking to herself. You know it is not good for her to be on her feet so much, doctor, dear. She did not see fit to tell me what her news was, and I am no pry, doctor, dear, and never was, but it is plain something has upset her. And it is not good for her to be upset."

Gilbert hurried rather anxiously to the garden. Had anything happened at Green Gables? But Anne, sitting on the rustic seat by the brook, did not look troubled, though she was certainly much excited. Her eyes were their grayest, and scarlet spots burned on her cheeks.

"What has happened, Anne?"

Anne gave a queer little laugh.

"I think you'll hardly believe it when I tell you, Gilbert. *I* can't believe it yet. As Susan said the other day, 'I feel like a fly coming to live in the sun—dazed-like.' It's all so incredible. I've read the letter a score of times and every time it's just the same—I can't believe my own eyes. Oh, Gilbert, you were right—so right. I can see that clearly enough now—and I'm so ashamed of myself—and will you ever really forgive me?"

"Anne, I'll shake you if you don't grow coherent. Redmond would be ashamed of you. WHAT has happened?"

"You won't believe it—you won't believe it—"

"I'm going to phone for Uncle Dave," said Gilbert, pretending to start for the house.

"Sit down, Gilbert. I'll try to tell you. I've had a letter, and oh, Gilbert, it's all so amazing—so incredibly amazing—we never thought—not one of us ever dreamed—"

"I suppose," said Gilbert, sitting down with a resigned air, "the only thing to do in a case of this kind is to have patience and go at the matter categorically. Whom is your letter from?"

"Leslie—and, oh, Gilbert—"

"Leslie! Whew! What has she to say? What's the news about Dick?"

Anne lifted the letter and held it out, calmly dramatic in a moment.

"There is NO Dick! The man we have thought Dick Moore—whom everybody in Four Winds has believed for twelve years to be Dick Moore—is his cousin, George Moore, of Nova Scotia, who, it seems, always resembled him very strikingly. Dick Moore died of yellow fever thirteen years ago in Cuba."

32. MISS CORNELIA DISCUSSES THE AFFAIR

"And do you mean to tell me, Anne, dearie, that Dick Moore has turned out not to be Dick Moore at all but somebody else? Is THAT what you phoned up to me today?"

"Yes, Miss Cornelia. It is very amazing, isn't it?"

"It's—it's—just like a man," said Miss Cornelia helplessly. She took off her hat with trembling fingers. For once in her life Miss Cornelia was undeniably staggered.

"I can't seem to sense it, Anne," she said. "I've heard you say it—and I believe you—but I can't take it in. Dick Moore is dead—has been dead all these years—and Leslie is free?"

"Yes. The truth has made her free. Gilbert was right when he said that verse was the grandest in the Bible."

"Tell me everything, Anne, dearie. Since I got your phone I've been in a regular muddle, believe ME. Cornelia Bryant was never so kerflummuxed before."

"There isn't a very great deal to tell. Leslie's letter was short. She didn't go into particulars. This man—George Moore—has recovered his memory and knows who he is. He says Dick took yellow fever in Cuba, and the Four Sisters had to sail without him. George stayed behind to nurse him. But he died very shortly afterwards.

"George did not write Leslie because he intended to come right home and tell her himself."

"And why didn't he?"

"I suppose his accident must have intervened. Gilbert says it is quite likely that George Moore remembers nothing of his accident, or what led to it, and may never remember it. It probably happened very soon after Dick's death. We may find out more particulars when Leslie writes again."

"Does she say what she is going to do? When is she coming home?"

"She says she will stay with George Moore until he can leave the hospital. She has written to his people in Nova Scotia. It seems that George's only near relative is a married sister much older than himself. She was living when George sailed on the Four Sisters, but of course we do not know what may have happened since. Did you ever see George Moore, Miss Cornelia?"

"I did. It is all coming back to me. He was here visiting his Uncle Abner eighteen years ago, when he and Dick would be about seventeen. They were double cousins, you see. Their fathers were brothers and their mothers were twin sisters, and they did look a terrible lot alike. Of course," added Miss Cornelia scornfully, "it wasn't one of those freak resemblances you read of in novels where two people are so much alike that they can fill each other's places and their nearest and dearest can't tell between them. In those days you could tell easy enough which was George and which was Dick, if you saw them together and near at hand. Apart, or some distance away, it wasn't so easy. They played lots of tricks on people and thought it great fun, the two scamps. George Moore was a little taller and a good deal fatter than Dick—though neither of them was what you would call fat—they were both of the lean kind. Dick had higher color than George, and his hair was a shade lighter. But their features were just alike, and they both had that queer freak of eyes—one blue and one hazel. They weren't much alike in any other way, though. George was a real nice fellow, though he was a scalawag for mischief, and some said he had a liking for a glass even then. But everybody liked him better than Dick. He spent about a month here. Leslie never saw him; she was only about eight or nine then and I remember now that she spent that whole winter over harbor with her grandmother West. Captain Jim was away, too—that was the winter he was wrecked on the Magdalens. I don't suppose either he or Leslie had ever heard about the Nova Scotia cousin looking so much like Dick. Nobody ever thought of him when Captain Jim brought Dick—George, I should say—home. Of course, we all thought Dick had changed considerable—he'd got so lumpish and fat. But we put that down to what had happened to him, and no doubt that was the reason, for, as I've said, George wasn't fat to begin with either. And there was no other way we could have guessed, for the man's senses were clean gone. I can't see that it is any wonder we were all deceived. But it's a staggering thing. And Leslie has sacrificed the best years of her life to nursing a man who hadn't any claim on her! Oh, drat the men! No matter what they do, it's the wrong thing. And no matter who they are, it's somebody they shouldn't be. They do exasperate me."

"Gilbert and Captain Jim are men, and it is through them that the truth has been discovered at last," said Anne.

"Well, I admit that," conceded Miss Cornelia reluctantly. "I'm sorry I raked the doctor off so. It's the first time in my life I've ever felt ashamed of anything I said to a man. I don't know as I shall tell him so, though. He'll just have to take it for granted. Well, Anne, dearie, it's a mercy the Lord doesn't answer all our prayers. I've been praying hard right along that the operation wouldn't cure Dick. Of course I didn't put it just quite so plain. But that was what was in the back of my mind, and I have no doubt the Lord knew it."

"Well, He has answered the spirit of your prayer. You really wished that things shouldn't be made any harder for Leslie. I'm afraid that in my secret heart I've been hoping the operation wouldn't succeed, and I am wholesomely ashamed of it."

"How does Leslie seem to take it?"

"She writes like one dazed. I think that, like ourselves, she hardly realises it yet. She says, 'It all seems like a strange dream to me, Anne.' That is the only reference she makes to herself."

"Poor child! I suppose when the chains are struck off a prisoner he'd feel queer and lost without them for a while. Anne, dearie, here's a thought keeps coming into my mind. What about Owen Ford? We both know Leslie was fond of him. Did it ever occur to you that he was fond of her?"

"It—did—once," admitted Anne, feeling that she might say so much.

"Well, I hadn't any reason to think he was, but it just appeared to me he MUST be. Now, Anne, dearie, the Lord knows I'm not a match-maker, and I scorn all such doings. But if I were you and writing to that Ford man I'd just mention, casual-like, what has happened. That is what *I'd* do."

"Of course I will mention it when I write him," said Anne, a trifle distantly. Somehow, this was a thing she could not discuss with Miss Cornelia. And yet, she had to admit that the same thought had been lurking in her mind ever since she had heard of Leslie's freedom. But she would not desecrate it by free speech.

"Of course there is no great rush, dearie. But Dick Moore's been dead for thirteen years and Leslie has wasted enough of her life for him. We'll just see what comes of it. As for this George

Moore, who's gone and come back to life when everyone thought he was dead and done for, just like a man, I'm real sorry for him. He won't seem to fit in anywhere."

"He is still a young man, and if he recovers completely, as seems likely, he will be able to make a place for himself again. It must be very strange for him, poor fellow. I suppose all these years since his accident will not exist for him."

33. LESLIE RETURNS

A fortnight later Leslie Moore came home alone to the old house where she had spent so many bitter years. In the June twilight she went over the fields to Anne's, and appeared with ghost-like suddenness in the scented garden.

"Leslie!" cried Anne in amazement. "Where have you sprung from? We never knew you were coming. Why didn't you write? We would have met you."

"I couldn't write somehow, Anne. It seemed so futile to try to say anything with pen and ink. And I wanted to get back quietly and unobserved."

Anne put her arms about Leslie and kissed her. Leslie returned the kiss warmly. She looked pale and tired, and she gave a little sigh as she dropped down on the grasses beside a great bed of daffodils that were gleaming through the pale, silvery twilight like golden stars.

"And you have come home alone, Leslie?"

"Yes. George Moore's sister came to Montreal and took him home with her. Poor fellow, he was sorry to part with me—though I was a stranger to him when his memory first came back. He clung to me in those first hard days when he was trying to realise that Dick's death was not the thing of yesterday that it seemed to him. It was all very hard for him. I helped him all I could. When his sister came it was easier for him, because it seemed to him only the other day that he had seen her last. Fortunately she had not changed much, and that helped him, too."

"It is all so strange and wonderful, Leslie. I think we none of us realise it yet."

"I cannot. When I went into the house over there an hour ago, I felt that it MUST be a dream—that Dick must be there, with his childish smile, as he had been for so long. Anne, I seem stunned yet. I'm not glad or sorry—or ANYTHING. I feel as if something had been torn suddenly out of my life and left a terrible hole. I feel as if I couldn't be *I*—as if I must have changed into somebody else and couldn't get used to it. It gives me a horrible lonely, dazed, helpless feeling. It's good to see you again—it seems as if you were a sort of anchor for my drifting soul. Oh, Anne, I dread it all—the gossip and wonderment and questioning. When I think of that, I wish that I need not have come home at all. Dr. Dave was at the station when I came off the train—he brought me home. Poor old man, he feels very badly because he told me years ago that nothing could be done for Dick. 'I honestly thought so, Leslie,' he said to me today. 'But I should have told you not to depend on my opinion—I should have told you to go to a specialist. If I had, you would have been saved many bitter years, and poor George Moore many wasted ones. I blame myself very much, Leslie.' I told him not to do that—he had done what he thought right. He has always been so kind to me—I couldn't bear to see him worrying over it."

"And Dick—George, I mean? Is his memory fully restored?"

"Practically. Of course, there are a great many details he can't recall yet—but he remembers more and more every day. He went out for a walk on the evening after Dick was buried. He had Dick's money and watch on him; he meant to bring them home to me, along with my letter. He admits he went to a place where the sailors resorted—and he remembers drinking—and nothing else. Anne, I shall never forget the moment he remembered his own name. I saw him looking at me with an intelligent but puzzled expression. I said, 'Do you know me, Dick?' He answered, 'I never saw you before. Who are you? And my name is not Dick. I am George Moore, and Dick died of yellow fever yesterday! Where am I? What has happened to me?' I—I fainted, Anne. And ever since I have felt as if I were in a dream."

"You will soon adjust yourself to this new state of things, Leslie. And you are young—life is before you—you will have many beautiful years yet."

"Perhaps I shall be able to look at it in that way after a while, Anne. Just now I feel too tired and indifferent to think about the future. I'm—I'm—Anne, I'm lonely. I miss Dick. Isn't it all very strange? Do you know, I was really fond of poor Dick—George, I suppose I should say—just as I would have been fond of a helpless child who depended on me for everything. I would never have admitted it—I was really ashamed of it—because, you see, I had hated and despised Dick so much before he went away. When I heard that Captain Jim was bringing him home I expected I would just feel the same to him. But I never did—although I continued to loathe him as I remembered him before. From the time he came home I felt only pity—a pity that hurt and wrung me. I supposed then that it was just because his accident had made him so helpless and changed. But now I believe it was because there was really a different personality there. Carlo knew it, Anne—I know now that Carlo knew it. I always thought it strange that Carlo shouldn't have known Dick. Dogs are usually so faithful. But HE knew it was not his master who had come back, although none of the rest of us did. I had never seen George Moore, you know. I remember now that Dick once mentioned casually that he had a cousin in Nova Scotia who looked as much like him as a twin; but the thing had gone out of my memory, and in any case I would never have thought it of any importance. You see, it never occurred to me to question Dick's identity. Any change in him seemed to me just the result of the accident.

"Oh, Anne, that night in April when Gilbert told me he thought Dick might be cured! I can never forget it. It seemed to me that I had once been a prisoner in a hideous cage of torture, and then the door had been opened and I could get out. I was still chained to the cage but I was not in it. And that night I felt that a merciless hand was drawing me back into the cage—back to a torture even more terrible than it had once been. I didn't blame Gilbert. I felt he was right. And he had been very good—he said that if, in view of the expense and uncertainty of the operation, I should decide not to risk it, he would not blame me in the least. But I knew how I ought to decide—and I couldn't face it. All night I walked the floor like a mad woman, trying to compel myself to face it. I couldn't, Anne—I thought I couldn't—and when morning broke I set my teeth and resolved that I WOULDN'T. I would let things remain as they were. It was very wicked, I know. It would have been just punishment for such wickedness if I had just been left to abide by that decision. I kept to it all day. That afternoon I had to go up to the Glen to do some shopping. It was one of Dick's quiet, drowsy days, so I left him alone. I was gone a little longer than I had expected, and he missed me. He felt lonely. And when I got home, he ran to meet me just like a child, with such a pleased smile on his face. Somehow, Anne, I just gave way then. That smile on his poor vacant face was more than I could endure. I felt as if I were denying a child the chance to grow and develop. I knew that I must give him his chance, no matter what the consequences might be. So I came over and told Gilbert. Oh, Anne, you must have thought me hateful in those weeks before I went away. I didn't mean to be—but I couldn't think of anything except what I had to do, and everything and everybody about me were like shadows."

"I know—I understood, Leslie. And now it is all over—your chain is broken—there is no cage."

"There is no cage," repeated Leslie absently, plucking at the fringing grasses with her slender, brown hands. "But—it doesn't seem as if there were anything else, Anne. You—you remember what I told you of my folly that night on the sand-bar? I find one doesn't get over being a fool very quickly. Sometimes I think there are people who are fools forever. And to be a fool—of that kind—is almost as bad as being a—a dog on a chain."

"You will feel very differently after you get over being tired and bewildered," said Anne, who, knowing a certain thing that Leslie did not know, did not feel herself called upon to waste overmuch sympathy.

Leslie laid her splendid golden head against Anne's knee.

"Anyhow, I have YOU," she said. "Life can't be altogether empty with such a friend. Anne, pat my head—just as if I were a little girl—MOTHER me a bit—and let me tell you while my stubborn tongue is loosed a little just what you and your comradeship have meant to me since that night I met you on the rock shore."

34. THE SHIP O'DREAMS COMES TO HARBOR

One morning, when a windy golden sunrise was billowing over the gulf in waves of light, a certain weary stork flew over the bar of Four Winds Harbor on his way from the Land of Evening Stars. Under his wing was tucked a sleepy, starry-eyed, little creature. The stork was tired, and he looked wistfully about him. He knew he was somewhere near his destination, but he could not yet see it. The big, white light-house on the red sandstone cliff had its good points; but no stork possessed of any gumption would leave a new, velvet baby there. An old gray house, surrounded by willows, in a blossomy brook valley, looked more promising, but did not seem quite the thing either. The staring green abode further on was manifestly out of the question. Then the stork brightened up. He had caught sight of the very place—a little white house nestled against a big, whispering firwood, with a spiral of blue smoke winding up from its kitchen chimney—a house which just looked as if it were meant for babies. The stork gave a sigh of satisfaction, and softly alighted on the ridge-pole.

Half an hour later Gilbert ran down the hall and tapped on the spare-room door. A drowsy voice answered him and in a moment Marilla's pale, scared face peeped out from behind the door.

"Marilla, Anne has sent me to tell you that a certain young gentleman has arrived here. He hasn't brought much luggage with him, but he evidently means to stay."

"For pity's sake!" said Marilla blankly. "You don't mean to tell me, Gilbert, that it's all over. Why wasn't I called?"

"Anne wouldn't let us disturb you when there was no need. Nobody was called until about two hours ago. There was no 'passage perilous' this time."

"And—and—Gilbert—will this baby live?"

"He certainly will. He weighs ten pounds and—why, listen to him. Nothing wrong with his lungs, is there? The nurse says his hair will be red. Anne is furious with her, and I'm tickled to death."

That was a wonderful day in the little house of dreams.

"The best dream of all has come true," said Anne, pale and rapturous. "Oh, Marilla, I hardly dare believe it, after that horrible day last summer. I have had a heartache ever since then—but it is gone now."

"This baby will take Joy's place," said Marilla.

"Oh, no, no, NO, Marilla. He can't—nothing can ever do that. He has his own place, my dear, wee man-child. But little Joy has hers, and always will have it. If she had lived she would have been over a year old. She would have been toddling around on her tiny feet and lisping a few words. I can see her so plainly, Marilla. Oh, I know now that Captain Jim was right when he said God would manage better than that my baby would seem a stranger to me when I found her Beyond. I've learned THAT this past year. I've followed her development day by day and week by week—I always shall. I shall know just how she grows from year to year—and when I meet her again I'll know her—she won't be a stranger. Oh, Marilla, LOOK at his dear, darling toes! Isn't it strange they should be so perfect?"

"It would be stranger if they weren't," said Marilla crisply. Now that all was safely over, Marilla was herself again.

"Oh, I know—but it seems as if they couldn't be quite FINISHED, you know—and they are, even to the tiny nails. And his hands—JUST look at his hands, Marilla."

"They appear to be a good deal like hands," Marilla conceded.

"See how he clings to my finger. I'm sure he knows me already. He cries when the nurse takes him away. Oh, Marilla, do you think—you don't think, do you—that his hair is going to be red?"

"I don't see much hair of any color," said Marilla. "I wouldn't worry about it, if I were you, until it becomes visible."

"Marilla, he HAS hair—look at that fine little down all over his head. Anyway, nurse says his eyes will be hazel and his forehead is exactly like Gilbert's."

"And he has the nicest little ears, Mrs. Doctor, dear," said Susan. "The first thing I did was to look at his ears. Hair is deceitful and noses and eyes change, and you cannot tell what is going to come of them, but ears is ears from start to finish, and you always know where you are with them. Just look at their shape—and they are set right back against his precious head. You will never need to be ashamed of his ears, Mrs. Doctor, dear."

Anne's convalescence was rapid and happy. Folks came and worshipped the baby, as people have bowed before the kingship of the new-born since long before the Wise Men of the East knelt in homage to the Royal Babe of the Bethlehem manger. Leslie, slowly finding herself amid the new conditions of her life, hovered over it, like a beautiful, golden-crowned Madonna. Miss Cornelia nursed it as knackily as could any mother in Israel. Captain Jim held the small creature in his big brown hands and gazed tenderly at it, with eyes that saw the children who had never been born to him.

"What are you going to call him?" asked Miss Cornelia.

"Anne has settled his name," answered Gilbert.

"James Matthew—after the two finest gentlemen I've ever known—not even saving your presence," said Anne with a saucy glance at Gilbert.

Gilbert smiled.

"I never knew Matthew very well; he was so shy we boys couldn't get acquainted with him—but I quite agree with you that Captain Jim is one of the rarest and finest souls God ever clothed in clay. He is so delighted over the fact that we have given his name to our small lad. It seems he has no other namesake."

"Well, James Matthew is a name that will wear well and not fade in the washing," said Miss Cornelia. "I'm glad you didn't load him down with some highfalutin, romantic name that he'd be ashamed of when he gets to be a grandfather. Mrs. William Drew at the Glen has called her baby Bertie Shakespeare. Quite a combination, isn't it? And I'm glad you haven't had much trouble picking on a name. Some folks have an awful time. When the Stanley Flaggs' first boy was born there was so much rivalry as to who the child should be named for that the poor little soul had to go for two years without a name. Then a brother came along and there it was—'Big Baby' and 'Little Baby.' Finally they called Big Baby Peter and Little Baby Isaac, after the two grandfathers, and had them both christened together. And each tried to see if it couldn't howl the other down. You know that Highland Scotch family of MacNabs back of the Glen? They've got twelve boys and the oldest and the youngest are both called Neil—Big Neil and Little Neil in the same family. Well, I s'pose they ran out of names."

"I have read somewhere," laughed Anne, "that the first child is a poem but the tenth is very prosy prose. Perhaps Mrs. MacNab thought that the twelfth was merely an old tale re-told."

"Well, there's something to be said for large families," said Miss Cornelia, with a sigh. "I was an only child for eight years and I did long for a brother and sister. Mother told me to pray for one—and pray I did, believe ME. Well, one day Aunt Nellie came to me and said, 'Cornelia, there is a little brother for you upstairs in your ma's room. You can go up and see him.' I was so excited and delighted I just flew upstairs. And old Mrs. Flagg lifted up the baby for me to see. Lord, Anne, dearie, I never was so disappointed in my life. You see, I'd been praying for A BROTHER TWO YEARS OLDER THAN MYSELF."

"How long did it take you to get over your disappointment?" asked Anne, amid her laughter.

"Well, I had a spite at Providence for a good spell, and for weeks I wouldn't even look at the baby. Nobody knew why, for I never told. Then he began to get real cute, and held out his wee hands to me and I began to get fond of him. But I didn't get really reconciled to him until one day a school chum came to see him and said she thought he was awful small for his age. I just got boiling mad, and I sailed right into her, and told her she didn't know a nice baby when she saw one, and ours was the nicest baby in the world. And after that I just worshipped him. Mother died before he was three years old and I was sister and mother to him both. Poor little lad, he was never strong, and he died when he wasn't much over twenty. Seems to me I'd have given anything on earth, Anne, dearie, if he'd only lived."

Miss Cornelia sighed. Gilbert had gone down and Leslie, who had been crooning over the small James Matthew in the dormer window, laid him asleep in his basket and went her way. As soon as she was safely out of earshot, Miss Cornelia bent forward and said in a conspirator's whisper:

"Anne, dearie, I'd a letter from Owen Ford yesterday. He's in Vancouver just now, but he wants to know if I can board him for a month later on. YOU know what that means. Well, I hope we're doing right."

"We've nothing to do with it—we couldn't prevent him from coming to Four Winds if he wanted to," said Anne quickly. She did not like the feeling of match-making Miss Cornelia's whispers gave her; and then she weakly succumbed herself.

"Don't let Leslie know he is coming until he is here," she said. "If she found out I feel sure she would go away at once. She intends to go in the fall anyhow—she told me so the other day. She is going to Montreal to take up nursing and make what she can of her life."

"Oh, well, Anne, dearie," said Miss Cornelia, nodding sagely "that is all as it may be. You and I have done our part and we must leave the rest to Higher Hands."

35. POLITICS AT FOUR WINDS

When Anne came downstairs again, the Island, as well as all Canada, was in the throes of a campaign preceding a general election. Gilbert, who was an ardent Conservative, found himself caught in the vortex, being much in demand for speech-making at the various county rallies. Miss Cornelia did not approve of his mixing up in politics and told Anne so.

"Dr. Dave never did it. Dr. Blythe will find he is making a mistake, believe ME. Politics is something no decent man should meddle with."

"Is the government of the country to be left solely to the rogues then?" asked Anne.

"Yes—so long as it's Conservative rogues," said Miss Cornelia, marching off with the honors of war. "Men and politicians are all tarred with the same brush. The Grits have it laid on thicker than the Conservatives, that's all—CONSIDERABLY thicker. But Grit or Tory, my advice to Dr. Blythe is to steer clear of politics. First thing you know, he'll be running an election himself, and going off to Ottawa for half the year and leaving his practice to go to the dogs."

"Ah, well, let's not borrow trouble," said Anne. "The rate of interest is too high. Instead, let's look at Little Jem. It should be spelled with a G. Isn't he perfectly beautiful? Just see the dimples in his elbows. We'll bring him up to be a good Conservative, you and I, Miss Cornelia."

"Bring him up to be a good man," said Miss Cornelia. "They're scarce and valuable; though, mind you, I wouldn't like to see him a Grit. As for the election, you and I may be thankful we don't live over harbor. The air there is blue these days. Every Elliott and Crawford and MacAllister is on the warpath, loaded for bear. This side is peaceful and calm, seeing there's so few men. Captain Jim's a Grit, but it's my opinion he's ashamed of it, for he never talks politics. There isn't any earthly doubt that the Conservatives will be returned with a big majority again."

Miss Cornelia was mistaken. On the morning after the election Captain Jim dropped in at the little house to tell the news. So virulent is the microbe of party politics, even in a peaceable old man, that Captain Jim's cheeks were flushed and his eyes were flashing with all his old-time fire.

"Mistress Blythe, the Liberals are in with a sweeping majority. After eighteen years of Tory mismanagement this down-trodden country is going to have a chance at last."

"I never heard you make such a bitter partisan speech before, Captain Jim. I didn't think you had so much political venom in you," laughed Anne, who was not much excited over the tidings. Little Jem had said "Wow-ga" that morning. What were principalities and powers, the rise and fall of dynasties, the overthrow of Grit or Tory, compared with that miraculous occurrence?

"It's been accumulating for a long while," said Captain Jim, with a deprecating smile. "I thought I was only a moderate Grit, but when the news came that we were in I found out how Gritty I really was."

"You know the doctor and I are Conservatives."

"Ah, well, it's the only bad thing I know of either of you, Mistress Blythe. Cornelia is a Tory, too. I called in on my way from the Glen to tell her the news."

"Didn't you know you took your life in your hands?"

"Yes, but I couldn't resist the temptation."

"How did she take it?"

"Comparatively calm, Mistress Blythe, comparatively calm. She says, says she, 'Well, Providence sends seasons of humiliation to a country, same as to individuals. You Grits have been cold and hungry for many a year. Make haste to get warmed and fed, for you won't be in long.' 'Well, now Cornelia,' I says, 'mebbe Providence thinks Canada needs a real long spell of humiliation.' Ah, Susan, have YOU heard the news? The Liberals are in."

Susan had just come in from the kitchen, attended by the odor of delectable dishes which always seemed to hover around her.

"Now, are they?" she said, with beautiful unconcern. "Well, I never could see but that my bread rose just as light when Grits were in as when they were not. And if any party, Mrs. Doctor, dear, will make it rain before the week is out, and save our kitchen garden from entire ruination, that is the party Susan will vote for. In the meantime, will you just step out and give me your opinion on the meat for dinner? I am fearing that it is very tough, and I think that we had better change our butcher as well as our government."

One evening, a week later, Anne walked down to the Point, to see if she could get some fresh fish from Captain Jim, leaving Little Jem for the first time. It was quite a tragedy. Suppose he cried? Suppose Susan did not know just exactly what to do for him? Susan was calm and serene.

"I have had as much experience with him as you, Mrs. Doctor, dear, have I not?"

"Yes, with him—but not with other babies. Why, I looked after three pairs of twins, when I was a child, Susan. When they cried, I gave them peppermint or castor oil quite coolly. It's quite curious now to recall how lightly I took all those babies and their woes."

"Oh, well, if Little Jem cries, I will just clap a hot water bag on his little stomach," said Susan.

"Not too hot, you know," said Anne anxiously. Oh, was it really wise to go?

"Do not you fret, Mrs. Doctor, dear. Susan is not the woman to burn a wee man. Bless him, he has no notion of crying."

Anne tore herself away finally and enjoyed her walk to the Point after all, through the long shadows of the sun-setting. Captain Jim was not in the living room of the lighthouse, but another man was—a handsome, middle-aged man, with a strong, clean-shaven chin, who was unknown to Anne. Nevertheless, when she sat down, he began to talk to her with all the assurance of an old acquaintance. There was nothing amiss in what he said or the way he said it, but Anne rather resented such a cool taking-for-granted in a complete stranger. Her replies were frosty, and as few as decency required. Nothing daunted, her companion talked on for several minutes, then excused himself and went away. Anne could have sworn there was a twinkle in his eye and it annoyed her. Who was the creature? There was something vaguely familiar about him but she was certain she had never seen him before.

"Captain Jim, who was that who just went out?" she asked, as Captain Jim came in.

"Marshall Elliott," answered the captain.

"Marshall Elliott!" cried Anne. "Oh, Captain Jim—it wasn't—yes, it WAS his voice—oh, Captain Jim, I didn't know him—and I was quite insulting to him! WHY didn't he tell me? He must have seen I didn't know him."

"He wouldn't say a word about it—he'd just enjoy the joke. Don't worry over snubbing him—he'll think it fun. Yes, Marshall's shaved off his beard at last and cut his hair. His party is in, you know. I didn't know him myself first time I saw him. He was up in Carter Flagg's store at the Glen the night after election day, along with a crowd of others, waiting for the news. About twelve the 'phone came through—the Liberals were in. Marshall just got up and walked out—he didn't cheer or shout—he left the others to do that, and they nearly lifted the roof off Carter's store, I reckon. Of course, all the Tories were over in Raymond Russell's store. Not much cheering THERE. Marshall went straight down the street to the side door of Augustus Palmer's barber shop. Augustus was in bed asleep, but Marshall hammered on the door until he got up and come down, wanting to know what all the racket was about.

"Come into your shop and do the best job you ever did in your life, Gus,' said Marshall. 'The Liberals are in and you're going to barber a good Grit before the sun rises.'

"Gus was mad as hops—partly because he'd been dragged out of bed, but more because he's a Tory. He vowed he wouldn't shave any man after twelve at night.

"'You'll do what I want you to do, sonny,' said Marshall, 'or I'll jest turn you over my knee and give you one of those spankings your mother forgot.'

"He'd have done it, too, and Gus knew it, for Marshall is as strong as an ox and Gus is only a midget of a man. So he gave in and towed Marshall in to the shop and went to work. 'Now,' says he, 'I'll barber you up, but if you say one word to me about the Grits getting in while I'm doing it I'll cut your throat with this razor,' says he. You wouldn't have thought mild little Gus could be so bloodthirsty, would you? Shows what party politics will do for a man. Marshall kept quiet and got his hair and beard disposed of and went home. When his old housekeeper heard him come upstairs she peeked out of her bedroom door to see whether 'twas him or the hired boy. And when she saw a strange man striding down the hall with a candle in his hand she screamed blue murder and fainted dead away. They had to send for the doctor before they could bring her to, and it was several days before she could look at Marshall without shaking all over."

Captain Jim had no fish. He seldom went out in his boat that summer, and his long tramping expeditions were over. He spent a great deal of his time sitting by his seaward window, looking out over the gulf, with his swiftly-whitening head leaning on his hand. He sat there tonight for many silent minutes, keeping some tryst with the past which Anne would not disturb. Presently he pointed to the iris of the West:

"That's beautiful, isn't, it, Mistress Blythe? But I wish you could have seen the sunrise this morning. It was a wonderful thing—wonderful. I've seen all kinds of sunrises come over that gulf. I've been all over the world, Mistress Blythe, and take it all in all, I've never seen a finer sight than a summer sunrise over the gulf. A man can't pick his time for dying, Mistress Blythe—jest got to go when the Great Captain gives His sailing orders. But if I could I'd go out when the morning comes across that water. I've watched it many a time and thought what a thing it would be to pass out through that great white glory to whatever was waiting beyant, on a sea that ain't mapped out on any airthly chart. I think, Mistress Blythe, that I'd find lost Margaret there."

Captain Jim had often talked to Anne of lost Margaret since he had told her the old story. His love for her trembled in every tone—that love that had never grown faint or forgetful.

"Anyway, I hope when my time comes I'll go quick and easy. I don't think I'm a coward, Mistress Blythe—I've looked an ugly death in the face more than once without blenching. But the thought of a lingering death does give me a queer, sick feeling of horror."

"Don't talk about leaving us, dear, DEAR Captain, Jim," pleaded Anne, in a choked voice, patting the old brown hand, once so strong, but now grown very feeble. "What would we do without you?"

Captain Jim smiled beautifully.

"Oh, you'd get along nicely—nicely—but you wouldn't forget the old man altogether, Mistress Blythe—no, I don't think you'll ever quite forget him. The race of Joseph always remembers one another. But it'll be a memory that won't hurt—I like to think that my memory won't hurt my friends—it'll always be kind of pleasant to them, I hope and believe. It won't be very long now before lost Margaret calls me, for the last time. I'll be all ready to answer. I jest spoke of this because there's a little favor I want to ask you. Here's this poor old Matey of mine"—Captain Jim reached out a hand and poked the big, warm, velvety, golden ball on the sofa. The First Mate uncoiled himself like a spring with a nice, throaty, comfortable sound, half purr, half meow, stretched his paws in air, turned over and coiled himself up again. "HE'll miss me when I start on the V'yage. I can't bear to think of leaving the poor critter to starve, like he was left before. If anything happens to me will you give Matey a bite and a corner, Mistress Blythe?"

"Indeed I will."

"Then that is all I had on my mind. Your Little Jem is to have the few curious things I picked up—I've seen to that. And now I don't like to see tears in those pretty eyes, Mistress Blythe. I'll mebbe hang on for quite a spell yet. I heard you reading a piece of poetry one day last winter—one of Tennyson's pieces. I'd sorter like to hear it again, if you could recite it for me."

Softly and clearly, while the seawind blew in on them, Anne repeated the beautiful lines of

Tennyson's wonderful swan song—"Crossing the Bar." The old captain kept time gently with his sinewy hand.

"Yes, yes, Mistress Blythe," he said, when she had finished, "that's it, that's it. He wasn't a sailor, you tell me—I dunno how he could have put an old sailor's feelings into words like that, if he wasn't one. He didn't want any 'sadness o' farewells' and neither do I, Mistress Blythe—for all will be well with me and mine beyant the bar."

36. BEAUTY FOR ASHES

"Any news from Green Gables, Anne?"

"Nothing very especial," replied Anne, folding up Marilla's letter. "Jake Donnell has been there shingling the roof. He is a full-fledged carpenter now, so it seems he has had his own way in regard to the choice of a life-work. You remember his mother wanted him to be a college professor. I shall never forget the day she came to the school and rated me for failing to call him St. Clair."

"Does anyone ever call him that now?"

"Evidently not. It seems that he has completely lived it down. Even his mother has succumbed. I always thought that a boy with Jake's chin and mouth would get his own way in the end. Diana writes me that Dora has a beau. Just think of it—that child!"

"Dora is seventeen," said Gilbert. "Charlie Sloane and I were both mad about you when you were seventeen, Anne."

"Really, Gilbert, we must be getting on in years," said Anne, with a half-rueful smile, "when children who were six when we thought ourselves grown up are old enough now to have beaux. Dora's is Ralph Andrews—Jane's brother. I remember him as a little, round, fat, white-headed fellow who was always at the foot of his class. But I understand he is quite a fine-looking young man now."

"Dora will probably marry young. She's of the same type as Charlotta the Fourth—she'll never miss her first chance for fear she might not get another."

"Well; if she marries Ralph I hope he will be a little more up-and-coming than his brother Billy," mused Anne.

"For instance," said Gilbert, laughing, "let us hope he will be able to propose on his own account. Anne, would you have married Billy if he had asked you himself, instead of getting Jane to do it for him?"

"I might have." Anne went off into a shriek of laughter over the recollection of her first proposal. "The shock of the whole thing might have hypnotized me into some such rash and foolish act. Let us be thankful he did it by proxy."

"I had a letter from George Moore yesterday," said Leslie, from the corner where she was reading.

"Oh, how is he?" asked Anne interestedly, yet with an unreal feeling that she was inquiring about some one whom she did not know.

"He is well, but he finds it very hard to adapt himself to all the changes in his old home and friends. He is going to sea again in the spring. It's in his blood, he says, and he longs for it. But he told me something that made me glad for him, poor fellow. Before he sailed on the Four Sisters he was engaged to a girl at home. He did not tell me anything about her in Montreal, because he said he supposed she would have forgotten him and married someone else long ago, and with him, you see, his engagement and love was still a thing of the present. It was pretty hard on him, but when he got home he found she had never married and still cared for him. They are to be married this fall. I'm going to ask him to bring her over here for a little trip; he says he wants to come and see the place where he lived so many years without knowing it."

"What a nice little romance," said Anne, whose love for the romantic was immortal. "And to think," she added with a sigh of self-reproach, "that if I had had my way George Moore would never have come up from the grave in which his identity was buried. How I did fight against Gilbert's suggestion! Well, I am punished: I shall never be able to have a different opinion from Gilbert's again! If I try to have, he will squelch me by casting George Moore's case up to me!"

"As if even that would squelch a woman!" mocked Gilbert. "At least do not become my echo, Anne. A little opposition gives spice to life. I do not want a wife like John MacAllister's over the harbor. No matter what he says, she at once remarks in that drab, lifeless little voice of hers, 'That is very true, John, dear me!'"

Anne and Leslie laughed. Anne's laughter was silver and Leslie's golden, and the combination of the two was as satisfactory as a perfect chord in music.

Susan, coming in on the heels of the laughter, echoed it with a resounding sigh.

"Why, Susan, what is the matter?" asked Gilbert.

"There's nothing wrong with little Jem, is there, Susan?" cried Anne, starting up in alarm.

"No, no, calm yourself, Mrs. Doctor, dear. Something has happened, though. Dear me, everything has gone catawampus with me this week. I spoiled the bread, as you know too well—and I scorched the doctor's best shirt bosom—and I broke your big platter. And now, on the top of all this, comes word that my sister Matilda has broken her leg and wants me to go and stay with her for a spell."

"Oh, I'm very sorry—sorry that your sister has met with such an accident, I mean," exclaimed Anne.

"Ah, well, man was made to mourn, Mrs. Doctor, dear. That sounds as if it ought to be in the Bible, but they tell me a person named Burns wrote it. And there is no doubt that we are born to trouble as the sparks fly upward. As for Matilda, I do not know what to think of her. None of our family ever broke their legs before. But whatever she has done she is still my sister, and I feel that it is my duty to go and wait on her, if you can spare me for a few weeks, Mrs. Doctor, dear."

"Of course, Susan, of course. I can get someone to help me while you are gone."

"If you cannot I will not go, Mrs. Doctor, dear, Matilda's leg to the contrary notwithstanding. I will not have you worried, and that blessed child upset in consequence, for any number of legs."

"Oh, you must go to your sister at once, Susan. I can get a girl from the cove, who will do for a time."

"Anne, will you let me come and stay with you while Susan is away?" exclaimed Leslie. "Do! I'd love to—and it would be an act of charity on your part. I'm so horribly lonely over there in that big barn of a house. There's so little to do—and at night I'm worse than lonely—I'm frightened and nervous in spite of locked doors. There was a tramp around two days ago."

Anne joyfully agreed, and next day Leslie was installed as an inmate of the little house of dreams. Miss Cornelia warmly approved of the arrangement.

"It seems Providential," she told Anne in confidence. "I'm sorry for Matilda Clow, but since she had to break her leg it couldn't have happened at a better time. Leslie will be here while Owen Ford is in Four Winds, and those old cats up at the Glen won't get the chance to meow, as they would if she was living over there alone and Owen going to see her. They are doing enough of it as it is, because she doesn't put on mourning. I said to one of them, 'If you mean she should put on mourning for George Moore, it seems to me more like his resurrection than his funeral; and if it's Dick you mean, I confess *I* can't see the propriety of going into weeds for a man who died thirteen years ago and good riddance then!' And when old Louisa Baldwin remarked to me that she thought it very strange that Leslie should never have suspected it wasn't her own husband *I* said, 'YOU never suspected it wasn't Dick Moore, and you were next-door neighbor to him all his life, and by nature you're ten times as suspicious as Leslie.' But you can't stop some people's tongues, Anne, dearie, and I'm real thankful Leslie will be under your roof while Owen is courting her."

Owen Ford came to the little house one August evening when Leslie and Anne were absorbed in worshipping the baby. He paused at the open door of the living room, unseen by the two within, gazing with greedy eyes at the beautiful picture. Leslie sat on the floor with the baby in her lap, making ecstatic dabs at his fat little hands as he fluttered them in the air.

"Oh, you dear, beautiful, beloved baby," she mumbled, catching one wee hand and covering it with kisses.

"Isn't him ze darlingest itty sing," crooned Anne, hanging over the arm of her chair adoringly. "Dem itty wee pads are ze very tweetest handies in ze whole big world, isn't dey, you darling itty man."

Anne, in the months before Little Jem's coming, had pored diligently over several wise volumes, and pinned her faith to one in especial, "Sir Oracle on the Care and Training of Children." Sir Oracle implored parents by all they held sacred never to talk "baby talk" to their children. Infants should invariably be addressed in classical language from the moment of their birth. So should they learn to speak English undefiled from their earliest utterance. "How," demanded Sir Oracle, "can a mother reasonably expect her child to learn correct speech, when she continually accustoms its impressionable gray matter to such absurd expressions and distortions of our noble tongue as thoughtless mothers inflict every day on the helpless creatures committed to their care? Can a child who is constantly called 'tweet itty wee singie' ever attain to any proper conception of his own being and possibilities and destiny?"

Anne was vastly impressed with this, and informed Gilbert that she meant to make it an inflexible rule never, under any circumstances, to talk "baby talk" to her children. Gilbert agreed with her, and they made a solemn compact on the subject—a compact which Anne shamelessly violated the very first moment Little Jem was laid in her arms. "Oh, the darling itty wee sing!" she had exclaimed. And she had continued to violate it ever since. When Gilbert teased her she laughed Sir Oracle to scorn.

"He never had any children of his own, Gilbert—I am positive he hadn't or he would never have written such rubbish. You just can't help talking baby talk to a baby. It comes natural—and it's RIGHT. It would be inhuman to talk to those tiny, soft, velvety little creatures as we do to great big boys and girls. Babies want love and cuddling and all the sweet baby talk they can get, and Little Jem is going to have it, bless his dear itty heartums."

"But you're the worst I ever heard, Anne," protested Gilbert, who, not being a mother but only a father, was not wholly convinced yet that Sir Oracle was wrong. "I never heard anything like the way you talk to that child."

"Very likely you never did. Go away—go away. Didn't I bring up three pairs of Hammond twins before I was eleven? You and Sir Oracle are nothing but cold-blooded theorists. Gilbert, JUST look at him! He's smiling at me—he knows what we're talking about. And oo dest agwees wif evy word muzzer says, don't oo, angel-lover?"

Gilbert put his arm about them. "Oh you mothers!" he said. "You mothers! God knew what He was about when He made you."

So Little Jem was talked to and loved and cuddled; and he throve as became a child of the house of dreams. Leslie was quite as foolish over him as Anne was. When their work was done and Gilbert was out of the way, they gave themselves over to shameless orgies of love-making and ecstasies of adoration, such as that in which Owen Ford had surprised them.

Leslie was the first to become aware of him. Even in the twilight Anne could see the sudden whiteness that swept over her beautiful face, blotting out the crimson of lip and cheeks.

Owen came forward, eagerly, blind for a moment to Anne.

"Leslie!" he said, holding out his hand. It was the first time he had ever called her by her name; but the hand Leslie gave him was cold; and she was very quiet all the evening, while Anne and Gilbert and Owen laughed and talked together. Before his call ended she excused herself and went upstairs. Owen's gay spirits flagged and he went away soon after with a downcast air.

Gilbert looked at Anne.

"Anne, what are you up to? There's something going on that I don't understand. The whole air here tonight has been charged with electricity. Leslie sits like the muse of tragedy; Owen Ford jokes and laughs on the surface, and watches Leslie with the eyes of his soul. You seem all the time to be bursting with some suppressed excitement. Own up. What secret have you been keeping from your deceived husband?"

"Don't be a goose, Gilbert," was Anne's conjugal reply. "As for Leslie, she is absurd and I'm going up to tell her so."

Anne found Leslie at the dormer window of her room. The little place was filled with the rhythmic thunder of the sea. Leslie sat with locked hands in the misty moonshine—a beautiful, accusing presence.

"Anne," she said in a low, reproachful voice, "did you know Owen Ford was coming to Four Winds?"

"I did," said Anne brazenly.

"Oh, you should have told me, Anne," Leslie cried passionately. "If I had known I would have gone away—I wouldn't have stayed here to meet him. You should have told me. It wasn't fair of you, Anne—oh, it wasn't fair!"

Leslie's lips were trembling and her whole form was tense with emotion. But Anne laughed heartlessly. She bent over and kissed Leslie's upturned reproachful face.

"Leslie, you are an adorable goose. Owen Ford didn't rush from the Pacific to the Atlantic from a burning desire to see ME. Neither do I believe that he was inspired by any wild and frenzied passion for Miss Cornelia. Take off your tragic airs, my dear friend, and fold them up and put them away in lavender. You'll never need them again. There are some people who can see through a grindstone when there is a hole in it, even if you cannot. I am not a prophetess, but I shall venture on a prediction. The bitterness of life is over for you. After this you are going to have the joys and hopes—and I daresay the sorrows, too—of a happy woman. The omen of the shadow of Venus did come true for you, Leslie. The year in which you saw it brought your life's best gift for you—your love for Owen Ford. Now, go right to bed and have a good sleep."

Leslie obeyed orders in so far that she went to bed: but it may be questioned if she slept much. I do not think she dared to dream wakingly; life had been so hard for this poor Leslie, the path on which she had had to walk had been so strait, that she could not whisper to her own heart the hopes that might wait on the future. But she watched the great revolving light bestarring the short hours of the summer night, and her eyes grew soft and bright and young once more. Nor, when Owen Ford came next day, to ask her to go with him to the shore, did she say him nay.

37. MISS CORNELIA MAKES A STARTLING ANNOUNCEMENT

Miss Cornelia sailed down to the little house one drowsy afternoon, when the gulf was the faint, bleached blue of the August seas, and the orange lilies at the gate of Anne's garden held up their imperial cups to be filled with the molten gold of August sunshine. Not that Miss Cornelia concerned herself with painted oceans or sun-thirsty lilies. She sat in her favorite rocker in unusual idleness. She sewed not, neither did she spin. Nor did she say a single derogatory word concerning any portion of mankind. In short, Miss Cornelia's conversation was singularly devoid of spice that day, and Gilbert, who had stayed home to listen to her, instead of going a-fishing, as he had intended, felt himself aggrieved. What had come over Miss Cornelia? She did not look cast down or worried. On the contrary, there was a certain air of nervous exultation about her.

"Where is Leslie?" she asked—not as if it mattered much either.

"Owen and she went raspberrying in the woods back of her farm," answered Anne. "They won't be back before supper time—if then."

"They don't seem to have any idea that there is such a thing as a clock," said Gilbert. "I can't get to the bottom of that affair. I'm certain you women pulled strings. But Anne, undutiful wife, won't tell me. Will you, Miss Cornelia?"

"No, I shall not. But," said Miss Cornelia, with the air of one determined to take the plunge and have it over, "I will tell you something else. I came today on purpose to tell it. I am going to be married."

Anne and Gilbert were silent. If Miss Cornelia had announced her intention of going out to the channel and drowning herself the thing might have been believable. This was not. So they waited. Of course Miss Cornelia had made a mistake.

"Well, you both look sort of kerflummexed," said Miss Cornelia, with a twinkle in her eyes. Now that the awkward moment of revelation was over, Miss Cornelia was her own woman again. "Do you think I'm too young and inexperienced for matrimony?"

"You know—it IS rather staggering," said Gilbert, trying to gather his wits together. "I've heard you say a score of times that you wouldn't marry the best man in the world."

"I'm not going to marry the best man in the world," retorted Miss Cornelia. "Marshall Elliott is a long way from being the best."

"Are you going to marry Marshall Elliott?" exclaimed Anne, recovering her power of speech under this second shock.

"Yes. I could have had him any time these twenty years if I'd lifted my finger. But do you suppose I was going to walk into church beside a perambulating haystack like that?"

"I am sure we are very glad—and we wish you all possible happiness," said Anne, very flatly and inadequately, as she felt. She was not prepared for such an occasion. She had never imagined herself offering betrothal felicitations to Miss Cornelia.

"Thanks, I knew you would," said Miss Cornelia. "You are the first of my friends to know it."

"We shall be so sorry to lose you, though, dear Miss Cornelia," said Anne, beginning to be a little sad and sentimental.

"Oh, you won't lose me," said Miss Cornelia unsentimentally. "You don't suppose I would live over harbor with all those MacAllisters and Elliotts and Crawfords, do you? 'From the conceit of the Elliotts, the pride of the MacAllisters and the vain-glory of the Crawfords, good Lord deliver us.' Marshall is coming to live at my place. I'm sick and tired of hired men. That Jim Hastings I've got this summer is positively the worst of the species. He would drive anyone to getting married. What do you think? He upset the churn yesterday and spilled a big churning of cream over the yard. And not one whit concerned about it was he! Just gave a foolish laugh and said cream was good for the land. Wasn't that like a man? I told him I wasn't in the habit of fertilising my back yard with cream."

"Well, I wish you all manner of happiness too, Miss Cornelia," said Gilbert, solemnly; "but," he added, unable to resist the temptation to tease Miss Cornelia, despite Anne's imploring eyes, "I fear your day of independence is done. As you know, Marshall Elliott is a very determined man."

"I like a man who can stick to a thing," retorted Miss Cornelia. "Amos Grant, who used to be after me long ago, couldn't. You never saw such a weather-vane. He jumped into the pond to drown himself once and then changed his mind and swum out again. Wasn't that like a man? Marshall would have stuck to it and drowned."

"And he has a bit of a temper, they tell me," persisted Gilbert.

"He wouldn't be an Elliott if he hadn't. I'm thankful he has. It will be real fun to make him mad. And you can generally do something with a tempery man when it comes to repenting time. But you can't do anything with a man who just keeps placid and aggravating."

"You know he's a Grit, Miss Cornelia."

"Yes, he IS," admitted Miss Cornelia rather sadly. "And of course there is no hope of making a Conservative of him. But at least he is a Presbyterian. So I suppose I shall have to be satisfied with that."

"Would you marry him if he were a Methodist, Miss Cornelia?"

"No, I would not. Politics is for this world, but religion is for both."

"And you may be a 'relict' after all, Miss Cornelia."

"Not I. Marshall will live me out. The Elliotts are long-lived, and the Bryants are not."

"When are you to be married?" asked Anne.

"In about a month's time. My wedding dress is to be navy blue silk. And I want to ask you, Anne, dearie, if you think it would be all right to wear a veil with a navy blue dress. I've always thought I'd like to wear a veil if I ever got married. Marshall says to have it if I want to. Isn't that like a man?"

"Why shouldn't you wear it if you want to?" asked Anne.

"Well, one doesn't want to be different from other people," said Miss Cornelia, who was not noticeably like anyone else on the face of the earth. "As I say, I do fancy a veil. But maybe it shouldn't be worn with any dress but a white one. Please tell me, Anne, dearie, what you really think. I'll go by your advice."

"I don't think veils are usually worn with any but white dresses," admitted Anne, "but that is merely a convention; and I am like Mr. Elliott, Miss Cornelia. I don't see any good reason why you shouldn't have a veil if you want one."

But Miss Cornelia, who made her calls in calico wrappers, shook her head.

"If it isn't the proper thing I won't wear it," she said, with a sigh of regret for a lost dream.

"Since you are determined to be married, Miss Cornelia," said Gilbert solemnly, "I shall give you the excellent rules for the management of a husband which my grandmother gave my mother when she married my father."

"Well, I reckon I can manage Marshall Elliott," said Miss Cornelia placidly. "But let us hear your rules."

"The first one is, catch him."

"He's caught. Go on."

"The second one is, feed him well."

"With enough pie. What next?"

"The third and fourth are—keep your eye on him."

"I believe you," said Miss Cornelia emphatically.

38. RED ROSES

The garden of the little house was a haunt beloved of bees and reddened by late roses that August. The little house folk lived much in it, and were given to taking picnic suppers in the grassy corner beyond the brook and sitting about in it through the twilights when great night moths sailed athwart the velvet gloom. One evening Owen Ford found Leslie alone in it. Anne and Gilbert were away, and Susan, who was expected back that night, had not yet returned.

The northern sky was amber and pale green over the fir tops. The air was cool, for August was nearing September, and Leslie wore a crimson scarf over her white dress. Together they wandered through the little, friendly, flower-crowded paths in silence. Owen must go soon. His holiday was nearly over. Leslie found her heart beating wildly. She knew that this beloved garden was to be the scene of the binding words that must seal their as yet unworded understanding.

"Some evenings a strange odor blows down the air of this garden, like a phantom perfume," said Owen. "I have never been able to discover from just what flower it comes. It is elusive and haunting and wonderfully sweet. I like to fancy it is the soul of Grandmother Selwyn passing on a little visit to the old spot she loved so well. There should be a lot of friendly ghosts about this little old house."

"I have lived under its roof only a month," said Leslie, "but I love it as I never loved the house over there where I have lived all my life."

"This house was builded and consecrated by love," said Owen. "Such houses, MUST exert an influence over those who live in them. And this garden—it is over sixty years old and the history of a thousand hopes and joys is written in its blossoms. Some of those flowers were actually set out by the schoolmaster's bride, and she has been dead for thirty years. Yet they bloom on every summer. Look at those red roses, Leslie—how they queen it over everything else!"

"I love the red roses," said Leslie. "Anne likes the pink ones best, and Gilbert likes the white. But I want the crimson ones. They satisfy some craving in me as no other flower does."

"These roses are very late—they bloom after all the others have gone—and they hold all the warmth and soul of the summer come to fruition," said Owen, plucking some of the glowing, half-opened buds.

"The rose is the flower of love—the world has acclaimed it so for centuries. The pink roses are love hopeful and expectant—the white roses are love dead or forsaken—but the red roses—ah, Leslie, what are the red roses?"

"Love triumphant," said Leslie in a low voice.

"Yes—love triumphant and perfect. Leslie, you know—you understand. I have loved you from the first. And I KNOW you love me—I don't need to ask you. But I want to hear you say it —my darling—my darling!"

Leslie said something in a very low and tremulous voice. Their hands and lips met; it was life's supreme moment for them and as they stood there in the old garden, with its many years of love and delight and sorrow and glory, he crowned her shining hair with the red, red rose of a love triumphant.

Anne and Gilbert returned presently, accompanied by Captain Jim. Anne lighted a few sticks of driftwood in the fireplace, for love of the pixy flames, and they sat around it for an hour of good fellowship.

"When I sit looking at a driftwood fire it's easy to believe I'm young again," said Captain Jim.

"Can you read futures in the fire, Captain Jim?" asked Owen.

Captain Jim looked at them all affectionately and then back again at Leslie's vivid face and glowing eyes.

"I don't need the fire to read your futures," he said. "I see happiness for all of you—all of you—for Leslie and Mr. Ford—and the doctor here and Mistress Blythe—and Little Jem—and children that ain't born yet but will be. Happiness for you all—though, mind you, I reckon you'll have your troubles and worries and sorrows, too. They're bound to come—and no house, whether it's a palace or a little house of dreams, can bar 'em out. But they won't get the better of you if you face 'em TOGETHER with love and trust. You can weather any storm with them two for compass and pilot."

The old man rose suddenly and placed one hand on Leslie's head and one on Anne's.

"Two good, sweet women," he said. "True and faithful and to be depended on. Your husbands will have honor in the gates because of you—your children will rise up and call you blessed in the years to come."

There was a strange solemnity about the little scene. Anne and Leslie bowed as those receiving a benediction. Gilbert suddenly brushed his hand over his eyes; Owen Ford was rapt as one who can see visions. All were silent for a space. The little house of dreams added another poignant and unforgettable moment to its store of memories.

"I must be going now," said Captain Jim slowly at last. He took up his hat and looked lingeringly about the room.

"Good night, all of you," he said, as he went out.

Anne, pierced by the unusual wistfulness of his farewell, ran to the door after him.

"Come back soon, Captain Jim," she called, as he passed through the little gate hung between the firs.

"Ay, ay," he called cheerily back to her. But Captain Jim had sat by the old fireside of the house of dreams for the last time.

Anne went slowly back to the others.

"It's so—so pitiful to think of him going all alone down to that lonely Point," she said. "And there is no one to welcome him there."

"Captain Jim is such good company for others that one can't imagine him being anything but good company for himself," said Owen. "But he must often be lonely. There was a touch of the seer about him tonight—he spoke as one to whom it had been given to speak. Well, I must be going, too."

Anne and Gilbert discreetly melted away; but when Owen had gone Anne returned, to find Leslie standing by the hearth.

"Oh, Leslie—I know—and I'm so glad, dear," she said, putting her arms about her.

"Anne, my happiness frightens me," whispered Leslie. "It seems too great to be real—I'm afraid to speak of it—to think of it. It seems to me that it must just be another dream of this house of dreams and it will vanish when I leave here."

"Well, you are not going to leave here—until Owen takes you. You are going to stay with me until that times comes. Do you think I'd let you go over to that lonely, sad place again?"

"Thank you, dear. I meant to ask you if I might stay with you. I didn't want to go back there—it would seem like going back into the chill and dreariness of the old life again. Anne, Anne, what a friend you've been to me—'a good, sweet woman—true and faithful and to be depended on'—Captain Jim summed you up."

"He said 'women,' not 'woman,'" smiled Anne. "Perhaps Captain Jim sees us both through the rose-colored spectacles of his love for us. But we can try to live up to his belief in us, at least."

"Do you remember, Anne," said Leslie slowly, "that I once said—that night we met on the shore—that I hated my good looks? I did—then. It always seemed to me that if I had been homely Dick would never have thought of me. I hated my beauty because it had attracted him, but now—oh, I'm glad that I have it. It's all I have to offer Owen,—his artist soul delights in it. I feel as if I do not come to him quite empty-handed."

"Owen loves your beauty, Leslie. Who would not? But it's foolish of you to say or think that that is all you bring him. HE will tell you that—I needn't. And now I must lock up. I expected Susan back tonight, but she has not come."

"Oh, yes, here I am, Mrs. Doctor, dear," said Susan, entering unexpectedly from the kitchen, "and puffing like a hen drawing rails at that! It's quite a walk from the Glen down here."

"I'm glad to see you back, Susan. How is your sister?"

"She is able to sit up, but of course she cannot walk yet. However, she is very well able to get on without me now, for her daughter has come home for her vacation. And I am thankful to be back, Mrs. Doctor, dear. Matilda's leg was broken and no mistake, but her tongue was not. She would talk the legs off an iron pot, that she would, Mrs. Doctor, dear, though I grieve to say it of my own sister. She was always a great talker and yet she was the first of our family to get married. She really did not care much about marrying James Clow, but she could not bear to disoblige him. Not but what James is a good man—the only fault I have to find with him is that he always starts in to say grace with such an unearthly groan, Mrs. Doctor, dear. It always frightens my appetite clear away. And speaking of getting married, Mrs. Doctor, dear, is it true that Cornelia Bryant is going to be married to Marshall Elliott?"

"Yes, quite true, Susan."

"Well, Mrs. Doctor, dear, it does NOT seem to me fair. Here is me, who never said a word against the men, and I cannot get married nohow. And there is Cornelia Bryant, who is never done abusing them, and all she has to do is to reach out her hand and pick one up, as it were. It is a very strange world, Mrs. Doctor, dear."

"There's another world, you know, Susan."

"Yes," said Susan with a heavy sigh, "but, Mrs. Doctor, dear, there is neither marrying nor giving in marriage there."

39. CAPTAIN JIM CROSSES THE BAR

One day in late September Owen Ford's book came at last. Captain Jim had gone faithfully to the Glen post office every day for a month, expecting it. This day he had not gone, and Leslie brought his copy home with hers and Anne's.

"We'll take it down to him this evening," said Anne, excited as a schoolgirl.

The long walk to the Point on that clear, beguiling evening along the red harbor road was very pleasant. Then the sun dropped down behind the western hills into some valley that must have been full of lost sunsets, and at the same instant the big light flashed out on the white tower of the point.

"Captain Jim is never late by the fraction of a second," said Leslie.

Neither Anne nor Leslie ever forgot Captain Jim's face when they gave him the book—HIS book, transfigured and glorified. The cheeks that had been blanched of late suddenly flamed with the color of boyhood; his eyes glowed with all the fire of youth; but his hands trembled as he opened it.

It was called simply The Life-Book of Captain Jim, and on the title page the names of Owen

Ford and James Boyd were printed as collaborators. The frontispiece was a photograph of Captain Jim himself, standing at the door of the lighthouse, looking across the gulf. Owen Ford had "snapped" him one day while the book was being written. Captain Jim had known this, but he had not known that the picture was to be in the book.

"Just think of it," he said, "the old sailor right there in a real printed book. This is the proudest day of my life. I'm like to bust, girls. There'll be no sleep for me tonight. I'll read my book clean through before sun-up."

"We'll go right away and leave you free to begin it," said Anne.

Captain Jim had been handling the book in a kind of reverent rapture. Now he decidedly closed it and laid it aside.

"No, no, you're not going away before you take a cup of tea with the old man," he protested. "I couldn't hear to that—could you, Matey? The life-book will keep, I reckon. I've waited for it this many a year. I can wait a little longer while I'm enjoying my friends."

Captain Jim moved about getting his kettle on to boil, and setting out his bread and butter. Despite his excitement he did not move with his old briskness. His movements were slow and halting. But the girls did not offer to help him. They knew it would hurt his feelings.

"You just picked the right evening to visit me," he said, producing a cake from his cupboard. "Leetle Joe's mother sent me down a big basket full of cakes and pies today. A blessing on all good cooks, says I. Look at this purty cake, all frosting and nuts. 'Tain't often I can entertain in such style. Set in, girls, set in! We'll 'tak a cup o' kindness yet for auld lang syne.'"

The girls "set in" right merrily. The tea was up to Captain Jim's best brewing. Little Joe's mother's cake was the last word in cakes; Captain Jim was the prince of gracious hosts, never even permitting his eyes to wander to the corner where the life-book lay, in all its bravery of green and gold. But when his door finally closed behind Anne and Leslie they knew that he went straight to it, and as they walked home they pictured the delight of the old man poring over the printed pages wherein his own life was portrayed with all the charm and color of reality itself.

"I wonder how he will like the ending—the ending I suggested," said Leslie.

She was never to know. Early the next morning Anne awakened to find Gilbert bending over her, fully dressed, and with an expression of anxiety on his face.

"Are you called out?" she asked drowsily.

"No. Anne, I'm afraid there's something wrong at the Point. It's an hour after sunrise now, and the light is still burning. You know it has always been a matter of pride with Captain Jim to start the light the moment the sun sets, and put it out the moment it rises."

Anne sat up in dismay. Through her window she saw the light blinking palely against the blue skies of dawn.

"Perhaps he has fallen asleep over his life-book," she said anxiously, "or become so absorbed in it that he has forgotten the light."

Gilbert shook his head.

"That wouldn't be like Captain Jim. Anyway, I'm going down to see."

"Wait a minute and I'll go with you," exclaimed Anne. "Oh, yes, I must—Little Jem will sleep for an hour yet, and I'll call Susan. You may need a woman's help if Captain Jim is ill."

It was an exquisite morning, full of tints and sounds at once ripe and delicate. The harbor was sparkling and dimpling like a girl; white gulls were soaring over the dunes; beyond the bar was a shining, wonderful sea. The long fields by the shore were dewy and fresh in that first fine, purely-tinted light. The wind came dancing and whistling up the channel to replace the beautiful silence with a music more beautiful still. Had it not been for the baleful star on the white tower that early walk would have been a delight to Anne and Gilbert. But they went softly with fear.

Their knock was not responded to. Gilbert opened the door and they went in.

The old room was very quiet. On the table were the remnants of the little evening feast. The lamp still burned on the corner stand. The First Mate was asleep in a square of sunshine by the sofa.

Captain Jim lay on the sofa, with his hands clasped over the life-book, open at the last page, lying on his breast. His eyes were closed and on his face was a look of the most perfect peace and happiness—the look of one who has long sought and found at last.

"He is asleep?" whispered Anne tremulously.

Gilbert went to the sofa and bent over him for a few moments. Then he straightened up.

"Yes, he sleeps—well," he added quietly. "Anne, Captain Jim has crossed the bar."

They could not know precisely at what hour he had died, but Anne always believed that he had had his wish, and went out when the morning came across the gulf. Out on that shining tide his spirit drifted, over the sunrise sea of pearl and silver, to the haven where lost Margaret waited, beyond the storms and calms.

40. FAREWELL TO THE HOUSE OF DREAMS

Captain Jim was buried in the little over-harbor graveyard, very near to the spot where the wee white lady slept. His relatives put up a very expensive, very ugly "monument"—a monument at which he would have poked sly fun had he seen it in life. But his real monument was in the hearts of those who knew him, and in the book that was to live for generations.

Leslie mourned that Captain Jim had not lived to see the amazing success of it.

"How he would have delighted in the reviews—they are almost all so kindly. And to have seen his life-book heading the lists of the best sellers—oh, if he could just have lived to see it, Anne!"

But Anne, despite her grief, was wiser.

"It was the book itself he cared for, Leslie—not what might be said of it—and he had it. He had read it all through. That last night must have been one of the greatest happiness for him—with the quick, painless ending he had hoped for in the morning. I am glad for Owen's sake and yours that the book is such a success—but Captain Jim was satisfied—I KNOW."

The lighthouse star still kept a nightly vigil; a substitute keeper had been sent to the Point, until such time as an all-wise government could decide which of many applicants was best fitted for the place—or had the strongest pull. The First Mate was at home in the little house, beloved by Anne and Gilbert and Leslie, and tolerated by a Susan who had small liking for cats.

"I can put up with him for the sake of Captain Jim, Mrs. Doctor, dear, for I liked the old man. And I will see that he gets bite and sup, and every mouse the traps account for. But do not ask me to do more than that, Mrs. Doctor, dear. Cats is cats, and take my word for it, they will never be anything else. And at least, Mrs. Doctor, dear, do keep him away from the blessed wee man. Picture to yourself how awful it would be if he was to suck the darling's breath."

"That might be fitly called a CAT-astrophe," said Gilbert.

"Oh, you may laugh, doctor, dear, but it would be no laughing matter."

"Cats never suck babies' breaths," said Gilbert. "That is only an old superstition, Susan."

"Oh, well, it may be a superstition or it may not, doctor, dear. All that I know is, it has happened. My sister's husband's nephew's wife's cat sucked their baby's breath, and the poor innocent was all but gone when they found it. And superstition or not, if I find that yellow beast lurking near our baby I will whack him with the poker, Mrs. Doctor, dear."

Mr. and Mrs. Marshall Elliott were living comfortably and harmoniously in the green house. Leslie was busy with sewing, for she and Owen were to be married at Christmas. Anne wondered what she would do when Leslie was gone.

"Changes come all the time. Just as soon as things get really nice they change," she said with a sigh.

"The old Morgan place up at the Glen is for sale," said Gilbert, apropos of nothing in especial.

"Is it?" asked Anne indifferently.

"Yes. Now that Mr. Morgan has gone, Mrs. Morgan wants to go to live with her children in Vancouver. She will sell cheaply, for a big place like that in a small village like the Glen will not be very easy to dispose of."

"Well, it's certainly a beautiful place, so it is likely she will find a purchaser," said Anne, absently, wondering whether she should hemstitch or feather-stitch little Jem's "short" dresses. He was to be shortened the next week, and Anne felt ready to cry at the thought of it.

"Suppose we buy it, Anne?" remarked Gilbert quietly.

Anne dropped her sewing and stared at him.

"You're not in earnest, Gilbert?"

"Indeed I am, dear."

"And leave this darling spot—our house of dreams?" said Anne incredulously. "Oh, Gilbert, it's—it's unthinkable!"

"Listen patiently to me, dear. I know just how you feel about it. I feel the same. But we've always known we would have to move some day."

"Oh, but not so soon, Gilbert—not just yet."

"We may never get such a chance again. If we don't buy the Morgan place someone else will—and there is no other house in the Glen we would care to have, and no other really good site on which to build. This little house is—well, it is and has been what no other house can ever be to us, I admit, but you know it is out-of-the-way down here for a doctor. We have felt the inconvenience, though we've made the best of it. And it's a tight fit for us now. Perhaps, in a few years, when Jem wants a room of his own, it will be entirely too small."

"Oh, I know—I know," said Anne, tears filling her eyes. "I know all that can be said against it, but I love it so—and it's so beautiful here."

"You would find it very lonely here after Leslie goes—and Captain Jim has gone too. The Morgan place is beautiful, and in time we would love it. You know you have always admired it, Anne."

"Oh, yes, but—but—this has all seemed to come up so suddenly, Gilbert. I'm dizzy. Ten minutes ago I had no thought of leaving this dear spot. I was planning what I meant to do for it in the spring—what I meant to do in the garden. And if we leave this place who will get it? It IS out-of-the-way, so it's likely some poor, shiftless, wandering family will rent it—and over-run it—and oh, that would be desecration. It would hurt me horribly."

"I know. But we cannot sacrifice our own interests to such considerations, Anne-girl. The Morgan place will suit us in every essential particular—we really can't afford to miss such a chance. Think of that big lawn with those magnificent old trees; and of that splendid hardwood grove behind it—twelve acres of it. What a play place for our children! There's a fine orchard, too, and you've always admired that high brick wall around the garden with the door in it—you've thought it was so like a story-book garden. And there is almost as fine a view of the harbor and the dunes from the Morgan place as from here."

"You can't see the lighthouse star from it."

"Yes, You can see it from the attic window. THERE'S another advantage, Anne-girl—you love big garrets."

"There's no brook in the garden."

"Well, no, but there is one running through the maple grove into the Glen pond. And the pond itself isn't far away. You'll be able to fancy you have your own Lake of Shining Waters again."

"Well, don't say anything more about it just now, Gilbert. Give me time to think—to get used to the idea."

"All right. There is no great hurry, of course. Only—if we decide to buy, it would be well to be moved in and settled before winter."

Gilbert went out, and Anne put away Little Jem's short dresses with trembling hands. She could not sew any more that day. With tear-wet eyes she wandered over the little domain where she had reigned so happy a queen. The Morgan place was all that Gilbert claimed. The grounds were beautiful, the house old enough to have dignity and repose and traditions, and new enough to be comfortable and up-to-date. Anne had always admired it; but admiring is not loving; and she loved this house of dreams so much. She loved EVERYTHING about it—the garden she had tended, and which so many women had tended before her—the gleam and sparkle of the little brook that crept so roguishly across the corner—the gate between the creaking fir trees—the old red sandstone step—the stately Lombardies—the two tiny quaint glass cupboards over the chimney-piece in the living-room—the crooked pantry door in the kitchen—the two funny dormer windows upstairs—the little jog in the staircase—why, these things were a part of her! How could she leave them?

And how this little house, consecrated aforetime by love and joy, had been re-consecrated for her by her happiness and sorrow! Here she had spent her bridal moon; here wee Joyce had lived her one brief day; here the sweetness of motherhood had come again with Little Jem; here she had heard the exquisite music of her baby's cooing laughter; here beloved friends had sat by her fireside. Joy and grief, birth and death, had made sacred forever this little house of dreams.

And now she must leave it. She knew that, even while she had contended against the idea to Gilbert. The little house was outgrown. Gilbert's interests made the change necessary; his work, successful though it had been, was hampered by his location. Anne realised that the end of their life in this dear place drew nigh, and that she must face the fact bravely. But how her heart ached!

"It will be just like tearing something out of my life," she sobbed. "And oh, if I could hope that some nice folk would come here in our place—or even that it would be left vacant. That itself would be better than having it overrun with some horde who know nothing of the geography of dreamland, and nothing of the history that has given this house its soul and its identity. And if such a tribe come here the place will go to rack and ruin in no time—an old place goes down so quickly if it is not carefully attended to. They'll tear up my garden—and let the Lombardies get ragged—and the paling will come to look like a mouth with half the teeth missing—and the roof will leak—and the plaster fall—and they'll stuff pillows and rags in broken window panes—and everything will be out-at-elbows."

Anne's imagination pictured forth so vividly the coming degeneration of her dear little house that it hurt her as severely as if it had already been an accomplished fact. She sat down on the stairs and had a long, bitter cry. Susan found her there and enquired with much concern what the trouble was.

"You have not quarrelled with the doctor, have you now, Mrs. Doctor, dear? But if you have, do not worry. It is a thing quite likely to happen to married couples, I am told, although I have had no experience that way myself. He will be sorry, and you can soon make it up."

"No, no, Susan, we haven't quarrelled. It's only—Gilbert is going to buy the Morgan place, and we'll have to go and live at the Glen. And it will break my heart."

Susan did not enter into Anne's feelings at all. She was, indeed, quite rejoiced over the prospect of living at the Glen. Her one grievance against her place in the little house was its lonesome location.

"Why, Mrs. Doctor, dear, it will be splendid. The Morgan house is such a fine, big one."

"I hate big houses," sobbed Anne.

"Oh, well, you will not hate them by the time you have half a dozen children," remarked Susan calmly. "And this house is too small already for us. We have no spare room, since Mrs. Moore is here, and that pantry is the most aggravating place I ever tried to work in. There is a corner every way you turn. Besides, it is out-of-the-world down here. There is really nothing at all but scenery."

"Out of your world perhaps, Susan—but not out of mine," said Anne with a faint smile.

"I do not quite understand you, Mrs. Doctor, dear, but of course I am not well educated. But if Dr. Blythe buys the Morgan place he will make no mistake, and that you may tie to. They have water in it, and the pantries and closets are beautiful, and there is not another such cellar in P. E. Island, so I have been told. Why, the cellar here, Mrs. Doctor, dear, has been a heartbreak to me, as well you know."

"Oh, go away, Susan, go away," said Anne forlornly. "Cellars and pantries and closets don't make a HOME. Why don't you weep with those who weep?"

"Well, I never was much hand for weeping, Mrs. Doctor, dear. I would rather fall to and cheer people up than weep with them. Now, do not you cry and spoil your pretty eyes. This house is very well and has served your turn, but it is high time you had a better."

Susan's point of view seemed to be that of most people. Leslie was the only one who sympathised understandingly with Anne. She had a good cry, too, when she heard the news. Then they both dried their tears and went to work at the preparations for moving.

"Since we must go let us go as soon as we can and have it over," said poor Anne with bitter resignation.

"You know you will like that lovely old place at the Glen after you have lived in it long enough to have dear memories woven about it," said Leslie. "Friends will come there, as they have come here—happiness will glorify it for you. Now, it's just a house to you—but the years will make it a home."

Anne and Leslie had another cry the next week when they shortened Little Jem. Anne felt the tragedy of it until evening when in his long nightie she found her own dear baby again.

"But it will be rompers next—and then trousers—and in no time he will be grown-up," she sighed.

"Well, you would not want him to stay a baby always, Mrs. Doctor, dear, would you?" said Susan. "Bless his innocent heart, he looks too sweet for anything in his little short dresses, with his dear feet sticking out. And think of the save in the ironing, Mrs. Doctor, dear."

"Anne, I have just had a letter from Owen," said Leslie, entering with a bright face. "And, oh! I have such good news. He writes me that he is going to buy this place from the church trustees and keep it to spend our summer vacations in. Anne, are you not glad?"

"Oh, Leslie, 'glad' isn't the word for it! It seems almost too good to be true. I sha'n't feel half so badly now that I know this dear spot will never be desecrated by a vandal tribe, or left to tumble down in decay. Why, it's lovely! It's lovely!"

One October morning Anne wakened to the realisation that she had slept for the last time under the roof of her little house. The day was too busy to indulge regret and when evening came the house was stripped and bare. Anne and Gilbert were alone in it to say farewell. Leslie and Susan and Little Jem had gone to the Glen with the last load of furniture. The sunset light streamed in through the curtainless windows.

"It has all such a heart-broken, reproachful look, hasn't it?" said Anne. "Oh, I shall be so homesick at the Glen tonight!"

"We have been very happy here, haven't we, Anne-girl?" said Gilbert, his voice full of feeling.

Anne choked, unable to answer. Gilbert waited for her at the fir-tree gate, while she went over the house and said farewell to every room. She was going away; but the old house would still be there, looking seaward through its quaint windows. The autumn winds would blow around it mournfully, and the gray rain would beat upon it and the white mists would come in from the sea to enfold it; and the moonlight would fall over it and light up the old paths where the schoolmaster and his bride had walked. There on that old harbor shore the charm of story would linger; the wind would still whistle alluringly over the silver sand-dunes; the waves would still call from the red rock-coves.

"But we will be gone," said Anne through her tears.

She went out, closing and locking the door behind her. Gilbert was waiting for her with a smile. The lighthouse star was gleaming northward. The little garden, where only marigolds still bloomed, was already hooding itself in shadows.

Anne knelt down and kissed the worn old step which she had crossed as a bride.

"Good-bye, dear little house of dreams," she said.

RAINBOW VALLEY

RAINBOW VALLEY

I. HOME AGAIN

It was a clear, apple-green evening in May, and Four Winds Harbour was mirroring back the clouds of the golden west between its softly dark shores. The sea moaned eerily on the sand-bar, sorrowful even in spring, but a sly, jovial wind came piping down the red harbour road along which Miss Cornelia's comfortable, matronly figure was making its way towards the village of Glen St. Mary. Miss Cornelia was rightfully Mrs. Marshall Elliott, and had been Mrs. Marshall Elliott for thirteen years, but even yet more people referred to her as Miss Cornelia than as Mrs. Elliott. The old name was dear to her old friends, only one of them contemptuously dropped it. Susan Baker, the gray and grim and faithful handmaiden of the Blythe family at Ingleside, never lost an opportunity of calling her "Mrs. Marshall Elliott," with the most killing and pointed emphasis, as if to say "You wanted to be Mrs. and Mrs. you shall be with a vengeance as far as I am concerned."

Miss Cornelia was going up to Ingleside to see Dr. and Mrs. Blythe, who were just home from Europe. They had been away for three months, having left in February to attend a famous medical congress in London; and certain things, which Miss Cornelia was anxious to discuss, had taken place in the Glen during their absence. For one thing, there was a new family in the manse. And such a family! Miss Cornelia shook her head over them several times as she walked briskly along.

Susan Baker and the Anne Shirley of other days saw her coming, as they sat on the big veranda at Ingleside, enjoying the charm of the cat's light, the sweetness of sleepy robins whistling among the twilit maples, and the dance of a gusty group of daffodils blowing against the old, mellow, red brick wall of the lawn.

Anne was sitting on the steps, her hands clasped over her knee, looking, in the kind dusk, as girlish as a mother of many has any right to be; and the beautiful gray-green eyes, gazing down the harbour road, were as full of unquenchable sparkle and dream as ever. Behind her, in the hammock, Rilla Blythe was curled up, a fat, roly-poly little creature of six years, the youngest of the Ingleside children. She had curly red hair and hazel eyes that were now buttoned up after the funny, wrinkled fashion in which Rilla always went to sleep.

Shirley, "the little brown boy," as he was known in the family "Who's Who," was asleep in Susan's arms. He was brown-haired, brown-eyed and brown-skinned, with very rosy cheeks, and he was Susan's especial love. After his birth Anne had been very ill for a long time, and Susan "mothered" the baby with a passionate tenderness which none of the other children, dear as they were to her, had ever called out. Dr. Blythe had said that but for her he would never have lived.

"I gave him life just as much as you did, Mrs. Dr. dear," Susan was wont to say. "He is just as much my baby as he is yours." And, indeed, it was always to Susan that Shirley ran, to be kissed for bumps, and rocked to sleep, and protected from well-deserved spankings. Susan had conscientiously spanked all the other Blythe children when she thought they needed it for their souls' good, but she would not spank Shirley nor allow his mother to do it. Once, Dr. Blythe had spanked him and Susan had been stormily indignant.

"That man would spank an angel, Mrs. Dr. dear, that he would," she had declared bitterly; and she would not make the poor doctor a pie for weeks.

She had taken Shirley with her to her brother's home during his parents' absence, while all the other children had gone to Avonlea, and she had three blessed months of him all to herself. Nevertheless, Susan was very glad to find herself back at Ingleside, with all her darlings around her again. Ingleside was her world and in it she reigned supreme. Even Anne seldom questioned her decisions, much to the disgust of Mrs. Rachel Lynde of Green Gables, who gloomily told Anne, whenever she visited Four Winds, that she was letting Susan get to be entirely too much of a boss and would live to rue it.

"Here is Cornelia Bryant coming up the harbour road, Mrs. Dr. dear," said Susan. "She will be coming up to unload three months' gossip on us."

"I hope so," said Anne, hugging her knees. "I'm starving for Glen St. Mary gossip, Susan. I hope Miss Cornelia can tell me everything that has happened while we've been away—EVERYTHING—who has got born, or married, or drunk; who has died, or gone away, or come, or fought, or lost a cow, or found a beau. It's so delightful to be home again with all the dear Glen folks, and I want to know all about them. Why, I remember wondering, as I walked through Westminster Abbey which of her two especial beaux Millicent Drew would finally marry. Do you know, Susan, I have a dreadful suspicion that I love gossip."

"Well, of course, Mrs. Dr. dear," admitted Susan, "every proper woman likes to hear the news. I am rather interested in Millicent Drew's case myself. I never had a beau, much less two, and I do not mind now, for being an old maid does not hurt when you get used to it. Millicent's hair always looks to me as if she had swept it up with a broom. But the men do not seem to mind that."

"They see only her pretty, piquant, mocking, little face, Susan."

"That may very well be, Mrs. Dr. dear. The Good Book says that favour is deceitful and beauty is vain, but I should not have minded finding that out for myself, if it had been so ordained. I have no doubt we will all be beautiful when we are angels, but what good will it do us then? Speaking of gossip, however, they do say that poor Mrs. Harrison Miller over harbour tried to hang herself last week."

"Oh, Susan!"

"Calm yourself, Mrs. Dr. dear. She did not succeed. But I really do not blame her for trying, for her husband is a terrible man. But she was very foolish to think of hanging herself and leaving the way clear for him to marry some other woman. If I had been in her shoes, Mrs. Dr. dear, I would have gone to work to worry him so that he would try to hang himself instead of me. Not that I hold with people hanging themselves under any circumstances, Mrs. Dr. dear."

"What is the matter with Harrison Miller, anyway?" said Anne impatiently. "He is always driving some one to extremes."

"Well, some people call it religion and some call it cussedness, begging your pardon, Mrs. Dr. dear, for using such a word. It seems they cannot make out which it is in Harrison's case. There are days when he growls at everybody because he thinks he is fore-ordained to eternal punishment. And then there are days when he says he does not care and goes and gets drunk. My own opinion is that he is not sound in his intellect, for none of that branch of the Millers were. His grandfather went out of his mind. He thought he was surrounded by big black spiders. They crawled over him and floated in the air about him. I hope I shall never go insane, Mrs. Dr. dear, and I do not think I will, because it is not a habit of the Bakers. But, if an all-wise Providence should decree it, I hope it will not take the form of big black spiders, for I loathe the animals. As for Mrs. Miller, I do not know whether she really deserves pity or not. There are some who say she just married Harrison to spite Richard Taylor, which seems to me a very peculiar reason for getting married. But then, of course, *I* am no judge of things matrimonial, Mrs. Dr. dear. And there is Cornelia Bryant at the gate, so I will put this blessed brown baby on his bed and get my knitting."

2. SHEER GOSSIP

"Where are the other children?" asked Miss Cornelia, when the first greetings—cordial on her side, rapturous on Anne's, and dignified on Susan's—were over.

"Shirley is in bed and Jem and Walter and the twins are down in their beloved Rainbow Valley," said Anne. "They just came home this afternoon, you know, and they could hardly wait until supper was over before rushing down to the valley. They love it above every spot on earth. Even the maple grove doesn't rival it in their affections."

"I am afraid they love it too well," said Susan gloomily. "Little Jem said once he would rather go to Rainbow Valley than to heaven when he died, and that was not a proper remark."

"I suppose they had a great time in Avonlea?" said Miss Cornelia.

"Enormous. Marilla does spoil them terribly. Jem, in particular, can do no wrong in her eyes."

"Miss Cuthbert must be an old lady now," said Miss Cornelia, getting out her knitting, so that she could hold her own with Susan. Miss Cornelia held that the woman whose hands were employed always had the advantage over the woman whose hands were not.

"Marilla is eighty-five," said Anne with a sigh. "Her hair is snow-white. But, strange to say, her eyesight is better than it was when she was sixty."

"Well, dearie, I'm real glad you're all back. I've been dreadful lonesome. But we haven't been dull in the Glen, believe ME. There hasn't been such an exciting spring in my time, as far as church matters go. We've got settled with a minister at last, Anne dearie."

"The Reverend John Knox Meredith, Mrs. Dr. dear," said Susan, resolved not to let Miss Cornelia tell all the news.

"Is he nice?" asked Anne interestedly.

Miss Cornelia sighed and Susan groaned.

"Yes, he's nice enough if that were all," said the former. "He is VERY nice—and very learned—and very spiritual. But, oh Anne dearie, he has no common sense!

"How was it you called him, then?"

"Well, there's no doubt he is by far the best preacher we ever had in Glen St. Mary church," said Miss Cornelia, veering a tack or two. "I suppose it is because he is so moony and absent-minded that he never got a town call. His trial sermon was simply wonderful, believe ME. Every one went mad about it—and his looks."

"He is VERY comely, Mrs. Dr. dear, and when all is said and done, I DO like to see a well-looking man in the pulpit," broke in Susan, thinking it was time she asserted herself again.

"Besides," said Miss Cornelia, "we were anxious to get settled. And Mr. Meredith was the first candidate we were all agreed on. Somebody had some objection to all the others. There was some talk of calling Mr. Folsom. He was a good preacher, too, but somehow people didn't care for his appearance. He was too dark and sleek."

"He looked exactly like a great black tomcat, that he did, Mrs. Dr. dear," said Susan. "I never could abide such a man in the pulpit every Sunday."

"Then Mr. Rogers came and he was like a chip in porridge—neither harm nor good," resumed Miss Cornelia. "But if he had preached like Peter and Paul it would have profited him nothing, for that was the day old Caleb Ramsay's sheep strayed into church and gave a loud 'ba-a-a' just as he announced his text. Everybody laughed, and poor Rogers had no chance after that. Some thought we ought to call Mr. Stewart, because he was so well educated. He could read the New Testament in five languages."

"But I do not think he was any surer than other men of getting to heaven because of that," interjected Susan.

"Most of us didn't like his delivery," said Miss Cornelia, ignoring Susan. "He talked in grunts, so to speak. And Mr. Arnett couldn't preach AT ALL. And he picked about the worst candidating text there is in the Bible—'Curse ye Meroz.'"

"Whenever he got stuck for an idea, he would bang the Bible and shout very bitterly, 'Curse ye Meroz.' Poor Meroz got thoroughly cursed that day, whoever he was, Mrs. Dr. dear," said Susan.

"The minister who is candidating can't be too careful what text he chooses," said Miss Cornelia solemnly. "I believe Mr. Pierson would have got the call if he had picked a different text. But when he announced 'I will lift my eyes to the hills' HE was done for. Every one grinned, for every one knew that those two Hill girls from the Harbour Head have been setting their caps for every single minister who came to the Glen for the last fifteen years. And Mr. Newman had too large a family."

"He stayed with my brother-in-law, James Clow," said Susan. "'How many children have you got?' I asked him. 'Nine boys and a sister for each of them,' he said. 'Eighteen!' said I. 'Dear me, what a family!' And then he laughed and laughed. But I do not know why, Mrs. Dr. dear, and I am certain that eighteen children would be too many for any manse."

"He had only ten children, Susan," explained Miss Cornelia, with contemptuous patience. "And ten good children would not be much worse for the manse and congregation than the four who are there now. Though I wouldn't say, Anne dearie, that they are so bad, either. I like them—everybody likes them. It's impossible to help liking them. They would be real nice little souls if there was anyone to look after their manners and teach them what is right and proper. For instance, at school the teacher says they are model children. But at home they simply run wild."

"What about Mrs. Meredith?" asked Anne.

"There's NO Mrs. Meredith. That is just the trouble. Mr. Meredith is a widower. His wife died four years ago. If we had known that I don't suppose we would have called him, for a widower is even worse in a congregation than a single man. But he was heard to speak of his children and we all supposed there was a mother, too. And when they came there was nobody but old Aunt Martha, as they call her. She's a cousin of Mr. Meredith's mother, I believe, and he took her in to save her from the poorhouse. She is seventy-five years old, half blind, and very deaf and very cranky."

"And a very poor cook, Mrs. Dr. dear."

"The worst possible manager for a manse," said Miss Cornelia bitterly. "Mr. Meredith won't get any other housekeeper because he says it would hurt Aunt Martha's feelings. Anne dearie, believe me, the state of that manse is something terrible. Everything is thick with dust and nothing is ever in its place. And we had painted and papered it all so nice before they came."

"There are four children, you say?" asked Anne, beginning to mother them already in her heart.

"Yes. They run up just like the steps of a stair. Gerald's the oldest. He's twelve and they call him Jerry. He's a clever boy. Faith is eleven. She is a regular tomboy but pretty as a picture, I must say."

"She looks like an angel but she is a holy terror for mischief, Mrs. Dr. dear," said Susan solemnly. "I was at the manse one night last week and Mrs. James Millison was there, too. She had brought them up a dozen eggs and a little pail of milk—a VERY little pail, Mrs. Dr. dear. Faith took them and whisked down the cellar with them. Near the bottom of the stairs she caught her toe and fell the rest of the way, milk and eggs and all. You can imagine the result, Mrs. Dr. dear. But that child came up laughing. 'I don't know whether I'm myself or a custard pie,' she said. And Mrs. James Millison was very angry. She said she would never take another thing to the manse if it was to be wasted and destroyed in that fashion."

"Maria Millison never hurt herself taking things to the manse," sniffed Miss Cornelia. "She just took them that night as an excuse for curiosity. But poor Faith is always getting into scrapes. She is so heedless and impulsive."

"Just like me. I'm going to like your Faith," said Anne decidedly.

"She is full of spunk—and I do like spunk, Mrs. Dr. dear," admitted Susan.

"There's something taking about her," conceded Miss Cornelia. "You never see her but she's laughing, and somehow it always makes you want to laugh too. She can't even keep a straight face in church. Una is ten—she's a sweet little thing—not pretty, but sweet. And Thomas Carlyle is nine. They call him Carl, and he has a regular mania for collecting toads and bugs and frogs and bringing them into the house."

"I suppose he was responsible for the dead rat that was lying on a chair in the parlour the afternoon Mrs. Grant called. It gave her a turn," said Susan, "and I do not wonder, for manse parlours are no places for dead rats. To be sure it may have been the cat who left it, there. HE is as full of the old Nick as he can be stuffed, Mrs. Dr. dear. A manse cat should at least LOOK respectable, in my opinion, whatever he really is. But I never saw such a rakish-looking beast. And he walks along the ridgepole of the manse almost every evening at sunset, Mrs. Dr. dear, and waves his tail, and that is not becoming."

"The worst of it is, they are NEVER decently dressed," sighed Miss Cornelia. "And since the snow went they go to school barefooted. Now, you know Anne dearie, that isn't the right thing for manse children—especially when the Methodist minister's little girl always wears such nice buttoned boots. And I DO wish they wouldn't play in the old Methodist graveyard."

"It's very tempting, when it's right beside the manse," said Anne. "I've always thought graveyards must be delightful places to play in."

"Oh, no, you did not, Mrs. Dr. dear," said loyal Susan, determined to protect Anne from herself. "You have too much good sense and decorum."

"Why did they ever build that manse beside the graveyard in the first place?" asked Anne. "Their lawn is so small there is no place for them to play except in the graveyard."

"It WAS a mistake," admitted Miss Cornelia. "But they got the lot cheap. And no other manse children ever thought of playing there. Mr. Meredith shouldn't allow it. But he has always got his nose buried in a book, when he is home. He reads and reads, or walks about in his study in a day-dream. So far he hasn't forgotten to be in church on Sundays, but twice he has forgotten about the prayer-meeting and one of the elders had to go over to the manse and remind him. And he forgot about Fanny Cooper's wedding. They rang him up on the 'phone and then he rushed right over, just as he was, carpet slippers and all. One wouldn't mind if the Methodists didn't laugh so about it. But there's one comfort—they can't criticize his sermons. He wakes up when he's in the pulpit, believe ME. And the Methodist minister can't preach at all—so they tell me. *I* have never heard him, thank goodness."

Miss Cornelia's scorn of men had abated somewhat since her marriage, but her scorn of Methodists remained untinged of charity. Susan smiled slyly.

"They do say, Mrs. Marshall Elliott, that the Methodists and Presbyterians are talking of uniting," she said.

"Well, all I hope is that I'll be under the sod if that ever comes to pass," retorted Miss Cornelia. "I shall never have truck or trade with Methodists, and Mr. Meredith will find that he'd better steer clear of them, too. He is entirely too sociable with them, believe ME. Why, he went to the Jacob Drews' silver-wedding supper and got into a nice scrape as a result."

"What was it?"

"Mrs. Drew asked him to carve the roast goose—for Jacob Drew never did or could carve. Well, Mr. Meredith tackled it, and in the process he knocked it clean off the platter into Mrs. Reese's lap, who was sitting next him. And he just said dreamily. 'Mrs. Reese, will you kindly return me that goose?' Mrs. Reese 'returned' it, as meek as Moses, but she must have been furious, for she had on her new silk dress. The worst of it is, she was a Methodist."

"But I think that is better than if she was a Presbyterian," interjected Susan. "If she had been a Presbyterian she would mostly likely have left the church and we cannot afford to lose our members. And Mrs. Reese is not liked in her own church, because she gives herself such great airs, so that the Methodists would be rather pleased that Mr. Meredith spoiled her dress."

"The point is, he made himself ridiculous, and *I*, for one, do not like to see my minister made ridiculous in the eyes of the Methodists," said Miss Cornelia stiffly. "If he had had a wife it would not have happened."

"I do not see if he had a dozen wives how they could have prevented Mrs. Drew from using up her tough old gander for the wedding-feast," said Susan stubbornly.

"They say that was her husband's doing," said Miss Cornelia. "Jacob Drew is a conceited, stingy, domineering creature."

"And they do say he and his wife detest each other—which does not seem to me the proper way for married folks to get along. But then, of course, I have had no experience along that line," said Susan, tossing her head. "And *I* am not one to blame everything on the men. Mrs. Drew is mean enough herself. They say that the only thing she was ever known to give away was a crock of butter made out of cream a rat had fell into. She contributed it to a church social. Nobody found out about the rat until afterwards."

"Fortunately, all the people the Merediths have offended so far are Methodists," said Miss Cornelia. "That Jerry went to the Methodist prayer-meeting one night about a fortnight ago and sat beside old William Marsh who got up as usual and testified with fearful groans. 'Do you feel any better now?' whispered Jerry when William sat down. Poor Jerry meant to be sympathetic, but Mr. Marsh thought he was impertinent and is furious at him. Of course, Jerry had no business to be in a Methodist prayer-meeting at all. But they go where they like."

"I hope they will not offend Mrs. Alec Davis of the Harbour Head," said Susan. "She is a very touchy woman, I understand, but she is very well off and pays the most of any one to the salary. I have heard that she says the Merediths are the worst brought up children she ever saw."

"Every word you say convinces me more and more that the Merediths belong to the race that knows Joseph," said Mistress Anne decidedly.

"When all is said and done, they DO," admitted Miss Cornelia. "And that balances everything. Anyway, we've got them now and we must just do the best we can by them and stick up for them to the Methodists. Well, I suppose I must be getting down harbour. Marshall will soon be home—he went over-harbour to-day—and wanting his super, man-like. I'm sorry I haven't seen the other children. And where's the doctor?"

"Up at the Harbour Head. We've only been home three days and in that time he has spent three hours in his own bed and eaten two meals in his own house."

"Well, everybody who has been sick for the last six weeks has been waiting for him to come home—and I don't blame them. When that over-harbour doctor married the undertaker's daughter at Lowbridge people felt suspicious of him. It didn't look well. You and the doctor must come down soon and tell us all about your trip. I suppose you've had a splendid time."

"We had," agreed Anne. "It was the fulfilment of years of dreams. The old world is very lovely and very wonderful. But we have come back very well satisfied with our own land. Canada is the finest country in the world, Miss Cornelia."

"Nobody ever doubted that," said Miss Cornelia, complacently.

"And old P.E.I. is the loveliest province in it and Four Winds the loveliest spot in P.E.I.," laughed Anne, looking adoringly out over the sunset splendour of glen and harbour and gulf. She waved her hand at it. "I saw nothing more beautiful than that in Europe, Miss Cornelia. Must you go? The children will be sorry to have missed you."

"They must come and see me soon. Tell them the doughnut jar is always full."

"Oh, at supper they were planning a descent on you. They'll go soon; but they must settle down to school again now. And the twins are going to take music lessons."

"Not from the Methodist minister's wife, I hope?" said Miss Cornelia anxiously.

"No—from Rosemary West. I was up last evening to arrange it with her. What a pretty girl she is!"

"Rosemary holds her own well. She isn't as young as she once was."

"I thought her very charming. I've never had any real acquaintance with her, you know. Their house is so out of the way, and I've seldom ever seen her except at church."

"People always have liked Rosemary West, though they don't understand her," said Miss Cornelia, quite unconscious of the high tribute she was paying to Rosemary's charm. "Ellen has always kept her down, so to speak. She has tyrannized over her, and yet she has always indulged her in a good many ways. Rosemary was engaged once, you know—to young Martin Crawford. His ship was wrecked on the Magdalens and all the crew were drowned. Rosemary was just a child—only seventeen. But she was never the same afterwards. She and Ellen have stayed very close at home since their mother's death. They don't often get to their own church at Lowbridge and I understand Ellen doesn't approve of going too often to a Presbyterian church. To the Methodist she NEVER goes, I'll say that much for her. That family of Wests have always been strong Episcopalians. Rosemary and Ellen are pretty well off. Rosemary doesn't really need to give music lessons. She does it because she likes to. They are distantly related to Leslie, you know. Are the Fords coming to the harbour this summer?"

"No. They are going on a trip to Japan and will probably be away for a year. Owen's new novel is to have a Japanese setting. This will be the first summer that the dear old House of Dreams will be empty since we left it."

"I should think Owen Ford might find enough to write about in Canada without dragging his wife and his innocent children off to a heathen country like Japan," grumbled Miss Cornelia. "*The Life Book* was the best book he's ever written and he got the material for that right here in Four Winds."

"Captain Jim gave him the most of that, you know. And he collected it all over the world. But Owen's books are all delightful, I think."

"Oh, they're well enough as far as they go. I make it a point to read every one he writes, though I've always held, Anne dearie, that reading novels is a sinful waste of time. I shall write and tell him my opinion of this Japanese business, believe ME. Does he want Kenneth and Persis to be converted into pagans?"

With which unanswerable conundrum Miss Cornelia took her departure. Susan proceeded to put Rilla in bed and Anne sat on the veranda steps under the early stars and dreamed her incorrigible dreams and learned all over again for the hundredth happy time what a moonrise splendour and sheen could be on Four Winds Harbour.

3. THE INGLESIDE CHILDREN

In daytime the Blythe children liked very well to play in the rich, soft greens and glooms of the big maple grove between Ingleside and the Glen St. Mary pond; but for evening revels there was no place like the little valley behind the maple grove. It was a fairy realm of romance to them. Once, looking from the attic windows of Ingleside, through the mist and aftermath of a summer thunderstorm, they had seen the beloved spot arched by a glorious rainbow, one end of which seemed to dip straight down to where a corner of the pond ran up into the lower end of the valley.

"Let us call it Rainbow Valley," said Walter delightedly, and Rainbow Valley thenceforth it was.

Outside of Rainbow Valley the wind might be rollicking and boisterous. Here it always went gently. Little, winding, fairy paths ran here and there over spruce roots cushioned with moss. Wild cherry trees, that in blossom time would be misty white, were scattered all over the valley, mingling with the dark spruces. A little brook with amber waters ran through it from the Glen village. The houses of the village were comfortably far away; only at the upper end of the valley was a little tumble-down, deserted cottage, referred to as "the old Bailey house." It had not been occupied for many years, but a grass-grown dyke surrounded it and inside was an ancient garden where the Ingleside children could find violets and daisies and June lilies still blooming in season. For the rest, the garden was overgrown with caraway that swayed and foamed in the moonshine of summer eves like seas of silver.

To the sought lay the pond and beyond it the ripened distance lost itself in purple woods, save where, on a high hill, a solitary old gray homestead looked down on glen and harbour. There was a certain wild woodsiness and solitude about Rainbow Valley, in spite of its nearness to the village, which endeared it to the children of Ingleside.

The valley was full of dear, friendly hollows and the largest of these was their favourite stamping ground. Here they were assembled on this particular evening. There was a grove of young spruces in this hollow, with a tiny, grassy glade in its heart, opening on the bank of the brook. By the brook grew a silver birch-tree, a young, incredibly straight thing which Walter had named the "White Lady." In this glade, too, were the "Tree Lovers," as Walter called a spruce and maple which grew so closely together that their boughs were inextricably intertwined. Jem had hung an old string of sleigh-bells, given him by the Glen blacksmith, on the Tree Lovers, and every visitant breeze called out sudden fairy tinkles from it.

"How nice it is to be back!" said Nan. "After all, none of the Avonlea places are quite as nice as Rainbow Valley."

But they were very fond of the Avonlea places for all that. A visit to Green Gables was always considered a great treat. Aunt Marilla was very good to them, and so was Mrs. Rachel Lynde, who was spending the leisure of her old age in knitting cotton-warp quilts against the day when Anne's daughters should need a "setting-out." There were jolly playmates there, too —"Uncle" Davy's children and "Aunt" Diana's children. They knew all the spots their mother had loved so well in her girlhood at old Green Gables—the long Lover's Lane, that was pink-hedged in wild-rose time, the always neat yard, with its willows and poplars, the Dryad's Bubble, lucent and lovely as of yore, the Lake of Shining Waters, and Willowmere. The twins had their mother's old porch-gable room, and Aunt Marilla used to come in at night, when she thought they were asleep, to gloat over them. But they all knew she loved Jem the best.

Jem was at present busily occupied in frying a mess of small trout which he had just caught in the pond. His stove consisted of a circle of red stones, with a fire kindled in it, and his culinary utensils were an old tin can, hammered out flat, and a fork with only one tine left. Nevertheless, ripping good meals had before now been thus prepared.

Jem was the child of the House of Dreams. All the others had been born at Ingleside. He had curly red hair, like his mother's, and frank hazel eyes, like his father's; he had his mother's fine nose and his father's steady, humorous mouth. And he was the only one of the family who had ears nice enough to please Susan. But he had a standing feud with Susan because she would not give up calling him Little Jem. It was outrageous, thought thirteen-year-old Jem. Mother had more sense.

"I'm NOT little any more, Mother," he had cried indignantly, on his eighth birthday. "I'm AWFUL big."

Mother had sighed and laughed and sighed again; and she never called him Little Jem again —in his hearing at least.

He was and always had been a sturdy, reliable little chap. He never broke a promise. He was not a great talker. His teachers did not think him brilliant, but he was a good, all-round student. He never took things on faith; he always liked to investigate the truth of a statement for himself. Once Susan had told him that if he touched his tongue to a frosty latch all the skin would tear off it. Jem had promptly done it, "just to see if it was so." He found it was "so," at the cost of a very sore tongue for several days. But Jem did not grudge suffering in the interests of science. By constant experiment and observation he learned a great deal and his brothers and sisters thought his extensive knowledge of their little world quite wonderful. Jem always knew where the first and ripest berries grew, where the first pale violets shyly wakened from their winter's sleep, and how many blue eggs were in a given robin's nest in the maple grove. He could tell fortunes from daisy petals and suck honey from red clovers, and grub up all sorts of edible roots on the banks of the pond, while Susan went in daily fear that they would all be poisoned. He knew where the finest spruce-gum was to be found, in pale amber knots on the lichened bark, he knew where the nuts grew thickest in the beechwoods around the Harbour Head, and where the best trouting places up the brooks were. He could mimic the call of any wild bird or beast in Four Winds and he knew the haunt of every wild flower from spring to autumn.

Walter Blythe was sitting under the White Lady, with a volume of poems lying beside him, but he was not reading. He was gazing now at the emerald-misted willows by the pond, and now at a flock of clouds, like little silver sheep, herded by the wind, that were drifting over Rainbow Valley, with rapture in his wide splendid eyes. Walter's eyes were very wonderful. All the joy and sorrow and laughter and loyalty and aspiration of many generations lying under the sod looked out of their dark gray depths.

Walter was a "hop out of kin," as far as looks went. He did not resemble any known relative. He was quite the handsomest of the Ingleside children, with straight black hair and finely modelled features. But he had all his mother's vivid imagination and passionate love of beauty. Frost of winter, invitation of spring, dream of summer and glamour of autumn, all meant much to Walter.

In school, where Jem was a chieftain, Walter was not thought highly of. He was supposed to be "girly" and milk-soppish, because he never fought and seldom joined in the school sports, preferring to herd by himself in out of the way corners and read books—especially "po'try books." Walter loved the poets and pored over their pages from the time he could first read. Their music was woven into his growing soul—the music of the immortals. Walter cherished the ambition to be a poet himself some day. The thing could be done. A certain Uncle Paul—so called out of courtesy—who lived now in that mysterious realm called "the States," was Walter's model. Uncle Paul had once been a little school boy in Avonlea and now his poetry was read everywhere. But the Glen schoolboys did not know of Walter's dreams and would not have been greatly impressed if they had. In spite of his lack of physical prowess, however, he commanded a certain unwilling respect because of his power of "talking book talk." Nobody in Glen St. Mary school could talk like him. He "sounded like a preacher," one boy said; and for this reason he was generally left alone and not persecuted, as most boys were who were suspected of disliking or fearing fisticuffs.

The ten year old Ingleside twins violated twin tradition by not looking in the least alike. Anne, who was always called Nan, was very pretty, with velvety nut-brown eyes and silky nut-brown hair. She was a very blithe and dainty little maiden—Blythe by name and blithe by nature, one of her teachers had said. Her complexion was quite faultless, much to her mother's satisfaction.

"I'm so glad I have one daughter who can wear pink," Mrs. Blythe was wont to say jubilantly.

Diana Blythe, known as Di, was very like her mother, with gray-green eyes that always shone with a peculiar lustre and brilliancy in the dusk, and red hair. Perhaps this was why she was her father's favourite. She and Walter were especial chums; Di was the only one to whom he would ever read the verses he wrote himself—the only one who knew that he was secretly hard at work on an epic, strikingly resembling "Marmion" in some things, if not in others. She kept all his secrets, even from Nan, and told him all hers.

"Won't you soon have those fish ready, Jem?" said Nan, sniffing with her dainty nose. "The smell makes me awfully hungry."

"They're nearly ready," said Jem, giving one a dexterous turn. "Get out the bread and the plates, girls. Walter, wake up."

"How the air shines to-night," said Walter dreamily. Not that he despised fried trout either, by any means; but with Walter food for the soul always took first place. "The flower angel has been walking over the world to-day, calling to the flowers. I can see his blue wings on that hill by the woods."

"Any angels' wings I ever saw were white," said Nan.

"The flower angel's aren't. They are a pale misty blue, just like the haze in the valley. Oh, how I wish I could fly. It must be glorious."

"One does fly in dreams sometimes," said Di.

"I never dream that I'm flying exactly," said Walter. "But I often dream that I just rise up from the ground and float over the fences and the trees. It's delightful—and I always think,

'This ISN'T a dream like it's always been before. THIS is real'—and then I wake up after all, and it's heart-breaking."

"Hurry up, Nan," ordered Jem.

Nan had produced the banquet-board—a board literally as well as figuratively—from which many a feast, seasoned as no viands were elsewhere, had been eaten in Rainbow Valley. It was converted into a table by propping it on two large, mossy stones. Newspapers served as tablecloth, and broken plates and handleless cups from Susan's discard furnished the dishes. From a tin box secreted at the root of a spruce tree Nan brought forth bread and salt. The brook gave Adam's ale of unsurpassed crystal. For the rest, there was a certain sauce, compounded of fresh air and appetite of youth, which gave to everything a divine flavour. To sit in Rainbow Valley, steeped in a twilight half gold, half amethyst, rife with the odours of balsam-fir and woodsy growing things in their springtime prime, with the pale stars of wild strawberry blossoms all around you, and with the sough of the wind and tinkle of bells in the shaking tree tops, and eat fried trout and dry bread, was something which the mighty of earth might have envied them.

"Sit in," invited Nan, as Jem placed his sizzling tin platter of trout on the table. "It's your turn to say grace, Jem."

"I've done my part frying the trout," protested Jem, who hated saying grace. "Let Walter say it. He LIKES saying grace. And cut it short, too, Walt. I'm starving."

But Walter said no grace, short or long, just then. An interruption occurred.

"Who's coming down from the manse hill?" said Di.

4. THE MANSE CHILDREN

Aunt Martha might be, and was, a very poor housekeeper; the Rev. John Knox Meredith might be, and was, a very absent-minded, indulgent man. But it could not be denied that there was something very homelike and lovable about the Glen St. Mary manse in spite of its untidiness. Even the critical housewives of the Glen felt it, and were unconsciously mellowed in judgment because of it. Perhaps its charm was in part due to accidental circumstances—the luxuriant vines clustering over its gray, clap-boarded walls, the friendly acacias and balm-of-gileads that crowded about it with the freedom of old acquaintance, and the beautiful views of harbour and sand-dunes from its front windows. But these things had been there in the reign of Mr. Meredith's predecessor, when the manse had been the primmest, neatest, and dreariest house in the Glen. So much of the credit must be given to the personality of its new inmates. There was an atmosphere of laughter and comradeship about it; the doors were always open; and inner and outer worlds joined hands. Love was the only law in Glen St. Mary manse.

The people of his congregation said that Mr. Meredith spoiled his children. Very likely he did. It is certain that he could not bear to scold them. "They have no mother," he used to say to himself, with a sigh, when some unusually glaring peccadillo forced itself upon his notice. But he did not know the half of their goings-on. He belonged to the sect of dreamers. The windows of his study looked out on the graveyard but, as he paced up and down the room, reflecting deeply on the immortality of the soul, he was quite unaware that Jerry and Carl were playing leap-frog hilariously over the flat stones in that abode of dead Methodists. Mr. Meredith had occasional acute realizations that his children were not so well looked after, physically or morally, as they had been before his wife died, and he had always a dim sub-consciousness that house and meals were very different under Aunt Martha's management from what they had been under Cecilia's. For the rest, he lived in a world of books and abstractions; and, therefore, although his clothes were seldom brushed, and although the Glen housewives concluded, from the ivory-like pallor of his clear-cut features and slender hands, that he never got enough to eat, he was not an unhappy man.

If ever a graveyard could be called a cheerful place, the old Methodist graveyard at Glen St. Mary might be so called. The new graveyard, at the other side of the Methodist church, was a neat and proper and doleful spot; but the old one had been left so long to Nature's kindly and gracious ministries that it had become very pleasant.

It was surrounded on three sides by a dyke of stones and sod, topped by a gray and uncertain paling. Outside the dyke grew a row of tall fir trees with thick, balsamic boughs. The dyke, which had been built by the first settlers of the Glen, was old enough to be beautiful, with mosses and green things growing out of its crevices, violets purpling at its base in the early spring days, and asters and golden-rod making an autumnal glory in its corners. Little ferns clustered companionably between its stones, and here and there a big bracken grew.

On the eastern side there was neither fence nor dyke. The graveyard there straggled off into a young fir plantation, ever pushing nearer to the graves and deepening eastward into a thick wood. The air was always full of the harp-like voices of the sea, and the music of gray old trees, and in the spring mornings the choruses of birds in the elms around the two churches sang of life and not of death. The Meredith children loved the old graveyard.

Blue-eyed ivy, "garden-spruce," and mint ran riot over the sunken graves. Blueberry bushes grew lavishly in the sandy corner next to the fir wood. The varying fashions of tombstones for three generations were to be found there, from the flat, oblong, red sandstone slabs of old settlers, down through the days of weeping willows and clasped hands, to the latest monstrosities of tall "monuments" and draped urns. One of the latter, the biggest and ugliest in the graveyard, was sacred to the memory of a certain Alec Davis who had been born a Methodist but had taken to himself a Presbyterian bride of the Douglas clan. She had made him turn Presbyterian and kept him toeing the Presbyterian mark all his life. But when he died she did not dare to doom him to a lonely grave in the Presbyterian graveyard over-harbour. His people were all buried in the Methodist cemetery; so Alec Davis went back to his own in death and his widow consoled herself by erecting a monument which cost more than any of the Methodists could afford. The Meredith children hated it, without just knowing why, but they loved the old, flat, bench-like stones with the tall grasses growing rankly about them. They made jolly seats for one thing. They were all sitting on one now. Jerry, tired of leap frog, was playing on a jew's-harp. Carl was lovingly poring over a strange beetle he had found; Una was trying to make a doll's dress, and Faith, leaning back on her slender brown wrists, was swinging her bare feet in lively time to the jew's-harp.

Jerry had his father's black hair and large black eyes, but in him the latter were flashing instead of dreamy. Faith, who came next to him, wore her beauty like a rose, careless and glowing. She had golden-brown eyes, golden-brown curls and crimson cheeks. She laughed too much to please her father's congregation and had shocked old Mrs. Taylor, the disconsolate spouse of several departed husbands, by saucily declaring—in the church-porch at that—"The world ISN'T a vale of tears, Mrs. Taylor. It's a world of laughter."

Little dreamy Una was not given to laughter. Her braids of straight, dead-black hair betrayed no lawless kinks, and her almond-shaped, dark-blue eyes had something wistful and sorrowful in them. Her mouth had a trick of falling open over her tiny white teeth, and a shy, meditative smile occasionally crept over her small face. She was much more sensitive to public opinion than Faith, and had an uneasy consciousness that there was something askew in their way of living. She longed to put it right, but did not know how. Now and then she dusted the furniture—but it was so seldom she could find the duster because it was never in the same place twice. And when the clothes-brush was to be found she tried to brush her father's best suit on Saturdays, and once sewed on a missing button with coarse white thread. When Mr. Meredith went to church next day every female eye saw that button and the peace of the Ladies' Aid was upset for weeks.

Carl had the clear, bright, dark-blue eyes, fearless and direct, of his dead mother, and her brown hair with its glints of gold. He knew the secrets of bugs and had a sort of freemasonry with bees and beetles. Una never liked to sit near him because she never knew what uncanny creature might be secreted about him. Jerry refused to sleep with him because Carl had once taken a young garter snake to bed with him; so Carl slept in his old cot, which was so short that he could never stretch out, and had strange bed-fellows. Perhaps it was just as well that Aunt Martha was half blind when she made that bed. Altogether they were a jolly, lovable little crew, and Cecilia Meredith's heart must have ached bitterly when she faced the knowledge that she must leave them.

"Where would you like to be buried if you were a Methodist?" asked Faith cheerfully.

This opened up an interesting field of speculation.

"There isn't much choice. The place is full," said Jerry. "I'D like that corner near the road, I guess. I could hear the teams going past and the people talking."

"I'd like that little hollow under the weeping birch," said Una. "That birch is such a place for birds and they sing like mad in the mornings."

"I'd take the Porter lot where there's so many children buried. *I* like lots of company," said Faith. "Carl, where'd you?"

"I'd rather not be buried at all," said Carl, "but if I had to be I'd like the ant-bed. Ants are AWF'LY int'resting."

"How very good all the people who are buried here must have been," said Una, who had been reading the laudatory old epitaphs. "There doesn't seem to be a single bad person in the whole graveyard. Methodists must be better than Presbyterians after all."

"Maybe the Methodists bury their bad people just like they do cats," suggested Carl. "Maybe they don't bother bringing them to the graveyard at all."

"Nonsense," said Faith. "The people that are buried here weren't any better than other folks, Una. But when anyone is dead you mustn't say anything of him but good or he'll come back and ha'nt you. Aunt Martha told me that. I asked father if it was true and he just looked through me and muttered, 'True? True? What is truth? What IS truth, O jesting Pilate?' I concluded from that it must be true."

"I wonder if Mr. Alec Davis would come back and ha'nt me if I threw a stone at the urn on top of his tombstone," said Jerry.

"Mrs. Davis would," giggled Faith. "She just watches us in church like a cat watching mice. Last Sunday I made a face at her nephew and he made one back at me and you should have seen her glare. I'll bet she boxed HIS ears when they got out. Mrs. Marshall Elliott told me we mustn't offend her on any account or I'd have made a face at her, too!"

"They say Jem Blythe stuck out his tongue at her once and she would never have his father again, even when her husband was dying," said Jerry. "I wonder what the Blythe gang will be like."

"I liked their looks," said Faith. The manse children had been at the station that afternoon when the Blythe small fry had arrived. "I liked Jem's looks ESPECIALLY."

"They say in school that Walter's a sissy," said Jerry.

"I don't believe it," said Una, who had thought Walter very handsome.

"Well, he writes poetry, anyhow. He won the prize the teacher offered last year for writing a poem, Bertie Shakespeare Drew told me. Bertie's mother thought HE should have got the prize because of his name, but Bertie said he couldn't write poetry to save his soul, name or no name."

"I suppose we'll get acquainted with them as soon as they begin going to school," mused Faith. "I hope the girls are nice. I don't like most of the girls round here. Even the nice ones are poky. But the Blythe twins look jolly. I thought twins always looked alike, but they don't. I think the red-haired one is the nicest."

"I liked their mother's looks," said Una with a little sigh. Una envied all children their mothers. She had been only six when her mother died, but she had some very precious memories, treasured in her soul like jewels, of twilight cuddlings and morning frolics, of loving eyes, a tender voice, and the sweetest, gayest laugh.

"They say she isn't like other people," said Jerry.

"Mrs. Elliot says that is because she never really grew up," said Faith.

"She's taller than Mrs. Elliott."

"Yes, yes, but it is inside—Mrs. Elliot says Mrs. Blythe just stayed a little girl inside."

"What do I smell?" interrupted Carl, sniffing.

They all smelled it now. A most delectable odour came floating up on the still evening air from the direction of the little woodsy dell below the manse hill.

"That makes me hungry," said Jerry.

"We had only bread and molasses for supper and cold ditto for dinner," said Una plaintively.

Aunt Martha's habit was to boil a large slab of mutton early in the week and serve it up every day, cold and greasy, as long as it lasted. To this Faith, in a moment of inspiration, had give the name of "ditto", and by this it was invariably known at the manse.

"Let's go and see where that smell is coming from," said Jerry.

They all sprang up, frolicked over the lawn with the abandon of young puppies, climbed a fence, and tore down the mossy slope, guided by the savory lure that ever grew stronger. A few minutes later they arrived breathlessly in the sanctum sanctorum of Rainbow Valley where the Blythe children were just about to give thanks and eat.

They halted shyly. Una wished they had not been so precipitate: but Di Blythe was equal to that and any occasion. She stepped forward, with a comrade's smile.

"I guess I know who you are," she said. "You belong to the manse, don't you?"

Faith nodded, her face creased by dimples.

"We smelled your trout cooking and wondered what it was."

"You must sit down and help us eat them," said Di.

"Maybe you haven't more than you want yourselves," said Jerry, looking hungrily at the tin platter.

"We've heaps—three apiece," said Jem. "Sit down."

No more ceremony was necessary. Down they all sat on mossy stones. Merry was that feast and long. Nan and Di would probably have died of horror had they known what Faith and Una knew perfectly well—that Carl had two young mice in his jacket pocket. But they never knew it, so it never hurt them. Where can folks get better acquainted than over a meal table? When the last trout had vanished, the manse children and the Ingleside children were sworn friends and allies. They had always known each other and always would. The race of Joseph recognized its own.

They poured out the history of their little pasts. The manse children heard of Avonlea and Green Gables, of Rainbow Valley traditions, and of the little house by the harbour shore where Jem had been born. The Ingleside children heard of Maywater, where the Merediths had lived before coming to the Glen, of Una's beloved, one-eyed doll and Faith's pet rooster.

Faith was inclined to resent the fact that people laughed at her for petting a rooster. She liked the Blythes because they accepted it without question.

"A handsome rooster like Adam is just as nice a pet as a dog or cat, *I* think," she said. "If he was a canary nobody would wonder. And I brought him up from a little, wee, yellow chicken. Mrs. Johnson at Maywater gave him to me. A weasel had killed all his brothers and sisters. I called him after her husband. I never liked dolls or cats. Cats are too sneaky and dolls are DEAD."

"Who lives in that house away up there?" asked Jerry.

"The Miss Wests—Rosemary and Ellen," answered Nan. "Di and I are going to take music lessons from Miss Rosemary this summer."

Una gazed at the lucky twins with eyes whose longing was too gentle for envy. Oh, if she could only have music lessons! It was one of the dreams of her little hidden life. But nobody ever thought of such a thing.

"Miss Rosemary is so sweet and she always dresses so pretty," said Di. "Her hair is just the colour of new molasses taffy," she added wistfully—for Di, like her mother before her, was not resigned to her own ruddy tresses.

"I like Miss Ellen, too," said Nan. "She always used to give me candies when she came to church. But Di is afraid of her."

"Her brows are so black and she has such a great deep voice," said Di. "Oh, how scared of her Kenneth Ford used to be when he was little! Mother says the first Sunday Mrs. Ford brought him to church Miss Ellen happened to be there, sitting right behind them. And the minute Kenneth saw her he just screamed and screamed until Mrs. Ford had to carry him out."

"Who is Mrs. Ford?" asked Una wonderingly.

"Oh, the Fords don't live here. They only come here in the summer. And they're not coming this summer. They live in that little house 'way, 'way down on the harbour shore where father and mother used to lie. I wish you could see Persis Ford. She is just like a picture."

"I've heard of Mrs. Ford," broke in Faith. "Bertie Shakespeare Drew told me about her. She was married fourteen years to a dead man and then he came to life."

"Nonsense," said Nan. "That isn't the way it goes at all. Bertie Shakespeare can never get anything straight. I know the whole story and I'll tell it to you some time, but not now, for it's too long and it's time for us to go home. Mother doesn't like us to be out late these damp evenings."

Nobody cared whether the manse children were out in the damp or not. Aunt Martha was already in bed and the minister was still too deeply lost in speculations concerning the immortality of the soul to remember the mortality of the body. But they went home, too, with visions of good times coming in their heads.

"I think Rainbow Valley is even nicer than the graveyard," said Una. "And I just love those dear Blythes. It's SO nice when you can love people because so often you CAN'T. Father said in his sermon last Sunday that we should love everybody. But how can we? How could we love Mrs. Alec Davis?"

"Oh, father only said that in the pulpit," said Faith airily. "He has more sense than to really think it outside."

The Blythe children went up to Ingleside, except Jem, who slipped away for a few moments on a solitary expedition to a remote corner of Rainbow Valley. Mayflowers grew there and Jem never forgot to take his mother a bouquet as long as they lasted.

5. THE ADVENT OF MARY VANCE

"This is just the sort of day you feel as if things might happen," said Faith, responsive to the lure of crystal air and blue hills. She hugged herself with delight and danced a hornpipe on old Hezekiah Pollock's bench tombstone, much to the horror of two ancient maidens who happened to be driving past just as Faith hopped on one foot around the stone, waving the other and her arms in the air.

"And that," groaned one ancient maiden, "is our minister's daughter."

"What else could you expect of a widower's family?" groaned the other ancient maiden. And then they both shook their heads.

It was early on Saturday morning and the Merediths were out in the dew-drenched world with a delightful consciousness of the holiday. They had never had anything to do on a holiday. Even Nan and Di Blythe had certain household tasks for Saturday mornings, but the daughters of the manse were free to roam from blushing morn to dewy eve if so it pleased them. It DID please Faith, but Una felt a secret, bitter humiliation because they never learned to do anything. The other girls in her class at school could cook and sew and knit; she only was a little ignoramus.

Jerry suggested that they go exploring; so they went lingeringly through the fir grove, picking up Carl on the way, who was on his knees in the dripping grass studying his darling ants. Beyond the grove they came out in Mr. Taylor's pasture field, sprinkled over with the white ghosts of dandelions; in a remote corner was an old tumbledown barn, where Mr. Taylor sometimes stored his surplus hay crop but which was never used for any other purpose. Thither the Meredith children trooped, and prowled about the ground floor for several minutes.

"What was that?" whispered Una suddenly.

They all listened. There was a faint but distinct rustle in the hayloft above. The Merediths looked at each other.

"There's something up there," breathed Faith.

"I'm going up to see what it is," said Jerry resolutely.

"Oh, don't," begged Una, catching his arm.

"I'm going."

"We'll all go, too, then," said Faith.

The whole four climbed the shaky ladder, Jerry and Faith quite dauntless, Una pale from fright, and Carl rather absent-mindedly speculating on the possibility of finding a bat up in the loft. He longed to see a bat in daylight.

When they stepped off the ladder they saw what had made the rustle and the sight struck them dumb for a few moments.

In a little nest in the hay a girl was curled up, looking as if she had just wakened from sleep. When she saw them she stood up, rather shakily, as it seemed, and in the bright sunlight that streamed through the cobwebbed window behind her, they saw that her thin, sunburned face was very pale under its tan. She had two braids of lank, thick, tow-coloured hair and very odd eyes—"white eyes," the manse children thought, as she stared at them half defiantly, half piteously. They were really of so pale a blue that they did seem almost white, especially when contrasted with the narrow black ring that circled the iris. She was barefooted and bareheaded, and was clad in a faded, ragged, old plaid dress, much too short and tight for her. As for years, she might have been almost any age, judging from her wizened little face, but her height seemed to be somewhere in the neighbourhood of twelve.

"Who are you?" asked Jerry.

The girl looked about her as if seeking a way of escape. Then she seemed to give in with a little shiver of despair.

"I'm Mary Vance," she said.

"Where'd you come from?" pursued Jerry.

Mary, instead of replying, suddenly sat, or fell, down on the hay and began to cry. Instantly Faith had flung herself down beside her and put her arm around the thin, shaking shoulders.

"You stop bothering her," she commanded Jerry. Then she hugged the waif. "Don't cry, dear. Just tell us what's the matter. WE'RE friends."

"I'm so—so—hungry," wailed Mary. "I—I hain't had a thing to eat since Thursday morning, 'cept a little water from the brook out there."

The manse children gazed at each other in horror. Faith sprang up.

"You come right up to the manse and get something to eat before you say another word."

Mary shrank.

"Oh—I can't. What will your pa and ma say? Besides, they'd send me back."

"We've no mother, and father won't bother about you. Neither will Aunt Martha. Come, I say." Faith stamped her foot impatiently. Was this queer girl going to insist on starving to death almost at their very door?

Mary yielded. She was so weak that she could hardly climb down the ladder, but somehow they got her down and over the field and into the manse kitchen. Aunt Martha, muddling through her Saturday cooking, took no notice of her. Faith and Una flew to the pantry and ransacked it for such eatables as it contained—some "ditto," bread, butter, milk and a doubtful pie. Mary Vance attacked the food ravenously and uncritically, while the manse children stood around and watched her. Jerry noticed that she had a pretty mouth and very nice, even, white teeth. Faith decided, with secret horror, that Mary had not one stitch on her except that ragged, faded dress. Una was full of pure pity, Carl of amused wonder, and all of them of curiosity.

"Now come out to the graveyard and tell us about yourself," ordered Faith, when Mary's appetite showed signs of failing her. Mary was now nothing loath. Food had restored her natural vivacity and unloosed her by no means reluctant tongue.

"You won't tell your pa or anybody if I tell you?" she stipulated, when she was enthroned on Mr. Pollock's tombstone. Opposite her the manse children lined up on another. Here was spice and mystery and adventure. Something HAD happened.

"No, we won't."

"Cross your hearts?"

"Cross our hearts."

"Well, I've run away. I was living with Mrs. Wiley over-harbour. Do you know Mrs. Wiley?"

"No."

"Well, you don't want to know her. She's an awful woman. My, how I hate her! She worked me to death and wouldn't give me half enough to eat, and she used to larrup me 'most every day. Look a-here."

Mary rolled up her ragged sleeves, and held up her scrawny arms and thin hands, chapped almost to rawness. They were black with bruises. The manse children shivered. Faith flushed crimson with indignation. Una's blue eyes filled with tears.

"She licked me Wednesday night with a stick," said Mary, indifferently. "It was 'cause I let the cow kick over a pail of milk. How'd I know the darn old cow was going to kick?"

A not unpleasant thrill ran over her listeners. They would never dream of using such dubious words, but it was rather titivating to hear someone else use them—and a girl, at that. Certainly this Mary Vance was an interesting creature.

"I don't blame you for running away," said Faith.

"Oh, I didn't run away 'cause she licked me. A licking was all in the day's work with me. I was darn well used to it. Nope, I'd meant to run away for a week 'cause I'd found out that Mrs. Wiley was going to rent her farm and go to Lowbridge to live and give me to a cousin of hers up Charlottetown way. I wasn't going to stand for THAT. She was a worse sort than Mrs. Wiley even. Mrs. Wiley lent me to her for a month last summer and I'd rather live with the devil himself."

Sensation number two. But Una looked doubtful.

"So I made up my mind I'd beat it. I had seventy cents saved up that Mrs. John Crawford give me in the spring for planting potatoes for her. Mrs. Wiley didn't know about it. She was away visiting her cousin when I planted them. I thought I'd sneak up here to the Glen and buy a ticket to Charlottetown and try to get work there. I'm a hustler, let me tell you. There ain't a lazy bone in MY body. So I lit out Thursday morning 'fore Mrs. Wiley was up and walked to the Glen—six miles. And when I got to the station I found I'd lost my money. Dunno how—dunno where. Anyhow, it was gone. I didn't know what to do. If I went back to old Lady Wiley she'd take the hide off me. So I went and hid in that old barn."

"And what will you do now?" asked Jerry.

"Dunno. I s'pose I'll have to go back and take my medicine. Now that I've got some grub in my stomach I guess I can stand it."

But there was fear behind the bravado in Mary's eyes. Una suddenly slipped from the one tombstone to the other and put her arm about Mary.

"Don't go back. Just stay here with us."

"Oh, Mrs. Wiley'll hunt me up," said Mary. "It's likely she's on my trail before this. I might stay here till she finds me, I s'pose, if your folks don't mind. I was a darn fool ever to think of skipping out. She'd run a weasel to earth. But I was so misrebul."

Mary's voice quivered, but she was ashamed of showing her weakness.

"I hain't had the life of a dog for these four years," she explained defiantly.

"You've been four years with Mrs. Wiley?"

"Yip. She took me out of the asylum over in Hopetown when I was eight."

"That's the same place Mrs. Blythe came from," exclaimed Faith.

"I was two years in the asylum. I was put there when I was six. My ma had hung herself and my pa had cut his throat."

"Holy cats! Why?" said Jerry.

"Booze," said Mary laconically.

"And you've no relations?"

"Not a darn one that I know of. Must have had some once, though. I was called after half a dozen of them. My full name is Mary Martha Lucilla Moore Ball Vance. Can you beat that? My grandfather was a rich man. I'll bet he was richer than YOUR grandfather. But pa drunk it all up and ma, she did her part. THEY used to beat me, too. Laws, I've been licked so much I kind of like it."

Mary tossed her head. She divined that the manse children were pitying her for her many stripes and she did not want pity. She wanted to be envied. She looked gaily about her. Her strange eyes, now that the dullness of famine was removed from them, were brilliant. She would show these youngsters what a personage she was.

"I've been sick an awful lot," she said proudly. "There's not many kids could have come through what I have. I've had scarlet fever and measles and ersipelas and mumps and whooping cough and pewmonia."

"Were you ever fatally sick?" asked Una.

"I don't know," said Mary doubtfully.

"Of course she wasn't," scoffed Jerry. "If you're fatally sick you die."

"Oh, well, I never died exactly," said Mary, "but I come blamed near it once. They thought I was dead and they were getting ready to lay me out when I up and come to."

"What is it like to be half dead?" asked Jerry curiously.

"Like nothing. I didn't know it for days afterwards. It was when I had the pewmonia. Mrs. Wiley wouldn't have the doctor—said she wasn't going to no such expense for a home girl. Old Aunt Christina MacAllister nursed me with poultices. She brung me round. But sometimes I wish I'd just died the other half and done with it. I'd been better off."

"If you went to heaven I s'pose you would," said Faith, rather doubtfully.

"Well, what other place is there to go to?" demanded Mary in a puzzled voice.

"There's hell, you know," said Una, dropping her voice and hugging Mary to lessen the awfulness of the suggestion.

"Hell? What's that?"

"Why, it's where the devil lives," said Jerry. "You've heard of him—you spoke about him."

"Oh, yes, but I didn't know he lived anywhere. I thought he just roamed round. Mr. Wiley used to mention hell when he was alive. He was always telling folks to go there. I thought it was some place over in New Brunswick where he come from."

"Hell is an awful place," said Faith, with the dramatic enjoyment that is born of telling dreadful things. "Bad people go there when they die and burn in fire for ever and ever and ever."

"Who told you that?" demanded Mary incredulously.

"It's in the Bible. And Mr. Isaac Crothers at Maywater told us, too, in Sunday School. He was an elder and a pillar in the church and knew all about it. But you needn't worry. If you're good you'll go to heaven and if you're bad I guess you'd rather go to hell."

"I wouldn't," said Mary positively. "No matter how bad I was I wouldn't want to be burned and burned. *I* know what it's like. I picked up a red hot poker once by accident. What must you do to be good?"

"You must go to church and Sunday School and read your Bible and pray every night and give to missions," said Una.

"It sounds like a large order," said Mary. "Anything else?"

"You must ask God to forgive the sins you've committed.

"But I've never com—committed any," said Mary. "What's a sin any way?"

"Oh, Mary, you must have. Everybody does. Did you never tell a lie?"

"Heaps of 'em," said Mary.

"That's a dreadful sin," said Una solemnly.

"Do you mean to tell me," demanded Mary, "that I'd be sent to hell for telling a lie now and then? Why, I HAD to. Mr. Wiley would have broken every bone in my body one time if I hadn't told him a lie. Lies have saved me many a whack, I can tell you."

Una sighed. Here were too many difficulties for her to solve. She shuddered as she thought of being cruelly whipped. Very likely she would have lied too. She squeezed Mary's little calloused hand.

"Is that the only dress you've got?" asked Faith, whose joyous nature refused to dwell on disagreeable subjects.

"I just put on this dress because it was no good," cried Mary flushing. "Mrs. Wiley'd bought my clothes and I wasn't going to be beholden to her for anything. And I'm honest. If I was going to run away I wasn't going to take what belong to HER that was worth anything. When I grow up I'm going to have a blue sating dress. Your own clothes don't look so stylish. I thought ministers' children were always dressed up."

It was plain that Mary had a temper and was sensitive on some points. But there was a queer, wild charm about her which captivated them all. She was taken to Rainbow Valley that afternoon and introduced to the Blythes as "a friend of ours from over-harbour who is visiting us." The Blythes accepted her unquestioningly, perhaps because she was fairly respectable now. After dinner—through which Aunt Martha had mumbled and Mr. Meredith had been in a state of semi-unconsciousness while brooding his Sunday sermon—Faith had prevailed on Mary to put on one of her dresses, as well as certain other articles of clothing. With her hair neatly braided Mary passed muster tolerably well. She was an acceptable playmate, for she knew several new and exciting games, and her conversation lacked not spice. In fact, some of her expressions made Nan and Di look at her rather askance. They were not quite sure what their mother would have thought of her, but they knew quite well what Susan would. However, she was a visitor at the manse, so she must be all right.

When bedtime came there was the problem of where Mary should sleep.

"We can't put her in the spare room, you know," said Faith perplexedly to Una.

"I haven't got anything in my head," cried Mary in an injured tone.

"Oh, I didn't mean THAT," protested Faith. "The spare room is all torn up. The mice have gnawed a big hole in the feather tick and made a nest in it. We never found it out till Aunt Martha put the Rev. Mr. Fisher from Charlottetown there to sleep last week. HE soon found it out. Then father had to give him his bed and sleep on the study lounge. Aunt Martha hasn't had time to fix the spare room bed up yet, so she says; so NOBODY can sleep there, no matter how clean their heads are. And our room is so small, and the bed so small you can't sleep with us."

"I can go back to the hay in the old barn for the night if you'll lend me a quilt," said Mary philosophically. "It was kind of chilly last night, but 'cept for that I've had worse beds."

"Oh, no, no, you mustn't do that," said Una. "I've thought of a plan, Faith. You know that little trestle bed in the garret room, with the old mattress on it, that the last minister left there? Let's take up the spare room bedclothes and make Mary a bed there. You won't mind sleeping in the garret, will you, Mary? It's just above our room."

"Any place'll do me. Laws, I never had a decent place to sleep in my life. I slept in the loft over the kitchen at Mrs. Wiley's. The roof leaked rain in the summer and the snow druv in in winter. My bed was a straw tick on the floor. You won't find me a mite huffy about where *I* sleep."

The manse garret was a long, low, shadowy place, with one gable end partitioned off. Here a bed was made up for Mary of the dainty hemstitched sheets and embroidered spread which Cecilia Meredith had once so proudly made for her spare-room, and which still survived Aunt Martha's uncertain washings. The good nights were said and silence fell over the manse. Una was just falling asleep when she heard a sound in the room just above that made her sit up suddenly.

"Listen, Faith—Mary's crying," she whispered. Faith replied not, being already asleep. Una slipped out of bed, and made her way in her little white gown down the hall and up the garret stairs. The creaking floor gave ample notice of her coming, and when she reached the corner room all was moonlit silence and the trestle bed showed only a hump in the middle.

"Mary," whispered Una.

There was no response.

Una crept close to the bed and pulled at the spread. "Mary, I know you are crying. I heard you. Are you lonesome?"

Mary suddenly appeared to view but said nothing.

"Let me in beside you. I'm cold," said Una shivering in the chilly air, for the little garret window was open and the keen breath of the north shore at night blew in.

Mary moved over and Una snuggled down beside her.

"NOW you won't be lonesome. We shouldn't have left you here alone the first night."

"I wasn't lonesome," sniffed Mary.

"What were you crying for then?"

"Oh, I just got to thinking of things when I was here alone. I thought of having to go back to Mrs. Wiley—and of being licked for running away—and—and—and of going to hell for telling lies. It all worried me something scandalous."

"Oh, Mary," said poor Una in distress. "I don't believe God will send you to hell for telling lies when you didn't know it was wrong. He COULDN'T. Why, He's kind and good. Of course, you mustn't tell any more now that you know it's wrong."

"If I can't tell lies what's to become of me?" said Mary with a sob. "YOU don't understand. You don't know anything about it. You've got a home and a kind father—though it does seem to me that he isn't more'n about half there. But anyway he doesn't lick you, and you get enough to eat such as it is—though that old aunt of yours doesn't know ANYTHING about cooking. Why, this is the first day I ever remember of feeling 'sif I'd enough to eat. I've been knocked about all of my life, 'cept for the two years I was at the asylum. They didn't lick me there and it wasn't too bad, though the matron was cross. She always looked ready to bite my head off a nail. But Mrs. Wiley is a holy terror, that's what SHE is, and I'm just scared stiff when I think of going back to her."

"Perhaps you won't have to. Perhaps we'll be able to think of a way out. Let's both ask God to keep you from having to go back to Mrs. Wiley. You say your prayers, don't you Mary?"

"Oh, yes, I always go over an old rhyme 'fore I get into bed," said Mary indifferently. "I never thought of asking for anything in particular though. Nobody in this world ever bothered themselves about me so I didn't s'pose God would. He MIGHT take more trouble for you, seeing you're a minister's daughter."

"He'd take every bit as much trouble for you, Mary, I'm sure," said Una. "It doesn't matter whose child you are. You just ask Him—and I will, too."

"All right," agreed Mary. "It won't do any harm if it doesn't do much good. If you knew Mrs. Wiley as well as I do you wouldn't think God would want to meddle with her. Anyhow, I won't cry any more about it. This is a big sight better'n last night down in that old barn, with the mice running about. Look at the Four Winds light. Ain't it pretty?"

"This is the only window we can see it from," said Una. "I love to watch it."

"Do you? So do I. I could see it from the Wiley loft and it was the only comfort I had. When I was all sore from being licked I'd watch it and forget about the places that hurt. I'd think of the ships sailing away and away from it and wish I was on one of them sailing far away too—away from everything. On winter nights when it didn't shine, I just felt real lonesome. Say, Una, what makes all you folks so kind to me when I'm just a stranger?"

"Because it's right to be. The bible tells us to be kind to everybody."

"Does it? Well, I guess most folks don't mind it much then. I never remember of any one being kind to me before—true's you live I don't. Say, Una, ain't them shadows on the walls pretty? They look just like a flock of little dancing birds. And say, Una, I like all you folks and them Blythe boys and Di, but I don't like that Nan. She's a proud one."

"Oh, no, Mary, she isn't a bit proud," said Una eagerly. "Not a single bit."

"Don't tell me. Any one that holds her head like that IS proud. I don't like her."

"WE all like her very much."

"Oh, I s'pose you like her better'n me?" said Mary jealously. "Do you?"

"Why, Mary—we've known her for weeks and we've only known you a few hours," stammered Una.

"So you do like her better then?" said Mary in a rage. "All right! Like her all you want to. *I* don't care. *I* can get along without you."

She flung herself over against the wall of the garret with a slam.

"Oh, Mary," said Una, pushing a tender arm over Mary's uncompromising back, "don't talk like that. I DO like you ever so much. And you make me feel so bad."

No answer. Presently Una gave a sob. Instantly Mary squirmed around again and engulfed Una in a bear's hug.

"Hush up," she ordered. "Don't go crying over what I said. I was as mean as the devil to talk that way. I orter to be skinned alive—and you all so good to me. I should think you WOULD like any one better'n me. I deserve every licking I ever got. Hush, now. If you cry any more I'll go and walk right down to the harbour in this night-dress and drown myself."

This terrible threat made Una choke back her sobs. Her tears were wiped away by Mary with the lace frill of the spare-room pillow and forgiver and forgiven cuddled down together again, harmony restored, to watch the shadows of the vine leaves on the moonlit wall until they fell asleep.

And in the study below Rev. John Meredith walked the floor with rapt face and shining eyes, thinking out his message of the morrow, and knew not that under his own roof there was a little forlorn soul, stumbling in darkness and ignorance, beset by terror and compassed about with difficulties too great for it to grapple in its unequal struggle with a big indifferent world.

6. MARY STAYS AT THE MANSE

The manse children took Mary Vance to church with them the next day. At first Mary objected to the idea.

"Didn't you go to church over-harbour?" asked Una.

"You bet. Mrs. Wiley never troubled church much, but I went every Sunday I could get off. I was mighty thankful to go to some place where I could sit down for a spell. But I can't go to church in this old ragged dress."

This difficulty was removed by Faith offering the loan of her second best dress.

"It's faded a little and two of the buttons are off, but I guess it'll do."

"I'll sew the buttons on in a jiffy," said Mary.

"Not on Sunday," said Una, shocked.

"Sure. The better the day the better the deed. You just gimme a needle and thread and look the other way if you're squeamish."

Faith's school boots, and an old black velvet cap that had once been Cecilia Meredith's, completed Mary's costume, and to church she went. Her behaviour was quite conventional, and though some wondered who the shabby little girl with the manse children was she did not attract much attention. She listened to the sermon with outward decorum and joined lustily in the singing. She had, it appeared, a clear, strong voice and a good ear.

"His blood can make the VIOLETS clean," carolled Mary blithely. Mrs. Jimmy Milgrave, whose pew was just in front of the manse pew, turned suddenly and looked the child over from top to toe. Mary, in a mere superfluity of naughtiness, stuck out her tongue at Mrs. Milgrave, much to Una's horror.

"I couldn't help it," she declared after church. "What'd she want to stare at me like that for? Such manners! I'm GLAD stuck my tongue out at her. I wish I'd stuck it farther out. Say, I saw Rob MacAllister from over-harbour there. Wonder if he'll tell Mrs. Wiley on me."

No Mrs. Wiley appeared, however, and in a few day the children forgot to look for her. Mary was apparently a fixture at the manse. But she refused to go to school with the others.

"Nope. I've finished my education," she said, when Faith urged her to go. "I went to school four winters since I come to Mrs. Wiley's and I've had all I want of THAT. I'm sick and tired of being everlastingly jawed at 'cause I didn't get my home-lessons done. I'D no time to do home-lessons."

"Our teacher won't jaw you. He is awfully nice," said Faith.

"Well, I ain't going. I can read and write and cipher up to fractions. That's all I want. You fellows go and I'll stay home. You needn't be scared I'll steal anything. I swear I'm honest."

Mary employed herself while the others were at school in cleaning up the manse. In a few days it was a different place. Floors were swept, furniture dusted, everything straightened out. She mended the spare-room bed-tick, she sewed on missing buttons, she patched clothes neatly, she even invaded the study with broom and dustpan and ordered Mr. Meredith out while she put it to rights. But there was one department with which Aunt Martha refused to let her interfere. Aunt Martha might be deaf and half blind and very childish, but she was resolved to keep the commissariat in her own hands, in spite of all Mary's wiles and stratagems.

"I can tell you if old Martha'd let ME cook you'd have some decent meals," she told the manse children indignantly. "There'd be no more 'ditto'—and no more lumpy porridge and blue milk either. What DOES she do with all the cream?"

"She gives it to the cat. He's hers, you know," said Faith.

"I'd like to CAT her," exclaimed Mary bitterly. "I've no use for cats anyhow. They belong to the old Nick. You can tell that by their eyes. Well, if old Martha won't, she won't, I s'pose. But it gits on my nerves to see good vittles spoiled."

When school came out they always went to Rainbow Valley. Mary refused to play in the graveyard. She declared she was afraid of ghosts.

"There's no such thing as ghosts," declared Jem Blythe.

"Oh, ain't there?"

"Did you ever see any?"

"Hundreds of 'em," said Mary promptly.

"What are they like?" said Carl.

"Awful-looking. Dressed all in white with skellington hands and heads," said Mary.

"What did you do?" asked Una.

"Run like the devil," said Mary. Then she caught Walter's eyes and blushed. Mary was a good deal in awe of Walter. She declared to the manse girls that his eyes made her nervous.

"I think of all the lies I've ever told when I look into them," she said, "and I wish I hadn't."

Jem was Mary's favourite. When he took her to the attic at Ingleside and showed her the museum of curios that Captain Jim Boyd had bequeathed to him she was immensely pleased and flattered. She also won Carl's heart entirely by her interest in his beetles and ants. It could not be denied that Mary got on rather better with the boys than with the girls. She quarrelled bitterly with Nan Blythe the second day.

"Your mother is a witch," she told Nan scornfully. "Red-haired women are always witches." Then she and Faith fell out about the rooster. Mary said its tail was too short. Faith angrily retorted that she guessed God know what length to make a rooster's tail. They did not "speak" for a day over this. Mary treated Una's hairless, one-eyed doll with consideration; but when Una showed her other prized treasure—a picture of an angel carrying a baby, presumably to heaven, Mary declared that it looked too much like a ghost for her. Una crept away to her room and cried over this, but Mary hunted her out, hugged her repentantly and implored forgiveness. No one could keep up a quarrel long with Mary—not even Nan, who was rather prone to hold grudges and never quite forgave the insult to her mother. Mary was jolly. She could and did tell the most thrilling ghost stories. Rainbow Valley seances were undeniably more exciting after Mary came. She learned to play on the jew's-harp and soon eclipsed Jerry.

"Never struck anything yet I couldn't do if I put my mind to it," she declared. Mary seldom lost a chance of tooting her own horn. She taught them how to make "blow-bags" out of the thick leaves of the "live-forever" that flourished in the old Bailey garden, she initiated them into the toothsome qualities of the "sours" that grew in the niches of the graveyard dyke, and she could make the most wonderful shadow pictures on the walls with her long, flexible fingers. And when they all went picking gum in Rainbow Valley Mary always got "the biggest chew" and bragged about it. There were times when they hated her and times when they loved her. But at all times they found her interesting. So they submitted quite meekly to her bossing, and by the end of a fortnight had come to feel that she must always have been with them.

"It's the queerest thing that Mrs. Wiley hain't been after me," said Mary. "I can't understand it."

"Maybe she isn't going to bother about you at all," said Una. "Then you can just go on staying here."

"This house ain't hardly big enough for me and old Martha," said Mary darkly. "It's a very fine thing to have enough to eat—I've often wondered what it would be like—but I'm p'ticler about my cooking. And Mrs. Wiley'll be here yet. SHE'S got a rod in pickle for me all right. I don't think about it so much in daytime but say, girls, up there in that garret at night I git to thinking and thinking of it, till I just almost wish she'd come and have it over with. I dunno's one real good whipping would be much worse'n all the dozen I've lived through in my mind ever since I run away. Were any of you ever licked?"

"No, of course not," said Faith indignantly. "Father would never do such a thing."

"You don't know you're alive," said Mary with a sigh half of envy, half of superiority. "You don't know what I've come through. And I s'pose the Blythes were never licked either?"

"No-o-o, I guess not. But I THINK they were sometimes spanked when they were small."

"A spanking doesn't amount to anything," said Mary contemptuously. "If my folks had just spanked me I'd have thought they were petting me. Well, it ain't a fair world. I wouldn't mind taking my share of wallopings but I've had a darn sight too many."

"It isn't right to say that word, Mary," said Una reproachfully. "You promised me you wouldn't say it."

"G'way," responded Mary. "If you knew some of the words I COULD say if I liked you wouldn't make such a fuss over darn. And you know very well I hain't ever told any lies since I come here."

"What about all those ghosts you said you saw?" asked Faith.

Mary blushed.

"That was diff'runt," she said defiantly. "I knew you wouldn't believe them yarns and I didn't intend you to. And I really did see something queer one night when I was passing the over-harbour graveyard, true's you live. I dunno whether 'twas a ghost or Sandy Crawford's old white nag, but it looked blamed queer and I tell you I scooted at the rate of no man's business."

7. A FISHY EPISODE

Rilla Blythe walked proudly, and perhaps a little primly, through the main "street" of the Glen and up the manse hill, carefully carrying a small basketful of early strawberries, which Susan had coaxed into lusciousness in one of the sunny nooks of Ingleside. Susan had charged Rilla to give the basket to nobody except Aunt Martha or Mr. Meredith, and Rilla, very proud of being entrusted with such an errand, was resolved to carry out her instructions to the letter.

Susan had dressed her daintily in a white, starched, and embroidered dress, with sash of blue and beaded slippers. Her long ruddy curls were sleek and round, and Susan had let her put on her best hat, out of compliment to the manse. It was a somewhat elaborate affair, wherein Susan's taste had had more to say than Anne's, and Rilla's small soul gloried in its splendours of silk and lace and flowers. She was very conscious of her hat, and I am afraid she strutted up the manse hill. The strut, or the hat, or both, got on the nerves of Mary Vance, who was swinging on the lawn gate. Mary's temper was somewhat ruffled just then, into the bargain. Aunt Martha had refused to let her peel the potatoes and had ordered her out of the kitchen.

"Yah! You'll bring the potatoes to the table with strips of skin hanging to them and half boiled as usual! My, but it'll be nice to go to your funeral," shrieked Mary. She went out of the kitchen, giving the door such a bang that even Aunt Martha heard it, and Mr. Meredith in his study felt the vibration and thought absently that there must have been a slight earthquake shock. Then he went on with his sermon.

Mary slipped from the gate and confronted the spick-and-span damsel of Ingleside.

"What you got there?" she demanded, trying to take the basket.

Rilla resisted. "It'th for Mithter Meredith," she lisped.

"Give it to me. I'LL give it to him," said Mary.

"No. Thuthan thaid that I wathn't to give it to anybody but Mithter Mer'dith or Aunt Martha," insisted Rilla.

Mary eyed her sourly.

"You think you're something, don't you, all dressed up like a doll! Look at me. My dress is all rags and *I* don't care! I'd rather be ragged than a doll baby. Go home and tell them to put you in a glass case. Look at me—look at me—look at me!"

Mary executed a wild dance around the dismayed and bewildered Rilla, flirting her ragged skirt and vociferating "Look at me—look at me" until poor Rilla was dizzy. But as the latter tried to edge away towards the gate Mary pounced on her again.

"You give me that basket," she ordered with a grimace. Mary was past mistress in the art of "making faces." She could give her countenance a most grotesque and unearthly appearance out of which her strange, brilliant, white eyes gleamed with weird effect.

"I won't," gasped Rilla, frightened but staunch. "You let me go, Mary Vanth."

Mary let go for a minute and looked around here. Just inside the gate was a small "flake," on which a half a dozen large codfish were drying. One of Mr. Meredith's parishioners had presented him with them one day, perhaps in lieu of the subscription he was supposed to pay to the stipend and never did. Mr. Meredith had thanked him and then forgotten all about the fish, which would have promptly spoiled had not the indefatigable Mary prepared them for drying and rigged up the "flake" herself on which to dry them.

Mary had a diabolical inspiration. She flew to the "flake" and seized the largest fish there—a huge, flat thing, nearly as big as herself. With a whoop she swooped down on the terrified Rilla, brandishing her weird missile. Rilla's courage gave way. To be lambasted with a dried codfish was such an unheard-of thing that Rilla could not face it. With a shriek she dropped her basket and fled. The beautiful berries, which Susan had so tenderly selected for the minister, rolled in a rosy torrent over the dusty road and were trodden on by the flying feet of pursuer and pursued. The basket and contents were no longer in Mary's mind. She thought only of the delight of giving Rilla Blythe the scare of her life. She would teach HER to come giving herself airs because of her fine clothes.

Rilla flew down the hill and along the street. Terror lent wings to her feet, and she just managed to keep ahead of Mary, who was somewhat hampered by her own laughter, but who had breath enough to give occasional blood-curdling whoops as she ran, flourishing her codfish in the air. Through the Glen street they swept, while everybody ran to the windows and gates to see them. Mary felt she was making a tremendous sensation and enjoyed it. Rilla, blind with terror and spent of breath, felt that she could run no longer. In another instant that terrible girl would be on her with the codfish. At this point the poor mite stumbled and fell into the mud-puddle at the end of the street just as Miss Cornelia came out of Carter Flagg's store.

Miss Cornelia took the whole situation in at a glance. So did Mary. The latter stopped short in her mad career and before Miss Cornelia could speak she had whirled around and was running up as fast as she had run down. Miss Cornelia's lips tightened ominously, but she knew it was no use to think of chasing her. So she picked up poor, sobbing, dishevelled Rilla instead and took her home. Rilla was heart-broken. Her dress and slippers and hat were ruined and her six year old pride had received terrible bruises.

Susan, white with indignation, heard Miss Cornelia's story of Mary Vance's exploit.

"Oh, the hussy—oh, the littly hussy!" she said, as she carried Rilla away for purification and comfort.

"This thing has gone far enough, Anne dearie," said Miss Cornelia resolutely. "Something must be done. WHO is this creature who is staying at the manse and where does she come from?"

"I understood she was a little girl from over-harbour who was visiting at the manse," answered Anne, who saw the comical side of the codfish chase and secretly thought Rilla was rather vain and needed a lesson or two.

"I know all the over-harbour families who come to our church and that imp doesn't belong to any of them," retorted Miss Cornelia. "She is almost in rags and when she goes to church she wears Faith Meredith's old clothes. There's some mystery here, and I'm going to investigate it, since it seems nobody else will. I believe she was at the bottom of their goings-on in Warren Mead's spruce bush the other day. Did you hear of their frightening his mother into a fit?"

"No. I knew Gilbert had been called to see her, but I did not hear what the trouble was."

"Well, you know she has a weak heart. And one day last week, when she was all alone on the veranda, she heard the most awful shrieks of 'murder' and 'help' coming from the bush—positively frightful sounds, Anne dearie. Her heart gave out at once. Warren heard them himself at the barn, and went straight to the bush to investigate, and there he found all the manse children sitting on a fallen tree and screaming 'murder' at the top of their lungs. They told him they were only in fun and didn't think anyone would hear them. They were just playing Indian ambush. Warren went back to the house and found his poor mother unconscious on the veranda."

Susan, who had returned, sniffed contemptuously.

"I think she was very far from being unconscious, Mrs. Marshall Elliott, and that you may tie to. I have been hearing of Amelia Warren's weak heart for forty years. She had it when she was twenty. She enjoys making a fuss and having the doctor, and any excuse will do."

"I don't think Gilbert thought her attack very serious," said Anne.

"Oh, that may very well be," said Miss Cornelia. "But the matter has made an awful lot of talk and the Meads being Methodists makes it that much worse. What is going to become of those children? Sometimes I can't sleep at nights for thinking about them, Anne dearie. I really do question if they get enough to eat, even, for their father is so lost in dreams that he doesn't often remember he has a stomach, and that lazy old woman doesn't bother cooking what she ought. They are just running wild and now that school is closing they'll be worse than ever."

"They do have jolly times," said Anne, laughing over the recollections of some Rainbow Valley happenings that had come to her ears. "And they are all brave and frank and loyal and truthful."

"That's a true word, Anne dearie, and when you come to think of all the trouble in the church those two tattling, deceitful youngsters of the last minister's made, I'm inclined to overlook a good deal in the Merediths."

"When all is said and done, Mrs. Dr. dear, they are very nice children," said Susan. "They have got plenty of original sin in them and that I will admit, but maybe it is just as well, for if they had not they might spoil from over-sweetness. Only I do think it is not proper for them to play in a graveyard and that I will maintain."

"But they really play quite quietly there," excused Anne. "They don't run and yell as they do elsewhere. Such howls as drift up here from Rainbow Valley sometimes! Though I fancy my own small fry bear a valiant part in them. They had a sham battle there last night and had to 'roar' themselves, because they had no artillery to do it, so Jem says. Jem is passing through the stage where all boys hanker to be soldiers."

"Well, thank goodness, he'll never be a soldier," said Miss Cornelia. "I never approved of our boys going to that South African fracas. But it's over, and not likely anything of the kind will ever happen again. I think the world is getting more sensible. As for the Merediths, I've said many a time and I say it again, if Mr. Meredith had a wife all would be well."

"He called twice at the Kirks' last week, so I am told," said Susan.

"Well," said Miss Cornelia thoughtfully, "as a rule, I don't approve of a minister marrying in his congregation. It generally spoils him. But in this case it would do no harm, for every one likes Elizabeth Kirk and nobody else is hankering for the job of stepmothering those youngsters. Even the Hill girls balk at that. They haven't been found laying traps for Mr. Meredith. Elizabeth would make him a good wife if he only thought so. But the trouble is, she really is homely and, Anne dearie, Mr. Meredith, abstracted as he is, has an eye for a good-looking woman, man-like. He isn't SO other-worldly when it comes to that, believe ME."

"Elizabeth Kirk is a very nice person, but they do say that people have nearly frozen to death in her mother's spare-room bed before now, Mrs. Dr. dear," said Susan darkly. "If I felt I had any right to express an opinion concerning such a solemn matter as a minister's marriage I would say that I think Elizabeth's cousin Sarah, over-harbour, would make Mr. Meredith a better wife."

"Why, Sarah Kirk is a Methodist," said Miss Cornelia, much as if Susan had suggested a Hottentot as a manse bride.

"She would likely turn Presbyterian if she married Mr. Meredith," retorted Susan.

Miss Cornelia shook her head. Evidently with her it was, once a Methodist, always a Methodist.

"Sarah Kirk is entirely out of the question," she said positively. "And so is Emmeline Drew —though the Drews are all trying to make the match. They are literally throwing poor Emmeline at his head, and he hasn't the least idea of it."

"Emmeline Drew has no gumption, I must allow," said Susan. "She is the kind of woman, Mrs. Dr. dear, who would put a hot-water bottle in your bed on a dog-night and then have her feelings hurt because you were not grateful. And her mother was a very poor housekeeper. Did you ever hear the story of her dishcloth? She lost her dishcloth one day. But the next day she found it. Oh, yes, Mrs. Dr. dear, she found it, in the goose at the dinner-table, mixed up with the stuffing. Do you think a woman like that would do for a minister's mother-in-law? I do not. But no doubt I would be better employed in mending little Jem's trousers than in talking gossip about my neighbours. He tore them something scandalous last night in Rainbow Valley."

"Where is Walter?" asked Anne.

"He is up to no good, I fear, Mrs. Dr. dear. He is in the attic writing something in an exercise book. And he has not done as well in arithmetic this term as he should, so the teacher tells me. Too well I know the reason why. He has been writing silly rhymes when he should have been doing his sums. I am afraid that boy is going to be a poet, Mrs. Dr. dear."

"He is a poet now, Susan."

"Well, you take it real calm, Mrs. Dr. dear. I suppose it is the best way, when a person has the strength. I had an uncle who began by being a poet and ended up by being a tramp. Our family were dreadfully ashamed of him."

"You don't seem to think very highly of poets, Susan," said Anne, laughing.

"Who does, Mrs. Dr. dear?" asked Susan in genuine astonishment.

"What about Milton and Shakespeare? And the poets of the Bible?"

"They tell me Milton could not get along with his wife, and Shakespeare was no more than respectable by times. As for the Bible, of course things were different in those sacred days—although I never had a high opinion of King David, say what you will. I never knew any good to come of writing poetry, and I hope and pray that blessed boy will outgrow the tendency. If he does not—we must see what emulsion of cod-liver oil will do."

8. MISS CORNELIA INTERVENES

Miss Cornelia descended upon the manse the next day and cross-questioned Mary, who, being a young person of considerable discernment and astuteness, told her story simple and truthfully, with an entire absence of complaint or bravado. Miss Cornelia was more favourably impressed than she had expected to be, but deemed it her duty to be severe.

"Do you think," she said sternly, "that you showed your gratitude to this family, who have been far too kind to you, by insulting and chasing one of their little friends as you did yesterday?"

"Say, it was rotten mean of me," admitted Mary easily. "I dunno what possessed me. That old codfish seemed to come in so blamed handy. But I was awful sorry—I cried last night after I went to bed about it, honest I did. You ask Una if I didn't. I wouldn't tell her what for 'cause I was ashamed of it, and then she cried, too, because she was afraid someone had hurt my feelings. Laws, *I* ain't got any feelings to hurt worth speaking of. What worries me is why Mrs. Wiley hain't been hunting for me. It ain't like her."

Miss Cornelia herself thought it rather peculiar, but she merely admonished Mary sharply not to take any further liberties with the minister's codfish, and went to report progress at Ingleside.

"If the child's story is true the matter ought to be looked into," she said. "I know something about that Wiley woman, believe ME. Marshall used to be well acquainted with her when he lived over-harbour. I heard him say something last summer about her and a home child she had—likely this very Mary-creature. He said some one told him she was working the child to death and not half feeding and clothing it. You know, Anne dearie, it has always been my habit neither to make nor meddle with those over-harbour folks. But I shall send Marshall over to-morrow to find out the rights of this if he can. And THEN I'll speak to the minister. Mind you, Anne dearie, the Merediths found this girl literally starving in James Taylor's old hay barn. She had been there all night, cold and hungry and alone. And us sleeping warm in our beds after good suppers."

"The poor little thing," said Anne, picturing one of her own dear babies, cold and hungry and alone in such circumstances. "If she has been ill-used, Miss Cornelia, she mustn't be taken back to such a place. *I* was an orphan once in a very similar situation."

"We'll have to consult the Hopetown asylum folks," said Miss Cornelia. "Anyway, she can't be left at the manse. Dear knows what those poor children might learn from her. I understand that she has been known to swear. But just think of her being there two whole weeks and Mr Meredith never waking up to it! What business has a man like that to have a family? Why, Anne dearie, he ought to be a monk."

Two evenings later Miss Cornelia was back at Ingleside.

"It's the most amazing thing!" she said. "Mrs. Wiley was found dead in her bed the very morning after this Mary-creature ran away. She has had a bad heart for years and the doctor had warned her it might happen at any time. She had sent away her hired man and there was nobody in the house. Some neighbours found her the next day. They missed the child, it seems, but supposed Mrs. Wiley had sent her to her cousin near Charlottetown as she had said she was going to do. The cousin didn't come to the funeral and so nobody ever knew that Mary wasn't with her. The people Marshall talked to told him some things about the way Mrs. Wiley used this Mary that made his blood boil, so he declares. You know, it puts Marshall in a regular fury to hear of a child being ill-used. They said she whipped her mercilessly for every little fault or mistake. Some folks talked of writing to the asylum authorities but everybody's business is nobody's business and it was never done."

"I am sorry that Wiley person is dead," said Susan fiercely. "I should like to go over-harbour and give her a piece of my mind. Starving and beating a child, Mrs. Dr. dear! As you know, I hold with lawful spanking, but I go no further. And what is to become of this poor child now, Mrs. Marshall Elliott?"

"I suppose she must be sent back to Hopetown," said Miss Cornelia. "I think every one hereabouts who wants a home child has one. I'll see Mr. Meredith to-morrow and tell him my opinion of the whole affair."

"And no doubt she will, Mrs. Dr. dear," said Susan, after Miss Cornelia had gone. "She would stick at nothing, not even at shingling the church spire if she took it into her head. But I cannot understand how even Cornelia Bryant can talk to a minister as she does. You would think he was just any common person."

When Miss Cornelia had gone, Nan Blythe uncurled herself from the hammock where she had been studying her lessons and slipped away to Rainbow Valley. The others were already there. Jem and Jerry were playing quoits with old horseshoes borrowed from the Glen blacksmith. Carl was stalking ants on a sunny hillock. Walter, lying on his stomach among the fern, was reading aloud to Mary and Di and Faith and Una from a wonderful book of myths wherein were fascinating accounts of Prester John and the Wandering Jew, divining rods and tailed men, of Schamir, the worm that split rocks and opened the way to golden treasure, of Fortunate Isles and swan-maidens. It was a great shock to Walter to learn that William Tell and Gelert were myths also; and the story of Bishop Hatto was to keep him awake all that night; but best of all he loved the stories of the Pied Piper and the San Greal. He read them thrillingly, while the bells on the Tree Lovers tinkled in the summer wind and the coolness of the evening shadows crept across the valley.

"Say, ain't them in'resting lies?" said Mary admiringly when Walter had closed the book.

"They aren't lies," said Di indignantly.

"You don't mean they're true?" asked Mary incredulously.

"No—not exactly. They're like those ghost-stories of yours. They weren't true—but you didn't expect us to believe them, so they weren't lies."

"That yarn about the divining rod is no lie, anyhow," said Mary. "Old Jake Crawford over-harbour can work it. They send for him from everywhere when they want to dig a well. And I believe I know the Wandering Jew."

"Oh, Mary," said Una, awe-struck.

"I do—true's you're alive. There was an old man at Mrs. Wiley's one day last fall. He looked old enough to be ANYTHING. She was asking him about cedar posts, if he thought they'd last well. And he said, 'Last well? They'll last a thousand years. I know, for I've tried them twice.' Now, if he was two thousand years old who was he but your Wandering Jew?"

"I don't believe the Wandering Jew would associate with a person like Mrs. Wiley," said Faith decidedly.

"I love the Pied Piper story," said Di, "and so does mother. I always feel so sorry for the poor little lame boy who couldn't keep up with the others and got shut out of the mountain. He must have been so disappointed. I think all the rest of his life he'd be wondering what wonderful thing he had missed and wishing he could have got in with the others."

"But how glad his mother must have been," said Una softly. "I think she had been sorry all her life that he was lame. Perhaps she even used to cry about it. But she would never be sorry again—never. She would be glad he was lame because that was why she hadn't lost him."

"Some day," said Walter dreamily, looking afar into the sky, "the Pied Piper will come over the hill up there and down Rainbow Valley, piping merrily and sweetly. And I will follow him —follow him down to the shore—down to the sea—away from you all. I don't think I'll want to go—Jem will want to go—it will be such an adventure—but I won't. Only I'll HAVE to—the music will call and call and call me until I MUST follow."

"We'll all go," cried Di, catching fire at the flame of Walter's fancy, and half-believing she could see the mocking, retreating figure of the mystic piper in the far, dim end of the valley.

"No. You'll sit here and wait," said Walter, his great, splendid eyes full of strange glamour. "You'll wait for us to come back. And we may not come—for we cannot come as long as the Piper plays. He may pipe us round the world. And still you'll sit here and wait—and WAIT."

"Oh, dry up," said Mary, shivering. "Don't look like that, Walter Blythe. You give me the creeps. Do you want to set me bawling? I could just see that horrid old Piper going away on, and you boys following him, and us girls sitting here waiting all alone. I dunno why it is—I never was one of the blubbering kind—but as soon as you start your spieling I always want to cry."

Walter smiled in triumph. He liked to exercise this power of his over his companions—to play on their feelings, waken their fears, thrill their souls. It satisfied some dramatic instinct in him. But under his triumph was a queer little chill of some mysterious dread. The Pied Piper had seemed very real to him—as if the fluttering veil that hid the future had for a moment been blown aside in the starlit dusk of Rainbow Valley and some dim glimpse of coming years granted to him.

Carl, coming up to their group with a report of the doings in ant-land, brought them all back to the realm of facts.

"Ants ARE darned in'resting," exclaimed Mary, glad to escape the shadowy Piper's thrall. "Carl and me watched that bed in the graveyard all Saturday afternoon. I never thought there was so much in bugs. Say, but they're quarrelsome little cusses—some of 'em like to start a fight 'thout any reason, far's we could see. And some of 'em are cowards. They got so scared they just doubled theirselves up into a ball and let the other fellows bang 'em. They wouldn't put up a fight at all. Some of 'em are lazy and won't work. We watched 'em shirking. And there was one ant died of grief 'cause another ant got killed—wouldn't work—wouldn't eat—just died—it did, honest to Go—oodness."

A shocked silence prevailed. Every one knew that Mary had not started out to say "goodness." Faith and Di exchanged glances that would have done credit to Miss Cornelia herself. Walter and Carl looked uncomfortable and Una's lip trembled.

Mary squirmed uncomfortably.

"That slipped out 'fore I thought—it did, honest to—I mean, true's you live, and I swallowed half of it. You folks over here are mighty squeamish seems to me. Wish you could have heard the Wileys when they had a fight."

"Ladies don't say such things," said Faith, very primly for her.

"It isn't right," whispered Una.

"I ain't a lady," said Mary. "What chance've I ever had of being a lady? But I won't say that again if I can help it. I promise you."

"Besides," said Una, "you can't expect God to answer your prayers if you take His name in vain, Mary."

"I don't expect Him to answer 'em anyhow," said Mary of little faith. "I've been asking Him for a week to clear up this Wiley affair and He hasn't done a thing. I'm going to give up."

At this juncture Nan arrived breathless.

"Oh, Mary, I've news for you. Mrs. Elliott has been over-harbour and what do you think she found out? Mrs. Wiley is dead—she was found dead in bed the morning after you ran away. So you'll never have to go back to her."

"Dead!" said Mary stupefied. Then she shivered.

"Do you s'pose my praying had anything to do with that?" she cried imploringly to Una. "If it had I'll never pray again as long as I live. Why, she may come back and ha'nt me."

"No, no, Mary," said Una comfortingly, "it hadn't. Why, Mrs. Wiley died long before you ever began to pray about it at all."

"That's so," said Mary recovering from her panic. "But I tell you it gave me a start. I wouldn't like to think I'd prayed anybody to death. I never thought of such a thing as her dying when I was praying. She didn't seem much like the dying kind. Did Mrs. Elliott say anything about me?"

"She said you would likely have to go back to the asylum."

"I thought as much," said Mary drearily. "And then they'll give me out again—likely to some one just like Mrs. Wiley. Well, I s'pose I can stand it. I'm tough."

"I'm going to pray that you won't have to go back," whispered Una, as she and Mary walked home to the manse.

"You can do as you like," said Mary decidedly, "but I vow *I* won't. I'm good and scared of this praying business. See what's come of it. If Mrs. Wiley HAD died after I started praying it would have been my doings."

"Oh, no, it wouldn't," said Una. "I wish I could explain things better—father could, I know, if you'd talk to him, Mary."

"Catch me! I don't know what to make of your father, that's the long and short of it. He goes by me and never sees me in broad daylight. I ain't proud—but I ain't a door-mat, neither!"

"Oh, Mary, it's just father's way. Most of the time he never sees us, either. He is thinking deeply, that is all. And I AM going to pray that God will keep you in Four Winds—because I like you, Mary."

"All right. Only don't let me hear of any more people dying on account of it," said Mary. "I'd like to stay in Four Winds fine. I like it and I like the harbour and the light house—and you and the Blythes. You're the only friends I ever had and I'd hate to leave you."

9. UNA INTERVENES

Miss Cornelia had an interview with Mr. Meredith which proved something of a shock to that abstracted gentleman. She pointed out to him, none too respectfully, his dereliction of duty in allowing a waif like Mary Vance to come into his family and associate with his children without knowing or learning anything about her.

"I don't say there is much harm done, of course," she concluded. "This Mary-creature isn't what you might call bad, when all is said and done. I've been questioning your children and the Blythes, and from what I can make out there's nothing much to be said against the child except that she's slangy and doesn't use very refined language. But think what might have happened if she'd been like some of those home children we know of. You know yourself what that poor little creature the Jim Flaggs' had, taught and told the Flagg children."

Mr. Meredith did know and was honestly shocked over his own carelessness in the matter.

"But what is to be done, Mrs. Elliott?" he asked helplessly. "We can't turn the poor child out. She must be cared for."

"Of course. We'd better write to the Hopetown authorities at once. Meanwhile, I suppose she might as well stay here for a few more days till we hear from them. But keep your eyes and ears open, Mr. Meredith."

Susan would have died of horror on the spot if she had heard Miss Cornelia so admonishing a minister. But Miss Cornelia departed in a warm glow of satisfaction over duty done, and that night Mr. Meredith asked Mary to come into his study with him. Mary obeyed, looking literally ghastly with fright. But she got the surprise of her poor, battered little life. This man, of whom she had stood so terribly in awe, was the kindest, gentlest soul she had ever met. Before she knew what happened Mary found herself pouring all her troubles into his ear and receiving in return such sympathy and tender understanding as it had never occurred to her to imagine. Mary left the study with her face and eyes so softened that Una hardly knew her.

"Your father's all right, when he does wake up," she said with a sniff that just escaped being a sob. "It's a pity he doesn't wake up oftener. He said I wasn't to blame for Mrs. Wiley dying, but that I must try to think of her good points and not of her bad ones. I dunno what good points she had, unless it was keeping her house clean and making first-class butter. I know I 'most wore my arms out scrubbing her old kitchen floor with the knots in it. But anything your father says goes with me after this."

Mary proved a rather dull companion in the following days, however. She confided to Una that the more she thought of going back to the asylum the more she hated it. Una racked her small brains for some way of averting it, but it was Nan Blythe who came to the rescue with a somewhat startling suggestion.

"Mrs. Elliott might take Mary herself. She has a great big house and Mr. Elliott is always wanting her to have help. It would be just a splendid place for Mary. Only she'd have to behave herself."

"Oh, Nan, do you think Mrs. Elliott would take her?"

"It wouldn't do any harm if you asked her," said Nan. At first Una did not think she could. She was so shy that to ask a favour of anybody was agony to her. And she was very much in awe of the bustling, energetic Mrs. Elliott. She liked her very much and always enjoyed a visit to her house; but to go and ask her to adopt Mary Vance seemed such a height of presumption that Una's timid spirit quailed.

When the Hopetown authorities wrote to Mr. Meredith to send Mary to them without delay Mary cried herself to sleep in the manse attic that night and Una found a desperate courage. The next evening she slipped away from the manse to the harbour road. Far down in Rainbow

Valley she heard joyous laughter but her way lay not there. She was terribly pale and terribly in earnest—so much so that she took no notice of the people she met—and old Mrs. Stanley Flagg was quite huffed and said Una Meredith would be as absentminded as her father when she grew up.

Miss Cornelia lived half way between the Glen and Four Winds Point, in a house whose original glaring green hue had mellowed down to an agreeable greenish gray. Marshall Elliott had planted trees about it and set out a rose garden and a spruce hedge. It was quite a different place from what it had been in years agone. The manse children and the Ingleside children liked to go there. It was a beautiful walk down the old harbour road, and there was always a well-filled cooky jar at the end.

The misty sea was lapping softly far down on the sands. Three big boats were skimming down the harbour like great white sea-birds. A schooner was coming up the channel. The world of Four Winds was steeped in glowing colour, and subtle music, and strange glamour, and everybody should have been happy in it. But when Una turned in at Miss Cornelia's gate her very legs had almost refused to carry her.

Miss Cornelia was alone on the veranda. Una had hoped Mr. Elliott would be there. He was so big and hearty and twinkly that there would be encouragement in his presence. She sat on the little stool Miss Cornelia brought out and tried to eat the doughnut Miss Cornelia gave her. It stuck in her throat, but she swallowed desperately lest Miss Cornelia be offended. She could not talk; she was still pale; and her big, dark-blue eyes looked so piteous that Miss Cornelia concluded the child was in some trouble.

"What's on your mind, dearie?" she asked. "There's something, that's plain to be seen."

Una swallowed the last twist of doughnut with a desperate gulp.

"Mrs. Elliott, won't you take Mary Vance?" she said beseechingly.

Miss Cornelia stared blankly.

"Me! Take Mary Vance! Do you mean keep her?"

"Yes—keep her—adopt her," said Una eagerly, gaining courage now that the ice was broken. "Oh, Mrs. Elliott, PLEASE do. She doesn't want to go back to the asylum—she cries every night about it. She's so afraid of being sent to another hard place. And she's SO smart—there isn't anything she can't do. I know you wouldn't be sorry if you took her."

"I never thought of such a thing," said Miss Cornelia rather helplessly.

"WON'T you think of it?" implored Una.

"But, dearie, I don't want help. I'm quite able to do all the work here. And I never thought I'd like to have a home girl if I did need help."

The light went out of Una's eyes. Her lips trembled. She sat down on her stool again, a pathetic little figure of disappointment, and began to cry.

"Don't—dearie—don't," exclaimed Miss Cornelia in distress. She could never bear to hurt a child. "I don't say I WON'T take her—but the idea is so new it has just kerflummuxed me. I must think it over."

"Mary is SO smart," said Una again.

"Humph! So I've heard. I've heard she swears, too. Is that true?"

"I've never heard her swear EXACTLY," faltered Una uncomfortably. "But I'm afraid she COULD."

"I believe you! Does she always tell the truth?"

"I think she does, except when she's afraid of a whipping."

"And yet you want me to take her!"

"SOME ONE has to take her," sobbed Una. "SOME ONE has to look after her, Mrs. Elliott."

"That's true. Perhaps it IS my duty to do it," said Miss Cornelia with a sigh. "Well, I'll have to talk it over with Mr. Elliott. So don't say anything about it just yet. Take another doughnut, dearie."

Una took it and ate it with a better appetite.

"I'm very fond of doughnuts," she confessed "Aunt Martha never makes any. But Miss Susan at Ingleside does, and sometimes she lets us have a plateful in Rainbow Valley. Do you know what I do when I'm hungry for doughnuts and can't get any, Mrs. Elliott?"

"No, dearie. What?"

"I get out mother's old cook book and read the doughnut recipe—and the other recipes. They sound SO nice. I always do that when I'm hungry—especially after we've had ditto for dinner. THEN I read the fried chicken and the roast goose recipes. Mother could make all those nice things."

"Those manse children will starve to death yet if Mr. Meredith doesn't get married," Miss Cornelia told her husband indignantly after Una had gone. "And he won't—and what's to be done? And SHALL we take this Mary-creature, Marshall?"

"Yes, take her," said Marshall laconically.

"Just like a man," said his wife, despairingly. "'Take her'—as if that was all. There are a hundred things to be considered, believe ME."

"Take her—and we'll consider them afterwards, Cornelia," said her husband.

In the end Miss Cornelia did take her and went up to announce her decision to the Ingleside people first.

"Splendid!" said Anne delightedly. "I've been hoping you would do that very thing, Miss Cornelia. I want that poor child to get a good home. I was a homeless little orphan just like her once."

"I don't think this Mary-creature is or ever will be much like you," retorted Miss Cornelia gloomily. "She's a cat of another colour. But she's also a human being with an immortal soul to save. I've got a shorter catechism and a small tooth comb and I'm going to do my duty by her, now that I've set my hand to the plough, believe me."

Mary received the news with chastened satisfaction.

"It's better luck than I expected," she said.

"You'll have to mind your p's and q's with Mrs. Elliott," said Nan.

"Well, I can do that," flashed Mary. "I know how to behave when I want to just as well as you, Nan Blythe."

"You mustn't use bad words, you know, Mary," said Una anxiously.

"I s'pose she'd die of horror if I did," grinned Mary, her white eyes shining with unholy glee over the idea. "But you needn't worry, Una. Butter won't melt in my mouth after this. I'll be all prunes and prisms."

"Nor tell lies," added Faith.

"Not even to get off from a whipping?" pleaded Mary.

"Mrs. Elliott will NEVER whip you—NEVER," exclaimed Di.

"Won't she?" said Mary skeptically. "If I ever find myself in a place where I ain't licked I'll think it's heaven all right. No fear of me telling lies then. I ain't fond of telling 'em—I'd ruther not, if it comes to that."

The day before Mary's departure from the manse they had a picnic in her honour in Rainbow Valley, and that evening all the manse children gave her something from their scanty store of treasured things for a keepsake. Carl gave her his Noah's ark and Jerry his second best jew's-harp. Faith gave her a little hairbrush with a mirror in the back of it, which Mary had always considered very wonderful. Una hesitated between an old beaded purse and a gay picture of Daniel in the lion's den, and finally offered Mary her choice. Mary really hankered after the beaded purse, but she knew Una loved it, so she said,

"Give me Daniel. I'd rusher have it 'cause I'm partial to lions. Only I wish they'd et Daniel up. It would have been more exciting."

At bedtime Mary coaxed Una to sleep with her.

"It's for the last time," she said, "and it's raining tonight, and I hate sleeping up there alone when it's raining on account of that graveyard. I don't mind it on fine nights, but a night like this I can't see anything but the rain pouring down on them old white stones, and the wind round the window sounds as if them dead people were trying to get in and crying 'cause they couldn't."

"I like rainy nights," said Una, when they were cuddled down together in the little attic room, "and so do the Blythe girls."

"I don't mind 'em when I'm not handy to graveyards," said Mary. "If I was alone here I'd cry my eyes out I'd be so lonesome. I feel awful bad to be leaving you all."

"Mrs. Elliott will let you come up and play in Rainbow Valley quite often I'm sure," said Una. "And you WILL be a good girl, won't you, Mary?"

"Oh, I'll try," sighed Mary. "But it won't be as easy for me to be good—inside, I mean, as well as outside—as it is for you. You hadn't such scalawags of relations as I had."

"But your people must have had some good qualities as well as bad ones," argued Una. "You must live up to them and never mind their bad ones."

"I don't believe they had any good qualities," said Mary gloomily. "I never heard of any. My grandfather had money, but they say he was a rascal. No, I'll just have to start out on my own hook and do the best I can."

"And God will help you, you know, Mary, if you ask Him."

"I don't know about that."

"Oh, Mary. You know we asked God to get a home for you and He did."

"I don't see what He had to do with it," retorted Mary. "It was you put it into Mrs. Elliott's head."

"But God put it into her HEART to take you. All my putting it into her HEAD wouldn't have done any good if He hadn't."

"Well, there may be something in that," admitted Mary. "Mind you, I haven't got anything against God, Una. I'm willing to give Him a chance. But, honest, I think He's an awful lot like your father—just absent-minded and never taking any notice of a body most of the time, but sometimes waking up all of a suddent and being awful good and kind and sensible."

"Oh, Mary, no!" exclaimed horrified Una. "God isn't a bit like father—I mean He's a thousand times better and kinder."

"If He's as good as your father He'll do for me," said Mary. "When your father was talking to me I felt as if I never could be bad any more."

"I wish you'd talk to father about Him," sighed Una. "He can explain it all so much better than I can."

"Why, so I will, next time he wakes up," promised Mary. "That night he talked to me in the study he showed me real clear that my praying didn't kill Mrs. Wiley. My mind's been easy since, but I'm real cautious about praying. I guess the old rhyme is the safest. Say, Una, it seems to me if one has to pray to anybody it'd be better to pray to the devil than to God. God's good, anyhow so you say, so He won't do you any harm, but from all I can make out the devil needs to be pacified. I think the sensible way would be to say to HIM, 'Good devil, please don't tempt me. Just leave me alone, please.' Now, don't you?"

"Oh, no, no, Mary. I'm sure it couldn't be right to pray to the devil. And it wouldn't do any good because he's bad. It might aggravate him and he'd be worse than ever."

"Well, as to this God-matter," said Mary stubbornly, "since you and I can't settle it, there ain't no use in talking more about it until we've a chanct to find out the rights of it. I'll do the best I can alone till then."

"If mother was alive she could tell us everything," said Una with a sigh.

"I wisht she was alive," said Mary. "I don't know what's going to become of you youngsters when I'm gone. Anyhow, DO try and keep the house a little tidy. The way people talks about it is scandalous. And the first thing you know your father will be getting married again and then your noses will be out of joint."

Una was startled. The idea of her father marrying again had never presented itself to her before. She did not like it and she lay silent under the chill of it.

"Stepmothers are AWFUL creatures," Mary went on. "I could make your blood run cold if I was to tell you all I know about 'em. The Wilson kids across the road from Wiley's had a stepmother. She was just as bad to 'em as Mrs. Wiley was to me. It'll be awful if you get a stepmother."

"I'm sure we won't," said Una tremulously. "Father won't marry anybody else."

"He'll be hounded into it, I expect," said Mary darkly. "All the old maids in the settlement are after him. There's no being up to them. And the worst of stepmothers is, they always set your father against you. He'd never care anything about you again. He'd always take her part and her children's part. You see, she'd make him believe you were all bad."

"I wish you hadn't told me this, Mary," cried Una. "It makes me feel so unhappy."

"I only wanted to warn you," said Mary, rather repentantly. "Of course, your father's so absent-minded he mightn't happen to think of getting married again. But it's better to be prepared."

Long after Mary slept serenely little Una lay awake, her eyes smarting with tears. On, how dreadful it would be if her father should marry somebody who would make him hate her and Jerry and Faith and Carl! She couldn't bear it—she couldn't!

Mary had not instilled any poison of the kind Miss Cornelia had feared into the manse children's minds. Yet she had certainly contrived to do a little mischief with the best of intentions. But she slept dreamlessly, while Una lay awake and the rain fell and the wind wailed around the old gray manse. And the Rev. John Meredith forgot to go to bed at all because he was absorbed in reading a life of St. Augustine. It was gray dawn when he finished it and went upstairs, wrestling with the problems of two thousand years ago. The door of the girls' room was open and he saw Faith lying asleep, rosy and beautiful. He wondered where Una was. Perhaps she had gone over to "stay all night" with the Blythe girls. She did this occasionally, deeming it a great treat. John Meredith sighed. He felt that Una's whereabouts ought not to be a mystery to him. Cecelia would have looked after her better than that.

If only Cecelia were still with him! How pretty and gay she had been! How the old manse up at Maywater had echoed to her songs! And she had gone away so suddenly, taking her laughter and music and leaving silence—so suddenly that he had never quite got over his feeling of amazement. How could SHE, the beautiful and vivid, have died?

The idea of a second marriage had never presented itself seriously to John Meredith. He had loved his wife so deeply that he believed he could never care for any woman again. He had a vague idea that before very long Faith would be old enough to take her mother's place. Until then, he must do the best he could alone. He sighed and went to his room, where the bed was still unmade. Aunt Martha had forgotten it, and Mary had not dared to make it because Aunt

Martha had forbidden her to meddle with anything in the minister's room. But Mr. Meredith did not notice that it was unmade. His last thoughts were of St. Augustine.

10. THE MANSE GIRLS CLEAN HOUSE

"Ugh," said Faith, sitting up in bed with a shiver. "It's raining. I do hate a rainy Sunday. Sunday is dull enough even when it's fine."

"We oughtn't to find Sunday dull," said Una sleepily, trying to pull her drowsy wits together with an uneasy conviction that they had overslept.

"But we DO, you know," said Faith candidly. "Mary Vance says most Sundays are so dull she could hang herself."

"We ought to like Sunday better than Mary Vance," said Una remorsefully. "We're the minister's children."

"I wish we were a blacksmith's children," protested Faith angrily, hunting for her stockings. "THEN people wouldn't expect us to be better than other children. JUST look at the holes in my heels. Mary darned them all up before she went away, but they're as bad as ever now. Una, get up. I can't get the breakfast alone. Oh, dear. I wish father and Jerry were home. You wouldn't think we'd miss father much—we don't see much of him when he is home. And yet EVERYTHING seems gone. I must run in and see how Aunt Martha is."

"Is she any better?" asked Una, when Faith returned.

"No, she isn't. She's groaning with the misery still. Maybe we ought to tell Dr. Blythe. But she says not—she never had a doctor in her life and she isn't going to begin now. She says doctors just live by poisoning people. Do you suppose they do?"

"No, of course not," said Una indignantly. "I'm sure Dr. Blythe wouldn't poison anybody."

"Well, we'll have to rub Aunt Martha's back again after breakfast. We'd better not make the flannels as hot as we did yesterday."

Faith giggled over the remembrance. They had nearly scalded the skin off poor Aunt Martha's back. Una sighed. Mary Vance would have known just what the precise temperature of flannels for a misery back should be. Mary knew everything. They knew nothing. And how could they learn, save by bitter experience for which, in this instance, unfortunate Aunt Martha had paid?

The preceding Monday Mr. Meredith had left for Nova Scotia to spend his short vacation, taking Jerry with him. On Wednesday Aunt Martha was suddenly seized with a recurring and mysterious ailment which she always called "the misery," and which was tolerably certain to attack her at the most inconvenient times. She could not rise from her bed, any movement causing agony. A doctor she flatly refused to have. Faith and Una cooked the meals and waited on her. The less said about the meals the better—yet they were not much worse than Aunt Martha's had been. There were many women in the village who would have been glad to come and help, but Aunt Martha refused to let her plight be known.

"You must worry on till I kin git around," she groaned. "Thank goodness, John isn't here. There's a plenty o' cold biled meat and bread and you kin try your hand at making porridge."

The girls had tried their hand, but so far without much success. The first day it had been too thin. The next day so thick that you could cut it in slices. And both days it had been burned.

"I hate porridge," said Faith viciously. "When I have a house of my own I'm NEVER going to have a single bit of porridge in it."

"What'll your children do then?" asked Una. "Children have to have porridge or they won't grow. Everybody says so."

"They'll have to get along without it or stay runts," retorted Faith stubbornly. "Here, Una, you stir it while I set the table. If I leave it for a minute the horrid stuff will burn. It's half past nine. We'll be late for Sunday School."

"I haven't seen anyone going past yet," said Una. "There won't likely be many out. Just see how it's pouring. And when there's no preaching the folks won't come from a distance to bring the children."

"Go and call Carl," said Faith.

Carl, it appeared, had a sore throat, induced by getting wet in the Rainbow Valley marsh the previous evening while pursuing dragon-flies. He had come home with dripping stockings and boots and had sat out the evening in them. He could not eat any breakfast and Faith made him go back to bed again. She and Una left the table as it was and went to Sunday School. There was no one in the school room when they got there and no one came. They waited until eleven and then went home.

"There doesn't seem to be anybody at the Methodist Sunday School either," said Una.

"I'm GLAD," said Faith. "I'd hate to think the Methodists were better at going to Sunday School on rainy Sundays than the Presbyterians. But there's no preaching in their Church to-day, either, so likely their Sunday School is in the afternoon."

Una washed the dishes, doing them quite nicely, for so much had she learned from Mary Vance. Faith swept the floor after a fashion and peeled the potatoes for dinner, cutting her finger in the process.

"I wish we had something for dinner besides ditto," sighed Una. "I'm so tired of it. The Blythe children don't know what ditto is. And we NEVER have any pudding. Nan says Susan would faint if they had no pudding on Sundays. Why aren't we like other people, Faith?"

"I don't want to be like other people," laughed Faith, tying up her bleeding finger. "I like being myself. It's more interesting. Jessie Drew is as good a housekeeper as her mother, but would you want to be as stupid as she is?"

"But our house isn't right. Mary Vance says so. She says people talk about it being so untidy."

Faith had an inspiration.

"We'll clean it all up," she cried. "We'll go right to work to-morrow. It's a real good chance when Aunt Martha is laid up and can't interfere with us. We'll have it all lovely and clean when father comes home, just like it was when Mary went away. ANY ONE can sweep and dust and wash windows. People won't be able to talk about us any more. Jem Blythe says it's only old cats that talk, but their talk hurts just as much as anybody's."

"I hope it will be fine to-morrow," said Una, fired with enthusiasm. "Oh, Faith, it will be splendid to be all cleaned up and like other people."

"I hope Aunt Martha's misery will last over to-morrow," said Faith. "If it doesn't we won't get a single thing done."

Faith's amiable wish was fulfilled. The next day found Aunt Martha still unable to rise. Carl, too, was still sick and easily prevailed on to stay in bed. Neither Faith nor Una had any idea how sick the boy really was; a watchful mother would have had a doctor without delay; but there was no mother, and poor little Carl, with his sore throat and aching head and crimson cheeks, rolled himself up in his twisted bedclothes and suffered alone, somewhat comforted by the companionship of a small green lizard in the pocket of his ragged nighty.

The world was full of summer sunshine after the rain. It was a peerless day for house-cleaning and Faith and Una went gaily to work.

"We'll clean the dining-room and the parlour," said Faith. "It wouldn't do to meddle with the study, and it doesn't matter much about the upstairs. The first thing is to take everything out."

Accordingly, everything was taken out. The furniture was piled on the veranda and lawn and the Methodist graveyard fence was gaily draped with rugs. An orgy of sweeping followed, with an attempt at dusting on Una's part, while Faith washed the windows of the dining-room, breaking one pane and cracking two in the process. Una surveyed the streaked result dubiously.

"They don't look right, somehow," she said. "Mrs. Elliott's and Susan's windows just shine and sparkle."

"Never mind. They let the sunshine through just as well," said Faith cheerfully. "They MUST be clean after all the soap and water I've used, and that's the main thing. Now, it's past eleven, so I'll wipe up this mess on the floor and we'll go outside. You dust the furniture and I'll shake the rugs. I'm going to do it in the graveyard. I don't want to send dust flying all over the lawn."

Faith enjoyed the rug shaking. To stand on Hezekiah Pollock's tombstone, flapping and shaking rugs, was real fun. To be sure, Elder Abraham Clow and his wife, driving past in their capacious double-seated buggy, seemed to gaze at her in grim disapproval.

"Isn't that a terrible sight?" said Elder Abraham solemnly.

"I would never have believed it if I hadn't seen it with my own eyes," said Mrs. Elder Abraham, more solemnly still.

Faith waved a door mat cheerily at the Clow party. It did not worry her that the elder and his wife did not return her greeting. Everybody knew that Elder Abraham had never been known to smile since he had been appointed Superintendent of the Sunday School fourteen years previously. But it hurt her that Minnie and Adella Clow did not wave back. Faith liked Minnie and Adella. Next to the Blythes, they were her best friends in school and she always helped Adella with her sums. This was gratitude for you. Her friends cut her because she was shaking rugs in an old graveyard where, as Mary Vance said, not a living soul had been buried for years. Faith flounced around to the veranda, where she found Una grieved in spirit because the Clow girls had not waved to her, either.

"I suppose they're mad over something," said Faith. "Perhaps they're jealous because we play so much in Rainbow Valley with the Blythes. Well, just wait till school opens and Adella wants me to show her how to do her sums! We'll get square then. Come on, let's put the things back in. I'm tired to death and I don't believe the rooms will look much better than before we started—though I shook out pecks of dust in the graveyard. I HATE house-cleaning."

It was two o'clock before the tired girls finished the two rooms. They got a dreary bite in the kitchen and intended to wash the dishes at once. But Faith happened to pick up a new story-book Di Blythe had lent her and was lost to the world until sunset. Una took a cup of rank tea up to Carl but found him asleep; so she curled herself up on Jerry's bed and went to sleep too. Meanwhile, a weird story flew through Glen St. Mary and folks asked each other seriously what was to be done with those manse youngsters.

"That is past laughing at, believe ME," said Miss Cornelia to her husband, with a heavy sigh. "I couldn't believe it at first. Miranda Drew brought the story home from the Methodist Sunday School this afternoon and I simply scoffed at it. But Mrs. Elder Abraham says she and the Elder saw it with their own eyes."

"Saw what?" asked Marshall.

"Faith and Una Meredith stayed home from Sunday School this morning and CLEANED HOUSE," said Miss Cornelia, in accents of despair. "When Elder Abraham went home from the church—he had stayed behind to straighten out the library books—he saw them shaking rugs in the Methodist graveyard. I can never look a Methodist in the face again. Just think what a scandal it will make!"

A scandal it assuredly did make, growing more scandalous as it spread, until the over-harbour people heard that the manse children had not only cleaned house and put out a washing on Sunday, but had wound up with an afternoon picnic in the graveyard while the Methodist Sunday School was going on. The only household which remained in blissful ignorance of the terrible thing was the manse itself; on what Faith and Una fondly believed to be Tuesday it rained again; for the next three days it rained; nobody came near the manse; the manse folk went nowhere; they might have waded through the misty Rainbow Valley up to Ingleside, but all the Blythe family, save Susan and the doctor, were away on a visit to Avonlea.

"This is the last of our bread," said Faith, "and the ditto is done. If Aunt Martha doesn't get better soon WHAT will we do?"

"We can buy some bread in the village and there's the codfish Mary dried," said Una. "But we don't know how to cook it."

"Oh, that's easy," laughed Faith. "You just boil it."

Boil it they did; but as it did not occur to them to soak it beforehand it was too salty to eat. That night they were very hungry; but by the following day their troubles were over. Sunshine returned to the world; Carl was well and Aunt Martha's misery left her as suddenly as it had come; the butcher called at the manse and chased famine away. To crown all, the Blythes returned home, and that evening they and the manse children and Mary Vance kept sunset tryst once more in Rainbow Valley, where the daisies were floating upon the grass like spirits of the dew and the bells on the Tree Lovers rang like fairy chimes in the scented twilight.

11. A DREADFUL DISCOVERY

"Well, you kids have gone and done it now," was Mary's greeting, as she joined them in the Valley. Miss Cornelia was up at Ingleside, holding agonized conclave with Anne and Susan, and Mary hoped that the session might be a long one, for it was all of two weeks since she had been allowed to revel with her chums in the dear valley of rainbows.

"Done what?" demanded everybody but Walter, who was day-dreaming as usual.

"It's you manse young ones, I mean," said Mary. "It was just awful of you. *I* wouldn't have done such a thing for the world, and *I* weren't brought up in a manse—weren't brought up ANYWHERE—just COME up."

"What have WE done?" asked Faith blankly.

"Done! You'd BETTER ask! The talk is something terrible. I expect it's ruined your father in this congregation. He'll never be able to live it down, poor man! Everybody blames him for it, and that isn't fair. But nothing IS fair in this world. You ought to be ashamed of yourselves."

"What HAVE we done?" asked Una again, despairingly. Faith said nothing, but her eyes flashed golden-brown scorn at Mary.

"Oh, don't pretend innocence," said Mary, witheringly. "Everybody knows what you have done."

"*I* don't," interjected Jem Blythe indignantly. "Don't let me catch you making Una cry, Mary Vance. What are you talking about?"

"I s'pose you don't know, since you're just back from up west," said Mary, somewhat subdued. Jem could always manage her. "But everybody else knows, you'd better believe."

"Knows what?"

"That Faith and Una stayed home from Sunday School last Sunday and CLEANED HOUSE."

"We didn't," cried Faith and Una, in passionate denial.

Mary looked haughtily at them.

"I didn't suppose you'd deny it, after the way you've combed ME down for lying," she said. "What's the good of saying you didn't? Everybody knows you DID. Elder Clow and his wife saw you. Some people say it will break up the church, but *I* don't go that far. You ARE nice ones."

Nan Blythe stood up and put her arms around the dazed Faith and Una.

"They were nice enough to take you in and feed you and clothe you when you were starving in Mr. Taylor's barn, Mary Vance," she said. "You are VERY grateful, I must say."

"I AM grateful," retorted Mary. "You'd know it if you'd heard me standing up for Mr. Meredith through thick and thin. I've blistered my tongue talking for him this week. I've said again and again that he isn't to blame if his young ones did clean house on Sunday. He was away—and they knew better."

"But we didn't," protested Una. "It was MONDAY we cleaned house. Wasn't it, Faith?"

"Of course it was," said Faith, with flashing eyes. "We went to Sunday School in spite of the rain—and no one came—not even Elder Abraham, for all his talk about fair-weather Christians."

"It was Saturday it rained," said Mary. "Sunday was as fine as silk. I wasn't at Sunday School because I had toothache, but every one else was and they saw all your stuff out on the lawn. And Elder Abraham and Mrs. Elder Abraham saw you shaking rugs in the graveyard."

Una sat down among the daisies and began to cry.

"Look here," said Jem resolutely, "this thing must be cleared up. SOMEBODY has made a mistake. Sunday WAS fine, Faith. How could you have thought Saturday was Sunday?"

"Prayer-meeting was Thursday night," cried Faith, "and Adam flew into the soup-pot on Friday when Aunt Martha's cat chased him, and spoiled our dinner; and Saturday there was a snake in the cellar and Carl caught it with a forked stick and carried it out, and Sunday it rained. So there!"

"Prayer-meeting was Wednesday night," said Mary. "Elder Baxter was to lead and he couldn't go Thursday night and it was changed to Wednesday. You were just a day out, Faith Meredith, and you DID work on Sunday."

Suddenly Faith burst into a peal of laughter.

"I suppose we did. What a joke!"

"It isn't much of a joke for your father," said Mary sourly.

"It'll be all right when people find out it was just a mistake," said Faith carelessly. "We'll explain."

"You can explain till you're black in the face," said Mary, "but a lie like that'll travel faster'n further than you ever will. I'VE seen more of the world than you and *I* know. Besides, there are plenty of folks won't believe it was a mistake."

"They will if I tell them," said Faith.

"You can't tell everybody," said Mary. "No, I tell you you've disgraced your father."

Una's evening was spoiled by this dire reflection, but Faith refused to be made uncomfortable. Besides, she had a plan that would put everything right. So she put the past with its mistake behind her and gave herself over to enjoyment of the present. Jem went away to fish and Walter came out of his reverie and proceeded to describe the woods of heaven. Mary pricked up her ears and listened respectfully. Despite her awe of Walter she revelled in his "book talk." It always gave her a delightful sensation. Walter had been reading his Coleridge that day, and he pictured a heaven where

"There were gardens bright with sinuous rills
Where blossomed many an incense bearing tree,

And there were forests ancient as the hills
Enfolding sunny spots of greenery."

"I didn't know there was any woods in heaven," said Mary, with a long breath. "I thought it was all streets—and streets—AND streets."

"Of course there are woods," said Nan. "Mother can't live without trees and I can't, so what would be the use of going to heaven if there weren't any trees?"

"There are cities, too," said the young dreamer, "splendid cities—coloured just like the sunset, with sapphire towers and rainbow domes. They are built of gold and diamonds—whole streets of diamonds, flashing like the sun. In the squares there are crystal fountains kissed by the light, and everywhere the asphodel blooms—the flower of heaven."

"Fancy!" said Mary. "I saw the main street in Charlottetown once and I thought it was real grand, but I s'pose it's nothing to heaven. Well, it all sounds gorgeous the way you tell it, but won't it be kind of dull, too?"

"Oh, I guess we can have some fun when the angels' backs are turned," said Faith comfortably.

"Heaven is ALL fun," declared Di.

"The Bible doesn't say so," cried Mary, who had read so much of the Bible on Sunday afternoons under Miss Cornelia's eye that she now considered herself quite an authority on it.

"Mother says the Bible language is figurative," said Nan.

"Does that mean that it isn't true?" asked Mary hopefully.

"No—not exactly—but I think it means that heaven will be just like what you'd like it to be."

"I'd like it to be just like Rainbow Valley," said Mary, "with all you kids to gas and play with. THAT'S good enough for me. Anyhow, we can't go to heaven till we're dead and maybe not then, so what's the use of worrying? Here's Jem with a string of trout and it's my turn to fry them."

"We ought to know more about heaven than Walter does when we're the minister's family," said Una, as they walked home that night.

"We KNOW just as much, but Walter can IMAGINE," said Faith. "Mrs. Elliott says he gets it from his mother."

"I do wish we hadn't made that mistake about Sunday," sighed Una.

"Don't worry over that. I've thought of a great plan to explain so that everybody will know," said Faith. "Just wait till to-morrow night."

12. AN EXPLANATION AND A DARE

The Rev. Dr. Cooper preached in Glen St. Mary the next evening and the Presbyterian Church was crowded with people from near and far. The Reverend Doctor was reputed to be a very eloquent speaker; and, bearing in mind the old dictum that a minister should take his best clothes to the city and his best sermons to the country, he delivered a very scholarly and impressive discourse. But when the folks went home that night it was not of Dr. Cooper's sermon they talked. They had completely forgotten all about it.

Dr. Cooper had concluded with a fervent appeal, had wiped the perspiration from his massive brow, had said "Let us pray" as he was famed for saying it, and had duly prayed. There was a slight pause. In Glen St. Mary church the old fashion of taking the collection after the sermon instead of before still held—mainly because the Methodists had adopted the new fashion first, and Miss Cornelia and Elder Clow would not hear of following where Methodists had led. Charles Baxter and Thomas Douglas, whose duty it was to pass the plates, were on the point of rising to their feet. The organist had got out the music of her anthem and the choir had cleared its throat. Suddenly Faith Meredith rose in the manse pew, walked up to the pulpit platform, and faced the amazed audience.

Miss Cornelia half rose in her seat and then sat down again. Her pew was far back and it occurred to her that whatever Faith meant to do or say would be half done or said before she could reach her. There was no use making the exhibition worse than it had to be. With an anguished glance at Mrs. Dr. Blythe, and another at Deacon Warren of the Methodist Church, Miss Cornelia resigned herself to another scandal.

"If the child was only dressed decently itself," she groaned in spirit.

Faith, having spilled ink on her good dress, had serenely put on an old one of faded pink print. A caticornered rent in the skirt had been darned with scarlet tracing cotton and the hem had been let down, showing a bright strip of unfaded pink around the skirt. But Faith was not thinking of her clothes at all. She was feeling suddenly nervous. What had seemed easy in imagination was rather hard in reality. Confronted by all those staring questioning eyes Faith's courage almost failed her. The lights were so bright, the silence so awesome. She thought she could not speak after all. But she MUST—her father MUST be cleared of suspicion. Only—the words would NOT come.

Una's little pearl-pure face gleamed up at her beseechingly from the manse pew. The Blythe children were lost in amazement. Back under the gallery Faith saw the sweet graciousness of Miss Rosemary West's smile and the amusement of Miss Ellen's. But none of these helped her. It was Bertie Shakespeare Drew who saved the situation. Bertie Shakespeare sat in the front seat of the gallery and he made a derisive face at Faith. Faith promptly made a dreadful one back at him, and, in her anger over being grimaced at by Bertie Shakespeare, forgot her stage fright. She found her voice and spoke out clearly and bravely.

"I want to explain something," she said, "and I want to do it now because everybody will hear it that heard the other. People are saying that Una and I stayed home last Sunday and cleaned house instead of going to Sunday School. Well, we did—but we didn't mean to. We got mixed up in the days of the week. It was all Elder Baxter's fault"—sensation in Baxter's pew—"because he went and changed the prayer-meeting to Wednesday night and then we thought Thursday was Friday and so on till we thought Saturday was Sunday. Carl was laid up sick and so was Aunt Martha, so they couldn't put us right. We went to Sunday School in all that rain on Saturday and nobody came. And then we thought we'd clean house on Monday and stop old cats from talking about how dirty the manse was"—general sensation all over the church—"and we did. I shook the rugs in the Methodist graveyard because it was such a convenient place and not because I meant to be disrespectful of the dead. It isn't the dead folks who have made the fuss over this—it's the living folks. And it isn't right for any of you to blame my father for this, because he was away and didn't know, and anyhow we thought it was Monday. He's just the best father that ever lived in the world and we love him with all our hearts."

Faith's bravado ebbed out in a sob. She ran down the steps and flashed out of the side door of the church. There the friendly starlit, summer night comforted her and the ache went out of her eyes and throat. She felt very happy. The dreadful explanation was over and everybody knew now that her father wasn't to blame and that she and Una were not so wicked as to have cleaned house knowingly on Sunday.

Inside the church people gazed blankly at each other, but Thomas Douglas rose and walked up the aisle with a set face. HIS duty was clear; the collection must be taken if the skies fell. Taken it was; the choir sang the anthem, with a dismal conviction that it fell terribly flat, and Dr. Cooper gave out the concluding hymn and pronounced the benediction with considerably less unction than usual. The Reverend Doctor had a sense of humour and Faith's performance tickled him. Besides, John Meredith was well known in Presbyterian circles.

Mr. Meredith returned home the next afternoon, but before his coming Faith contrived to scandalize Glen St. Mary again. In the reaction from Sunday evening's intensity and strain she was especially full of what Miss Cornelia would have called "devilment" on Monday. This led her to dare Walter Blythe to ride through Main Street on a pig, while she rode another one.

The pigs in question were two tall, lank animals, supposed to belong to Bertie Shakespeare Drew's father, which had been haunting the roadside by the manse for a couple of weeks. Walter did not want to ride a pig through Glen St. Mary, but whatever Faith Meredith dared him to do must be done. They tore down the hill and through the village, Faith bent double with laughter over her terrified courser, Walter crimson with shame. They tore past the minister himself, just coming home from the station; he, being a little less dreamy and abstracted than usual—owing to having had a talk on the train with Miss Cornelia who always wakened him up temporarily—noticed them, and thought he really must speak to Faith about it and tell her that such conduct was not seemly. But he had forgotten the trifling incident by the time he reached home. They passed Mrs. Alec Davis, who shrieked in horror, and they passed Miss Rosemary West who laughed and sighed. Finally, just before the pigs swooped into Bertie Shakespeare Drew's back yard, never to emerge therefrom again, so great had been the shock to their nerves—Faith and Walter jumped off, as Dr. and Mrs. Blythe drove swiftly by.

"So that is how you bring up your boys," said Gilbert with mock severity.

"Perhaps I do spoil them a little," said Anne contritely, "but, oh, Gilbert, when I think of my own childhood before I came to Green Gables I haven't the heart to be very strict. How hungry for love and fun I was—an unloved little drudge with never a chance to play! They do have such good times with the manse children."

"What about the poor pigs?" asked Gilbert.

Anne tried to look sober and failed.

"Do you really think it hurt them?" she said. "I don't think anything could hurt those animals. They've been the plague of the neighbourhood this summer and the Drews WON'T shut them up. But I'll talk to Walter—if I can keep from laughing when I do it."

Miss Cornelia came up to Ingleside that evening to relieve her feelings over Sunday night. To her surprise she found that Anne did not view Faith's performance in quite the same light as she did.

"I thought there was something brave and pathetic in her getting up there before that churchful of people, to confess," she said. "You could see she was frightened to death—yet she was bound to clear her father. I loved her for it."

"Oh, of course, the poor child meant well," sighed Miss Cornelia, "but just the same it was a terrible thing to do, and is making more talk than the house-cleaning on Sunday. THAT had begun to die away, and this has started it all up again. Rosemary West is like you—she said last night as she left the church that it was a plucky thing for Faith to do, but it made her feel sorry for the child, too. Miss Ellen thought it all a good joke, and said she hadn't had as much fun in church for years. Of course THEY don't care—they are Episcopalians. But we Presbyterians feel it. And there were so many hotel people there that night and scores of Methodists. Mrs. Leander Crawford cried, she felt so bad. And Mrs. Alec Davis said the little hussy ought to be spanked."

"Mrs. Leander Crawford is always crying in church," said Susan contemptuously. "She cries over every affecting thing the minister says. But you do not often see her name on a subscription list, Mrs. Dr. dear. Tears come cheaper. She tried to talk to me one day about Aunt Martha being such a dirty housekeeper; and I wanted to say, 'Every one knows that YOU have been seen mixing up cakes in the kitchen wash-pan, Mrs. Leander Crawford!' But I did not say it, Mrs. Dr. dear, because I have too much respect for myself to condescend to argue with the likes of her. But I could tell worse things than THAT of Mrs. Leander Crawford, if I was disposed to gossip. And as for Mrs. Alec Davis, if she had said that to me, Mrs. Dr. dear, do you know what I would have said? I would have said, 'I have no doubt you would like to spank Faith, Mrs. Davis, but you will never have the chance to spank a minister's daughter either in this world or in that which is to come.'"

"If poor Faith had only been decently dressed," lamented Miss Cornelia again, "it wouldn't have been quite that bad. But that dress looked dreadful, as she stood there upon the platform."

"It was clean, though, Mrs. Dr. dear," said Susan. "They ARE clean children. They may be very heedless and reckless, Mrs. Dr. dear, and I am not saying they are not, but they NEVER forget to wash behind their ears."

"The idea of Faith forgetting what day was Sunday," persisted Miss Cornelia. "She will grow up just as careless and impractical as her father, believe ME. I suppose Carl would have known better if he hadn't been sick. I don't know what was wrong with him, but I think it very likely he had been eating those blueberries that grew in the graveyard. No wonder they made him sick. If I was a Methodist I'd try to keep my graveyard cleaned up at least."

"I am of the opinion that Carl only ate the sours that grow on the dyke," said Susan hopefully. "I do not think ANY minister's son would eat blueberries that grew on the graves of dead people. You know it would not be so bad, Mrs. Dr. dear, to eat things that grew on the dyke."

"The worst of last night's performance was the face Faith made made at somebody in the congregation before she started in," said Miss Cornelia. "Elder Clow declares she made it at him. And DID you hear that she was seen riding on a pig to-day?"

"I saw her. Walter was with her. I gave him a little—a VERY little—scolding about it. He did not say much, but he gave me the impression that it had been his idea and that Faith was not to blame."

"I do not not believe THAT, Mrs. Dr. dear," cried Susan, up in arms. "That is just Walter's way—to take the blame on himself. But you know as well as I do, Mrs. Dr. dear, that that blessed child would never have thought of riding on a pig, even if he does write poetry."

"Oh, there's no doubt the notion was hatched in Faith Meredith's brain," said Miss Cornelia. "And I don't say that I'm sorry that Amos Drew's old pigs did get their come-uppance for once. But the minister's daughter!"

"AND the doctor's son!" said Anne, mimicking Miss Cornelia's tone. Then she laughed. "Dear Miss Cornelia, they're only little children. And you KNOW they've never yet done anything bad—they're just heedless and impulsive—as I was myself once. They'll grow sedate and sober—as I've done."

Miss Cornelia laughed, too.

"There are times, Anne dearie, when I know by your eyes that YOUR soberness is put on like a garment and you're really aching to do something wild and young again. Well, I feel encouraged. Somehow, a talk with you always does have that effect on me. Now, when I go to see Barbara Samson, it's just the opposite. She makes me feel that everything's wrong and always will be. But of course living all your life with a man like Joe Samson wouldn't be exactly cheering."

"It is a very strange thing to think that she married Joe Samson after all her chances," remarked Susan. "She was much sought after when she was a girl. She used to boast to me that she had twenty-one beaus and Mr. Pethick."

"What was Mr. Pethick?"

"Well, he was a sort of hanger-on, Mrs. Dr. dear, but you could not exactly call him a beau. He did not really have any intentions. Twenty-one beaus—and me that never had one! But Barbara went through the woods and picked up the crooked stick after all. And yet they say her husband can make better baking powder biscuits than she can, and she always gets him to make them when company comes to tea."

"Which reminds ME that I have company coming to tea to-morrow and I must go home and set my bread," said Miss Cornelia. "Mary said she could set it and no doubt she could. But while I live and move and have my being *I* set my own bread, believe me."

"How is Mary getting on?" asked Anne.

"I've no fault to find with Mary," said Miss Cornelia rather gloomily. "She's getting some flesh on her bones and she's clean and respectful—though there's more in her than *I* can fathom. She's a sly puss. If you dug for a thousand years you couldn't get to the bottom of that child's mind, believe ME! As for work, I never saw anything like her. She EATS it up. Mrs. Wiley may have been cruel to her, but folks needn't say she made Mary work. Mary's a born worker. Sometimes I wonder which will wear out first—her legs or her tongue. I don't have enough to do to keep me out of mischief these days. I'll be real glad when school opens, for then I'll have something to do again. Mary doesn't want to go to school, but I put my foot down and said that go she must. I shall NOT have the Methodists saying that I kept her out of school while I lolled in idleness."

13. THE HOUSE ON THE HILL

There was a little unfailing spring, always icy cold and crystal pure, in a certain birch-screened hollow of Rainbow Valley in the lower corner near the marsh. Not a great many people knew of its existence. The manse and Ingleside children knew, of course, as they knew everything else about the magic valley. Occasionally they went there to get a drink, and it figured in many of their plays as a fountain of old romance. Anne knew of it and loved it because it somehow reminded her of the beloved Dryad's Bubble at Green Gables. Rosemary West knew of it; it was her fountain of romance, too. Eighteen years ago she had sat behind it one spring twilight and heard young Martin Crawford stammer out a confession of fervent, boyish love. She had whispered her own secret in return, and they had kissed and promised by the wild wood spring. They had never stood together by it again—Martin had sailed on his fatal voyage soon after; but to Rosemary West it was always a sacred spot, hallowed by that immortal hour of youth and love. Whenever she passed near it she turned aside to hold a secret tryst with an old dream—a dream from which the pain had long gone, leaving only its unforgettable sweetness.

The spring was a hidden thing. You might have passed within ten feet of it and never have suspected its existence. Two generations past a huge old pine had fallen almost across it. Nothing was left of the tree but its crumbling trunk out of which the ferns grew thickly, making a green roof and a lacy screen for the water. A maple-tree grew beside it with a curiously gnarled and twisted trunk, creeping along the ground for a little way before shooting up into the air, and so forming a quaint seat; and September had flung a scarf of pale smoke-blue asters around the hollow.

John Meredith, taking the cross-lots road through Rainbow Valley on his way home from some pastoral visitations around the Harbour head one evening, turned aside to drink of the little spring. Walter Blythe had shown it to him one afternoon only a few days before, and they had had a long talk together on the maple seat. John Meredith, under all his shyness and aloofness, had the heart of a boy. He had been called Jack in his youth, though nobody in Glen St. Mary would ever have believed it. Walter and he had taken to each other and had talked unreservedly. Mr. Meredith found his way into some sealed and sacred chambers of the lad's soul wherein not even Di had ever looked. They were to be chums from that friendly hour and Walter knew that he would never be frightened of the minister again.

"I never believed before that it was possible to get really acquainted with a minister," he told his mother that night.

John Meredith drank from his slender white hand, whose grip of steel always surprised people who were unacquainted with it, and then sat down on the maple seat. He was in no hurry to go home; this was a beautiful spot and he was mentally weary after a round of rather uninspiring conversations with many good and stupid people. The moon was rising. Rainbow Valley was wind-haunted and star-sentinelled only where he was, but afar from the upper end came the gay notes of children's laughter and voices.

The ethereal beauty of the asters in the moonlight, the glimmer of the little spring, the soft croon of the brook, the wavering grace of the brackens all wove a white magic round John Meredith. He forgot congregational worries and spiritual problems; the years slipped away from him; he was a young divinity student again and the roses of June were blooming red and fragrant on the dark, queenly head of his Cecilia. He sat there and dreamed like any boy. And it was at this propitious moment that Rosemary West stepped aside from the by-path and stood beside him in that dangerous, spell-weaving place. John Meredith stood up as she came in and saw her—REALLY saw her—for the first time.

He had met her in his church once or twice and shaken hands with her abstractedly as he did with anyone he happened to encounter on his way down the aisle. He had never met her elsewhere, for the Wests were Episcopalians, with church affinities in Lowbridge, and no occasion for calling upon them had ever arisen. Before to-night, if anyone had asked John Meredith what Rosemary West looked like he would not have had the slightest notion. But he was never to forget her, as she appeared to him in the glamour of kind moonlight by the spring.

She was certainly not in the least like Cecilia, who had always been his ideal of womanly beauty. Cecilia had been small and dark and vivacious—Rosemary West was tall and fair and placid, yet John Meredith thought he had never seen so beautiful a woman.

She was bareheaded and her golden hair—hair of a warm gold, "molasses taffy" colour as Di Blythe had said—was pinned in sleek, close coils over her head; she had large, tranquil, blue eyes that always seemed full of friendliness, a high white forehead and a finely shaped face.

Rosemary West was always called a "sweet woman." She was so sweet that even her high-bred, stately air had never gained for her the reputation of being "stuck-up," which it would inevitably have done in the case of anyone else in Glen St. Mary. Life had taught her to be brave, to be patient, to love, to forgive. She had watched the ship on which her lover went sailing out of Four Winds Harbour into the sunset. But, though she watched long, she had never seen it coming sailing back. That vigil had taken girlhood from her eyes, yet she kept her youth to a marvellous degree. Perhaps this was because she always seemed to preserve that attitude of delighted surprise towards life which most of us leave behind in childhood—an attitude which not only made Rosemary herself seem young, but flung a pleasing illusion of youth over the consciousness of every one who talked to her.

John Meredith was startled by her loveliness and Rosemary was startled by his presence. She had never thought she would find anyone by that remote spring, least of all the recluse of Glen St. Mary manse. She almost dropped the heavy armful of books she was carrying home from the Glen lending library, and then, to cover her confusion, she told one of those small fibs which even the best of women do tell at times.

"I—I came for a drink," she said, stammering a little, in answer to Mr. Meredith's grave "good evening, Miss West." She felt that she was an unpardonable goose and she longed to shake herself. But John Meredith was not a vain man and he knew she would likely have been as much startled had she met old Elder Clow in that unexpected fashion. Her confusion put him at ease and he forgot to be shy; besides, even the shyest of men can sometimes be quite audacious in moonlight.

"Let me get you a cup," he said smiling. There was a cup near by, if he had only known it, a cracked, handleless blue cup secreted under the maple by the Rainbow Valley children; but he did not know it, so he stepped out to one of the birch-trees and stripped a bit of its white skin away. Deftly he fashioned this into a three-cornered cup, filled it from the spring, and handed it to Rosemary.

Rosemary took it and drank every drop to punish herself for her fib, for she was not in the least thirsty, and to drink a fairly large cupful of water when you are not thirsty is somewhat of an ordeal. Yet the memory of that draught was to be very pleasant to Rosemary. In after years it seemed to her that there was something sacramental about it. Perhaps this was because of what the minister did when she handed him back the cup. He stooped again and filled it and drank of it himself. It was only by accident that he put his lips just where Rosemary had put hers, and Rosemary knew it. Nevertheless, it had a curious significance for her. They two had drunk of the same cup. She remembered idly that an old aunt of hers used to say that when two people did this their after-lives would be linked in some fashion, whether for good or ill.

John Meredith held the cup uncertainly. He did not know what to do with it. The logical thing would have been to toss it away, but somehow he was disinclined to do this. Rosemary held out her hand for it.

"Will you let me have it?" she said. "You made it so knackily. I never saw anyone make a birch cup so since my little brother used to make them long ago—before he died."

"I learned how to make them when *I* was a boy, camping out one summer. An old hunter taught me," said Mr. Meredith. "Let me carry your books, Miss West."

Rosemary was startled into another fib and said oh, they were not heavy. But the minister took them from her with quite a masterful air and they walked away together. It was the first time Rosemary had stood by the valley spring without thinking of Martin Crawford. The mystic tryst had been broken.

The little by-path wound around the marsh and then struck up the long wooded hill on the top of which Rosemary lived. Beyond, through the trees, they could see the moonlight shining across the level summer fields. But the little path was shadowy and narrow. Trees crowded over it, and trees are never quite as friendly to human beings after nightfall as they are in daylight. They wrap themselves away from us. They whisper and plot furtively. If they reach out a hand to us it has a hostile, tentative touch. People walking amid trees after night always draw closer together instinctively and involuntarily, making an alliance, physical and mental, against certain alien powers around them. Rosemary's dress brushed against John Meredith as they walked. Not even an absent-minded minister, who was after all a young man still, though he firmly believed he had outlived romance, could be insensible to the charm of the night and the path and the companion.

It is never quite safe to think we have done with life. When we imagine we have finished our story fate has a trick of turning the page and showing us yet another chapter. These two people each thought their hearts belonged irrevocably to the past; but they both found their walk up that hill very pleasant. Rosemary thought the Glen minister was by no means as shy and tongue-tied as he had been represented. He seemed to find no difficulty in talking easily and freely. Glen housewives would have been amazed had they heard him. But then so many Glen housewives talked only gossip and the price of eggs, and John Meredith was not interested in either. He talked to Rosemary of books and music and wide-world doings and something of his own history, and found that she could understand and respond. Rosemary, it appeared, possessed a book which Mr. Meredith had not read and wished to read. She offered to lend it to him and when they reached the old homestead on the hill he went in to get it.

The house itself was an old-fashioned gray one, hung with vines, through which the light in the sitting-room winked in friendly fashion. It looked down the Glen, over the harbour, silvered in the moonlight, to the sand-dunes and the moaning ocean. They walked in through a garden that always seemed to smell of roses, even when no roses were in bloom. There was a sisterhood of lilies at the gate and a ribbon of asters on either side of the broad walk, and a lacery of fir trees on the hill's edge beyond the house.

"You have the whole world at your doorstep here," said John Meredith, with a long breath. "What a view—what an outlook! At times I feel stifled down there in the Glen. You can breathe up here."

"It is calm to-night," said Rosemary laughing. "If there were a wind it would blow your breath away. We get 'a' the airts the wind can blow' up here. This place should be called Four Winds instead of the Harbour."

"I like wind," he said. "A day when there is no wind seems to me DEAD. A windy day wakes me up." He gave a conscious laugh. "On a calm day I fall into day dreams. No doubt you know my reputation, Miss West. If I cut you dead the next time we meet don't put it down to bad manners. Please understand that it is only abstraction and forgive me—and speak to me."

They found Ellen West in the sitting room when they went in. She laid her glasses down on the book she had been reading and looked at them in amazement tinctured with something else. But she shook hands amiably with Mr. Meredith and he sat down and talked to her, while Rosemary hunted out his book.

Ellen West was ten years older than Rosemary, and so different from her that it was hard to believe they were sisters. She was dark and massive, with black hair, thick, black eyebrows and eyes of the clear, slaty blue of the gulf water in a north wind. She had a rather stern, forbidding look, but she was in reality very jolly, with a hearty, gurgling laugh and a deep, mellow, pleasant voice with a suggestion of masculinity about it. She had once remarked to Rosemary that she would really like to have a talk with that Presbyterian minister at the Glen, to see if he could find a word to say to a woman when he was cornered. She had her chance now and she tackled him on world politics. Miss Ellen, who was a great reader, had been devouring a book on the Kaiser of Germany, and she demanded Mr. Meredith's opinion of him.

"A dangerous man," was his answer.

"I believe you!" Miss Ellen nodded. "Mark my words, Mr. Meredith, that man is going to fight somebody yet. He's ACHING to. He is going to set the world on fire."

"If you mean that he will wantonly precipitate a great war I hardly think so," said Mr. Meredith. "The day has gone by for that sort of thing."

"Bless you, it hasn't," rumbled Ellen. "The day never goes by for men and nations to make asses of themselves and take to the fists. The millenniun isn't THAT near, Mr. Meredith, and YOU don't think it is any more than I do. As for this Kaiser, mark my words, he is going to make a heap of trouble"—and Miss Ellen prodded her book emphatically with her long finger. "Yes, if he isn't nipped in the bud he's going to make trouble. WE'LL live to see it—you and I will live to see it, Mr. Meredith. And who is going to nip him? England should, but she won't. WHO is going to nip him? Tell me that, Mr. Meredith."

Mr. Meredith couldn't tell her, but they plunged into a discussion of German militarism that lasted long after Rosemary had found the book. Rosemary said nothing, but sat in a little rocker behind Ellen and stroked an important black cat meditatively. John Meredith hunted big game in Europe with Ellen, but he looked oftener at Rosemary than at Ellen, and Ellen noticed it. After Rosemary had gone to the door with him and come back Ellen rose and looked at her accusingly.

"Rosemary West, that man has a notion of courting you."

Rosemary quivered. Ellen's speech was like a blow to her. It rubbed all the bloom off the pleasant evening. But she would not let Ellen see how it hurt her.

"Nonsense," she said, and laughed, a little too carelessly. "You see a beau for me in every bush, Ellen. Why he told me all about his wife to-night—how much she was to him—how empty her death had left the world."

"Well, that may be HIS way of courting," retorted Ellen. "Men have all kinds of ways, I understand. But don't forget your promise, Rosemary."

"There is no need of my either forgetting or remembering it," said Rosemary, a little wearily. "YOU forget that I'm an old maid, Ellen. It is only your sisterly delusion that I am still young and blooming and dangerous. Mr. Meredith merely wants to be a friend—if he wants that much itself. He'll forget us both long before he gets back to the manse."

"I've no objection to your being friends with him," conceded Ellen, "but it musn't go beyond friendship, remember. I'm always suspicious of widowers. They are not given to romantic ideas about friendship. They're apt to mean business. As for this Presbyterian man, what do they call him shy for? He's not a bit shy, though he may be absent-minded—so absent-minded that he forgot to say goodnight to ME when you started to go to the door with him. He's got brains, too. There's so few men round here that can talk sense to a body. I've enjoyed the evening. I wouldn't mind seeing more of him. But no philandering, Rosemary, mind you—no philandering."

Rosemary was quite used to being warned by Ellen from philandering if she so much as talked five minutes to any marriageable man under eighty or over eighteen. She had always laughed at the warning with unfeigned amusement. This time it did not amuse her—it irritated her a little. Who wanted to philander?

"Don't be such a goose, Ellen," she said with unaccustomed shortness as she took her lamp. She went upstairs without saying goodnight.

Ellen shook her head dubiously and looked at the black cat.

"What is she so cross about, St. George?" she asked. "When you howl you're hit, I've always heard, George. But she promised, Saint—she promised, and we Wests always keep our word. So it won't matter if he does want to philander, George. She promised. I won't worry."

Upstairs, in her room, Rosemary sat for a long while looking out of the window across the moonlit garden to the distant, shining harbour. She felt vaguely upset and unsettled. She was suddenly tired of outworn dreams. And in the garden the petals of the last red rose were scattered by a sudden little wind. Summer was over—it was autumn.

14. MRS. ALEC DAVIS MAKES A CALL

John Meredith walked slowly home. At first he thought a little about Rosemary, but by the time he reached Rainbow Valley he had forgotten all about her and was meditating on a point regarding German theology which Ellen had raised. He passed through Rainbow Valley and knew it not. The charm of Rainbow Valley had no potency against German theology. When he reached the manse he went to his study and took down a bulky volume in order to see which had been right, he or Ellen. He remained immersed in its mazes until dawn, struck a new trail of speculation and pursued it like a sleuth hound for the next week, utterly lost to the world, his parish and his family. He read day and night; he forgot to go to his meals when Una was not there to drag him to them; he never thought about Rosemary or Ellen again. Old Mrs. Marshall, over-harbour, was very ill and sent for him, but the message lay unheeded on his desk and gathered dust. Mrs. Marshall recovered but never forgave him. A young couple came to the manse to be married and Mr. Meredith, with unbrushed hair, in carpet slippers and faded dressing gown, married them. To be sure, he began by reading the funeral service to them and got along as far as "ashes to ashes and dust to dust" before he vaguely suspected that something was wrong.

"Dear me," he said absently, "that is strange—very strange."

The bride, who was very nervous, began to cry. The bridegroom, who was not in the least nervous, giggled.

"Please, sir, I think you're burying us instead of marrying us," he said.

"Excuse me," said Mr. Meredith, as it it did not matter much. He turned up the marriage service and got through with it, but the bride never felt quite properly married for the rest of her life.

He forgot his prayer-meeting again—but that did not matter, for it was a wet night and nobody came. He might even have forgotten his Sunday service if it had not been for Mrs. Alec Davis. Aunt Martha came in on Saturday afternoon and told him that Mrs. Davis was in the parlour and wanted to see him. Mr. Meredith sighed. Mrs. Davis was the only woman in Glen St. Mary church whom he positively detested. Unfortunately, she was also the richest, and his board of managers had warned Mr. Meredith against offending her. Mr. Meredith seldom thought of such a worldly matter as his stipend; but the managers were more practical. Also, they were astute. Without mentioning money, they contrived to instil into Mr. Meredith's mind a conviction that he should not offend Mrs. Davis. Otherwise, he would likely have forgotten all about her as soon as Aunt Martha had gone out. As it was, he turned down his Ewald with a feeling of annoyance and went across the hall to the parlour.

Mrs. Davis was sitting on the sofa, looking about her with an air of scornful disapproval.

What a scandalous room! There were no curtains on the window. Mrs. Davis did not know that Faith and Una had taken them down the day before to use as court trains in one of their plays and had forgotten to put them up again, but she could not have accused those windows more fiercely if she had known. The blinds were cracked and torn. The pictures on the walls were crooked; the rugs were awry; the vases were full of faded flowers; the dust lay in heaps—literally in heaps.

"What are we coming to?" Mrs. Davis asked herself, and then primmed up her unbeautiful mouth.

Jerry and Carl had been whooping and sliding down the banisters as she came through the hall. They did not see her and continued whooping and sliding, and Mrs. Davis was convinced they did it on purpose. Faith's pet rooster ambled through the hall, stood in the parlour doorway and looked at her. Not liking her looks, he did not venture in. Mrs. Davis gave a scornful sniff. A pretty manse, indeed, where roosters paraded the halls and stared people out of countenance.

"Shoo, there," commanded Mrs. Davis, poking her flounced, changeable-silk parasol at him.

Adam shooed. He was a wise rooster and Mrs. Davis had wrung the necks of so many roosters with her own fair hands in the course of her fifty years that an air of the executioner seemed to hang around her. Adam scuttled through the hall as the minister came in.

Mr. Meredith still wore slippers and dressing gown, and his dark hair still fell in uncared-for locks over his high brow. But he looked the gentleman he was; and Mrs. Alec Davis, in her silk dress and beplumed bonnet, and kid gloves and gold chain looked the vulgar, coarse-souled woman she was. Each felt the antagonisn of the other's personality. Mr. Meredith shrank, but

Mrs. Davis girded up her loins for the fray. She had come to the manse to propose a certain thing to the minister and she meant to lose no time in proposing it. She was going to do him a favour—a great favour—and the sooner he was made aware of it the better. She had been thinking about it all summer and had come to a decision at last. This was all that mattered, Mrs. Davis thought. When she decided a thing it WAS decided. Nobody else had any say in the matter. That had always been her attitude. When she had made her mind up to marry Alec Davis she had married him and that was the end to it. Alec had never known how it happened, but what odds? So in this case—Mrs. Davis had arranged everything to her own satisfaction. Now it only remained to inform Mr. Meredith.

"Will you please shut that door?" said Mrs. Davis, unprimming her mouth slightly to say it, but speaking with asperity. "I have something important to say, and I can't say it with that racket in the hall."

Mr. Meredith shut the door meekly. Then he sat down before Mrs. Davis. He was not wholly aware of her yet. His mind was still wrestling with Ewald's arguments. Mrs. Davis sensed this detachment and it annoyed her.

"I have come to tell you, Mr. Meredith," she said aggressively, "that I have decided to adopt Una."

"To—adopt—Una!" Mr. Meredith gazed at her blankly, not understanding in the least.

"Yes. I've been thinking it over for some time. I have often thought of adopting a child, since my husband's death. But it seemed so hard to get a suitable one. It is very few children I would want to take into MY home. I wouldn't think of taking a home child—some outcast of the slums in all probability. And there is hardly ever any other child to be got. One of the fishermen down at the harbour died last fall and left six youngsters. They tried to get me to take one, but I soon gave them to understand that I had no idea of adopting trash like that. Their grandfather stole a horse. Besides, they were all boys and I wanted a girl—a quiet, obedient girl that I could train up to be a lady. Una will suit me exactly. She would be a nice little thing if she was properly looked after—so different from Faith. I would never dream of adopting Faith. But I'll take Una and I'll give her a good home, and up-bringing, Mr. Meredith, and if she behaves herself I'll leave her all my money when I die. Not one of my own relatives shall have a cent of it in any case, I'm determined on that. It was the idea of aggravating them that set me to thinking of adopting a child as much as anything in the first place. Una shall be well dressed and educated and trained, Mr. Meredith, and I shall give her music and painting lessons and treat her as if she was my own."

Mr. Meredith was wide enough awake by this time. There was a faint flush in his pale cheek and a dangerous light in his fine dark eyes. Was this woman, whose vulgarity and consciousness of money oozed out of her at every pore, actually asking him to give her Una—his dear little wistful Una with Cecilia's own dark-blue eyes—the child whom the dying mother had clasped to her heart after the other children had been led weeping from the room. Cecilia had clung to her baby until the gates of death had shut between them. She had looked over the little dark head to her husband.

"Take good care of her, John," she had entreated. "She is so small—and sensitive. The others can fight their way—but the world will hurt HER. Oh, John, I don't know what you and she are going to do. You both need me so much. But keep her close to you—keep her close to you."

These had been almost her last words except a few unforgettable ones for him alone. And it was this child whom Mrs. Davis had coolly announced her intention of taking from him. He sat up straight and looked at Mrs. Davis. In spite of the worn dressing gown and the frayed slippers there was something about him that made Mrs. Davis feel a little of the old reverence for "the cloth" in which she had been brought up. After all, there WAS a certain divinity hedging a minister, even a poor, unworldly, abstracted one.

"I thank you for your kind intentions, Mrs. Davis," said Mr. Meredith with a gentle, final, quite awful courtesy, "but I cannot give you my child."

Mrs. Davis looked blank. She had never dreamed of his refusing.

"Why, Mr. Meredith," she said in astonishment. "You must be cr—you can't mean it. You must think it over—think of all the advantages I can give her."

"There is no need to think it over, Mrs. Davis. It is entirely out of the question. All the worldly advantages it is in your power to bestow on her could not compensate for the loss of a father's love and care. I thank you again—but it is not to be thought of."

Disappointment angered Mrs. Davis beyond the power of old habit to control. Her broad red face turned purple and her voice trembled.

"I thought you'd be only too glad to let me have her," she sneered.

"Why did you think that?" asked Mr. Meredith quietly.

"Because nobody ever supposed you cared anything about any of your children," retorted Mrs. Davis contemptuously. "You neglect them scandalously. It is the talk of the place. They aren't fed and dressed properly, and they're not trained at all. They have no more manners than a pack of wild Indians. You never think of doing your duty as a father. You let a stray child come here among them for a fortnight and never took any notice of her—a child that swore like a trooper I'm told. YOU wouldn't have cared if they'd caught small-pox from her. And Faith made an exhibition of herself getting up in preaching and making that speech! And she rid a pig down the street—under your very eyes I understand. The way they act is past belief and you never lift a finger to stop them or try to teach them anything. And now when I offer one of them a good home and good prospects you refuse it and insult me. A pretty father you, to talk of loving and caring for your children!"

"That will do, woman!" said Mr. Meredith. He stood up and looked at Mrs. Davis with eyes that made her quail. "That will do," he repeated. "I desire to hear no more, Mrs. Davis. You have said too much. It may be that I have been remiss in some respects in my duty as a parent, but it is not for you to remind me of it in such terms as you have used. Let us say good afternoon."

Mrs. Davis did not say anything half so amiable as good afternoon, but she took her departure. As she swept past the minister a large, plump toad, which Carl had secreted under the lounge, hopped out almost under her feet. Mrs. Davis gave a shriek and in trying to avoid treading on the awful thing, lost her balance and her parasol. She did not exactly fall, but she staggered and reeled across the room in a very undignified fashion and brought up against the door with a thud that jarred her from head to foot. Mr. Meredith, who had not seen the toad, wondered if she had been attacked with some kind of apoplectic or paralytic seizure, and ran in alarm to her assistance. But Mrs. Davis, recovering her feet, waved him back furiously.

"Don't you dare to touch me," she almost shouted. "This is some more of your children's doings, I suppose. This is no fit place for a decent woman. Give me my umbrella and let me go. I'll never darken the doors of your manse or your church again."

Mr. Meredith picked up the gorgeous parasol meekly enough and gave it to her. Mrs. Davis seized it and marched out. Jerry and Carl had given up banister sliding and were sitting on the edge of the veranda with Faith. Unfortunately, all three were singing at the tops of their healthy young voices "There'll be a hot time in the old town to-night." Mrs. Davis believed the song was meant for her and her only. She stopped and shook her parasol at them.

"Your father is a fool," she said, "and you are three young varmints that ought to be whipped within an inch of your lives."

"He isn't," cried Faith. "We're not," cried the boys. But Mrs. Davis was gone.

"Goodness, isn't she mad!" said Jerry. "And what is a 'varmint' anyhow?"

John Meredith paced up and down the parlour for a few minutes; then he went back to his study and sat down. But he did not return to his German theology. He was too grievously disturbed for that. Mrs. Davis had wakened him up with a vengeance. WAS he such a remiss, careless father as she had accused him of being? HAD he so scandalously neglected the bodily and spiritual welfare of the four little motherless creatures dependent on him? WERE his people talking of it as harshly as Mrs. Davis had declared? It must be so, since Mrs. Davis had come to ask for Una in the full and confident belief that he would hand the child over to her as unconcernedly and gladly as one might hand over a strayed, unwelcome kitten. And, if so, what then?

John Meredith groaned and resumed his pacing up and down the dusty, disordered room. What could he do? He loved his children as deeply as any father could and he knew, past the power of Mrs. Davis or any of her ilk, to disturb his conviction, that they loved him devotedly. But WAS he fit to have charge of them? He knew—none better—his weaknesses and limitations. What was needed was a good woman's presence and influence and common sense. But how could that be arranged? Even were he able to get such a housekeeper it would cut Aunt Martha to the quick. She believed she could still do all that was meet and necessary. He could not so hurt and insult the poor old woman who had been so kind to him and his. How devoted she had been to Cecilia! And Cecilia had asked him to be very considerate of Aunt Martha. To be sure, he suddenly remembered that Aunt Martha had once hinted that he ought to marry again. He felt she would not resent a wife as she would a housekeeper. But that was out of the question. He did not wish to marry—he did not and could not care for anyone. Then what could he do? It suddenly occurred to him that he would go over to Ingleside and talk over his difficulties with Mrs. Blythe. Mrs. Blythe was one of the few women he never felt shy or tongue-tied with. She was always so sympathetic and refreshing. It might be that she could suggest some solution of his problems. And even if she could not Mr. Meredith felt that he needed a little decent human companionship after his dose of Mrs. Davis—something to take the taste of her out of his soul.

He dressed hurriedly and ate his supper less abstractedly than usual. It occurred to him that it was a poor meal. He looked at his children; they were rosy and healthy looking enough—except Una, and she had never been very strong even when her mother was alive. They were all laughing and talking—certainly they seemed happy. Carl was especially happy because he had two most beautiful spiders crawling around his supper plate. Their voices were pleasant, their manners did not seem bad, they were considerate of and gentle to one another. Yet Mrs. Davis had said their behaviour was the talk of the congregation.

As Mr. Meredith went through his gate Dr. Blythe and Mrs. Blythe drove past on the road that led to Lowbridge. The minister's face fell. Mrs. Blythe was going away—there was no use in going to Ingleside. And he craved a little companionship more than ever. As he gazed rather hopelessly over the landscape the sunset light struck on a window of the old West homestead on the hill. It flared out rosily like a beacon of good hope. He suddenly remembered Rosemary and Ellen West. He thought that he would relish some of Ellen's pungent conversation. He thought it would be pleasant to see Rosemary's slow, sweet smile and calm, heavenly blue eyes again. What did that old poem of Sir Philip Sidney's say?—"continual comfort in a face"—that just suited her. And he needed comfort. Why not go and call? He remembered that Ellen had asked him to drop in sometimes and there was Rosemary's book to take back—he ought to take it back before he forgot. He had an uneasy suspicion that there were a great many books in his library which he had borrowed at sundry times and in divers places and had forgotten to take back. It was surely his duty to guard against that in this case. He went back into his study, got the book, and plunged downward into Rainbow Valley.

15. MORE GOSSIP

On the evening after Mrs. Myra Murray of the over-harbour section had been buried Miss Cornelia and Mary Vance came up to Ingleside. There were several things concerning which Miss Cornelia wished to unburden her soul. The funeral had to be all talked over, of course. Susan and Miss Cornelia thrashed this out between them; Anne took no part or delight in such goulish conversations. She sat a little apart and watched the autumnal flame of dahlias in the garden, and the dreaming, glamorous harbour of the September sunset. Mary Vance sat beside her, knitting meekly. Mary's heart was down in the Rainbow Valley, whence came sweet, distance-softened sounds of children's laughter, but her fingers were under Miss Cornelia's eye. She had to knit so many rounds of her stocking before she might go to the valley. Mary knit and held her tongue, but used her ears.

"I never saw a nicer looking corpse," said Miss Cornelia judicially. "Myra Murray was always a pretty woman—she was a Corey from Lowbridge and the Coreys were noted for their good looks."

"I said to the corpse as I passed it, 'poor woman. I hope you are as happy as you look.'" sighed Susan. "She had not changed much. That dress she wore was the black satin she got for her daughter's wedding fourteen years ago. Her Aunt told her then to keep it for her funeral, but Myra laughed and said, 'I may wear it to my funeral, Aunty, but I will have a good time out of it first.' And I may say she did. Myra Murray was not a woman to attend her own funeral before she died. Many a time afterwards when I saw her enjoying herself out in company I thought to myself, 'You are a handsome woman, Myra Murray, and that dress becomes you, but it will likely be your shroud at last.' And you see my words have come true, Mrs. Marshall Elliott."

Susan sighed again heavily. She was enjoying herself hugely. A funeral was really a delightful subject of conversation.

"I always liked to meet Myra," said Miss Cornelia. "She was always so gay and cheerful—she made you feel better just by her handshake. Myra always made the best of things."

"That is true," asserted Susan. "Her sister-in-law told me that when the doctor told her at last that he could do nothing for her and she would never rise from that bed again, Myra said quite cheerfully, 'Well, if that is so, I'm thankful the preserving is all done, and I will not have to face the fall house-cleaning. I always liked house-cleaning in spring,' she says, 'but I always hated it in the fall. I will get clear of it this year, thank goodness.' There are people who would call that levity, Mrs. Marshall Elliott, and I think her sister-in-law was a little ashamed of it. She said perhaps her sickness had made Myra a little light-headed. But I said, 'No, Mrs. Murray, do not worry over it. It was just Myra's way of looking at the bright side.'"

"Her sister Luella was just the opposite," said Miss Cornelia. "There was no bright side for Luella—there was just black and shades of gray. For years she used always to be declaring she was going to die in a week or so. 'I won't be here to burden you long,' she would tell her family with a groan. And if any of them ventured to talk about their little future plans she'd groan also and say, 'Ah, *I* won't be here then.' When I went to see her I always agreed with her and it made her so mad that she was always quite a lot better for several days afterwards. She has better health now but no more cheerfulness. Myra was so different. She was always doing or saying something to make some one feel good. Perhaps the men they married had something to do with it. Luella's man was a Tartar, believe ME, while Jim Murray was decent, as men go. He looked heart-broken to-day. It isn't often I feel sorry for a man at his wife's funeral, but I did feel for Jim Murray."

"No wonder he looked sad. He will not get a wife like Myra again in a hurry," said Susan. "Maybe he will not try, since his children are all grown up and Mirabel is able to keep house. But there is no predicting what a widower may or may not do and I, for one, will not try."

"We'll miss Myra terrible in church," said Miss Cornelia. "She was such a worker. Nothing ever stumped HER. If she couldn't get over a difficulty she'd get around it, and if she couldn't get around it she'd pretend it wasn't there—and generally it wasn't. 'I'll keep a stiff upper lip to my journey's end,' said she to me once. Well, she has ended her journey."

"Do you think so?" asked Anne suddenly, coming back from dreamland. "I can't picture HER journey as being ended. Can YOU think of her sitting down and folding her hands—that eager, asking spirit of hers, with its fine adventurous outlook? No, I think in death she just opened a gate and went through—on—on—to new, shining adventures."

"Maybe—maybe," assented Miss Cornelia. "Do you know, Anne dearie, I never was much taken with this everlasting rest doctrine myself—though I hope it isn't heresy to say so. I want to bustle round in heaven the same as here. And I hope there'll be a celestial substitute for pies and doughnuts—something that has to be MADE. Of course, one does get awful tired at times—and the older you are the tireder you get. But the very tiredest could get rested in something short of eternity, you'd think—except, perhaps, a lazy man."

"When I meet Myra Murray again," said Anne, "I want to see her coming towards me, brisk and laughing, just as she always did here."

"Oh, Mrs. Dr. dear," said Susan, in a shocked tone, "you surely do not think that Myra will be laughing in the world to come?"

"Why not, Susan? Do you think we will be crying there?"

"No, no, Mrs. Dr. dear, do not misunderstand me. I do not think we shall be either crying or laughing."

"What then?"

"Well," said Susan, driven to it, "it is my opinion, Mrs. Dr. dear, that we shall just look solemn and holy."

"And do you really think, Susan," said Anne, looking solemn enough, "that either Myra Murray or I could look solemn and holy all the time—ALL the time, Susan?"

"Well," admitted Susan reluctantly, "I might go so far as to say that you both would have to smile now and again, but I can never admit that there will be laughing in heaven. The idea seems really irreverent, Mrs. Dr. dear."

"Well, to come back to earth," said Miss Cornelia, "who can we get to take Myra's class in Sunday School? Julia Clow has been teaching it since Myra took ill, but she's going to town for the winter and we'll have to get somebody else."

"I heard that Mrs. Laurie Jamieson wanted it," said Anne. "The Jamiesons have come to church very regularly since they moved to the Glen from Lowbridge."

"New brooms!" said Miss Cornelia dubiously. "Wait till they've gone regularly for a year."

"You cannot depend on Mrs. Jamieson a bit, Mrs. Dr. dear," said Susan solemnly. "She died once and when they were measuring her for her coffin, after laying her out just beautiful, did she not go and come back to life! Now, Mrs. Dr. dear, you know you CANNOT depend on a woman like that."

"She might turn Methodist at any moment," said Miss Cornelia. "They tell me they went to the Methodist Church at Lowbridge quite as often as to the Presbyterian. I haven't caught them at it here yet, but I would not approve of taking Mrs. Jamieson into the Sunday School. Yet we must not offend them. We are losing too many people, by death or bad temper. Mrs. Alec Davis has left the church, no one knows why. She told the managers that she would never pay another cent to Mr. Meredith's salary. Of course, most people say that the children offended her, but somehow I don't think so. I tried to pump Faith, but all I could get out of her was that Mrs. Davis had come, seemingly in high good humour, to see her father, and had left in an awful rage, calling them all 'varmints!'"

"Varmints, indeed!" said Susan furiously. "Does Mrs. Alec Davis forget that her uncle on her mother's side was suspected of poisoning his wife? Not that it was ever proved, Mrs. Dr. dear, and it does not do to believe all you hear. But if *I* had an uncle whose wife died without any satisfactory reason, *I* would not go about the country calling innocent children varmints."

"The point is," said Miss Cornelia, "that Mrs. Davis paid a large subscription, and how its loss is going to be made up is a problem. And if she turns the other Douglases against Mr. Meredith, as she will certainly try to do, he will just have to go."

"I do not think Mrs. Alec Davis is very well liked by the rest of the clan," said Susan. "It is not likely she will be able to influence them."

"But those Douglases all hang together so. If you touch one, you touch all. We can't do without them, so much is certain. They pay half the salary. They are not mean, whatever else may be said of them. Norman Douglas used to give a hundred a year long ago before he left."

"What did he leave for?" asked Anne.

"He declared a member of the session cheated him in a cow deal. He hasn't come to church for twenty years. His wife used to come regular while she was alive, poor thing, but he never would let her pay anything, except one red cent every Sunday. She felt dreadfully humiliated. I don't know that he was any too good a husband to her, though she was never heard to complain. But she always had a cowed look. Norman Douglas didn't get the woman he wanted thirty years ago and the Douglases never liked to put up with second best."

"Who was the woman he did want."

"Ellen West. They weren't engaged exactly, I believe, but they went about together for two years. And then they just broke off—nobody ever know why. Just some silly quarrel, I suppose. And Norman went and married Hester Reese before his temper had time to cool—married her just to spite Ellen, I haven't a doubt. So like a man! Hester was a nice little thing, but she never had much spirit and he broke what little she had. She was too meek for Norman. He needed a woman who could stand up to him. Ellen would have kept him in fine order and he would have liked her all the better for it. He despised Hester, that is the truth, just because she always gave in to him. I used to hear him say many a time, long ago when he was a young fellow 'Give me a spunky woman—spunk for me every time.' And then he went and married a girl who couldn't say boo to a goose—man-like. That family of Reeses were just vegetables. They went through the motions of living, but they didn't LIVE."

"Russell Reese used his first wife's wedding-ring to marry his second," said Susan reminiscently. "That was TOO economical in my opinion, Mrs. Dr. dear. And his brother John has his own tombstone put up in the over-harbour graveyard, with everything on it but the date of death, and he goes and looks at it every Sunday. Most folks would not consider that much fun, but it is plain he does. People do have such different ideas of enjoyment. As for Norman Douglas, he is a perfect heathen. When the last minister asked him why he never went to church he said 'Too many ugly women there, parson—too many ugly women!' I should like to go to such a man, Mrs. Dr. dear, and say to him solemnly, 'There is a hell!'"

"Oh, Norman doesn't believe there is such a place," said Miss Cornelia. "I hope he'll find out his mistake when he comes to die. There, Mary, you've knit your three inches and you can go and play with the children for half an hour."

Mary needed no second bidding. She flew to Rainbow Valley with a heart as light as her heels, and in the course of conversation told Faith Meredith all about Mrs. Alec Davis.

"And Mrs. Elliott says that she'll turn all the Douglases against your father and then he'll have to leave the Glen because his salary won't be paid," concluded Mary. "*I* don't know what is to be done, honest to goodness. If only old Norman Douglas would come back to church and pay, it wouldn't be so bad. But he won't—and the Douglases will leave—and you all will have to go."

Faith carried a heavy heart to bed with her that night. The thought of leaving the Glen was unbearable. Nowhere else in the world were there such chums as the Blythes. Her little heart had been wrung when they had left Maywater—she had shed many bitter tears when she parted with Maywater chums and the old manse there where her mother had lived and died. She could not contemplate calmly the thought of such another and harder wrench. She COULDN'T leave Glen St. Mary and dear Rainbow Valley and that delicious graveyard.

"It's awful to be minister's family," groaned Faith into her pillow. "Just as soon as you get fond of a place you are torn up by the roots. I'll never, never, NEVER marry a minister, no matter how nice he is."

Faith sat up in bed and looked out of the little vine-hung window. The night was very still, the silence broken only by Una's soft breathing. Faith felt terribly alone in the world. She could see Glen St. Mary lying under the starry blue meadows of the autumn night. Over the valley a light shone from the girls' room at Ingleside, and another from Walter's room. Faith wondered if poor Walter had toothache again. Then she sighed, with a little passing sigh of envy of Nan and Di. They had a mother and a settled home—THEY were not at the mercy of people who got angry without any reason and called you a varmint. Away beyond the Glen, amid fields that were very quiet with sleep, another light was burning. Faith knew it shone in the house where Norman Douglas lived. He was reputed to sit up all hours of the night reading. Mary had said if he could only be induced to return to the church all would be well. And why not? Faith looked at a big, low star hanging over the tall, pointed spruce at the gate of the Methodist Church and had an inspiration. She knew what ought to be done and she, Faith Meredith, would do it. She would make everything right. With a sigh of satisfaction, she turned from the lonely, dark world and cuddled down beside Una.

16. TIT FOR TAT

With Faith, to decide was to act. She lost no time in carrying out the idea. As soon as she came home from school the next day she left the manse and made her way down the Glen. Walter Blythe joined her as she passed the post office.

"I'm going to Mrs. Elliott's on an errand for mother," he said. "Where are you going, Faith?"

"I am going somewhere on church business," said Faith loftily. She did not volunteer any further information and Walter felt rather snubbed. They walked on in silence for a little while. It was a warm, windy evening with a sweet, resinous air. Beyond the sand dunes were gray seas, soft and beautiful. The Glen brook bore down a freight of gold and crimson leaves, like fairy shallops. In Mr. James Reese's buckwheat stubble-land, with its beautiful tones of red and brown, a crow parliament was being held, whereat solemn deliberations regarding the welfare of crowland were in progress. Faith cruelly broke up the august assembly by climbing up on the fence and hurling a broken rail at it. Instantly the air was filled with flapping black wings and indignant caws.

"Why did you do that?" said Walter reproachfully. "They were having such a good time."

"Oh, I hate crows," said Faith airily. "The are so black and sly I feel sure they're hypocrites.

They steal little birds' eggs out of their nests, you know. I saw one do it on our lawn last spring. Walter, what makes you so pale to-day? Did you have the toothache again last night?"

Walter shivered.

"Yes—a raging one. I couldn't sleep a wink—so I just paced up and down the floor and imagined I was an early Christian martyr being tortured at the command of Nero. That helped ever so much for a while—and then I got so bad I couldn't imagine anything."

"Did you cry?" asked Faith anxiously.

"No—but I lay down on the floor and groaned," admitted Walter. "Then the girls came in and Nan put cayenne pepper in it—and that made it worse—Di made me hold a swallow of cold water in my mouth—and I couldn't stand it, so they called Susan. Susan said it served me right for sitting up in the cold garret yesterday writing poetry trash. But she started up the kitchen fire and got me a hot-water bottle and it stopped the toothache. As soon as I felt better I told Susan my poetry wasn't trash and she wasn't any judge. And she said no, thank goodness she was not and she did not know anything about poetry except that it was mostly a lot of lies. Now you know, Faith, that isn't so. That is one reason why I like writing poetry—you can say so many things in it that are true in poetry but wouldn't be true in prose. I told Susan so, but she said to stop my jawing and go to sleep before the water got cold, or she'd leave me to see if rhyming would cure toothache, and she hoped it would be a lesson to me."

"Why don't you go to the dentist at Lowbridge and get the tooth out?"

Walter shivered again.

"They want me to—but I can't. It would hurt so."

"Are you afraid of a little pain?" asked Faith contemptuously.

Walter flushed.

"It would be a BIG pain. I hate being hurt. Father said he wouldn't insist on my going—he'd wait until I'd made up my own mind to go."

"It wouldn't hurt as long as the toothache," argued Faith, "You've had five spells of toothache. If you'd just go and have it out there'd be no more bad nights. *I* had a tooth out once. I yelled for a moment, but it was all over then—only the bleeding."

"The bleeding is worst of all—it's so ugly," cried Walter. "It just made me sick when Jem cut his foot last summer. Susan said I looked more like fainting than Jem did. But I couldn't hear to see Jem hurt, either. Somebody is always getting hurt, Faith—and it's awful. I just can't BEAR to see things hurt. It makes me just want to run—and run—and run—till I can't hear or see them."

"There's no use making a fuss over anyone getting hurt," said Faith, tossing her curls. "Of course, if you've hurt yourself very bad, you have to yell—and blood IS messy—and I don't like seeing other people hurt, either. But I don't want to run—I want to go to work and help them. Your father HAS to hurt people lots of times to cure them. What would they do if HE ran away?"

"I didn't say I WOULD run. I said I WANTED to run. That's a different thing. I want to help people, too. But oh, I wish there weren't any ugly, dreadful things in the world. I wish everything was glad and beautiful."

"Well, don't let's think of what isn't," said Faith. "After all, there's lots of fun in being alive. You wouldn't have toothache if you were dead, but still, wouldn't you lots rather be alive than dead? I would, a hundred times. Oh, here's Dan Reese. He's been down to the harbour for fish."

"I hate Dan Reese," said Walter.

"So do I. All us girls do. I'm just going to walk past and never take the least notice of him. You watch me!"

Faith accordingly stalked past Dan with her chin out and an expression of scorn that bit into his soul. He turned and shouted after her.

"Pig-girl! Pig-girl!! Pig-girl!!!" in a crescendo of insult.

Faith walked on, seemingly oblivious. But her lip trembled slightly with a sense of outrage. She knew she was no match for Dan Reese when it came to an exchange of epithets. She wished Jem Blythe had been with her instead of Walter. If Dan Reese had dared to call her a pig-girl in Jem's hearing, Jem would have wiped up the dust with him. But it never occurred to Faith to expect Walter to do it, or blame him for not doing it. Walter, she knew, never fought other boys. Neither did Charlie Clow of the north road. The strange part was that, while she despised Charlie for a coward, it never occurred to her to disdain Walter. It was simply that he seemed to her an inhabitant of a world of his own, where different traditions prevailed. Faith would as soon have expected a starry-eyed young angel to pummel dirty, freckled Dan Reese for her as Walter Blythe. She would not have blamed the angel and she did not blame Walter Blythe. But she wished that sturdy Jem or Jerry had been there and Dan's insult continued to rankle in her soul.

Walter was pale no longer. He had flushed crimson and his beautiful eyes were clouded with shame and anger. He knew that he ought to have avenged Faith. Jem would have sailed right in and made Dan eat his words with bitter sauce. Ritchie Warren would have overwhelmed Dan with worse "names" than Dan had called Faith. But Walter could not—simply could not—"call names." He knew he would get the worst of it. He could never conceive or utter the vulgar, ribald insults of which Dan Reese had unlimited command. And as for the trial by fist, Walter couldn't fight. He hated the idea. It was rough and painful—and, worst of all, it was ugly. He never could understand Jem's exultation in an occasional conflict. But he wished he COULD fight Dan Reese. He was horribly ashamed because Faith Meredith had been insulted in his presence and he had not tried to punish her insulter. He felt sure she must despise him. She had not even spoken to him since Dan had called her pig-girl. He was glad when they came to the parting of the ways.

Faith, too, was relieved, though for a different reason. She wanted to be alone because she suddenly felt rather nervous about her errand. Impulse had cooled, especially since Dan had bruised her self-respect. She must go through with it, but she no longer had enthusiasm to sustain her. She was going to see Norman Douglas and ask him to come back to church, and she began to be afraid of him. What had seemed so easy and simple up at the Glen seemed very different down here. She had heard a good deal about Norman Douglas, and she knew that even the biggest boys in school were afraid of him. Suppose he called her something nasty—she had heard he was given to that. Faith could not endure being called names—they subdued her far more quickly than a physical blow. But she would go on—Faith Meredith always went on. If she did not her father might have to leave the Glen.

At the end of the long lane Faith came to the house—a big, old-fashioned one with a row of soldierly Lombardies marching past it. On the back veranda Norman Douglas himself was sitting, reading a newspaper. His big dog was beside him. Behind, in the kitchen, where his housekeeper, Mrs. Wilson, was getting supper, there was a clatter of dishes—an angry clatter, for Norman Douglas had just had a quarrel with Mrs. Wilson, and both were in a very bad temper over it. Consequently, when Faith stepped on the veranda and Norman Douglas lowered his newspaper she found herself looking into the choleric eyes of an irritated man.

Norman Douglas was rather a fine-looking personage in his way. He had a sweep of long red beard over his broad chest and a mane of red hair, ungrizzled by the years, on his massive head. His high, white forehead was unwrinkled and his blue eyes could flash still with all the fire of his tempestuous youth. He could be very amiable when he liked, and he could be very terrible. Poor Faith, so anxiously bent on retrieving the situation in regard to the church, had caught him in one of his terrible moods.

He did not know who she was and he gazed at her with disfavour. Norman Douglas liked girls of spirit and flame and laughter. At this moment Faith was very pale. She was of the type to which colour means everything. Lacking her crimson cheeks she seemed meek and even insignificant. She looked apologetic and afraid, and the bully in Norman Douglas's heart stirred.

"Who the dickens are you? And what do you want here?" he demanded in his great resounding voice, with a fierce scowl.

For once in her life Faith had nothing to say. She had never supposed Norman Douglas was like THIS. She was paralyzed with terror of him. He saw it and it made him worse.

"What's the matter with you?" he boomed. "You look as if you wanted to say something and was scared to say it. What's troubling you? Confound it, speak up, can't you?"

No. Faith could not speak up. No words would come. But her lips began to tremble.

"For heaven's sake, don't cry," shouted Norman. "I can't stand snivelling. If you've anything to say, say it and have done. Great Kitty, is the girl possessed of a dumb spirit? Don't look at me like that—I'm human—I haven't got a tail! Who are you—who are you, I say?"

Norman's voice could have been heard at the harbour. Operations in the kitchen were suspended. Mrs. Wilson was listening open-eared and eyed. Norman put his huge brown hands on his knees and leaned forward, staring into Faith's pallid, shrinking face. He seemed to loom over her like some evil giant out of a fairy tale. She felt as if he would eat her up next thing, body and bones.

"I—am—Faith—Meredith," she said, in little more than a whisper.

"Meredith, hey? One of the parson's youngsters, hey? I've heard of you—I've heard of you! Riding on pigs and breaking the Sabbath! A nice lot! What do you want here, hey? What do you want of the old pagan, hey? *I* don't ask favours of parsons—and I don't give any. What do you want, I say?"

Faith wished herself a thousand miles away. She stammered out her thought in its naked simplicity.

"I came—to ask you—to go to church—and pay—to the salary."

Norman glared at her. Then he burst forth again.

"You impudent hussy—you! Who put you up to it, jade? Who put you up to it?"

"Nobody," said poor Faith.

"That's a lie. Don't lie to me! Who sent you here? It wasn't your father—he hasn't the smeddum of a flea—but he wouldn't send you to do what he dassn't do himself. I suppose it was some of them confounded old maids at the Glen, was it—was it, hey?"

"No—I—I just came myself."

"Do you take me for a fool?" shouted Norman.

"No—I thought you were a gentleman," said Faith faintly, and certainly without any thought of being sarcastic.

Norman bounced up.

"Mind your own business. I don't want to hear another word from you. If you wasn't such a kid I'd teach you to interfere in what doesn't concern you. When I want parsons or pill-dosers I'll send for them. Till I do I'll have no truck with them. Do you understand? Now, get out, cheese-face."

Faith got out. She stumbled blindly down the steps, out of the yard gate and into the lane. Half way up the lane her daze of fear passed away and a reaction of tingling anger possessed her. By the time she reached the end of the lane she was in such a furious temper as she had never experienced before. Norman Douglas' insults burned in her soul, kindling a scorching flame. Go home! Not she! She would go straight back and tell that old ogre just what she thought of him—she would show him—oh, wouldn't she! Cheese-face, indeed!

Unhesitatingly she turned and walked back. The veranda was deserted and the kitchen door shut. Faith opened the door without knocking, and went in. Norman Douglas had just sat down at the supper table, but he still held his newspaper. Faith walked inflexibly across the room, caught the paper from his hand, flung it on the floor and stamped on it. Then she faced him, with her flashing eyes and scarlet cheeks. She was such a handsome young fury that Norman Douglas hardly recognized her.

"What's brought you back?" he growled, but more in bewilderment than rage.

Unquailingly she glared back into the angry eyes against which so few people could hold their own.

"I have come back to tell you exactly what I think of you," said Faith in clear, ringing tones. "I am not afraid of you. You are a rude, unjust, tyrannical, disagreeable old man. Susan says you are sure to go to hell, and I was sorry for you, but I am not now. Your wife never had a new hat for ten years—no wonder she died. I am going to make faces at you whenever I see you after this. Every time I am behind you you will know what is happening. Father has a picture of the devil in a book in his study, and I mean to go home and write your name under it. You are an old vampire and I hope you'll have the Scotch fiddle!"

Faith did not know what a vampire meant any more than she knew what the Scotch fiddle was. She had heard Susan use the expressions and gathered from her tone that both were dire things. But Norman Douglas knew what the latter meant at least. He had listened in absolute silence to Faith's tirade. When she paused for breath, with a stamp of her foot, he suddenly burst into loud laughter. With a mighty slap of hand on knee he exclaimed,

"I vow you've got spunk, after all—I like spunk. Come, sit down—sit down!"

"I will not." Faith's eyes flashed more passionately. She thought she was being made fun of—treated contemptuously. She would have enjoyed another explosion of rage, but this cut deep. "I will not sit down in your house. I am going home. But I am glad I came back here and told you exactly what my opinion of you is."

"So am I—so am I," chuckled Norman. "I like you—you're fine—you're great. Such roses—such vim! Did I call her cheese-face? Why, she never smelt a cheese. Sit down. If you'd looked like that at the first, girl! So you'll write my name under the devil's picture, will you? But he's black, girl, he's black—and I'm red. It won't do—it won't do! And you hope I'll have the Scotch fiddle, do you? Lord love you, girl, I had IT when I was a boy. Don't wish it on me again. Sit down—sit in. We'll tak' a cup o' kindness."

"No, thank you," said Faith haughtily.

"Oh, yes, you will. Come, come now, I apologize, girl—I apologize. I made a fool of myself and I'm sorry. Man can't say fairer. Forget and forgive. Shake hands, girl—shake hands. She won't—no, she won't! But she must! Look-a-here, girl, if you'll shake hands and break bread with me I'll pay what I used to to the salary and I'll go to church the first Sunday in every month and I'll make Kitty Alec hold her jaw. I'm the only one in the clan can do it. Is it a bargain, girl?"

It seemed a bargain. Faith found herself shaking hands with the ogre and then sitting at his board. Her temper was over—Faith's tempers never lasted very long—but its excitement still sparkled in her eyes and crimsoned her cheeks. Norman Douglas looked at her admiringly.

"Go, get some of your best preserves, Wilson," he ordered, "and stop sulking, woman, stop sulking. What if we did have a quarrel, woman? A good squall clears the air and briskens things up. But no drizzling and fogging afterwards—no drizzling and fogging, woman. I can't stand that. Temper in a woman but no tears for me. Here, girl, is some messed up meat and potatoes for you. Begin on that. Wilson has some fancy name for it, but I call lit macanaccady. Anything I can't analyze in the eating line I call macanaccady and anything wet that puzzles me I call shallamagouslem. Wilson's tea is shallamagouslem. I swear she makes it out of burdocks. Don't take any of the ungodly black liquid—here's some milk for you. What did you say your name was?"

"Faith."

"No name that—no name that! I can't stomach such a name. Got any other?"

"No, sir."

"Don't like the name, don't like it. There's no smeddum to it. Besides, it makes me think of my Aunt Jinny. She called her three girls Faith, Hope, and Charity. Faith didn't believe in anything—Hope was a born pessimist—and Charity was a miser. You ought to be called Red Rose—you look like one when you're mad. I'LL call you Red Rose. And you've roped me into promising to go to church? But only once a month, remember—only once a month. Come now, girl, will you let me off? I used to pay a hundred to the salary every year and go to church. If I promise to pay two hundred a year will you let me off going to church? Come now!"

"No, no, sir," said Faith, dimpling roguishly. "I want you to go to church, too."

"Well, a bargain is a bargain. I reckon I can stand it twelve times a year. What a sensation it'll make the first Sunday I go! And old Susan Baker says I'm going to hell, hey? Do you believe I'll go there—come, now, do you?"

"I hope not, sir," stammered Faith in some confusion.

"WHY do you hope not? Come, now, WHY do you hope not? Give us a reason, girl—give us a reason."

"It—it must be a very—uncomfortable place, sir."

"Uncomfortable? All depends on your taste in comfortable, girl. I'd soon get tired of angels. Fancy old Susan in a halo, now!"

Faith did fancy it, and it tickled her so much that she had to laugh. Norman eyed her approvingly.

"See the fun of it, hey? Oh, I like you—you're great. About this church business, now—can your father preach?"

"He is a splendid preacher," said loyal Faith.

"He is, hey? I'll see—I'll watch out for flaws. He'd better be careful what he says before ME. I'll catch him—I'll trip him up—I'll keep tabs on his arguments. I'm bound to have some fun out of this church going business. Does he ever preach hell?"

"No—o—o—I don't think so."

"Too bad. I like sermons on that subject. You tell him that if he wants to keep me in good humour to preach a good rip-roaring sermon on hell once every six months—and the more brimstone the better. I like 'em smoking. And think of all the pleasure he'd give the old maids, too. They'd all keep looking at old Norman Douglas and thinking, 'That's for you, you old reprobate. That's what's in store for YOU!' I'll give an extra ten dollars every time you get your father to preach on hell. Here's Wilson and the jam. Like that, hey? IT isn't macanaccady. Taste!"

Faith obediently swallowed the big spoonful Norman held out to her. Luckily it WAS good.

"Best plum jam in the world," said Norman, filling a large saucer and plumping it down before her. "Glad you like it. I'll give you a couple of jars to take home with you. There's nothing mean about me—never was. The devil can't catch me at THAT corner, anyhow. It wasn't my fault that Hester didn't have a new hat for ten years. It was her own—she pinched on hats to save money to give yellow fellows over in China. *I* never gave a cent to missions in my life—never will. Never you try to bamboozle me into that! A hundred a year to the salary and church once a month—but no spoiling good heathens to make poor Christians! Why, girl, they wouldn't be fit for heaven or hell—clean spoiled for either place—clean spoiled. Hey, Wilson, haven't you got a smile on yet? Beats all how you women can sulk! *I* never sulked in my life—it's just one big flash and crash with me and then—pouf—the squall's over and the sun is out and you could eat out of my hand."

Norman insisted on driving Faith home after supper and he filled the buggy up with apples, cabbages, potatoes and pumpkins and jars of jam.

"There's a nice little tom-pussy out in the barn. I'll give you that too, if you'd like it. Say the word," he said.

"No, thank you," said Faith decidedly. "I don't like cats, and besides, I have a rooster."

"Listen to her. You can't cuddle a rooster as you can a kitten. Who ever heard of petting a rooster? Better take little Tom. I want to find a good home for him."

"No. Aunt Martha has a cat and he would kill a strange kitten."

Norman yielded the point rather reluctantly. He gave Faith an exciting drive home, behind his wild two-year old, and when he had let her out at the kitchen door of the manse and dumped his cargo on the back veranda he drove away shouting,

"It's only once a month—only once a month, mind!"

Faith went up to bed, feeling a little dizzy and breathless, as if she had just escaped from the grasp of a genial whirlwind. She was happy and thankful. No fear now that they would have to leave the Glen and the graveyard and Rainbow Valley. But she fell asleep troubled by a disagreeable subconsciousness that Dan Reese had called her pig-girl and that, having stumbled on such a congenial epithet, he would continue to call her so whenever opportunity offered.

17. A DOUBLE VICTORY

Norman Douglas came to church the first Sunday in November and made all the sensation he desired. Mr. Meredith shook hands with him absently on the church steps and hoped dreamily that Mrs. Douglas was well.

"She wasn't very well just before I buried her ten years ago, but I reckon she has better health now," boomed Norman, to the horror and amusement of every one except Mr. Meredith, who was absorbed in wondering if he had made the last head of his sermon as clear as he might have, and hadn't the least idea what Norman had said to him or he to Norman.

Norman intercepted Faith at the gate.

"Kept my word, you see—kept my word, Red Rose. I'm free now till the first Sunday in December. Fine sermon, girl—fine sermon. Your father has more in his head than he carries on his face. But he contradicted himself once—tell him he contradicted himself. And tell him I want that brimstone sermon in December. Great way to wind up the old year—with a taste of hell, you know. And what's the matter with a nice tasty discourse on heaven for New Year's? Though it wouldn't be half as interesting as hell, girl—not half. Only I'd like to know what your father thinks about heaven—he CAN think—rarest thing in the world—a person who can think. But he DID contradict himself. Ha, ha! Here's a question you might ask him sometime when he's awake, girl. 'Can God make a stone so big He couldn't lift it Himself?' Don't forget now. I want to hear his opinion on it. I've stumped many a minister with that, girl."

Faith was glad to escape him and run home. Dan Reese, standing among the crowd of boys at the gate, looked at her and shaped his mouth into "pig-girl," but dared not utter it aloud just there. Next day in school was a different matter. At noon recess Faith encountered Dan in the little spruce plantation behind the school and Dan shouted once more,

"Pig-girl! Pig-girl! ROOSTER-GIRL!"

Walter Blythe suddenly rose from a mossy cushion behind a little clump of firs where he had been reading. He was very pale, but his eyes blazed.

"You hold your tongue, Dan Reese!" he said.

"Oh, hello, Miss Walter," retorted Dan, not at all abashed. He vaulted airily to the top of the rail fence and chanted insultingly,

"Cowardy, cowardy-custard
Stole a pot of mustard,
Cowardy, cowardy-custard!"

"You are a coincidence!" said Walter scornfully, turning still whiter. He had only a very hazy idea what a coincidence was, but Dan had none at all and thought it must be something peculiarly opprobrious.

"Yah! Cowardy!" he yelled gain. "Your mother writes lies—lies—lies! And Faith Meredith is a pig-girl—a—pig-girl—a pig-girl! And she's a rooster-girl—a rooster-girl—a rooster-girl! Yah! Cowardy—cowardy—cust—"

Dan got no further. Walter had hurled himself across the intervening space and knocked Dan off the fence backward with one well-directed blow. Dan's sudden inglorious sprawl was greeted with a burst of laughter and a clapping of hands from Faith. Dan sprang up, purple with rage, and began to climb the fence. But just then the school-bell rang and Dan knew what happened to boys who were late during Mr. Hazard's regime.

"We'll fight this out," he howled. "Cowardy!"

"Any time you like," said Walter.

"Oh, no, no, Walter," protested Faith. "Don't fight him. *I* don't mind what he says—I wouldn't condescend to mind the like of HIM."

"He insulted you and he insulted my mother," said Walter, with the same deadly calm. "Tonight after school, Dan."

"I've got to go right home from school to pick taters after the harrows, dad says," answered Dan sulkily. "But to-morrow night'll do."

"All right—here to-morrow night," agreed Walter.

"And I'll smash your sissy-face for you," promised Dan.

Walter shuddered—not so much from fear of the threat as from repulsion over the ugliness and vulgarity of it. But he held his head high and marched into school. Faith followed in a conflict of emotions. She hated to think of Walter fighting that little sneak, but oh, he had been splendid! And he was going to fight for HER—Faith Meredith—to punish her insulter! Of course he would win—such eyes spelled victory.

Faith's confidence in her champion had dimmed a little by evening, however. Walter had seemed so very quiet and dull the rest of the day in school.

"If it were only Jem," she sighed to Una, as they sat on Hezekiah Pollock's tombstone in the graveyard. "HE is such a fighter—he could finish Dan off in no time. But Walter doesn't know much about fighting."

"I'm so afraid he'll be hurt," sighed Una, who hated fighting and couldn't understand the subtle, secret exultation she divined in Faith.

"He oughtn't to be," said Faith uncomfortably. "He's every bit as big as Dan."

"But Dan's so much older," said Una. "Why, he's nearly a year older."

"Dan hasn't done much fighting when you come to count up," said Faith. "I believe he's really a coward. He didn't think Walter would fight, or he wouldn't have called names before him. Oh, if you could just have seen Walter's face when he looked at him, Una! It made me shiver—with a nice shiver. He looked just like Sir Galahad in that poem father read us on Saturday."

"I hate the thought of them fighting and I wish it could be stopped," said Una.

"Oh, it's got to go on now," cried Faith. "It's a matter of honour. Don't you DARE tell anyone, Una. If you do I'll never tell you secrets again!"

"I won't tell," agreed Una. "But I won't stay to-morrow to watch the fight. I'm coming right home."

"Oh, all right. *I* have to be there—it would be mean not to, when Walter is fighting for me. I'm going to tie my colours on his arm—that's the thing to do when he's my knight. How lucky Mrs. Blythe gave me that pretty blue hair-ribbon for my birthday! I've only worn it twice so it will be almost new. But I wish I was sure Walter would win. It will be so—so HUMILIATING if he doesn't."

Faith would have been yet more dubious if she could have seen her champion just then. Walter had gone home from school with all his righteous anger at a low ebb and a very nasty feeling in its place. He had to fight Dan Reese the next night—and he didn't want to—he hated the thought of it. And he kept thinking of it all the time. Not for a minute could he get away from the thought. Would it hurt much? He was terribly afraid that it would hurt. And would he be defeated and shamed?

He could not eat any supper worth speaking of. Susan had made a big batch of his favourite monkey-faces, but he could choke only one down. Jem ate four. Walter wondered how he could. How could ANYBODY eat? And how could they all talk gaily as they were doing? There was mother, with her shining eyes and pink cheeks. SHE didn't know her son had to fight next day. Would she be so gay if she knew, Walter wondered darkly. Jem had taken Susan's picture with his new camera and the result was passed around the table and Susan was terribly indignant over it.

"I am no beauty, Mrs. Dr. dear, and well I know it, and have always known it," she said in an aggrieved tone, "but that I am as ugly as that picture makes me out I will never, no, never believe."

Jem laughed over this and Anne laughed again with him. Walter couldn't endure it. He got up and fled to his room.

"That child has got something on his mind, Mrs. Dr. dear," said Susan. "He has et next to nothing. Do you suppose he is plotting another poem?"

Poor Walter was very far removed in spirit from the starry realms of poesy just then. He propped his elbow on his open window-sill and leaned his head drearily on his hands.

"Come on down to the shore, Walter," cried Jem, busting in. "The boys are going to burn the sand-hill grass to-night. Father says we can go. Come on."

At any other time Walter would have been delighted. He gloried in the burning of the sand-hill grass. But now he flatly refused to go, and no arguments or entreaties could move him. Disappointed Jem, who did not care for the long dark walk to Four Winds Point alone, retreated to his museum in the garret and buried himself in a book. He soon forgot his disappointment, revelling with the heroes of old romance, and pausing occasionally to picture himself a famous general, leading his troops to victory on some great battlefield.

Walter sat at his window until bedtime. Di crept in, hoping to be told what was wrong, but Walter could not talk of it, even to Di. Talking of it seemed to give it a reality from which he shrank. It was torture enough to think of it. The crisp, withered leaves rustled on the maple trees outside his window. The glow of rose and flame had died out of the hollow, silvery sky, and the full moon was rising gloriously over Rainbow Valley. Afar off, a ruddy woodfire was painting a page of glory on the horizon beyond the hills. It was a sharp, clear evening when far-away sounds were heard distinctly. A fox was barking across the pond; an engine was puffing down at the Glen station; a blue-jay was screaming madly in the maple grove; there was laughter over on the manse lawn. How could people laugh? How could foxes and blue-jays and engines behave as if nothing were going to happen on the morrow?

"Oh, I wish it was over," groaned Walter.

He slept very little that night and had hard work choking down his porridge in the morning. Susan WAS rather lavish in her platefuls. Mr. Hazard found him an unsatisfactory pupil that day. Faith Meredith's wits seemed to be wool-gathering, too. Dan Reese kept drawing surreptitious pictures of girls, with pig or rooster heads, on his slate and holding them up for all to see. The news of the coming battle had leaked out and most of the boys and many of the girls were in the spruce plantation when Dan and Walter sought it after school. Una had gone home, but Faith was there, having tied her blue ribbon around Walter's arm. Walter was thankful that neither Jem nor Di nor Nan were among the crowd of spectators. Somehow they had not heard of what was in the wind and had gone home, too. Walter faced Dan quite undauntedly now. At the last moment all his fear had vanished, but he still felt disgust at the idea of fighting. Dan, it was noted, was really paler under his freckles than Walter was. One of the older boys gave the word and Dan struck Walter in the face.

Walter reeled a little. The pain of the blow tingled through all his sensitive frame for a moment. Then he felt pain no longer. Something, such as he had never experienced before, seemed to roll over him like a flood. His face flushed crimson, his eyes burned like flame. The scholars of Glen St. Mary school had never dreamed that "Miss Walter" could look like that. He hurled himself forward and closed with Dan like a young wildcat.

There were no particular rules in the fights of the Glen school boys. It was catch-as-catch can, and get your blows in anyhow. Walter fought with a savage fury and a joy in the struggle against which Dan could not hold his ground. It was all over very speedily. Walter had no clear consciousness of what he was doing until suddenly the red mist cleared from his sight and he found himself kneeling on the body of the prostrate Dan whose nose—oh, horror!—was spouting blood.

"Have you had enough?" demanded Walter through his clenched teeth.

Dan sulkily admitted that he had.

"My mother doesn't write lies?"

"No."

"Faith Meredith isn't a pig-girl?"

"No."

"Nor a rooster-girl?"

"No."

"And I'm not a coward?"

"No."

Walter had intended to ask, "And you are a liar?" but pity intervened and he did not humiliate Dan further. Besides, that blood was so horrible.

"You can go, then," he said contemptuously.

There was a loud clapping from the boys who were perched on the rail fence, but some of the girls were crying. They were frightened. They had seen schoolboy fights before, but nothing like Walter as he had grappled with Dan. There had been something terrifying about him. They thought he would kill Dan. Now that all was over they sobbed hysterically—except Faith, who still stood tense and crimson cheeked.

Walter did not stay for any conqueror's meed. He sprang over the fence and rushed down the spruce hill to Rainbow Valley. He felt none of the victor's joy, but he felt a certain calm satisfaction in duty done and honour avenged—mingled with a sickish qualm when he thought of Dan's gory nose. It had been so ugly, and Walter hated ugliness.

Also, he began to realize that he himself was somewhat sore and battered up. His lip was cut and swollen and one eye felt very strange. In Rainbow Valley he encountered Mr. Meredith, who was coming home from an afternoon call on the Miss Wests. That reverend gentleman looked gravely at him.

"It seems to me that you have been fighting, Walter?"

"Yes, sir," said Walter, expecting a scolding.

"What was it about?"

"Dan Reese said my mother wrote lies and that that Faith was a pig-girl," answered Walter bluntly.

"Oh—h! Then you were certainly justified, Walter."

"Do you think it's right to fight, sir?" asked Walter curiously.

"Not always—and not often—but sometimes—yes, sometimes," said John Meredith. "When womenkind are insulted for instance—as in your case. My motto, Walter, is, don't fight till you're sure you ought to, and THEN put every ounce of you into it. In spite of sundry discolorations I infer that you came off best."

"Yes. I made him take it all back."

"Very good—very good, indeed. I didn't think you were such a fighter, Walter."

"I never fought before—and I didn't want to right up to the last—and then," said Walter, determined to make a clean breast of it, "I liked it while I was at it."

The Rev. John's eyes twinkled.

"You were—a little frightened—at first?"

"I was a whole lot frightened," said honest Walter. "But I'm not going to be frightened any more, sir. Being frightened of things is worse than the things themselves. I'm going to ask father to take me over to Lowbridge to-morrow to get my tooth out."

"Right again. 'Fear is more pain than is the pain it fears.' Do you know who wrote that, Walter? It was Shakespeare. Was there any feeling or emotion or experience of the human heart that that wonderful man did not know? When you go home tell your mother I am proud of you."

Walter did not tell her that, however; but he told her all the rest, and she sympathized with him and told him she was glad he had stood up for her and Faith, and she anointed his sore spots and rubbed cologne on his aching head.

"Are all mothers as nice as you?" asked Walter, hugging her. "You're WORTH standing up for."

Miss Cornelia and Susan were in the living room when Anne came downstairs, and listened to the story with much enjoyment. Susan in particular was highly gratified.

"I am real glad to hear he has had a good fight, Mrs. Dr. dear. Perhaps it may knock that poetry nonsense out of him. And I never, no, never could bear that little viper of a Dan Reese. Will you not sit nearer to the fire, Mrs. Marshall Elliott? These November evenings are very chilly."

"Thank you, Susan, I'm not cold. I called at the manse before I came here and got quite warm—though I had to go to the kitchen to do it, for there was no fire anywhere else. The kitchen looked as if it had been stirred up with a stick, believe ME. Mr. Meredith wasn't home. I couldn't find out where he was, but I have an idea that he was up at the Wests'. Do you know, Anne dearie, they say he has been going there frequently all the fall and people are beginning to think he is going to see Rosemary."

"He would get a very charming wife if he married Rosemary," said Anne, piling driftwood on the fire. "She is one of the most delightful girls I've ever known—truly one of the race of Joseph."

"Ye—s—only she is an Episcopalian," said Miss Cornelia doubtfully. "Of course, that is better than if she was a Methodist—but I do think Mr. Meredith could find a good enough wife in his own denomination. However, very likely there is nothing in it. It's only a month ago that I said to him, 'You ought to marry again, Mr. Meredith.' He looked as shocked as if I had suggested something improper. 'My wife is in her grave, Mrs. Elliott,' he said, in that gentle, saintly way of his. 'I suppose so,' I said, 'or I wouldn't be advising you to marry again.' Then he looked more shocked than ever. So I doubt if there is much in this Rosemary story. If a single minister calls twice at a house where there is a single woman all the gossips have it he is courting her."

"It seems to me—if I may presume to say so—that Mr. Meredith is too shy to go courting a second wife," said Susan solemnly.

"He ISN'T shy, believe ME," retorted Miss Cornelia. "Absent-minded,—yes—but shy, no. And for all he is so abstracted and dreamy he has a very good opinion of himself, man-like, and when he is really awake he wouldn't think it much of a chore to ask any woman to have him. No, the trouble is, he's deluding himself into believing that his heart is buried, while all the time it's beating away inside of him just like anybody else's. He may have a notion of Rosemary West and he may not. If he has, we must make the best of it. She is a sweet girl and a fine housekeeper, and would make a good mother for those poor, neglected children. And," concluded Miss Cornelia resignedly, "my own grandmother was an Episcopalian."

18. MARY BRINGS EVIL TIDINGS

Mary Vance, whom Mrs. Elliott had sent up to the manse on an errand, came tripping down Rainbow Valley on her way to Ingleside where she was to spend the afternoon with Nan and Di as a Saturday treat. Nan and Di had been picking spruce gum with Faith and Una in the manse woods and the four of them were now sitting on a fallen pine by the brook, all, it must be admitted, chewing rather vigorously. The Ingleside twins were not allowed to chew spruce gum anywhere but in the seclusion of Rainbow Valley, but Faith and Una were unrestricted by such rules of etiquette and cheerfully chewed it everywhere, at home and abroad, to the very proper horror of the Glen. Faith had been chewing it in church one day; but Jerry had realized the enormity of THAT, and had given her such an older-brotherly scolding that she never did it again.

"I was so hungry I just felt as if I had to chew something," she protested. "You know well enough what breakfast was like, Jerry Meredith. I COULDN'T eat scorched porridge and my stomach just felt so queer and empty. The gum helped a lot—and I didn't chew VERY hard. I didn't make any noise and I never cracked the gum once."

"You mustn't chew gum in church, anyhow," insisted Jerry. "Don't let me catch you at it again."

"You chewed yourself in prayer-meeting last week," cried Faith.

"THAT'S different," said Jerry loftily. "Prayer-meeting isn't on Sunday. Besides, I sat away at the back in a dark seat and nobody saw me. You were sitting right up front where every one saw you. And I took the gum out of my mouth for the last hymn and stuck it on the back of the pew right up in front where every one saw you. Then I came away and forgot it. I went back to get it next morning, but it was gone. I suppose Rod Warren swiped it. And it was a dandy chew."

Mary Vance walked down the Valley with her head held high. She had on a new blue velvet cap with a scarlet rosette in it, a coat of navy blue cloth and a little squirrel-fur muff. She was very conscious of her new clothes and very well pleased with herself. Her hair was elaborately crimped, her face was quite plump, her cheeks rosy, her white eyes shining. She did not look much like the forlorn and ragged waif the Merediths had found in the old Taylor barn. Una tried not to feel envious. Here was Mary with a new velvet cap, but she and Faith had to wear their shabby old gray tams again this winter. Nobody ever thought of getting them new ones and they were afraid to ask their father for them for fear that he might be short of money and then he would feel badly. Mary had told them once that ministers were always short of money, and found it "awful hard" to make ends meet. Since then Faith and Una would have gone in rags rather than ask their father for anything if they could help it. They did not worry a great deal over their shabbiness; but it was rather trying to see Mary Vance coming out in such style and putting on such airs about it, too. The new squirrel muff was really the last straw. Neither Faith nor Una had ever had a muff, counting themselves lucky if they could compass mittens without holes in them. Aunt Martha could not see to darn holes and though Una tried to, she made sad cobbling. Somehow, they could not make their greeting of Mary very cordial. But Mary did not mind or notice that; she was not overly sensitive. She vaulted lightly to a seat on the pine tree, and laid the offending muff on a bough. Una saw that it was lined with shirred red satin and had red tassels. She looked down at her own rather purple, chapped, little hands and wondered if she would ever, EVER be able to put them into a muff like that.

"Give us a chew," said Mary companionably. Nan, Di and Faith all produced an amber-hued knot or two from their pockets and passed them to Mary. Una sat very still. She had four lovely big knots in the pocket of her tight, thread-bare little jacket, but she wasn't going to give one of them to Mary Vance—not one Let Mary pick her own gum! People with squirrel muffs needn't expect to get everything in the world.

"Great day, isn't it?" said Mary, swinging her legs, the better, perhaps, to display new boots with very smart cloth tops. Una tucked HER feet under her. There was a hole in the toe of one of her boots and both laces were much knotted. But they were the best she had. Oh, this Mary Vance! Why hadn't they left her in the old barn?

Una never felt badly because the Ingleside twins were better dressed than she and Faith were. THEY wore their pretty clothes with careless grace and never seemed to think about them at all. Somehow, they did not make other people feel shabby. But when Mary Vance was dressed up she seemed fairly to exude clothes—to walk in an atmosphere of clothes—to make everybody else feel and think clothes. Una, as she sat there in the honey-tinted sunshine of the gracious December afternoon, was acutely and miserably conscious of everything she had on—the faded tam, which was yet her best, the skimpy jacket she had worn for three winters, the holes in her skirt and her boots, the shivering insufficiency of her poor little undergarments. Of course, Mary was going out for a visit and she was not. But even if she had been she had nothing better to put on and in this lay the sting.

"Say, this is great gum. Listen to me cracking it. There ain't any gum spruces down at Four Winds," said Mary. "Sometimes I just hanker after a chew. Mrs. Elliott won't let me chew gum if she sees me. She says it ain't lady-like. This lady-business puzzles me. I can't get on to all its kinks. Say, Una, what's the matter with you? Cat got your tongue?"

"No," said Una, who could not drag her fascinated eyes from that squirrel muff. Mary leaned past her, picked it up and thrust it into Una's hands.

"Stick your paws in that for a while," she ordered. "They look sorter pinched. Ain't that a dandy muff? Mrs. Elliott give it to me last week for a birthday present. I'm to get the collar at Christmas. I heard her telling Mr. Elliott that."

"Mrs. Elliott is very good to you," said Faith.

"You bet she is. And I'M good to her, too," retorted Mary. "I work like a nigger to make it easy for her and have everything just as she likes it. We was made for each other. 'Tisn't every one could get along with her as well as I do. She's pizen neat, but so am I, and so we agree fine."

"I told you she would never whip you."

"So you did. She's never tried to lay a finger on me and I ain't never told a lie to her—not one, true's you live. She combs me down with her tongue sometimes though, but that just slips off ME like water off a duck's back. Say, Una, why didn't you hang on to the muff?"

Una had put it back on the bough.

"My hands aren't cold, thank you," she said stiffly.

"Well, if you're satisfied, *I* am. Say, old Kitty Alec has come back to church as meek as Moses and nobody knows why. But everybody is saying it was Faith brought Norman Douglas out. His housekeeper says you went there and gave him an awful tongue-lashing. Did you?"

"I went and asked him to come to church," said Faith uncomfortably.

"Fancy your spunk!" said Mary admiringly. "*I* wouldn't have dared do that and I'm not so slow. Mrs. Wilson says the two of you jawed something scandalous, but you come off best and then he just turned round and like to eat you up. Say, is your father going to preach here to-morrow?"

"No. He's going to exchange with Mr. Perry from Charlottetown. Father went to town this morning and Mr. Perry is coming out to-night."

"I THOUGHT there was something in the wind, though old Martha wouldn't give me any satisfaction. But I felt sure she wouldn't have been killing that rooster for nothing."

"What rooster? What do you mean?" cried Faith, turning pale.

"*I* don't know what rooster. I didn't see it. When she took the butter Mrs. Elliott sent up she said she'd been out to the barn killing a rooster for dinner tomorrow."

Faith sprang down from the pine.

"It's Adam—we have no other rooster—she has killed Adam."

"Now, don't fly off the handle. Martha said the butcher at the Glen had no meat this week and she had to have something and the hens were all laying and too poor."

"If she has killed Adam—" Faith began to run up the hill.

Mary shrugged her shoulders.

"She'll go crazy now. She was so fond of that Adam. He ought to have been in the pot long ago—he'll be as tough as sole leather. But *I* wouldn't like to be in Martha's shoes. Faith's just white with rage; Una, you'd better go after her and try to peacify her."

Mary had gone a few steps with the Blythe girls when Una suddenly turned and ran after her.

"Here's some gum for you, Mary," she said, with a little repentant catch in her voice, thrusting all her four knots into Mary's hands, "and I'm glad you have such a pretty muff."

"Why, thanks," said Mary, rather taken by surprise. To the Blythe girls, after Una had gone, she said, "Ain't she a queer little mite? But I've always said she had a good heart."

19. POOR ADAM!

When Una got home Faith was lying face downwards on her bed, utterly refusing to be comforted. Aunt Martha had killed Adam. He was reposing on a platter in the pantry that very minute, trussed and dressed, encircled by his liver and heart and gizzard. Aunt Martha heeded Faith's passion of grief and anger not a whit.

"We had to have something for the strange minister's dinner," she said. "You're too big a girl to make such a fuss over an old rooster. You knew he'd have to be killed sometime."

"I'll tell father when he comes home what you've done," sobbed Faith.

"Don't you go bothering your poor father. He has troubles enough. And I'M housekeeper here."

"Adam was MINE—Mrs. Johnson gave him to me. You had no business to touch him," stormed Faith.

"Don't you get sassy now. The rooster's killed and there's an end of it. I ain't going to set no strange minister down to a dinner of cold b'iled mutton. I was brought up to know better than that, if I have come down in the world."

Faith would not go down to supper that night and she would not go to church the next morning. But at dinner time she went to the table, her eyes swollen with crying, her face sullen.

The Rev. James Perry was a sleek, rubicund man, with a bristling white moustache, bushy white eyebrows, and a shining bald head. He was certainly not handsome and he was a very tiresome, pompous sort of person. But if he had looked like the Archangel Michael and talked with the tongues of men and angels Faith would still have utterly detested him. He carved Adam up dexterously, showing off his plump white hands and very handsome diamond ring. Also, he made jovial remarks all through the performance. Jerry and Carl giggled, and even Una smiled wanly, because she thought politeness demanded it. But Faith only scowled darkly. The Rev. James thought her manners shockingly bad. Once, when he was delivering himself of an unctuous remark to Jerry, Faith broke in rudely with a flat contradiction. The Rev. James drew his bushy eyebrows together at her.

"Little girls should not interrupt," he said, "and they should not contradict people who know far more than they do."

This put Faith in a worse temper than ever. To be called "little girl" as if she were no bigger than chubby Rilla Blythe over at Ingleside! It was insufferable. And how that abominable Mr. Perry did eat! He even picked poor Adam's bones. Neither Faith nor Una would touch a mouthful, and looked upon the boys as little better than cannibals. Faith felt that if that awful repast did not soon come to an end she would wind it up by throwing something at Mr. Perry's gleaming head. Fortunately, Mr. Perry found Aunt Martha's leathery apple pie too much even for his powers of mastication and the meal came to an end, after a long grace in which Mr. Perry offered up devout thanks for the food which a kind and beneficent Providence had provided for sustenance and temperate pleasure.

"God hadn't a single thing to do with providing Adam for you," muttered Faith rebelliously under her breath.

The boys gladly made their escape to outdoors, Una went to help Aunt Martha with the dishes—though that rather grumpy old dame never welcomed her timid assistance—and Faith betook herself to the study where a cheerful wood fire was burning in the grate. She thought she would thereby escape from the hated Mr. Perry, who had announced his intention of taking a nap in his room during the afternoon. But scarcely had Faith settled herself in a corner, with a book, when he walked in and, standing before the fire, proceeded to survey the disorderly study with an air of disapproval.

"You father's books seem to be in somewhat deplorable confusion, my little girl," he said severely.

Faith darkled in her corner and said not a word. She would NOT talk to this—this creature.

"You should try to put them in order," Mr. Perry went on, playing with his handsome watch chain and smiling patronizingly on Faith. "You are quite old enough to attend to such duties. MY little daughter at home is only ten and she is already an excellent little housekeeper and the greatest help and comfort to her mother. She is a very sweet child. I wish you had the privilege of her acquaintance. She could help you in many ways. Of course, you have not had the inestimable privilege of a good mother's care and training. A sad lack—a very sad lack. I have spoken more than once to your father in this connection and pointed out his duty to him faithfully, but so far with no effect. I trust he may awaken to a realization of his responsibility before it is too late. In the meantime, it is your duty and privilege to endeavour to take your sainted mother's place. You might exercise a great influence over your brothers and your little sister—you might be a true mother to them. I fear that you do not think of these things as you should. My dear child, allow me to open your eyes in regard to them."

Mr. Perry's oily, complacent voice trickled on. He was in his element. Nothing suited him better than to lay down the law, patronize and exhort. He had no idea of stopping, and he did not stop. He stood before the fire, his feet planted firmly on the rug, and poured out a flood of pompous platitudes. Faith heard not a word. She was really not listening to him at all. But she was watching his long black coat-tails with impish delight growing in her brown eyes. Mr. Perry was standing VERY near the fire. His coat-tails began to scorch—his coat-tails began to smoke. He still prosed on, wrapped up in his own eloquence. The coat-tails smoked worse. A tiny spark flew up from the burning wood and alighted in the middle of one. It clung and caught and spread into a smouldering flame. Faith could restrain herself no longer and broke into a stifled giggle.

Mr. Perry stopped short, angered over this impertinence. Suddenly he became conscious that a reek of burning cloth filled the room. He whirled round and saw nothing. Then he clapped his hands to his coat-tails and brought them around in front of him. There was already quite a hole in one of them—and this was his new suit. Faith shook with helpless laughter over his pose and expression.

"Did you see my coat-tails burning?" he demanded angrily.

"Yes, sir," said Faith demurely.

"Why didn't you tell me?" he demanded, glaring at her.

"You said it wasn't good manners to interrupt, sir," said Faith, more demurely still.

"If—if I was your father, I would give you a spanking that you would remember all your life, Miss," said a very angry reverend gentleman, as he stalked out of the study. The coat of Mr. Meredith's second best suit would not fit Mr. Perry, so he had to go to the evening service with his singed coat-tail. But he did not walk up the aisle with his usual consciousness of the honour he was conferring on the building. He never would agree to an exchange of pulpits with Mr. Meredith again, and he was barely civil to the latter when they met for a few minutes at the station the next morning. But Faith felt a certain gloomy satisfaction. Adam was partially avenged.

20. FAITH MAKES A FRIEND

Next day in school was a hard one for Faith. Mary Vance had told the tale of Adam, and all the scholars, except the Blythes, thought it quite a joke. The girls told Faith, between giggles, that it was too bad, and the boys wrote sardonic notes of condolence to her. Poor Faith went home from school feeling her very soul raw and smarting within her.

"I'm going over to Ingleside to have a talk with Mrs. Blythe," she sobbed. "SHE won't laugh at me, as everybody else does. I've just GOT to talk to somebody who understands how bad I feel."

She ran down through Rainbow Valley. Enchantment had been at work the night before. A light snow had fallen and the powdered firs were dreaming of a spring to come and a joy to be.

The long hill beyond was richly purple with leafless beeches. The rosy light of sunset lay over the world like a pink kiss. Of all the airy, fairy places, full of weird, elfin grace, Rainbow Valley that winter evening was the most beautiful. But all its dreamlike loveliness was lost on poor, sore-hearted little Faith.

By the brook she came suddenly upon Rosemary West, who was sitting on the old pine tree. She was on her way home from Ingleside, where she had been giving the girls their music lesson. She had been lingering in Rainbow Valley quite a little time, looking across its white beauty and roaming some by-ways of dream. Judging from the expression of her face, her thoughts were pleasant ones. Perhaps the faint, occasional tinkle from the bells on the Tree Lovers brought the little lurking smile to her lips. Or perhaps it was occasioned by the consciousness that John Meredith seldom failed to spend Monday evening in the gray house on the white wind-swept hill.

Into Rosemary's dreams burst Faith Meredith full of rebellious bitterness. Faith stopped abruptly when she saw Miss West. She did not know her very well—just well enough to speak to when they met. And she did not want to see any one just then—except Mrs. Blythe. She knew her eyes and nose were red and swollen and she hated to have a stranger know she had been crying.

"Good evening, Miss West," she said uncomfortably.

"What is the matter, Faith?" asked Rosemary gently.

"Nothing," said Faith rather shortly.

"Oh!" Rosemary smiled. "You mean nothing that you can tell to outsiders, don't you?"

Faith looked at Miss West with sudden interest. Here was a person who understood things. And how pretty she was! How golden her hair was under her plumy hat! How pink her cheeks were over her velvet coat! How blue and companionable her eyes were! Faith felt that Miss West could be a lovely friend—if only she were a friend instead of a stranger!

"I—I'm going up to tell Mrs. Blythe," said Faith. "She always understands—she never laughs at us. I always talk things over with her. It helps."

"Dear girlie, I'm sorry to have to tell you that Mrs. Blythe isn't home," said Miss West, sympathetically. "She went to Avonlea to-day and isn't coming back till the last of the week."

Faith's lip quivered.

"Then I might as well go home again," she said miserably.

"I suppose so—unless you think you could bring yourself to talk it over with me instead," said Miss Rosemary gently. "It IS such a help to talk things over. *I* know. I don't suppose I can be as good at understanding as Mrs. Blythe—but I promise you that I won't laugh."

"You wouldn't laugh outside," hesitated Faith. "But you might—inside."

"No, I wouldn't laugh inside, either. Why should I? Something has hurt you—it never amuses me to see anybody hurt, no matter what hurts them. If you feel that you'd like to tell me what has hurt you I'll be glad to listen. But if you think you'd rather not—that's all right, too, dear."

Faith took another long, earnest look into Miss West's eyes. They were very serious—there was no laughter in them, not even far, far back. With a little sigh she sat down on the old pine beside her new friend and told her all about Adam and his cruel fate.

Rosemary did not laugh or feel like laughing. She understood and sympathized—really, she was almost as good as Mrs. Blythe—yes, quite as good.

"Mr. Perry is a minister, but he should have been a BUTCHER," said Faith bitterly. "He is so fond of carving things up. He ENJOYED cutting poor Adam to pieces. He just sliced into him as if he were any common rooster."

"Between you and me, Faith, *I* don't like Mr. Perry very well myself," said Rosemary, laughing a little—but at Mr. Perry, not at Adam, as Faith clearly understood. "I never did like him. I went to school with him—he was a Glen boy, you know—and he was a most detestable little prig even then. Oh, how we girls used to hate holding his fat, clammy hands in the ring-around games. But we must remember, dear, that he didn't know that Adam had been a pet of yours. He thought he WAS just a common rooster. We must be just, even when we are terribly hurt."

"I suppose so," admitted Faith. "But why does everybody seem to think it funny that I should have loved Adam so much, Miss West? If it had been a horrid old cat nobody would have thought it queer. When Lottie Warren's kitten had its legs cut off by the binder everybody was sorry for her. She cried two days in school and nobody laughed at her, not even Dan Reese. And all her chums went to the kitten's funeral and helped her bury it—only they couldn't bury its poor little paws with it, because they couldn't find them. It was a horrid thing to have happen, of course, but I don't think it was as dreadful as seeing your pet EATEN UP. Yet everybody laughs at ME."

"I think it is because the name 'rooster' seems rather a funny one," said Rosemary gravely. "There IS something in it that is comical. Now, 'chicken' is different. It doesn't sound so funny to talk of loving a chicken."

"Adam was the dearest little chicken, Miss West. He was just a little golden ball. He would run up to me and peck out of my hand. And he was handsome when he grew up, too —white as snow, with such a beautiful curving white tail, though Mary Vance said it was too short. He knew his name and always came when I called him—he was a very intelligent rooster. And Aunt Martha had no right to kill him. He was mine. It wasn't fair, was it, Miss West?"

"No, it wasn't," said Rosemary decidedly. "Not a bit fair. I remember I had a pet hen when I was a little girl. She was such a pretty little thing—all golden brown and speckly. I loved her as much as I ever loved any pet. She was never killed—she died of old age. Mother wouldn't have her killed because she was my pet."

"If MY mother had been living she wouldn't have let Adam be killed," said Faith. "For that matter, father wouldn't have either, if he'd been home and known of it. I'm SURE he wouldn't, Miss West."

"I'm sure, too," said Rosemary. There was a little added flush on her face. She looked rather conscious but Faith noticed nothing.

"Was it VERY wicked of me not to tell Mr. Perry his coat-tails were scorching?" she asked anxiously.

"Oh, terribly wicked," answered Rosemary, with dancing eyes. "But *I* would have been just as naughty, Faith—*I* wouldn't have told him they were scorching—and I don't believe I would ever have been a bit sorry for my wickedness, either."

"Una thought I should have told him because he was a minister."

"Dearest, if a minister doesn't behave as a gentleman we are not bound to respect his coat-tails. I know *I* would just have loved to see Jimmy Perry's coat-tails burning up. It must have been fun."

Both laughed; but Faith ended with a bitter little sigh.

"Well, anyway, Adam is dead and I am NEVER going to love anything again."

"Don't say that, dear. We miss so much out of life if we don't love. The more we love the richer life is—even if it is only some little furry or feathery pet. Would you like a canary, Faith—a little golden bit of a canary? If you would I'll give you one. We have two up home."

"Oh, I WOULD like that," cried Faith. "I love birds. Only—would Aunt Martha's cat eat it? It's so TRAGIC to have your pets eaten. I don't think I could endure it a second time."

"If you hang the cage far enough from the wall I don't think the cat could harm it. I'll tell you just how to take care of it and I'll bring it to Ingleside for you the next time I come down."

To herself, Rosemary was thinking,

"It will give every gossip in the Glen something to talk of, but I WILL not care. I want to comfort this poor little heart."

Faith was comforted. Sympathy and understanding were very sweet. She and Miss Rosemary sat on the old pine until the twilight crept softly down over the white valley and the evening star shone over the gray maple grove. Faith told Rosemary all her small history and hopes, her likes and dislikes, the ins and outs of life at the manse, the ups and downs of school society. Finally they parted firm friends.

Mr. Meredith was, as usual, lost in dreams when supper began that evening, but presently a name pierced his abstraction and brought him back to reality. Faith was telling Una of her meeting with Rosemary.

"She is just lovely, I think," said Faith. "Just as nice as Mrs. Blythe—but different. I felt as if I wanted to hug her. She did hug ME—such a nice, velvety hug. And she called me 'dearest.' It THRILLED me. I could tell her ANYTHING."

"So you liked Miss West, Faith?" Mr. Meredith asked, with a rather odd intonation.

"I love her," cried Faith.

"Ah!" said Mr. Meredith. "Ah!"

21. THE IMPOSSIBLE WORD

John Meredith walked meditatively through the clear crispness of a winter night in Rainbow Valley. The hills beyond glistened with the chill splendid lustre of moonlight on snow. Every little fir tree in the long valley sang its own wild song to the harp of wind and frost. His children and the Blythe lads and lasses were coasting down the eastern slope and whizzing over the glassy pond. They were having a glorious time and their gay voices and gayer laughter echoed up and down the valley, dying away in elfin cadences among the trees. On the right the lights of Ingleside gleamed through the maple grove with the genial lure and invitation which seems always to glow in the beacons of a home where we know there is love and good-cheer and a welcome for all kin, whether of flesh or spirit. Mr. Meredith liked very well on occasion to spend an evening arguing with the doctor by the drift wood fire, where the famous china dogs of Ingleside kept ceaseless watch and ward, as became deities of the hearth, but to-night he did not look that way. Far on the western hill gleamed a paler but more alluring star. Mr. Meredith was on his way to see Rosemary West, and he meant to tell her something which had been slowly blossoming in his heart since their first meeting and had sprung into full flower on the evening when Faith had so warmly voiced her admiration for Rosemary.

He had come to realize that he had learned to care for Rosemary. Not as he had cared for Cecilia, of course. THAT was entirely different. That love of romance and dream and glamour could never, he thought, return. But Rosemary was beautiful and sweet and dear—very dear. She was the best of companions. He was happier in her company than he had ever expected to be again. She would be an ideal mistress for his home, a good mother to his children.

During the years of his widowhood Mr. Meredith had received innumerable hints from brother members of Presbytery and from many parishioners who could not be suspected of any ulterior motive, as well as from some who could, that he ought to marry again: But these hints never made any impression on him. It was commonly thought he was never aware of them. But he was quite acutely aware of them. And in his own occasional visitations of common sense he knew that the common sensible thing for him to do was to marry. But common sense was not the strong point of John Meredith, and to choose out, deliberately and cold-bloodedly, some "suitable" woman, as one might choose a housekeeper or a business partner, was something he was quite incapable of doing. How he hated that word "suitable." It reminded him so strongly of James Perry. "A SUIT able woman of SUIT able age," that unctuous brother of the cloth had said, in his far from subtle hint. For the moment John Meredith had had a perfectly unbelievable desire to rush madly away and propose marriage to the youngest, most unsuitable woman it was possible to discover.

Mrs. Marshall Elliott was his good friend and he liked her. But when she had bluntly told him he should marry again he felt as if she had torn away the veil that hung before some sacred shrine of his innermost life, and he had been more or less afraid of her ever since. He knew there were women in his congregation "of suitable age" who would marry him quite readily. That fact had seeped through all his abstraction very early in his ministry in Glen St. Mary. They were good, substantial, uninteresting women, one or two fairly comely, the others not exactly so and John Meredith would as soon have thought of marrying any one of them as of hanging himself. He had some ideals to which no seeming necessity could make him false. He could ask no woman to fill Cecilia's place in his home unless he could offer her at least some of the affection and homage he had given to his girlish bride. And where, in his limited feminine acquaintance, was such a woman to be found?

Rosemary West had come into his life on that autumn evening bringing with her an atmosphere in which his spirit recognized native air. Across the gulf of strangerhood they clasped hands of friendship. He knew her better in that ten minutes by the hidden spring than he knew Emmeline Drew or Elizabeth Kirk or Amy Annetta Douglas in a year, or could know them, in a century. He had fled to her for comfort when Mrs. Alec Davis had outraged his mind and soul and had found it. Since then he had gone often to the house on the hill, slipping through the shadowy paths of night in Rainbow Valley so astutely that Glen gossip could never be absolutely certain that he DID go to see Rosemary West. Once or twice he had been caught in the West living room by other visitors; that was all the Ladies' Aid had to go by. But when Elizabeth Kirk heard it she put away a secret hope she had allowed herself to cherish, without a change of expression on her kind plain face, and Emmeline Drew resolved that the next time she saw a certain old bachelor of Lowbridge she would not snub him as she had done at a previous meeting. Of course, if Rosemary West was out to catch the minister she would catch him; she looked younger than she was and MEN thought her pretty; besides, the West girls had money!

"It is to be hoped that he won't be so absent-minded as to propose to Ellen by mistake," was the only malicious thing she allowed herself to say to a sympathetic sister Drew. Emmeline bore no further grudge towards Rosemary. When all was said and done, an unencumbered bachelor was far better than a widower with four children. It had been only the glamour of the manse that had temporarily blinded Emmeline's eyes to the better part.

A sled with three shrieking occupants sped past Mr. Meredith to the pond. Faith's long curls streamed in the wind and her laughter rang above that of the others. John Meredith looked after them kindly and longingly. He was glad that his children had such chums as the Blythes—glad that they had so wise and gay and tender a friend as Mrs. Blythe. But they needed something more, and that something would be supplied when he brought Rosemary West as a bride to the old manse. There was in her a quality essentially maternal.

It was Saturday night and he did not often go calling on Saturday night, which was supposed to be dedicated to a thoughtful revision of Sunday's sermon. But he had chosen this night because he had learned that Ellen West was going to be away and Rosemary would be alone. Often as he had spent pleasant evenings in the house on the hill he had never, since that first meeting at the spring, seen Rosemary alone. Ellen had always been there.

He did not precisely object to Ellen being there. He liked Ellen West very much and they were the best of friends. Ellen had an almost masculine understanding and a sense of humour which his own shy, hidden appreciation of fun found very agreeable. He liked her interest in politics and world events. There was no man in the Glen, not even excepting Dr. Blythe, who had a better grasp of such things.

"I think it is just as well to be interested in things as long as you live," she had said. "If you're not, it doesn't seem to me that there's much difference between the quick and the dead."

He liked her pleasant, deep, rumbly voice; he liked the hearty laugh with which she always ended up some jolly and well-told story. She never gave him digs about his children as other Glen women did; she never bored him with local gossip; she had no malice and no pettiness. She was always splendidly sincere. Mr. Meredith, who had picked up Miss Cornelia's way of classifying people, considered that Ellen belonged to the race of Joseph. Altogether, an admirable woman for a sister-in-law. Nevertheless, a man did not want even the most admirable of women around when he was proposing to another woman. And Ellen was always around. She did not insist on talking to Mr. Meredith herself all the time. She let Rosemary have a fair share of him. Many evenings, indeed, Ellen effaced herself almost totally, sitting back in the corner with St. George in her lap, and letting Mr. Meredith and Rosemary talk and sing and read books together. Sometimes they quite forgot her presence. But if their conversation or choice of duets ever betrayed the least tendency to what Ellen considered philandering, Ellen promptly nipped that tendency in the bud and blotted Rosemary out for the rest of the evening. But not even the grimmest of amiable dragons can altogether prevent a certain subtle language of eye and smile and eloquent silence; and so the minister's courtship progressed after a fashion.

But if it was ever to reach a climax that climax must come when Ellen was away. And Ellen was so seldom away, especially in winter. She found her own fireside the pleasantest place in the world, she vowed. Gadding had no attraction for her. She was fond of company but she wanted it at home. Mr. Meredith had almost been driven to the conclusion that he must write to Rosemary what he wanted to say, when Ellen casually announced one evening that she was going to a silver wedding next Saturday night. She had been bridesmaid when the principals were married. Only old guests were invited, so Rosemary was not included. Mr. Meredith pricked up his ears a trifle and a gleam flashed into his dreamy dark eyes. Both Ellen and Rosemary saw it; and both Ellen and Rosemary felt, with a tingling shock, that Mr. Meredith would certainly come up the hill next Saturday night.

"Might as well have it over with, St. George," Ellen sternly told the black cat, after Mr. Meredith had gone home and Rosemary had silently gone upstairs. "He means to ask her, St. George—I'm perfectly sure of that. So he might as well have his chance to do it and find out he can't get her, George. She'd rather like to take him, Saint. I know that—but she promised, and she's got to keep her promise. I'm rather sorry in some ways, St. George. I don't know of a man I'd sooner have for a brother-in-law if a brother-in-law was convenient. I haven't a thing against him, Saint—not a thing except that he won't see and can't be made to see that the Kaiser is a menace to the peace of Europe. That's HIS blind spot. But he's good company and I like him. A woman can say anything she likes to a man with a mouth like John Meredith's and be sure of not being misunderstood. Such a man is more precious than rubies, Saint—and much rarer, George. But he can't have Rosemary—and I suppose when he finds out he can't have her he'll drop us both. And we'll miss him, Saint—we'll miss him something scandalous, George. But she promised, and I'll see that she keeps her promise!"

Ellen's face looked almost ugly in its lowering resolution. Upstairs Rosemary was crying into her pillow.

So Mr. Meredith found his lady alone and looking very beautiful. Rosemary had not made any special toilet for the occasion; she wanted to, but she thought it would be absurd to dress up for a man you meant to refuse. So she wore her plain dark afternoon dress and looked like a queen in it. Her suppressed excitement coloured her face to brilliancy, her great blue eyes were pools of light less placid than usual.

She wished the interview were over. She had looked forward to it all day with dread. She felt quite sure that John Meredith cared a great deal for her after a fashion—and she felt just as sure that he did not care for her as he had cared for his first love. She felt that her refusal would disappoint him considerably, but she did not think it would altogether overwhelm him. Yet she hated to make it; hated for his sake and—Rosemary was quite honest with herself—for her own. She knew she could have loved John Meredith if—if it had been permissible. She knew that life would be a blank thing if, rejected as lover, he refused longer to be a friend. She knew that she could be very happy with him and that she could make him happy. But between her and happiness stood the prison gate of the promise she had made to Ellen years ago. Rosemary could not remember her father. He had died when she was only three years old. Ellen, who had been thirteen, remembered him, but with no special tenderness. He had been a stern, reserved man many years older than his fair, pretty wife. Five years later their brother of twelve died also; since his death the two girls had always lived alone with their mother. They had never mingled very freely in the social life of the Glen or Lowbridge, though where they went the wit and spirit of Ellen and the sweetness and beauty of Rosemary made them welcome guests. Both had what was called "a disappointment" in their girlhood. The sea had not given up Rosemary's lover; and Norman Douglas, then a handsome, red-haired young giant, noted for wild driving and noisy though harmless escapades, had quarrelled with Ellen and left her in a fit of pique.

There were not lacking candidates for both Martin's and Norman's places, but none seemed to find favour in the eyes of the West girls, who drifted slowly out of youth and bellehood without any seeming regret. They were devoted to their mother, who was a chronic invalid. The three had a little circle of home interests—books and pets and flowers—which made them happy and contented.

Mrs. West's death, which occurred on Rosemary's twenty-fifth birthday, was a bitter grief to them. At first they were intolerably lonely. Ellen, especially, continued to grieve and brood, her long, moody musings broken only by fits of stormy, passionate weeping. The old Lowbridge doctor told Rosemary that he feared permanent melancholy or worse.

Once, when Ellen had sat all day, refusing either to speak or eat, Rosemary had flung herself on her knees by her sister's side.

"Oh, Ellen, you have me yet," she said imploringly. "Am I nothing to you? We have always loved each other so."

"I won't have you always," Ellen had said, breaking her silence with harsh intensity. "You will marry and leave me. I shall be left all alone. I cannot bear the thought—I CANNOT. I would rather die."

"I will never marry," said Rosemary, "never, Ellen."

Ellen bent forward and looked searchingly into Rosemary's eyes.

"Will you promise me that solemnly?" she said. "Promise it on mother's Bible."

Rosemary assented at once, quite willing to humour Ellen. What did it matter? She knew quite well she would never want to marry any one. Her love had gone down with Martin Crawford to the deeps of the sea; and without love she could not marry any one. So she promised readily, though Ellen made rather a fearsome rite of it. They clasped hands over the Bible, in their mother's vacant room, and both vowed to each other that they would never marry and would always live together.

Ellen's condition improved from that hour. She soon regained her normal cheery poise. For ten years she and Rosemary lived in the old house happily, undisturbed by any thought of marrying or giving in marriage. Their promise sat very lightly on them. Ellen never failed to remind her sister of it whenever any eligible male creature crossed their paths, but she had never been really alarmed until John Meredith came home that night with Rosemary. As for Rosemary, Ellen's obsession regarding that promise had always been a little matter of mirth to her—until lately. Now, it was a merciless fetter, self-imposed but never to be shaken off. Because of it to-night she must turn her face from happiness.

It was true that the shy, sweet, rosebud love she had given to her boy-lover she could never give to another. But she knew now that she could give to John Meredith a love richer and more womanly. She knew that he touched deeps in her nature that Martin had never touched—that had not, perhaps, been in the girl of seventeen to touch. And she must send him away to-night—send him back to his lonely hearth and his empty life and his heart-breaking problems, because she had promised Ellen, ten years before, on their mother's Bible, that she would never marry.

John Meredith did not immediately grasp his opportunity. On the contrary, he talked for two good hours on the least lover-like of subjects. He even tried politics, though politics always bored Rosemary. The later began to think that she had been altogether mistaken, and her fears and expectations suddenly seemed to her grotesque. She felt flat and foolish. The glow went out of her face and the lustre out of her eyes. John Meredith had not the slightest intention of asking her to marry him.

And then, quite suddenly, he rose, came across the room, and standing by her chair, he asked it. The room had grown terribly still. Even St. George ceased to purr. Rosemary heard her own heart beating and was sure John Meredith must hear it too.

Now was the time for her to say no, gently but firmly. She had been ready for days with her stilted, regretful little formula. And now the words of it had completely vanished from her mind. She had to say no—and she suddenly found she could not say it. It was the impossible word. She knew now that it was not that she COULD have loved John Meredith, but that she DID love him. The thought of putting him from her life was agony.

She must say SOMETHING; she lifted her bowed golden head and asked him stammeringly to give her a few days for—for consideration.

John Meredith was a little surprised. He was not vainer than any man has a right to be, but he had expected that Rosemary West would say yes. He had been tolerably sure she cared for him. Then why this doubt—this hesitation? She was not a school girl to be uncertain as to her own mind. He felt an ugly shock of disappointment and dismay. But he assented to her request with his unfailing gentle courtesy and went away at once.

"I will tell you in a few days," said Rosemary, with downcast eyes and burning face.

When the door shut behind him she went back into the room and wrung her hands.

22. ST. GEORGE KNOWS ALL ABOUT IT

At midnight Ellen West was walking home from the Pollock silver wedding. She had stayed a little while after the other guests had gone, to help the gray-haired bride wash the dishes. The distance between the two houses was not far and the road good, so that Ellen was enjoying the walk back home in the moonlight.

The evening had been a pleasant one. Ellen, who had not been to a party for years, found it very pleasant. All the guests had been members of her old set and there was no intrusive youth to spoil the flavour, for the only son of the bride and groom was far away at college and could not be present. Norman Douglas had been there and they had met socially for the first time in years, though she had seen him once or twice in church that winter. Not the least sentiment was awakened in Ellen's heart by their meeting. She was accustomed to wonder, when she thought about it at all, how she could ever have fancied him or felt so badly over his sudden marriage. But she had rather liked meeting him again. She had forgotten how bracing and stimulating he could be. No gathering was ever stagnant when Norman Douglas was present. Everybody had been surprised when Norman came. It was well known he never went anywhere. The Pollocks had invited him because he had been one of the original guests, but they never thought he would come. He had taken his second cousin, Amy Annetta Douglas, out to supper and seemed rather attentive to her. But Ellen sat across the table from him and had a spirited argument with him—an argument during which all his shouting and banter could not fluster her and in which she came off best, flooring Norman so composedly and so completely that he was silent for ten minutes. At the end of which time he had muttered in his ruddy beard —"spunky as ever—spunky as ever"—and began to hector Amy Annetta, who giggled foolishly over his sallies where Ellen would have retorted bitingly.

Ellen thought these things over as she walked home, tasting them with reminiscent relish. The moonlit air sparkled with frost. The snow crisped under her feet. Below her lay the Glen with the white harbour beyond. There was a light in the manse study. So John Meredith had gone home. Had he asked Rosemary to marry him? And after what fashion had she made her refusal known? Ellen felt that she would never know this, though she was quite curious. She was sure Rosemary would never tell her anything about it and she would not dare to ask. She must just be content with the fact of the refusal. After all, that was the only thing that really mattered.

"I hope he'll have sense enough to come back once in a while and be friendly," she said to herself. She disliked so much to be alone that thinking aloud was one of her devices for circumventing unwelcome solitude. "It's awful never to have a man-body with some brains to talk to once in a while. And like as not he'll never come near the house again. There's Norman Douglas, too—I like that man, and I'd like to have a good rousing argument with him now and then. But he'd never dare come up for fear people would think he was courting me again—for fear I'D think it, too, most likely—though he's more a stranger to me now than John Meredith. It seems like a dream that we could ever have been beaus. But there it is—there's only two men in the Glen I'd ever want to talk to—and what with gossip and this wretched love-making business it's not likely I'll ever see either of them again. I could," said Ellen, addressing the unmoved stars with a spiteful emphasis, "I could have made a better world myself."

She paused at her gate with a sudden vague feeling of alarm. There was still a light in the living-room and to and fro across the window-shades went the shadow of a woman walking restlessly up and down. What was Rosemary doing up at this hour of the night? And why was she striding about like a lunatic?

Ellen went softly in. As she opened the hall door Rosemary came out of the room. She was flushed and breathless. An atmosphere of stress and passion hung about her like a garment.

"Why aren't you in bed, Rosemary?" demanded Ellen.

"Come in here," said Rosemary intensely. "I want to tell you something."

Ellen composedly removed her wraps and overshoes, and followed her sister into the warm, fire-lighted room. She stood with her hand on the table and waited. She was looking very handsome herself, in her own grim, black-browed style. The new black velvet dress, with its train and V-neck, which she had made purposely for the party, became her stately, massive figure. She wore coiled around her neck the rich heavy necklace of amber beads which was a family heirloom. Her walk in the frosty air had stung her cheeks into a glowing scarlet. But her steel-blue eyes were as icy and unyielding as the sky of the winter night. She stood waiting in a silence which Rosemary could break only by a convulsive effort.

"Ellen, Mr. Meredith was here this evening."

"Yes?"

"And—and—he asked me to marry him."

"So I expected. Of course, you refused him?"

"No."

"Rosemary." Ellen clenched her hands and took an involuntary step forward. "Do you mean to tell me that you accepted him?"

"No—no."

Ellen recovered her self-command.

"What DID you do then?"

"I—I asked him to give me a few days to think it over."

"I hardly see why that was necessary," said Ellen, coldly contemptuous, "when there is only the one answer you can make him."

Rosemary held out her hands beseechingly.

"Ellen," she said desperately, "I love John Meredith—I want to be his wife. Will you set me free from that promise?"

"No," said Ellen, merciless, because she was sick from fear.

"Ellen—Ellen—"

"Listen," interrupted Ellen. "I did not ask you for that promise. You offered it."

"I know—I know. But I did not think then that I could ever care for anyone again."

"You offered it," went on Ellen unmovably. "You promised it over our mother's Bible. It was more than a promise—it was an oath. Now you want to break it."

"I only asked you to set me free from it, Ellen."

"I will not do it. A promise is a promise in my eyes. I will not do it. Break your promise—be forsworn if you will—but it shall not be with any assent of mine."

"You are very hard on me, Ellen."

"Hard on you! And what of me? Have you ever given a thought to what my loneliness would be here if you left me? I could not bear it—I would go crazy. I CANNOT live alone. Haven't I been a good sister to you? Have I ever opposed any wish of yours? Haven't I indulged you in everything?"

"Yes—yes."

"Then why do you want to leave me for this man whom you hadn't seen a year ago?"

"I love him, Ellen."

"Love! You talk like a school miss instead of a middle-aged woman. He doesn't love you. He wants a housekeeper and a governess. You don't love him. You want to be 'Mrs.'—you are one of those weak-minded women who think it's a disgrace to be ranked as an old maid. That's all there is to it."

Rosemary quivered. Ellen could not, or would not, understand. There was no use arguing with her.

"So you won't release me, Ellen?"

"No, I won't. And I won't talk of it again. You promised and you've got to keep your word. That's all. Go to bed. Look at the time! You're all romantic and worked up. To-morrow you'll be more sensible. At any rate, don't let me hear any more of this nonsense. Go."

Rosemary went without another word, pale and spiritless. Ellen walked stormily about the room for a few minutes, then paused before the chair where St. George had been calmly sleeping through the whole evening. A reluctant smile overspread her dark face. There had been only one time in her life—the time of her mother's death—when Ellen had not been able to temper tragedy with comedy. Even in that long ago bitterness, when Norman Douglas had, after a fashion, jilted her, she had laughed at herself quite as often as she had cried.

"I expect there'll be some sulking, St. George. Yes, Saint, I expect we are in for a few unpleasant foggy days. Well, we'll weather them through, George. We've dealt with foolish children before, Saint. Rosemary'll sulk a while—and then she'll get over it—and all will be as before, George. She promised—and she's got to keep her promise. And that's the last word on the subject I'll say to you or her or anyone, Saint."

But Ellen lay savagely awake till morning.

There was no sulking, however. Rosemary was pale and quiet the next day, but beyond that Ellen could detect no difference in her. Certainly, she seemed to bear Ellen no grudge. It was stormy, so no mention was made of going to church. In the afternoon Rosemary shut herself in her room and wrote a note to John Meredith. She could not trust herself to say "no" in person. She felt quite sure that if he suspected she was saying "no" reluctantly he would not take it for an answer, and she could not face pleading or entreaty. She must make him think she cared nothing at all for him and she could do that only by letter. She wrote him the stiffest, coolest little refusal imaginable. It was barely courteous; it certainly left no loophole of hope for the boldest lover—and John Meredith was anything but that. He shrank into himself, hurt and mortified, when he read Rosemary's letter next day in his dusty study. But under his mortification a dreadful realization presently made itself felt. He had thought he did not love Rosemary as deeply as he had loved Cecilia. Now, when he had lost her, he knew that he did. She was everything to him—everything! And he must put her out of his life completely. Even friendship was impossible now. Life stretched before him in intolerable dreariness. He must go on—there was his work—his children—but the heart had gone out of him. He sat alone all that evening in his dark, cold, comfortless study with his head bowed on his hands. Up on the hill Rosemary had a headache and went early to bed, while Ellen remarked to St. George, purring his disdain of foolish humankind, who did not know that a soft cushion was the only thing that really mattered,

"What would women do if headaches had never been invented, St. George? But never mind, Saint. We'll just wink the other eye for a few weeks. I admit I don't feel comfortable myself, George. I feel as if I had drowned a kitten. But she promised, Saint—and she was the one to offer it, George. Bismillah!"

23. THE GOOD-CONDUCT CLUB

A light rain had been falling all day—a little, delicate, beautiful spring rain, that somehow seemed to hint and whisper of mayflowers and wakening violets. The harbour and the gulf and the low-lying shore fields had been dim with pearl-gray mists. But now in the evening the rain had ceased and the mists had blown out to sea. Clouds sprinkled the sky over the harbour like little fiery roses. Beyond it the hills were dark against a spendthrift splendour of daffodil and crimson. A great silvery evening star was watching over the bar. A brisk, dancing, new-sprung wind was blowing up from Rainbow Valley, resinous with the odours of fir and damp mosses. It crooned in the old spruces around the graveyard and ruffled Faith's splendid curls as she sat on Hezekiah Pollock's tombstone with her arms round Mary Vance and Una. Carl and Jerry were sitting opposite them on another tombstone and all were rather full of mischief after being cooped up all day.

"The air just SHINES to-night, doesn't it? It's been washed so clean, you see," said Faith happily.

Mary Vance eyed her gloomily. Knowing what she knew, or fancied she knew, Mary considered that Faith was far too light-hearted. Mary had something on her mind to say and she meant to say it before she went home. Mrs. Elliott had sent her up to the manse with some new-laid eggs, and had told her not to stay longer than half an hour. The half hour was nearly up, so Mary uncurled her cramped legs from under her and said abruptly,

"Never mind about the air. Just you listen to me. You manse young ones have just got to behave yourselves better than you've been doing this spring—that's all there is to it. I just come up to-night a-purpose to tell you so. The way people are talking about you is awful."

"What have we been doing now?" cried Faith in amazement, pulling her arm away from Mary. Una's lips trembled and her sensitive little soul shrank within her. Mary was always so brutally frank. Jerry began to whistle out of bravado. He meant to let Mary see he didn't care for HER tirades. Their behaviour was no business of HERS anyway. What right had SHE to lecture them on their conduct?

"Doing now! You're doing ALL the time," retorted Mary. "Just as soon as the talk about one of your didos fades away you do something else to start it up again. It seems to me you haven't any idea of how manse children ought to behave!"

"Maybe YOU can tell us," said Jerry, killingly sarcastic.

Sarcasm was quite thrown away on Mary.

"*I* can tell you what will happen if you don't learn to behave yourselves. The session will ask your father to resign. There now, Master Jerry-know-it-all. Mrs. Alec Davis said so to Mrs. Elliott. I heard her. I always have my ears pricked up when Mrs. Alec Davis comes to tea. She said you were all going from bad to worse and that though it was only what was to be expected when you had nobody to bring you up, still the congregation couldn't be expected to put up with it much longer, and something would have to be done. The Methodists just laugh and laugh at you, and that hurts the Presbyterian feelings. SHE says you all need a good dose of birch tonic. Lor', if that would make folks good *I* oughter be a young saint. I'm not telling you this because I want to hurt YOUR feelings. I'm sorry for you"—Mary was past mistress of the gentle art of condescension. "*I* understand that you haven't much chance, the way things are. But other people don't make as much allowance as *I* do. Miss Drew says Carl had a frog in his pocket in Sunday School last Sunday and it hopped out while she was hearing the lesson. She says she's going to give up the class. Why don't you keep your insecks home?"

"I popped it right back in again," said Carl. "It didn't hurt anybody—a poor little frog! And I wish old Jane Drew WOULD give up our class. I hate her. Her own nephew had a dirty plug of tobacco in his pocket and offered us fellows a chew when Elder Clow was praying. I guess that's worse than a frog."

"No, 'cause frogs are more unexpected-like. They make more of a sensation. 'Sides, he wasn't caught at it. And then that praying competition you had last week has made a fearful scandal. Everybody is talking about it."

"Why, the Blythes were in that as well as us," cried Faith, indignantly. "It was Nan Blythe who suggested it in the first place. And Walter took the prize."

"Well, you get the credit of it any way. It wouldn't have been so bad if you hadn't had it in the graveyard."

"I should think a graveyard was a very good place to pray in," retorted Jerry.

"Deacon Hazard drove past when YOU were praying," said Mary, "and he saw and heard you, with your hands folded over your stomach, and groaning after every sentence. He thought you were making fun of HIM."

"So I was," declared unabashed Jerry. "Only I didn't know he was going by, of course. That was just a mean accident. *I* wasn't praying in real earnest—I knew I had no chance of winning the prize. So I was just getting what fun I could out of it. Walter Blythe can pray bully. Why, he can pray as well as dad."

"Una is the only one of US who really likes praying," said Faith pensively.

"Well, if praying scandalizes people so much we mustn't do it any more," sighed Una.

"Shucks, you can pray all you want to, only not in the graveyard—and don't make a game of it. That was what made it so bad—that, and having a tea-party on the tombstones."

"We hadn't."

"Well, a soap-bubble party then. You had SOMETHING. The over-harbour people swear you had a tea-party, but I'm willing to take your word. And you used this tombstone as a table."

"Well, Martha wouldn't let us blow bubbles in the house. She was awful cross that day," explained Jerry. "And this old slab made such a jolly table."

"Weren't they pretty?" cried Faith, her eyes sparkling over the remembrance. "They reflected the trees and the hills and the harbour like little fairy worlds, and when we shook them loose they floated away down to Rainbow Valley."

"All but one and it went over and bust up on the Methodist spire," said Carl.

"I'm glad we did it once, anyhow, before we found out it was wrong," said Faith.

"It wouldn't have been wrong to blow them on the lawn," said Mary impatiently. "Seems like I can't knock any sense into your heads. You've been told often enough you shouldn't play in the graveyard. The Methodists are sensitive about it."

"We forget," said Faith dolefully. "And the lawn is so small—and so caterpillary—and so full of shrubs and things. We can't be in Rainbow Valley all the time—and where are we to go?"

"It's the things you DO in the graveyard. It wouldn't matter if you just sat here and talked quiet, same as we're doing now. Well, I don't know what is going to come of it all, but I DO know that Elder Warren is going to speak to your pa about it. Deacon Hazard is his cousin."

"I wish they wouldn't bother father about us," said Una.

"Well, people think he ought to bother himself about you a little more. *I* don't—*I* understand him. He's a child in some ways himself—that's what he is, and needs some one to look after him as bad as you do. Well, perhaps he'll have some one before long, if all tales is true."

"What do you mean?" asked Faith.

"Haven't you got any idea—honest?" demanded Mary.

"No, no. What DO you mean?"

"Well, you are a lot of innocents, upon my word. Why, EVERYbody is talking of it. Your pa goes to see Rosemary West. SHE is going to be your step-ma."

"I don't believe it," cried Una, flushing crimson.

"Well, *I* dunno. I just go by what folks say. *I* don't give it for a fact. But it would be a good thing. Rosemary West'd make you toe the mark if she came here, I'll bet a cent, for all she's so sweet and smiley on the face of her. They're always that way till they've caught them. But you need some one to bring you up. You're disgracing your pa and I feel for him. I've always thought an awful lot of your pa ever since that night he talked to me so nice. I've never said a single swear word since, or told a lie. And I'd like to see him happy and comfortable, with his buttons on and his meals decent, and you young ones licked into shape, and that old cat of a Martha put in HER proper place. The way she looked at the eggs I brought her to-night.

'I hope they're fresh,' says she. I just wished they WAS rotten. But you just mind that she gives you all one for breakfast, including your pa. Make a fuss if she doesn't. That was what they was sent up for—but I don't trust old Martha. She's quite capable of feeding 'em to her cat."

Mary's tongue being temporarily tired, a brief silence fell over the graveyard. The manse children did not feel like talking. They were digesting the new and not altogether palatable ideas Mary had suggested to them. Jerry and Carl were somewhat startled. But, after all, what did it matter? And it wasn't likely there was a word of truth in it. Faith, on the whole, was pleased. Only Una was seriously upset. She felt that she would like to get away and cry.

"Will there be any stars in my crown?" sang the Methodist choir, beginning to practise in the Methodist church.

"*I* want just three," said Mary, whose theological knowledge had increased notably since her residence with Mrs. Elliott. "Just three—setting up on my head, like a corownet, a big one in the middle and a small one each side."

"Are there different sizes in souls?" asked Carl.

"Of course. Why, little babies must have smaller ones than big men. Well, it's getting dark and I must scoot home. Mrs. Elliott doesn't like me to be out after dark. Laws, when I lived with Mrs. Wiley the dark was just the same as the daylight to me. I didn't mind it no more'n a gray cat. Them days seem a hundred years ago. Now, you mind what I've said and try to behave yourselves, for you pa's sake. I'LL always back you up and defend you—you can be dead sure of that. Mrs. Elliott says she never saw the like of me for sticking up for my friends. I was real sassy to Mrs. Alec Davis about you and Mrs. Elliott combed me down for it afterwards. The fair Cornelia has a tongue of her own and no mistake. But she was pleased underneath for all, 'cause she hates old Kitty Alec and she's real fond of you. *I* can see through folks."

Mary sailed off, excellently well pleased with herself, leaving a rather depressed little group behind her.

"Mary Vance always says something that makes us feel bad when she comes up," said Una resentfully.

"I wish we'd left her to starve in the old barn," said Jerry vindictively.

"Oh, that's wicked, Jerry," rebuked Una.

"May as well have the game as the name," retorted unrepentant Jerry. "If people say we're so bad let's BE bad."

"But not if it hurts father," pleaded Faith.

Jerry squirmed uncomfortably. He adored his father. Through the unshaded study window they could see Mr. Meredith at his desk. He did not seem to be either reading or writing. His head was in his hands and there was something in his whole attitude that spoke of weariness and dejection. The children suddenly felt it.

"I dare say somebody's been worrying him about us to-day," said Faith. "I wish we COULD get along without making people talk. Oh—Jem Blythe! How you scared me!"

Jem Blythe had slipped into the graveyard and sat down beside the girls. He had been prowling about Rainbow Valley and had succeeded in finding the first little star-white cluster of arbutus for his mother. The manse children were rather silent after his coming. Jem was beginning to grow away from them somewhat this spring. He was studying for the entrance examination of Queen's Academy and stayed after school with the older pupils for extra lessons. Also, his evenings were so full of work that he seldom joined the others in Rainbow Valley now. He seemed to be drifting away into grown-up land.

"What is the matter with you all to-night?" he asked. "There's no fun in you."

"Not much," agreed Faith dolefully. "There wouldn't be much fun in you either if YOU knew you were disgracing your father and making people talk about you."

"Who's been talking about you now?"

"Everybody—so Mary Vance says." And Faith poured out her troubles to sympathetic Jem. "You see," she concluded dolefully, "we've nobody to bring us up. And so we get into scrapes and people think we're bad."

"Why don't you bring yourselves up?" suggested Jem. "I'll tell you what to do. Form a Good-Conduct Club and punish yourselves every time you do anything that's not right."

"That's a good idea," said Faith, struck by it. "But," she added doubtfully, "things that don't seem a bit of harm to US seem simply dreadful to other people. How can we tell? We can't be bothering father all the time—and he has to be away a lot, anyhow."

"You could mostly tell if you stopped to think a thing over before doing it and ask yourselves what the congregation would say about it," said Jem. "The trouble is you just rush into things and don't think them over at all. Mother says you're all too impulsive, just as she used to be. The Good-Conduct Club would help you to think, if you were fair and honest about punishing yourselves when you broke the rules. You'd have to punish in some way that really HURT, or it wouldn't do any good."

"Whip each other?"

"Not exactly. You'd have to think up different ways of punishment to suit the person. You wouldn't punish each other—you'd punish YOURSELVES. I read all about such a club in a story-book. You try it and see how it works."

"Let's," said Faith; and when Jem was gone they agreed they would. "If things aren't right we've just got to make them right," said Faith, resolutely.

"We've got to be fair and square, as Jem says," said Jerry. "This is a club to bring ourselves up, seeing there's nobody else to do it. There's no use in having many rules. Let's just have one and any of us that breaks it has got to be punished hard."

"But HOW."

"We'll think that up as we go along. We'll hold a session of the club here in the graveyard every night and talk over what we've done through the day, and if we think we've done anything that isn't right or that would disgrace dad the one that does it, or is responsible for it, must be punished. That's the rule. We'll all decide on the kind of punishment—it must be made to fit the crime, as Mr. Flagg says. And the one that's, guilty will be bound to carry it out and no shirking. There's going to be fun in this," concluded Jerry, with a relish.

"You suggested the soap-bubble party," said Faith.

"But that was before we'd formed the club," said Jerry hastily. "Everything starts from to-night."

"But what if we can't agree on what's right, or what the punishment ought to be? S'pose two of us thought of one thing and two another. There ought to be five in a club like this."

"We can ask Jem Blythe to be umpire. He is the squarest boy in Glen St. Mary. But I guess we can settle our own affairs mostly. We want to keep this as much of a secret as we can. Don't breathe a word to Mary Vance. She'd want to join and do the bringing up."

"*I* think," said Faith, "that there's no use in spoiling every day by dragging punishments in. Let's have a punishment day."

"We'd better choose Saturday because there is no school to interfere," suggested Una.

"And spoil the one holiday in the week," cried Faith. "Not much! No, let's take Friday. That's fish day, anyhow, and we all hate fish. We may as well have all the disagreeable things in one day. Then other days we can go ahead and have a good time."

"Nonsense," said Jerry authoritatively. "Such a scheme wouldn't work at all. We'll just punish ourselves as we go along and keep a clear slate. Now, we all understand, don't we? This is a Good-Conduct Club, for the purpose of bringing ourselves up. We agree to punish ourselves for bad conduct, and always to stop before we do anything, no matter what, and ask ourselves if it is likely to hurt dad in any way, and any one who shirks is to be cast out of the club and never allowed to play with the rest of us in Rainbow Valley again. Jem Blythe to be umpire in case of disputes. No more taking bugs to Sunday School, Carl, and no more chewing gum in public, if you please, Miss Faith."

"No more making fun of elders praying or going to the Methodist prayer meeting," retorted Faith.

"Why, it isn't any harm to go to the Methodist prayer meeting," protested Jerry in amazement.

"Mrs. Elliott says it is, She says manse children have no business to go anywhere but to Presbyterian things."

"Darn it, I won't give up going to the Methodist prayer meeting," cried Jerry. "It's ten times more fun than ours is."

"You said a naughty word," cried Faith. "NOW, you've got to punish yourself."

"Not till it's all down in black and white. We're only talking the club over. It isn't really formed until we've written it out and signed it. There's got to be a constitution and by-laws. And you KNOW there's nothing wrong in going to a prayer meeting."

"But it's not only the wrong things we're to punish ourselves for, but anything that might hurt father."

"It won't hurt anybody. You know Mrs. Elliott is cracked on the subject of Methodists. Nobody else makes any fuss about my going. I always behave myself. You ask Jem or Mrs. Blythe and see what they say. I'll abide by their opinion. I'm going for the paper now and I'll bring out the lantern and we'll all sign."

Fifteen minutes later the document was solemnly signed on Hezekiah Pollock's tombstone, on the centre of which stood the smoky manse lantern, while the children knelt around it. Mrs. Elder Clow was going past at the moment and next day all the Glen heard that the manse children had been having another praying competition and had wound it up by chasing each other all over the graves with a lantern. This piece of embroidery was probably suggested by the fact that, after the signing and sealing was completed, Carl had taken the lantern and had walked circumspectly to the little hollow to examine his ant-hill. The others had gone quietly into the manse and to bed.

"Do you think it is true that father is going to marry Miss West?" Una had tremulously asked of Faith, after their prayers had been said.

"I don't know, but I'd like it," said Faith.

"Oh, I wouldn't," said Una, chokingly. "She is nice the way she is. But Mary Vance says it changes people ALTOGETHER to be made stepmothers. They get horrid cross and mean and hateful then, and turn your father against you. She says they're sure to do that. She never knew it to fail in a single case."

"I don't believe Miss West would EVER try to do that," cried Faith.

"Mary says ANYBODY would. She knows ALL about stepmothers, Faith—she says she's seen hundreds of them—and you've never seen one. Oh, Mary has told me blood-curdling things about them. She says she knew of one who whipped her husband's little girls on their bare shoulders till they bled, and then shut them up in a cold, dark coal cellar all night. She says they're ALL aching to do things like that."

"I don't believe Miss West would. You don't know her as well as I do, Una. Just think of that sweet little bird she sent me. I love it far more even than Adam."

"It's just being a stepmother changes them. Mary says they can't help it. I wouldn't mind the whippings so much as having father hate us."

"You know nothing could make father hate us. Don't be silly, Una. I dare say there's nothing to worry over. Likely if we run our club right and bring ourselves up properly father won't think of marrying any one. And if he does, I KNOW Miss West will be lovely to us."

But Una had no such conviction and she cried herself to sleep.

24. A CHARITABLE IMPULSE

For a fortnight things ran smoothly in the Good-Conduct Club. It seemed to work admirably. Not once was Jem Blythe called in as umpire. Not once did any of the manse children set the Glen gossips by the ears. As for their minor peccadilloes at home, they kept sharp tabs on each other and gamely underwent their self-imposed punishment—generally a voluntary absence from some gay Friday night frolic in Rainbow Valley, or a sojourn in bed on some spring evening when all young bones ached to be out and away. Faith, for whispering in Sunday School, condemned herself to pass a whole day without speaking a single word, unless it was absolutely necessary, and accomplished it. It was rather unfortunate that Mr. Baker from over-harbour should have chosen that evening for calling at the manse, and that Faith should have happened to go to the door. Not one word did she reply to his genial greeting, but went silently away to call her father briefly. Mr. Baker was slightly offended and told his wife when he went home that that the biggest Meredith girl seemed a very shy, sulky little thing, without manners enough to speak when she was spoken to. But nothing worse came of it, and generally their penances did no harm to themselves or anybody else. All of them were beginning to feel quite cocksure that after all, it was a very easy matter to bring yourself up.

"I guess people will soon see that we can behave ourselves properly as well as anybody," said Faith jubilantly. "It isn't hard when we put our minds to it."

She and Una were sitting on the Pollock tombstone. It had been a cold, raw, wet day of spring storm and Rainbow Valley was out of the question for girls, though the manse and the Ingleside boys were down there fishing. The rain had held up, but the east wind blew mercilessly in from the sea, cutting to bone and marrow. Spring was late in spite of its early promise, and there was even yet a hard drift of old snow and ice in the northern corner of the graveyard. Lida Marsh, who had come up to bring the manse a mess of herring, slipped in through the gate shivering. She belonged to the fishing village at the harbour mouth and her father had, for thirty years, made a practice of sending a mess from his first spring catch to the manse. He never darkened a church door; he was a hard drinker and a reckless man, but as long as he sent those herring up to the manse every spring, as his father had done before him, he felt comfortably sure that his account with the Powers That Govern was squared for the year. He would not have expected a good mackerel catch if he had not so sent the first fruits of the season.

Lida was a mite of ten and looked younger, because she was such a small, wizened little creature. To-night, as she sidled boldly enough up to the manse girls, she looked as if she had never been warm since she was born. Her face was purple and her pale-blue, bold little eyes were red and watery. She wore a tattered print dress and a ragged woollen comforter, tied across her thin shoulders and under her arms. She had walked the three miles from the harbour mouth barefooted, over a road where there was still snow and slush and mud. Her feet and legs were as purple as her face. But Lida did not mind this much. She was used to being cold, and she had been going barefooted for a month already, like all the other swarming young fry of the fishing village. There was no self-pity in her heart as she sat down on the tombstone and grinned cheerfully at Faith and Una. Faith and Una grinned cheerfully back. They knew Lida slightly, having met her once or twice the preceding summer when they had gone down the harbour with the Blythes.

"Hello!" said Lida, "ain't this a fierce kind of a night? 'T'ain't fit for a dog to be out, is it?"

"Then why are you out?" asked Faith.

"Pa made me bring you up some herring," returned Lida. She shivered, coughed, and stuck out her bare feet. Lida was not thinking about herself or her feet, and was making no bid for sympathy. She held her feet out instinctively to keep them from the wet grass around the tombstone. But Faith and Una were instantly swamped with a wave of pity for her. She looked so cold—so miserable.

"Oh, why are you barefooted on such a cold night?" cried Faith. "Your feet must be almost frozen."

"Pretty near," said Lida proudly. "I tell you it was fierce walking up that harbour road."

"Why didn't you put on your shoes and stockings?" asked Una.

"Hain't none to put on. All I had was wore out by the time winter was over," said Lida indifferently.

For a moment Faith stated in horror. This was terrible. Here was a little girl, almost a neighbour, half frozen because she had no shoes or stockings in this cruel spring weather. Impulsive Faith thought of nothing but the dreadfulness of it. In a moment she was pulling off her own shoes and stockings.

"Here, take these and put them right on," she said, forcing them into the hands of the astonished Lida. "Quick now. You'll catch your death of cold. I've got others. Put them right on."

Lida, recovering her wits, snatched at the offered gift, with a sparkle in her dull eyes. Sure she would put them on, and that mighty quick, before any one appeared with authority to recall them. In a minute she had pulled the stockings over her scrawny little legs and slipped Faith's shoes over her thick little ankles.

"I'm obliged to you," she said, "but won't your folks be cross?"

"No—and I don't care if they are," said Faith. "Do you think I could see any one freezing to death without helping them if I could? It wouldn't be right, especially when my father's a minister."

"Will you want them back? It's awful cold down at the harbour mouth—long after it's warm up here," said Lida slyly.

"No, you're to keep them, of course. That is what I meant when I gave them. I have another pair of shoes and plenty of stockings."

Lida had meant to stay awhile and talk to the girls about many things. But now she thought she had better get away before somebody came and made her yield up her booty. So she shuffled off through the bitter twilight, in the noiseless, shadowy way she had slipped in. As soon as she was out of sight of the manse she sat down, took off the shoes and stockings, and put them in her herring basket. She had no intention of keeping them on down that dirty harbour road. They were to be kept good for gala occasions. Not another little girl down at the harbour mouth had such fine black cashmere stockings and such smart, almost new shoes. Lida was furnished forth for the summer. She had no qualms in the matter. In her eyes the manse people were quite fabulously rich, and no doubt those girls had slathers of shoes and stockings. Then Lida ran down to the Glen village and played for an hour with the boys before Mr. Flagg's store, splashing about in a pool of slush with the maddest of them, until Mrs. Elliott came along and bade her begone home.

"I don't think, Faith, that you should have done that," said Una, a little reproachfully, after

Lida had gone. "You'll have to wear your good boots every day now and they'll soon scuff out."

"I don't care," cried Faith, still in the fine glow of having done a kindness to a fellow creature. "It isn't fair that I should have two pairs of shoes and poor little Lida Marsh not have any. NOW we both have a pair. You know perfectly well, Una, that father said in his sermon last Sunday that there was no real happiness in getting or having—only in giving. And it's true. I feel FAR happier now than I ever did in my whole life before. Just think of Lida walking home this very minute with her poor little feet all nice and warm and comfy."

"You know you haven't another pair of black cashmere stockings," said Una. "Your other pair were so full of holes that Aunt Martha said she couldn't darn them any more and she cut the legs up for stove dusters. You've nothing but those two pairs of striped stockings you hate so."

All the glow and uplift went out of Faith. Her gladness collapsed like a pricked balloon. She sat for a few dismal minutes in silence, facing the consequences of her rash act.

"Oh, Una, I never thought of that," she said dolefully. "I didn't stop to think at all."

The striped stockings were thick, heavy, coarse, ribbed stockings of blue and red which Aunt Martha had knit for Faith in the winter. They were undoubtedly hideous. Faith loathed them as she had never loathed anything before. Wear them she certainly would not. They were still unworn in her bureau drawer.

"You'll have to wear the striped stockings after this," said Una. "Just think how the boys in school will laugh at you. You know how they laugh at Mamie Warren for her striped stockings and call her barber pole and yours are far worse."

"I won't wear them," said Faith. "I'll go barefooted first, cold as it is."

"You can't go barefooted to church to-morrow. Think what people would say."

"Then I'll stay home."

"You can't. You know very well Aunt Martha will make you go."

Faith did know this. The one thing on which Aunt Martha troubled herself to insist was that they must all go to church, rain or shine. How they were dressed, or if they were dressed at all, never concerned her. But go they must. That was how Aunt Martha had been brought up seventy years ago, and that was how she meant to bring them up.

"Haven't you got a pair you can lend me, Una?" said poor Faith piteously.

Una shook her head. "No, you know I only have the one black pair. And they're so tight I can hardly get them on. They wouldn't go on you. Neither would my gray ones. Besides, the legs of THEM are all darned AND darned."

"I won't wear those striped stockings," said Faith stubbornly. "The feel of them is even worse than the looks. They make me feel as if my legs were as big as barrels and they're so SCRATCHY."

"Well, I don't know what you're going to do."

"If father was home I'd go and ask him to get me a new pair before the store closes. But he won't be home till too late. I'll ask him Monday—and I won't go to church tomorrow. I'll pretend I'm sick and Aunt Martha'll HAVE to let me stay home."

"That would be acting a lie, Faith," cried Una. "You CAN'T do that. You know it would be dreadful. What would father say if he knew? Don't you remember how he talked to us after mother died and told us we must always be TRUE, no matter what else we failed in. He said we must never tell or act a lie—he said he'd TRUST us not to. You CAN'T do it, Faith. Just wear the striped stockings. It'll only be for once. Nobody will notice them in church. It isn't like school. And your new brown dress is so long they won't show much. Wasn't it lucky Aunt

Martha made it big, so you'd have room to grow in it, for all you hated it so when she finished it?"

"I won't wear those stockings," repeated Faith. She uncoiled her bare, white legs from the tombstone and deliberately walked through the wet, cold grass to the bank of snow. Setting her teeth, she stepped upon it and stood there.

"What are you doing?" cried Una aghast. "You'll catch your death of cold, Faith Meredith."

"I'm trying to," answered Faith. "I hope I'll catch a fearful cold and be AWFUL sick to-morrow. Then I won't be acting a lie. I'm going to stand here as long as I can bear it."

"But, Faith, you might really die. You might get pneumonia. Please, Faith don't. Let's go into the house and get SOMETHING for your feet. Oh, here's Jerry. I'm so thankful. Jerry, MAKE Faith get off that snow. Look at her feet."

"Holy cats! Faith, what ARE you doing?" demanded Jerry. "Are you crazy?"

"No. Go away!" snapped Faith.

"Then are you punishing yourself for something? It isn't right, if you are. You'll be sick."

"I want to be sick. I'm not punishing myself. Go away."

"Where's her shoes and stockings?" asked Jerry of Una.

"She gave them to Lida Marsh."

"Lida Marsh? What for?"

"Because Lida had none—and her feet were so cold. And now she wants to be sick so that she won't have to go to church to-morrow and wear her striped stockings. But, Jerry, she may die."

"Faith," said Jerry, "get off that ice-bank or I'll pull you off."

"Pull away," dared Faith.

Jerry sprang at her and caught her arms. He pulled one way and Faith pulled another. Una ran behind Faith and pushed. Faith stormed at Jerry to leave her alone. Jerry stormed back at her not to be a dizzy idiot; and Una cried. They made no end of noise and they were close to the road fence of the graveyard. Henry Warren and his wife drove by and heard and saw them. Very soon the Glen heard that the manse children had been having an awful fight in the graveyard and using most improper language. Meanwhile, Faith had allowed herself to be pulled off the ice because her feet were aching so sharply that she was ready to get off any way. They all went in amiably and went to bed. Faith slept like a cherub and woke in the morning without a trace of a cold. She felt that she couldn't feign sickness and act a lie, after remembering that long-ago talk with her father. But she was still as fully determined as ever that she would not wear those abominable stockings to church.

25. ANOTHER SCANDAL AND ANOTHER "EXPLANATION"

Faith went early to Sunday School and was seated in the corner of her class pew before any one came. Therefore, the dreadful truth did not burst upon any one until Faith left the class pew near the door to walk up to the manse pew after Sunday School. The church was already half filled and all who were sitting near the aisle saw that the minister's daughter had boots on but no stockings!

Faith's new brown dress, which Aunt Martha had made from an ancient pattern, was absurdly long for her, but even so it did not meet her boot-tops. Two good inches of bare white leg showed plainly.

Faith and Carl sat alone in the manse pew. Jerry had gone into the gallery to sit with a chum and the Blythe girls had taken Una with them. The Meredith children were given to "sitting all over the church" in this fashion and a great many people thought it very improper. The gallery especially, where irresponsible lads congregated and were known to whisper and suspected of chewing tobacco during service, was no place, for a son of the manse. But Jerry hated the manse pew at the very top of the church, under the eyes of Elder Clow and his family. He escaped from it whenever he could.

Carl, absorbed in watching a spider spinning its web at the window, did not notice Faith's legs. She walked home with her father after church and he never noticed them. She got on the hated striped stockings before Jerry and Una arrived, so that for the time being none of the occupants of the manse knew what she had done. But nobody else in Glen St. Mary was ignorant of it. The few who had not seen soon heard. Nothing else was talked of on the way home from church. Mrs. Alec Davis said it was only what she expected, and the next thing you would see some of those young ones coming to church with no clothes on at all. The president of the Ladies' Aid decided that she would bring the matter up at the next Aid meeting, and suggest that they wait in a body on the minister and protest. Miss Cornelia said that she, for her part, gave up. There was no use worrying over the manse fry any longer. Even Mrs. Dr. Blythe felt a little shocked, though she attributed the occurrence solely to Faith's forgetfulness. Susan could not immediately begin knitting stockings for Faith because it was Sunday, but she had one set up before any one else was out of bed at Ingleside the next morning.

"You need not tell me anything but that it was old Martha's fault, Mrs. Dr. dear." she told Anne. "I suppose that poor little child had no decent stockings to wear. I suppose every stocking she had was in holes, as you know very well they generally are. And *I* think, Mrs. Dr. dear, that the Ladies' Aid would be better employed in knitting some for them than in fighting over the new carpet for the pulpit platform. *I* am not a Ladies' Aider, but I shall knit Faith two pairs of stockings, out of this nice black yarn, as fast as my fingers can move and that you may tie to. Never shall I forget my sensations, Mrs. Dr. dear, when I saw a minister's child walking up the aisle of our church with no stockings on. I really did not know what way to look."

"And the church was just full of Methodists yesterday, too," groaned Miss Cornelia, who had come up to the Glen to do some shopping and run into Ingleside to talk the affair over. "I don't know how it is, but just as sure as those manse children do something especially awful the church is sure to be crowded with Methodists. I thought Mrs. Deacon Hazard's eyes would drop out of her head. When she came out of church she said, 'Well, that exhibition was no more than decent. I do pity the Presbyterians.' And we just had to TAKE it. There was nothing one could say."

"There was something *I* could have said, Mrs. Dr. dear, if I had heard her," said Susan grimly. "I would have said, for one thing, that in my opinion clean bare legs were quite as decent as holes. And I would have said, for another, that the Presbyterians did not feel greatly in need of pity seeing that they had a minister who could PREACH and the Methodists had NOT. I could have squelched Mrs. Deacon Hazard, Mrs. Dr dear, and that you may tie to."

"I wish Mr. Meredith didn't preach quite so well and looked after his family a little better," retorted Miss Cornelia. "He could at least glance over his children before they went to church and see that they were quite properly clothed. I'm tired making excuses for him, believe ME."

Meanwhile, Faith's soul was being harrowed up in Rainbow Valley. Mary Vance was there and, as usual, in a lecturing mood. She gave Faith to understand that she had disgraced herself and her father beyond redemption and that she, Mary Vance, was done with her. "Everybody" was talking, and "everybody" said the same thing.

"I simply feel that I can't associate with you any longer," she concluded.

"WE are going to associate with her then," cried Nan Blythe. Nan secretly thought Faith HAD done a awful thing, but she wasn't going to let Mary Vance run matters in this high-handed fashion. "And if YOU are not you needn't come any more to Rainbow Valley, MISS Vance."

Nan and Di both put their arms around Faith and glared defiance at Mary. The latter suddenly crumpled up, sat down on a stump and began to cry.

"It ain't that I don't want to," she wailed. "But if I keep in with Faith people'll be saying I put her up to doing things. Some are saying it now, true's you live. I can't afford to have such things said of me, now that I'm in a respectable place and trying to be a lady. And *I* never went bare-legged in church in my toughest days. I'd never have thought of doing such a thing. But that hateful old Kitty Alec says Faith has never been the same girl since that time I stayed in the manse. She says Cornelia Elliott will live to rue the day she took me in. It hurts my feelings, I tell you. But it's Mr. Meredith I'm really worried over."

"I think you needn't worry about him," said Di scornfully. "It isn't likely necessary. Now, Faith darling, stop crying and tell us why you did it."

Faith explained tearfully. The Blythe girls sympathized with her, and even Mary Vance agreed that it was a hard position to be in. But Jerry, on whom the thing came like a thunderbolt, refused to be placated. So THIS was what some mysterious hints he had got in school that day meant! He marched Faith and Una home without ceremony, and the Good-Conduct Club held an immediate session in the graveyard to sit in judgment on Faith's case.

"I don't see that it was any harm," said Faith defiantly. "Not MUCH of my legs showed. It wasn't WRONG and it didn't hurt anybody."

"It will hurt Dad. You KNOW it will. You know people blame him whenever we do anything queer."

"I didn't think of that," muttered Faith.

"That's just the trouble. You didn't think and you SHOULD have thought. That's what our Club is for—to bring us up and MAKE us think. We promised we'd always stop and think before doing things. You didn't and you've got to be punished, Faith—and real hard, too. You'll wear those striped stockings to school for a week for punishment."

"Oh, Jerry, won't a day do—two days? Not a whole week!"

"Yes, a whole week," said inexorable Jerry. "It is fair—ask Jem Blythe if it isn't."

Faith felt she would rather submit then ask Jem Blythe about such a matter. She was beginning to realize that her offence was a quite shameful one.

"I'll do it, then," she muttered, a little sulkily.

"You're getting off easy," said, Jerry severely. "And no matter how we punish you it won't help father. People will always think you just did it for mischief, and they'll blame father for not stopping it. We can never explain it to everybody."

This aspect of the case weighed on Faith's mind. Her own condemnation she could bear, but it tortured her that her father should be blamed. If people knew the true facts of the case they would not blame him. But how could she make them known to all the world? Getting up in church, as she had once done, and explaining the matter was out of the question. Faith had heard from Mary Vance how the congregation had looked upon that performance and realized that she must not repeat it. Faith worried over the problem for half a week. Then she had an inspiration and promptly acted upon it. She spent that evening in the garret, with a lamp and an exercise book, writing busily, with flushed cheeks and shining eyes. It was the very thing! How clever she was to have thought of it! It would put everything right and explain everything and yet cause no scandal. It was eleven o'clock when she had finished to her satisfaction and crept down to bed, dreadfully tired, but perfectly happy.

In a few days the little weekly published in the Glen under the name of *The Journal* came out as usual, and the Glen had another sensation. A letter signed "Faith Meredith" occupied a prominent place on the front page and ran as follows:—

"To Whom It May Concern:

"I want to explain to everybody how it was I came to go to church without stockings on, so that everybody will know that father was not to blame one bit for it, and the old gossips need not say he is, because it is not true. I gave my only pair of black stockings to Lida Marsh, because she hadn't any and her poor little feet were awful cold and I was so sorry for her. No child ought to have to go without shoes and stockings in a Christian community before the snow is all gone, and I think the W. F. M. S. ought to have given her stockings. Of course, I know they are sending things to the little heathen children, and that is all right and a kind thing to do. But the little heathen children have lots more warm weather than we have, and I think the women of our church ought to look after Lida and not leave it all to me. When I gave her my stockings I forgot they were the only black pair I had without holes, but I am glad I did give them to her, because my conscience would have been uncomfortable if I hadn't. When she had gone away, looking so proud and happy, the poor little thing, I remembered that all I had to wear were the horrid red and blue things Aunt Martha knit last winter for me out of some yarn that Mrs. Joseph Burr of Upper Glen sent us. It was dreadfully coarse yarn and all knots, and I never saw any of Mrs. Burr's own children wearing things made of such yarn. But Mary Vance says Mrs. Burr gives the minister stuff that she can't use or eat herself, and thinks it ought to go as part of the salary her husband signed to pay, but never does.

"I just couldn't bear to wear those hateful stockings. They were so ugly and rough and felt so scratchy. Everybody would have made fun of me. I thought at first I'd pretend to be sick and not go to church next day, but I decided I couldn't do that, because it would be acting a lie, and father told us after mother died that was something we must never, never do. It is just as bad to act a lie as to tell one, though I know some people, right here in the Glen, who act them, and never seem to feel a bit bad about it. I will not mention any names, but I know who they are and so does father.

"Then I tried my best to catch cold and really be sick by standing on the snowbank in the Methodist graveyard with my bare feet until Jerry pulled me off. But it didn't hurt me a bit and so I couldn't get out of going to church. So I just decided I would put my boots on and go that way. I can't see why it was so wrong and I was so careful to wash my legs just as clean as my face, but, anyway, father wasn't to blame for it. He was in the study thinking of his sermon and other heavenly things, and I kept out of his way before I went to Sunday School. Father does not look at people's legs in church, so of course he did not notice mine, but all the gossips did and talked about it, and that is why I am writing this letter to the *Journal* to explain. I suppose I did very wrong, since everybody says so, and I am sorry and I am wearing those awful stockings to punish myself, although father bought me two nice new black pairs as soon as Mr. Flagg's store opened on Monday morning. But it was all my fault, and if people blame father for it after they read this they are not Christians and so I do not mind what they say.

"There is another thing I want to explain about before I stop. Mary Vance told me that Mr. Evan Boyd is blaming the Lew Baxters for stealing potatoes out of his field last fall. They did not touch his potatoes. They are very poor, but they are honest. It was us did it—Jerry and Carl and I. Una was not with us at the time. We never thought it was stealing. We just wanted a few potatoes to cook over a fire in Rainbow Valley one evening to eat with our fried trout. Mr. Boyd's field was the nearest, just between the valley and the village, so we climbed over his fence and pulled up some stalks. The potatoes were awful small, because Mr. Boyd did not put enough fertilizer on them and we had to pull up a lot of stalks before we got enough, and then they were not much bigger than marbles. Walter and Di Blythe helped us eat them, but they did not come along until we had them cooked and did not know where we got them, so they were not to blame at all, only us. We didn't mean any harm, but if it was stealing we are very sorry and we will pay Mr. Boyd for them if he will wait until we grow up. We never have any money now because we are not big enough to earn any, and Aunt Martha says it takes every cent of poor father's salary, even when it is paid up regularly—and it isn't often—to run this house. But Mr. Boyd must not blame the Lew Baxters any more, when they were quite innocent, and give them a bad name.

"Yours respectfully,

"Faith Meredith."

26. MISS CORNELIA GETS A NEW POINT OF VIEW

"Susan, after I'm dead I'm going to come back to earth every time when the daffodils blow in this garden," said Anne rapturously. "Nobody may see me, but I'll be here. If anybody is in the garden at the time—I THINK I'll come on an evening just like this, but it MIGHT be just at dawn—a lovely, pale-pinky spring dawn—they'll just see the daffodils nodding wildly as if an extra gust of wind had blown past them, but it will be *I*."

"Indeed, Mrs. Dr. dear, you will not be thinking of flaunting worldly things like daffies after you are dead," said Susan. "And I do NOT believe in ghosts, seen or unseen."

"Oh, Susan, I shall not be a ghost! That has such a horrible sound. I shall just be ME. And I shall run around in the twilight, whether it is morn or eve, and see all the spots I love. Do you remember how badly I felt when I left our little House of Dreams, Susan? I thought I could never love Ingleside so well. But I do. I love every inch of the ground and every stick and stone on it."

"I am rather fond of the place myself," said Susan, who would have died if she had been removed from it, "but we must not set our affections too much on earthly things, Mrs. Dr. dear. There are such things as fires and earthquakes. We should always be prepared. The Tom MacAllisters over-harbour were burned out three nights ago. Some say Tom MacAllister set the house on fire himself to get the insurance. That may or may not be. But I advise the doctor to have our chimneys seen to at once. An ounce of prevention is worth a pound of cure. But I see Mrs. Marshall Elliott coming in at the gate, looking as if she had been sent for and couldn't go."

"Anne dearie, have you seen the *Journal* to-day?"

Miss Cornelia's voice was trembling, partly from emotion, partly from the fact that she had hurried up from the store too fast and lost her breath.

Anne bent over the daffodils to hide a smile. She and Gilbert had laughed heartily and heartlessly over the front page of the *Journal* that day, but she knew that to dear Miss Cornelia it was almost a tragedy, and she must not wound her feelings by any display of levity.

"Isn't it dreadful? What IS to be done?" asked Miss Cornelia despairingly. Miss Cornelia had vowed that she was done with worrying over the pranks of the manse children, but she went on worrying just the same.

Anne led the way to the veranda, where Susan was knitting, with Shirley and Rilla conning their primers on either side. Susan was already on her second pair of stockings for Faith. Susan never worried over poor humanity. She did what in her lay for its betterment and serenely left the rest to the Higher Powers.

"Cornelia Elliott thinks she was born to run this world, Mrs. Dr. dear," she had once said to Anne, "and so she is always in a stew over something. I have never thought *I* was, and so I go calmly along. Not but what it has sometimes occurred to me that things might be run a little better than they are. But it is not for us poor worms to nourish such thoughts. They only make us uncomfortable and do not get us anywhere."

"I don't see that anything can be done—now—" said Anne, pulling out a nice, cushiony chair for Miss Cornelia. "But how in the world did Mr. Vickers allow that letter to be printed? Surely he should have known better."

"Why, he's away, Anne dearie—he's been away to New Brunswick for a week. And that young scalawag of a Joe Vickers is editing the *Journal* in his absence. Of course, Mr. Vickers would never have put it in, even if he is a Methodist, but Joe would just think it a good joke. As you say, I don't suppose there is anything to be done now, only live it down. But if I ever get Joe Vickers cornered somewhere I'll give him a talking to he won't forget in a hurry. I wanted Marshall to stop our subscription to the *Journal* instantly, but he only laughed and said that today's issue was the only one that had had anything readable in it for a year. Marshall never will take anything seriously—just like a man. Fortunately, Evan Boyd is like that, too. He takes it as a joke and is laughing all over the place about it. And he's another Methodist! As for Mrs. Burr of Upper Glen, of course she will be furious and they will leave the church. Not that it will be a great loss from any point of view. The Methodists are quite welcome to THEM."

"It serves Mrs. Burr right," said Susan, who had an old feud with the lady in question and had been hugely tickled over the reference to her in Faith's letter. "She will find that she will not be able to cheat the Methodist parson out of HIS salary with bad yarn."

"The worst of it is, there's not much hope of things getting any better," said Miss Cornelia gloomily. "As long as Mr. Meredith was going to see Rosemary West I did hope the manse would soon have a proper mistress. But that is all off. I suppose she wouldn't have him on account of the children—at least, everybody seems to think so."

"I do not believe that he ever asked her," said Susan, who could not conceive of any one refusing a minister.

"Well, nobody knows anything about THAT. But one thing is certain, he doesn't go there any longer. And Rosemary didn't look well all the spring. I hope her visit to Kingsport will do her good. She's been gone for a month and will stay another month, I understand. I can't remember when Rosemary was away from home before. She and Ellen could never bear to be parted. But I understand Ellen insisted on her going this time. And meanwhile Ellen and Norman Douglas are warming up the old soup."

"Is that really so?" asked Anne, laughing. "I heard a rumour of it, but I hardly believed it."

"Believe it! You may believe it all right, Anne, dearie. Nobody is in ignorance of it. Norman Douglas never left anybody in doubt as to his intentions in regard to anything. He always did his courting before the public. He told Marshall that he hadn't thought about Ellen for years, but the first time he went to church last fall he saw her and fell in love with her all over again. He said he'd clean forgot how handsome she was. He hadn't seen her for twenty years, if you can believe it. Of course he never went to church, and Ellen never went anywhere else round here. Oh, we all know what Norman means, but what Ellen means is a different matter. I shan't take it upon me to predict whether it will be a match or not."

"He jilted her once—but it seems that does not count with some people, Mrs. Dr. dear," Susan remarked rather acidly.

"He jilted her in a fit of temper and repented it all his life," said Miss Cornelia. "That is different from a cold-blooded jilting. For my part, I never detested Norman as some folks do. He could never over-crow ME. I DO wonder what started him coming to church. I have never been able to believe Mrs. Wilsons's story that Faith Meredith went there and bullied him into it. I've always intended to ask Faith herself, but I've never happened to think of it just when I saw her. What influence could SHE have over Norman Douglas? He was in the store when I left, bellowing with laughter over that scandalous letter. You could have heard him at Four Winds Point. 'The greatest girl in the world,' he was shouting. 'She's that full of spunk she's bursting with it. And all the old grannies want to tame her, darn them. But they'll never be able to do it —never! They might as well try to drown a fish. Boyd, see that you put more fertilizer on your potatoes next year. Ho, ho, ho!' And then he laughed till the roof shook."

"Mr. Douglas pays well to the salary, at least," remarked Susan.

"Oh, Norman isn't mean in some ways. He'd give a thousand without blinking a lash, and roar like a Bull of Bashan if he had to pay five cents too much for anything. Besides, he likes Mr. Meredith's sermons, and Norman Douglas was always willing to shell out if he got his brains tickled up. There is no more Christianity about him than there is about a black, naked heathen in Africa and never will be. But he's clever and well read and he judges sermons as he would lectures. Anyhow, it's well he backs up Mr. Meredith and the children as he does, for they'll need friends more than ever after this. I am tired of making excuses for them, believe ME."

"Do you know, dear Miss Cornelia," said Anne seriously, "I think we have all been making too many excuses. It is very foolish and we ought to stop it. I am going to tell you what I'd LIKE to do. I shan't do it, of course"—Anne had noted a glint of alarm in Susan's eye—"it would be too unconventional, and we must be conventional or die, after we reach what is supposed to be a dignified age. But I'd LIKE to do it. I'd like to call a meeting of the Ladies Aid and W.M.S. and the Girls Sewing Society, and include in the audience all and any Methodists who have been criticizing the Merediths—although I do think if we Presbyterians stopped criticizing and excusing we would find that other denominations would trouble themselves very little about our manse folks. I would say to them, 'Dear Christian friends'—with marked emphasis on 'Christian'—I have something to say to you and I want to say it good and hard, that you may take it home and repeat it to your families. You Methodists need not pity us, and we Presbyterians need not pity ourselves. We are not going to do it any more. And we are going to say, boldly and truthfully, to all critics and sympathizers, 'We are PROUD of our minister and his family. Mr. Meredith is the best preacher Glen St. Mary church ever had. Moreover, he is a sincere, earnest teacher of truth and Christian charity. He is a faithful friend, a judicious pastor in all essentials, and a refined, scholarly, well-bred man. His family are worthy of him. Gerald Meredith is the cleverest pupil in the Glen school, and Mr. Hazard says that he is destined to a brilliant career. He is a manly, honourable, truthful little fellow. Faith Meredith is a beauty, and as inspiring and original as she is beautiful. There is nothing commonplace about her. All the other girls in the Glen put together haven't the vim, and wit, and joyousness and 'spunk' she has. She has not an enemy in the world. Every one who knows her loves her. Of how many, children or grown-ups, can that be said? Una Meredith is sweetness personified. She will make a most lovable woman. Carl Meredith, with his love for ants and frogs and spiders, will some day be a naturalist whom all Canada—nay, all the world, will delight to honour. Do you know of any other family in the Glen, or out of it, of whom all these things can be said? Away with shamefaced excuses and apologies. We REJOICE in our minister and his splendid boys and girls!"

Anne stopped, partly because she was out of breath after her vehement speech and partly because she could not trust herself to speak further in view of Miss Cornelia's face. That good lady was staring helplessly at Anne, apparently engulfed in billows of new ideas. But she came up with a gasp and struck out for shore gallantly.

"Anne Blythe, I wish you WOULD call that meeting and say just that! You've made me ashamed of myself, for one, and far be it from me to refuse to admit it. OF COURSE, that is how we should have talked—especially to the Methodists. And it's every word of it true—every word. We've just been shutting our eyes to the big worth-while things and squinting them on the little things that don't really matter a pin's worth. Oh, Anne dearie, I can see a thing when it's hammered into my head. No more apologizing for Cornelia Marshall! *I* shall hold MY head up after this, believe ME—though I MAY talk things over with you as usual just to relieve my feelings if the Merediths do any more startling stunts. Even that letter I felt so bad about—why, it's only a good joke after all, as Norman says. Not many girls would have been cute enough to think of writing it—and all punctuated so nicely and not one word misspelled. Just let me hear any Methodist say one word about it—though all the same I'll never forgive Joe Vickers—believe ME! Where are the rest of your small fry to-night?"

"Walter and the twins are in Rainbow Valley. Jem is studying in the garret."

"They are all crazy about Rainbow Valley. Mary Vance thinks it's the only place in the world. She'd be off up here every evening if I'd let her. But I don't encourage her in gadding. Besides, I miss the creature when she isn't around, Anne dearie. I never thought I'd get so fond of her. Not but what I see her faults and try to correct them. But she has never said one saucy word to me since she came to my house and she is a GREAT help—for when all is said and done, Anne dearie, I am not so young as I once was, and there is no sense denying it. I was fifty-nine my last birthday. I don't FEEL it, but there is no gainsaying the Family Bible."

27. A SACRED CONCERT

In spite of Miss Cornelia's new point of view she could not help feeling a little disturbed over the next performance of the manse children. In public she carried off the situation splendidly, saying to all the gossips the substance of what Anne had said in daffodil time, and saying it so pointedly and forcibly that her hearers found themselves feeling rather foolish and began to think that, after all, they were making too much of a childish prank. But in private Miss Cornelia allowed herself the relief of bemoaning it to Anne.

"Anne dearie, they had a CONCERT IN THE GRAVEYARD last Thursday evening, while the Methodist prayer meeting was going on. There they sat, on Hezekiah Pollock's tombstone, and sang for a solid hour. Of course, I understand it was mostly hymns they sang, and it wouldn't have been quite so bad if they'd done nothing else. But I'm told they finished up with *Polly Wolly Doodle* at full length—and that just when Deacon Baxter was praying."

"I was there that night," said Susan, "and, although I did not say anything about it to you, Mrs. Dr. dear, I could not help thinking that it was a great pity they picked that particular evening. It was truly blood-curdling to hear them sitting there in that abode of the dead, shouting that frivolous song at the tops of their lungs."

"I don't know what YOU were doing in a Methodist prayer meeting," said Miss Cornelia acidly.

"I have never found that Methodism was catching," retorted Susan stiffly. "And, as I was going to say when I was interrupted, badly as I felt, I did NOT give in to the Methodists. When Mrs. Deacon Baxter said, as we came out, 'What a disgraceful exhibition!' *I* said, looking her fairly in the eye, 'They are all beautiful singers, and none of YOUR choir, Mrs. Baxter, ever bother themselves coming out to your prayer meeting, it seems. Their voices appear to be in tune only on Sundays!' She was quite meek and I felt that I had snubbed her properly. But I could have done it much more thoroughly, Mrs. Dr. dear, if only they had left out *Polly Wolly Doodle*. It is truly terrible to think of that being sung in a graveyard."

"Some of those dead folks sang *Polly Wolly Doodle* when they were living, Susan. Perhaps they like to hear it yet," suggested Gilbert.

Miss Cornelia looked at him reproachfully and made up her mind that, on some future occasion, she would hint to Anne that the doctor should be admonished not to say such things.

They might injure his practice. People might get it into their heads that he wasn't orthodox. To be sure, Marshall said even worse things habitually, but then HE was not a public man.

"I understand that their father was in his study all the time, with his windows open, but never noticed them at all. Of course, he was lost in a book as usual. But I spoke to him about it yesterday, when he called."

"How could you dare, Mrs. Marshall Elliott?" asked Susan rebukingly.

"Dare! It's time somebody dared something. Why, they say he knows nothing about that letter of Faith's to the JOURNAL because nobody liked to mention it to him. He never looks at a JOURNAL of course. But I thought he ought to know of this to prevent any such performances in future. He said he would 'discuss it with them.' But of course he'd never think of it again after he got out of our gate. That man has no sense of humour, Anne, believe ME. He preached last Sunday on 'How to Bring up Children.' A beautiful sermon it was, too—and everybody in church thinking 'what a pity you can't practise what you preach.'"

Miss Cornelia did Mr. Meredith an injustice in thinking he would soon forget what she had told him. He went home much disturbed and when the children came from Rainbow Valley that night, at a much later hour than they should have been prowling in it, he called them into his study.

They went in, somewhat awed. It was such an unusual thing for their father to do. What could he be going to say to them? They racked their memories for any recent transgression of sufficient importance, but could not recall any. Carl had spilled a saucerful of jam on Mrs. Peter Flagg's silk dress two evenings before, when, at Aunt Martha's invitation, she had stayed to supper. But Mr. Meredith had not noticed it, and Mrs. Flagg, who was a kindly soul, had made no fuss. Besides, Carl had been punished by having to wear Una's dress all the rest of the evening.

Una suddenly thought that perhaps her father meant to tell them that he was going to marry Miss West. Her heart began to beat violently and her legs trembled. Then she saw that Mr. Meredith looked very stern and sorrowful. No, it could not be that.

"Children," said Mr. Meredith, "I have heard something that has pained me very much. Is it true that you sat out in the graveyard all last Thursday evening and sang ribald songs while a prayer meeting was being held in the Methodist church?"

"Great Caesar, Dad, we forgot all about it being their prayer meeting night," exclaimed Jerry in dismay.

"Then it is true—you did do this thing?"

"Why, Dad, I don't know what you mean by ribald songs. We sang hymns—it was a sacred concert, you know. What harm was that? I tell you we never thought about it's being Methodist prayer meeting night. They used to have their meeting Tuesday nights and since they've changed to Thursdays it's hard to remember."

"Did you sing nothing but hymns?"

"Why," said Jerry, turning red, "we DID sing *Polly Wolly Doodle* at the last. Faith said, 'Let's have something cheerful to wind up with.' But we didn't mean any harm, Father—truly we didn't."

"The concert was my idea, Father," said Faith, afraid that Mr. Meredith might blame Jerry too much. "You know the Methodists themselves had a sacred concert in their church three Sunday nights ago. I thought it would be good fun to get one up in imitation of it. Only they had prayers at theirs, and we left that part out, because we heard that people thought it awful for us to pray in a graveyard. YOU were sitting in here all the time," she added, "and never said a word to us."

"I did not notice what you were doing. That is no excuse for me, of course. I am more to blame than you—I realize that. But why did you sing that foolish song at the end?"

"We didn't think," muttered Jerry, feeling that it was a very lame excuse, seeing that he had lectured Faith so strongly in the Good-Conduct Club sessions for her lack of thought. "We're sorry, Father—truly, we are. Pitch into us hard—we deserve a regular combing down."

But Mr. Meredith did no combing down or pitching into. He sat down and gathered his small culprits close to him and talked a little to them, tenderly and wisely. They were overcome with remorse and shame, and felt that they could never be so silly and thoughtless again.

"We've just got to punish ourselves good and hard for this," whispered Jerry as they crept upstairs. "We'll have a session of the Club first thing tomorrow and decide how we'll do it. I never saw father so cut up. But I wish to goodness the Methodists would stick to one night for their prayer meeting and not wander all over the week."

"Anyhow, I'm glad it wasn't what I was afraid it was," murmured Una to herself.

Behind them, in the study, Mr. Meredith had sat down at his desk and buried his face in his arms.

"God help me!" he said. "I'm a poor sort of father. Oh, Rosemary! If you had only cared!"

28. A FAST DAY

The Good-Conduct Club had a special session the next morning before school. After various suggestions, it was decided that a fast day would be an appropriate punishment.

"We won't eat a single thing for a whole day," said Jerry. "I'm kind of curious to see what fasting is like, anyhow. This will be a good chance to find out."

"What day will we choose for it?" asked Una, who thought it would be quite an easy punishment and rather wondered that Jerry and Faith had not devised something harder.

"Let's pick Monday," said Faith. "We mostly have a pretty FILLING dinner on Sundays, and Mondays meals never amount to much anyhow."

"But that's just the point," exclaimed Jerry. "We mustn't take the easiest day to fast, but the hardest—and that's Sunday, because, as you say, we mostly have roast beef that day instead of cold ditto. It wouldn't be much punishment to fast from ditto. Let's take next Sunday. It will be a good day, for father is going to exchange for the morning service with the Upper Lowbridge minister. Father will be away till evening. If Aunt Martha wonders what's got into us, we'll tell her right up that we're fasting for the good of our souls, and it is in the Bible and she is not to interfere, and I guess she won't."

Aunt Martha did not. She merely said in her fretful mumbling way, "What foolishness are you young rips up to now?" and thought no more about it. Mr. Meredith had gone away early in the morning before any one was up. He went without his breakfast, too, but that was, of course, of common occurrence. Half of the time he forgot it and there was no one to remind him of it. Breakfast—Aunt Martha's breakfast—was not a hard meal to miss. Even the hungry "young rips" did not feel it any great deprivation to abstain from the "lumpy porridge and blue milk" which had aroused the scorn of Mary Vance. But it was different at dinner time. They were furiously hungry then, and the odor of roast beef which pervaded the manse, and which was wholly delightful in spite of the fact that the roast beef was badly underdone, was almost more than they could stand. In desperation they rushed to the graveyard where they couldn't smell it. But Una could not keep her eyes from the dining room window, through which the Upper Lowbridge minister could be seen, placidly eating.

"If I could only have just a weeny, teeny piece," she sighed.

"Now, you stop that," commanded Jerry. "Of course it's hard—but that's the punishment of it. I could eat a graven image this very minute, but am I complaining? Let's think of something else. We've just got to rise above our stomachs."

At supper time they did not feel the pangs of hunger which they had suffered earlier in the day.

"I suppose we're getting used to it," said Faith. "I feel an awfully queer all-gone sort of feeling, but I can't say I'm hungry."

"My head is funny," said Una. "It goes round and round sometimes."

But she went gamely to church with the others. If Mr. Meredith had not been so wholly wrapped up in and carried away with his subject he might have noticed the pale little face and hollow eyes in the manse pew beneath. But he noticed nothing and his sermon was something longer than usual. Then, just before he gave out the final hymn, Una Meredith tumbled off the seat of the manse pew and lay in a dead faint on the floor.

Mrs. Elder Clow was the first to reach her. She caught the thin little body from the arms of white-faced, terrified Faith and carried it into the vestry. Mr. Meredith forgot the hymn and everything else and rushed madly after her. The congregation dismissed itself as best it could.

"Oh, Mrs. Clow," gasped Faith, "is Una dead? Have we killed her?"

"What is the matter with my child?" demanded the pale father.

"She has just fainted, I think," said Mrs. Clow. "Oh, here's the doctor, thank goodness."

Gilbert did not find it a very easy thing to bring Una back to consciousness. He worked over her for a long time before her eyes opened. Then he carried her over to the manse, followed by Faith, sobbing hysterically in her relief.

"She is just hungry, you know—she didn't eat a thing to-day—none of us did—we were all fasting."

"Fasting!" said Mr. Meredith, and "Fasting?" said the doctor.

"Yes—to punish ourselves for singing *Polly Wolly* in the graveyard," said Faith.

"My child, I don't want you to punish yourselves for that," said Mr. Meredith in distress. "I gave you your little scolding—and you were all penitent—and I forgave you."

"Yes, but we had to be punished," explained Faith. "It's our rule—in our Good-Conduct Club, you know—if we do anything wrong, or anything that is likely to hurt father in the congregation, we HAVE to punish ourselves. We are bringing ourselves up, you know, because there is nobody to do it."

Mr. Meredith groaned, but the doctor got up from Una's side with an air of relief.

"Then this child simply fainted from lack of food and all she needs is a good square meal," he said. "Mrs. Clow, will you be kind enough to see she gets it? And I think from Faith's story that they all would be the better for something to eat, or we shall have more faintings."

"I suppose we shouldn't have made Una fast," said Faith remorsefully. "When I think of it, only Jerry and I should have been punished. WE got up the concert and we were the oldest."

"I sang *Polly Wolly* just the same as the rest of you," said Una's weak little voice, "so I had to be punished, too."

Mrs. Clow came with a glass of milk, Faith and Jerry and Carl sneaked off to the pantry, and John Meredith went into his study, where he sat in the darkness for a long time, alone with his bitter thoughts. So his children were bringing themselves up because there was "nobody to do it"—struggling along amid their little perplexities without a hand to guide or a voice to counsel. Faith's innocently uttered phrase rankled in her father's mind like a barbed shaft. There was "nobody" to look after them—to comfort their little souls and care for their little bodies. How frail Una had looked, lying there on the vestry sofa in that long faint! How thin were her tiny hands, how pallid her little face! She looked as if she might slip away from him in a breath—sweet little Una, of whom Cecilia had begged him to take such special care. Since his wife's death he had not felt such an agony of dread as when he had hung over his little girl in her unconsciousness. He must do something—but what? Should he ask Elizabeth Kirk to marry him? She was a good woman—she would be kind to his children. He might bring himself to do it if it were not for his love for Rosemary West. But until he had crushed that out he could not seek another woman in marriage. And he could not crush it out—he had tried and he could not. Rosemary had been in church that evening, for the first time since her return from Kingsport. He had caught a glimpse of her face in the back of the crowded church, just as he had finished his sermon. His heart had given a fierce throb. He sat while the choir sang the "collection piece," with his bent head and tingling pulses. He had not seen her since the evening upon which he had asked her to marry him. When he had risen to give out the hymn his hands were trembling and his pale face was flushed. Then Una's fainting spell had banished everything from his mind for a time. Now, in the darkness and solitude of the study it rushed back. Rosemary was the only woman in the world for him. It was of no use for him to think of marrying any other. He could not commit such a sacrilege even for his children's sake. He must take up his burden alone—he must try to be a better, a more watchful father—he must tell his children not to be afraid to come to him with all their little problems. Then he lighted his lamp and took up a bulky new book which was setting the theological world by the ears. He would read just one chapter to compose his mind. Five minutes later he was lost to the world and the troubles of the world.

29. A WEIRD TALE

On an early June evening Rainbow Valley was an entirely delightful place and the children felt it to be so, as they sat in the open glade where the bells rang elfishly on the Tree Lovers, and the White Lady shook her green tresses. The wind was laughing and whistling about them like a leal, glad-hearted comrade. The young ferns were spicy in the hollow. The wild cherry trees scattered over the valley, among the dark firs, were mistily white. The robins were whistling over in the maples behind Ingleside. Beyond, on the slopes of the Glen, were blossoming orchards, sweet and mystic and wonderful, veiled in dusk. It was spring, and young things MUST be glad in spring. Everybody was glad in Rainbow Valley that evening—until Mary Vance froze their blood with the story of Henry Warren's ghost.

Jem was not there. Jem spent his evenings now studying for his entrance examination in the Ingleside garret. Jerry was down near the pond, trouting. Walter had been reading Longfellow's sea poems to the others and they were steeped in the beauty and mystery of the ships. Then they talked of what they would do when they were grown up—where they would travel—the far, fair shores they would see. Nan and Di meant to go to Europe. Walter longed for the Nile moaning past its Egyptian sands, and a glimpse of the sphinx. Faith opined rather dismally that she supposed she would have to be a missionary—old Mrs. Taylor told her she ought to be—and then she would at least see India or China, those mysterious lands of the Orient. Carl's heart was set on African jungles. Una said nothing. She thought she would just like to stay at home. It was prettier here than anywhere else. It would be dreadful when they were all grown up and had to scatter over the world. The very idea made Una feel lonesome and homesick. But the others dreamed on delightedly until Mary Vance arrived and vanished poesy and dreams at one fell swoop.

"Laws, but I'm out of puff," she exclaimed. "I've run down that hill like sixty. I got an awful scare up there at the old Bailey place."

"What frightened you?" asked Di.

"I dunno. I was poking about under them lilacs in the old garden, trying to see if there was any lilies-of-the-valley out yet. It was dark as a pocket there—and all at once I seen something stirring and rustling round at the other side of the garden, in those cherry bushes. It was WHITE. I tell you I didn't stop for a second look. I flew over the dyke quicker than quick. I was sure it was Henry Warren's ghost."

"Who was Henry Warren?" asked Di.

"And why should he have a ghost?" asked Nan.

"Laws, did you never hear the story? And you brought up in the Glen. Well, wait a minute till I get by breath all back and I'll tell you."

Walter shivered delightsomely. He loved ghost stories. Their mystery, their dramatic climaxes, their eeriness gave him a fearful, exquisite pleasure. Longfellow instantly grew tame and commonplace. He threw the book aside and stretched himself out, propped upon his elbows to listen whole-heartedly, fixing his great luminous eyes on Mary's face. Mary wished he wouldn't look at her so. She felt she could make a better job of the ghost story if Walter were not looking at her. She could put on several frills and invent a few artistic details to enhance the horror. As it was, she had to stick to the bare truth—or what had been told her for the truth.

"Well," she began, "you know old Tom Bailey and his wife used to live in that house up there thirty years ago. He was an awful old rip, they say, and his wife wasn't much better. They'd no children of their own, but a sister of old Tom's died and left a little boy—this Henry Warren—and they took him. He was about twelve when he came to them, and kind of undersized and delicate. They say Tom and his wife used him awful from the start—whipped him and starved him. Folks said they wanted him to die so's they could get the little bit of money his mother had left for him. Henry didn't die right off, but he begun having fits—epileps, they called 'em—and he grew up kind of simple, till he was about eighteen. His uncle used to thrash him in that garden up there 'cause it was back of the house where no one could see him. But folks could hear, and they say it was awful sometimes hearing poor Henry plead with his uncle not to kill him. But nobody dared interfere 'cause old Tom was such a reprobate he'd have been sure to get square with 'em some way. He burned the barns of a man at Harbour Head who offended him. At last Henry died and his uncle and aunt give out he died in one of his fits and that was all anybody ever knowed, but everybody said Tom had just up and killed him for keeps at last. And it wasn't long till it got around that Henry WALKED. That old garden was HA'NTED. He was heard there at nights, moaning and crying. Old Tom and his wife got out—went out West and never came back. The place got such a bad name nobody'd buy or rent it. That's why it's all gone to ruin. That was thirty years ago, but Henry Warren's ghost ha'nts it yet."

"Do you believe that?" asked Nan scornfully. "*I* don't."

"Well, GOOD people have seen him—and heard him." retorted Mary. "They say he appears and grovels on the ground and holds you by the legs and gibbers and moans like he did when he was alive. I thought of that as soon as I seen that white thing in the bushes and thought if it caught me like that and moaned I'd drop down dead on the spot. So I cut and run. It MIGHTN'T have been his ghost, but I wasn't going to take any chances with a ha'nt."

"It was likely old Mrs. Stimson's white calf," laughed Di. "It pastures in that garden—I've seen it."

"Maybe so. But I'M not going home through the Bailey garden any more. Here's Jerry with a big string of trout and it's my turn to cook them. Jem and Jerry both say I'm the best cook in the Glen. And Cornelia told me I could bring up this batch of cookies. I all but dropped them when I saw Henry's ghost."

Jerry hooted when he heard the ghost story—which Mary repeated as she fried the fish, touching it up a trifle or so, since Walter had gone to help Faith to set the table. It made no impression on Jerry, but Faith and Una and Carl had been secretly much frightened, though they would never have given in to it. It was all right as long as the others were with them in the valley: but when the feast was over and the shadows fell they quaked with remembrance. Jerry went up to Ingleside with the Blythes to see Jem about something, and Mary Vance went around that way home. So Faith and Una and Carl had to go back to the manse alone. They walked very close together and gave the old Bailey garden a wide berth. They did not believe that it was haunted, of course, but they would not go near it for all that.

30. THE GHOST ON THE DYKE

Somehow, Faith and Carl and Una could not shake off the hold which the story of Henry Warren's ghost had taken upon their imaginations. They had never believed in ghosts. Ghost tales they had heard a-plenty—Mary Vance had told some far more blood-curdling than this; but those tales were all of places and people and spooks far away and unknown. After the first half-awful, half-pleasant thrill of awe and terror they thought of them no more. But this story came home to them. The old Bailey garden was almost at their very door—almost in their beloved Rainbow Valley. They had passed and repassed it constantly; they had hunted for flowers in it; they had made short cuts through it when they wished to go straight from the village to the valley. But never again! After the night when Mary Vance told them its gruesome tale they would not have gone through or near it on pain of death. Death! What was death compared to the unearthly possibility of falling into the clutches of Henry Warren's grovelling ghost?

One warm July evening the three of them were sitting under the Tree Lovers, feeling a little lonely. Nobody else had come near the valley that evening. Jem Blythe was away in Charlottetown, writing on his entrance examinations. Jerry and Walter Blythe were off for a sail on the harbour with old Captain Crawford. Nan and Di and Rilla and Shirley had gone down the harbour road to visit Kenneth and Persis Ford, who had come with their parents for a flying visit to the little old House of Dreams. Nan had asked Faith to go with them, but Faith had declined. She would never have admitted it, but she felt a little secret jealousy of Persis Ford, concerning whose wonderful beauty and city glamour she had heard a great deal. No, she wasn't going to go down there and play second fiddle to anybody. She and Una took their story books to Rainbow Valley and read, while Carl investigated bugs along the banks of the brook, and all three were happy until they suddenly realized that it was twilight and that the old Bailey garden was uncomfortably near by. Carl came and sat down close to the girls. They all wished they had gone home a little sooner, but nobody said anything.

Great, velvety, purple clouds heaped up in the west and spread over the valley. There was no wind and everything was suddenly, strangely, dreadfully still. The marsh was full of thousands of fire-flies. Surely some fairy parliament was being convened that night. Altogether, Rainbow Valley was not a canny place just then.

Faith looked fearfully up the valley to the old Bailey garden. Then, if anybody's blood ever did freeze, Faith Meredith's certainly froze at that moment. The eyes of Carl and Una followed her entranced gaze and chills began gallopading up and down their spines also. For there, under the big tamarack tree on the tumble-down, grass-grown dyke of the Bailey garden, was something white—shapelessly white in the gathering gloom. The three Merediths sat and gazed as if turned to stone.

"It's—it's the—calf," whispered Una at last.

"It's—too—big—for the calf," whispered Faith. Her mouth and lips were so dry she could hardly articulate the words.

Suddenly Carl gasped,

"It's coming here."

The girls gave one last agonized glance. Yes, it was creeping down over the dyke, as no calf ever did or could creep. Reason fled before sudden, over-mastering panic. For the moment every one of the trio was firmly convinced that what they saw was Henry Warren's ghost. Carl sprang to his feet and bolted blindly. With a simultaneous shriek the girls followed him. Like mad creatures they tore up the hill, across the road and into the manse. They had left Aunt Martha sewing in the kitchen. She was not there. They rushed to the study. It was dark and tenantless. As with one impulse, they swung around and made for Ingleside—but not across Rainbow Valley. Down the hill and through the Glen street they flew on the wings of their wild terror, Carl in the lead, Una bringing up the rear. Nobody tried to stop them, though everybody who saw them wondered what fresh devilment those manse youngsters were up to now. But at the gate of Ingleside they ran into Rosemary West, who had just been in for a moment to return some borrowed books.

She saw their ghastly faces and staring eyes. She realized that their poor little souls were wrung with some awful and real fear, whatever its cause. She caught Carl with one arm and Faith with the other. Una stumbled against her and held on desperately.

"Children, dear, what has happened?" she said. "What has frightened you?"

"Henry Warren's ghost," answered Carl, through his chattering teeth.

"Henry—Warren's—ghost!" said amazed Rosemary, who had never heard the story.

"Yes," sobbed Faith hysterically. "It's there—on the Bailey dyke—we saw it—and it started to—chase us."

Rosemary herded the three distracted creatures to the Ingleside veranda. Gilbert and Anne were both away, having also gone to the House of Dreams, but Susan appeared in the doorway, gaunt and practical and unghostlike.

"What is all this rumpus about?" she inquired.

Again the children gasped out their awful tale, while Rosemary held them close to her and soothed them with wordless comfort.

"Likely it was an owl," said Susan, unstirred.

An owl! The Meredith children never had any opinion of Susan's intelligence after that!

"It was bigger than a million owls," said Carl, sobbing—oh, how ashamed Carl was of that sobbing in after days—"and it—it GROVELLED just as Mary said—and it was crawling down over the dyke to get at us. Do owls CRAWL?"

Rosemary looked at Susan.

"They must have seen something to frighten them so," she said.

"I will go and see," said Susan coolly. "Now, children, calm yourselves. Whatever you have seen, it was not a ghost. As for poor Henry Warren, I feel sure he would be only too glad to rest quietly in his peaceful grave once he got there. No fear of HIM venturing back, and that you may tie to. If you can make them see reason, Miss West, I will find out the truth of the matter."

Susan departed for Rainbow Valley, valiantly grasping a pitchfork which she found leaning against the back fence where the doctor had been working in his little hay-field. A pitchfork might not be of much use against "ha'nts," but it was a comforting sort of weapon. There was nothing to be seen in Rainbow Valley when Susan reached it. No white visitants appeared to be lurking in the shadowy, tangled old Bailey garden. Susan marched boldly through it and beyond it, and rapped with her pitchfork on the door of the little cottage on the other side, where Mrs. Stimson lived with her two daughters.

Back at Ingleside Rosemary had succeeded in calming the children. They still sobbed a little from shock, but they were beginning to feel a lurking and salutary suspicion that they had made dreadful geese of themselves. This suspicion became a certainty when Susan finally returned.

"I have found out what your ghost was," she said, with a grim smile, sitting down on a rocker and fanning herself. "Old Mrs. Stimson has had a pair of factory cotton sheets bleaching in the Bailey garden for a week. She spread them on the dyke under the tamarack tree because the grass was clean and short there. This evening she went out to take them in. She had her knitting in her hands so she hung the sheets over her shoulders by way of carrying them. And then she must have dropped one of her needles and find it she could not and has not yet. But she went down on her knees and crept about to hunt for it, and she was at that when she heard awful yells down in the valley and saw the three children tearing up the hill past her. She thought they had been bit by something and it gave her poor old heart such a turn that she could not move or speak, but just crouched there till they disappeared. Then she staggered back home and they have been applying stimulants to her ever since, and her heart is in a terrible condition and she says she will not get over this fright all summer."

The Merediths sat, crimson with a shame that even Rosemary's understanding sympathy could not remove. They sneaked off home, met Jerry at the manse gate and made remorseful confession. A session of the Good-Conduct Club was arranged for next morning.

"Wasn't Miss West sweet to us to-night?" whispered Faith in bed.

"Yes," admitted Una. "It is such a pity it changes people so much to be made stepmothers."

"I don't believe it does," said Faith loyally.

31. CARL DOES PENANCE

"I don't see why we should be punished at all," said Faith, rather sulkily. "We didn't do anything wrong. We couldn't help being frightened. And it won't do father any harm. It was just an accident."

"You were cowards," said Jerry with judicial scorn, "and you gave way to your cowardice. That is why you should be punished. Everybody will laugh at you about this, and that is a disgrace to the family."

"If you knew how awful the whole thing was," said Faith with a shiver, "you would think we had been punished enough already. I wouldn't go through it again for anything in the whole world."

"I believe you'd have run yourself if you'd been there," muttered Carl.

"From an old woman in a cotton sheet," mocked Jerry. "Ho, ho, ho!"

"It didn't look a bit like an old woman," cried Faith. "It was just a great, big, white thing crawling about in the grass just as Mary Vance said Henry Warren did. It's all very fine for you to laugh, Jerry Meredith, but you'd have laughed on the other side of your mouth if you'd been there. And how are we to be punished? *I* don't think it's fair, but let's know what we have to do, Judge Meredith!"

"The way I look at it," said Jerry, frowning, "is that Carl was the most to blame. He bolted first, as I understand it. Besides, he was a boy, so he should have stood his ground to protect you girls, whatever the danger was. You know that, Carl, don't you?"

"I s'pose so," growled Carl shamefacedly.

"Very well. This is to be your punishment. To-night you'll sit on Mr. Hezekiah Pollock's tombstone in the graveyard alone, until twelve o'clock."

Carl gave a little shudder. The graveyard was not so very far from the old Bailey garden. It would be a trying ordeal, but Carl was anxious to wipe out his disgrace and prove that he was not a coward after all.

"All right," he said sturdily. "But how'll I know when it is twelve?"

"The study windows are open and you'll hear the clock striking. And mind you that you are not to budge out of that graveyard until the last stroke. As for you girls, you've got to go without jam at supper for a week."

Faith and Una looked rather blank. They were inclined to think that even Carl's comparatively short though sharp agony was lighter punishment than this long drawn-out ordeal. A whole week of soggy bread without the saving grace of jam! But no shirking was permitted in the club. The girls accepted their lot with such philosophy as they could summon up.

That night they all went to bed at nine, except Carl, who was already keeping vigil on the tombstone. Una slipped in to bid him good night. Her tender heart was wrung with sympathy.

"Oh, Carl, are you much scared?" she whispered.

"Not a bit," said Carl airily.

"I won't sleep a wink till after twelve," said Una. "If you get lonesome just look up at our window and remember that I'm inside, awake, and thinking about you. That will be a little company, won't it?"

"I'll be all right. Don't you worry about me," said Carl.

But in spite of his dauntless words Carl was a pretty lonely boy when the lights went out in the manse. He had hoped his father would be in the study as he so often was. He would not feel alone then. But that night Mr. Meredith had been summoned to the fishing village at the harbour mouth to see a dying man. He would not likely be back until after midnight. Carl must dree his weird alone.

A Glen man went past carrying a lantern. The mysterious shadows caused by the lantern-light went hurtling madly over the graveyard like a dance of demons or witches. Then they passed and darkness fell again. One by one the lights in the Glen went out. It was a very dark night, with a cloudy sky, and a raw east wind that was cold in spite of the calendar. Far away on the horizon was the low dim lustre of the Charlottetown lights. The wind wailed and sighed in the old fir-trees. Mr. Alec Davis' tall monument gleamed whitely through the gloom. The willow beside it tossed long, writhing arms spectrally. At times, the gyrations of its boughs made it seem as if the monument were moving, too.

Carl curled himself up on the tombstone with his legs tucked under him. It wasn't precisely pleasant to hang them over the edge of the stone. Just suppose—just suppose—bony hands should reach up out of Mr. Pollock's grave under it and clutch him by the ankles. That had been one of Mary Vance's cheerful speculations one time when they had all been sitting there. It returned to haunt Carl now. He didn't believe those things; he didn't even really believe in Henry Warren's ghost. As for Mr. Pollock, he had been dead sixty years, so it wasn't likely he cared who sat on his tombstone now. But there is something very strange and terrible in being awake when all the rest of the world is asleep. You are alone then with nothing but your own feeble personality to pit against the mighty principalities and powers of darkness. Carl was only ten and the dead were all around him—and he wished, oh, he wished that the clock would strike twelve. Would it NEVER strike twelve? Surely Aunt Martha must have forgotten to wind it.

And then it struck eleven—only eleven! He must stay yet another hour in that grim place. If only there were a few friendly stars to be seen! The darkness was so thick it seemed to press against his face. There was a sound as of stealthy passing footsteps all over the graveyard. Carl shivered, partly with prickling terror, partly with real cold.

Then it began to rain—a chill, penetrating drizzle. Carl's thin little cotton blouse and shirt were soon wet through. He felt chilled to the bone. He forgot mental terrors in his physical discomfort. But he must stay there till twelve—he was punishing himself and he was on his honour. Nothing had been said about rain—but it did not make any difference. When the study clock finally struck twelve a drenched little figure crept stiffly down off Mr. Pollock's tombstone, made its way into the manse and upstairs to bed. Carl's teeth were chattering. He thought he would never get warm again.

He was warm enough when morning came. Jerry gave one startled look at his crimson face and then rushed to call his father. Mr. Meredith came hurriedly, his own face ivory white from the pallor of his long night vigil by a death bed. He had not got home until daylight. He bent over his little lad anxiously.

"Carl, are you sick?" he said.

"That—tombstone—over here," said Carl, "it's—moving—about—it's coming—at—me—keep it—away—please."

Mr. Meredith rushed to the telephone. In ten minutes Dr. Blythe was at the manse. Half an hour later a wire was sent to town for a trained nurse, and all the Glen knew that Carl Meredith was very ill with pneumonia and that Dr. Blythe had been seen to shake his head.

Gilbert shook his head more than once in the fortnight that followed. Carl developed double pneumonia. There was one night when Mr. Meredith paced his study floor, and Faith and Una huddled in their bedroom and cried, and Jerry, wild with remorse, refused to budge from the floor of the hall outside Carl's door. Dr. Blythe and the nurse never left the bedside. They fought death gallantly until the red dawn and they won the victory. Carl rallied and passed the crisis in safety. The news was phoned about the waiting Glen and people found out how much they really loved their minister and his children.

"I haven't had one decent night's sleep since I heard the child was sick," Miss Cornelia told Anne, "and Mary Vance has cried until those queer eyes of hers looked like burnt holes in a blanket. Is it true that Carl got pneumonia from straying out in the graveyard that wet night for a dare?"

"No. He was staying there to punish himself for cowardice in that affair of the Warren ghost. It seems they have a club for bringing themselves up, and they punish themselves when they do wrong. Jerry told Mr. Meredith all about it."

"The poor little souls," said Miss Cornelia.

Carl got better rapidly, for the congregation took enough nourishing things to the manse to furnish forth a hospital. Norman Douglas drove up every evening with a dozen fresh eggs and a jar of Jersey cream. Sometimes he stayed an hour and bellowed arguments on predestination with Mr. Meredith in the study; oftener he drove on up to the hill that overlooked the Glen.

When Carl was able to go again to Rainbow Valley they had a special feast in his honour and the doctor came down and helped them with the fireworks. Mary Vance was there, too, but she did not tell any ghost stories. Miss Cornelia had given her a talking on that subject which Mary would not forget in a hurry.

32. TWO STUBBORN PEOPLE

Rosemary West, on her way home from a music lesson at Ingleside, turned aside to the hidden spring in Rainbow Valley. She had not been there all summer; the beautiful little spot had no longer any allurement for her. The spirit of her young lover never came to the tryst now; and the memories connected with John Meredith were too painful and poignant. But she had happened to glance backward up the valley and had seen Norman Douglas vaulting as airily as a stripling over the old stone dyke of the Bailey garden and thought he was on his way up the hill. If he overtook her she would have to walk home with him and she was not going to do that. So she slipped at once behind the maples of the spring, hoping he had not seen her and would pass on.

But Norman had seen her and, what was more, was in pursuit of her. He had been wanting for some time to have talk with Rosemary, but she had always, so it seemed, avoided him. Rosemary had never, at any time, liked Norman Douglas very well. His bluster, his temper, his noisy hilarity, had always antagonized her. Long ago she had often wondered how Ellen could possibly be attracted to him. Norman Douglas was perfectly aware of her dislike and he chuckled over it. It never worried Norman if people did not like him. It did not even make him dislike them in return, for he took it as a kind of extorted compliment. He thought Rosemary a fine girl, and he meant to be an excellent, generous brother-in-law to her. But before he could be her brother-in-law he had to have a talk with her, so, having seen her leaving Ingleside as he stood in the doorway of a Glen store, he had straightway plunged into the valley to overtake her.

Rosemary was sitting pensively on the maple seat where John Meredith had been sitting on that evening nearly a year ago. The tiny spring shimmered and dimpled under its fringe of ferns. Ruby-red gleams of sunset fell through the arching boughs. A tall clump of perfect asters grew at her side. The little spot was as dreamy and witching and evasive as any retreat of fairies and dryads in ancient forests. Into it Norman Douglas bounced, scattering and annihilating its charm in a moment. His personality seemed to swallow the place up. There was simply nothing there but Norman Douglas, big, red-bearded, complacent.

"Good evening," said Rosemary coldly, standing up.

"'Evening, girl. Sit down again—sit down again. I want to have a talk with you. Bless the girl, what's she looking at me like that for? I don't want to eat you—I've had my supper. Sit down and be civil."

"I can hear what you have to say quite as well here," said Rosemary.

"So you can, girl, if you use your ears. I only wanted you to be comfortable. You look so durned uncomfortable, standing there. Well, I'LL sit anyway."

Norman accordingly sat down in the very place John Meredith had once sat. The contrast was so ludicrous that Rosemary was afraid she would go off into a peal of hysterical laughter over it. Norman cast his hat aside, placed his huge, red hands on his knees, and looked up at her with his eyes a-twinkle.

"Come, girl, don't be so stiff," he said, ingratiatingly. When he liked he could be very ingratiating. "Let's have a reasonable, sensible, friendly chat. There's something I want to ask you. Ellen says she won't, so it's up to me to do it."

Rosemary looked down at the spring, which seemed to have shrunk to the size of a dewdrop. Norman gazed at her in despair.

"Durn it all, you might help a fellow out a bit," he burst forth.

"What is it you want me to help you say?" asked Rosemary scornfully.

"You know as well as I do, girl. Don't be putting on your tragedy airs. No wonder Ellen was scared to ask you. Look here, girl, Ellen and I want to marry each other. That's plain English, isn't it? Got that? And Ellen says she can't unless you give her back some tom-fool promise she made. Come now, will you do it? Will you do it?"

"Yes," said Rosemary.

Norman bounced up and seized her reluctant hand.

"Good! I knew you would—I told Ellen you would. I knew it would only take a minute. Now, girl, you go home and tell Ellen, and we'll have a wedding in a fortnight and you'll come and live with us. We shan't leave you to roost on that hill-top like a lonely crow—don't you worry. I know you hate me, but, Lord, it'll be great fun living with some one that hates me.

Life'll have some spice in it after this. Ellen will roast me and you'll freeze me. I won't have a dull moment."

Rosemary did not condescend to tell him that nothing would ever induce her to live in his house. She let him go striding back to the Glen, oozing delight and complacency, and she walked slowly up the hill home. She had known this was coming ever since she had returned from Kingsport, and found Norman Douglas established as a frequent evening caller. His name was never mentioned between her and Ellen, but the very avoidance of it was significant. It was not in Rosemary's nature to feel bitter, or she would have felt very bitter. She was coldly civil to Norman, and she made no difference in any way with Ellen. But Ellen had not found much comfort in her second courtship.

She was in the garden, attended by St. George, when Rosemary came home. The two sisters met in the dahlia walk. St. George sat down on the gravel walk between them and folded his glossy black tail gracefully around his white paws, with all the indifference of a well-fed, well-bred, well-groomed cat.

"Did you ever see such dahlias?" demanded Ellen proudly. "They are just the finest we've ever had."

Rosemary had never cared for dahlias. Their presence in the garden was her concession to Ellen's taste. She noticed one huge mottled one of crimson and yellow that lorded it over all the others.

"That dahlia," she said, pointing to it, "is exactly like Norman Douglas. It might easily be his twin brother."

Ellen's dark-browed face flushed. She admired the dahlia in question, but she knew Rosemary did not, and that no compliment was intended. But she dared not resent Rosemary's speech—poor Ellen dared not resent anything just then. And it was the first time Rosemary had ever mentioned Norman's name to her. She felt that this portended something.

"I met Norman Douglas in the valley," said Rosemary, looking straight at her sister, "and he told me you and he wanted to be married—if I would give you permission."

"Yes? What did you say?" asked Ellen, trying to speak naturally and off-handedly, and failing completely. She could not meet Rosemary's eyes. She looked down at St. George's sleek back and felt horribly afraid. Rosemary had either said she would or she wouldn't. If she would Ellen would feel so ashamed and remorseful that she would be a very uncomfortable bride-elect; and if she wouldn't—well, Ellen had once learned to live without Norman Douglas, but she had forgotten the lesson and felt that she could never learn it again.

"I said that as far as I was concerned you were at full liberty to marry each other as soon as you liked," said Rosemary.

"Thank you," said Ellen, still looking at St. George.

Rosemary's face softened.

"I hope you'll be happy, Ellen," she said gently.

"Oh, Rosemary," Ellen looked up in distress, "I'm so ashamed—I don't deserve it—after all I said to you—"

"We won't speak about that," said Rosemary hurriedly and decidedly.

"But—but," persisted Ellen, "you are free now, too—and it's not too late—John Meredith—"

"Ellen West!" Rosemary had a little spark of temper under all her sweetness and it flashed forth now in her blue eyes. "Have you quite lost your senses in EVERY respect? Do you suppose for an instant that *I* am going to go to John Meredith and say meekly, 'Please, sir, I've changed my mind and please, sir, I hope you haven't changed yours.' Is that what you want me to do?"

"No—no—but a little—encouragement—he would come back—"

"Never. He despises me—and rightly. No more of this, Ellen. I bear you no grudge—marry whom you like. But no meddling in my affairs."

"Then you must come and live with me," said Ellen. "I shall not leave you here alone."

"Do you really think that I would go and live in Norman Douglas's house?"

"Why not?" cried Ellen, half angrily, despite her humiliation.

Rosemary began to laugh.

"Ellen, I thought you had a sense of humour. Can you see me doing it?"

"I don't see why you wouldn't. His house is big enough—you'd have your share of it to yourself—he wouldn't interfere."

"Ellen, the thing is not to be thought of. Don't bring this up again."

"Then," said Ellen coldly, and determinedly, "I shall not marry him. I shall not leave you here alone. That is all there is to be said about it."

"Nonsense, Ellen."

"It is not nonsense. It is my firm decision. It would be absurd for you to think of living here by yourself—a mile from any other house. If you won't come with me I'll stay with you. Now, we won't argue the matter, so don't try."

"I shall leave Norman to do the arguing," said Rosemary.

"I'LL deal with Norman. I can manage HIM. I would never have asked you to give me back my promise—never—but I had to tell Norman why I couldn't marry him and he said HE would ask you. I couldn't prevent him. You need not suppose you are the only person in the world who possesses self-respect. I never dreamed of marrying and leaving you here alone. And you'll find I can be as determined as yourself."

Rosemary turned away and went into the house, with a shrug of her shoulders. Ellen looked down at St. George, who had never blinked an eyelash or stirred a whisker during the whole interview.

"St. George, this world would be a dull place without the men, I'll admit, but I'm almost tempted to wish there wasn't one of 'em in it. Look at the trouble and bother they've made right here, George—torn our happy old life completely up by the roots, Saint. John Meredith began it and Norman Douglas has finished it. And now both of them have to go into limbo. Norman is the only man I ever met who agrees with me that the Kaiser of Germany is the most dangerous creature alive on this earth—and I can't marry this sensible person because my sister is stubborn and I'm stubborner. Mark my words, St. George, the minister would come back if she raised her little finger. But she won't George—she'll never do it—she won't even crook it—and I don't dare meddle, Saint. I won't sulk, George; Rosemary didn't sulk, so I'm determined I won't either, Saint; Norman will tear up the turf, but the long and short of it is, St. George, that all of us old fools must just stop thinking of marrying. Well, well, 'despair is a free man, hope is a slave,' Saint. So now come into the house, George, and I'll solace you with a saucerful of cream. Then there will be one happy and contented creature on this hill at least."

33. CARL IS—NOT—WHIPPED

"There is something I think I ought to tell you," said Mary Vance mysteriously.

She and Faith and Una were walking arm in arm through the village, having foregathered at Mr. Flagg's store. Una and Faith exchanged looks which said, "NOW something disagreeable is coming." When Mary Vance thought she ought to tell them things there was seldom much pleasure in the hearing. They often wondered why they kept on liking Mary Vance—for like her they did, in spite of everything. To be sure, she was generally a stimulating and agreeable companion. If only she would not have those convictions that it was her duty to tell them things!

"Do you know that Rosemary West won't marry your pa because she thinks you are such a wild lot? She's afraid she couldn't bring you up right and so she turned him down."

Una's heart thrilled with secret exultation. She was very glad to hear that Miss West would not marry her father. But Faith was rather disappointed.

"How do you know?" she asked.

"Oh, everybody's saying it. I heard Mrs. Elliott talking it over with Mrs. Doctor. They thought I was too far away to hear, but I've got ears like a cat's. Mrs. Elliott said she hadn't a doubt that Rosemary was afraid to try stepmothering you because you'd got such a reputation. Your pa never goes up the hill now. Neither does Norman Douglas. Folks say Ellen has jilted him just to get square with him for jilting her ages ago. But Norman is going about declaring he'll get her yet. And I think you ought to know you've spoiled your pa's match and *I*think it's a pity, for he's bound to marry somebody before long, and Rosemary West would have been the best wife *I* know of for him."

"You told me all stepmothers were cruel and wicked," said Una.

"Oh—well," said Mary rather confusedly, "they're mostly awful cranky, I know. But Rosemary West couldn't be very mean to any one. I tell you if your pa turns round and marries Emmeline Drew you'll wish you'd behaved yourselves better and not frightened Rosemary out of it. It's awful that you've got such a reputation that no decent woman'll marry your pa on account of you. Of course, *I* know that half the yarns that are told about you ain't true. But give a dog a bad name. Why, some folks are saying that it was Jerry and Carl that threw the stones through Mrs. Stimson's window the other night when it was really them two Boyd boys. But I'm afraid it was Carl that put the eel in old Mrs. Carr's buggy, though I said at first I wouldn't believe it until I'd better proof than old Kitty Alec's word. I told Mrs. Elliott so right to her face."

"What did Carl do?" cried Faith.

"Well, they say—now, mind, I'm only telling you what people say—so there's no use in your blaming me for it—that Carl and a lot of other boys were fishing eels over the bridge one evening last week. Mrs. Carr drove past in that old rattletrap buggy of hers with the open back. And Carl he just up and threw a big eel into the back. When poor old Mrs. Carr was driving up the hill by Ingleside that eel came squirming out between her feet. She thought it was a snake and she just give one awful screech and stood up and jumped clean over the wheels. The horse bolted, but it went home and no damage was done. But Mrs. Carr jarred her legs most terrible, and has had nervous spasms ever since whenever she thinks of the eel. Say, it was a rotten trick to play on the poor old soul. She's a decent body, if she is as queer as Dick's hat band."

Faith and Una looked at each other again. This was a matter for the Good-Conduct Club. They would not talk it over with Mary.

"There goes your pa," said Mary as Mr. Meredith passed them, "and never seeing us no more'n if we weren't here. Well, I'm getting so's I don't mind it. But there are folks who do."

Mr. Meredith had not seen them, but he was not walking along in his usual dreamy and abstracted fashion. He strode up the hill in agitation and distress. Mrs. Alec Davis had just told him the story of Carl and the eel. She had been very indignant about it. Old Mrs. Carr was her third cousin. Mr. Meredith was more than indignant. He was hurt and shocked. He had not thought Carl would do anything like this. He was not inclined to be hard on pranks of heedlessness or forgetfulness, but THIS was different. THIS had a nasty tang in it. When he reached home he found Carl on the lawn, patiently studying the habits and customs of a colony of wasps. Calling him into the study Mr. Meredith confronted him, with a sterner face than any of his children had ever seen before, and asked him if the story were true.

"Yes," said Carl, flushing, but meeting his father's eyes bravely.

Mr. Meredith groaned. He had hoped that there had been at least exaggeration.

"Tell me the whole matter," he said.

"The boys were fishing for eels over the bridge," said Carl. "Link Drew had caught a whopper—I mean an awful big one—the biggest eel I ever saw. He caught it right at the start and it had been lying in his basket a long time, still as still. I thought it was dead, honest I did. Then old Mrs. Carr drove over the bridge and she called us all young varmints and told us to go home. And we hadn't said a word to her, father, truly. So when she drove back again, after going to the store, the boys dared me to put Link's eel in her buggy. I thought it was so dead it couldn't hurt her and I threw it in. Then the eel came to life on the hill and we heard her scream and saw her jump out. I was awful sorry. That's all, father."

It was not quite as bad as Mr. Meredith had feared, but it was quite bad enough. "I must punish you, Carl," he said sorrowfully.

"Yes, I know, father."

"I—I must whip you."

Carl winced. He had never been whipped. Then, seeing how badly his father felt, he said cheerfully,

"All right, father."

Mr. Meredith misunderstood his cheerfulness and thought him insensible. He told Carl to come to the study after supper, and when the boy had gone out he flung himself into his chair and groaned again. He dreaded the evening sevenfold more than Carl did. The poor minister did not even know what he should whip his boy with. What was used to whip boys? Rods? Canes? No, that would be too brutal. A timber switch, then? And he, John Meredith, must hie him to the woods and cut one. It was an abominable thought. Then a picture presented itself unbidden to his mind. He saw Mrs. Carr's wizened, nut-cracker little face at the appearance of that reviving eel—he saw her sailing witch-like over the buggy wheels. Before he could prevent himself the minister laughed. Then he was angry with himself and angrier still with Carl. He would get that switch at once—and it must not be too limber, after all.

Carl was talking the matter over in the graveyard with Faith and Una, who had just come home. They were horrified at the idea of his being whipped—and by father, who had never done such a thing! But they agreed soberly that it was just.

"You know it was a dreadful thing to do," sighed Faith. "And you never owned up in the club."

"I forgot," said Carl. "Besides, I didn't think any harm came of it. I didn't know she jarred her legs. But I'm to be whipped and that will make things square."

"Will it hurt—very much?" said Una, slipping her hand into Carl's.

"Oh, not so much, I guess," said Carl gamely. "Anyhow, I'm not going to cry, no matter how much it hurts. It would make father feel so bad, if I did. He's all cut up now. I wish I could whip myself hard enough and save him doing it."

After supper, at which Carl had eaten little and Mr. Meredith nothing at all, both went silently into the study. The switch lay on the table. Mr. Meredith had had a bad time getting a switch to suit him. He cut one, then felt it was too slender. Carl had done a really indefensible thing. Then he cut another—it was far too thick. After all, Carl had thought the eel was dead. The third one suited him better; but as he picked it up from the table it seemed very thick and heavy—more like a stick than a switch.

"Hold out your hand," he said to Carl.

Carl threw back his head and held out his hand unflinchingly. But he was not very old and he could not quite keep a little fear out of his eyes. Mr. Meredith looked down into those eyes—why, they were Cecilia's eyes—her very eyes—and in them was the selfsame expression he had once seen in Cecilia's eyes when she had come to him to tell him something she had been a little afraid to tell him. Here were her eyes in Carl's little, white face—and six weeks ago he had thought, through one endless, terrible night, that his little lad was dying.

John Meredith threw down the switch.

"Go," he said, "I cannot whip you."

Carl fled to the graveyard, feeling that the look on his father's face was worse than any whipping.

"Is it over so soon?" asked Faith. She and Una had been holding hands and setting teeth on the Pollock tombstone.

"He—he didn't whip me at all," said Carl with a sob, "and—I wish he had—and he's in there, feeling just awful."

Una slipped away. Her heart yearned to comfort her father. As noiselessly as a little gray mouse she opened the study door and crept in. The room was dark with twilight. Her father was sitting at his desk. His back was towards her—his head was in his hands. He was talking to himself—broken, anguished words—but Una heard—heard and understood, with the sudden illumination that comes to sensitive, unmothered children. As silently as she had come in she slipped out and closed the door. John Meredith went on talking out his pain in what he deemed his undisturbed solitude.

34. UNA VISITS THE HILL

Una went upstairs. Carl and Faith were already on their way through the early moonlight to Rainbow Valley, having heard therefrom the elfin lilt of Jerry's jews-harp and having guessed that the Blythes were there and fun afoot. Una had no wish to go. She sought her own room first where she sat down on her bed and had a little cry. She did not want anybody to come in her dear mother's place. She did not want a stepmother who would hate her and make her father hate her. But father was so desperately unhappy—and if she could do any anything to make him happier she MUST do it. There was only one thing she could do—and she had known the moment she had left the study that she must do it. But it was a very hard thing to do.

After Una cried her heart out she wiped her eyes and went to the spare room. It was dark and rather musty, for the blind had not been drawn up nor the window opened for a long time. Aunt Martha was no fresh-air fiend. But as nobody ever thought of shutting a door in the manse this did not matter so much, save when some unfortunate minister came to stay all night and was compelled to breathe the spare room atmosphere.

There was a closet in the spare room and far back in the closet a gray silk dress was hanging. Una went into the closet and shut the door, went down on her knees and pressed her face against the soft silken folds. It had been her mother's wedding-dress. It was still full of a sweet, faint, haunting perfume, like lingering love. Una always felt very close to her mother there—as if she were kneeling at her feet with head in her lap. She went there once in a long while when life was TOO hard.

"Mother," she whispered to the gray silk gown, "*I* will never forget you, mother, and I'll ALWAYS love you best. But I have to do it, mother, because father is so very unhappy. I know you wouldn't want him to be unhappy. And I will be very good to her, mother, and try to love her, even if she is like Mary Vance said stepmothers always were."

Una carried some fine, spiritual strength away from her secret shrine. She slept peacefully that night with the tear stains still glistening on her sweet, serious, little face.

The next afternoon she put on her best dress and hat. They were shabby enough. Every other little girl in the Glen had new clothes that summer except Faith and Una. Mary Vance had a lovely dress of white embroidered lawn, with scarlet silk sash and shoulder bows. But to-day Una did not mind her shabbiness. She only wanted to be very neat. She washed her face carefully. She brushed her black hair until it was as smooth as satin. She tied her shoelaces carefully, having first sewed up two runs in her one pair of good stockings. She would have liked to black her shoes, but she could not find any blacking. Finally, she slipped away from the manse, down through Rainbow Valley, up through the whispering woods, and out to the road that ran past the house on the hill. It was quite a long walk and Una was tired and warm when she got there.

She saw Rosemary West sitting under a tree in the garden and stole past the dahlia beds to her. Rosemary had a book in her lap, but she was gazing afar across the harbour and her thoughts were sorrowful enough. Life had not been pleasant lately in the house on the hill. Ellen had not sulked—Ellen had been a brick. But things can be felt that are never said and at times the silence between the two women was intolerably eloquent. All the many familiar things that had once made life sweet had a flavour of bitterness now. Norman Douglas made periodical irruptions also, bullying and coaxing Ellen by turns. It would end, Rosemary believed, by his dragging Ellen off with him some day, and Rosemary felt that she would be almost glad when it happened. Existence would be horribly lonely then, but it would be no longer charged with dynamite.

She was roused from her unpleasant reverie by a timid little touch on her shoulder. Turning, she saw Una Meredith.

"Why, Una, dear, did you walk up here in all this heat?"

"Yes," said Una, "I came to—I came to—"

But she found it very hard to say what she had come to do. Her voice failed—her eyes filled with tears.

"Why, Una, little girl, what is the trouble? Don't be afraid to tell me."

Rosemary put her arm around the thin little form and drew the child close to her. Her eyes were very beautiful—her touch so tender that Una found courage.

"I came—to ask you—to marry father," she gasped.

Rosemary was silent for a moment from sheer dumbfounderment. She stared at Una blankly.

"Oh, don't be angry, please, dear Miss West," said Una, pleadingly. "You see, everybody is saying that you wouldn't marry father because we are so bad. He is VERY unhappy about it. So I thought I would come and tell you that we are never bad ON PURPOSE. And if you will only marry father we will all try to be good and do just what you tell us. I'm SURE you won't have any trouble with us. PLEASE, Miss West."

Rosemary had been thinking rapidly. Gossiping surmise, she saw, had put this mistaken idea into Una's mind. She must be perfectly frank and sincere with the child.

"Una, dear," she said softly. "It isn't because of you poor little souls that I cannot be your father's wife. I never thought of such a thing. You are not bad—I never supposed you were. There—there was another reason altogether, Una."

"Don't you like father?" asked Una, lifting reproachful eyes. "Oh, Miss West, you don't know how nice he is. I'm sure he'd make you a GOOD husband."

Even in the midst of her perplexity and distress Rosemary couldn't help a twisted, little smile.

"Oh, don't laugh, Miss West," Una cried passionately. "Father feels DREADFUL about it."

"I think you're mistaken, dear," said Rosemary.

"I'm not. I'm SURE I'm not. Oh, Miss West, father was going to whip Carl yesterday—Carl had been naughty—and father couldn't do it because you see he had no PRACTICE in whipping. So when Carl came out and told us father felt so bad, I slipped into the study to see if I could help him—he LIKES me to comfort him, Miss West—and he didn't hear me come in and I heard what he was saying. I'll tell you, Miss West, if you'll let me whisper it in your ear."

Una whispered earnestly. Rosemary's face turned crimson. So John Meredith still cared. HE hadn't changed his mind. And he must care intensely if he had said that—care more than she had ever supposed he did. She sat still for a moment, stroking Una's hair. Then she said,

"Will you take a little letter from me to your father, Una?"

"Oh, are you going to marry him, Miss West?" asked Una eagerly.

"Perhaps—if he really wants me to," said Rosemary, blushing again.

"I'm glad—I'm glad," said Una bravely. Then she looked up, with quivering lips. "Oh, Miss West, you won't turn father against us—you won't make him hate us, will you?" she said beseechingly.

Rosemary stared again.

"Una Meredith! Do you think I would do such a thing? Whatever put such an idea into your head?"

"Mary Vance said stepmothers were all like that—and that they all hated their stepchildren and made their father hate them—she said they just couldn't help it—just being stepmothers made them like that"—

"You poor child! And yet you came up here and asked me to marry your father because you wanted to make him happy? You're a darling—a heroine—as Ellen would say, you're a brick. Now listen to me, very closely, dearest. Mary Vance is a silly little girl who doesn't know very much and she is dreadfully mistaken about some things. I would never dream of trying to turn your father against you. I would love you all dearly. I don't want to take your own mother's place—she must always have that in your hearts. But neither have I any intention of being a stepmother. I want to be your friend and helper and CHUM. Don't you think that would be nice, Una—if you and Faith and Carl and Jerry could just think of me as a good jolly chum—a big older sister?"

"Oh, it would be lovely," cried Una, with a transfigured face. She flung her arms impulsively round Rosemary's neck. She was so happy that she felt as if she could fly on wings.

"Do the others—do Faith and the boys have the same idea you had about stepmothers?"

"No. Faith never believed Mary Vance. I was dreadfully foolish to believe her, either. Faith loves you already—she has loved you ever since poor Adam was eaten. And Jerry and Carl will think it is jolly. Oh, Miss West, when you come to live with us, will you—could you—teach me to cook—a little—and sew—and—and—and do things? I don't know anything. I won't be much trouble—I'll try to learn fast."

"Darling, I'll teach you and help you all I can. Now, you won't say a word to anybody about this, will you—not even to Faith, until your father himself tells you you may? And you'll stay and have tea with me?"

"Oh, thank you—but—but—I think I'd rather go right back and take the letter to father," faltered Una. "You see, he'll be glad that much SOONER, Miss West."

"I see," said Rosemary. She went to the house, wrote a note and gave it to Una. When that small damsel had run off, a palpitating bundle of happiness, Rosemary went to Ellen, who was shelling peas on the back porch.

"Ellen," she said, "Una Meredith has just been here to ask me to marry her father."

Ellen looked up and read her sister's face.

"And you're going to?" she said.

"It's quite likely."

Ellen went on shelling peas for a few minutes. Then she suddenly put her hands up to her own face. There were tears in her black-browed eyes.

"I—I hope we'll all be happy," she said between a sob and a laugh.

Down at the manse Una Meredith, warm, rosy, triumphant, marched boldly into her father's study and laid a letter on the desk before him. His pale face flushed as he saw the clear, fine handwriting he knew so well. He opened the letter. It was very short—but he shed twenty years as he read it. Rosemary asked him if he could meet her that evening at sunset by the spring in Rainbow Valley.

35. "LET THE PIPER COME"

"And so," said Miss Cornelia, "the double wedding is to be sometime about the middle of this month."

There was a faint chill in the air of the early September evening, so Anne had lighted her ever ready fire of driftwood in the big living room, and she and Miss Cornelia basked in its fairy flicker.

"It is so delightful—especially in regard to Mr. Meredith and Rosemary," said Anne. "I'm as happy in the thought of it, as I was when I was getting married myself. I felt exactly like a bride again last evening when I was up on the hill seeing Rosemary's trousseau."

"They tell me her things are fine enough for a princess," said Susan from a shadowy corner where she was cuddling her brown boy. "I have been invited up to see them also and I intend to go some evening. I understand that Rosemary is to wear white silk and a veil, but Ellen is to be married in navy blue. I have no doubt, Mrs. Dr. dear, that that is very sensible of her, but for my own part I have always felt that if I were ever married *I* would prefer the white and the veil, as being more bride-like."

A vision of Susan in "white and a veil" presented itself before Anne's inner vision and was almost too much for her.

"As for Mr. Meredith," said Miss Cornelia, "even his engagement has made a different man of him. He isn't half so dreamy and absent-minded, believe me. I was so relieved when I heard that he had decided to close the manse and let the children visit round while he was away on his honeymoon. If he had left them and old Aunt Martha there alone for a month I should have expected to wake every morning and see the place burned down."

"Aunt Martha and Jerry are coming here," said Anne. "Carl is going to Elder Clow's. I haven't heard where the girls are going."

"Oh, I'm going to take them," said Miss Cornelia. "Of course, I was glad to, but Mary would have given me no peace till I asked them any way. The Ladies' Aid is going to clean the manse from top to bottom before the bride and groom come back, and Norman Douglas has arranged to fill the cellar with vegetables. Nobody ever saw or heard anything quite like Norman Douglas these days, believe ME. He's so tickled that he's going to marry Ellen West after wanting her all his life. If *I* was Ellen—but then, I'm not, and if she is satisfied I can very well be. I heard her say years ago when she was a schoolgirl that she didn't want a tame puppy for a husband. There's nothing tame about Norman, believe ME."

The sun was setting over Rainbow Valley. The pond was wearing a wonderful tissue of purple and gold and green and crimson. A faint blue haze rested on the eastern hill, over which a great, pale, round moon was just floating up like a silver bubble.

They were all there, squatted in the little open glade—Faith and Una, Jerry and Carl, Jem and Walter, Nan and Di, and Mary Vance. They had been having a special celebration, for it would be Jem's last evening in Rainbow Valley. On the morrow he would leave for Charlottetown to attend Queen's Academy. Their charmed circle would be broken; and, in spite of the jollity of their little festival, there was a hint of sorrow in every gay young heart.

"See—there is a great golden palace over there in the sunset," said Walter, pointing. "Look at the shining tower—and the crimson banners streaming from them. Perhaps a conqueror is riding home from battle—and they are hanging them out to do honour to him."

"Oh, I wish we had the old days back again," exclaimed Jem. "I'd love to be a soldier—a great, triumphant general. I'd give EVERYTHING to see a big battle."

Well, Jem was to be a soldier and see a greater battle than had ever been fought in the world; but that was as yet far in the future; and the mother, whose first-born son he was, was wont to look on her boys and thank God that the "brave days of old," which Jem longed for, were gone for ever, and that never would it be necessary for the sons of Canada to ride forth to battle "for the ashes of their fathers and the temples of their gods."

The shadow of the Great Conflict had not yet made felt any forerunner of its chill. The lads who were to fight, and perhaps fall, on the fields of France and Flanders, Gallipoli and Palestine, were still roguish schoolboys with a fair life in prospect before them: the girls whose hearts were to be wrung were yet fair little maidens a-star with hopes and dreams.

Slowly the banners of the sunset city gave up their crimson and gold; slowly the conqueror's pageant faded out. Twilight crept over the valley and the little group grew silent. Walter had been reading again that day in his beloved book of myths and he remembered how he had once fancied the Pied Piper coming down the valley on an evening just like this.

He began to speak dreamily, partly because he wanted to thrill his companions a little, partly because something apart from him seemed to be speaking through his lips.

"The Piper is coming nearer," he said, "he is nearer than he was that evening I saw him before. His long, shadowy cloak is blowing around him. He pipes—he pipes—and we must follow—Jem and Carl and Jerry and I—round and round the world. Listen—listen—can't you hear his wild music?"

The girls shivered.

"You know you're only pretending," protested Mary Vance, "and I wish you wouldn't. You make it too real. I hate that old Piper of yours."

But Jem sprang up with a gay laugh. He stood up on a little hillock, tall and splendid, with his open brow and his fearless eyes. There were thousands like him all over the land of the maple.

"Let the Piper come and welcome," he cried, waving his hand. "I'LL follow him gladly round and round the world."

RILLA OF INGLESIDE

RILLA OF INGLESIDE

1. GLEN "NOTES" AND OTHER MATTERS

It was a warm, golden-cloudy, lovable afternoon. In the big living-room at Ingleside Susan Baker sat down with a certain grim satisfaction hovering about her like an aura; it was four o'clock and Susan, who had been working incessantly since six that morning, felt that she had fairly earned an hour of repose and gossip. Susan just then was perfectly happy; everything had gone almost uncannily well in the kitchen that day. Dr. Jekyll had not been Mr. Hyde and so had not grated on her nerves; from where she sat she could see the pride of her heart—the bed of peonies of her own planting and culture, blooming as no other peony plot in Glen St. Mary ever did or could bloom, with peonies crimson, peonies silvery pink, peonies white as drifts of winter snow.

Susan had on a new black silk blouse, quite as elaborate as anything Mrs. Marshall Elliott ever wore, and a white starched apron, trimmed with complicated crocheted lace fully five inches wide, not to mention insertion to match. Therefore Susan had all the comfortable consciousness of a well-dressed woman as she opened her copy of the Daily Enterprise and prepared to read the Glen "Notes" which, as Miss Cornelia had just informed her, filled half a column of it and mentioned almost everybody at Ingleside. There was a big, black headline on the front page of the Enterprise, stating that some Archduke Ferdinand or other had been assassinated at a place bearing the weird name of Sarajevo, but Susan tarried not over uninteresting, immaterial stuff like that; she was in quest of something really vital. Oh, here it was—"Jottings from Glen St. Mary." Susan settled down keenly, reading each one over aloud to extract all possible gratification from it.

Mrs. Blythe and her visitor, Miss Cornelia—alias Mrs. Marshall Elliott—were chatting together near the open door that led to the veranda, through which a cool, delicious breeze was blowing, bringing whiffs of phantom perfume from the garden, and charming gay echoes from the vine-hung corner where Rilla and Miss Oliver and Walter were laughing and talking. Wherever Rilla Blythe was, there was laughter.

There was another occupant of the living-room, curled up on a couch, who must not be overlooked, since he was a creature of marked individuality, and, moreover, had the distinction of being the only living thing whom Susan really hated.

All cats are mysterious but Dr. Jekyll-and-Mr. Hyde—"Doc" for short—was trebly so. He was a cat of double personality—or else, as Susan vowed, he was possessed by the devil. To begin with, there had been something uncanny about the very dawn of his existence. Four years previously Rilla Blythe had had a treasured darling of a kitten, white as snow, with a saucy black tip to its tail, which she called Jack Frost. Susan disliked Jack Frost, though she could not or would not give any valid reason therefor.

"Take my word for it, Mrs. Dr. dear," she was wont to say ominously, "that cat will come to no good."

"But why do you think so?" Mrs. Blythe would ask.

"I do not think—I know," was all the answer Susan would vouchsafe.

With the rest of the Ingleside folk Jack Frost was a favourite; he was so very clean and well groomed, and never allowed a spot or stain to be seen on his beautiful white suit; he had endearing ways of purring and snuggling; he was scrupulously honest.

And then a domestic tragedy took place at Ingleside. Jack Frost had kittens!

It would be vain to try to picture Susan's triumph. Had she not always insisted that that cat would turn out to be a delusion and a snare? Now they could see for themselves!

Rilla kept one of the kittens, a very pretty one, with peculiarly sleek glossy fur of a dark yellow crossed by orange stripes, and large, satiny, golden ears. She called it Goldie and the name seemed appropriate enough to the little frolicsome creature which, during its kittenhood, gave no indication of the sinister nature it really possessed. Susan, of course, warned the family that no good could be expected from any offspring of that diabolical Jack Frost; but Susan's Cassandra-like croakings were unheeded.

The Blythes had been so accustomed to regard Jack Frost as a member of the male sex that they could not get out of the habit. So they continually used the masculine pronoun, although the result was ludicrous. Visitors used to be quite electrified when Rilla referred casually to "Jack and his kitten," or told Goldie sternly, "Go to your mother and get him to wash your fur."

"It is not decent, Mrs. Dr. dear," poor Susan would say bitterly. She herself compromised by always referring to Jack as "it" or "the white beast," and one heart at least did not ache when "it" was accidentally poisoned the following winter.

In a year's time "Goldie" became so manifestly an inadequate name for the orange kitten that Walter, who was just then reading Stevenson's story, changed it to Dr. Jekyll-and-Mr. Hyde. In his Dr. Jekyll mood the cat was a drowsy, affectionate, domestic, cushion-loving puss, who liked petting and gloried in being nursed and patted. Especially did he love to lie on his back and have his sleek, cream-coloured throat stroked gently while he purred in somnolent satisfaction. He was a notable purrer; never had there been an Ingleside cat who purred so constantly and so ecstatically.

"The only thing I envy a cat is its purr," remarked Dr. Blythe once, listening to Doc's resonant melody. "It is the most contented sound in the world."

Doc was very handsome; his every movement was grace; his poses magnificent. When he folded his long, dusky-ringed tail about his feet and sat him down on the veranda to gaze steadily into space for long intervals the Blythes felt that an Egyptian sphinx could not have made a more fitting Deity of the Portal.

When the Mr. Hyde mood came upon him—which it invariably did before rain, or wind—he was a wild thing with changed eyes. The transformation always came suddenly. He would spring fiercely from a reverie with a savage snarl and bite at any restraining or caressing hand. His fur seemed to grow darker and his eyes gleamed with a diabolical light. There was really an unearthly beauty about him. If the change happened in the twilight all the Ingleside folk felt a certain terror of him. At such times he was a fearsome beast and only Rilla defended him, asserting that he was "such a nice prowly cat." Certainly he prowled.

Dr. Jekyll loved new milk; Mr. Hyde would not touch milk and growled over his meat. Dr. Jekyll came down the stairs so silently that no one could hear him. Mr. Hyde made his tread as heavy as a man's. Several evenings, when Susan was alone in the house, he "scared her stiff," as she declared, by doing this. He would sit in the middle of the kitchen floor, with his terrible eyes fixed unwinkingly upon hers for an hour at a time. This played havoc with her nerves, but poor Susan really held him in too much awe to try to drive him out. Once she had dared to throw a stick at him and he had promptly made a savage leap towards her. Susan rushed out of doors and never attempted to meddle with Mr. Hyde again—though she visited his misdeeds upon the innocent Dr. Jekyll, chasing him ignominiously out of her domain whenever he dared to poke his nose in and denying him certain savoury tidbits for which he yearned.

"'The many friends of Miss Faith Meredith, Gerald Meredith and James Blythe,'" read Susan, rolling the names like sweet morsels under her tongue, "'were very much pleased to welcome them home a few weeks ago from Redmond College. James Blythe, who was graduated in Arts in 1913, had just completed his first year in medicine.'"

"Faith Meredith has really got to be the most handsomest creature I ever saw," commented Miss Cornelia above her filet crochet. "It's amazing how those children came on after Rosemary West went to the manse. People have almost forgotten what imps of mischief they were once. Anne, dearie, will you ever forget the way they used to carry on? It's really surprising how well Rosemary got on with them. She's more like a chum than a step-mother. They all love her and Una adores her. As for that little Bruce, Una just makes a perfect slave of herself to him. Of course, he is a darling. But did you ever see any child look as much like an aunt as he looks like his Aunt Ellen? He's just as dark and just as emphatic. I can't see a feature of Rosemary in him. Norman Douglas always vows at the top of his voice that the stork meant Bruce for him and Ellen and took him to the manse by mistake."

"Bruce adores Jem," said Mrs Blythe. "When he comes over here he follows Jem about silently like a faithful little dog, looking up at him from under his black brows. He would do anything for Jem, I verily believe."

"Are Jem and Faith going to make a match of it?"

Mrs. Blythe smiled. It was well known that Miss Cornelia, who had been such a virulent man-hater at one time, had actually taken to match-making in her declining years.

"They are only good friends yet, Miss Cornelia."

"Very good friends, believe me," said Miss Cornelia emphatically. "I hear all about the doings of the young fry."

"I have no doubt that Mary Vance sees that you do, Mrs. Marshall Elliott," said Susan significantly, "but I think it is a shame to talk about children making matches."

"Children! Jem is twenty-one and Faith is nineteen," retorted Miss Cornelia. "You must not forget, Susan, that we old folks are not the only grown-up people in the world."

Outraged Susan, who detested any reference to her age—not from vanity but from a haunting dread that people might come to think her too old to work—returned to her "Notes."

"'Carl Meredith and Shirley Blythe came home last Friday evening from Queen's Academy. We understand that Carl will be in charge of the school at Harbour Head next year and we are sure he will be a popular and successful teacher.'"

"He will teach the children all there is to know about bugs, anyhow," said Miss Cornelia. "He is through with Queen's now and Mr. Meredith and Rosemary wanted him to go right on to Redmond in the fall, but Carl has a very independent streak in him and means to earn part of his own way through college. He'll be all the better for it."

"'Walter Blythe, who has been teaching for the past two years at Lowbridge, has resigned,'" read Susan. "'He intends going to Redmond this fall.'"

"Is Walter quite strong enough for Redmond yet?" queried Miss Cornelia anxiously.

"We hope that he will be by the fall," said Mrs. Blythe. "An idle summer in the open air and sunshine will do a great deal for him."

"Typhoid is a hard thing to get over," said Miss Cornelia emphatically, "especially when one has had such a close shave as Walter had. I think he'd do well to stay out of college another year. But then he's so ambitious. Are Di and Nan going too?"

"Yes. They both wanted to teach another year but Gilbert thinks they had better go to Redmond this fall."

"I'm glad of that. They'll keep an eye on Walter and see that he doesn't study too hard. I suppose," continued Miss Cornelia, with a side glance at Susan, "that after the snub I got a few minutes ago it will not be safe for me to suggest that Jerry Meredith is making sheep's eyes at Nan."

Susan ignored this and Mrs. Blythe laughed again.

"Dear Miss Cornelia, I have my hands full, haven't I?—with all these boys and girls sweethearting around me? If I took it seriously it would quite crush me. But I don't—it is too hard yet to realize that they're grown up. When I look at those two tall sons of mine I wonder if they can possibly be the fat, sweet, dimpled babies I kissed and cuddled and sang to slumber the other day—only the other day, Miss Cornelia. Wasn't Jem the dearest baby in the old House of Dreams? and now he's a B.A. and accused of courting."

"We're all growing older," sighed Miss Cornelia.

"The only part of me that feels old," said Mrs. Blythe, "is the ankle I broke when Josie Pye dared me to walk the Barry ridge-pole in the Green Gables days. I have an ache in it when the wind is east. I won't admit that it is rheumatism, but it does ache. As for the children, they and the Merediths are planning a gay summer before they have to go back to studies in the fall. They are such a fun-loving little crowd. They keep this house in a perpetual whirl of merriment."

"Is Rilla going to Queen's when Shirley goes back?"

"It isn't decided yet. I rather fancy not. Her father thinks she is not quite strong enough—she has rather outgrown her strength—she's really absurdly tall for a girl not yet fifteen. I am not anxious to have her go—why, it would be terrible not to have a single one of my babies home with me next winter. Susan and I would fall to fighting with each other to break the monotony."

Susan smiled at this pleasantry. The idea of her fighting with "Mrs. Dr. dear!"

"Does Rilla herself want to go?" asked Miss Cornelia.

"No. The truth is, Rilla is the only one of my flock who isn't ambitious. I really wish she had a little more ambition. She has no serious ideals at all—her sole aspiration seems to be to have a good time."

"And why should she not have it, Mrs. Dr. dear?" cried Susan, who could not bear to hear a single word against anyone of the Ingleside folk, even from one of themselves. "A young girl should have a good time, and that I will maintain. There will be time enough for her to think of Latin and Greek."

"I should like to see a little sense of responsibility in her, Susan. And you know yourself that she is abominably vain."

"She has something to be vain about," retorted Susan. "She is the prettiest girl in Glen St.

Mary. Do you think that all those over-harbour MacAllisters and Crawfords and Elliotts could scare up a skin like Rilla's in four generations? They could not. No, Mrs. Dr. dear, I know my place but I cannot allow you to run down Rilla. Listen to this, Mrs. Marshall Elliott."

Susan had found a chance to get square with Miss Cornelia for her digs at the children's love affairs. She read the item with gusto.

"'Miller Douglas has decided not to go West. He says old P.E.I. is good enough for him and he will continue to farm for his aunt, Mrs. Alec Davis.'"

Susan looked keenly at Miss Cornelia.

"I have heard, Mrs. Marshall Elliott, that Miller is courting Mary Vance."

This shot pierced Miss Cornelia's armour. Her sonsy face flushed.

"I won't have Miller Douglas hanging round Mary," she said crisply. "He comes of a low family. His father was a sort of outcast from the Douglases—they never really counted him in—and his mother was one of those terrible Dillons from the Harbour Head."

"I think I have heard, Mrs. Marshall Elliott, that Mary Vance's own parents were not what you could call aristocratic."

"Mary Vance has had a good bringing up and she is a smart, clever, capable girl," retorted Miss Cornelia. "She is not going to throw herself away on Miller Douglas, believe me! She knows my opinion on the matter and Mary has never disobeyed me yet."

"Well, I do not think you need worry, Mrs. Marshall Elliott, for Mrs. Alec Davis is as much against it as you could be, and says no nephew of hers is ever going to marry a nameless nobody like Mary Vance."

Susan returned to her mutton, feeling that she had got the best of it in this passage of arms, and read another "note."

"'We are pleased to hear that Miss Oliver has been engaged as teacher for another year. Miss Oliver will spend her well-earned vacation at her home in Lowbridge.'"

"I'm so glad Gertrude is going to stay," said Mrs. Blythe. "We would miss her horribly. And she has an excellent influence over Rilla who worships her. They are chums, in spite of the difference in their ages."

"I thought I heard she was going to be married?"

"I believe it was talked of but I understand it is postponed for a year."

"Who is the young man?"

"Robert Grant. He is a young lawyer in Charlottetown. I hope Gertrude will be happy. She has had a sad life, with much bitterness in it, and she feels things with a terrible keenness. Her first youth is gone and she is practically alone in the world. This new love that has come into her life seems such a wonderful thing to her that I think she hardly dares believe in its permanence. When her marriage had to be put off she was quite in despair—though it certainly wasn't Mr. Grant's fault. There were complications in the settlement of his father's estate—his father died last winter—and he could not marry till the tangles were unravelled. But I think Gertrude felt it was a bad omen and that her happiness would somehow elude her yet."

"It does not do, Mrs. Dr. dear, to set your affections too much on a man," remarked Susan solemnly.

"Mr. Grant is quite as much in love with Gertrude as she is with him, Susan. It is not he whom she distrusts—it is fate. She has a little mystic streak in her—I suppose some people would call her superstitious. She has an odd belief in dreams and we have not been able to laugh it out of her. I must own, too, that some of her dreams—but there, it would not do to let Gilbert hear me hinting such heresy. What have you found of much interest, Susan?"

Susan had given an exclamation.

"Listen to this, Mrs. Dr. dear. 'Mrs. Sophia Crawford has given up her house at Lowbridge and will make her home in future with her niece, Mrs. Albert Crawford.' Why that is my own cousin Sophia, Mrs. Dr. dear. We quarrelled when we were children over who should get a Sunday-school card with the words 'God is Love,' wreathed in rosebuds, on it, and have never spoken to each other since. And now she is coming to live right across the road from us."

"You will have to make up the old quarrel, Susan. It will never do to be at outs with your neighbours."

"Cousin Sophia began the quarrel, so she can begin the making up also, Mrs. Dr. dear," said Susan loftily. "If she does I hope I am a good enough Christian to meet her half-way. She is not a cheerful person and has been a wet blanket all her life. The last time I saw her, her face had a thousand wrinkles—maybe more, maybe less—from worrying and foreboding. She howled dreadful at her first husband's funeral but she married again in less than a year. The next note, I see, describes the special service in our church last Sunday night and says the decorations were very beautiful."

"Speaking of that reminds me that Mr. Pryor strongly disapproves of flowers in church," said Miss Cornelia. "I always said there would be trouble when that man moved here from Lowbridge. He should never have been put in as elder—it was a mistake and we shall live to rue it, believe me! I have heard that he has said that if the girls continue to 'mess up the pulpit with weeds' that he will not go to church."

"The church got on very well before old Whiskers-on-the-moon came to the Glen and it is my opinion it will get on without him after he is gone," said Susan.

"Who in the world ever gave him that ridiculous nickname?" asked Mrs. Blythe.

"Why, the Lowbridge boys have called him that ever since I can remember, Mrs. Dr. dear—I suppose because his face is so round and red, with that fringe of sandy whisker about it. It does not do for anyone to call him that in his hearing, though, and that you may tie to. But worse than his whiskers, Mrs. Dr. dear, he is a very unreasonable man and has a great many queer ideas. He is an elder now and they say he is very religious; but I can well remember the time, Mrs. Dr. dear, twenty years ago, when he was caught pasturing his cow in the Lowbridge graveyard. Yes, indeed, I have not forgotten that, and I always think of it when he is praying in meeting. Well, that is all the notes and there is not much else in the paper of any importance. I never take much interest in foreign parts. Who is this Archduke man who has been murdered?"

"What does it matter to us?" asked Miss Cornelia, unaware of the hideous answer to her question which destiny was even then preparing. "Somebody is always murdering or being murdered in those Balkan States. It's their normal condition and I don't really think that our papers ought to print such shocking things. The Enterprise is getting far too sensational with its big headlines. Well, I must be getting home. No, Anne dearie, it's no use asking me to stay to supper. Marshall has got to thinking that if I'm not home for a meal it's not worth eating—just like a man. So off I go. Merciful goodness, Anne dearie, what is the matter with that cat? Is he having a fit?"—this, as Doc suddenly bounded to the rug at Miss Cornelia's feet, laid back his ears, swore at her, and then disappeared with one fierce leap through the window.

"Oh, no. He's merely turning into Mr. Hyde—which means that we shall have rain or high wind before morning. Doc is as good as a barometer."

"Well, I am thankful he has gone on the rampage outside this time and not into my kitchen," said Susan. "And I am going out to see about supper. With such a crowd as we have at Ingleside now it behooves us to think about our meals betimes."

2. DEW OF MORNING

Outside, the Ingleside lawn was full of golden pools of sunshine and plots of alluring shadows. Rilla Blythe was swinging in the hammock under the big Scotch pine, Gertrude Oliver sat at its roots beside her, and Walter was stretched at full length on the grass, lost in a romance of chivalry wherein old heroes and beauties of dead and gone centuries lived vividly again for him.

Rilla was the "baby" of the Blythe family and was in a chronic state of secret indignation because nobody believed she was grown up. She was so nearly fifteen that she called herself that, and she was quite as tall as Di and Nan; also, she was nearly as pretty as Susan believed her to be. She had great, dreamy, hazel eyes, a milky skin dappled with little golden freckles, and delicately arched eyebrows, giving her a demure, questioning look which made people, especially lads in their teens, want to answer it. Her hair was ripely, ruddily brown and a little dent in her upper lip looked as if some good fairy had pressed it in with her finger at Rilla's christening. Rilla, whose best friends could not deny her share of vanity, thought her face would do very well, but worried over her figure, and wished her mother could be prevailed upon to let her wear longer dresses. She, who had been so plump and roly-poly in the old Rainbow Valley days, was incredibly slim now, in the arms-and-legs period. Jem and Shirley harrowed her soul by calling her "Spider." Yet she somehow escaped awkwardness. There was something in her movements that made you think she never walked but always danced. She had been much petted and was a wee bit spoiled, but still the general opinion was that Rilla Blythe was a very sweet girl, even if she were not so clever as Nan and Di.

Miss Oliver, who was going home that night for vacation, had boarded for a year at Ingleside. The Blythes had taken her to please Rilla who was fathoms deep in love with her teacher and was even willing to share her room, since no other was available. Gertrude Oliver was twenty-eight and life had been a struggle for her. She was a striking-looking girl, with rather sad, almond-shaped brown eyes, a clever, rather mocking mouth, and enormous masses of black hair twisted about her head. She was not pretty but there was a certain charm of interest and mystery in her face, and Rilla found her fascinating. Even her occasional moods of gloom and cynicism had allurement for Rilla. These moods came only when Miss Oliver was tired. At all other times she was a stimulating companion, and the gay set at Ingleside never remembered that she was so much older than themselves. Walter and Rilla were her favourites and she was the confidante of the secret wishes and aspirations of both. She knew that Rilla longed to be "out"—to go to parties as Nan and Di did, and to have dainty evening dresses and —yes, there is no mincing matters—beaux! In the plural, at that! As for Walter, Miss Oliver knew that he had written a sequence of sonnets "to Rosamond"—i.e., Faith Meredith—and that he aimed at a Professorship of English literature in some big college. She knew his passionate love of beauty and his equally passionate hatred of ugliness; she knew his strength and his weakness.

Walter was, as ever, the handsomest of the Ingleside boys. Miss Oliver found pleasure in looking at him for his good looks—he was so exactly like what she would have liked her own son to be. Glossy black hair, brilliant dark grey eyes, faultless features. And a poet to his fingertips! That sonnet sequence was really a remarkable thing for a lad of twenty to write. Miss Oliver was no partial critic and she knew that Walter Blythe had a wonderful gift.

Rilla loved Walter with all her heart. He never teased her as Jem and Shirley did. He never called her "Spider." His pet name for her was "Rilla-my-Rilla"—a little pun on her real name, Marilla. She had been named after Aunt Marilla of Green Gables, but Aunt Marilla had died before Rilla was old enough to know her very well, and Rilla detested the name as being horribly old-fashioned and prim. Why couldn't they have called her by her first name, Bertha, which was beautiful and dignified, instead of that silly "Rilla"? She did not mind Walter's version, but nobody else was allowed to call her that, except Miss Oliver now and then. "Rilla-my-Rilla" in Walter's musical voice sounded very beautiful to her—like the lilt and ripple of some silvery brook. She would have died for Walter if it would have done him any good, so she told Miss Oliver. Rilla was as fond of italics as most girls of fifteen are—and the bitterest drop in her cup was her suspicion that he told Di more of his secrets than he told her.

"He thinks I'm not grown up enough to understand," she had once lamented rebelliously to Miss Oliver, "but I am! And I would never tell them to a single soul—not even to you, Miss Oliver. I tell you all my own—I just couldn't be happy if I had any secret from you, dearest—but I would never betray his. I tell him everything—I even show him my diary. And it hurts me dreadfully when he doesn't tell me things. He shows me all his poems, though—they are marvellous, Miss Oliver. Oh, I just live in the hope that some day I shall be to Walter what Wordsworth's sister Dorothy was to him. Wordsworth never wrote anything like Walter's poems—nor Tennyson, either."

"I wouldn't say just that. Both of them wrote a great deal of trash," said Miss Oliver dryly. Then, repenting, as she saw a hurt look in Rilla's eye, she added hastily,

"But I believe Walter will be a great poet, too—some day—and you will have more of his confidence as you grow older."

"When Walter was in the hospital with typhoid last year I was almost crazy," sighed Rilla, a little importantly. "They never told me how ill he really was until it was all over—father wouldn't let them. I'm glad I didn't know—I couldn't have borne it. I cried myself to sleep every night as it was. But sometimes," concluded Rilla bitterly—she liked to speak bitterly now and then in imitation of Miss Oliver—"sometimes I think Walter cares more for Dog Monday than he does for me."

Dog Monday was the Ingleside dog, so called because he had come into the family on a Monday when Walter had been reading Robinson Crusoe. He really belonged to Jem but was much attached to Walter also. He was lying beside Walter now with nose snuggled against his arm, thumping his tail rapturously whenever Walter gave him an absent pat. Monday was not a collie or a setter or a hound or a Newfoundland. He was just, as Jem said, "plain dog"—very plain dog, uncharitable people added. Certainly, Monday's looks were not his strong point. Black spots were scattered at random over his yellow carcass, one of them, apparently, blotting out an eye. His ears were in tatters, for Monday was never successful in affairs of honour. But he possessed one talisman. He knew that not all dogs could be handsome or eloquent or victorious, but that every dog could love. Inside his homely hide beat the most affectionate, loyal, faithful heart of any dog since dogs were; and something looked out of his brown eyes that was nearer akin to a soul than any theologian would allow. Everybody at Ingleside was fond of him, even Susan, although his one unfortunate propensity of sneaking into the spare room and going to sleep on the bed tried her affection sorely.

On this particular afternoon Rilla had no quarrel on hand with existing conditions.

"Hasn't June been a delightful month?" she asked, looking dreamily afar at the little quiet silvery clouds hanging so peacefully over Rainbow Valley. "We've had such lovely times—and such lovely weather. It has just been perfect every way."

"I don't half like that," said Miss Oliver, with a sigh. "It's ominous—somehow. A perfect thing is a gift of the gods—a sort of compensation for what is coming afterwards. I've seen that so often that I don't care to hear people say they've had a perfect time. June has been delightful, though."

"Of course, it hasn't been very exciting," said Rilla. "The only exciting thing that has happened in the Glen for a year was old Miss Mead fainting in Church. Sometimes I wish something dramatic would happen once in a while."

"Don't wish it. Dramatic things always have a bitterness for some one. What a nice summer all you gay creatures will have! And me moping at Lowbridge!"

"You'll be over often, won't you? I think there's going to be lots of fun this summer, though I'll just be on the fringe of things as usual, I suppose. Isn't it horrid when people think you're a little girl when you're not?"

"There's plenty of time for you to be grown up, Rilla. Don't wish your youth away. It goes too quickly. You'll begin to taste life soon enough."

"Taste life! I want to eat it," cried Rilla, laughing. "I want everything—everything a girl can have. I'll be fifteen in another month, and then nobody can say I'm a child any longer. I heard someone say once that the years from fifteen to nineteen are the best years in a girl's life. I'm going to make them perfectly splendid—just fill them with fun."

"There's no use thinking about what you're going to do—you are tolerably sure not to do it."

"Oh, but you do get a lot of fun out of the thinking," cried Rilla.

"You think of nothing but fun, you monkey," said Miss Oliver indulgently, reflecting that Rilla's chin was really the last word in chins. "Well, what else is fifteen for? But have you any notion of going to college this fall?"

"No—nor any other fall. I don't want to. I never cared for all those ologies and isms Nan and Di are so crazy about. And there's five of us going to college already. Surely that's enough. There's bound to be one dunce in every family. I'm quite willing to be a dunce if I can be a pretty, popular, delightful one. I can't be clever. I have no talent at all, and you can't imagine how comfortable it is. Nobody expects me to do anything so I'm never pestered to do it. And I can't be a housewifely, cookly creature, either. I hate sewing and dusting, and when Susan couldn't teach me to make biscuits nobody could. Father says I toil not neither do I spin. Therefore, I must be a lily of the field," concluded Rilla, with another laugh.

"You are too young to give up your studies altogether, Rilla."

"Oh, mother will put me through a course of reading next winter. It will polish up her B.A. degree. Luckily I like reading. Don't look at me so sorrowfully and so disapprovingly, dearest. I can't be sober and serious—everything looks so rosy and rainbowy to me. Next month I'll be fifteen—and next year sixteen—and the year after that seventeen. Could anything be more enchanting?"

"Rap wood," said Gertrude Oliver, half laughingly, half seriously. "Rap wood, Rilla-my-Rilla."

3. MOONLIT MIRTH

Rilla, who still buttoned up her eyes when she went to sleep so that she always looked as if she were laughing in her slumber, yawned, stretched, and smiled at Gertrude Oliver. The latter had come over from Lowbridge the previous evening and had been prevailed upon to remain for the dance at the Four Winds lighthouse the next night.

"The new day is knocking at the window. What will it bring us, I wonder."

Miss Oliver shivered a little. She never greeted the days with Rilla's enthusiasm. She had lived long enough to know that a day may bring a terrible thing.

"I think the nicest thing about days is their unexpectedness," went on Rilla. "It's jolly to wake up like this on a golden-fine morning and wonder what surprise packet the day will hand you. I always day-dream for ten minutes before I get up, imagining the heaps of splendid things that may happen before night."

"I hope something very unexpected will happen today," said Gertrude. "I hope the mail will bring us news that war has been averted between Germany and France."

"Oh—yes," said Rilla vaguely. "It will be dreadful if it isn't, I suppose. But it won't really matter much to us, will it? I think a war would be so exciting. The Boer war was, they say, but I don't remember anything about it, of course. Miss Oliver, shall I wear my white dress tonight or my new green one? The green one is by far the prettier, of course, but I'm almost afraid to wear it to a shore dance for fear something will happen to it. And will you do my hair the new way? None of the other girls in the Glen wear it yet and it will make such a sensation."

"How did you induce your mother to let you go to the dance?"

"Oh, Walter coaxed her over. He knew I would be heart-broken if I didn't go. It's my first really-truly grown-up party, Miss Oliver, and I've just lain awake at nights for a week thinking it over. When I saw the sun shining this morning I wanted to whoop for joy. It would be simply terrible if it rained tonight. I think I'll wear the green dress and risk it. I want to look my nicest at my first party. Besides, it's an inch longer than my white one. And I'll wear my silver slippers too. Mrs. Ford sent them to me last Christmas and I've never had a chance to wear them yet. They're the dearest things. Oh, Miss Oliver, I do hope some of the boys will ask me to dance. I shall die of mortification—truly I will, if nobody does and I have to sit stuck up against the wall all the evening. Of course Carl and Jerry can't dance because they're the minister's sons, or else I could depend on them to save me from utter disgrace."

"You'll have plenty of partners—all the over-harbour boys are coming—there'll be far more boys than girls."

"I'm glad I'm not a minister's daughter," laughed Rilla. "Poor Faith is so furious because she won't dare to dance tonight. Una doesn't care, of course. She has never hankered after dancing. Somebody told Faith there would be a taffy-pull in the kitchen for those who didn't dance and you should have seen the face she made. She and Jem will sit out on the rocks most of the evening, I suppose. Did you know that we are all to walk down as far as that little creek below the old House of Dreams and then sail to the lighthouse? Won't it just be absolutely divine?"

"When I was fifteen I talked in italics and superlatives too," said Miss Oliver sarcastically. "I think the party promises to be pleasant for young fry. I expect to be bored. None of those boys will bother dancing with an old maid like me. Jem and Walter will take me out once out of charity. So you can't expect me to look forward to it with your touching young rapture."

"Didn't you have a good time at your first party, though, Miss Oliver?"

"No. I had a hateful time. I was shabby and homely and nobody asked me to dance except one boy, homelier and shabbier than myself. He was so awkward I hated him—and even he didn't ask me again. I had no real girlhood, Rilla. It's a sad loss. That's why I want you to have a splendid, happy girlhood. And I hope your first party will be one you'll remember all your life with pleasure."

"I dreamed last night I was at the dance and right in the middle of things I discovered I was dressed in my kimono and bedroom shoes," sighed Rilla. "I woke up with a gasp of horror."

"Speaking of dreams—I had an odd one," said Miss Oliver absently. "It was one of those vivid dreams I sometimes have—they are not the vague jumble of ordinary dreams—they are as clear cut and real as life."

"What was your dream?"

"I was standing on the veranda steps, here at Ingleside, looking down over the fields of the Glen. All at once, far in the distance, I saw a long, silvery, glistening wave breaking over them. It came nearer and nearer—just a succession of little white waves like those that break on the sandshore sometimes. The Glen was being swallowed up. I thought, 'Surely the waves will not come near Ingleside'—but they came nearer and nearer—so rapidly—before I could move or call they were breaking right at my feet—and everything was gone—there was nothing but a waste of stormy water where the Glen had been. I tried to draw back—and I saw that the edge of my dress was wet with blood—and I woke—shivering. I don't like the dream. There was some sinister significance in it. That kind of vivid dream always 'comes true' with me."

"I hope it doesn't mean there's a storm coming up from the east to spoil the party," murmured Rilla.

"Incorrigible fifteen!" said Miss Oliver dryly. "No, Rilla-my-Rilla, I don't think there is any danger that it foretells anything so awful as that."

There had been an undercurrent of tension in the Ingleside existence for several days. Only Rilla, absorbed in her own budding life, was unaware of it. Dr. Blythe had taken to looking grave and saying little over the daily paper. Jem and Walter were keenly interested in the news it brought. Jem sought Walter out in excitement that evening.

"Oh, boy, Germany has declared war on France. This means that England will fight too, probably—and if she does—well, the Piper of your old fancy will have come at last."

"It wasn't a fancy," said Walter slowly. "It was a presentiment—a vision—Jem, I really saw him for a moment that evening long ago. Suppose England does fight?"

"Why, we'll all have to turn in and help her," cried Jem gaily. "We couldn't let the 'old grey mother of the northern sea' fight it out alone, could we? But you can't go—the typhoid has done you out of that. Sort of a shame, eh?"

Walter did not say whether it was a shame or not. He looked silently over the Glen to the dimpling blue harbour beyond.

"We're the cubs—we've got to pitch in tooth and claw if it comes to a family row," Jem went on cheerfully, rumpling up his red curls with a strong, lean, sensitive brown hand—the hand of the born surgeon, his father often thought. "What an adventure it would be! But I suppose Grey or some of those wary old chaps will patch matters up at the eleventh hour. It'll be a rotten shame if they leave France in the lurch, though. If they don't, we'll see some fun. Well, I suppose it's time to get ready for the spree at the light."

Jem departed whistling "Wi' a hundred pipers and a' and a'," and Walter stood for a long time where he was. There was a little frown on his forehead. This had all come up with the blackness and suddenness of a thundercloud. A few days ago nobody had even thought of such a thing. It was absurd to think of it now. Some way out would be found. War was a hellish, horrible, hideous thing—too horrible and hideous to happen in the twentieth century between civilized nations. The mere thought of it was hideous, and made Walter unhappy in its threat to the beauty of life. He would not think of it—he would resolutely put it out of his mind. How beautiful the old Glen was, in its August ripeness, with its chain of bowery old homesteads, tilled meadows and quiet gardens. The western sky was like a great golden pearl. Far down the harbour was frosted with a dawning moonlight. The air was full of exquisite sounds—sleepy robin whistles, wonderful, mournful, soft murmurs of wind in the twilit trees, rustle of aspen poplars talking in silvery whispers and shaking their dainty, heart-shaped leaves, lilting young laughter from the windows of rooms where the girls were making ready for the dance. The world was steeped in maddening loveliness of sound and colour. He would think only of these things and of the deep, subtle joy they gave him. "Anyhow, no one will expect me to go," he thought. "As Jem says, typhoid has seen to that."

Rilla was leaning out of her room window, dressed for the dance. A yellow pansy slipped from her hair and fell out over the sill like a falling star of gold. She caught at it vainly—but there were enough left. Miss Oliver had woven a little wreath of them for her pet's hair.

"It's so beautifully calm—isn't that splendid? We'll have a perfect night. Listen, Miss Oliver—I can hear those old bells in Rainbow Valley quite clearly. They've been hanging there for over ten years."

"Their wind chime always makes me think of the aerial, celestial music Adam and Eve heard in Milton's Eden," responded Miss Oliver.

"We used to have such fun in Rainbow Valley when we were children," said Rilla dreamily.

Nobody ever played in Rainbow Valley now. It was very silent on summer evenings. Walter liked to go there to read. Jem and Faith trysted there considerably; Jerry and Nan went there to pursue uninterruptedly the ceaseless wrangles and arguments on profound subjects that seemed to be their preferred method of sweethearting. And Rilla had a beloved little sylvan dell of her own there where she liked to sit and dream.

"I must run down to the kitchen before I go and show myself off to Susan. She would never forgive me if I didn't."

Rilla whirled into the shadowy kitchen at Ingleside, where Susan was prosaically darning socks, and lighted it up with her beauty. She wore her green dress with its little pink daisy garlands, her silk stockings and silver slippers. She had golden pansies in her hair and at her creamy throat. She was so pretty and young and glowing that even Cousin Sophia Crawford was compelled to admire her—and Cousin Sophia Crawford admired few transient earthly things. Cousin Sophia and Susan had made up, or ignored, their old feud since the former had come to live in the Glen, and Cousin Sophia often came across in the evenings to make a neighbourly call. Susan did not always welcome her rapturously for Cousin Sophia was not what could be called an exhilarating companion. "Some calls are visits and some are visitations, Mrs. Dr. dear," Susan said once, and left it to be inferred that Cousin Sophia's were the latter.

Cousin Sophia had a long, pale, wrinkled face, a long, thin nose, a long, thin mouth, and very long, thin, pale hands, generally folded resignedly on her black calico lap. Everything about her seemed long and thin and pale. She looked mournfully upon Rilla Blythe and said sadly,

"Is your hair all your own?"

"Of course it is," cried Rilla indignantly.

"Ah, well!" Cousin Sophia sighed. "It might be better for you if it wasn't! Such a lot of hair takes from a person's strength. It's a sign of consumption, I've heard, but I hope it won't turn out like that in your case. I s'pose you'll all be dancing tonight—even the minister's boys most likely. I s'pose his girls won't go that far. Ah, well, I never held with dancing. I knew a girl once who dropped dead while she was dancing. How any one could ever dance aga' after a judgment like that I cannot comprehend."

"Did she ever dance again?" asked Rilla pertly.

"I told you she dropped dead. Of course she never danced again, poor creature. She was a Kirke from Lowbridge. You ain't a-going off like that with nothing on your bare neck, are you?"

"It's a hot evening," protested Rilla. "But I'll put on a scarf when we go on the water."

"I knew of a boat load of young folks who went sailing on that harbour forty years ago just such a night as this—just exactly such a night as this," said Cousin Sophia lugubriously, "and they were upset and drowned—every last one of them. I hope nothing like that'll happen to you tonight. Do you ever try anything for the freckles? I used to find plantain juice real good."

"You certainly should be a judge of freckles, Cousin Sophia," said Susan, rushing to Rilla's defence. "You were more speckled than any toad when you was a girl. Rilla's only come in summer but yours stayed put, season in and season out; and you had not a ground colour like hers behind them neither. You look real nice, Rilla, and that way of fixing your hair is becoming. But you are not going to walk to the harbour in those slippers, are you?"

"Oh, no. We'll all wear our old shoes to the harbour and carry our slippers. Do you like my dress, Susan?"

"It minds me of a dress I wore when I was a girl," sighed Cousin Sophia before Susan could reply. "It was green with pink posies on it, too, and it was flounced from the waist to the hem. We didn't wear the skimpy things girls wear nowadays. Ah me, times has changed and not for the better I'm afraid. I tore a big hole in it that night and someone spilled a cup of tea all over it. Ruined it completely. But I hope nothing will happen to your dress. It orter to be a bit longer I'm thinking—your legs are so terrible long and thin."

"Mrs. Dr. Blythe does not approve of little girls dressing like grown-up ones," said Susan stiffly, intending merely a snub to Cousin Sophia. But Rilla felt insulted. A little girl indeed! She whisked out of the kitchen in high dudgeon. Another time she wouldn't go down to show herself off to Susan—Susan, who thought nobody was grown up until she was sixty! And that horrid Cousin Sophia with her digs about freckles and legs! What business had an old—an old beanpole like that to talk of anybody else being long and thin? Rilla felt all her pleasure in herself and her evening clouded and spoiled. The very teeth of her soul were set on edge and she could have sat down and cried.

But later on her spirits rose again when she found herself one of the gay crowd bound for the Four Winds light.

The Blythes left Ingleside to the melancholy music of howls from Dog Monday, who was locked up in the barn lest he make an uninvited guest at the light. They picked up the Merediths in the village, and others joined them as they walked down the old harbour road. Mary Vance, resplendent in blue crepe, with lace overdress, came out of Miss Cornelia's gate and attached herself to Rilla and Miss Oliver who were walking together and who did not welcome her over-warmly. Rilla was not very fond of Mary Vance. She had never forgotten the humiliating day when Mary had chased her through the village with a dried codfish. Mary Vance, to tell the truth, was not exactly popular with any of her set. Still, they enjoyed her society—she had such a biting tongue that it was stimulating. "Mary Vance is a habit of ours—we can't do without her even when we are furious with her," Di Blythe had once said.

Most of the little crowd were paired off after a fashion. Jem walked with Faith Meredith, of course, and Jerry Meredith with Nan Blythe. Di and Walter were together, deep in confidential conversation which Rilla envied.

Carl Meredith was walking with Miranda Pryor, more to torment Joe Milgrave than for any other reason. Joe was known to have a strong hankering for the said Miranda, which shyness prevented him from indulging on all occasions. Joe might summon enough courage to amble up beside Miranda if the night were dark, but here, in this moonlit dusk, he simply could not do it. So he trailed along after the procession and thought things not lawful to be uttered of Carl Meredith. Miranda was the daughter of Whiskers-on-the-moon; she did not share her father's unpopularity but she was not much run after, being a pale, neutral little creature, somewhat addicted to nervous giggling. She had silvery blonde hair and her eyes were big china blue orbs that looked as if she had been badly frightened when she was little and had never got over it. She would much rather have walked with Joe than with Carl, with whom she did not feel in the least at home. Yet it was something of an honour, too, to have a college boy beside her, and a son of the manse at that.

Shirley Blythe was with Una Meredith and both were rather silent because such was their nature. Shirley was a lad of sixteen, sedate, sensible, thoughtful, full of a quiet humour. He was Susan's "little brown boy" yet, with his brown hair, brown eyes, and clear brown skin. He liked to walk with Una Meredith because she never tried to make him talk or badgered him with chatter. Una was as sweet and shy as she had been in the Rainbow Valley days, and her large, dark-blue eyes were as dreamy and wistful. She had a secret, carefully-hidden fancy for Walter Blythe that nobody but Rilla ever suspected. Rilla sympathized with it and wished Walter would return it. She liked Una better than Faith, whose beauty and aplomb rather overshadowed other girls—and Rilla did not enjoy being overshadowed.

But just now she was very happy. It was so delightful to be tripping with her friends down that dark, gleaming road sprinkled with its little spruces and firs, whose balsam made all the air resinous around them. Meadows of sunset afterlight were behind the westerning hills. Before them was the shining harbour. A bell was ringing in the little church over-harbour and the lingering dream-notes died around the dim, amethystine points. The gulf beyond was still silvery blue in the afterlight. Oh, it was all glorious—the clear air with its salt tang, the balsam of the firs, the laughter of her friends. Rilla loved life—its bloom and brilliance; she loved the ripple of music, the hum of merry conversation; she wanted to walk on forever over this road of silver and shadow. It was her first party and she was going to have a splendid time. There was nothing in the world to worry about—not even freckles and over-long legs—nothing except one little haunting fear that nobody would ask her to dance. It was beautiful and satisfying just to be alive—to be fifteen—to be pretty. Rilla drew a long breath of rapture—and caught it midway rather sharply. Jem was telling some story to Faith—something that had happened in the Balkan War.

"The doctor lost both his legs—they were smashed to pulp—and he was left on the field to die. And he crawled about from man to man, to all the wounded men round him, as long as he could, and did everything possible to relieve their sufferings—never thinking of himself—he was tying a bit of bandage round another man's leg when he went under. They found them there, the doctor's dead hands still held the bandage tight, the bleeding was stopped and the other man's life was saved. Some hero, wasn't he, Faith? I tell you when I read that—"

Jem and Faith moved on out of hearing. Gertrude Oliver suddenly shivered. Rilla pressed her arm sympathetically.

"Wasn't it dreadful, Miss Oliver? I don't know why Jem tells such gruesome things at a time like this when we're all out for fun."

"Do you think it dreadful, Rilla? I thought it wonderful—beautiful. Such a story makes one ashamed of ever doubting human nature. That man's action was godlike. And how humanity responds to the ideal of self-sacrifice. As for my shiver, I don't know what caused it. The evening is certainly warm enough. Perhaps someone is walking over the dark, starshiny spot that is to be my grave. That is the explanation the old superstition would give. Well, I won't think of that on this lovely night. Do you know, Rilla, that when night-time comes I'm always glad I live in the country. We know the real charm of night here as town dwellers never do. Every night is beautiful in the country—even the stormy ones. I love a wild night storm on this old gulf shore. As for a night like this, it is almost too beautiful—it belongs to youth and dreamland and I'm half afraid of it."

"I feel as if I were part of it," said Rilla.

"Ah yes, you're young enough not to be afraid of perfect things. Well, here we are at the House of Dreams. It seems lonely this summer. The Fords didn't come?"

"Mr. and Mrs. Ford and Persis didn't. Kenneth did—but he stayed with his mother's people over-harbour. We haven't seen a great deal of him this summer. He's a little lame, so didn't go about very much."

"Lame? What happened to him?"

"He broke his ankle in a football game last fall and was laid up most of the winter. He has limped a little ever since but it is getting better all the time and he expects it will be all right before long. He has been up to Ingleside only twice."

"Ethel Reese is simply crazy about him," said Mary Vance. "She hasn't got the sense she was born with where he is concerned. He walked home with her from the over-harbour church last prayer-meeting night and the airs she has put on since would really make you weary of life. As if a Toronto boy like Ken Ford would ever really think of a country girl like Ethel!"

Rilla flushed. It did not matter to her if Kenneth Ford walked home with Ethel Reese a dozen times—it did not! Nothing that he did mattered to her. He was ages older than she was. He chummed with Nan and Di and Faith, and looked upon her, Rilla, as a child whom he never noticed except to tease. And she detested Ethel Reese and Ethel Reese hated her—always had hated her since Walter had pummelled Dan so notoriously in Rainbow Valley days; but why need she be thought beneath Kenneth Ford's notice because she was a country girl, pray? As for Mary Vance, she was getting to be an out-and-out gossip and thought of nothing but who walked home with people!

There was a little pier on the harbour shore below the House of Dreams, and two boats were moored there. One boat was skippered by Jem Blythe, the other by Joe Milgrave, who knew all about boats and was nothing loth to let Miranda Pryor see it. They raced down the harbour and Joe's boat won. More boats were coming down from the Harbour Head and across the harbour from the western side. Everywhere there was laughter. The big white tower on Four Winds Point was overflowing with light, while its revolving beacon flashed overhead. A family from Charlottetown, relatives of the light's keeper, were summering at the light, and they were giving the party to which all the young people of Four Winds and Glen St. Mary and over-harbour had been invited. As Jem's boat swung in below the lighthouse Rilla desperately snatched off her shoes and donned her silver slippers behind Miss Oliver's screening back. A glance had told her that the rock-cut steps climbing up to the light were lined with boys, and lighted by Chinese lanterns, and she was determined she would not walk up those steps in the heavy shoes her mother had insisted on her wearing for the road. The slippers pinched abominably, but nobody would have suspected it as Rilla tripped smilingly up the steps, her soft dark eyes glowing and questioning, her colour deepening richly on her round, creamy cheeks. The very minute she reached the top of the steps an over-harbour boy asked her to dance and the next moment they were in the pavilion that had been built seaward of the lighthouse for dances. It was a delightful spot, roofed over with fir-boughs and hung with lanterns. Beyond was the sea in a radiance that glowed and shimmered, to the left the moonlit crests and hollows of the sand-dunes, to the right the rocky shore with its inky shadows and its crystalline coves. Rilla and her partner swung in among the dancers; she drew a long breath of delight; what witching music Ned Burr of the Upper Glen was coaxing from his fiddle—it was really like the magical pipes of the old tale which compelled all who heard them to dance. How cool and fresh the gulf breeze blew; how white and wonderful the moonlight was over everything! This was life—enchanting life. Rilla felt as if her feet and her soul both had wings.

4. THE PIPER PIPES

Rilla's first party was a triumph—or so it seemed at first. She had so many partners that she had to split her dances. Her silver slippers seemed verily to dance of themselves and though they continued to pinch her toes and blister her heels that did not interfere with her enjoyment in the least. Ethel Reese gave her a bad ten minutes by beckoning her mysteriously out of the pavilion and whispering, with a Reese-like smirk, that her dress gaped behind and that there was a stain on the flounce. Rilla rushed miserably to the room in the lighthouse which was fitted up for a temporary ladies' dressing-room, and discovered that the stain was merely a tiny grass smear and that the gap was equally tiny where a hook had pulled loose. Irene Howard fastened it up for her and gave her some over-sweet, condescending compliments. Rilla felt flattered by Irene's condescension. She was an Upper Glen girl of nineteen who seemed to like the society of the younger girls—spiteful friends said because she could queen it over them without rivalry. But Rilla thought Irene quite wonderful and loved her for her patronage. Irene was pretty and stylish; she sang divinely and spent every winter in Charlottetown taking music lessons. She had an aunt in Montreal who sent her wonderful things to wear; she was reported to have had a sad love affair—nobody knew just what, but its very mystery allured. Rilla felt that Irene's compliments crowned her evening. She ran gaily back to the pavilion and lingered for a moment in the glow of the lanterns at the entrance looking at the dancers. A momentary break in the whirling throng gave her a glimpse of Kenneth Ford standing at the other side.

Rilla's heart skipped a beat—or, if that be a physiological impossibility, she thought it did. So he was here, after all. She had concluded he was not coming—not that it mattered in the least. Would he see her? Would he take any notice of her? Of course, he wouldn't ask her to dance—that couldn't be hoped for. He thought her just a mere child. He had called her "Spider" not three weeks ago when he had been at Ingleside one evening. She had cried about it upstairs afterwards and hated him. But her heart skipped a beat when she saw that he was edging his way round the side of the pavilion towards her. Was he coming to her—was he?—was he?—yes, he was! He was looking for her—he was here beside her—he was gazing down at her with something in his dark grey eyes that Rilla had never seen in them. Oh, it was almost too much to bear! and everything was going on as before—the dancers were spinning round, the boys who couldn't get partners were hanging about the pavilion, canoodling couples were sitting out on the rocks—nobody seemed to realize what a stupendous thing had happened.

Kenneth was a tall lad, very good looking, with a certain careless grace of bearing that somehow made all the other boys seem stiff and awkward by contrast. He was reported to be awesomely clever, with the glamour of a far-away city and a big university hanging around him. He had also the reputation of being a bit of a lady-killer. But that probably accrued to him from his possession of a laughing, velvety voice which no girl could hear without a heartbeat, and a dangerous way of listening as if she were saying something that he had longed all his life to hear.

"Is this Rilla-my-Rilla?" he asked in a low tone.

"Yeth," said Rilla, and immediately wished she could throw herself headlong down the lighthouse rock or otherwise vanish from a jeering world.

Rilla had lisped in early childhood; but she had grown out of it. Only on occasions of stress and strain did the tendency re-assert itself. She hadn't lisped for a year; and now at this very moment, when she was so especially desirous of appearing grown up and sophisticated, she must go and lisp like a baby! It was too mortifying; she felt as if tears were going to come into her eyes; the next minute she would be—blubbering—yes, just blubbering—she wished Kenneth would go away—she wished he had never come. The party was spoiled. Everything had turned to dust and ashes.

And he had called her "Rilla-my-Rilla"—not "Spider" or "Kid" or "Puss," as he had been used to call her when he took any notice whatever of her. She did not at all resent his using Walter's pet name for her; it sounded beautifully in his low caressing tones, with just the faintest suggestion of emphasis on the "my." It would have been so nice if she had not made a fool of herself. She dared not look up lest she should see laughter in his eyes. So she looked down; and as her lashes were very long and dark and her lids very thick and creamy, the effect was quite charming and provocative, and Kenneth reflected that Rilla Blythe was going to be the beauty of the Ingleside girls after all. He wanted to make her look up—to catch again that little, demure, questioning glance. She was the prettiest thing at the party, there was no doubt of that.

What was he saying? Rilla could hardly believe her ears.

"Can we have a dance?"

"Yes," said Rilla. She said it with such a fierce determination not to lisp that she fairly blurted the word out. Then she writhed in spirit again. It sounded so bold—so eager—as if she were fairly jumping at him! What would he think of her? Oh, why did dreadful things like this happen, just when a girl wanted to appear at her best?

Kenneth drew her in among the dancers.

"I think this game ankle of mine is good for one hop around, at least," he said.

"How is your ankle?" said Rilla. Oh, why couldn't she think of something else to say? She knew he was sick of inquiries about his ankle. She had heard him say so at Ingleside—heard him tell Di he was going to wear a placard on his breast announcing to all and sundry that the ankle was improving, etc. And now she must go and ask this stale question again.

Kenneth was tired of inquiries about his ankle. But then he had not often been asked about it by lips with such an adorable kissable dent just above them. Perhaps that was why he answered very patiently that it was getting on well and didn't trouble him much, if he didn't walk or stand too long at a time.

"They tell me it will be as strong as ever in time, but I'll have to cut football out this fall."

They danced together and Rilla knew every girl in sight envied her. After the dance they went down the rock steps and Kenneth found a little flat and they rowed across the moonlit channel to the sand-shore; they walked on the sand till Kenneth's ankle made protest and then they sat down among the dunes. Kenneth talked to her as he had talked to Nan and Di. Rilla, overcome with a shyness she did not understand, could not talk much, and thought he would think her frightfully stupid; but in spite of this it was all very wonderful—the exquisite moonlit night, the shining sea, the tiny little wavelets swishing on the sand, the cool and freakish wind of night crooning in the stiff grasses on the crest of the dunes, the music sounding faintly and sweetly over the channel.

"'A merry lilt o' moonlight for mermaiden revelry,'" quoted Kenneth softly from one of Walter's poems.

And just he and she alone together in the glamour of sound and sight! If only her slippers didn't bite so! and if only she could talk cleverly like Miss Oliver—nay, if she could only talk as she did herself to other boys! But words would not come, she could only listen and murmur little commonplace sentences now and again. But perhaps her dreamy eyes and her dented lip and her slender throat talked eloquently for her. At any rate Kenneth seemed in no hurry to suggest going back and when they did go back supper was in progress. He found a seat for her near the window of the lighthouse kitchen and sat on the sill beside her while she ate her ices and cake. Rilla looked about her and thought how lovely her first party had been. She would never forget it. The room re-echoed to laughter and jest. Beautiful young eyes sparkled and shone. From the pavilion outside came the lilt of the fiddle and the rhythmic steps of the dancers.

There was a little disturbance among a group of boys crowded about the door; a young fellow pushed through and halted on the threshold, looking about him rather sombrely. It was Jack Elliott from over-harbour—a McGill medical student, a quiet chap not much addicted to social doings. He had been invited to the party but had not been expected to come since he had to go to Charlottetown that day and could not be back until late. Yet here he was—and he carried a folded paper in his hand.

Gertrude Oliver looked at him from her corner and shivered again. She had enjoyed the party herself, after all, for she had foregathered with a Charlottetown acquaintance who, being a stranger and much older than most of the guests, felt himself rather out of it, and had been glad to fall in with this clever girl who could talk of world doings and outside events with the zest and vigour of a man. In the pleasure of his society she had forgotten some of her misgivings of the day. Now they suddenly returned to her. What news did Jack Elliott bring? Lines from an old poem flashed unbidden into her mind—"there was a sound of revelry by night"—"Hush! Hark! A deep sound strikes like a rising knell"—why should she think of that now? Why didn't Jack Elliott speak—if he had anything to tell? Why did he just stand there, glowering importantly?

"Ask him—ask him," she said feverishly to Allan Daly. But somebody else had already asked him. The room grew very silent all at once. Outside the fiddler had stopped for a rest and there was silence there too. Afar off they heard the low moan of the gulf—the presage of a storm already on its way up the Atlantic. A girl's laugh drifted up from the rocks and died away as if frightened out of existence by the sudden stillness.

"England declared war on Germany today," said Jack Elliott slowly. "The news came by wire just as I left town."

"God help us," whispered Gertrude Oliver under her breath. "My dream—my dream! The first wave has broken." She looked at Allan Daly and tried to smile.

"Is this Armageddon?" she asked.

"I am afraid so," he said gravely.

A chorus of exclamations had arisen round them—light surprise and idle interest for the most part. Few there realized the import of the message—fewer still realized that it meant anything to them. Before long the dancing was on again and the hum of pleasure was as loud as ever. Gertrude and Allan Daly talked the news over in low, troubled tones. Walter Blythe had turned pale and left the room. Outside he met Jem, hurrying up the rock steps.

"Have you heard the news, Jem?"

"Yes. The Piper has come. Hurrah! I knew England wouldn't leave France in the lurch. I've been trying to get Captain Josiah to hoist the flag but he says it isn't the proper caper till sunrise. Jack says they'll be calling for volunteers tomorrow."

"What a fuss to make over nothing," said Mary Vance disdainfully as Jem dashed off. She was sitting out with Miller Douglas on a lobster trap which was not only an unromantic but an uncomfortable seat. But Mary and Miller were both supremely happy on it. Miller Douglas was a big, strapping, uncouth lad, who thought Mary Vance's tongue uncommonly gifted and Mary Vance's white eyes stars of the first magnitude; and neither of them had the least inkling why Jem Blythe wanted to hoist the lighthouse flag. "What does it matter if there's going to be a war over there in Europe? I'm sure it doesn't concern us."

Walter looked at her and had one of his odd visitations of prophecy.

"Before this war is over," he said—or something said through his lips—"every man and woman and child in Canada will feel it—you, Mary, will feel it—feel it to your heart's core. You will weep tears of blood over it. The Piper has come—and he will pipe until every corner of the world has heard his awful and irresistible music. It will be years before the dance of death is over—years, Mary. And in those years millions of hearts will break."

"Fancy now!" said Mary who always said that when she couldn't think of anything else to say. She didn't know what Walter meant but she felt uncomfortable. Walter Blythe was always saying odd things. That old Piper of his—she hadn't heard anything about him since their playdays in Rainbow Valley—and now here he was bobbing up again. She didn't like it, and that was the long and short of it.

"Aren't you painting it rather strong, Walter?" asked Harvey Crawford, coming up just then. "This war won't last for years—it'll be over in a month or two. England will just wipe Germany off the map in no time."

"Do you think a war for which Germany has been preparing for twenty years will be over in a few weeks?" said Walter passionately. "This isn't a paltry struggle in a Balkan corner, Harvey. It is a death grapple. Germany comes to conquer or to die. And do you know what will happen if she conquers? Canada will be a German colony."

"Well, I guess a few things will happen before that," said Harvey shrugging his shoulders. "The British navy would have to be licked for one; and for another, Miller here, now, and I, we'd raise a dust, wouldn't we, Miller? No Germans need apply for this old country, eh?"

Harvey ran down the steps laughing.

"I declare, I think all you boys talk the craziest stuff," said Mary Vance in disgust. She got up and dragged Miller off to the rock-shore. It didn't happen often that they had a chance for a talk together; Mary was determined that this one shouldn't be spoiled by Walter Blythe's silly blather about Pipers and Germans and such like absurd things. They left Walter standing alone on the rock steps, looking out over the beauty of Four Winds with brooding eyes that saw it not.

The best of the evening was over for Rilla, too. Ever since Jack Elliott's announcement, she had sensed that Kenneth was no longer thinking about her. She felt suddenly lonely and unhappy. It was worse than if he had never noticed her at all. Was life like this—something delightful happening and then, just as you were revelling in it, slipping away from you? Rilla told herself pathetically that she felt years older than when she had left home that evening. Perhaps she did—perhaps she was. Who knows? It does not do to laugh at the pangs of youth. They are very terrible because youth has not yet learned that "this, too, will pass away." Rilla sighed and wished she were home, in bed, crying into her pillow.

"Tired?" said Kenneth, gently but absently—oh, so absently. He really didn't care a bit whether she were tired or not, she thought.

"Kenneth," she ventured timidly, "you don't think this war will matter much to us in Canada, do you?"

"Matter? Of course it will matter to the lucky fellows who will be able to take a hand. I won't—thanks to this confounded ankle. Rotten luck, I call it."

"I don't see why we should fight England's battles," cried Rilla. "She's quite able to fight them herself."

"That isn't the point. We are part of the British Empire. It's a family affair. We've got to stand by each other. The worst of it is, it will be over before I can be of any use."

"Do you mean that you would really volunteer to go if it wasn't for your ankle? asked Rilla incredulously.

"Sure I would. You see they'll go by thousands. Jem'll be off, I'll bet a cent—Walter won't be strong enough yet, I suppose. And Jerry Meredith—he'll go! And I was worrying about being out of football this year!"

Rilla was too startled to say anything. Jem—and Jerry! Nonsense! Why father and Mr. Meredith wouldn't allow it. They weren't through college. Oh, why hadn't Jack Elliott kept his horrid news to himself?

Mark Warren came up and asked her to dance. Rilla went, knowing Kenneth didn't care whether she went or stayed. An hour ago on the sand-shore he had been looking at her as if she were the only being of any importance in the world. And now she was nobody. His thoughts were full of this Great Game which was to be played out on bloodstained fields with empires for stakes—a Game in which womenkind could have no part. Women, thought Rilla miserably, just had to sit and cry at home. But all this was foolishness. Kenneth couldn't go—he admitted that himself—and Walter couldn't—thank goodness for that—and Jem and Jerry would have more sense. She wouldn't worry—she would enjoy herself. But how awkward Mark Warren was! How he bungled his steps! Why, for mercy's sake, did boys try to dance who didn't know the first thing about dancing; and who had feet as big as boats? There, he had bumped her into somebody! She would never dance with him again!

She danced with others, though the zest was gone out of the performance and she had begun to realize that her slippers hurt her badly. Kenneth seemed to have gone—at least nothing was to be seen of him. Her first party was spoiled, though it had seemed so beautiful at one time. Her head ached—her toes burned. And worse was yet to come. She had gone down with some over-harbour friends to the rock-shore where they all lingered as dance after dance went on above them. It was cool and pleasant and they were tired. Rilla sat silent, taking no part in the gay conversation. She was glad when someone called down that the over-harbour boats were leaving. A laughing scramble up the lighthouse rock followed. A few couples still whirled about in the pavilion but the crowd had thinned out. Rilla looked about her for the Glen group. She could not see one of them. She ran into the lighthouse. Still, no sign of anybody. In dismay she ran to the rock steps, down which the over-harbour guests were hurrying. She could see the boats below—where was Jem's—where was Joe's?

"Why, Rilla Blythe, I thought you'd be gone home long ago," said Mary Vance, who was waving her scarf at a boat skimming up the channel, skippered by Miller Douglas.

"Where are the rest?" gasped Rilla.

"Why, they're gone—Jem went an hour ago—Una had a headache. And the rest went with Joe about fifteen minutes ago. See—they're just going around Birch Point. I didn't go because it's getting rough and I knew I'd be seasick. I don't mind walking home from here. It's only a mile and a half. I s'posed you'd gone. Where were you?"

"Down on the rocks with Jem and Mollie Crawford. Oh, why didn't they look for me?"

"They did—but you couldn't be found. Then they concluded you must have gone in the other boat. Don't worry. You can stay all night with me and we'll 'phone up to Ingleside where you are."

Rilla realized that there was nothing else to do. Her lips trembled and tears came into her eyes. She blinked savagely—she would not let Mary Vance see her crying. But to be forgotten like this! To think nobody had thought it worth while to make sure where she was—not even Walter. Then she had a sudden dismayed recollection.

"My shoes," she exclaimed. "I left them in the boat."

"Well, I never," said Mary. "You're the most thoughtless kid I ever saw. You'll have to ask Hazel Lewison to lend you a pair of shoes."

"I won't." cried Rilla, who didn't like the said Hazel. "I'll go barefoot first."

Mary shrugged her shoulders.

"Just as you like. Pride must suffer pain. It'll teach you to be more careful. Well, let's hike."

Accordingly they hiked. But to "hike" along a deep-rutted, pebbly lane in frail, silver-hued slippers with high French heels, is not an exhilarating performance. Rilla managed to limp and totter along until they reached the harbour road; but she could go no farther in those detestable slippers. She took them and her dear silk stockings off and started barefoot. That was not pleasant either; her feet were very tender and the pebbles and ruts of the road hurt them. Her blistered heels smarted. But physical pain was almost forgotten in the sting of humiliation. This was a nice predicament! If Kenneth Ford could see her now, limping along like a little girl with a stone bruise! Oh, what a horrid way for her lovely party to end! She just had to cry—it was too terrible. Nobody cared for her—nobody bothered about her at all. Well, if she caught cold from walking home barefoot on a dew-wet road and went into a decline perhaps they would be sorry. She furtively wiped her tears away with her scarf—handkerchiefs seemed to have vanished like shoes!—but she could not help sniffling. Worse and worse!

"You've got a cold, I see," said Mary. "You ought to have known you would, sitting down in the wind on those rocks. Your mother won't let you go out again in a hurry I can tell you. It's certainly been something of a party. The Lewisons know how to do things, I'll say that for them, though Hazel Lewison is no choice of mine. My, how black she looked when she saw you dancing with Ken Ford. And so did that little hussy of an Ethel Reese. What a flirt he is!"

"I don't think he's a flirt," said Rilla as defiantly as two desperate sniffs would let her.

"You'll know more about men when you're as old as I am," said Mary patronizingly. "Mind you, it doesn't do to believe all they tell you. Don't let Ken Ford think that all he has to do to get you on a string is to drop his handkerchief. Have more spirit than that, child."

To be thus hectored and patronized by Mary Vance was unendurable! And it was unendurable to walk on stony roads with blistered heels and bare feet! And it was unendurable to be crying and have no handkerchief and not to be able to stop crying!

"I'm not thinking"—sniff—"about Kenneth"—sniff—"Ford"—two sniffs—"at all," cried tortured Rilla.

"There's no need to fly off the handle, child. You ought to be willing to take advice from older people. I saw how you slipped over to the sands with Ken and stayed there ever so long with him. Your mother wouldn't like it if she knew."

"I'll tell my mother all about it—and Miss Oliver—and Walter," Rilla gasped between sniffs. "You sat for hours with Miller Douglas on that lobster trap, Mary Vance! What would Mrs. Elliott say to that if she knew?"

"Oh, I'm not going to quarrel with you," said Mary, suddenly retreating to high and lofty ground. "All I say is, you should wait until you're grown-up before you do things like that."

Rilla gave up trying to hide the fact that she was crying. Everything was spoiled—even that beautiful, dreamy, romantic, moonlit hour with Kenneth on the sands was vulgarized and cheapened. She loathed Mary Vance.

"Why, whatever's wrong?" cried mystified Mary. "What are you crying for?"

"My feet—hurt so—" sobbed Rilla clinging to the last shred of her pride. It was less humiliating to admit crying because of your feet than because—because somebody had been amusing himself with you, and your friends had forgotten you, and other people patronized you.

"I daresay they do," said Mary, not unkindly. "Never mind. I know where there's a pot of goose-grease in Cornelia's tidy pantry and it beats all the fancy cold creams in the world. I'll put some on your heels before you go to bed."

Goose-grease on your heels! So this was what your first party and your first beau and your first moonlit romance ended in!

Rilla gave over crying in sheer disgust at the futility of tears and went to sleep in Mary Vance's bed in the calm of despair. Outside, the dawn came greyly in on wings of storm; Captain Josiah, true to his word, ran up the Union Jack at the Four Winds Light and it streamed on the fierce wind against the clouded sky like a gallant unquenchable beacon.

5. "THE SOUND OF A GOING"

Rilla ran down through the sunlit glory of the maple grove behind Ingleside, to her favourite nook in Rainbow Valley. She sat down on a green-mossed stone among the fern, propped her chin on her hands and stared unseeingly at the dazzling blue sky of the August afternoon—so blue, so peaceful, so unchanged, just as it had arched over the valley in the mellow days of late summer ever since she could remember.

She wanted to be alone—to think things out—to adjust herself, if it were possible, to the new world into which she seemed to have been transplanted with a suddenness and completeness that left her half bewildered as to her own identity. Was she—could she be—the same Rilla Blythe who had danced at Four Winds Light six days ago—only six days ago? It seemed to Rilla that she had lived as much in those six days as in all her previous life—and if it be true that we should count time by heart-throbs she had. That evening, with its hopes and fears and triumphs and humiliations, seemed like ancient history now. Could she really ever have cried just because she had been forgotten and had to walk home with Mary Vance? Ah, thought Rilla sadly, how trivial and absurd such a cause of tears now appeared to her. She could cry now with a right good will—but she would not—she must not. What was it mother had said, looking, with her white lips and stricken eyes, as Rilla had never seen her mother look before,

"When our women fail in courage,
Shall our men be fearless still?"

Yes, that was it. She must be brave—like mother—and Nan—and Faith—Faith, who had cried with flashing eyes, "Oh, if I were only a man, to go too!" Only, when her eyes ached and her throat burned like this she had to hide herself in Rainbow Valley for a little, just to think things out and remember that she wasn't a child any longer—she was grown-up and women had to face things like this. But it was—nice—to get away alone now and then, where nobody could see her and where she needn't feel that people thought her a little coward if some tears came in spite of her.

How sweet and woodsey the ferns smelled! How softly the great feathery boughs of the firs waved and murmured over her! How elfinly rang the bells of the "Tree Lovers"—just a tinkle now and then as the breeze swept by! How purple and elusive the haze where incense was being offered on many an altar of the hills! How the maple leaves whitened in the wind until the grove seemed covered with pale silvery blossoms! Everything was just the same as she had seen it hundreds of times; and yet the whole face of the world seemed changed.

"How wicked I was to wish that something dramatic would happen!" she thought. "Oh, if we could only have those dear, monotonous, pleasant days back again! I would never, never grumble about them again."

Rilla's world had tumbled to pieces the very day after the party. As they lingered around the dinner table at Ingleside, talking of the war, the telephone had rung. It was a long-distance call from Charlottetown for Jem. When he had finished talking he hung up the receiver and turned around, with a flushed face and glowing eyes. Before he had said a word his mother and Nan and Di had turned pale. As for Rilla, for the first time in her life she felt that every one must hear her heart beating and that something had clutched at her throat.

"They are calling for volunteers in town, father," said Jem. "Scores have joined up already. I'm going in tonight to enlist."

"Oh—Little Jem," cried Mrs. Blythe brokenly. She had not called him that for many years—not since the day he had rebelled against it. "Oh—no—no—Little Jem."

"I must, mother. I'm right—am I not, father?" said Jem.

Dr. Blythe had risen. He was very pale, too, and his voice was husky. But he did not hesitate.

"Yes, Jem, yes—if you feel that way, yes—"

Mrs. Blythe covered her face. Walter stared moodily at his plate. Nan and Di clasped each others' hands. Shirley tried to look unconcerned. Susan sat as if paralysed, her piece of pie half-eaten on her plate. Susan never did finish that piece of pie—a fact which bore eloquent testimony to the upheaval in her inner woman for Susan considered it a cardinal offence against civilized society to begin to eat anything and not finish it. That was wilful waste, hens to the contrary notwithstanding.

Jem turned to the phone again. "I must ring the manse. Jerry will want to go, too."

At this Nan had cried out "Oh!" as if a knife had been thrust into her, and rushed from the room. Di followed her. Rilla turned to Walter for comfort but Walter was lost to her in some reverie she could not share.

"All right," Jem was saying, as coolly as if he were arranging the details of a picnic. "I thought you would—yes, tonight—the seven o'clock—meet me at the station. So long."

"Mrs. Dr. dear," said Susan. "I wish you would wake me up. Am I dreaming—or am I awake? Does that blessed boy realize what he is saying? Does he mean that he is going to enlist as a soldier? You do not mean to tell me that they want children like him! It is an outrage. Surely you and the doctor will not permit it."

"We can't stop him," said Mrs. Blythe, chokingly. "Oh, Gilbert!"

Dr. Blythe came up behind his wife and took her hand gently, looking down into the sweet grey eyes that he had only once before seen filled with such imploring anguish as now. They both thought of that other time—the day years ago in the House of Dreams when little Joyce had died.

"Would you have him stay, Anne—when the others are going—when he thinks it his duty—would you have him so selfish and small-souled?"

"No—no! But—oh—our first-born son—he's only a lad—Gilbert—I'll try to be brave after a while—just now I can't. It's all come so suddenly. Give me time."

The doctor and his wife went out of the room. Jem had gone—Walter had gone—Shirley got up to go. Rilla and Susan remained staring at each other across the deserted table. Rilla had not yet cried—she was too stunned for tears. Then she saw that Susan was crying—Susan, whom she had never seen shed a tear before.

"Oh, Susan, will he really go?" she asked.

"It—it—it is just ridiculous, that is what it is," said Susan.

She wiped away her tears, gulped resolutely and got up.

"I am going to wash the dishes. That has to be done, even if everybody has gone crazy. There now, dearie, do not you cry. Jem will go, most likely—but the war will be over long before he gets anywhere near it. Let us take a brace and not worry your poor mother."

"In the Enterprise today it was reported that Lord Kitchener says the war will last three years," said Rilla dubiously.

"I am not acquainted with Lord Kitchener," said Susan, composedly, "but I dare say he makes mistakes as often as other people. Your father says it will be over in a few months and I have as much faith in his opinion as I have in Lord Anybody's. So just let us be calm and trust in the Almighty and get this place tidied up. I am done with crying which is a waste of time and discourages everybody."

Jem and Jerry went to Charlottetown that night and two days later they came back in khaki. The Glen hummed with excitement over it. Life at Ingleside had suddenly become a tense, strained, thrilling thing. Mrs. Blythe and Nan were brave and smiling and wonderful. Already Mrs. Blythe and Miss Cornelia were organizing a Red Cross. The doctor and Mr. Meredith were rounding up the men for a Patriotic Society. Rilla, after the first shock, reacted to the romance of it all, in spite of her heartache. Jem certainly looked magnificent in his uniform. It was splendid to think of the lads of Canada answering so speedily and fearlessly and uncalculatingly to the call of their country. Rilla carried her head high among the girls whose brothers had not so responded. In her diary she wrote:

"He goes to do what I had done
Had Douglas's daughter been his son,"

and was sure she meant it. If she were a boy of course she would go, too! She hadn't the least doubt of that.

She wondered if it was very dreadful of her to feel glad that Walter hadn't got strong as soon as they had wished after the fever.

"I couldn't bear to have Walter go," she wrote. "I love Jem ever so much but Walter means more to me than anyone in the world and I would die if he had to go. He seems so changed these days. He hardly ever talks to me. I suppose he wants to go, too, and feels badly because he can't. He doesn't go about with Jem and Jerry at all. I shall never forget Susan's face when Jem came home in his khaki. It worked and twisted as if she were going to cry, but all she said was, 'You look almost like a man in that, Jem.' Jem laughed. He never minds because Susan thinks him just a child still. Everybody seems busy but me. I wish there was something I could do but there doesn't seem to be anything. Mother and Nan and Di are busy all the time and I just wander about like a lonely ghost. What hurts me terribly, though, is that mother's smiles, and Nan's, just seem put on from the outside. Mother's eyes never laugh now. It makes me feel that I shouldn't laugh either—that it's wicked to feel laughy. And it's so hard for me to keep from laughing, even if Jem is going to be a soldier. But when I laugh I don't enjoy it either, as I used to do. There's something behind it all that keeps hurting me—especially when I wake up in the night. Then I cry because I am afraid that Kitchener of Khartoum is right and the war will last for years and Jem may be—but no, I won't write it. It would make me feel as if it were really going to happen. The other day Nan said, 'Nothing can ever be quite the same for any of us again.' It made me feel rebellious. Why shouldn't things be the same again—when everything is over and Jem and Jerry are back? We'll all be happy and jolly again and these days will seem just like a bad dream.

"The coming of the mail is the most exciting event of every day now. Father just snatches the paper—I never saw father snatch before—and the rest of us crowd round and look at the headlines over his shoulder. Susan vows she does not and will not believe a word the papers say but she always comes to the kitchen door, and listens and then goes back, shaking her head. She is terribly indignant all the time, but she cooks up all the things Jem likes especially, and she did not make a single bit of fuss when she found Monday asleep on the spare-room bed yesterday right on top of Mrs. Rachel Lynde's apple-leaf spread. 'The Almighty only knows where your master will be having to sleep before long, you poor dumb beast,' she said as she put him quite gently out. But she never relents towards Doc. She says the minute he saw Jem in khaki he turned into Mr. Hyde then and there and she thinks that ought to be proof enough of what he really is. Susan is funny, but she is an old dear. Shirley says she is one half angel and the other half good cook. But then Shirley is the only one of us she never scolds.

"Faith Meredith is wonderful. I think she and Jem are really engaged now. She goes about with a shining light in her eyes, but her smiles are a little stiff and starched, just like mother's. I wonder if I could be as brave as she is if I had a lover and he was going to the war. It is bad enough when it is your brother. Bruce Meredith cried all night, Mrs. Meredith says, when he heard Jem and Jerry were going. And he wanted to know if the 'K of K.' his father talked about was the King of Kings. He is the dearest kiddy. I just love him—though I don't really care much for children. I don't like babies one bit—though when I say so people look at me as if I had said something perfectly shocking. Well, I don't, and I've got to be honest about it. I don't mind looking at a nice clean baby if somebody else holds it—but I wouldn't touch it for anything and I don't feel a single real spark of interest in it. Gertrude Oliver says she just feels the same. (She is the most honest person I know. She never pretends anything.) She says babies bore her until they are old enough to talk and then she likes them—but still a good ways off. Mother and Nan and Di all adore babies and seem to think I'm unnatural because I don't.

"I haven't seen Kenneth since the night of the party. He was here one evening after Jem came back but I happened to be away. I don't think he mentioned me at all—at least nobody told me he did and I was determined I wouldn't ask—but I don't care in the least. All that matters absolutely nothing to me now. The only thing that does matter is that Jem has volunteered for active service and will be going to Valcartier in a few more days—my big, splendid brother Jem. Oh, I'm so proud of him!

"I suppose Kenneth would enlist too if it weren't for his ankle. I think that is quite providential. He is his mother's only son and how dreadful she would feel if he went. Only sons should never think of going!"

Walter came wandering through the valley as Rilla sat there, with his head bent and his hands clasped behind him. When he saw Rilla he turned abruptly away; then as abruptly he turned and came back to her.

"Rilla-my-Rilla, what are you thinking of?"

"Everything is so changed, Walter," said Rilla wistfully. "Even you—you're changed. A week ago we were all so happy—and—and—now I just can't find myself at all. I'm lost."

Walter sat down on a neighbouring stone and took Rilla's little appealing hand.

"I'm afraid our old world has come to an end, Rilla. We've got to face that fact."

"It's so terrible to think of Jem," pleaded Rilla. "Sometimes I forget for a little while what it really means and feel excited and proud—and then it comes over me again like a cold wind."

"I envy Jem!" said Walter moodily.

"Envy Jem! Oh, Walter you—you don't want to go too."

"No," said Walter, gazing straight before him down the emerald vistas of the valley, "no, I don't want to go. That's just the trouble. Rilla, I'm afraid to go. I'm a coward."

"You're not!" Rilla burst out angrily. "Why, anybody would be afraid to go. You might be—why, you might be killed."

"I wouldn't mind that if it didn't hurt," muttered Walter. "I don't think I'm afraid of death itself—it's of the pain that might come before death—it wouldn't be so bad to die and have it over—but to keep on dying! Rilla, I've always been afraid of pain—you know that. I can't help it—I shudder when I think of the possibility of being mangled or—or blinded. Rilla, I cannot face that thought. To be blind—never to see the beauty of the world again—moonlight on Four Winds—the stars twinkling through the fir-trees—mist on the gulf. I ought to go—I ought to want to go—but I don't—I hate the thought of it—I'm ashamed—ashamed."

"But, Walter, you couldn't go anyhow," said Rilla piteously. She was sick with a new terror that Walter would go after all. "You're not strong enough."

"I am. I've felt as fit as ever I did this last month. I'd pass any examination—I know it. Everybody thinks I'm not strong yet—and I'm skulking behind that belief. I—I should have been a girl," Walter concluded in a burst of passionate bitterness.

"Even if you were strong enough, you oughtn't to go," sobbed Rilla. "What would mother do? She's breaking her heart over Jem. It would kill her to see you both go."

"Oh, I'm not going—don't worry. I tell you I'm afraid to go—afraid. I don't mince the matter to myself. It's a relief to own up even to you, Rilla. I wouldn't confess it to anybody else—Nan and Di would despise me. But I hate the whole thing—the horror, the pain, the ugliness.

War isn't a khaki uniform or a drill parade—everything I've read in old histories haunts me. I lie awake at night and see things that have happened—see the blood and filth and misery of it all. And a bayonet charge! If I could face the other things I could never face that. It turns me sick to think of it—sicker even to think of giving it than receiving it—to think of thrusting a bayonet through another man." Walter writhed and shuddered. "I think of these things all the time—and it doesn't seem to me that Jem and Jerry ever think of them. They laugh and talk about 'potting Huns'! But it maddens me to see them in the khaki. And they think I'm grumpy because I'm not fit to go."

Walter laughed bitterly. "It is not a nice thing to feel yourself a coward." But Rilla got her arms about him and cuddled her head on his shoulder. She was so glad he didn't want to go—for just one minute she had been horribly frightened. And it was so nice to have Walter confiding his troubles to her—to her, not Di. She didn't feel so lonely and superfluous any longer.

"Don't you despise me, Rilla-my-Rilla?" asked Walter wistfully. Somehow, it hurt him to think Rilla might despise him—hurt him as much as if it had been Di. He realized suddenly how very fond he was of this adoring kid sister with her appealing eyes and troubled, girlish face.

"No, I don't. Why, Walter, hundreds of people feel just as you do. You know what that verse of Shakespeare in the old Fifth Reader says—'the brave man is not he who feels no fear.'"

"No—but it is 'he whose noble soul its fear subdues.' I don't do that. We can't gloss it over, Rilla. I'm a coward."

"You're not. Think of how you fought Dan Reese long ago."

"One spurt of courage isn't enough for a lifetime."

"Walter, one time I heard father say that the trouble with you was a sensitive nature and a vivid imagination. You feel things before they really come—feel them all alone when there isn't anything to help you bear them—to take away from them. It isn't anything to be ashamed of. When you and Jem got your hands burned when the grass was fired on the sand-hills two years ago Jem made twice the fuss over the pain that you did. As for this horrid old war, there'll be plenty to go without you. It won't last long."

"I wish I could believe it. Well, it's supper-time, Rilla. You'd better run. I don't want anything."

"Neither do I. I couldn't eat a mouthful. Let me stay here with you, Walter. It's such a comfort to talk things over with someone. The rest all think that I'm too much of a baby to understand."

So they two sat there in the old valley until the evening star shone through a pale-grey, gauzy cloud over the maple grove, and a fragrant dewy darkness filled their little sylvan dell. It was one of the evenings Rilla was to treasure in remembrance all her life—the first one on which Walter had ever talked to her as if she were a woman and not a child. They comforted and strengthened each other. Walter felt, for the time being at least, that it was not such a despicable thing after all to dread the horror of war; and Rilla was glad to be made the confidante of his struggles—to sympathize with and encourage him. She was of importance to somebody.

When they went back to Ingleside they found callers sitting on the veranda. Mr. and Mrs. Meredith had come over from the manse, and Mr. and Mrs. Norman Douglas had come up from the farm. Cousin Sophia was there also, sitting with Susan in the shadowy background. Mrs. Blythe and Nan and Di were away, but Dr. Blythe was home and so was Dr. Jekyll, sitting in golden majesty on the top step. And of course they were all talking of the war, except Dr. Jekyll who kept his own counsel and looked contempt as only a cat can. When two people foregathered in those days they talked of the war; and old Highland Sandy of the Harbour Head talked of it when he was alone and hurled anathemas at the Kaiser across all the acres of his farm. Walter slipped away, not caring to see or be seen, but Rilla sat down on the steps, where the garden mint was dewy and pungent. It was a very calm evening with a dim, golden afterlight irradiating the glen. She felt happier than at any time in the dreadful week that had passed. She was no longer haunted by the fear that Walter would go.

"I'd go myself if I was twenty years younger," Norman Douglas was shouting. Norman always shouted when he was excited. "I'd show the Kaiser a thing or two! Did I ever say there wasn't a hell? Of course there's a hell—dozens of hells—hundreds of hells—where the Kaiser and all his brood are bound for."

"I knew this war was coming," said Mrs. Norman triumphantly. "I saw it coming right along. I could have told all those stupid Englishmen what was ahead of them. I told you, John Meredith, years ago what the Kaiser was up to but you wouldn't believe it. You said he would never plunge the world in war. Who was right about the Kaiser, John? You—or I? Tell me that."

"You were, I admit," said Mr. Meredith.

"It's too late to admit it now," said Mrs. Norman, shaking her head, as if to intimate that if John Meredith had admitted it sooner there might have been no war.

"Thank God, England's navy is ready," said the doctor.

"Amen to that," nodded Mrs. Norman. "Bat-blind as most of them were somebody had foresight enough to see to that."

"Maybe England'll manage not to get into trouble over it," said Cousin Sophia plaintively. "I dunno. But I'm much afraid."

"One would suppose that England was in trouble over it already, up to her neck, Sophia Crawford," said Susan. "But your ways of thinking are beyond me and always were. It is my opinion that the British Navy will settle Germany in a jiffy and that we are all getting worked up over nothing."

Susan spat out the words as if she wanted to convince herself more than anybody else. She had her little store of homely philosophies to guide her through life, but she had nothing to buckler her against the thunderbolts of the week that had just passed. What had an honest, hard-working, Presbyterian old maid of Glen St. Mary to do with a war thousands of miles away? Susan felt that it was indecent that she should have to be disturbed by it.

"The British army will settle Germany," shouted Norman. "Just wait till it gets into line and the Kaiser will find that real war is a different thing from parading round Berlin with your moustaches cocked up."

"Britain hasn't got an army," said Mrs. Norman emphatically. "You needn't glare at me, Norman. Glaring won't make soldiers out of timothy stalks. A hundred thousand men will just be a mouthful for Germany's millions."

"There'll be some tough chewing in the mouthful, I reckon," persisted Norman valiantly. "Germany'll break her teeth on it. Don't you tell me one Britisher isn't a match for ten foreigners. I could polish off a dozen of 'em myself with both hands tied behind my back!"

"I am told," said Susan, "that old Mr. Pryor does not believe in this war. I am told that he says England went into it just because she was jealous of Germany and that she did not really care in the least what happened to Belgium."

"I believe he's been talking some such rot," said Norman. "I haven't heard him. When I do, Whiskers-on-the-moon won't know what happened to him. That precious relative of mine, Kitty Alec, holds forth to the same effect, I understand. Not before me, though—somehow, folks don't indulge in that kind of conversation in my presence. Lord love you, they've a kind of presentiment, so to speak, that it wouldn't be healthy for their complaint."

"I am much afraid that this war has been sent as a punishment for our sins," said Cousin Sophia, unclasping her pale hands from her lap and reclasping them solemnly over her stomach. "'The world is very evil—the times are waxing late.'"

"Parson here's got something of the same idea," chuckled Norman. "Haven't you, Parson? That's why you preached t'other night on the text 'Without shedding of blood there is no remission of sins.' I didn't agree with you—wanted to get up in the pew and shout out that there wasn't a word of sense in what you were saying, but Ellen, here, she held me down. I never have any fun sassing parsons since I got married."

"Without shedding of blood there is no anything," said Mr. Meredith, in the gentle dreamy way which had an unexpected trick of convincing his hearers. "Everything, it seems to me, has to be purchased by self-sacrifice. Our race has marked every step of its painful ascent with blood. And now torrents of it must flow again. No, Mrs. Crawford, I don't think the war has been sent as a punishment for sin. I think it is the price humanity must pay for some blessing—some advance great enough to be worth the price—which we may not live to see but which our children's children will inherit."

"If Jerry is killed will you feel so fine about it?" demanded Norman, who had been saying things like that all his life and never could be made to see any reason why he shouldn't. "Now, never mind kicking me in the shins, Ellen. I want to see if Parson meant what he said or if it was just a pulpit frill."

Mr. Meredith's face quivered. He had had a terrible hour alone in his study on the night Jem and Jerry had gone to town. But he answered quietly.

"Whatever I felt, it could not alter my belief—my assurance that a country whose sons are ready to lay down their lives in her defence will win a new vision because of their sacrifice."

"You do mean it, Parson. I can always tell when people mean what they say. It's a gift that was born in me. Makes me a terror to most parsons, that! But I've never caught you yet saying anything you didn't mean. I'm always hoping I will—that's what reconciles me to going to church. It'd be such a comfort to me—such a weapon to batter Ellen here with when she tries to civilize me. Well, I'm off over the road to see Ab. Crawford a minute. The gods be good to you all."

"The old pagan!" muttered Susan, as Norman strode away. She did not care if Ellen Douglas did hear her. Susan could never understand why fire did not descend from heaven upon Norman Douglas when he insulted ministers the way he did. But the astonishing thing was Mr. Meredith seemed really to like his brother-in-law.

Rilla wished they would talk of something besides war. She had heard nothing else for a week and she was really a little tired of it. Now that she was relieved from her haunting fear that Walter would want to go it made her quite impatient. But she supposed—with a sigh—that there would be three or four months of it yet.

6. SUSAN, RILLA, AND DOG MONDAY MAKE A RESOLUTION

The big living-room at Ingleside was snowed over with drifts of white cotton. Word had come from Red Cross headquarters that sheets and bandages would be required. Nan and Di and Rilla were hard at work. Mrs. Blythe and Susan were upstairs in the boys' room, engaged in a more personal task. With dry, anguished eyes they were packing up Jem's belongings. He must leave for Valcartier the next morning. They had been expecting the word but it was none the less dreadful when it came.

Rilla was basting the hem of a sheet for the first time in her life. When the word had come that Jem must go she had her cry out among the pines in Rainbow Valley and then she had gone to her mother.

"Mother, I want to do something. I'm only a girl—I can't do anything to win the war—but I must do something to help at home."

"The cotton has come up for the sheets," said Mrs. Blythe. "You can help Nan and Di make them up. And Rilla, don't you think you could organize a Junior Red Cross among the young girls? I think they would like it better and do better work by themselves than if mixed up with the older people."

"But, mother—I've never done anything like that."

"We will all have to do a great many things in the months ahead of us that we have never done before, Rilla."

"Well"—Rilla took the plunge—"I'll try, mother—if you'll tell me how to begin. I have been thinking it all over and I have decided that I must be as brave and heroic and unselfish as I can possibly be."

Mrs. Blythe did not smile at Rilla's italics. Perhaps she did not feel like smiling or perhaps she detected a real grain of serious purpose behind Rilla's romantic pose. So here was Rilla hemming sheets and organizing a Junior Red Cross in her thoughts as she hemmed; moreover, she was enjoying it—the organizing that is, not the hemming. It was interesting and Rilla discovered a certain aptitude in herself for it that surprised her. Who would be president? Not she. The older girls would not like that. Irene Howard? No, somehow Irene was not quite as popular as she deserved to be. Marjorie Drew? No, Marjorie hadn't enough backbone. She was too prone to agree with the last speaker. Betty Mead—calm, capable, tactful Betty—the very one! And Una Meredith for treasurer; and, if they were very insistent, they might make her, Rilla, secretary. As for the various committees, they must be chosen after the Juniors were organized, but Rilla knew just who should be put on which. They would meet around—and there must be no eats—Rilla knew she would have a pitched battle with Olive Kirk over that—and everything should be strictly business-like and constitutional. Her minute book should be covered in white with a Red Cross on the cover—and wouldn't it be nice to have some kind of uniform which they could all wear at the concerts they would have to get up to raise money—something simple but smart?

"You have basted the top hem of that sheet on one side and the bottom hem on the other," said Di.

Rilla picked out her stitches and reflected that she hated sewing. Running the Junior Reds would be much more interesting.

Mrs. Blythe was saying upstairs, "Susan, do you remember that first day Jem lifted up his little arms to me and called me 'mo'er'—the very first word he ever tried to say?"

"You could not mention anything about that blessed baby that I do not and will not remember till my dying day," said Susan drearily.

"Susan, I keep thinking today of once when he cried for me in the night. He was just a few months old. Gilbert didn't want me to go to him—he said the child was well and warm and that it would be fostering bad habits in him. But I went—and took him up—I can feel that tight clinging of his little arms round my neck yet. Susan, if I hadn't gone that night, twenty-one years ago, and taken my baby up when he cried for me I couldn't face tomorrow morning."

"I do not know how we are going to face it anyhow, Mrs. Dr. dear. But do not tell me that it will be the final farewell. He will be back on leave before he goes overseas, will he not?"

"We hope so but we are not very sure. I am making up my mind that he will not, so that there will be no disappointment to bear. Susan, I am determined that I will send my boy off tomorrow with a smile. He shall not carry away with him the remembrance of a weak mother who had not the courage to send when he had the courage to go. I hope none of us will cry."

"I am not going to cry, Mrs. Dr. dear, and that you may tie to, but whether I shall manage to smile or not will be as Providence ordains and as the pit of my stomach feels. Have you room there for this fruit-cake? And the shortbread? And the mince-pie? That blessed boy shall not starve, whether they have anything to eat in that Quebec place or not. Everything seems to be changing all at once, does it not? Even the old cat at the manse has passed away. He breathed his last at a quarter to ten last night and Bruce is quite heart-broken, they tell me."

"It's time that pussy went where good cats go. He must be at least fifteen years old. He has seemed so lonely since Aunt Martha died."

"I should not have lamented, Mrs. Dr. dear, if that Hyde-beast had died also. He has been Mr. Hyde most of the time since Jem came home in khaki, and that has a meaning I will maintain. I do not know what Monday will do when Jem is gone. The creature just goes about with a human look in his eyes that takes all the good out of me when I see it. Ellen West used to be always railing at the Kaiser and we thought her crazy, but now I see that there was a method in her madness. This tray is packed, Mrs. Dr. dear, and I will go down and put in my best licks preparing supper. I wish I knew when I would cook another supper for Jem but such things are hidden from our eyes."

Jem Blythe and Jerry Meredith left next morning. It was a dull day, threatening rain, and the clouds lay in heavy grey rolls over the sky; but almost everybody in the Glen and Four Winds and Harbour Head and Upper Glen and over-harbour—except Whiskers-on-the-moon—was there to see them off. The Blythe family and the Meredith family were all smiling. Even Susan, as Providence did ordain, wore a smile, though the effect was somewhat more painful than tears would have been. Faith and Nan were very pale and very gallant. Rilla thought she would get on very well if something in her throat didn't choke her, and if her lips didn't take such spells of trembling. Dog Monday was there, too. Jem had tried to say good-bye to him at Ingleside but Monday implored so eloquently that Jem relented and let him go to the station. He kept close to Jem's legs and watched every movement of his beloved master.

"I can't bear that dog's eyes," said Mrs. Meredith.

"The beast has more sense than most humans," said Mary Vance. "Well, did we any of us ever think we'd live to see this day? I bawled all night to think of Jem and Jerry going like this. I think they're plumb deranged. Miller got a maggot in his head about going but I soon talked him out of it—likewise his aunt said a few touching things. For once in our lives Kitty Alec and I agree. It's a miracle that isn't likely to happen again. There's Ken, Rilla."

Rilla knew Kenneth was there. She had been acutely conscious of it from the moment he had sprung from Leo West's buggy. Now he came up to her smiling.

"Doing the brave-smiling-sister-stunt, I see. What a crowd for the Glen to muster! Well, I'm off home in a few days myself."

A queer little wind of desolation that even Jem's going had not caused blew over Rilla's spirit.

"Why? You have another month of vacation."

"Yes—but I can't hang around Four Winds and enjoy myself when the world's on fire like this. It's me for little old Toronto where I'll find some way of helping in spite of this bally ankle. I'm not looking at Jem and Jerry—makes me too sick with envy. You girls are great—no crying, no grim endurance. The boys'll go off with a good taste in their mouths. I hope Persis and mother will be as game when my turn comes."

"Oh, Kenneth—the war will be over before your turn cometh."

There! She had lisped again. Another great moment of life spoiled! Well, it was her fate. And anyhow, nothing mattered. Kenneth was off already—he was talking to Ethel Reese, who was dressed, at seven in the morning, in the gown she had worn to the dance, and was crying. What on earth had Ethel to cry about? None of the Reeses were in khaki. Rilla wanted to cry, too—but she would not. What was that horrid old Mrs. Drew saying to mother, in that melancholy whine of hers? "I don't know how you can stand this, Mrs. Blythe. I couldn't if it was my pore boy." And mother—oh, mother could always be depended on! How her grey eyes flashed in her pale face. "It might have been worse, Mrs. Drew. I might have had to urge him to go." Mrs. Drew did not understand but Rilla did. She flung up her head. Her brother did not have to be urged to go.

Rilla found herself standing alone and listening to disconnected scraps of talk as people walked up and down past her.

"I told Mark to wait and see if they asked for a second lot of men. If they did I'd let him go—but they won't," said Mrs. Palmer Burr.

"I think I'll have it made with a crush girdle of velvet," said Bessie Clow.

"I'm frightened to look at my husband's face for fear I'll see in it that he wants to go too," said a little over-harbour bride.

"I'm scared stiff," said whimsical Mrs. Jim Howard. "I'm scared Jim will enlist—and I'm scared he won't."

"The war will be over by Christmas," said Joe Vickers.

"Let them European nations fight it out between them," said Abner Reese.

"When he was a boy I gave him many a good trouncing," shouted Norman Douglas, who seemed to be referring to some one high in military circles in Charlottetown. "Yes, sir, I walloped him well, big gun as he is now."

"The existence of the British Empire is at stake," said the Methodist minister.

"There's certainly something about uniforms," sighed Irene Howard.

"It's a commercial war when all is said and done and not worth one drop of good Canadian blood," said a stranger from the shore hotel.

"The Blythe family are taking it easy," said Kate Drew.

"Them young fools are just going for adventure," growled Nathan Crawford.

"I have absolute confidence in Kitchener," said the over-harbour doctor.

In these ten minutes Rilla passed through a dizzying succession of anger, laughter, contempt, depression and inspiration. Oh, people were—funny! How little they understood. "Taking it easy," indeed—when even Susan hadn't slept a wink all night! Kate Drew always was a minx.

Rilla felt as if she were in some fantastic nightmare. Were these the people who, three weeks ago, were talking of crops and prices and local gossip?

There—the train was coming—mother was holding Jem's hand—Dog Monday was licking it—everybody was saying good-bye—the train was in! Jem kissed Faith before everybody—old Mrs. Drew whooped hysterically—the men, led by Kenneth, cheered—Rilla felt Jem seize her hand—"Good-bye, Spider"—somebody kissed her cheek—she believed it was Jerry but never was sure—they were off—the train was pulling out—Jem and Jerry were waving to everybody—everybody was waving back—mother and Nan were smiling still, but as if they had just forgotten to take the smile off—Monday was howling dismally and being forcibly restrained by the Methodist minister from tearing after the train—Susan was waving her best bonnet and hurrahing like a man—had she gone crazy?—the train rounded a curve. They had gone.

Rilla came to herself with a gasp. There was a sudden quiet. Nothing to do now but to go home—and wait. The doctor and Mrs. Blythe walked off together—so did Nan and Faith—so did John Meredith and Rosemary. Walter and Una and Shirley and Di and Carl and Rilla went in a group. Susan had put her bonnet back on her head, hindside foremost, and stalked grimly off alone. Nobody missed Dog Monday at first. When they did Shirley went back for him. He found Dog Monday curled up in one of the shipping-sheds near the station and tried to coax him home. Dog Monday would not move. He wagged his tail to show he had no hard feelings but no blandishments availed to budge him.

"Guess Monday has made up his mind to wait there till Jem comes back," said Shirley, trying to laugh as he rejoined the rest. This was exactly what Dog Monday had done. His dear master had gone—he, Monday, had been deliberately and of malice aforethought prevented from going with him by a demon disguised in the garb of a Methodist minister. Wherefore, he, Monday, would wait there until the smoking, snorting monster, which had carried his hero off, carried him back.

Ay, wait there, little faithful dog with the soft, wistful, puzzled eyes. But it will be many a long bitter day before your boyish comrade comes back to you.

The doctor was away on a case that night and Susan stalked into Mrs. Blythe's room on her way to bed to see if her adored Mrs. Dr. dear were "comfortable and composed." She paused solemnly at the foot of the bed and solemnly declared,

"Mrs. Dr. dear, I have made up my mind to be a heroine."

"Mrs. Dr. dear" found herself violently inclined to laugh—which was manifestly unfair, since she had not laughed when Rilla had announced a similar heroic determination. To be sure, Rilla was a slim, white-robed thing, with a flower-like face and starry young eyes aglow with feeling; whereas Susan was arrayed in a grey flannel nightgown of strait simplicity, and had a strip of red woollen worsted tied around her grey hair as a charm against neuralgia. But that should not make any vital difference. Was it not the spirit that counted? Yet Mrs. Blythe was hard put to it not to laugh.

"I am not," proceeded Susan firmly, "going to lament or whine or question the wisdom of the Almighty any more as I have been doing lately. Whining and shirking and blaming Providence do not get us anywhere. We have just got to grapple with whatever we have to do whether it is weeding the onion patch, or running the Government. I shall grapple. Those blessed boys have gone to war; and we women, Mrs. Dr. dear, must tarry by the stuff and keep a stiff upper lip."

7. A WAR-BABY AND A SOUP TUREEN

"Liege and Namur—and now Brussels!" The doctor shook his head. "I don't like it—I don't like it."

"Do not you lose heart, Dr. dear; they were just defended by foreigners," said Susan superbly. "Wait you till the Germans come against the British; there will be a very different story to tell and that you may tie to."

The doctor shook his head again, but a little less gravely; perhaps they all shared subconsciously in Susan's belief that "the thin grey line" was unbreakable, even by the victorious rush of Germany's ready millions. At any rate, when the terrible day came—the first of many terrible days—with the news that the British army was driven back they stared at each other in blank dismay.

"It—it can't be true," gasped Nan, taking a brief refuge in temporary incredulity.

"I felt that there was to be bad news today," said Susan, "for that cat-creature turned into Mr. Hyde this morning without rhyme or reason for it, and that was no good omen."

"'A broken, a beaten, but not a demoralized, army,'" muttered the doctor, from a London dispatch. "Can it be England's army of which such a thing is said?"

"It will be a long time now before the war is ended," said Mrs. Blythe despairingly.

Susan's faith, which had for a moment been temporarily submerged, now reappeared triumphantly.

"Remember, Mrs. Dr. dear, that the British army is not the British navy. Never forget that. And the Russians are on their way, too, though Russians are people I do not know much about and consequently will not tie to."

"The Russians will not be in time to save Paris," said Walter gloomily. "Paris is the heart of France—and the road to it is open. Oh, I wish"—he stopped abruptly and went out.

After a paralysed day the Ingleside folk found it was possible to "carry on" even in the face of ever-darkening bad news. Susan worked fiercely in her kitchen, the doctor went out on his round of visits, Nan and Di returned to their Red Cross activities; Mrs. Blythe went to Charlottetown to attend a Red Cross Convention; Rilla after relieving her feelings by a stormy fit of tears in Rainbow Valley and an outburst in her diary, remembered that she had elected to be brave and heroic. And, she thought, it really was heroic to volunteer to drive about the Glen and Four Winds one day, collecting promised Red Cross supplies with Abner Crawford's old grey horse. One of the Ingleside horses was lame and the doctor needed the other, so there was nothing for it but the Crawford nag, a placid, unhasting, thick-skinned creature with an amiable habit of stopping every few yards to kick a fly off one leg with the foot of the other. Rilla felt that this, coupled with the fact that the Germans were only fifty miles from Paris, was hardly to be endured. But she started off gallantly on an errand fraught with amazing results.

Late in the afternoon she found herself, with a buggy full of parcels, at the entrance to a grassy, deep-rutted lane leading to the harbour shore, wondering whether it was worth while to call down at the Anderson house. The Andersons were desperately poor and it was not likely Mrs. Anderson had anything to give. On the other hand, her husband, who was an Englishman by birth and who had been working in Kingsport when the war broke out, had promptly sailed for England to enlist there, without, it may be said, coming home or sending much hard cash to represent him. So possibly Mrs. Anderson might feel hurt if she were overlooked. Rilla decided to call. There were times afterwards when she wished she hadn't, but in the long run she was very thankful that she did.

The Anderson house was a small and tumbledown affair, crouching in a grove of battered spruces near the shore as if rather ashamed of itself and anxious to hide. Rilla tied her grey nag to the rickety fence and went to the door. It was open; and the sight she saw bereft her temporarily of the power of speech or motion.

Through the open door of the small bedroom opposite her, Rilla saw Mrs. Anderson lying on the untidy bed; and Mrs. Anderson was dead. There was no doubt of that; neither was there any doubt that the big, frowzy, red-headed, red-faced, over-fat woman sitting near the doorway, smoking a pipe quite comfortably, was very much alive. She rocked idly back and forth amid her surroundings of squalid disorder, and paid no attention whatever to the piercing wails proceeding from a cradle in the middle of the room.

Rilla knew the woman by sight and reputation. Her name was Mrs. Conover; she lived down at the fishing village; she was a great-aunt of Mrs. Anderson; and she drank as well as smoked.

Rilla's first impulse was to turn and flee. But that would never do. Perhaps this woman, repulsive as she was, needed help—though she certainly did not look as if she were worrying over the lack of it.

"Come in," said Mrs. Conover, removing her pipe and staring at Rilla with her little, rat-like eyes.

"Is—is Mrs. Anderson really dead?" asked Rilla timidly, as she stepped over the sill.

"Dead as a door nail," responded Mrs. Conover cheerfully. "Kicked the bucket half an hour ago. I've sent Jen Conover to 'phone for the undertaker and get some help up from the shore. You're the doctor's miss, ain't ye? Have a cheer?"

Rilla did not see any chair which was not cluttered with something. She remained standing.

"Wasn't it—very sudden?"

"Well, she's been a-pining ever since that worthless Jim lit out for England—which I say it's a pity as he ever left. It's my belief she was took for death when she heard the news. That young un there was born a fortnight ago and since then she's just gone down and today she up and died, without a soul expecting it."

"Is there anything I can do to—to help?" hesitated Rilla.

"Bless yez, no—unless ye've a knack with kids. I haven't. That young un there never lets up squalling, day or night. I've just got that I take no notice of it."

Rilla tiptoed gingerly over to the cradle and more gingerly still pulled down the dirty blanket. She had no intention of touching the baby—she had no "knack with kids" either. She saw an ugly midget with a red, distorted little face, rolled up in a piece of dingy old flannel. She had never seen an uglier baby. Yet a feeling of pity for the desolate, orphaned mite which had "come out of the everywhere" into such a dubious "here", took sudden possession of her.

"What is going to become of the baby?" she asked.

"Lord knows," said Mrs. Conover candidly. "Min worried awful over that before she died. She kept on a-saying 'Oh, what will become of my pore baby' till it really got on my nerves. I ain't a-going to trouble myself with it, I can tell yez. I brung up a boy that my sister left and he skinned out as soon as he got to be some good and won't give me a mite o' help in my old age, ungrateful whelp as he is. I told Min it'd have to be sent to an orphan asylum till we'd see if Jim ever came back to look after it. Would yez believe it, she didn't relish the idee. But that's the long and short of it."

"But who will look after it until it can be taken to the asylum?" persisted Rilla. Somehow the baby's fate worried her.

"S'pose I'll have to," grunted Mrs. Conover. She put away her pipe and took an unblushing swig from a black bottle she produced from a shelf near her. "It's my opinion the kid won't live long. It's sickly. Min never had no gimp and I guess it hain't either. Likely it won't trouble any one long and good riddance, sez I."

Rilla drew the blanket down a little farther.

"Why, the baby isn't dressed!" she exclaimed, in a shocked tone.

"Who was to dress him I'd like to know," demanded Mrs. Conover truculently. "I hadn't time—took me all the time there was looking after Min. 'Sides, as I told yez, I don't know nithing about kids. Old Mrs. Billy Crawford, she was here when it was born and she washed it and rolled it up in that flannel, and Jen she's tended it a bit since. The critter is warm enough. This weather would melt a brass monkey."

Rilla was silent, looking down at the crying baby. She had never encountered any of the tragedies of life before and this one smote her to the core of her heart. The thought of the poor mother going down into the valley of the shadow alone, fretting about her baby, with no one near but this abominable old woman, hurt her terribly. If she had only come a little sooner! Yet what could she have done—what could she do now? She didn't know, but she must do something. She hated babies—but she simply could not go away and leave that poor little creature with Mrs. Conover—who was applying herself again to her black bottle and would probably be helplessly drunk before anybody came.

"I can't stay," thought Rilla. "Mr. Crawford said I must be home by supper-time because he wanted the pony this evening himself. Oh, what can I do?"

She made a sudden, desperate, impulsive resolution.

"I'll take the baby home with me," she said. "Can I?"

"Sure, if yez wants to," said Mrs. Conover amiably. "I hain't any objection. Take it and welcome."

"I—I can't carry it," said Rilla. "I have to drive the horse and I'd be afraid I'd drop it. Is there a—a basket anywhere that I could put it in?"

"Not as I knows on. There ain't much here of anything, I kin tell yez. Min was pore and as shiftless as Jim. Ef ye opens that drawer over there yez'll find a few baby clo'es. Best take them along."

Rilla got the clothes—the cheap, sleazy garments the poor mother had made ready as best she could. But this did not solve the pressing problem of the baby's transportation. Rilla looked helplessly round. Oh, for mother—or Susan! Her eyes fell on an enormous blue soup tureen at the back of the dresser.

"May I have this to—to lay him in?" she asked.

"Well, 'tain't mine but I guess yez kin take it. Don't smash it if yez can help—Jim might make a fuss about it if he comes back alive—which he sure will, seein' he ain't any good. He brung that old tureen out from England with him—said it'd always been in the family. Him and Min never used it—never had enough soup to put in it—but Jim thought the world of it. He was mighty perticuler about some things but didn't worry him none that there weren't much in the way o' eatables to put in the dishes."

For the first time in her life Rilla Blythe touched a baby—lifted it—rolled it in a blanket, trembling with nervousness lest she drop it or—or—break it. Then she put it in the soup tureen.

"Is there any fear of it smothering?" she asked anxiously.

"Not much odds if it do," said Mrs. Conover.

Horrified Rilla loosened the blanket round the baby's face a little. The mite had stopped crying and was blinking up at her. It had big dark eyes in its ugly little face.

"Better not let the wind blow on it," admonished Mrs. Conover. "Take its breath if it do."

Rilla wrapped the tattered little quilt around the soup tureen.

"Will you hand this to me after I get into the buggy, please?"

"Sure I will," said Mrs. Conover, getting up with a grunt.

And so it was that Rilla Blythe, who had driven to the Anderson house a self-confessed hater of babies, drove away from it carrying one in a soup tureen on her lap!

Rilla thought she would never get to Ingleside. In the soup tureen there was an uncanny silence. In one way she was thankful the baby did not cry but she wished it would give an occasional squeak to prove that it was alive. Suppose it were smothered! Rilla dared not unwrap it to see, lest the wind, which was now blowing a hurricane, should "take its breath," whatever dreadful thing that might be. She was a thankful girl when at last she reached harbour at Ingleside.

Rilla carried the soup tureen to the kitchen, and set it on the table under Susan's eyes. Susan looked into the tureen and for once in her life was so completely floored that she had not a word to say.

"What in the world is this?" asked the doctor, coming in.

Rilla poured out her story. "I just had to bring it, father," she concluded. "I couldn't leave it there."

"What are you going to do with it?" asked the doctor coolly.

Rilla hadn't exactly expected this kind of question.

"We—we can keep it here for awhile—can't we—until something can be arranged?" she stammered confusedly.

Dr. Blythe walked up and down the kitchen for a moment or two while the baby stared at the white walls of the soup tureen and Susan showed signs of returning animation.

Presently the doctor confronted Rilla.

"A young baby means a great deal of additional work and trouble in a household, Rilla. Nan and Di are leaving for Redmond next week and neither your mother nor Susan is able to assume so much extra care under present conditions. If you want to keep that baby here you must attend to it yourself."

"Me!" Rilla was dismayed into being ungrammatical. "Why—father—I—I couldn't!"

"Younger girls than you have had to look after babies. My advice and Susan's is at your disposal. If you cannot, then the baby must go back to Meg Conover. Its lease of life will be short if it does for it is evident that it is a delicate child and requires particular care. I doubt if it would survive even if sent to an orphans' home. But I cannot have your mother and Susan over-taxed."

The doctor walked out of the kitchen, looking very stern and immovable. In his heart he knew quite well that the small inhabitant of the big soup tureen would remain at Ingleside, but he meant to see if Rilla could not be induced to rise to the occasion.

Rilla sat looking blankly at the baby. It was absurd to think she could take care of it. But—that poor little, frail, dead mother who had worried about it—that dreadful old Meg Conover.

"Susan, what must be done for a baby?" she asked dolefully.

"You must keep it warm and dry and wash it every day, and be sure the water is neither too hot nor too cold, and feed it every two hours. If it has colic, you put hot things on its stomach," said Susan, rather feebly and flatly for her.

The baby began to cry again.

"It must be hungry—it has to be fed anyhow," said Rilla desperately. "Tell me what to get for it, Susan, and I'll get it."

Under Susan's directions a ration of milk and water was prepared, and a bottle obtained from the doctor's office. Then Rilla lifted the baby out of the soup tureen and fed it. She brought down the old basket of her own infancy from the attic and laid the now sleeping baby in it. She put the soup tureen away in the pantry. Then she sat down to think things over.

The result of her thinking things over was that she went to Susan when the baby woke.

"I'm going to see what I can do, Susan. I can't let that poor little thing go back to Mrs. Conover. Tell me how to wash and dress it."

Under Susan's supervision Rilla bathed the baby. Susan dared not help, other than by suggestion, for the doctor was in the living-room and might pop in at any moment. Susan had learned by experience that when Dr. Blythe put his foot down and said a thing must be, that thing was. Rilla set her teeth and went ahead. In the name of goodness, how many wrinkles and kinks did a baby have? Why, there wasn't enough of it to take hold of. Oh, suppose she let it slip into the water—it was so wobbly! If it would only stop howling like that! How could such a tiny morsel make such an enormous noise. Its shrieks could be heard over Ingleside from cellar to attic.

"Am I really hurting it much, Susan, do you suppose?" she asked piteously.

"No, dearie. Most new babies hate like poison to be washed. You are real knacky for a beginner. Keep your hand under its back, whatever you do, and keep cool."

Keep cool! Rilla was oozing perspiration at every pore. When the baby was dried and dressed and temporarily quieted with another bottle she was as limp as a rag.

"What must I do with it tonight, Susan?"

A baby by day was dreadful enough; a baby by night was unthinkable.

"Set the basket on a chair by your bed and keep it covered. You will have to feed it once or twice in the night, so you would better take the oil heater upstairs. If you cannot manage it call me and I will go, doctor or no doctor."

"But, Susan, if it cries?"

The baby, however, did not cry. It was surprisingly good—perhaps because its poor little stomach was filled with proper food. It slept most of the night but Rilla did not. She was afraid to go to sleep for fear something would happen to the baby. She prepared its three o'clock ration with a grim determination that she would not call Susan. Oh, was she dreaming? Was it really she, Rilla Blythe, who had got into this absurd predicament? She did not care if the Germans were near Paris—she did not care if they were in Paris—if only the baby wouldn't cry or choke or smother or have convulsions. Babies did have convulsions, didn't they? Oh, why had she forgotten to ask Susan what she must do if the baby had convulsions? She reflected rather bitterly that father was very considerate of mother's and Susan's health, but what about hers? Did he think she could continue to exist if she never got any sleep? But she was not going to back down now—not she. She would look after this detestable little animal if it killed her. She would get a book on baby hygiene and be beholden to nobody. She would never go to father for advice—she wouldn't bother mother—and she would only condescend to Susan in dire extremity. They would all see!

Thus it came about that Mrs. Blythe, when she returned home two nights later and asked Susan where Rilla was, was electrified by Susan's composed reply.

"She's upstairs, Mrs. Dr. dear, putting her baby to bed."

8. RILLA DECIDES

Families and individuals alike soon become used to new conditions and accept them unquestioningly. By the time a week had elapsed it seemed as it the Anderson baby had always been at Ingleside. After the first three distracted nights Rilla began to sleep again, waking automatically to attend to her charge on schedule time. She bathed and fed and dressed it as skilfully as if she had been doing it all her life. She liked neither her job nor the baby any the better; she still handled it as gingerly as if it were some kind of a small lizard, and a breakable lizard at that; but she did her work thoroughly and there was not a cleaner, better-cared-for infant in Glen St. Mary. She even took to weighing the creature every day and jotting the result down in her diary; but sometimes she asked herself pathetically why unkind destiny had ever led her down the Anderson lane on that fatal day. Shirley, Nan, and Di did not tease her as much as she had expected. They all seemed rather stunned by the mere fact of Rilla adopting a war-baby; perhaps, too, the doctor had issued instructions. Walter, of course, never had teased her over anything; one day he told her she was a brick.

"It took more courage for you to tackle that five pounds of new infant, Rilla-my-Rilla, than it would be for Jem to face a mile of Germans. I wish I had half your pluck," he said ruefully.

Rilla was very proud of Walter's approval; nevertheless, she wrote gloomily in her diary that night:—

"I wish I could like the baby a little bit. It would make things easier. But I don't. I've heard people say that when you took care of a baby you got fond of it—but you don't—I don't, anyway. And it's a nuisance—it interferes with everything. It just ties me down—and now of all times when I'm trying to get the Junior Reds started. And I couldn't go to Alice Clow's party last night and I was just dying to. Of course father isn't really unreasonable and I can always get an hour or two off in the evening when it's necessary; but I knew he wouldn't stand for my being out half the night and leaving Susan or mother to see to the baby. I suppose it was just as well, because the thing did take colic—or something—about one o'clock. It didn't kick or stiffen out, so I knew that, according to Morgan, it wasn't crying for temper; and it wasn't hungry and no pins were sticking in it. It screamed till it was black in the face; I got up and heated water and put the hot-water bottle on its stomach, and it howled worse than ever and drew up its poor wee thin legs. I was afraid I had burnt it but I don't believe I did. Then I walked the floor with it although 'Morgan on Infants' says that should never be done. I walked miles, and oh, I was so tired and discouraged and mad—yes, I was. I could have shaken the creature if it had been big enough to shake, but it wasn't. Father was out on a case, and mother had had a headache and Susan is squiffy because when she and Morgan differ I insist upon going by what Morgan says, so I was determined I wouldn't call her unless I had to.

"Finally, Miss Oliver came in. She has rooms with Nan now, not me, all because of the baby, and I am broken-hearted about it. I miss our long talks after we went to bed, so much. It was the only time I ever had her to myself. I hated to think the baby's yells had wakened her up, for she has so much to bear now. Mr. Grant is at Valcartier, too, and Miss Oliver feels it dreadfully, though she is splendid about it. She thinks he will never come back and her eyes just break my heart—they are so tragic. She said it wasn't the baby that woke her—she hadn't been able to sleep because the Germans are so near Paris; she took the little wretch and laid it flat on its stomach across her knee and thumped its back gently a few times, and it stopped shrieking and went right off to sleep and slept like a lamb the rest of the night. I didn't—I was too worn out.

"I'm having a perfectly dreadful time getting the Junior Reds started. I succeeded in getting Betty Mead as president, and I am secretary, but they put Jen Vickers in as treasurer and I despise her. She is the sort of girl who calls any clever, handsome, or distinguished people she knows slightly by their first names—behind their backs. And she is sly and two-faced. Una doesn't mind, of course. She is willing to do anything that comes to hand and never minds whether she has an office or not. She is just a perfect angel, while I am only angelic in spots and demonic in other spots. I wish Walter would take a fancy to her, but he never seems to think about her in that way, although I heard him say once she was like a tea rose. She is too. And she gets imposed upon, just because she is so sweet and willing; but I don't allow people to impose on Rilla Blythe and 'that you may tie to,' as Susan says.

"Just as I expected, Olive was determined we should have lunch served at our meetings. We had a battle royal over it. The majority was against eats and now the minority is sulking. Irene Howard was on the eats side and she has been very cool to me ever since and it makes me feel miserable. I wonder if mother and Mrs. Elliott have problems in the Senior Society too. I suppose they have, but they just go on calmly in spite of everything. I go on—but not calmly—I rage and cry—but I do it all in private and blow off steam in this diary; and when it's over I vow I'll show them. I never sulk. I detest people who sulk. Anyhow, we've got the society started and we're to meet once a week, and we're all going to learn to knit.

"Shirley and I went down to the station again to try to induce Dog Monday to come home but we failed. All the family have tried and failed. Three days after Jem had gone Walter went down and brought Monday home by main force in the buggy and shut him up for three days. Then Monday went on a hunger strike and howled like a Banshee night and day. We had to let him out or he would have starved to death.

"So we have decided to let him alone and father has arranged with the butcher near the station to feed him with bones and scraps. Besides, one of us goes down nearly every day to take him something. He just lies curled up in the shipping-shed, and every time a train comes in he will rush over to the platform, wagging his tail expectantly, and tear around to every one who comes off the train. And then, when the train goes and he realizes that Jem has not come, he creeps dejectedly back to his shed, with his disappointed eyes, and lies down patiently to wait for the next train. Mr. Gray, the station master, says there are times when he can hardly help crying from sheer sympathy. One day some boys threw stones at Monday and old Johnny Mead, who never was known to take notice of anything before, snatched up a meat axe in the butcher's shop and chased them through the village. Nobody has molested Monday since.

"Kenneth Ford has gone back to Toronto. He came up two evenings ago to say good-bye. I wasn't home—some clothes had to be made for the baby and Mrs. Meredith offered to help me, so I was over at the manse, and I didn't see Kenneth. Not that it matters; he told Nan to say good-bye to Spider for him and tell me not to forget him wholly in my absorbing maternal duties. If he could leave such a frivolous, insulting message as that for me it shows plainly that our beautiful hour on the sandshore meant nothing to him and I am not going to think about him or it again.

"Fred Arnold was at the manse and walked home with me. He is the new Methodist minister's son and very nice and clever, and would be quite handsome if it were not for his nose. It is a really dreadful nose. When he talks of commonplace things it does not matter so much, but when he talks of poetry and ideals the contrast between his nose and his conversation is too much for me and I want to shriek with laughter. It is really not fair, because everything he said was perfectly charming and if somebody like Kenneth had said it I would have been enraptured. When I listened to him with my eyes cast down I was quite fascinated; but as soon as I looked up and saw his nose the spell was broken. He wants to enlist, too, but can't because he is only seventeen. Mrs. Elliott met us as we were walking through the village and could not have looked more horrified if she caught me walking with the Kaiser himself. Mrs. Elliott detests the Methodists and all their works. Father says it is an obsession with her."

About 1st September there was an exodus from Ingleside and the manse. Faith, Nan, Di and Walter left for Redmond; Carl betook himself to his Harbour Head school and Shirley was off to Queen's. Rilla was left alone at Ingleside and would have been very lonely if she had had time to be. She missed Walter keenly; since their talk in Rainbow Valley they had grown very near together and Rilla discussed problems with Walter which she never mentioned to others. But she was so busy with the Junior Reds and her baby that there was rarely a spare minute for loneliness; sometimes, after she went to bed, she cried a little in her pillow over Walter's absence and Jem at Valcartier and Kenneth's unromantic farewell message, but she was generally asleep before the tears got fairly started.

"Shall I make arrangements to have the baby sent to Hopetown?" the doctor asked one day two weeks after the baby's arrival at Ingleside.

For a moment Rilla was tempted to say "Yes." The baby could be sent to Hopetown—it would be decently looked after—she could have her free days and untrammelled nights back again. But—but—that poor young mother who hadn't wanted it to go to the asylum! Rilla couldn't get that out of her thoughts. And that very morning she discovered that the baby had gained eight ounces since its coming to Ingleside. Rilla had felt such a thrill of pride over this.

"You—you said it mightn't live if it went to Hopetown," she said.

"It mightn't. Somehow, institutional care, no matter how good it may be, doesn't always succeed with delicate babies. But you know what it means if you want it kept here, Rilla."

"I've taken care of it for a fortnight—and it has gained half a pound," cried Rilla. "I think we'd better wait until we hear from its father anyhow. He mightn't want to have it sent to an orphan asylum, when he is fighting the battles of his country."

The doctor and Mrs. Blythe exchanged amused, satisfied smiles behind Rilla's back; and nothing more was said about Hopetown.

Then the smile faded from the doctor's face; the Germans were twenty miles from Paris. Horrible tales were beginning to appear in the papers of deeds done in martyred Belgium. Life was very tense at Ingleside for the older people.

"We eat up the war news," Gertrude Oliver told Mrs. Meredith, trying to laugh and failing. "We study the maps and nip the whole Hun army in a few well-directed strategic moves. But Papa Joffre hasn't the benefit of our advice—and so Paris—must—fall."

"Will they reach it—will not some mighty hand yet intervene?" murmured John Meredith.

"I teach school like one in a dream," continued Gertrude; "then I come home and shut myself in my room and walk the floor. I am wearing a path right across Nan's carpet. We are so horribly near this war."

"Them German men are at Senlis. Nothing nor nobody can save Paris now," wailed Cousin Sophia. Cousin Sophia had taken to reading the newspapers and had learned more about the geography of northern France, if not about the pronunciation of French names, in her seventy-first year than she had ever known in her schooldays.

"I have not such a poor opinion of the Almighty, or of Kitchener," said Susan stubbornly. "I see there is a Bernstoff man in the States who says that the war is over and Germany has won—and they tell me Whiskers-on-the-moon says the same thing and is quite pleased about it, but I could tell them both that it is chancy work counting chickens even the day before they are hatched, and bears have been known to live long after their skins were sold."

"Why ain't the British navy doing more?" persisted Cousin Sophia.

"Even the British navy cannot sail on dry land, Sophia Crawford. I have not given up hope, and I shall not, Tomascow and Mobbage and all such barbarous names to the contrary notwithstanding. Mrs. Dr. dear, can you tell me if R-h-e-i-m-s is Rimes or Reems or Rames or Rems?"

"I believe it's really more like 'Rhangs,' Susan."

"Oh, those French names," groaned Susan.

"They tell me the Germans has about ruined the church there," sighed Cousin Sophia. "I always thought the Germans was Christians."

"A church is bad enough but their doings in Belgium are far worse," said Susan grimly. "When I heard the doctor reading about them bayonetting the babies, Mrs. Dr. dear, I just thought, 'Oh, what if it were our little Jem!' I was stirring the soup when that thought came to me and I just felt that if I could have lifted that saucepan full of that boiling soup and thrown it at the Kaiser I would not have lived in vain."

"Tomorrow—tomorrow—will bring the news that the Germans are in Paris," said Gertrude Oliver, through her tense lips. She had one of those souls that are always tied to the stake, burning in the suffering of the world around them. Apart from her own personal interest in the war, she was racked by the thought of Paris falling into the ruthless hands of the hordes who had burned Louvain and ruined the wonder of Rheims.

But on the morrow and the next morrow came the news of the miracle of the Marne. Rilla rushed madly home from the office waving the Enterprise with its big red headlines. Susan ran out with trembling hands to hoist the flag. The doctor stalked about muttering "Thank God." Mrs. Blythe cried and laughed and cried again.

"God just put out His hand and touched them—'thus far—no farther'," said Mr. Meredith that evening.

Rilla was singing upstairs as she put the baby to bed. Paris was saved—the war was over—Germany had lost—there would soon be an end now—Jem and Jerry would be back. The black clouds had rolled by.

"Don't you dare have colic this joyful night," she told the baby. "If you do I'll clap you back into your soup tureen and ship you off to Hopetown—by freight—on the early train. You have got beautiful eyes—and you're not quite as red and wrinkled as you were—but you haven't a speck of hair—and your hands are like little claws—and I don't like you a bit better than I ever did. But I hope your poor little white mother knows that you're tucked in a soft basket with a bottle of milk as rich as Morgan allows instead of perishing by inches with old Meg Conover. And I hope she doesn't know that I nearly drowned you that first morning when Susan wasn't there and I let you slip right out of my hands into the water. Why will you be so slippery? No, I don't like you and I never will but for all that I'm going to make a decent, upstanding infant of you. You are going to get as fat as a self-respecting child should be, for one thing. I am not going to have people saying 'what a puny little thing that baby of Rilla Blythe's is' as old Mrs. Drew said at the senior Red Cross yesterday. If I can't love you I mean to be proud of you at least."

9. DOC HAS A MISADVENTURE

"The war will not be over before next spring now," said Dr. Blythe, when it became apparent that the long battle of the Aisne had resulted in a stalemate.

Rilla was murmuring "knit four, purl one" under her breath, and rocking the baby's cradle with one foot. Morgan disapproved of cradles for babies but Susan did not, and it was worth while to make some slight sacrifice of principle to keep Susan in good humour. She laid down her knitting for a moment and said, "Oh, how can we bear it so long?"—then picked up her sock and went on. The Rilla of two months before would have rushed off to Rainbow Valley and cried.

Miss Oliver sighed and Mrs. Blythe clasped her hands for a moment. Then Susan said briskly, "Well, we must just gird up our loins and pitch in. Business as usual is England's motto, they tell me, Mrs. Dr. dear, and I have taken it for mine, not thinking I could easily find a better. I shall make the same kind of pudding today I always make on Saturday. It is a good deal of trouble to make, and that is well, for it will employ my thoughts. I will remember that Kitchener is at the helm and Joffer is doing very well for a Frenchman. I shall get that box of cake off to little Jem and finish that pair of socks today likewise. A sock a day is my allowance. Old Mrs. Albert Mead of Harbour Head manages a pair and a half a day but she has nothing to do but knit. You know, Mrs. Dr. dear, she has been bed-rid for years and she has been worrying terrible because she was no good to anybody and a dreadful expense, and yet could not die and be out of the way. And now they tell me she is quite chirked up and resigned to living because there is something she can do, and she knits for the soldiers from daylight to dark. Even Cousin Sophia has taken to knitting, Mrs. Dr. dear, and it is a good thing, for she cannot think of quite so many doleful speeches to make when her hands are busy with her needles instead of being folded on her stomach. She thinks we will all be Germans this time next year but I tell her it will take more than a year to make a German out of me. Do you know that Rick MacAllister has enlisted, Mrs. Dr. dear? And they say Joe Milgrave would too, only he is afraid that if he does that Whiskers-on-the-moon will not let him have Miranda. Whiskers says that he will believe the stories of German atrocities when he sees them, and that it is a good thing that Rangs Cathedral has been destroyed because it was a Roman Catholic church. Now, I am not a Roman Catholic, Mrs. Dr. dear, being born and bred a good Presbyterian and meaning to live and die one, but I maintain that the Catholics have as good a right to their churches as we have to ours and that the Huns had no kind of business to destroy them. Just think, Mrs. Dr. dear," concluded Susan pathetically, "how we would feel if a German shell knocked down the spire of our church here in the glen, and I'm sure it is every bit as bad to think of Rangs cathedral being hammered to pieces."

And, meanwhile, everywhere, the lads of the world rich and poor, low and high, white and brown, were following the Piper's call.

"Even Billy Andrews' boy is going—and Jane's only son—and Diana's little Jack," said Mrs. Blythe. "Priscilla's son has gone from Japan and Stella's from Vancouver—and both the Rev. Jo's boys. Philippa writes that her boys 'went right away, not being afflicted with her indecision.'"

"Jem says that he thinks they will be leaving very soon now, and that he will not be able to get leave to come so far before they go, as they will have to start at a few hours' notice," said the doctor, passing the letter to his wife.

"That is not fair," said Susan indignantly. "Has Sir Sam Hughes no regard for our feelings? The idea of whisking that blessed boy away to Europe without letting us even have a last glimpse of him! If I were you, doctor dear, I would write to the papers about it."

"Perhaps it is as well," said the disappointed mother. "I don't believe I could bear another parting from him—now that I know the war will not be over as soon as we hoped when he left first. Oh, if only—but no, I won't say it! Like Susan and Rilla," concluded Mrs. Blythe, achieving a laugh, "I am determined to be a heroine."

"You're all good stuff," said the doctor, "I'm proud of my women folk. Even Rilla here, my 'lily of the field,' is running a Red Cross Society full blast and saving a little life for Canada. That's a good piece of work. Rilla, daughter of Anne, what are you going to call your war-baby?"

"I'm waiting to hear from Jim Anderson," said Rilla. "He may want to name his own child."

But as the autumn weeks went by no word came from Jim Anderson, who had never been heard from since he sailed from Halifax, and to whom the fate of wife and child seemed a matter of indifference. Eventually Rilla decided to call the baby James, and Susan opined that Kitchener should be added thereto. So James Kitchener Anderson became the possessor of a name somewhat more imposing than himself. The Ingleside family promptly shortened it to Jims, but Susan obstinately called him "Little Kitchener" and nothing else.

"Jims is no name for a Christian child, Mrs. Dr. dear," she said disapprovingly. "Cousin Sophia says it is too flippant, and for once I consider she utters sense, though I would not please her by openly agreeing with her. As for the child, he is beginning to look something like a baby, and I must admit that Rilla is wonderful with him, though I would not pamper pride by saying so to her face. Mrs. Dr. dear, I shall never, no never, forget the first sight I had of that infant, lying in that big soup tureen, rolled up in dirty flannel. It is not often that Susan Baker is flabbergasted, but flabbergasted I was then, and that you may tie to. For one awful moment I thought my mind had given way and that I was seeing visions. Then thinks I, 'No, I never heard of anyone having a vision of a soup tureen, so it must be real at least,' and I plucked up confidence. When I heard the doctor tell Rilla that she must take care of the baby I thought he was joking, for I did not believe for a minute she would or could do it. But you see what has happened and it is making a woman of her. When we have to do a thing, Mrs. Dr. dear, we can do it."

Susan added another proof to this concluding dictum of hers one day in October. The doctor and his wife were away. Rilla was presiding over Jims' afternoon siesta upstairs, purling four and knitting one with ceaseless vim. Susan was seated on the back veranda, shelling beans, and Cousin Sophia was helping her. Peace and tranquility brooded over the Glen; the sky was fleeced over with silvery, shining clouds. Rainbow Valley lay in a soft, autumnal haze of fairy purple. The maple grove was a burning bush of colour and the hedge of sweet-briar around the kitchen yard was a thing of wonder in its subtle tintings. It did not seem that strife could be in the world, and Susan's faithful heart was lulled into a brief forgetfulness, although she had lain awake most of the preceding night thinking of little Jem far out on the Atlantic, where the great fleet was carrying Canada's first army across the ocean. Even Cousin Sophia looked less melancholy than usual and admitted that there was not much fault to be found in the day, although there was no doubt it was a weather-breeder and there would be an awful storm on its heels.

"Things is too calm to last," she said.

As if in confirmation of her assertion, a most unearthly din suddenly arose behind them. It was quite impossible to describe the confused medley of bangs and rattles and muffled shrieks and yowls that proceeded from the kitchen, accompanied by occasional crashes. Susan and Cousin Sophia stared at each other in dismay.

"What upon airth has bruk loose in there?" gasped Cousin Sophia.

"It must be that Hyde-cat gone clean mad at last," muttered Susan. "I have always expected it."

Rilla came flying out of the side door of the living-room.

"What has happened?" she demanded.

"It is beyond me to say, but that possessed beast of yours is evidently at the bottom of it," said Susan. "Do not go near him, at least. I will open the door and peep in. There goes some more of the crockery. I have always said that the devil was in him and that I will tie to."

"It is my opinion that the cat has hydrophobia," said Cousin Sophia solemnly. "I once heard of a cat that went mad and bit three people—and they all died a most terrible death, and turned black as ink."

Undismayed by this, Susan opened the door and looked in. The floor was littered with fragments of broken dishes, for it seemed that the fatal tragedy had taken place on the long dresser where Susan's array of cooking bowls had been marshalled in shining state. Around the kitchen tore a frantic cat, with his head wedged tightly in an old salmon can. Blindly he careered about with shrieks and profanity commingled, now banging the can madly against anything he encountered, now trying vainly to wrench it off with his paws.

The sight was so funny that Rilla doubled up with laughter. Susan looked at her reproachfully.

"I see nothing to laugh at. That beast has broken your ma's big blue mixing-bowl that she brought from Green Gables when she was married. That is no small calamity, in my opinion. But the thing to consider now is how to get that can off Hyde's head."

"Don't you dast go touching it," exclaimed Cousin Sophia, galvanized into animation. "It might be your death. Shut the kitchen up and send for Albert."

"I am not in the habit of sending for Albert during family difficulties," said Susan loftily. "That beast is in torment, and whatever my opinion of him may be, I cannot endure to see him suffering pain. You keep away, Rilla, for little Kitchener's sake, and I will see what I can do."

Susan stalked undauntedly into the kitchen, seized an old storm coat of the doctor's and after a wild pursuit and several fruitless dashes and pounces, managed to throw it over the cat and can. Then she proceeded to saw the can loose with a can-opener, while Rilla held the squirming animal, rolled in the coat. Anything like Doc's shrieks while the process was going on was never heard at Ingleside. Susan was in mortal dread that the Albert Crawfords would hear it and conclude she was torturing the creature to death. Doc was a wrathful and indignant cat when he was freed. Evidently he thought the whole thing was a put-up job to bring him low. He gave Susan a baleful glance by way of gratitude and rushed out of the kitchen to take sanctuary in the jungle of the sweet-briar hedge, where he sulked for the rest of the day. Susan swept up her broken dishes grimly.

"The Huns themselves couldn't have worked more havoc here," she said bitterly. "But when people will keep a Satanic animal like that, in spite of all warnings, they cannot complain when their wedding bowls get broken. Things have come to a pretty pass when an honest woman cannot leave her kitchen for a few minutes without a fiend of a cat rampaging through it with his head in a salmon can."

10. THE TROUBLES OF RILLA

October passed out and the dreary days of November and December dragged by. The world shook with the thunder of contending armies; Antwerp fell—Turkey declared war—gallant little Serbia gathered herself together and struck a deadly blow at her oppressor; and in quiet, hill-girdled Glen St. Mary, thousands of miles away, hearts beat with hope and fear over the varying dispatches from day to day.

"A few months ago," said Miss Oliver, "we thought and talked in terms of Glen St. Mary. Now, we think and talk in terms of military tactics and diplomatic intrigue."

There was just one great event every day—the coming of the mail. Even Susan admitted that from the time the mail-courier's buggy rumbled over the little bridge between the station and the village until the papers were brought home and read, she could not work properly.

"I must take up my knitting then and knit hard till the papers come, Mrs. Dr. dear. Knitting is something you can do, even when your heart is going like a trip-hammer and the pit of your stomach feels all gone and your thoughts are catawampus. Then when I see the headlines, be they good or be they bad, I calm down and am able to go about my business again. It is an unfortunate thing that the mail comes in just when our dinner rush is on, and I think the Government could arrange things better. But the drive on Calais has failed, as I felt perfectly sure it would, and the Kaiser will not eat his Christmas dinner in London this year. Do you know, Mrs. Dr. dear,"—Susan's voice lowered as a token that she was going to impart a very shocking piece of information,—"I have been told on good authority—or else you may be sure I would not be repeating it when it concerns a minster—that the Rev. Mr. Arnold goes to Charlottetown every week and takes a Turkish bath for his rheumatism. The idea of him doing that when we are at war with Turkey? One of his own deacons has always insisted that Mr. Arnold's theology was not sound and I am beginning to believe that there is some reason to fear it. Well, I must bestir myself this afternoon and get little Jem's Christmas cake packed up for him. He will enjoy it, if the blessed boy is not drowned in mud before that time."

Jem was in camp on Salisbury Plain and was writing gay, cheery letters home in spite of the mud. Walter was at Redmond and his letters to Rilla were anything but cheerful. She never opened one without a dread tugging at her heart that it would tell her he had enlisted. His unhappiness made her unhappy. She wanted to put her arm round him and comfort him, as she had done that day in Rainbow Valley. She hated everybody who was responsible for Walter's unhappiness.

"He will go yet," she murmured miserably to herself one afternoon, as she sat alone in Rainbow Valley, reading a letter from him, "he will go yet—and if he does I just can't bear it."

Walter wrote that some one had sent him an envelope containing a white feather.

"I deserved it, Rilla. I felt that I ought to put it on and wear it—proclaiming myself to all Redmond the coward I know I am. The boys of my year are going—going. Every day two or three of them join up. Some days I almost make up my mind to do it—and then I see myself thrusting a bayonet through another man—some woman's husband or sweetheart or son—perhaps the father of little children—I see myself lying alone torn and mangled, burning with thirst on a cold, wet field, surrounded by dead and dying men—and I know I never can. I can't face even the thought of it. How could I face the reality? There are times when I wish I had never been born. Life has always seemed such a beautiful thing to me—and now it is a hideous thing. Rilla-my-Rilla, if it weren't for your letters—your dear, bright, merry, funny, comical, believing letters—I think I'd give up. And Una's! Una is really a little brick, isn't she? There's a wonderful fineness and firmness under all that shy, wistful girlishness of her. She hasn't your knack of writing laugh-provoking epistles, but there's something in her letters—I don't know what—that makes me feel at least while I'm reading them, that I could even go to the front. Not that she ever says a word about my going—or hints that I ought to go—she isn't that kind. It's just the spirit of them—the personality that is in them. Well, I can't go. You have a brother and Una has a friend who is a coward."

"Oh, I wish Walter wouldn't write such things," sighed Rilla. "It hurts me. He isn't a coward—he isn't—he isn't!"

She looked wistfully about her—at the little woodland valley and the grey, lonely fallows beyond. How everything reminded her of Walter! The red leaves still clung to the wild sweet-briars that overhung a curve of the brook; their stems were gemmed with the pearls of the gentle rain that had fallen a little while before. Walter had once written a poem describing them. The wind was sighing and rustling among the frosted brown bracken ferns, then lessening sorrowfully away down the brook. Walter had said once that he loved the melancholy of the autumn wind on a November day. The old Tree Lovers still clasped each other in a faithful embrace, and the White Lady, now a great white-branched tree, stood out beautifully fine, against the grey velvet sky. Walter had named them long ago; and last November, when he had walked with her and Miss Oliver in the Valley, he had said, looking at the leafless Lady, with a young silver moon hanging over her, "A white birch is a beautiful Pagan maiden who has never lost the Eden secret of being naked and unashamed." Miss Oliver had said, "Put that into a poem, Walter," and he had done so, and read it to them the next day—just a short thing with goblin imagination in every line of it. Oh, how happy they had been then!

Well—Rilla scrambled to her feet—time was up. Jims would soon be awake—his lunch had to be prepared—his little slips had to be ironed—there was a committee meeting of the Junior Reds that night—there was her new knitting bag to finish—it would be the handsomest bag in the Junior Society—handsomer even than Irene Howard's—she must get home and get to work. She was busy these days from morning till night. That little monkey of a Jims took so much time. But he was growing—he was certainly growing. And there were times when Rilla felt sure that it was not merely a pious hope but an absolute fact that he was getting decidedly better looking. Sometimes she felt quite proud of him; and sometimes she yearned to spank him. But she never kissed him or wanted to kiss him.

"The Germans captured Lodz today," said Miss Oliver, one December evening, when she, Mrs. Blythe, and Susan were busy sewing or knitting in the cosy living-room. "This war is at least extending my knowledge of geography. Schoolma'am though I am, three months ago I didn't know there was such a place in the world such as Lodz. Had I heard it mentioned I would have known nothing about it and cared as little. I know all about it now—its size, its standing, its military significance. Yesterday the news that the Germans have captured it in their second rush to Warsaw made my heart sink into my boots. I woke up in the night and worried over it. I don't wonder babies always cry when they wake up in the night. Everything presses on my soul then and no cloud has a silver lining."

"When I wake up in the night and cannot go to sleep again," remarked Susan, who was knitting and reading at the same time, "I pass the moments by torturing the Kaiser to death. Last night I fried him in boiling oil and a great comfort it was to me, remembering those Belgian babies."

"If the Kaiser were here and had a pain in his shoulder you'd be the first to run for the liniment bottle to rub him down," laughed Miss Oliver.

"Would I?" cried outraged Susan. "Would I, Miss Oliver? I would rub him down with coal oil, Miss Oliver—and leave it to blister. That is what I would do and that you may tie to. A pain in his shoulder, indeed! He will have pains all over him before he is through with what he has started."

"We are told to love our enemies, Susan," said the doctor solemnly.

"Yes, our enemies, but not King George's enemies, doctor dear," retorted Susan crushingly. She was so well pleased with herself over this flattening out of the doctor completely that she even smiled as she polished her glasses. Susan had never given in to glasses before, but she had done so at last in order to be able to read the war news—and not a dispatch got by her. "Can you tell me, Miss Oliver, how to pronounce M-l-a-w-a and B-z-u-r-a and P-r-z-e-m-y-s-l?"

"That last is a conundrum which nobody seems to have solved yet, Susan. And I can make only a guess at the others."

"These foreign names are far from being decent, in my opinion," said disgusted Susan.

"I dare say the Austrians and Russians would think Saskatchewan and Musquodoboit about as bad, Susan," said Miss Oliver. "The Serbians have done wonderfully of late. They have captured Belgrade."

"And sent the Austrian creatures packing across the Danube with a flea in their ear," said Susan with a relish, as she settled down to examine a map of Eastern Europe, prodding each locality with the knitting needle to brand it on her memory. "Cousin Sophia said awhile ago that Serbia was done for, but I told her there was still such a thing as an over-ruling Providence, doubt it who might. It says here that the slaughter was terrible. For all they were foreigners it is awful to think of so many men being killed, Mrs. Dr. dear—for they are scarce enough as it is."

Rilla was upstairs relieving her over-charged feelings by writing in her diary.

"Things have all 'gone catawampus,' as Susan says, with me this week. Part of it was my own fault and part of it wasn't, and I seem to be equally unhappy over both parts.

"I went to town the other day to buy a new winter hat. It was the first time nobody insisted on coming with me to help me select it, and I felt that mother had really given up thinking of me as a child. And I found the dearest hat—it was simply bewitching. It was a velvet hat, of the very shade of rich green that was made for me. It just goes with my hair and complexion beautifully, bringing out the red-brown shades and what Miss Oliver calls my 'creaminess' so well. Only once before in my life have I come across that precise shade of green. When I was twelve I had a little beaver hat of it, and all the girls in school were wild over it. Well, as soon as I saw this hat I felt that I simply must have it—and have it I did. The price was dreadful. I will not put it down here because I don't want my descendants to know I was guilty of paying so much for a hat, in war-time, too, when everybody is—or should be—trying to be economical.

"When I got home and tried on the hat again in my room I was assailed by qualms. Of course, it was very becoming; but somehow it seemed too elaborate and fussy for church going and our quiet little doings in the Glen—too conspicuous, in short. It hadn't seemed so at the milliner's but here in my little white room it did. And that dreadful price tag! And the starving Belgians! When mother saw the hat and the tag she just looked at me. Mother is some expert at looking. Father says she looked him into love with her years ago in Avonlea school and I can well believe it—though I have heard a weird tale of her banging him over the head with a slate at the very beginning of their acquaintance. Mother was a limb when she was a little girl, I understand, and even up to the time when Jem went away she was full of ginger. But let me return to my mutton—that is to say, my new green velvet hat.

"'Do you think, Rilla,' mother said quietly—far too quietly—'that it was right to spend so much for a hat, especially when the need of the world is so great?'

"'I paid for it out of my own allowance, mother,' I exclaimed.

"'That is not the point. Your allowance is based on the principle of a reasonable amount for each thing you need. If you pay too much for one thing you must cut off somewhere else and that is not satisfactory. But if you think you did right, Rilla, I have no more to say. I leave it to your conscience.'

"I wish mother would not leave things to my conscience! And anyway, what was I to do? I couldn't take that hat back—I had worn it to a concert in town—I had to keep it! I was so uncomfortable that I flew into a temper—a cold, calm, deadly temper.

"'Mother,' I said haughtily, 'I am sorry you disapprove of my hat—'

"'Not of the hat exactly,' said mother, 'though I consider it in doubtful taste for so young a girl—but of the price you paid for it.'

"Being interrupted didn't improve my temper, so I went on, colder and calmer and deadlier than ever, just as if mother had not spoken.

"'—but I have to keep it now. However, I promise you that I will not get another hat for three years or for the duration of the war, if it lasts longer than that. Even you'—oh, the sarcasm I put into the 'you'—'cannot say that what I paid was too much when spread over at least three years.'

"'You will be very tired of that hat before three years, Rilla,' said mother, with a provoking grin, which, being interpreted, meant that I wouldn't stick it out.

"'Tired or not, I will wear it that long,' I said: and then I marched upstairs and cried to think that I had been sarcastic to mother.

"I hate that hat already. But three years or the duration of the war, I said, and three years or the duration of the war it shall be. I vowed and I shall keep my vow, cost what it will.

"That is one of the 'catawampus' things. The other is that I have quarrelled with Irene Howard—or she quarrelled with me—or, no, we both quarrelled.

"The Junior Red Cross met here yesterday. The hour of meeting was half-past two but Irene came at half-past one, because she got the chance of a drive down from the Upper Glen. Irene hasn't been a bit nice to me since the fuss about the eats; and besides I feel sure she resents not being president. But I have been determined that things should go smoothly, so I have never taken any notice, and when she came yesterday she seemed so nice and sweet again that I hoped she had got over her huffiness and we could be the chums we used to be.

"But as soon as we sat down Irene began to rub me the wrong way. I saw her cast a look at my new knitting-bag. All the girls have always said Irene was jealous-minded and I would never believe them before. But now I feel that perhaps she is.

"The first thing she did was to pounce on Jims—Irene pretends to adore babies—pick him out of his cradle and kiss him all over his face. Now, Irene knows perfectly well that I don't like to have Jims kissed like that. It is not hygienic. After she had worried him till he began to fuss, she looked at me and gave quite a nasty little laugh but she said, oh, so sweetly,

"'Why, Rilla, darling, you look as if you thought I was poisoning the baby.'

"'Oh, no, I don't, Irene,' I said—every bit as sweetly, 'but you know Morgan says that the only place a baby should be kissed is on its forehead, for fear of germs, and that is my rule with Jims.'

"'Dear me, am I so full of germs?' said Irene plaintively. I knew she was making fun of me and I began to boil inside—but outside no sign of a simmer. I was determined I would not scrap with Irene.

"Then she began to bounce Jims. Now, Morgan says bouncing is almost the worst thing that can be done to a baby. I never allow Jims to be bounced. But Irene bounced him and that exasperating child liked it. He smiled—for the very first time. He is four months old and he has never smiled once before. Not even mother or Susan have been able to coax that thing to smile, try as they would. And here he was smiling because Irene Howard bounced him! Talk of gratitude!

"I admit that smile made a big difference in him. Two of the dearest dimples came out in his cheeks and his big brown eyes seemed full of laughter. The way Irene raved over those dimples was silly, I consider. You would have supposed she thought she had really brought them into existence. But I sewed steadily and did not enthuse, and soon Irene got tired of bouncing Jims and put him back in his cradle. He did not like that after being played with, and he began to cry and was fussy the rest of the afternoon, whereas if Irene had only left him alone he would not have been a bit of trouble.

"Irene looked at him and said, 'Does he often cry like that?' as if she had never heard a baby crying before.

"I explained patiently that children have to cry so many minutes per day in order to expand their lungs. Morgan says so.

"'If Jims didn't cry at all I'd have to make him cry for at least twenty minutes,' I said.

"'Oh, indeed!' said Irene, laughing as if she didn't believe me. 'Morgan on the Care of Infants' was upstairs or I would soon have convinced her. Then she said Jims didn't have much hair—she had never seen a four months' old baby so bald.

"Of course, I knew Jims hadn't much hair—yet; but Irene said it in a tone that seemed to imply it was my fault that he hadn't any hair. I said I had seen dozens of babies every bit as bald as Jims, and Irene said, Oh very well, she hadn't meant to offend me—when I wasn't offended.

"It went on like that the rest of the hour—Irene kept giving me little digs all the time. The girls have always said she was revengeful like that if she were peeved about anything; but I never believed it before; I used to think Irene just perfect, and it hurt me dreadfully to find she could stoop to this. But I corked up my feelings and sewed away for dear life on a Belgian child's nightgown.

"Then Irene told me the meanest, most contemptible thing that someone had said about Walter. I won't write it down—I can't. Of course, she said it made her furious to hear it and all that—but there was no need for her to tell me such a thing even if she did hear it. She simply did it to hurt me.

"I just exploded. 'How dare you come here and repeat such a thing about my brother, Irene Howard?' I exclaimed. 'I shall never forgive you—never. Your brother hasn't enlisted—hasn't any idea of enlisting.'

"'Why Rilla, dear, I didn't say it,' said Irene. 'I told you it was Mrs. George Burr. And I told her—'

"'I don't want to hear what you told her. Don't you ever speak to me again, Irene Howard.'

"Oh course, I shouldn't have said that. But it just seemed to say itself. Then the other girls all came in a bunch and I had to calm down and act the hostess' part as well as I could. Irene paired off with Olive Kirk all the rest of the afternoon and went away without so much as a look. So I suppose she means to take me at my word and I don't care, for I do not want to be friends with a girl who could repeat such a falsehood about Walter. But I feel unhappy over it for all that. We've always been such good chums and until lately Irene was lovely to me; and now another illusion has been stripped from my eyes and I feel as if there wasn't such a thing as real true friendship in the world.

"Father got old Joe Mead to build a kennel for Dog Monday in the corner of the shipping-shed today. We thought perhaps Monday would come home when the cold weather came but he wouldn't. No earthly influence can coax Monday away from that shed even for a few minutes. There he stays and meets every train. So we had to do something to make him comfortable. Joe built the kennel so that Monday could lie in it and still see the platform, so we hope he will occupy it.

"Monday has become quite famous. A reporter of the Enterprise came out from town and photographed him and wrote up the whole story of his faithful vigil. It was published in the Enterprise and copied all over Canada. But that doesn't matter to poor little Monday, Jem has gone away—Monday doesn't know where or why—but he will wait until he comes back. Somehow it comforts me: it's foolish, I suppose, but it gives me a feeling that Jem will come back or else Monday wouldn't keep on waiting for him.

"Jims is snoring beside me in his cradle. It is just a cold that makes him snore—not adenoids. Irene had a cold yesterday and I know she gave it to him, kissing him. He is not quite such a nuisance as he was; he has got some backbone and can sit up quite nicely, and he loves his bath now and splashes unsmilingly in the water instead of twisting and shrieking. Oh, shall I ever forget those first two months! I don't know how I lived through them. But here I am and here is Jims and we both are going to 'carry on.' I tickled him a little bit tonight when I undressed him—I wouldn't bounce him but Morgan doesn't mention tickling—just to see if he would smile for me as well as Irene. And he did—and out popped the dimples. What a pity his mother couldn't have seen them!

"I finished my sixth pair of socks today. With the first three I got Susan to set the heel for me. Then I thought that was a bit of shirking, so I learned to do it myself. I hate it—but I have done so many things I hate since 4th of August that one more or less doesn't matter. I just think of Jem joking about the mud on Salisbury Plain and I go at them."

11. DARK AND BRIGHT

At Christmas the college boys and girls came home and for a little while Ingleside was gay again. But all were not there—for the first time one was missing from the circle round the Christmas table. Jem, of the steady lips and fearless eyes, was far away, and Rilla felt that the sight of his vacant chair was more than she could endure. Susan had taken a stubborn freak and insisted on setting out Jem's place for him as usual, with the twisted little napkin ring he had always had since a boy, and the odd, high Green Gables goblet that Aunt Marilla had once given him and from which he always insisted on drinking.

"That blessed boy shall have his place, Mrs. Dr. dear," said Susan firmly, "and do not you feel over it, for you may be sure he is here in spirit and next Christmas he will be here in the body. Wait you till the Big Push comes in the spring and the war will be over in a jiffy."

They tried to think so, but a shadow stalked in the background of their determined merrymaking. Walter, too, was quiet and dull, all through the holidays. He showed Rilla a cruel, anonymous letter he had received at Redmond—a letter far more conspicuous for malice than for patriotic indignation.

"Nevertheless, all it says is true, Rilla."

Rilla had caught it from him and thrown it into the fire.

"There isn't one word of truth in it," she declared hotly. "Walter, you've got morbid—as Miss Oliver says she gets when she broods too long over one thing."

"I can't get away from it at Redmond, Rilla. The whole college is aflame over the war. A perfectly fit fellow, of military age, who doesn't join up is looked upon as a shirker and treated accordingly. Dr. Milne, the English professor, who has always made a special pet of me, has two sons in khaki; and I can feel the change in his manner towards me."

"It's not fair—you're not fit."

"Physically I am. Sound as a bell. The unfitness is in the soul and it's a taint and a disgrace.

There, don't cry, Rilla. I'm not going if that's what you're afraid of. The Piper's music rings in my ears day and night—but I cannot follow."

"You would break mother's heart and mine if you did," sobbed Rilla. "Oh, Walter, one is enough for any family."

The holidays were an unhappy time for her. Still, having Nan and Di and Walter and Shirley home helped in the enduring of things. A letter and book came for her from Kenneth Ford, too; some sentences in the letter made her cheeks burn and her heart beat—until the last paragraph, which sent an icy chill over everything.

"My ankle is about as good as new. I'll be fit to join up in a couple of months more, Rilla-my-Rilla. It will be some feeling to get into khaki all right. Little Ken will be able to look the whole world in the face then and owe not any man. It's been rotten lately, since I've been able to walk without limping. People who don't know look at me as much as to say 'Slacker!' Well, they won't have the chance to look it much longer."

"I hate this war," said Rilla bitterly, as she gazed out into the maple grove that was a chill glory of pink and gold in the winter sunset.

"Nineteen-fourteen has gone," said Dr. Blythe on New Year's Day. "Its sun, which rose fairly, has set in blood. What will nineteen-fifteen bring?"

"Victory!" said Susan, for once laconic.

"Do you really believe we'll win the war, Susan?" said Miss Oliver drearily. She had come over from Lowbridge to spend the day and see Walter and the girls before they went back to Redmond. She was in a rather blue and cynical mood and inclined to look on the dark side.

"'Believe' we'll win the war!" exclaimed Susan. "No, Miss Oliver, dear, I do not believe—I know. That does not worry me. What does worry me is the trouble and expense of it all. But then you cannot make omelets without breaking eggs, so we must just trust in God and make big guns."

"Sometimes I think the big guns are better to trust in than God," said Miss Oliver defiantly.

"No, no, dear, you do not. The Germans had the big guns at the Marne, had they not? But Providence settled them. Do not ever forget that. Just hold on to that when you feel inclined to doubt. Clutch hold of the sides of your chair and sit tight and keep saying, 'Big guns are good but the Almighty is better, and He is on our side, no matter what the Kaiser says about it.' I would have gone crazy many a day lately, Miss Oliver, dear, if I had not sat tight and repeated that to myself. My cousin Sophia is, like you, somewhat inclined to despond. 'Oh, dear me, what will we do if the Germans ever get here,' she wailed to me yesterday. 'Bury them,' said I, just as off-hand as that. 'There is plenty of room for the graves.' Cousin Sophia said that I was flippant but I was not flippant, Miss Oliver, dear, only calm and confident in the British navy and our Canadian boys. I am like old Mr. William Pollock of the Harbour Head. He is very old and has been ill for a long time, and one night last week he was so low that his daughter-in-law whispered to some one that she thought he was dead. 'Darn it, I ain't,' he called right out—only, Miss Oliver, dear, he did not use so mild a word as 'darn'—'darn it, I ain't, and I don't mean to die until the Kaiser is well licked.' Now, that, Miss Oliver, dear," concluded Susan, "is the kind of spirit I admire."

"I admire it but I can't emulate it," sighed Gertrude. "Before this, I have always been able to escape from the hard things of life for a little while by going into dreamland, and coming back like a giant refreshed. But I can't escape from this."

"Nor I," said Mrs. Blythe. "I hate going to bed now. All my life I've liked going to bed, to have a gay, mad, splendid half-hour of imagining things before sleeping. Now I imagine them still. But such different things."

"I am rather glad when the time comes to go to bed," said Miss Oliver. "I like the darkness because I can be myself in it—I needn't smile or talk bravely. But sometimes my imagination gets out of hand, too, and I see what you do—terrible things—terrible years to come."

"I am very thankful that I never had any imagination to speak of," said Susan. "I have been spared that. I see by this paper that the Crown Prince is killed again. Do you suppose there is any hope of his staying dead this time? And I also see that Woodrow Wilson is going to write another note. I wonder," concluded Susan, with the bitter irony she had of late begun to use when referring to the poor President, "if that man's schoolmaster is alive."

In January Jims was five months old and Rilla celebrated the anniversary by shortening him.

"He weighs fourteen pounds," she announced jubilantly. "Just exactly what he should weigh at five months, according to Morgan."

There was no longer any doubt in anybody's mind that Jims was getting positively pretty. His little cheeks were round and firm and faintly pink, his eyes were big and bright, his tiny paws had dimples at the root of every finger. He had even begun to grow hair, much to Rilla's unspoken relief. There was a pale golden fuzz all over his head that was distinctly visible in some lights. He was a good infant, generally sleeping and digesting as Morgan decreed. Occasionally he smiled but he had never laughed, in spite of all efforts to make him. This worried Rilla also, because Morgan said that babies usually laughed aloud from the third to the fifth month. Jims was five months and had no notion of laughing. Why hadn't he? Wasn't he normal?

One night Rilla came home late from a recruiting meeting at the Glen where she had been giving patriotic recitations. Rilla had never been willing to recite in public before. She was afraid of her tendency to lisp, which had a habit of reviving if she were doing anything that made her nervous. When she had first been asked to recite at the Upper Glen meeting she had refused. Then she began to worry over her refusal. Was it cowardly? What would Jem think if he knew? After two days of worry Rilla phoned to the president of the Patriotic Society that she would recite. She did, and lisped several times, and lay awake most of the night in an agony of wounded vanity. Then two nights after she recited again at Harbour Head. She had been at Lowbridge and over-harbour since then and had become resigned to an occasional lisp. Nobody except herself seemed to mind it. And she was so earnest and appealing and shining-eyed! More than one recruit joined up because Rilla's eyes seemed to look right at him when she passionately demanded how could men die better than fighting for the ashes of their fathers and the temples of their gods, or assured her audience with thrilling intensity that one crowded hour of glorious life was worth an age without a name. Even stolid Miller Douglas was so fired one night that it took Mary Vance a good hour to talk him back to sense. Mary Vance said bitterly that if Rilla Blythe felt as bad as she had pretended to feel over Jem's going to the front she wouldn't be urging other girls' brothers and friends to go.

On this particular night Rilla was tired and cold and very thankful to creep into her warm nest and cuddle down between her blankets, though as usual with a sorrowful wonder how Jem and Jerry were faring. She was just getting warm and drowsy when Jims suddenly began to cry—and kept on crying.

Rilla curled herself up in her bed and determined she would let him cry. She had Morgan behind her for justification. Jims was warm, physically comfortable—his cry wasn't the cry of pain—and had his little tummy as full as was good for him. Under such circumstances it would be simply spoiling him to fuss over him, and she wasn't going to do it. He could cry until he got good and tired and ready to go to sleep again.

Then Rilla's imagination began to torment her. Suppose, she thought, I was a tiny, helpless creature only five months old, with my father somewhere in France and my poor little mother, who had been so worried about me, in the graveyard. Suppose I was lying in a basket in a big, black room, without one speck of light, and nobody within miles of me, for all I could see or know. Suppose there wasn't a human being anywhere who loved me—for a father who had never seen me couldn't love me very much, especially when he had never written a word to or about me. Wouldn't I cry, too? Wouldn't I feel just so lonely and forsaken and frightened that I'd have to cry?

Rilla hopped out. She picked Jims out of his basket and took him into her own bed. His hands were cold, poor mite. But he had promptly ceased to cry. And then, as she held him close to her in the darkness, suddenly Jims laughed—a real, gurgly, chuckly, delighted, delightful laugh.

"Oh, you dear little thing!" exclaimed Rilla. "Are you so pleased at finding you're not all alone, lost in a huge, big, black room?" Then she knew she wanted to kiss him and she did. She kissed his silky, scented little head, she kissed his chubby little cheek, she kissed his little cold hands. She wanted to squeeze him—to cuddle him, just as she used to squeeze and cuddle her kittens. Something delightful and yearning and brooding seemed to have taken possession of her. She had never felt like this before.

In a few minutes Jims was sound asleep; and, as Rilla listened to his soft, regular breathing and felt the little body warm and contented against her, she realized that—at last—she loved her war-baby.

"He has got to be—such—a—darling," she thought drowsily, as she drifted off to slumberland herself.

In February Jem and Jerry and Robert Grant were in the trenches and a little more tension and dread was added to the Ingleside life. In March "Yiprez," as Susan called it, had come to have a bitter significance. The daily list of casualties had begun to appear in the papers and no one at Ingleside ever answered the telephone without a horrible cold shrinking—for it might be the station-master phoning up to say a telegram had come from overseas. No one at Ingleside ever got up in the morning without a sudden piercing wonder over what the day might bring.

"And I used to welcome the mornings so," thought Rilla.

Yet the round of life and duty went steadily on and every week or so one of the Glen lads who had just the other day been a rollicking schoolboy went into khaki.

"It is bitter cold out tonight, Mrs. Dr. dear," said Susan, coming in out of the clear starlit crispness of the Canadian winter twilight. "I wonder if the boys in the trenches are warm."

"How everything comes back to this war," cried Gertrude Oliver. "We can't get away from it —not even when we talk of the weather. I never go out these dark cold nights myself without thinking of the men in the trenches—not only our men but everybody's men. I would feel the same if there were nobody I knew at the front. When I snuggle down in my comfortable bed I am ashamed of being comfortable. It seems as if it were wicked of me to be so when many are not."

"I saw Mrs. Meredith down at the store," said Susan, "and she tells me that they are really troubled over Bruce, he takes things so much to heart. He has cried himself to sleep for a week, over the starving Belgians. 'Oh, mother,' he will say to her, so beseeching-like, 'surely the babies are never hungry—oh, not the babies, mother! Just say the babies are not hungry, mother.' And she cannot say it because it would not be true, and she is at her wits' end. They try to keep such things from him but he finds them out and then they cannot comfort him. It breaks my heart to read about them myself, Mrs. Dr. dear, and I cannot console myself with the thought that the tales are not true. When I read a novel that makes me want to weep I just say severely to myself, 'Now, Susan Baker, you know that is all a pack of lies.' But we must carry on. Jack Crawford says he is going to the war because he is tired of farming. I hope he will find it a pleasant change. And Mrs. Richard Elliott over-harbour is worrying herself sick because she used to be always scolding her husband about smoking up the parlour curtains. Now that he has enlisted she wishes she had never said a word to him. You know Josiah Cooper and William Daley, Mrs. Dr. dear. They used to be fast friends but they quarrelled twenty years ago and have never spoken since. Well, the other day Josiah went to William and said right out, 'Let us be friends. 'Tain't any time to be holding grudges.' William was real glad and held out his hand, and they sat down for a good talk. And in less than half an hour they had quarrelled again, over how the war ought to be fought, Josiah holding that the Dardanelles expedition was rank folly and William maintaining that it was the one sensible thing the Allies had done. And now they are madder at each other than ever and William says Josiah is as bad a pro-German as Whiskers-on-the-Moon. Whiskers-on-the-moon vows he is no pro-German but calls himself a pacifist, whatever that may be. It is nothing proper or Whiskers would not be it and that you may tie to. He says that the big British victory at New Chapelle cost more than it was worth and he has forbid Joe Milgrave to come near the house because Joe ran up his father's flag when the news came. Have you noticed, Mrs. Dr. dear, that the Czar has changed that Prish name to Premysl, which proves that the man had good sense, Russian though he is? Joe Vickers told me in the store that he saw a very queer looking thing in the sky tonight over Lowbridge way. Do you suppose it could have been a Zeppelin, Mrs. Dr. dear?"

"I do not think it very likely, Susan."

"Well, I would feel easier about it if Whiskers-on-the-moon were not living in the Glen. They say he was seen going through strange manoeuvres with a lantern in his back yard one night lately. Some people think he was signalling."

"To whom—or what?"

"Ah, that is the mystery, Mrs. Dr. dear. In my opinion the Government would do well to keep an eye on that man if it does not want us to be all murdered in our beds some night. Now I shall just look over the papers a minute before going to write a letter to little Jem. Two things I never did, Mrs. Dr. dear, were write letters and read politics. Yet here I am doing both regular and I find there is something in politics after all. Whatever Woodrow Wilson means I cannot fathom but I am hoping I will puzzle it out yet."

Susan, in her pursuit of Wilson and politics, presently came upon something that disturbed her and exclaimed in a tone of bitter disappointment,

"That devilish Kaiser has only a boil after all."

"Don't swear, Susan," said Dr. Blythe, pulling a long face.

"'Devilish' is not swearing, doctor, dear. I have always understood that swearing was taking the name of the Almighty in vain?"

"Well, it isn't—ahem—refined," said the doctor, winking at Miss Oliver.

"No, doctor, dear, the devil and the Kaiser—if so be that they are really two different people —are not refined. And you cannot refer to them in a refined way. So I abide by what I said, although you may notice that I am careful not to use such expressions when young Rilla is about. And I maintain that the papers have no right to say that the Kaiser has pneumonia and raise people's hopes, and then come out and say he has nothing but a boil. A boil, indeed! I wish he was covered with them."

Susan stalked out to the kitchen and settled down to write to Jem; deeming him in need of some home comfort from certain passages in his letter that day.

"We're in an old wine cellar tonight, dad," he wrote, "in water to our knees. Rats everywhere—no fire—a drizzling rain coming down—rather dismal. But it might be worse. I got Susan's box today and everything was in tip-top order and we had a feast. Jerry is up the line somewhere and he says the rations are rather worse than Aunt Martha's ditto used to be.

But here they're not bad—only monotonous. Tell Susan I'd give a year's pay for a good batch of her monkey-faces; but don't let that inspire her to send any for they wouldn't keep.

"We have been under fire since the last week in February. One boy—he was a Nova Scotian—was killed right beside me yesterday. A shell burst near us and when the mess cleared away he was lying dead—not mangled at all—he just looked a little startled. It was the first time I'd been close to anything like that and it was a nasty sensation, but one soon gets used to horrors here. We're in an absolutely different world. The only things that are the same are the stars—and they are never in their right places, somehow.

"Tell mother not to worry—I'm all right—fit as a fiddle—and glad I came. There's something across from us here that has got to be wiped out of the world, that's all—an emanation of evil that would otherwise poison life for ever. It's got to be done, dad, however long it takes, and whatever it costs, and you tell the Glen people this for me. They don't realize yet what it is has broken loose—I didn't when I first joined up. I thought it was fun. Well, it isn't! But I'm in the right place all right—make no mistake about that. When I saw what had been done here to homes and gardens and people—well, dad, I seemed to see a gang of Huns marching through Rainbow Valley and the Glen, and the garden at Ingleside. There were gardens over here—beautiful gardens with the beauty of centuries—and what are they now? Mangled, desecrated things! We are fighting to make those dear old places where we had played as children, safe for other boys and girls—fighting for the preservation and safety of all sweet, wholesome things.

"Whenever any of you go to the station be sure to give Dog Monday a double pat for me. Fancy the faithful little beggar waiting there for me like that! Honestly, dad, on some of these dark cold nights in the trenches, it heartens and braces me up no end to think that thousands of miles away at the old Glen station there is a small spotted dog sharing my vigil.

"Tell Rilla I'm glad her war-baby is turning out so well, and tell Susan that I'm fighting a good fight against both Huns and cooties."

"Mrs. Dr. dear," whispered Susan solemnly, "what are cooties?"

Mrs. Blythe whispered back and then said in reply to Susan's horrified ejaculations, "It's always like that in the trenches, Susan."

Susan shook her head and went away in grim silence to re-open a parcel she had sewed up for Jem and slip in a fine tooth comb.

12. IN THE DAYS OF LANGEMARCK

"How can spring come and be beautiful in such a horror," wrote Rilla in her diary. "When the sun shines and the fluffy yellow catkins are coming out on the willow-trees down by the brook, and the garden is beginning to be beautiful I can't realize that such dreadful things are happening in Flanders. But they are!

"This past week has been terrible for us all, since the news came of the fighting around Ypres and the battles of Langemarck and St. Julien. Our Canadian boys have done splendidly—General French says they 'saved the situation,' when the Germans had all but broken through. But I can't feel pride or exultation or anything but a gnawing anxiety over Jem and Jerry and Mr. Grant. The casualty lists are coming out in the papers every day—oh, there are so many of them. I can't bear to read them for fear I'd find Jem's name—for there have been cases where people have seen their boys' names in the casualty lists before the official telegram came. As for the telephone, for a day or two I just refused to answer it, because I thought I could not endure the horrible moment that came between saying 'Hello' and hearing the response. That moment seemed a hundred years long, for I was always dreading to hear 'There is a telegram for Dr.

Blythe.' Then, when I had shirked for a while, I was ashamed of leaving it all for mother or Susan, and now I make myself go. But it never gets any easier. Gertrude teaches school and reads compositions and sets examination papers just as she always has done, but I know her thoughts are over in Flanders all the time. Her eyes haunt me.

"And Kenneth is in khaki now, too. He has got a lieutenant's commission and expects to go overseas in midsummer, so he wrote me. There wasn't much else in the letter—he seemed to be thinking of nothing but going overseas. I shall not see him again before he goes—perhaps I will never see him again. Sometimes I ask myself if that evening at Four Winds was all a dream. It might as well be—it seems as if it happened in another life lived years ago—and everybody has forgotten it but me.

"Walter and Nan and Di came home last night from Redmond. When Walter stepped off the train Dog Monday rushed to meet him, frantic with joy. I suppose he thought Jem would be there, too. After the first moment, he paid no attention to Walter and his pats, but just stood there, wagging his tail nervously and looking past Walter at the other people coming out, with eyes that made me choke up, for I couldn't help thinking that, for all we knew, Monday might never see Jem come off that train again. Then, when all the people were out, Monday looked up at Walter, gave his hand a little lick as if to say, 'I know it isn't your fault he didn't come—excuse me for feeling disappointed,' and then he trotted back to his shed, with that funny little sidelong waggle of his that always makes it seem that his hind legs are travelling directly away from the point at which his forelegs are aiming.

"We tried to coax him home with us—Di even got down and kissed him between the eyes and said, 'Monday, old duck, won't you come up with us just for the evening?' And Monday said—he did!—'I am very sorry but I can't. I've got a date to meet Jem here, you know, and there's a train goes through at eight.'

"It's lovely to have Walter back again though he seems quiet and sad, just as he was at Christmas. But I'm going to love him hard and cheer him up and make him laugh as he used to. It seems to me that every day of my life Walter means more to me.

"The other evening Susan happened to say that the mayflowers were out in Rainbow Valley. I chanced to be looking at mother when Susan spoke. Her face changed and she gave a queer little choked cry. Most of the time mother is so spunky and gay you would never guess what she feels inside; but now and then some little thing is too much for her and we see under the surface. 'Mayflowers!' she said. 'Jem brought me mayflowers last year!' and she got up and went out of the room. I would have rushed off to Rainbow Valley and brought her an armful of mayflowers, but I knew that wasn't what she wanted. And after Walter got home last night he slipped away to the valley and brought mother home all the mayflowers he could find. Nobody had said a word to him about it—he just remembered himself that Jem used to bring mother the first mayflowers and so he brought them in Jem's place. It shows how tender and thoughtful he is. And yet there are people who send him cruel letters!

"It seems strange that we can go in with ordinary life just as if nothing were happening overseas that concerned us, just as if any day might not bring us awful news. But we can and do. Susan is putting in the garden, and mother and she are housecleaning, and we Junior Reds are getting up a concert in aid of the Belgians. We have been practising for a month and having no end of trouble and bother with cranky people. Miranda Pryor promised to help with a dialogue and when she had her part all learnt her father put his foot down and refused to allow her to help at all. I am not blaming Miranda exactly, but I do think she might have a little more spunk sometimes. If she put her foot down once in a while she might bring her father to terms, for she is all the housekeeper he has and what would he do if she 'struck'? If I were in Miranda's shoes I'd find some way of managing Whiskers-on-the-moon. I would horse-whip him, or bite him, if nothing else would serve. But Miranda is a meek and obedient daughter whose days should be long in the land.

"I couldn't get anyone else to take the part, because nobody liked it, so finally I had to take it myself. Olive Kirk is on the concert committee and goes against me in every single thing. But I got my way in asking Mrs. Channing to come out from town and sing for us, anyhow. She is a beautiful singer and will draw such a crowd that we will make more than we will have to pay her. Olive Kirk thought our local talent good enough and Minnie Clow won't sing at all now in the choruses because she would be so nervous before Mrs. Channing. And Minnie is the only good alto we have! There are times when I am so exasperated that I feel tempted to wash my hands of the whole affair; but after I dance round my room a few times in sheer rage I cool down and have another whack at it. Just at present I am racked with worry for fear the Isaac Reeses are taking whooping-cough. They have all got a dreadful cold and there are five of them who have important parts in the programme and if they go and develop whooping-cough what shall I do? Dick Reese's violin solo is to be one of our titbits and Kit Reese is in every tableau and the three small girls have the cutest flag-drill. I've been toiling for weeks to train them in it, and now it seems likely that all my trouble will go for nothing.

"Jims cut his first tooth today. I am very glad, for he is nearly nine months old and Mary Vance has been insinuating that he is awfully backward about cutting his teeth. He has begun to creep but doesn't crawl as most babies do. He trots about on all fours and carries things in his mouth like a little dog. Nobody can say he isn't up to schedule time in the matter of creeping anyway—away ahead of it indeed, since ten months is Morgan's average for creeping. He is so cute, it will be a shame if his dad never sees him. His hair is coming on nicely too, and I am not without hope that it will be curly.

"Just for a few minutes, while I've been writing of Jims and the concert, I've forgotten Ypres and the poison gas and the casualty lists. Now it all rushes back, worse than ever. Oh, if we could just know that Jem is all right! I used to be so furious with Jem when he called me Spider. And now, if he would just come whistling through the hall and call out, 'Hello, Spider,' as he used to do, I would think it the loveliest name in the world."

Rilla put away her diary and went out to the garden. The spring evening was very lovely. The long, green, seaward-looking glen was filled with dusk, and beyond it were meadows of sunset. The harbour was radiant, purple here, azure there, opal elsewhere. The maple grove was beginning to be misty green. Rilla looked about her with wistful eyes. Who said that spring was the joy of the year? It was the heart-break of the year. And the pale-purply mornings and the daffodil stars and the wind in the old pine were so many separate pangs of the heart-break. Would life ever be free from dread again?

"It's good to see P.E.I. twilight once more," said Walter, joining her. "I didn't really remember that the sea was so blue and the roads so red and the wood nooks so wild and fairy haunted. Yes, the fairies still abide here. I vow I could find scores of them under the violets in Rainbow Valley."

Rilla was momentarily happy. This sounded like the Walter of yore. She hoped he was forgetting certain things that had troubled him.

"And isn't the sky blue over Rainbow Valley?" she said, responding to his mood. "Blue—blue—you'd have to say 'blue' a hundred times before you could express how blue it is."

Susan wandered by, her head tied up with a shawl, her hands full of garden implements. Doc, stealthy and wild-eyed, was shadowing her steps among the spirea bushes.

"The sky may be blue," said Susan, "but that cat has been Hyde all day so we will likely have rain tonight and by the same token I have rheumatism in my shoulder."

"It may rain—but don't think rheumatism, Susan—think violets," said Walter gaily—rather too gaily, Rilla thought.

Susan considered him unsympathetic.

"Indeed, Walter dear, I do not know what you mean by thinking violets," she responded stiffly, "and rheumatism is not a thing to be joked about, as you may some day realize for yourself. I hope I am not of the kind that is always complaining of their aches and pains, especially now when the news is so terrible. Rheumatism is bad enough but I realize, and none better, that it is not to be compared to being gassed by the Huns."

"Oh, my God, no!" exclaimed Walter passionately. He turned and went back to the house.

Susan shook her head. She disapproved entirely of such ejaculations. "I hope he will not let his mother hear him talking like that," she thought as she stacked the hoes and rake away.

Rilla was standing among the budding daffodils with tear-filled eyes. Her evening was spoiled; she detested Susan, who had somehow hurt Walter; and Jem—had Jem been gassed? Had he died in torture?

"I can't endure this suspense any longer," said Rilla desperately.

But she endured it as the others did for another week. Then a letter came from Jem. He was all right.

"I've come through without a scratch, dad. Don't know how I or any of us did it. You'll have seen all about it in the papers—I can't write of it. But the Huns haven't got through—they won't get through. Jerry was knocked stiff by a shell one time, but it was only the shock. He was all right in a few days. Grant is safe, too."

Nan had a letter from Jerry Meredith. "I came back to consciousness at dawn," he wrote. "Couldn't tell what had happened to me but thought that I was done for. I was all alone and afraid—terribly afraid. Dead men were all around me, lying on the horrible grey, slimy fields. I was woefully thirsty—and I thought of David and the Bethlehem water—and of the old spring in Rainbow Valley under the maples. I seemed to see it just before me—and you standing laughing on the other side of it—and I thought it was all over with me. And I didn't care. Honestly, I didn't care. I just felt a dreadful childish fear of loneliness and of those dead men around me, and a sort of wonder how this could have happened to me. Then they found me and carted me off and before long I discovered that there wasn't really anything wrong with me. I'm going back to the trenches tomorrow. Every man is needed there that can be got."

"Laughter is gone out of the world," said Faith Meredith, who had come over to report on her letters. "I remember telling old Mrs. Taylor long ago that the world was a world of laughter. But it isn't so any longer."

"It's a shriek of anguish," said Gertrude Oliver.

"We must keep a little laughter, girls," said Mrs. Blythe. "A good laugh is as good as a prayer sometimes—only sometimes," she added under her breath. She had found it very hard to laugh during the three weeks she had just lived through—she, Anne Blythe, to whom laughter had always come so easily and freshly. And what hurt most was that Rilla's laughter had grown so rare—Rilla whom she used to think laughed over-much. Was all the child's girlhood to be so clouded? Yet how strong and clever and womanly she was growing! How patiently she knitted and sewed and manipulated those uncertain Junior Reds! And how wonderful she was with Jims.

"She really could not do better for that child than if she had raised a baker's dozen, Mrs. Dr. dear," Susan had avowed solemnly. "Little did I ever expect it of her on the day she landed here with that soup tureen."

13. A SLICE OF HUMBLE PIE

"I am very much afraid, Mrs. Dr. dear," said Susan, who had been on a pilgrimage to the station with some choice bones for Dog Monday, "that something terrible has happened. Whiskers-on-the-moon came off the train from Charlottetown and he was looking pleased. I do not remember that I ever saw him with a smile on in public before. Of course he may have just been getting the better of somebody in a cattle deal but I have an awful presentiment that the Huns have broken through somewhere."

Perhaps Susan was unjust in connecting Mr. Pryor's smile with the sinking of the Lusitania, news of which circulated an hour later when the mail was distributed. But the Glen boys turned out that night in a body and broke all his windows in a fine frenzy of indignation over the Kaiser's doings.

"I do not say they did right and I do not say they did wrong," said Susan, when she heard of it. "But I will say that I wouldn't have minded throwing a few stones myself. One thing is certain—Whiskers-on-the-moon said in the post office the day the news came, in the presence of witnesses, that folks who could not stay home after they had been warned deserved no better fate. Norman Douglas is fairly foaming at the mouth over it all. 'If the devil doesn't get those men who sunk the Lusitania then there is no use in there being a devil,' he was shouting in Carter's store last night. Norman Douglas always has believed that anybody who opposed him was on the side of the devil, but a man like that is bound to be right once in a while. Bruce Meredith is worrying over the babies who were drowned. And it seems he prayed for something very special last Friday night and didn't get it, and was feeling quite disgruntled over it. But when he heard about the Lusitania he told his mother that he understood now why God didn't answer his prayer—He was too busy attending to the souls of all the people who went down on the Lusitania. That child's brain is a hundred years older than his body, Mrs. Dr. dear. As for the Lusitania, it is an awful occurrence, whatever way you look at it. But Woodrow Wilson is going to write a note about it, so why worry? A pretty president!" and Susan banged her pots about wrathfully. President Wilson was rapidly becoming anathema in Susan's kitchen.

Mary Vance dropped in one evening to tell the Ingleside folks that she had withdrawn all opposition to Miller Douglas's enlisting.

"This Lusitania business was too much for me," said Mary brusquely. "When the Kaiser takes to drowning innocent babies it's high time somebody told him where he gets off at. This thing must be fought to a finish. It's been soaking into my mind slow but I'm on now. So I up and told Miller he could go as far as I was concerned. Old Kitty Alec won't be converted though. If every ship in the world was submarined and every baby drowned, Kitty wouldn't turn a hair. But I flatter myself that it was me kept Miller back all along and not the fair Kitty. I may have deceived myself—but we shall see."

They did see. The next Sunday Miller Douglas walked into the Glen Church beside Mary Vance in khaki. And Mary was so proud of him that her white eyes fairly blazed. Joe Milgrave, back under the gallery, looked at Miller and Mary and then at Miranda Pryor, and sighed so heavily that every one within a radius of three pews heard him and knew what his trouble was. Walter Blythe did not sigh. But Rilla, scanning his face anxiously, saw a look that cut into her heart. It haunted her for the next week and made an undercurrent of soreness in her soul, which was externally being harrowed up by the near approach of the Red Cross concert and the worries connected therewith. The Reese cold had not developed into whooping-cough, so that tangle was straightened out. But other things were hanging in the balance; and on the very day before the concert came a regretful letter from Mrs. Channing saying that she could not come to sing. Her son, who was in Kingsport with his regiment, was seriously ill with pneumonia, and she must go to him at once.

The members of the concert committee looked at each other in blank dismay. What was to be done?

"This comes of depending on outside help," said Olive Kirk, disagreeably.

"We must do something," said Rilla, too desperate to care for Olive's manner. "We've advertised the concert everywhere—and crowds are coming—there's even a big party coming out from town—and we were short enough of music as it was. We must get some one to sing in Mrs. Channing's place."

"I don't know who you can get at this late date," said Olive. "Irene Howard could do it; but it is not likely she will after the way she was insulted by our society."

"How did our society insult her?" asked Rilla, in what she called her 'cold-pale tone.' Its coldness and pallor did not daunt Olive.

"You insulted her," she answered sharply. "Irene told me all about it—she was literally heart-broken. You told her never to speak to you again—and Irene told me she simply could not imagine what she had said or done to deserve such treatment. That was why she never came to our meetings again but joined in with the Lowbridge Red Cross. I do not blame her in the least, and I, for one, will not ask her to lower herself by helping us out of this scrape."

"You don't expect me to ask her?" giggled Amy MacAllister, the other member of the committee. "Irene and I haven't spoken for a hundred years. Irene is always getting 'insulted' by somebody. But she is a lovely singer, I'll admit that, and people would just as soon hear her as Mrs. Channing."

"It wouldn't do any good if you did ask her," said Olive significantly. "Soon after we began planning this concert, back in April, I met Irene in town one day and asked her if she wouldn't help us out. She said she'd love to but she really didn't see how she could when Rilla Blythe was running the programme, after the strange way Rilla had behaved to her. So there it is and here we are, and a nice failure our concert will be."

Rilla went home and shut herself up in her room, her soul in a turmoil. She would not humiliate herself by apologizing to Irene Howard! Irene had been as much in the wrong as she had been; and she had told such mean, distorted versions of their quarrel everywhere, posing as a puzzled, injured martyr. Rilla could never bring herself to tell her side of it. The fact that a slur at Walter was mixed up in it tied her tongue. So most people believed that Irene had been badly used, except a few girls who had never liked her and sided with Rilla. And yet—the concert over which she had worked so hard was going to be a failure. Mrs. Channing's four solos were the feature of the whole programme.

"Miss Oliver, what do you think about it?" she asked in desperation.

"I think Irene is the one who should apologize," said Miss Oliver. "But unfortunately my opinion will not fill the blanks in your programme."

"If I went and apologized meekly to Irene she would sing, I am sure," sighed Rilla. "She really loves to sing in public. But I know she'll be nasty about it—I feel I'd rather do anything than go. I suppose I should go—if Jem and Jerry can face the Huns surely I can face Irene Howard, and swallow my pride to ask a favour of her for the good of the Belgians. Just at present I feel that I cannot do it but for all that I have a presentiment that after supper you'll see me meekly trotting through Rainbow Valley on my way to the Upper Glen Road."

Rilla's presentiment proved correct. After supper she dressed herself carefully in her blue, beaded crepe—for vanity is harder to quell than pride and Irene always saw any flaw or shortcoming in another girl's appearance. Besides, as Rilla had told her mother one day when she was nine years old, "It is easier to behave nicely when you have your good clothes on."

Rilla did her hair very becomingly and donned a long raincoat for fear of a shower. But all the while her thoughts were concerned with the coming distasteful interview, and she kept rehearsing mentally her part in it. She wished it were over—she wished she had never tried to get up a Belgian Relief concert—she wished she had not quarreled with Irene. After all, disdainful silence would have been much more effective in meeting the slur upon Walter. It was foolish and childish to fly out as she had done—well, she would be wiser in the future, but meanwhile a large and very unpalatable slice of humble pie had to be eaten, and Rilla Blythe was no fonder of that wholesome article of diet than the rest of us.

By sunset she was at the door of the Howard house—a pretentious abode, with white scroll-work round the eaves and an eruption of bay-windows on all its sides. Mrs. Howard, a plump, voluble dame, met Rilla gushingly and left her in the parlour while she went to call Irene. Rilla threw off her rain-coat and looked at herself critically in the mirror over the mantel. Hair, hat, and dress were satisfactory—nothing there for Miss Irene to make fun of. Rilla remembered how clever and amusing she used to think Irene's biting little comments about other girls. Well, it had come home to her now.

Presently, Irene skimmed down, elegantly gowned, with her pale, straw-coloured hair done in the latest and most extreme fashion, and an over-luscious atmosphere of perfume enveloping her.

"Why how do you do, Miss Blythe?" she said sweetly. "This is a very unexpected pleasure."

Rilla had risen to take Irene's chilly finger-tips and now, as she sat down again, she saw something that temporarily stunned her. Irene saw it too, as she sat down, and a little amused, impertinent smile appeared on her lips and hovered there during the rest of the interview.

On one of Rilla's feet was a smart little steel-buckled shoe and a filmy blue silk stocking. The other was clad in a stout and rather shabby boot and black lisle!

Poor Rilla! She had changed, or begun to change her boots and stockings after she had put on her dress. This was the result of doing one thing with your hands and another with your brain. Oh, what a ridiculous position to be in—and before Irene Howard of all people—Irene, who was staring at Rilla's feet as if she had never seen feet before! And once she had thought Irene's manner perfection! Everything that Rilla had prepared to say vanished from her memory. Vainly trying to tuck her unlucky foot under her chair, she blurted out a blunt statement.

"I have come to athk a favour of you, Irene."

There—lisping! Oh, she had been prepared for humiliation but not to this extent! Really, there were limits!

"Yes?" said Irene in a cool, questioning tone, lifting her shallowly-set, insolent eyes to Rilla's crimson face for a moment and then dropping them again as if she could not tear them from their fascinated gaze at the shabby boot and the gallant shoe.

Rilla gathered herself together. She would not lisp—she would be calm and composed.

"Mrs. Channing cannot come because her son is ill in Kingsport, and I have come on behalf of the committee to ask you if you will be so kind as to sing for us in her place." Rilla enunciated every word so precisely and carefully that she seemed to be reciting a lesson.

"It's something of a fiddler's invitation, isn't it?" said Irene, with one of her disagreeable smiles.

"Olive Kirk asked you to help when we first thought of the concert and you refused," said Rilla.

"Why, I could hardly help—then—could I?" asked Irene plaintively. "After you ordered me never to speak to you again? It would have been very awkward for us both, don't you think?"

Now for the humble pie.

"I want to apologize to you for saying that, Irene." said Rilla steadily. "I should not have said it and I have been very sorry ever since. Will you forgive me?"

"And sing at your concert?" said Irene sweetly and insultingly.

"If you mean," said Rilla miserably, "that I would not be apologizing to you if it were not for the concert perhaps that is true. But it is also true that I have felt ever since it happened that I should not have said what I did and that I have been sorry for it all winter. That is all I can say. If you feel you can't forgive me I suppose there is nothing more to be said."

"Oh, Rilla dear, don't snap me up like that," pleaded Irene. "Of course I'll forgive you—though I did feel awfully about it—how awfully I hope you'll never know. I cried for weeks over it. And I hadn't said or done a thing!"

Rilla choked back a retort. After all, there was no use in arguing with Irene, and the Belgians were starving.

"Don't you think you can help us with the concert," she forced herself to say. Oh, if only Irene would stop looking at that boot! Rilla could just hear her giving Olive Kirk an account of it.

"I don't see how I really can at the last moment like this," protested Irene. "There isn't time to learn anything new."

"Oh, you have lots of lovely songs that nobody in the Glen ever heard before," said Rilla, who knew Irene had been going to town all winter for lessons and that this was only a pretext. "They will all be new down there."

"But I have no accompanist," protested Irene.

"Una Meredith can accompany you," said Rilla.

"Oh, I couldn't ask her," sighed Irene. "We haven't spoken since last fall. She was so hateful to me the time of our Sunday-school concert that I simply had to give her up."

Dear, dear, was Irene at feud with everybody? As for Una Meredith being hateful to anybody, the idea was so farcical that Rilla had much ado to keep from laughing in Irene's very face.

"Miss Oliver is a beautiful pianist and can play any accompaniment at sight," said Rilla desperately. "She will play for you and you could run over your songs easily tomorrow evening at Ingleside before the concert."

"But I haven't anything to wear. My new evening-dress isn't home from Charlottetown yet, and I simply cannot wear my old one at such a big affair. It is too shabby and old-fashioned."

"Our concert," said Rilla slowly, "is in aid of Belgian children who are starving to death. Don't you think you could wear a shabby dress once for their sake, Irene?"

"Oh, don't you think those accounts we get of the conditions of the Belgians are very much exaggerated?" said Irene. "I'm sure they can't be actually starving you know, in the twentieth century. The newspapers always colour things so highly."

Rilla concluded that she had humiliated herself enough. There was such a thing as self-respect. No more coaxing, concert or no concert. She got up, boot and all.

"I am sorry you can't help us, Irene, but since you cannot we must do the best we can."

Now this did not suit Irene at all. She desired exceedingly to sing at that concert, and all her hesitations were merely by way of enhancing the boon of her final consent. Besides, she really wanted to be friends with Rilla again. Rilla's whole-hearted, ungrudging adoration had been very sweet incense to her. And Ingleside was a very charming house to visit, especially when a handsome college student like Walter was home. She stopped looking at Rilla's feet.

"Rilla, darling, don't be so abrupt. I really want to help you, if I can manage it. Just sit down and let's talk it over."

"I'm sorry, but I can't. I have to be home soon—Jims has to be settled for the night, you know."

"Oh, yes—the baby you are bringing up by the book. It's perfectly sweet of you to do it when you hate children so. How cross you were just because I kissed him! But we'll forget all that and be chums again, won't we? Now, about the concert—I dare say I can run into town on the morning train after my dress, and out again on the afternoon one in plenty of time for the concert, if you'll ask Miss Oliver to play for me. I couldn't—she's so dreadfully haughty and supercilious that she simply paralyses poor little me."

Rilla did not waste time or breath defending Miss Oliver. She coolly thanked Irene, who had suddenly become very amiable and gushing, and got away. She was very thankful the interview was over. But she knew now that she and Irene could never be the friends they had been. Friendly, yes—but friends, no. Nor did she wish it. All winter she had felt under her other and more serious worries, a little feeling of regret for her lost chum. Now it was suddenly gone. Irene was not as Mrs. Elliott would say, of the race that knew Joseph. Rilla did not say or think that she had outgrown Irene. Had the thought occurred to her she would have considered it absurd when she was not yet seventeen and Irene was twenty. But it was the truth. Irene was just what she had been a year ago—just what she would always be. Rilla Blythe's nature in that year had changed and matured and deepened. She found herself seeing through Irene with a disconcerting clearness—discerning under all her superficial sweetness, her pettiness, her vindictiveness, her insincerity, her essential cheapness. Irene had lost for ever her faithful worshipper.

But not until Rilla had traversed the Upper Glen Road and found herself in the moon-dappled solitude of Rainbow Valley did she fully recover her composure of spirit. Then she stopped under a tall wild plum that was ghostly white and fair in its misty spring bloom and laughed.

"There is only one thing of importance just now—and that is that the Allies win the war," she said aloud. "Therefore, it follows without dispute that the fact that I went to see Irene Howard with odd shoes and stockings on is of no importance whatever. Nevertheless, I, Bertha Marilla Blythe, swear solemnly with the moon as witness"—Rilla lifted her hand dramatically to the said moon—"that I will never leave my room again without looking carefully at both my feet."

14. THE VALLEY OF DECISION

Susan kept the flag flying at Ingleside all the next day, in honour of Italy's declaration of war.

"And not before it was time, Mrs. Dr. dear, considering the way things have begun to go on the Russian front. Say what you will, those Russians are kittle cattle, the grand duke Nicholas to the contrary notwithstanding. It is a fortunate thing for Italy that she has come in on the right side, but whether it is as fortunate for the Allies I will not predict until I know more about Italians than I do now. However, she will give that old reprobate of a Francis Joseph something to think about. A pretty Emperor indeed—with one foot in the grave and yet plotting wholesale murder"—and Susan thumped and kneaded her bread with as much vicious energy as she could have expended in punching Francis Joseph himself if he had been so unlucky as to fall into her clutches.

Walter had gone to town on the early train, and Nan offered to look after Jims for the day and so set Rilla free. Rilla was wildly busy all day, helping to decorate the Glen hall and seeing to a hundred last things. The evening was beautiful, in spite of the fact that Mr. Pryor was reported to have said that he "hoped it would rain pitch forks points down," and to have wantonly kicked Miranda's dog as he said it. Rilla, rushing home from the hall, dressed hurriedly. Everything had gone surprisingly well at the last; Irene was even then downstairs practising her songs with Miss Oliver; Rilla was excited and happy, forgetful even of the Western front for the moment. It gave her a sense of achievement and victory to have brought her efforts of weeks to such a successful conclusion. She knew that there had not lacked people who thought and hinted that Rilla Blythe had not the tact or patience to engineer a concert programme. She had shown them! Little snatches of song bubbled up from her lips as she dressed. She thought she was looking very well. Excitement brought a faint, becoming pink into her round creamy cheeks, quite drowning out her few freckles, and her hair gleamed with red-brown lustre. Should she wear crab-apple blossoms in it, or her little fillet of pearls? After some agonised wavering she decided on the crab-apple blossoms and tucked the white waxen cluster behind her left ear. Now for a final look at her feet. Yes, both slippers were on. She gave the sleeping Jims a kiss—what a dear little warm, rosy, satin face he had—and hurried down the hill to the hall. Already it was filling—soon it was crowded. Her concert was going to be a brilliant success.

The first three numbers were successfully over. Rilla was in the little dressing-room behind the platform, looking out on the moonlit harbour and rehearsing her own recitations. She was alone, the rest of the performers being in the larger room on the other side. Suddenly she felt two soft bare arms slipping round her waist, then Irene Howard dropped a light kiss on her cheek.

"Rilla, you sweet thing, you're looking simply angelic to-night. You have spunk—I thought you would feel so badly over Walter's enlisting that you'd hardly be able to bear up at all, and here you are as cool as a cucumber. I wish I had half your nerve."

Rilla stood perfectly still. She felt no emotion whatever—she felt nothing. The world of feeling had just gone blank.

"Walter—enlisting"—she heard herself saying—then she heard Irene's affected little laugh.

"Why, didn't you know? I thought you did of course, or I wouldn't have mentioned it. I am always putting my foot in it, aren't I? Yes, that is what he went to town for to-day—he told me coming out on the train to-night, I was the first person he told. He isn't in khaki yet—they were out of uniforms—but he will be in a day or two. I always said Walter had as much pluck as anybody. I assure you I felt proud of him, Rilla, when he told me what he'd done. Oh, there's an end of Rick MacAllister's reading. I must fly. I promised I'd play for the next chorus—Alice Clow has such a headache."

She was gone—oh, thank God, she was gone! Rilla was alone again, staring out at the unchanged, dream-like beauty of moonlit Four Winds. Feeling was coming back to her—a pang of agony so acute as to be almost physical seemed to rend her apart.

"I cannot bear it," she said. And then came the awful thought that perhaps she could bear it and that there might be years of this hideous suffering before her.

She must get away—she must rush home—she must be alone. She could not go out there and play for drills and give readings and take part in dialogues now. It would spoil half the concert; but that did not matter—nothing mattered. Was this she, Rilla Blythe—this tortured thing, who had been quite happy a few minutes ago? Outside, a quartette was singing "We'll never let the old flag fall"—the music seemed to be coming from some remote distance. Why couldn't she cry, as she had cried when Jem told them he must go? If she could cry perhaps this horrible something that seemed to have seized on her very life might let go. But no tears came! Where were her scarf and coat? She must get away and hide herself like an animal hurt to the death.

Was it a coward's part to run away like this? The question came to her suddenly as if someone else had asked it. She thought of the shambles of the Flanders front—she thought of her brother and her playmate helping to hold those fire-swept trenches. What would they think of her if she shirked her little duty here—the humble duty of carrying the programme through for her Red Cross? But she couldn't stay—she couldn't—yet what was it mother had said when Jem went: "When our women fail in courage shall our men be fearless still?" But this—this was unbearable.

Still, she stopped half-way to the door and went back to the window. Irene was singing now; her beautiful voice—the only real thing about her—soared clear and sweet through the building. Rilla knew that the girls' Fairy Drill came next. Could she go out there and play for it? Her head was aching now—her throat was burning. Oh, why had Irene told her just then, when telling could do no good? Irene had been very cruel. Rilla remembered now that more than once that day she had caught her mother looking at her with an odd expression. She had been too busy to wonder what it meant. She understood now. Mother had known why Walter went to town but wouldn't tell her until the concert was over. What spirit and endurance mother had!

"I must stay here and see things through," said Rilla, clasping her cold hands together.

The rest of the evening always seemed like a fevered dream to her. Her body was crowded by people but her soul was alone in a torture-chamber of its own. Yet she played steadily for the drills and gave her readings without faltering. She even put on a grotesque old Irish woman's costume and acted the part in the dialogue which Miranda Pryor had not taken. But she did not give her "brogue" the inimitable twist she had given it in the practices, and her readings lacked their usual fire and appeal. As she stood before the audience she saw one face only—that of the handsome, dark-haired lad sitting beside her mother—and she saw that same face in the trenches—saw it lying cold and dead under the stars—saw it pining in prison—saw the light of its eyes blotted out—saw a hundred horrible things as she stood there on the beflagged platform of the Glen hall with her own face whiter than the milky crab-blossoms in her hair. Between her numbers she walked restlessly up and down the little dressing-room. Would the concert never end!

It ended at last. Olive Kirk rushed up and told her exultantly that they had made a hundred dollars. "That's good," Rilla said mechanically. Then she was away from them all—oh, thank God, she was away from them all—Walter was waiting for her at the door. He put his arm through hers silently and they went together down the moonlit road. The frogs were singing in the marshes, the dim, ensilvered fields of home lay all around them. The spring night was lovely and appealing. Rilla felt that its beauty was an insult to her pain. She would hate moonlight for ever.

"You know?" said Walter.

"Yes. Irene told me," answered Rilla chokingly.

"We didn't want you to know till the evening was over. I knew when you came out for the drill that you had heard. Little sister, I had to do it. I couldn't live any longer on such terms with myself as I have been since the Lusitania was sunk. When I pictured those dead women and children floating about in that pitiless, ice-cold water—well, at first I just felt a sort of nausea with life. I wanted to get out of the world where such a thing could happen—shake its accursed dust from my feet for ever. Then I knew I had to go."

"There are—plenty—without you."

"That isn't the point, Rilla-my-Rilla. I'm going for my own sake—to save my soul alive. It will shrink to something small and mean and lifeless if I don't go. That would be worse than blindness or mutilation or any of the things I've feared."

"You may—be—killed," Rilla hated herself for saying it—she knew it was a weak and cowardly thing to say—but she had rather gone to pieces after the tension of the evening.

"'Comes he slow or comes he fast
It is but death who comes at last.'"

quoted Walter. "It's not death I fear—I told you that long ago. One can pay too high a price for mere life, little sister. There's so much hideousness in this war—I've got to go and help wipe it out of the world. I'm going to fight for the beauty of life, Rilla-my-Rilla—that is my duty. There may be a higher duty, perhaps—but that is mine. I owe life and Canada that, and I've got to pay it. Rilla, tonight for the first time since Jem left I've got back my self-respect. I could write poetry," Walter laughed. "I've never been able to write a line since last August. Tonight I'm full of it. Little sister, be brave—you were so plucky when Jem went."

"This—is—different," Rilla had to stop after every word to fight down a wild outburst of sobs. "I loved—Jem—of course—but—when—he went—away—we thought—the war—would soon—be over—and you are—everything to me, Walter."

"You must be brave to help me, Rilla-my-Rilla. I'm exalted tonight—drunk with the excitement of victory over myself—but there will be other times when it won't be like this—I'll need your help then."

"When—do—you—go?" She must know the worst at once.

"Not for a week—then we go to Kingsport for training. I suppose we'll go overseas about the middle of July—we don't know."

One week—only one week more with Walter! The eyes of youth did not see how she was to go on living.

When they turned in at the Ingleside gate Walter stopped in the shadows of the old pines and drew Rilla close to him.

"Rilla-my-Rilla, there were girls as sweet and pure as you in Belgium and Flanders. You—even you—know what their fate was. We must make it impossible for such things to happen again while the world lasts. You'll help me, won't you?"

"I'll try, Walter," she said. "Oh, I will try."

As she clung to him with her face pressed against his shoulder she knew that it had to be. She accepted the fact then and there. He must go—her beautiful Walter with his beautiful soul and dreams and ideals. And she had known all along that it would come sooner or later. She had seen it coming to her—coming—coming—as one sees the shadow of a cloud drawing near over a sunny field, swiftly and inescapably. Amid all her pain she was conscious of an odd feeling of relief in some hidden part of her soul, where a little dull, unacknowledged soreness had been lurking all winter. No one—no one could ever call Walter a slacker now.

Rilla did not sleep that night. Perhaps no one at Ingleside did except Jims. The body grows slowly and steadily, but the soul grows by leaps and bounds. It may come to its full stature in an hour. From that night Rilla Blythe's soul was the soul of a woman in its capacity for suffering, for strength, for endurance.

When the bitter dawn came she rose and went to her window. Below her was a big apple-tree, a great swelling cone of rosy blossom. Walter had planted it years ago when he was a little boy. Beyond Rainbow Valley there was a cloudy shore of morning with little ripples of sunrise breaking over it. The far, cold beauty of a lingering star shone above it. Why, in this world of springtime loveliness, must hearts break?

Rilla felt arms go about her lovingly, protectingly. It was mother—pale, large-eyed mother.

"Oh, mother, how can you bear it?" she cried wildly. "Rilla, dear, I've known for several days that Walter meant to go. I've had time to—to rebel and grow reconciled. We must give him up. There is a Call greater and more insistent than the call of our love—he has listened to it. We must not add to the bitterness of his sacrifice."

"Our sacrifice is greater than his," cried Rilla passionately. "Our boys give only themselves. We give them."

Before Mrs. Blythe could reply Susan stuck her head in at the door, never troubling over such frills of etiquette as knocking. Her eyes were suspiciously red but all she said was,

"Will I bring up your breakfast, Mrs. Dr. dear."

"No, no, Susan. We will all be down presently. Do you know—that Walter has joined up."

"Yes, Mrs. Dr. dear. The doctor told me last night. I suppose the Almighty has His own reasons for allowing such things. We must submit and endeavour to look on the bright side. It may cure him of being a poet, at least"—Susan still persisted in thinking that poets and tramps were tarred with the same brush—"and that would be something. But thank God," she muttered in a lower tone, "that Shirley is not old enough to go."

"Isn't that the same thing as thanking Him that some other woman's son has to go in Shirley's place?" asked the doctor, pausing on the threshold.

"No, it is not, doctor dear," said Susan defiantly, as she picked up Jims, who was opening his big dark eyes and stretching up his dimpled paws. "Do not you put words in my mouth that I would never dream of uttering. I am a plain woman and cannot argue with you, but I do not thank God that anybody has to go. I only know that it seems they do have to go, unless we all want to be Kaiserised—for I can assure you that the Monroe doctrine, whatever it is, is nothing to tie to, with Woodrow Wilson behind it. The Huns, Dr. dear, will never be brought to book by notes. And now," concluded Susan, tucking Jims in the crook of her gaunt arms and marching downstairs, "having cried my cry and said my say I shall take a brace, and if I cannot look pleasant I will look as pleasant as I can."

15. UNTIL THE DAY BREAK

"The Germans have recaptured Premysl," said Susan despairingly, looking up from her newspaper, "and now I suppose we will have to begin calling it by that uncivilised name again. Cousin Sophia was in when the mail came and when she heard the news she hove a sigh up from the depths of her stomach, Mrs. Dr. dear, and said, 'Ah yes, and they will get Petrograd next I have no doubt.' I said to her, 'My knowledge of geography is not so profound as I wish it was but I have an idea that it is quite a walk from Premysl to Petrograd.' Cousin Sophia sighed again and said, 'The Grand Duke Nicholas is not the man I took him to be.' 'Do not let him know that,' said I. 'It might hurt his feelings and he has likely enough to worry him as it is. But you cannot cheer Cousin Sophia up, no matter how sarcastic you are, Mrs. Dr. dear. She sighed for the third time and groaned out, 'But the Russians are retreating fast,' and I said, 'Well, what of it? They have plenty of room for retreating, have they not?' But all the same, Mrs. Dr. dear, though I would never admit it to Cousin Sophia, I do not like the situation on the eastern front."

Nobody else liked it either; but all summer the Russian retreat went on—a long-drawn-out agony.

"I wonder if I shall ever again be able to await the coming of the mail with feelings of composure—never to speak of pleasure," said Gertrude Oliver. "The thought that haunts me night and day is—will the Germans smash Russia completely and then hurl their eastern army, flushed with victory, against the western front?"

"They will not, Miss Oliver dear," said Susan, assuming the role of prophetess.

"In the first place, the Almighty will not allow it, in the second, Grand Duke Nicholas, though he may have been a disappointment to us in some respects, knows how to run away decently and in order, and that is a very useful knowledge when Germans are chasing you. Norman Douglas declares he is just luring them on and killing ten of them to one he loses. But I am of the opinion he cannot help himself and is just doing the best he can under the circumstances, the same as the rest of us. So do not go so far afield to borrow trouble, Miss Oliver dear, when there is plenty of it already camping on our very doorstep."

Walter had gone to Kingsport the first of June. Nan, Di and Faith had gone also to do Red Cross work in their vacation. In mid-July Walter came home for a week's leave before going overseas. Rilla had lived through the days of his absence on the hope of that week, and now that it had come she drank every minute of it thirstily, hating even the hours she had to spend in sleep, they seemed such a waste of precious moments. In spite of its sadness, it was a beautiful week, full of poignant, unforgettable hours, when she and Walter had long walks and talks and silences together. He was all her own and she knew that he found strength and comfort in her sympathy and understanding. It was very wonderful to know she meant so much to him—the knowledge helped her through moments that would otherwise have been unendurable, and gave her power to smile—and even to laugh a little. When Walter had gone she might indulge in the comfort of tears, but not while he was here. She would not even let herself cry at night, lest her eyes should betray her to him in the morning.

On his last evening at home they went together to Rainbow Valley and sat down on the bank of the brook, under the White Lady, where the gay revels of olden days had been held in the cloudless years. Rainbow Valley was roofed over with a sunset of unusual splendour that night; a wonderful grey dusk just touched with starlight followed it; and then came moonshine, hinting, hiding, revealing, lighting up little dells and hollows here, leaving others in dark, velvet shadow.

"When I am 'somewhere in France,'" said Walter, looking around him with eager eyes on all the beauty his soul loved, "I shall remember these still, dewy, moon-drenched places. The balsam of the fir-trees; the peace of those white pools of moonshine; the 'strength of the hills'—what a beautiful old Biblical phrase that is. Rilla! Look at those old hills around us—the hills we looked up at as children, wondering what lay for us in the great world beyond them. How calm and strong they are—how patient and changeless—like the heart of a good woman. Rilla-my-Rilla, do you know what you have been to me the past year? I want to tell you before I go. I could not have lived through it if it had not been for you, little loving, believing heart."

Rilla dared not try to speak. She slipped her hand into Walter's and pressed it hard.

"And when I'm over there, Rilla, in that hell upon earth which men who have forgotten God have made, it will be the thought of you that will help me most. I know you'll be as plucky and patient as you have shown yourself to be this past year—I'm not afraid for you. I know that no matter what happens, you'll be Rilla-my-Rilla—no matter what happens."

Rilla repressed tear and sigh, but she could not repress a little shiver, and Walter knew that he had said enough. After a moment of silence, in which each made an unworded promise to each other, he said, "Now we won't be sober any more. We'll look beyond the years—to the time when the war will be over and Jem and Jerry and I will come marching home and we'll all be happy again."

"We won't be—happy—in the same way," said Rilla.

"No, not in the same way. Nobody whom this war has touched will ever be happy again in quite the same way. But it will be a better happiness, I think, little sister—a happiness we've earned. We were very happy before the war, weren't we? With a home like Ingleside, and a father and mother like ours we couldn't help being happy. But that happiness was a gift from life and love; it wasn't really ours—life could take it back at any time. It can never take away the happiness we win for ourselves in the way of duty. I've realised that since I went into khaki. In spite of my occasional funks, when I fall to living over things beforehand, I've been happy since that night in May. Rilla, be awfully good to mother while I'm away. It must be a horrible thing to be a mother in this war—the mothers and sisters and wives and sweethearts have the hardest times. Rilla, you beautiful little thing, are you anybody's sweetheart? If you are, tell me before I go."

"No," said Rilla. Then, impelled by a wish to be absolutely frank with Walter in this talk that might be the last they would ever have, she added, blushing wildly in the moonlight, "but if—Kenneth Ford—wanted me to be—"

"I see," said Walter. "And Ken's in khaki, too. Poor little girlie, it's a bit hard for you all round. Well, I'm not leaving any girl to break her heart about me—thank God for that."

Rilla glanced up at the Manse on the hill. She could see a light in Una Meredith's window. She felt tempted to say something—then she knew she must not. It was not her secret: and, anyway, she did not know—she only suspected.

Walter looked about him lingeringly and lovingly. This spot had always been so dear to him. What fun they all had had here lang syne. Phantoms of memory seemed to pace the dappled paths and peep merrily through the swinging boughs—Jem and Jerry, bare-legged, sunburned schoolboys, fishing in the brook and frying trout over the old stone fireplace; Nan and Di and Faith, in their dimpled, fresh-eyed childish beauty; Una the sweet and shy, Carl, poring over ants and bugs, little slangy, sharp-tongued, good-hearted Mary Vance—the old Walter that had been himself lying on the grass reading poetry or wandering through palaces of fancy. They were all there around him—he could see them almost as plainly as he saw Rilla—as plainly as he had once seen the Pied Piper piping down the valley in a vanished twilight. And they said to him, those gay little ghosts of other days, "We were the children of yesterday, Walter—fight a good fight for the children of to-day and to-morrow."

"Where are you, Walter," cried Rilla, laughing a little. "Come back—come back."

Walter came back with a long breath. He stood up and looked about him at the beautiful valley of moonlight, as if to impress on his mind and heart every charm it possessed—the great dark plumes of the firs against the silvery sky, the stately White Lady, the old magic of the dancing brook, the faithful Tree Lovers, the beckoning, tricksy paths.

"I shall see it so in my dreams," he said, as he turned away.

They went back to Ingleside. Mr. and Mrs. Meredith were there, with Gertrude Oliver, who had come from Lowbridge to say good-bye. Everybody was quite cheerful and bright, but nobody said much about the war being soon over, as they had said when Jem went away. They did not talk about the war at all—and they thought of nothing else. At last they gathered around the piano and sang the grand old hymn:

"Oh God, our help in ages past
Our hope for years to come.
Our shelter from the stormy blast
And our eternal home."

"We all come back to God in these days of soul-sifting," said Gertrude to John Meredith. "There have been many days in the past when I didn't believe in God—not as God—only as the impersonal Great First Cause of the scientists. I believe in Him now—I have to—there's nothing else to fall back on but God—humbly, starkly, unconditionally."

"'Our help in ages past'—'the same yesterday, to-day and for ever,'" said the minister gently. "When we forget God—He remembers us."

There was no crowd at the Glen Station the next morning to see Walter off. It was becoming a commonplace for a khaki clad boy to board that early morning train after his last leave. Besides his own, only the Manse folk were there, and Mary Vance. Mary had sent her Miller off the week before, with a determined grin, and now considered herself entitled to give expert opinion on how such partings should be conducted.

"The main thing is to smile and act as if nothing was happening," she informed the Ingleside group. "The boys all hate the sob act like poison. Miller told me I wasn't to come near the station if I couldn't keep from bawling. So I got through with my crying beforehand, and at the last I said to him, 'Good luck, Miller, and if you come back you'll find I haven't changed any, and if you don't come back I'll always be proud you went, and in any case don't fall in love with a French girl.' Miller swore he wouldn't, but you never can tell about those fascinating foreign hussies. Anyhow, the last sight he had of me I was smiling to my limit. Gee, all the rest of the day my face felt as if it had been starched and ironed into a smile."

In spite of Mary's advice and example Mrs. Blythe, who had sent Jem off with a smile, could not quite manage one for Walter. But at least no one cried. Dog Monday came out of his lair in the shipping-shed and sat down close to Walter, thumping his tail vigorously on the boards of the platform whenever Walter spoke to him, and looking up with confident eyes, as if to say, "I know you'll find Jem and bring him back to me."

"So long, old fellow," said Carl Meredith cheerfully, when the good-byes had to be said. "Tell them over there to keep their spirits up—I am coming along presently."

"Me too," said Shirley laconically, proffering a brown paw. Susan heard him and her face turned very grey.

Una shook hands quietly, looking at him with wistful, sorrowful, dark-blue eyes. But then Una's eyes had always been wistful. Walter bent his handsome black head in its khaki cap and kissed her with the warm, comradely kiss of a brother. He had never kissed her before, and for a fleeting moment Una's face betrayed her, if anyone had noticed. But nobody did; the conductor was shouting "all aboard"; everybody was trying to look very cheerful. Walter turned to Rilla; she held his hands and looked up at him. She would not see him again until the day broke and the shadows vanished—and she knew not if that daybreak would be on this side of the grave or beyond it.

"Good-bye," she said.

On her lips it lost all the bitterness it had won through the ages of parting and bore instead all the sweetness of the old loves of all the women who had ever loved and prayed for the beloved.

"Write me often and bring Jims up faithfully, according to the gospel of Morgan," Walter said lightly, having said all his serious things the night before in Rainbow Valley. But at the last moment he took her face between his hands and looked deep into her gallant eyes. "God bless you, Rilla-my-Rilla," he said softly and tenderly. After all it was not a hard thing to fight for a land that bore daughters like this.

He stood on the rear platform and waved to them as the train pulled out. Rilla was standing by herself, but Una Meredith came to her and the two girls who loved him most stood together and held each other's cold hands as the train rounded the curve of the wooded hill.

Rilla spent an hour in Rainbow Valley that morning about which she never said a word to anyone; she did not even write in her diary about it; when it was over she went home and made rompers for Jims. In the evening she went to a Junior Red Cross committee meeting and was severely businesslike.

"You would never suppose," said Irene Howard to Olive Kirk afterwards, "that Walter had left for the front only this morning. But some people really have no depth of feeling. I often wish I could take things as lightly as Rilla Blythe."

16. REALISM AND ROMANCE

"Warsaw has fallen," said Dr. Blythe with a resigned air, as he brought the mail in one warm August day.

Gertrude and Mrs. Blythe looked dismally at each other, and Rilla, who was feeding Jims a Morganized diet from a carefully sterilized spoon, laid the said spoon down on his tray, utterly regardless of germs, and said, "Oh, dear me," in as tragic a tone as if the news had come as a thunderbolt instead of being a foregone conclusion from the preceding week's dispatches. They had thought they were quite resigned to Warsaw's fall but now they knew they had, as always, hoped against hope.

"Now, let us take a brace," said Susan. "It is not the terrible thing we have been thinking. I read a dispatch three columns long in the Montreal Herald yesterday that proved that Warsaw was not important from a military point of view at all. So let us take the military point of view, doctor dear."

"I read that dispatch, too, and it has encouraged me immensely," said Gertrude. "I knew then and I know now that it was a lie from beginning to end. But I am in that state of mind where even a lie is a comfort, providing it is a cheerful lie."

"In that case, Miss Oliver dear, the German official reports ought to be all you need," said Susan sarcastically. "I never read them now because they make me so mad I cannot put my thoughts properly on my work after a dose of them. Even this news about Warsaw has taken the edge off my afternoon's plans. Misfortunes never come singly. I spoiled my baking of bread today—and now Warsaw has fallen—and here is little Kitchener bent on choking himself to death."

Jims was evidently trying to swallow his spoon, germs and all. Rilla rescued him mechanically and was about to resume the operation of feeding him when a casual remark of her father's sent such a shock and thrill over her that for the second time she dropped that doomed spoon.

"Kenneth Ford is down at Martin West's over-harbour," the doctor was saying. "His regiment was on its way to the front but was held up in Kingsport for some reason, and Ken got leave of absence to come over to the Island."

"I hope he will come up to see us," exclaimed Mrs. Blythe.

"He only has a day or two off, I believe," said the doctor absently.

Nobody noticed Rilla's flushed face and trembling hands. Even the most thoughtful and watchful of parents do not see everything that goes on under their very noses. Rilla made a third attempt to give the long-suffering Jims his dinner, but all she could think of was the question—Would Ken come to see her before he went away? She had not heard from him for a long while. Had he forgotten her completely? If he did not come she would know that he had. Perhaps there was even—some other girl back there in Toronto. Of course there was. She was a little fool to be thinking about him at all. She would not think about him. If he came, well and good. It would only be courteous of him to make a farewell call at Ingleside where he had often been a guest. If he did not come—well and good, too. It did not matter very much. Nobody was going to fret. That was all settled comfortably—she was quite indifferent—but meanwhile Jims was being fed with a haste and recklessness that would have filled the soul of Morgan with horror. Jims himself didn't like it, being a methodical baby, accustomed to swallowing spoonfuls with a decent interval for breath between each. He protested, but his protests availed him nothing. Rilla, as far as the care and feeding of infants was concerned, was utterly demoralized.

Then the telephone-bell rang. There was nothing unusual about the telephone ringing. It rang on an average every ten minutes at Ingleside. But Rilla dropped Jims' spoon again—on the carpet this time—and flew to the 'phone as if life depended on her getting there before anybody else. Jims, his patience exhausted, lifted up his voice and wept.

"Hello, is this Ingleside?"

"Yes."

"That you, Rilla?" "Yeth—yeth." Oh, why couldn't Jims stop howling for just one little minute? Why didn't somebody come in and choke him?

"Know who's speaking?"

Oh, didn't she know! Wouldn't she know that voice anywhere—at any time?

"It's Ken—isn't it?"

"Sure thing. I'm here for a look-in. Can I come up to Ingleside tonight and see you?"

"Of courthe."

Had he used "you" in the singular or plural sense? Presently she would wring Jims' neck—oh, what was Ken saying?

"See here, Rilla, can you arrange that there won't be more than a few dozen people round? Understand? I can't make my meaning clearer over this bally rural line. There are a dozen receivers down."

Did she understand! Yes, she understood.

"I'll try," she said.

"I'll be up about eight then. By-by."

Rilla hung up the 'phone and flew to Jims. But she did not wring that injured infant's neck. Instead she snatched him bodily out of his chair, crushed him against her face, kissed him rapturously on his milky mouth, and danced wildly around the room with him in her arms. After this Jims was relieved to find that she returned to sanity, gave him the rest of his dinner properly, and tucked him away for his afternoon nap with the little lullaby he loved best of all. She sewed at Red Cross shirts for the rest of the afternoon and built a crystal castle of dreams, all a-quiver with rainbows. Ken wanted to see her—to see her alone. That could be easily managed. Shirley wouldn't bother them, father and mother were going to the Manse, Miss Oliver never played gooseberry, and Jims always slept the clock round from seven to seven. She would entertain Ken on the veranda—it would be moonlight—she would wear her white georgette dress and do her hair up—yes, she would—at least in a low knot at the nape of her neck. Mother couldn't object to that, surely. Oh, how wonderful and romantic it would be! Would Ken say anything—he must mean to say something or why should he be so particular about seeing her alone? What if it rained—Susan had been complaining about Mr. Hyde that morning! What if some officious Junior Red called to discuss Belgians and shirts? Or, worst of all, what if Fred Arnold dropped in? He did occasionally.

The evening came at last and was all that could be desired in an evening. The doctor and his wife went to the Manse, Shirley and Miss Oliver went they alone knew where, Susan went to the store for household supplies, and Jims went to Dreamland. Rilla put on her georgette gown, knotted up her hair and bound a little double string of pearls around it. Then she tucked a cluster of pale pink baby roses at her belt. Would Ken ask her for a rose for a keepsake? She knew that Jem had carried to the trenches in Flanders a faded rose that Faith Meredith had kissed and given him the night before he left.

Rilla looked very sweet when she met Ken in the mingled moonlight and vine shadows of the big veranda. The hand she gave him was cold and she was so desperately anxious not to lisp that her greeting was prim and precise. How handsome and tall Kenneth looked in his lieutenant's uniform! It made him seem older, too—so much so that Rilla felt rather foolish. Hadn't it been the height of absurdity for her to suppose that this splendid young officer had anything special to say to her, little Rilla Blythe of Glen St. Mary? Likely she hadn't understood him after all—he had only meant that he didn't want a mob of folks around making a fuss over him and trying to lionize him, as they had probably done over-harbour. Yes, of course, that was all he meant—and she, little idiot, had gone and vainly imagined that he didn't want anybody but her. And he would think she had manoeuvred everybody away so that they could be alone together, and he would laugh to himself at her.

"This is better luck than I hoped for," said Ken, leaning back in his chair and looking at her with very unconcealed admiration in his eloquent eyes. "I was sure someone would be hanging about and it was just you I wanted to see, Rilla-my-Rilla."

Rilla's dream castle flashed into the landscape again. This was unmistakable enough certainly—not much doubt as to his meaning here.

"There aren't—so many of us—to poke around as there used to be," she said softly.

"No, that's so," said Ken gently. "Jem and Walter and the girls away—it makes a big blank, doesn't it? But—" he leaned forward until his dark curls almost brushed her hair—"doesn't Fred Arnold try to fill the blank occasionally. I've been told so."

At this moment, before Rilla could make any reply, Jims began to cry at the top of his voice in the room whose open window was just above them—Jims, who hardly ever cried in the evening. Moreover, he was crying, as Rilla knew from experience, with a vim and energy that betokened that he had been already whimpering softly unheard for some time and was thoroughly exasperated. When Jims started in crying like that he made a thorough job of it. Rilla knew that there was no use to sit still and pretend to ignore him. He wouldn't stop; and conversation of any kind was out of the question when such shrieks and howls were floating over your head. Besides, she was afraid Kenneth would think she was utterly unfeeling if she sat still and let a baby cry like that. He was not likely acquainted with Morgan's invaluable volume.

She got up. "Jims has had a nightmare, I think. He sometimes has one and he is always badly frightened by it. Excuse me for a moment."

Rilla flew upstairs, wishing quite frankly that soup tureens had never been invented. But when Jims, at sight of her, lifted his little arms entreatingly and swallowed several sobs, with tears rolling down his cheeks, resentment went out of her heart. After all, the poor darling was frightened. She picked him up gently and rocked him soothingly until his sobs ceased and his eyes closed. Then she essayed to lay him down in his crib. Jims opened his eyes and shrieked a protest. This performance was repeated twice. Rilla grew desperate. She couldn't leave Ken down there alone any longer—she had been away nearly half an hour already. With a resigned air she marched downstairs, carrying Jims, and sat down on the veranda. It was, no doubt, a ridiculous thing to sit and cuddle a contrary war-baby when your best young man was making his farewell call, but there was nothing else to be done.

Jims was supremely happy. He kicked his little pink-soled feet rapturously out under his white nighty and gave one of his rare laughs. He was beginning to be a very pretty baby; his golden hair curled in silken ringlets all over his little round head and his eyes were beautiful.

"He's a decorative kiddy all right, isn't he?" said Ken.

"His looks are very well," said Rilla, bitterly, as if to imply that they were much the best of him. Jims, being an astute infant, sensed trouble in the atmosphere and realized that it was up to him to clear it away. He turned his face up to Rilla, smiled adorably and said, clearly and beguilingly, "Will—Will."

It was the very first time he had spoken a word or tried to speak. Rilla was so delighted that she forgot her grudge against him. She forgave him with a hug and kiss. Jims, understanding that he was restored to favour, cuddled down against her just where a gleam of light from the lamp in the living-room struck across his hair and turned it into a halo of gold against her breast.

Kenneth sat very still and silent, looking at Rilla—at the delicate, girlish silhouette of her, her long lashes, her dented lip, her adorable chin. In the dim moonlight, as she sat with her head bent a little over Jims, the lamplight glinting on her pearls until they glistened like a slender nimbus, he thought she looked exactly like the Madonna that hung over his mother's desk at home. He carried that picture of her in his heart to the horror of the battlefields of France. He had had a strong fancy for Rilla Blythe ever since the night of the Four Winds dance; but it was when he saw her there, with little Jims in her arms, that he loved her and realized it. And all the while, poor Rilla was sitting, disappointed and humiliated, feeling that her last evening with Ken was spoiled and wondering why things always had to go so contrarily outside of books. She felt too absurd to try to talk. Evidently Ken was completely disgusted, too, since he was sitting there in such stony silence.

Hope revived momentarily when Jims went so thoroughly asleep that she thought it would be safe to lay him down on the couch in the living-room. But when she came out again Susan was sitting on the veranda, loosening her bonnet strings with the air of one who meant to stay where she was for some time.

"Have you got your baby to sleep?" she asked kindly.

Your baby! Really, Susan might have more tact.

"Yes," said Rilla shortly.

Susan laid her parcels on the reed table, as one determined to do her duty. She was very tired but she must help Rilla out. Here was Kenneth Ford who had come to call on the family and they were all unfortunately out, and "the poor child" had had to entertain him alone. But Susan had come to her rescue—Susan would do her part no matter how tired she was.

"Dear me, how you have grown up," she said, looking at Ken's six feet of khaki uniform without the least awe. Susan had grown used to khaki now, and at sixty-four even a lieutenant's uniform is just clothes and nothing else. "It is an amazing thing how fast children do grow up. Rilla here, now, is almost fifteen."

"I'm going on seventeen, Susan," cried Rilla almost passionately. She was a whole month past sixteen. It was intolerable of Susan.

"It seems just the other day that you were all babies," said Susan, ignoring Rilla's protest. "You were really the prettiest baby I ever saw, Ken, though your mother had an awful time trying to cure you of sucking your thumb. Do you remember the day I spanked you?"

"No," said Ken.

"Oh well, I suppose you would be too young—you were only about four and you were here with your mother and you insisted on teasing Nan until she cried. I had tried several ways of stopping you but none availed, and I saw that a spanking was the only thing that would serve. So I picked you up and laid you across my knee and lambasted you well. You howled at the top of your voice but you left Nan alone after that."

Rilla was writhing. Hadn't Susan any realization that she was addressing an officer of the Canadian Army? Apparently she had not. Oh, what would Ken think? "I suppose you do not remember the time your mother spanked you either," continued Susan, who seemed to be bent on reviving tender reminiscences that evening. "I shall never, no never, forget it. She was up here one night with you when you were about three, and you and Walter were playing out in the kitchen yard with a kitten. I had a big puncheon of rainwater by the spout which I was reserving for making soap. And you and Walter began quarrelling over the kitten. Walter was at one side of the puncheon standing on a chair, holding the kitten, and you were standing on a chair at the other side. You leaned across that puncheon and grabbed the kitten and pulled. You were always a great hand for taking what you wanted without too much ceremony. Walter held on tight and the poor kitten yelled but you dragged Walter and the kitten half over and then you both lost your balance and tumbled into that puncheon, kitten and all. If I had not been on the spot you would both have been drowned. I flew to the rescue and hauled you all three out before much harm was done, and your mother, who had seen it all from the upstairs window, came down and picked you up, dripping as you were, and gave you a beautiful spanking. Ah," said Susan with a sigh, "those were happy old days at Ingleside."

"Must have been," said Ken. His voice sounded queer and stiff. Rilla supposed he was hopelessly enraged. The truth was he dared not trust his voice lest it betray his frantic desire to laugh.

"Rilla here, now," said Susan, looking affectionately at that unhappy damsel, "never was much spanked. She was a real well-behaved child for the most part. But her father did spank her once. She got two bottles of pills out of his office and dared Alice Clow to see which of them could swallow all the pills first, and if her father had not happened in the nick of time those two children would have been corpses by night. As it was, they were both sick enough shortly after. But the doctor spanked Rilla then and there and he made such a thorough job of it that she never meddled with anything in his office afterwards. We hear a great deal nowadays of something that is called 'moral persuasion,' but in my opinion a good spanking and no nagging afterwards is a much better thing."

Rilla wondered viciously whether Susan meant to relate all the family spankings. But Susan had finished with the subject and branched off to another cheerful one.

"I remember little Tod MacAllister over-harbour killed himself that very way, eating up a whole box of fruitatives because he thought they were candy. It was a very sad affair. He was," said Susan earnestly, "the very cutest little corpse I ever laid my eyes on. It was very careless of his mother to leave the fruitatives where he could get them, but she was well-known to be a heedless creature. One day she found a nest of five eggs as she was going across the fields to church with a brand new blue silk dress on. So she put them in the pocket of her petticoat and when she got to church she forgot all about them and sat down on them and her dress was ruined, not to speak of the petticoat. Let me see—would not Tod be some relation of yours? Your great grandmother West was a MacAllister. Her brother Amos was a MacDonaldite in religion. I am told he used to take the jerks something fearful. But you look more like your great grandfather West than the MacAllisters. He died of a paralytic stroke quite early in life."

"Did you see anybody at the store?" asked Rilla desperately, in the faint hope of directing Susan's conversation into more agreeable channels.

"Nobody except Mary Vance," said Susan, "and she was stepping round as brisk as the Irishman's flea."

What terrible similes Susan used! Would Kenneth think she acquired them from the family!

"To hear Mary talk about Miller Douglas you would think he was the only Glen boy who had enlisted," Susan went on. "But of course she always did brag and she has some good qualities I am willing to admit, though I did not think so that time she chased Rilla here through the village with a dried codfish till the poor child fell, heels over head, into the puddle before Carter Flagg's store."

Rilla went cold all over with wrath and shame. Were there any more disgraceful scenes in her past that Susan could rake up? As for Ken, he could have howled over Susan's speeches, but he would not so insult the duenna of his lady, so he sat with a preternaturally solemn face which seemed to poor Rilla a haughty and offended one.

"I paid eleven cents for a bottle of ink tonight," complained Susan. "Ink is twice as high as it was last year. Perhaps it is because Woodrow Wilson has been writing so many notes. It must cost him considerable. My cousin Sophia says Woodrow Wilson is not the man she expected him to be—but then no man ever was. Being an old maid, I do not know much about men and have never pretended to, but my cousin Sophia is very hard on them, although she married two of them, which you might think was a fair share. Albert Crawford's chimney blew down in that big gale we had last week, and when Sophia heard the bricks clattering on the roof she thought it was a Zeppelin raid and went into hysterics. And Mrs. Albert Crawford says that of the two things she would have preferred the Zeppelin raid."

Rilla sat limply in her chair like one hypnotized. She knew Susan would stop talking when she was ready to stop and that no earthly power could make her stop any sooner. As a rule, she was very fond of Susan but just now she hated her with a deadly hatred. It was ten o'clock. Ken would soon have to go—the others would soon be home—and she had not even had a chance to explain to Ken that Fred Arnold filled no blank in her life nor ever could. Her rainbow castle lay in ruins round her.

Kenneth got up at last. He realized that Susan was there to stay as long as he did, and it was a three mile walk to Martin West's over-harbour. He wondered if Rilla had put Susan up to this, not wanting to be left alone with him, lest he say something Fred Arnold's sweetheart did not want to hear. Rilla got up, too, and walked silently the length of the veranda with him. They stood there for a moment, Ken on the lower step. The step was half sunk into the earth and mint grew thickly about and over its edge. Often crushed by so many passing feet it gave out its essence freely, and the spicy odour hung round them like a soundless, invisible benediction. Ken looked up at Rilla, whose hair was shining in the moonlight and whose eyes were pools of allurement. All at once he felt sure there was nothing in that gossip about Fred Arnold.

"Rilla," he said in a sudden, intense whisper, "you are the sweetest thing."

Rilla flushed and looked at Susan. Ken looked, too, and saw that Susan's back was turned. He put his arm about Rilla and kissed her. It was the first time Rilla had ever been kissed. She thought perhaps she ought to resent it but she didn't. Instead, she glanced timidly into Kenneth's seeking eyes and her glance was a kiss.

"Rilla-my-Rilla," said Ken, "will you promise that you won't let anyone else kiss you until I come back?"

"Yes," said Rilla, trembling and thrilling.

Susan was turning round. Ken loosened his hold and stepped to the walk.

"Good-bye," he said casually. Rilla heard herself saying it just as casually. She stood and watched him down the walk, out of the gate, and down the road. When the fir wood hid him from her sight she suddenly said "Oh," in a choked way and ran down to the gate, sweet blossomy things catching at her skirts as she ran. Leaning over the gate she saw Kenneth walking briskly down the road, over the bars of tree shadows and moonlight, his tall, erect figure grey in the white radiance. As he reached the turn he stopped and looked back and saw her standing amid the tall white lilies by the gate. He waved his hand—she waved hers—he was gone around the turn.

Rilla stood there for a little while, gazing across the fields of mist and silver. She had heard her mother say that she loved turns in roads—they were so provocative and alluring. Rilla thought she hated them. She had seen Jem and Jerry vanish from her around a bend in the road

—then Walter—and now Ken. Brothers and playmate and sweetheart—they were all gone, never, it might be, to return. Yet still the Piper piped and the dance of death went on.

When Rilla walked slowly back to the house Susan was still sitting by the veranda table and Susan was sniffing suspiciously.

"I have been thinking, Rilla dear, of the old days in the House of Dreams, when Kenneth's mother and father were courting and Jem was a little baby and you were not born or thought of. It was a very romantic affair and she and your mother were such chums. To think I should have lived to see her son going to the front. As if she had not had enough trouble in her early life without this coming upon her! But we must take a brace and see it through."

All Rilla's anger against Susan had evaporated. With Ken's kiss still burning on her lips, and the wonderful significance of the promise he had asked thrilling heart and soul, she could not be angry with anyone. She put her slim white hand into Susan's brown, work-hardened one and gave it a squeeze. Susan was a faithful old dear and would lay down her life for any one of them.

"You are tired, Rilla dear, and had better go to bed," Susan said, patting her hand. "I noticed you were too tired to talk tonight. I am glad I came home in time to help you out. It is very tiresome trying to entertain young men when you are not accustomed to it."

Rilla carried Jims upstairs and went to bed, but not before she had sat for a long time at her window reconstructing her rainbow castle, with several added domes and turrets.

"I wonder," she said to herself, "if I am, or am not, engaged to Kenneth Ford."

17. THE WEEKS WEAR BY

Rilla read her first love letter in her Rainbow Valley fir-shadowed nook, and a girl's first love letter, whatever blase, older people may think of it, is an event of tremendous importance in the teens. After Kenneth's regiment had left Kingsport there came a fortnight of dully-aching anxiety and when the congregation sang in Church on Sunday evenings,

"Oh, hear us when we cry to Thee
For those in peril on the sea,"

Rilla's voice always failed her; for with the words came a horribly vivid mind picture of a submarined ship sinking beneath pitiless waves amid the struggles and cries of drowning men. Then word came that Kenneth's regiment had arrived safely in England; and now, at last, here was his letter. It began with something that made Rilla supremely happy for the moment and ended with a paragraph that crimsoned her cheeks with the wonder and thrill and delight of it. Between beginning and ending the letter was just such a jolly, newsy epistle as Ken might have written to anyone; but for the sake of that beginning and ending Rilla slept with the letter under her pillow for weeks, sometimes waking in the night to slip her fingers under and just touch it, and looked with secret pity on other girls whose sweethearts could never have written them anything half so wonderful and exquisite. Kenneth was not the son of a famous novelist for nothing. He "had a way" of expressing things in a few poignant, significant words that seemed to suggest far more than they uttered, and never grew stale or flat or foolish with ever so many scores of readings. Rilla went home from Rainbow Valley as if she flew rather than walked.

But such moments of uplift were rare that autumn. To be sure, there was one day in September when great news came of a big Allied victory in the west and Susan ran out to hoist the flag—the first time she had hoisted it since the Russian line broke and the last time she was to hoist it for many dismal moons.

"Likely the Big Push has begun at last, Mrs. Dr. dear," she exclaimed, "and we will soon see the finish of the Huns. Our boys will be home by Christmas now. Hurrah!"

Susan was ashamed of herself for hurrahing the minute she had done it, and apologized meekly for such an outburst of juvenility. "But indeed, Mrs. Dr. dear, this good news has gone to my head after this awful summer of Russian slumps and Gallipoli setbacks."

"Good news!" said Miss Oliver bitterly. "I wonder if the women whose men have been killed for it will call it good news. Just because our own men are not on that part of the front we are rejoicing as if the victory had cost no lives."

"Now, Miss Oliver dear, do not take that view of it," deprecated Susan. "We have not had much to rejoice over of late and yet men were being killed just the same. Do not let yourself slump like poor Cousin Sophia. She said, when the word came, 'Ah, it is nothing but a rift in the clouds. We are up this week but we will be down the next.' 'Well, Sophia Crawford,' said I, —for I will never give in to her, Mrs. Dr. dear—'God himself cannot make two hills without a hollow between them, as I have heard it said, but that is no reason why we should not take the good of the hills when we are on them.' But Cousin Sophia moaned on. 'Here is the Gallipolly expedition a failure and the Grand Duke Nicholas sent off, and everyone knows the Czar of Rooshia is a pro-German and the Allies have no ammunition and Bulgaria is going against us. And the end is not yet, for England and France must be punished for their deadly sins until they repent in sackcloth and ashes.' 'I think myself,' I said, 'that they will do their repenting in khaki and trench mud, and it seems to me that the Huns should have a few sins to repent of also.' 'They are instruments in the hands of the Almighty, to purge the garner,' said Sophia. And then I got mad, Mrs. Dr. dear, and told her I did not and never would believe that the Almighty ever took such dirty instruments in hand for any purpose whatever, and that I did not consider it decent for her to be using the words of Holy Writ as glibly as she was doing in ordinary conversation. She was not, I told her, a minister or even an elder. And for the time being I squelched her, Mrs. Dr. dear. Cousin Sophia has no spirit. She is very different from her niece, Mrs. Dean Crawford over-harbour. You know the Dean Crawfords had five boys and now the new baby is another boy. All the connection and especially Dean Crawford were much disappointed because their hearts had been set on a girl; but Mrs. Dean just laughed and said, 'Everywhere I went this summer I saw the sign "MEN WANTED" staring me in the face. Do you think I could go and have a girl under such circumstances?' There is spirit for you, Mrs. Dr. dear. But Cousin Sophia would say the child was just so much more cannon fodder."

Cousin Sophia had full range for her pessimism that gloomy autumn, and even Susan, incorrigible old optimist as she was, was hard put to it for cheer. When Bulgaria lined up with Germany Susan only remarked scornfully, "One more nation anxious for a licking," but the Greek tangle worried her beyond her powers of philosophy to endure calmly.

"Constantine of Greece has a German wife, Mrs. Dr. dear, and that fact squelches hope. To think that I should have lived to care what kind of a wife Constantine of Greece had! The miserable creature is under his wife's thumb and that is a bad place for any man to be. I am an old maid and an old maid has to be independent or she will be squashed out. But if I had been a married woman, Mrs. Dr. dear, I would have been meek and humble. It is my opinion that this Sophia of Greece is a minx."

Susan was furious when the news came that Venizelos had met with defeat. "I could spank Constantine and skin him alive afterwards, that I could," she exclaimed bitterly.

"Oh, Susan, I'm surprised at you," said the doctor, pulling a long face. "Have you no regard for the proprieties? Skin him alive by all means but omit the spanking."

"If he had been well spanked in his younger days he might have more sense now," retorted Susan. "But I suppose princes are never spanked, more is the pity. I see the Allies have sent him an ultimatum. I could tell them that it will take more than ultimatums to skin a snake like Constantine. Perhaps the Allied blockade will hammer sense into his head; but that will take some time I am thinking, and in the meantime what is to become of poor Serbia?"

They saw what became of Serbia, and during the process Susan was hardly to be lived with. In her exasperation she abused everything and everybody except Kitchener, and she fell upon poor President Wilson tooth and claw.

"If he had done his duty and gone into the war long ago we should not have seen this mess in Serbia," she avowed.

"It would be a serious thing to plunge a great country like the United States, with its mixed population, into the war, Susan," said the doctor, who sometimes came to the defence of the President, not because he thought Wilson needed it especially, but from an unholy love of baiting Susan.

"Maybe, doctor dear—maybe! But that makes me think of the old story of the girl who told her grandmother she was going to be married. 'It is a solemn thing to be married,' said the old lady. 'Yes, but it is a solemner thing not to be,' said the girl. And I can testify to that out of my own experience, doctor dear. And I think it is a solemner thing for the Yankees that they have kept out of the war than it would have been if they had gone into it. However, though I do not know much about them, I am of the opinion that we will see them starting something yet, Woodrow Wilson or no Woodrow Wilson, when they get it into their heads that this war is not a correspondence school. They will not," said Susan, energetically waving a saucepan with one hand and a soup ladle with the other, "be too proud to fight then."

On a pale-yellow, windy evening in October Carl Meredith went away. He had enlisted on his eighteenth birthday. John Meredith saw him off with a set face. His two boys were gone—there was only little Bruce left now. He loved Bruce and Bruce's mother dearly; but Jerry and Carl were the sons of the bride of his youth and Carl was the only one of all his children who had Cecilia's very eyes. As they looked lovingly out at him above Carl's uniform the pale minister suddenly remembered the day when for the first and last time he had tried to whip Carl for his prank with the eel. That was the first time he had realised how much Carl's eyes were like Cecilia's. Now he realised it again once more. Would he ever again see his dead wife's eyes looking at him from his son's face? What a bonny, clean, handsome lad he was! It was—hard—to see him go. John Meredith seemed to be looking at a torn plain strewed with the bodies of "able-bodied men between the ages of eighteen and forty-five." Only the other day Carl had been a little scrap of a boy, hunting bugs in Rainbow Valley, taking lizards to bed with him, and scandalizing the Glen by carrying frogs to Sunday School. It seemed hardly—right—somehow that he should be an "able-bodied man" in khaki. Yet John Meredith had said no word to dissuade him when Carl had told him he must go.

Rilla felt Carl's going keenly. They had always been cronies and playmates. He was only a little older than she was and they had been children in Rainbow Valley together. She recalled all their old pranks and escapades as she walked slowly home alone. The full moon peeped through the scudding clouds with sudden floods of weird illumination, the telephone wires sang a shrill weird song in the wind, and the tall spikes of withered, grey-headed golden-rod in the fence corners swayed and beckoned wildly to her like groups of old witches weaving unholy spells. On such a night as this, long ago, Carl would come over to Ingleside and whistle her out to the gate. "Let's go on a moon-spree, Rilla," he would say, and the two of them would scamper off to Rainbow Valley. Rilla had never been afraid of his beetles and bugs, though she drew a hard and fast line at snakes. They used to talk together of almost everything and were teased about each other at school; but one evening when they were about ten years of age they had solemnly promised, by the old spring in Rainbow Valley, that they would never marry each other. Alice Clow had "crossed out" their names on her slate in school that day, and it came out that "both married." They did not like the idea at all, hence the mutual vow in Rainbow Valley. There was nothing like an ounce of prevention. Rilla laughed over the old memory—and then sighed. That very day a dispatch from some London paper had contained the cheerful announcement that "the present moment is the darkest since the war began." It was dark enough, and Rilla wished desperately that she could do something besides waiting and serving at home, as day after day the Glen boys she had known went away. If she were only a boy, speeding in khaki by Carl's side to the Western front! She had wished that in a burst of romance when Jem had gone, without, perhaps, really meaning it. She meant it now. There were moments when waiting at home, in safety and comfort, seemed an unendurable thing.

The moon burst triumphantly through an especially dark cloud and shadow and silver chased each other in waves over the Glen. Rilla remembered one moonlit evening of childhood when she had said to her mother, "The moon just looks like a sorry, sorry face." She thought it looked like that still—an agonised, care-worn face, as though it looked down on dreadful sights. What did it see on the Western front? In broken Serbia? On shell-swept Gallipoli?

"I am tired," Miss Oliver had said that day, in a rare outburst of impatience, "of this horrible rack of strained emotions, when every day brings a new horror or the dread of it. No, don't look reproachfully at me, Mrs. Blythe. There's nothing heroic about me today. I've slumped. I wish England had left Belgium to her fate—I wish Canada had never sent a man—I wish we'd tied our boys to our apron strings and not let one of them go. Oh—I shall be ashamed of myself in half an hour—but at this very minute I mean every word of it. Will the Allies never strike?"

"Patience is a tired mare but she jogs on," said Susan.

"While the steeds of Armageddon thunder, trampling over our hearts," retorted Miss Oliver. "Susan, tell me—don't you ever—didn't you ever—take spells of feeling that you must scream—or swear—or smash something—just because your torture reaches a point when it becomes unbearable?"

"I have never sworn or desired to swear, Miss Oliver dear, but I will admit," said Susan, with the air of one determined to make a clean breast of it once and for all, "that I have experienced occasions when it was a relief to do considerable banging."

"Don't you think that is a kind of swearing, Susan? What is the difference between slamming a door viciously and saying d——"

"Miss Oliver dear," interrupted Susan, desperately determined to save Gertrude from herself, if human power could do it, "you are all tired out and unstrung—and no wonder, teaching those obstreperous youngsters all day and coming home to bad war news. But just you go upstairs and lie down and I will bring you up a cup of hot tea and a bite of toast and very soon you will not want to slam doors or swear."

"Susan, you're a good soul—a very pearl of Susans! But, Susan, it would be such a relief—to say just one soft, low, little tiny d—-"

"I will bring you a hot-water bottle for the soles of your feet, also," interposed Susan resolutely, "and it would not be any relief to say that word you are thinking of, Miss Oliver, and that you may tie to."

"Well, I'll try the hot-water bottle first," said Miss Oliver, repenting herself on teasing Susan and vanishing upstairs, to Susan's intense relief. Susan shook her head ominously as she filled the hot-water bottle. The war was certainly relaxing the standards of behaviour woefully. Here was Miss Oliver admittedly on the point of profanity.

"We must draw the blood from her brain," said Susan, "and if this bottle is not effective I will see what can be done with a mustard plaster."

Gertrude rallied and carried on. Lord Kitchener went to Greece, whereat Susan foretold that Constantine would soon experience a change of heart. Lloyd George began to heckle the Allies regarding equipment and guns and Susan said you would hear more of Lloyd George yet. The gallant Anzacs withdrew from Gallipoli and Susan approved the step, with reservations. The siege of Kut-El-Amara began and Susan pored over maps of Mesopotamia and abused the Turks. Henry Ford started for Europe and Susan flayed him with sarcasm. Sir John French was superseded by Sir Douglas Haig and Susan dubiously opined that it was poor policy to swap horses crossing a stream, "though, to be sure, Haig was a good name and French had a foreign sound, say what you might." Not a move on the great chess-board of king or bishop or pawn escaped Susan, who had once read only Glen St. Mary notes. "There was a time," she said sorrowfully, "when I did not care what happened outside of P.E. Island, and now a king cannot have a toothache in Russia or China but it worries me. It may be broadening to the mind, as the doctor said, but it is very painful to the feelings."

When Christmas came again Susan did not set any vacant places at the festive board. Two empty chairs were too much even for Susan who had thought in September that there would not be one.

"This is the first Christmas that Walter was not home," Rilla wrote in her diary that night. "Jem used to be away for Christmases up in Avonlea, but Walter never was. I had letters from Ken and him today. They are still in England but expect to be in the trenches very soon. And then—but I suppose we'll be able to endure it somehow. To me, the strangest of all the strange things since 1914 is how we have all learned to accept things we never thought we could—to go on with life as a matter of course. I know that Jem and Jerry are in the trenches—that Ken and Walter will be soon—that if one of them does not come back my heart will break—yet I go on and work and plan—yes, and even enjoy life by times. There are moments when we have real fun because, just for the moment, we don't think about things and then—we remember—and the remembering is worse than thinking of it all the time would have been.

"Today was dark and cloudy and tonight is wild enough, as Gertrude says, to please any novelist in search of suitable matter for a murder or elopement. The raindrops streaming over the panes look like tears running down a face, and the wind is shrieking through the maple grove.

"This hasn't been a nice Christmas Day in any way. Nan had toothache and Susan had red eyes, and assumed a weird and gruesome flippancy of manner to deceive us into thinking she hadn't; and Jims had a bad cold all day and I'm afraid of croup. He has had croup twice since October. The first time I was nearly frightened to death, for father and mother were both away—father always is away, it seems to me, when any of this household gets sick. But Susan was cool as a fish and knew just what to do, and by morning Jims was all right. That child is a cross between a duck and an imp. He's a year and four months old, trots about everywhere, and says quite a few words. He has the cutest little way of calling me "Willa-will." It always brings back that dreadful, ridiculous, delightful night when Ken came to say good-bye, and I was so furious and happy. Jims is pink and white and big-eyed and curly-haired and every now and then I discover a new dimple in him. I can never quite believe he is really the same creature as that scrawny, yellow, ugly little changeling I brought home in the soup tureen. Nobody has ever heard a word from Jim Anderson. If he never comes back I shall keep Jims always. Everybody here worships and spoils him—or would spoil him if Morgan and I didn't stand remorselessly in the way. Susan says Jims is the cleverest child she ever saw and can recognize Old Nick when he sees him—this because Jims threw poor Doc out of an upstairs window one day. Doc turned into Mr. Hyde on his way down and landed in a currant bush, spitting and swearing. I tried to console his inner cat with a saucer of milk but he would have none of it, and remained Mr. Hyde the rest of the day. Jims's latest exploit was to paint the cushion of the big arm-chair in the sun parlour with molasses; and before anybody found it out Mrs. Fred Clow came in on Red Cross business and sat down on it. Her new silk dress was ruined and nobody could blame her for being vexed. But she went into one of her tempers and said nasty things and gave me such slams about 'spoiling' Jims that I nearly boiled over, too. But I kept the lid on till she had waddled away and then I exploded.

"'The fat, clumsy, horrid old thing,' I said—and oh, what a satisfaction it was to say it.

"'She has three sons at the front,' mother said rebukingly.

"'I suppose that covers all her shortcomings in manners,' I retorted. But I was ashamed—for it is true that all her boys have gone and she was very plucky and loyal about it too; and she is a perfect tower of strength in the Red Cross. It's a little hard to remember all the heroines. Just the same, it was her second new silk dress in one year and that when everybody is—or should be—trying to 'save and serve.'

"I had to bring out my green velvet hat again lately and begin wearing it. I hung on to my blue straw sailor as long as I could. How I hate the green velvet hat! It is so elaborate and conspicuous. I don't see how I could ever have liked it. But I vowed to wear it and wear it I will.

"Shirley and I went down to the station this morning to take Little Dog Monday a bang-up Christmas dinner. Dog Monday waits and watches there still, with just as much hope and confidence as ever. Sometimes he hangs around the station house and talks to people and the rest of his time he sits at his little kennel door and watches the track unwinkingly. We never try to coax him home now: we know it is of no use. When Jem comes back, Monday will come home with him; and if Jem—never comes back—Monday will wait there for him as long as his dear dog heart goes on beating.

"Fred Arnold was here last night. He was eighteen in November and is going to enlist just as soon as his mother is over an operation she has to have. He has been coming here very often lately and though I like him so much it makes me uncomfortable, because I am afraid he is thinking that perhaps I could care something for him. I can't tell him about Ken—because, after all, what is there to tell? And yet I don't like to behave coldly and distantly when he will be going away so soon. It is very perplexing. I remember I used to think it would be such fun to have dozens of beaux—and now I'm worried to death because two are too many.

"I am learning to cook. Susan is teaching me. I tried to learn long ago—but no, let me be honest—Susan tried to teach me, which is a very different thing. I never seemed to succeed with anything and I got discouraged. But since the boys have gone away I wanted to be able to make cake and things for them myself and so I started in again and this time I'm getting on surprisingly well. Susan says it is all in the way I hold my mouth and father says my subconscious mind is desirous of learning now, and I dare say they're both right. Anyhow, I can make dandy short-bread and fruitcake. I got ambitious last week and attempted cream puffs, but made an awful failure of them. They came out of the oven flat as flukes. I thought maybe the cream would fill them up again and make them plump but it didn't. I think Susan was secretly pleased. She is past mistress in the art of making cream puffs and it would break her heart if anyone else here could make them as well. I wonder if Susan tampered—but no, I won't suspect her of such a thing.

"Miranda Pryor spent an afternoon here a few days ago, helping me cut out certain Red Cross garments known by the charming name of 'vermin shirts.' Susan thinks that name is not quite decent, so I suggested she call them 'cootie sarks,' which is old Highland Sandy's version of it. But she shook her head and I heard her telling mother later that, in her opinion, 'cooties' and 'sarks' were not proper subjects for young girls to talk about. She was especially horrified when Jem wrote in his last letter to mother, 'Tell Susan I had a fine cootie hunt this morning and caught fifty-three!' Susan positively turned pea-green. 'Mrs. Dr. dear,' she said, 'when I was young, if decent people were so unfortunate as to get—those insects—they kept it a secret if possible. I do not want to be narrow-minded, Mrs. Dr. dear, but I still think it is better not to mention such things.'

"Miranda grew confidential over our vermin shirts and told me all her troubles. She is desperately unhappy. She is engaged to Joe Milgrave and Joe joined up in October and has been training in Charlottetown ever since. Her father was furious when he joined and forbade Miranda ever to have any dealing or communication with him again. Poor Joe expects to go overseas any day and wants Miranda to marry him before he goes, which shows that there have been 'communications' in spite of Whiskers-on-the-moon. Miranda wants to marry him but cannot, and she declares it will break her heart.

"'Why don't you run away and marry him?' I said. It didn't go against my conscience in the least to give her such advice. Joe Milgrave is a splendid fellow and Mr. Pryor fairly beamed on him until the war broke out and I know Mr. Pryor would forgive Miranda very quickly, once it was over and he wanted his housekeeper back. But Miranda shook her silvery head dolefully.

"'Joe wants me to but I can't. Mother's last words to me, as she lay on her dying-bed, were, "Never, never run away, Miranda," and I promised.'

"Miranda's mother died two years ago, and it seems, according to Miranda, that her mother and father actually ran away to be married themselves. To picture Whiskers-on-the-moon as the hero of an elopement is beyond my power. But such was the case and Mrs. Pryor at least lived to repent it. She had a hard life of it with Mr. Pryor, and she thought it was a punishment on her for running away. So she made Miranda promise she would never, for any reason whatever, do it.

"Of course, you cannot urge a girl to break a promise made to a dying mother, so I did not see what Miranda could do unless she got Joe to come to the house when her father was away and marry her there. But Miranda said that couldn't be managed. Her father seemed to suspect she might be up to something of the sort and he never went away for long at a time, and, of course, Joe couldn't get leave of absence at an hour's notice.

"'No, I shall just have to let Joe go, and he will be killed—I know he will be killed—and my heart will break,' said Miranda, her tears running down and copiously bedewing the vermin shirts!

"I am not writing like this for lack of any real sympathy with poor Miranda. I've just got into the habit of giving things a comical twist if I can, when I'm writing to Jem and Walter and Ken, to make them laugh. I really felt sorry for Miranda who is as much in love with Joe as a china-blue girl can be with anyone and who is dreadfully ashamed of her father's pro-German sentiments. I think she understood that I did, for she said she had wanted to tell me all about her worries because I had grown so sympathetic this past year. I wonder if I have. I know I used to be a selfish, thoughtless creature—how selfish and thoughtless I am ashamed to remember now, so I can't be quite so bad as I was.

"I wish I could help Miranda. It would be very romantic to contrive a war-wedding and I should dearly love to get the better of Whiskers-on-the-moon. But at present the oracle has not spoken."

18. A WAR-WEDDING

"I can tell you this Dr. dear," said Susan, pale with wrath, "that Germany is getting to be perfectly ridiculous."

They were all in the big Ingleside kitchen. Susan was mixing biscuits for supper. Mrs. Blythe was making shortbread for Jem, and Rilla was compounding candy for Ken and Walter—it had once been "Walter and Ken" in her thoughts but somehow, quite unconsciously, this had changed until Ken's name came naturally first. Cousin Sophia was also there, knitting. All the boys were going to be killed in the long run, so Cousin Sophia felt in her bones, but they might better die with warm feet than cold ones, so Cousin Sophia knitted faithfully and gloomily.

Into this peaceful scene erupted the doctor, wrathful and excited over the burning of the Parliament Buildings in Ottawa. And Susan became automatically quite as wrathful and excited.

"What will those Huns do next?" she demanded. "Coming over here and burning our Parliament building! Did anyone ever hear of such an outrage?"

"We don't know that the Germans are responsible for this," said the doctor—much as if he felt quite sure they were. "Fires do start without their agency sometimes. And Uncle Mark MacAllister's barn was burnt last week. You can hardly accuse the Germans of that, Susan."

"Indeed, Dr. dear, I do not know." Susan nodded slowly and portentously. "Whiskers-on-the-moon was there that very day. The fire broke out half an hour after he was gone. So much is a fact—but I shall not accuse a Presbyterian elder of burning anybody's barn until I have proof. However, everybody knows, Dr. dear, that both Uncle Mark's boys have enlisted, and that Uncle Mark himself makes speeches at all the recruiting meetings. So no doubt Germany is anxious to get square with him."

"I could never speak at a recruiting meeting," said Cousin Sophia solemnly. "I could never reconcile it to my conscience to ask another woman's son to go, to murder and be murdered."

"Could you not?" said Susan. "Well, Sophia Crawford, I felt as if I could ask anyone to go when I read last night that there were no children under eight years of age left alive in Poland. Think of that, Sophia Crawford"—Susan shook a floury finger at Sophia—"not—one—child—under—eight—years—of—age!"

"I suppose the Germans has et 'em all," sighed Cousin Sophia.

"Well, no-o-o," said Susan reluctantly, as if she hated to admit that there was any crime the Huns couldn't be accused of. "The Germans have not turned cannibal yet—as far as I know. They have died of starvation and exposure, the poor little creatures. There is murdering for you, Cousin Sophia Crawford. The thought of it poisons every bite and sup I take."

"I see that Fred Carson of Lowbridge has been awarded a Distinguished Conduct Medal," remarked the doctor, over his local paper.

"I heard that last week," said Susan. "He is a battalion runner and he did something extra brave and daring. His letter, telling his folks about it, came when his old Grandmother Carson was on her dying-bed. She had only a few minutes more to live and the Episcopal minister, who was there, asked her if she would not like him to pray. 'Oh yes, yes, you can pray,' she said impatient-like—she was a Dean, Dr. dear, and the Deans were always high-spirited—'you can pray, but for pity's sake pray low and don't disturb me. I want to think over this splendid news and I have not much time left to do it.' That was Almira Carson all over. Fred was the apple of her eye. She was seventy-five years of age and had not a grey hair in her head, they tell me."

"By the way, that reminds me—I found a grey hair this morning—my very first," said Mrs. Blythe.

"I have noticed that grey hair for some time, Mrs. Dr. dear, but I did not speak of it. Thought

I to myself, 'She has enough to bear.' But now that you have discovered it let me remind you that grey hairs are honourable."

"I must be getting old, Gilbert." Mrs. Blythe laughed a trifle ruefully. "People are beginning to tell me I look so young. They never tell you that when you are young. But I shall not worry over my silver thread. I never liked red hair. Gilbert, did I ever tell you of that time, years ago at Green Gables, when I dyed my hair? Nobody but Marilla and I knew about it."

"Was that the reason you came out once with your hair shingled to the bone?"

"Yes. I bought a bottle of dye from a German Jew pedlar. I fondly expected it would turn my hair black—and it turned it green. So it had to be cut off."

"You had a narrow escape, Mrs. Dr. dear," exclaimed Susan. "Of course you were too young then to know what a German was. It was a special mercy of Providence that it was only green dye and not poison."

"It seems hundreds of years since those Green Gables days," sighed Mrs. Blythe. "They belonged to another world altogether. Life has been cut in two by the chasm of war. What is ahead I don't know—but it can't be a bit like the past. I wonder if those of us who have lived half our lives in the old world will ever feel wholly at home in the new."

"Have you noticed," asked Miss Oliver, glancing up from her book, "how everything written before the war seems so far away now, too? One feels as if one was reading something as ancient as the Iliad. This poem of Wordsworth's—the Senior class have it in their entrance work—I've been glancing over it. Its classic calm and repose and the beauty of the lines seem to belong to another planet, and to have as little to do with the present world-welter as the evening star."

"The only thing that I find much comfort in reading nowadays is the Bible," remarked Susan, whisking her biscuits into the oven. "There are so many passages in it that seem to me exactly descriptive of the Huns. Old Highland Sandy declares that there is no doubt that the Kaiser is the Anti-Christ spoken of in Revelations, but I do not go as far as that. It would, in my humble opinion, Mrs. Dr. dear, be too great an honour for him."

Early one morning, several days later, Miranda Pryor slipped up to Ingleside, ostensibly to get some Red Cross sewing, but in reality to talk over with sympathetic Rilla troubles that were past bearing alone. She brought her dog with her—an over-fed, bandy-legged little animal very dear to her heart because Joe Milgrave had given it to her when it was a puppy. Mr. Pryor regarded all dogs with disfavour; but in those days he had looked kindly upon Joe as a suitor for Miranda's hand and so he had allowed her to keep the puppy. Miranda was so grateful that she endeavoured to please her father by naming her dog after his political idol, the great Liberal chieftain, Sir Wilfrid Laurier—though his title was soon abbreviated to Wilfy. Sir Wilfrid grew and flourished and waxed fat; but Miranda spoiled him absurdly and nobody else liked him. Rilla especially hated him because of his detestable trick of lying flat on his back and entreating you with waving paws to tickle his sleek stomach. When she saw that Miranda's pale eyes bore unmistakable testimony of her having cried all night, Rilla asked her to come up to her room, knowing Miranda had a tale of woe to tell, but she ordered Sir Wilfrid to remain below.

"Oh, can't he come, too?" said Miranda wistfully. "Poor Wilfy won't be any bother—and I wiped his paws so carefully before I brought him in. He is always so lonesome in a strange place without me—and very soon he'll be—all—I'll have left—to remind me—of Joe."

Rilla yielded, and Sir Wilfrid, with his tail curled at a saucy angle over his brindled back, trotted triumphantly up the stairs before them.

"Oh, Rilla," sobbed Miranda, when they had reached sanctuary. "I'm so unhappy. I can't begin to tell you how unhappy I am. Truly, my heart is breaking."

Rilla sat down on the lounge beside her. Sir Wilfrid squatted on his haunches before them, with his impertinent pink tongue stuck out, and listened. "What is the trouble, Miranda?"

"Joe is coming home tonight on his last leave. I had a letter from him on Saturday—he sends my letters in care of Bob Crawford, you know, because of father—and, oh, Rilla, he will only have four days—he has to go away Friday morning—and I may never see him again."

"Does he still want you to marry him?" asked Rilla.

"Oh, yes. He implored me in his letter to run away and be married. But I cannot do that, Rilla, not even for Joe. My only comfort is that I will be able to see him for a little while tomorrow afternoon. Father has to go to Charlottetown on business. At least we will have one good farewell talk. But oh—afterwards—why, Rilla, I know father won't even let me go to the station Friday morning to see Joe off."

"Why in the world don't you and Joe get married tomorrow afternoon at home?" demanded Rilla.

Miranda swallowed a sob in such amazement that she almost choked.

"Why—why—that is impossible, Rilla."

"Why?" briefly demanded the organizer of the Junior Red Cross and the transporter of babies in soup tureens.

"Why—why—we never thought of such a thing—Joe hasn't a license—I have no dress—I couldn't be married in black—I—I—we—you—you—" Miranda lost herself altogether and Sir Wilfrid, seeing that she was in dire distress threw back his head and emitted a melancholy yelp.

Rilla Blythe thought hard and rapidly for a few minutes. Then she said, "Miranda, if you will put yourself into my hands I'll have you married to Joe before four o'clock tomorrow afternoon."

"Oh, you couldn't."

"I can and I will. But you'll have to do exactly as I tell you."

"Oh—I—don't think—oh, father will kill me—"

"Nonsense. He'll be very angry I suppose. But are you more afraid of your father's anger than you are of Joe's never coming back to you?"

"No," said Miranda, with sudden firmness, "I'm not."

"Will you do as I tell you then?"

"Yes, I will."

"Then get Joe on the long-distance at once and tell him to bring out a license and ring tonight."

"Oh, I couldn't," wailed the aghast Miranda, "it—it would be so—so indelicate."

Rilla shut her little white teeth together with a snap. "Heaven grant me patience," she said under her breath. "I'll do it then," she said aloud, "and meanwhile, you go home and make what preparations you can. When I 'phone down to you to come up and help me sew come at once."

As soon as Miranda, pallid, scared, but desperately resolved, had gone, Rilla flew to the telephone and put in a long-distance call for Charlottetown. She got through with such surprising quickness that she was convinced Providence approved of her undertaking, but it was a good hour before she could get in touch with Joe Milgrave at his camp. Meanwhile, she paced impatiently about, and prayed that when she did get Joe there would be no listeners on the line to carry news to Whiskers-on-the-moon.

"Is that you, Joe? Rilla Blythe is speaking—Rilla—Rilla—oh, never mind. Listen to this. Before you come home tonight get a marriage license—a marriage license—yes, a marriage license—and a wedding-ring. Did you get that? And will you do it? Very well, be sure you do it—it is your only chance."

Flushed with triumph—for her only fear was that she might not be able to locate Joe in time—Rilla rang the Pryor ring. This time she had not such good luck for she drew Whiskers-on-the-moon.

"Is that Miranda? Oh—Mr. Pryor! Well, Mr. Pryor, will you kindly ask Miranda if she can come up this afternoon and help me with some sewing. It is very important, or I would not trouble her. Oh—thank you."

Mr. Pryor had consented somewhat grumpily, but he had consented—he did not want to offend Dr. Blythe, and he knew that if he refused to allow Miranda to do any Red Cross work public opinion would make the Glen too hot for comfort. Rilla went out to the kitchen, shut all the doors with a mysterious expression which alarmed Susan, and then said solemnly, "Susan can you make a wedding-cake this afternoon?"

"A wedding-cake!" Susan stared. Rilla had, without any warning, brought her a war-baby once upon a time. Was she now, with equal suddenness, going to produce a husband?

"Yes, a wedding-cake—a scrumptious wedding-cake, Susan—a beautiful, plummy, eggy, citron-peely wedding-cake. And we must make other things too. I'll help you in the morning. But I can't help you in the afternoon for I have to make a wedding-dress and time is the essence of the contract, Susan."

Susan felt that she was really too old to be subjected to such shocks.

"Who are you going to marry, Rilla?" she asked feebly.

"Susan, darling, I am not the happy bride. Miranda Pryor is going to marry Joe Milgrave tomorrow afternoon while her father is away in town. A war-wedding, Susan—isn't that thrilling and romantic? I never was so excited in my life."

The excitement soon spread over Ingleside, infecting even Mrs. Blythe and Susan.

"I'll go to work on that cake at once," vowed Susan, with a glance at the clock. "Mrs. Dr. dear, will you pick over the fruit and beat up the eggs? If you will I can have that cake ready for the oven by the evening. Tomorrow morning we can make salads and other things. I will work all night if necessary to get the better of Whiskers-on-the-moon."

Miranda arrived, tearful and breathless.

"We must fix over my white dress for you to wear," said Rilla. "It will fit you very nicely with a little alteration."

To work went the two girls, ripping, fitting, basting, sewing for dear life. By dint of unceasing effort they got the dress done by seven o'clock and Miranda tried it on in Rilla's room.

"It's very pretty—but oh, if I could just have a veil," sighed Miranda. "I've always dreamed of being married in a lovely white veil."

Some good fairy evidently waits on the wishes of war-brides. The door opened and Mrs. Blythe came in, her arms full of a filmy burden.

"Miranda dear," she said, "I want you to wear my wedding-veil tomorrow. It is twenty-four years since I was a bride at old Green Gables—the happiest bride that ever was—and the wedding-veil of a happy bride brings good luck, they say."

"Oh, how sweet of you, Mrs. Blythe," said Miranda, the ready tears starting to her eyes.

The veil was tried on and draped. Susan dropped in to approve but dared not linger.

"I've got that cake in the oven," she said, "and I am pursuing a policy of watchful waiting. The evening news is that the Grand Duke has captured Erzerum. That is a pill for the Turks. I wish I had a chance to tell the Czar just what a mistake he made when he turned Nicholas down."

Susan disappeared downstairs to the kitchen, whence a dreadful thud and a piercing shriek presently sounded. Everybody rushed to the kitchen—the doctor and Miss Oliver, Mrs. Blythe,

Rilla, Miranda in her wedding-veil. Susan was sitting flatly in the middle of the kitchen floor with a dazed, bewildered look on her face, while Doc, evidently in his Hyde incarnation, was standing on the dresser, with his back up, his eyes blazing, and his tail the size of three tails.

"Susan, what has happened?" cried Mrs. Blythe in alarm. "Did you fall? Are you hurt?"

Susan picked herself up.

"No," she said grimly, "I am not hurt, though I am jarred all over. Do not be alarmed. As for what has happened—I tried to kick that darned cat with both feet, that is what happened."

Everybody shrieked with laughter. The doctor was quite helpless.

"Oh, Susan, Susan," he gasped. "That I should live to hear you swear."

"I am sorry," said Susan in real distress, "that I used such an expression before two young girls. But I said that beast was darned, and darned it is. It belongs to Old Nick."

"Do you expect it will vanish some of these days with a bang and the odour of brimstone, Susan?"

"It will go to its own place in due time and that you may tie to," said Susan dourly, shaking out her raddled bones and going to her oven. "I suppose my plunking down like that has shaken my cake so that it will be as heavy as lead."

But the cake was not heavy. It was all a bride's cake should be, and Susan iced it beautifully. Next day she and Rilla worked all the forenoon, making delicacies for the wedding-feast, and as soon as Miranda phoned up that her father was safely off everything was packed in a big hamper and taken down to the Pryor house. Joe soon arrived in his uniform and a state of violent excitement, accompanied by his best man, Sergeant Malcolm Crawford. There were quite a few guests, for all the Manse and Ingleside folk were there, and a dozen or so of Joe's relatives, including his mother, "Mrs. Dead Angus Milgrave," so called, cheerfully, to distinguish her from another lady whose Angus was living. Mrs. Dead Angus wore a rather disapproving expression, not caring over-much for this alliance with the house of Whiskers-on-the-moon.

So Miranda Pryor was married to Private Joseph Milgrave on his last leave. It should have been a romantic wedding but it was not. There were too many factors working against romance, as even Rilla had to admit. In the first place, Miranda, in spite of her dress and veil, was such a flat-faced, commonplace, uninteresting little bride. In the second place, Joe cried bitterly all through the ceremony, and this vexed Miranda unreasonably. Long afterwards she told Rilla, "I just felt like saying to him then and there, 'If you feel so bad over having to marry me you don't have to.' But it was just because he was thinking all the time of how soon he would have to leave me."

In the third place, Jims, who was usually so well-behaved in public, took a fit of shyness and contrariness combined and began to cry at the top of his voice for "Willa." Nobody wanted to take him out, because everybody wanted to see the marriage, so Rilla who was a bridesmaid, had to take him and hold him during the ceremony.

In the fourth place, Sir Wilfrid Laurier took a fit.

Sir Wilfrid was entrenched in a corner of the room behind Miranda's piano. During his seizure he made the weirdest, most unearthly noises. He would begin with a series of choking, spasmodic sounds, continuing into a gruesome gurgle, and ending up with a strangled howl. Nobody could hear a word Mr. Meredith was saying, except now and then, when Sir Wilfrid stopped for breath. Nobody looked at the bride except Susan, who never dragged her fascinated eyes from Miranda's face—all the others were gazing at the dog. Miranda had been trembling with nervousness but as soon as Sir Wilfrid began his performance she forgot it. All that she could think of was that her dear dog was dying and she could not go to him. She never remembered a word of the ceremony.

Rilla, who in spite of Jims, had been trying her best to look rapt and romantic, as beseemed a war bridesmaid, gave up the hopeless attempt, and devoted her energies to choking down untimely merriment. She dared not look at anybody in the room, especially Mrs. Dead Angus, for fear all her suppressed mirth should suddenly explode in a most un-young-ladylike yell of laughter.

But married they were, and then they had a wedding-supper in the dining-room which was so lavish and bountiful that you would have thought it was the product of a month's labour. Everybody had brought something. Mrs. Dead Angus had brought a large apple-pie, which she placed on a chair in the dining-room and then absently sat down on it. Neither her temper nor her black silk wedding garment was improved thereby, but the pie was never missed at the gay bridal feast. Mrs. Dead Angus eventually took it home with her again. Whiskers-on-the-moon's pacifist pig should not get it, anyhow.

That evening Mr. and Mrs. Joe, accompanied by the recovered Sir Wilfrid, departed for the Four Winds Lighthouse, which was kept by Joe's uncle and in which they meant to spend their brief honeymoon. Una Meredith and Rilla and Susan washed the dishes, tidied up, left a cold supper and Miranda's pitiful little note on the table for Mr. Pryor, and walked home, while the mystic veil of dreamy, haunted winter twilight wrapped itself over the Glen.

"I would really not have minded being a war-bride myself," remarked Susan sentimentally.

But Rilla felt rather flat—perhaps as a reaction to all the excitement and rush of the past thirty-six hours. She was disappointed somehow—the whole affair had been so ludicrous, and Miranda and Joe so lachrymose and commonplace.

"If Miranda hadn't given that wretched dog such an enormous dinner he wouldn't have had that fit," she said crossly. "I warned her—but she said she couldn't starve the poor dog—he would soon be all she had left, etc. I could have shaken her."

"The best man was more excited than Joe was," said Susan. "He wished Miranda many happy returns of the day. She did not look very happy, but perhaps you could not expect that under the circumstances."

"Anyhow," thought Rilla, "I can write a perfectly killing account of it all to the boys. How Jem will howl over Sir Wilfrid's part in it!"

But if Rilla was rather disappointed in the war wedding she found nothing lacking on Friday morning when Miranda said good-bye to her bridegroom at the Glen station. The dawn was white as a pearl, clear as a diamond. Behind the station the balsamy copse of young firs was frost-misted. The cold moon of dawn hung over the westering snow fields but the golden fleeces of sunrise shone above the maples up at Ingleside. Joe took his pale little bride in his arms and she lifted her face to his. Rilla choked suddenly. It did not matter that Miranda was insignificant and commonplace and flat-featured. It did not matter that she was the daughter of Whiskers-on-the-moon. All that mattered was that rapt, sacrificial look in her eyes—that ever-burning, sacred fire of devotion and loyalty and fine courage that she was mutely promising Joe she and thousands of other women would keep alive at home while their men held the Western front. Rilla walked away, realising that she must not spy on such a moment. She went down to the end of the platform where Sir Wilfrid and Dog Monday were sitting, looking at each other.

Sir Wilfrid remarked condescendingly: "Why do you haunt this old shed when you might lie on the hearthrug at Ingleside and live on the fat of the land? Is it a pose? Or a fixed idea?"

Whereat Dog Monday, laconically: "I have a tryst to keep."

When the train had gone Rilla rejoined the little trembling Miranda. "Well, he's gone," said Miranda, "and he may never come back—but I'm his wife, and I'm going to be worthy of him. I'm going home."

"Don't you think you had better come with me now?" asked Rilla doubtfully. Nobody knew yet how Mr. Pryor had taken the matter.

"No. If Joe can face the Huns I guess I can face father," said Miranda daringly. "A soldier's wife can't be a coward. Come on, Wilfy. I'll go straight home and meet the worst."

There was nothing very dreadful to face, however. Perhaps Mr. Pryor had reflected that housekeepers were hard to get and that there were many Milgrave homes open to Miranda—also, that there was such a thing as a separation allowance. At all events, though he told her grumpily that she had made a nice fool of herself, and would live to regret it, he said nothing worse, and Mrs. Joe put on her apron and went to work as usual, while Sir Wilfrid Laurier, who had a poor opinion of lighthouses for winter residences, went to sleep in his pet nook behind the woodbox, a thankful dog that he was done with war-weddings.

19. "THEY SHALL NOT PASS"

One cold grey morning in February Gertrude Oliver wakened with a shiver, slipped into Rilla's room, and crept in beside her.

"Rilla—I'm frightened—frightened as a baby—I've had another of my strange dreams. Something terrible is before us—I know."

"What was it?" asked Rilla.

"I was standing again on the veranda steps—just as I stood in that dream on the night before the lighthouse dance, and in the sky a huge black, menacing thunder cloud rolled up from the east. I could see its shadow racing before it and when it enveloped me I shivered with icy cold. Then the storm broke—and it was a dreadful storm—blinding flash after flash and deafening peal after peal, driving torrents of rain. I turned in panic and tried to run for shelter, and as I did so a man—a soldier in the uniform of a French army officer—dashed up the steps and stood beside me on the threshold of the door. His clothes were soaked with blood from a wound in his breast, he seemed spent and exhausted; but his white face was set and his eyes blazed in his hollow face. 'They shall not pass,' he said, in low, passionate tones which I heard distinctly amid all the turmoil of the storm. Then I awakened. Rilla, I'm frightened—the spring will not bring the Big Push we've all been hoping for—instead it is going to bring some dreadful blow to France. I am sure of it. The Germans will try to smash through somewhere."

"But he told you that they would not pass," said Rilla, seriously. She never laughed at Gertrude's dreams as the doctor did.

"I do not know if that was prophecy or desperation, Rilla, the horror of that dream holds me yet in an icy grip. We shall need all our courage before long."

Dr. Blythe did laugh at the breakfast table—but he never laughed at Miss Oliver's dreams again; for that day brought news of the opening of the Verdun offensive, and thereafter through all the beautiful weeks of spring the Ingleside family, one and all, lived in a trance of dread. There were days when they waited in despair for the end as foot by foot the Germans crept nearer and nearer to the grim barrier of desperate France.

Susan's deeds were in her spotless kitchen at Ingleside, but her thoughts were on the hills around Verdun. "Mrs. Dr. dear," she would stick her head in at Mrs. Blythe's door the last thing at night to remark, "I do hope the French have hung onto the Crow's Wood today," and she woke at dawn to wonder if Dead Man's Hill—surely named by some prophet—was still held by the "poyloos." Susan could have drawn a map of the country around Verdun that would have satisfied a chief of staff.

"If the Germans capture Verdun the spirit of France will be broken," Miss Oliver said bitterly.

"But they will not capture it," staunchly said Susan, who could not eat her dinner that day for fear lest they do that very thing. "In the first place, you dreamed they would not—you dreamed the very thing the French are saying before they ever said it—'they shall not pass.' I declare to you, Miss Oliver, dear, when I read that in the paper, and remembered your dream, I went cold all over with awe. It seemed to me like Biblical times when people dreamed things like that quite frequently.

"I know—I know," said Gertrude, walking restlessly about. "I cling to a persistent faith in my dream, too—but every time bad news comes it fails me. Then I tell myself 'mere coincidence'—'subconscious memory' and so forth."

"I do not see how any memory could remember a thing before it was ever said at all," persisted Susan, "though of course I am not educated like you and the doctor. I would rather not be, if it makes anything as simple as that so hard to believe. But in any case we need not worry over Verdun, even if the Huns get it. Joffre says it has no military significance."

"That old sop of comfort has been served up too often already when reverses came," retorted Gertrude. "It has lost its power to charm."

"Was there ever a battle like this in the world before?" said Mr. Meredith, one evening in mid-April.

"It's such a titanic thing we can't grasp it," said the doctor. "What were the scraps of a few Homeric handfuls compared to this? The whole Trojan war might be fought around a Verdun fort and a newspaper correspondent would give it no more than a sentence. I am not in the confidence of the occult powers"—the doctor threw Gertrude a twinkle—"but I have a hunch that the fate of the whole war hangs on the issue of Verdun. As Susan and Joffre say, it has no real military significance; but it has the tremendous significance of an Idea. If Germany wins there she will win the war. If she loses, the tide will set against her."

"Lose she will," said Mr. Meredith: emphatically. "The Idea cannot be conquered. France is certainly very wonderful. It seems to me that in her I see the white form of civilization making a determined stand against the black powers of barbarism. I think our whole world realizes this and that is why we all await the issue so breathlessly. It isn't merely the question of a few forts changing hands or a few miles of blood-soaked ground lost and won."

"I wonder," said Gertrude dreamily, "if some great blessing, great enough for the price, will be the meed of all our pain? Is the agony in which the world is shuddering the birth-pang of some wondrous new era? Or is it merely a futile

struggle of ants
In the gleam of a million million of suns?

We think very lightly, Mr. Meredith, of a calamity which destroys an ant-hill and half its inhabitants. Does the Power that runs the universe think us of more importance than we think ants?"

"You forget," said Mr. Meredith, with a flash of his dark eyes, "that an infinite Power must be infinitely little as well as infinitely great. We are neither, therefore there are things too little as well as too great for us to apprehend. To the infinitely little an ant is of as much importance as a mastodon. We are witnessing the birth-pangs of a new era—but it will be born a feeble, wailing life like everything else. I am not one of those who expect a new heaven and a new earth as the immediate result of this war. That is not the way God works. But work He does, Miss Oliver, and in the end His purpose will be fulfilled."

"Sound and orthodox—sound and orthodox," muttered Susan approvingly in the kitchen. Susan liked to see Miss Oliver sat upon by the minister now and then. Susan was very fond of her but she thought Miss Oliver liked saying heretical things to ministers far too well, and deserved an occasional reminder that these matters were quite beyond her province.

In May Walter wrote home that he had been awarded a D.C. Medal. He did not say what for, but the other boys took care that the Glen should know the brave thing Walter had done. "In any war but this," wrote Jerry Meredith, "it would have meant a V.C. But they can't make V.C.'s as common as the brave things done every day here."

"He should have had the V.C.," said Susan, and was very indignant over it. She was not quite sure who was to blame for his not getting it, but if it were General Haig she began for the first time to entertain serious doubts as to his fitness for being Commander-in-Chief.

Rilla was beside herself with delight. It was her dear Walter who had done this thing—Walter, to whom someone had sent a white feather at Redmond—it was Walter who had dashed back from the safety of the trench to drag in a wounded comrade who had fallen on No-man's-land. Oh, she could see his white beautiful face and wonderful eyes as he did it! What a thing to be the sister of such a hero! And he hadn't thought it worth while writing about. His letter was full of other things—little intimate things that they two had known and loved together in the dear old cloudless days of a century ago.

"I've been thinking of the daffodils in the garden at Ingleside," he wrote. "By the time you get this they will be out, blowing there under that lovely rosy sky. Are they really as bright and golden as ever, Rilla? It seems to me that they must be dyed red with blood—like our poppies here. And every whisper of spring will be falling as a violet in Rainbow Valley.

"There is a young moon tonight—a slender, silver, lovely thing hanging over these pits of torment. Will you see it tonight over the maple grove?

"I'm enclosing a little scrap of verse, Rilla. I wrote it one evening in my trench dug-out by the light of a bit of candle—or rather it came to me there—I didn't feel as if I were writing it—something seemed to use me as an instrument. I've had that feeling once or twice before, but very rarely and never so strongly as this time. That was why I sent it over to the London Spectator. It printed it and the copy came today. I hope you'll like it. It's the only poem I've written since I came overseas."

The poem was a short, poignant little thing. In a month it had carried Walter's name to every corner of the globe. Everywhere it was copied—in metropolitan dailies and little village weeklies—in profound reviews and "agony columns," in Red Cross appeals and Government recruiting propaganda. Mothers and sisters wept over it, young lads thrilled to it, the whole great heart of humanity caught it up as an epitome of all the pain and hope and pity and purpose of the mighty conflict, crystallized in three brief immortal verses. A Canadian lad in the Flanders trenches had written the one great poem of the war. "The Piper," by Pte. Walter Blythe, was a classic from its first printing.

Rilla copied it in her diary at the beginning of an entry in which she poured out the story of the hard week that had just passed.

"It has been such a dreadful week," she wrote, "and even though it is over and we know that it was all a mistake that does not seem to do away with the bruises left by it. And yet it has in some ways been a very wonderful week and I have had some glimpses of things I never realized before—of how fine and brave people can be even in the midst of horrible suffering. I am sure I could never be as splendid as Miss Oliver was.

"Just a week ago today she had a letter from Mr. Grant's mother in Charlottetown. And it told her that a cable had just come saying that Major Robert Grant had been killed in action a few days before.

"Oh, poor Gertrude! At first she was crushed. Then after just a day she pulled herself together and went back to her school. She did not cry—I never saw her shed a tear—but oh, her face and her eyes!

"'I must go on with my work,' she said. 'That is my duty just now.'

"I could never have risen to such a height.

"She never spoke bitterly except once, when Susan said something about spring being here at last, and Gertrude said,

"'Can the spring really come this year?'

"Then she laughed—such a dreadful little laugh, just as one might laugh in the face of death, I think, and said,

"'Observe my egotism. Because I, Gertrude Oliver, have lost a friend, it is incredible that the spring can come as usual. The spring does not fail because of the million agonies of others—but for mine—oh, can the universe go on?'

"'Don't feel bitter with yourself, dear,' mother said gently. 'It is a very natural thing to feel as if things couldn't go on just the same when some great blow has changed the world for us. We all feel like that.'

"Then that horrid old Cousin Sophia of Susan's piped up. She was sitting there, knitting and croaking like an old 'raven of bode and woe' as Walter used to call her.

"'You ain't as bad off as some, Miss Oliver,' she said, 'and you shouldn't take it so hard. There's some as has lost their husbands; that's a hard blow; and there's some as has lost their sons. You haven't lost either husband or son.'

"'No,' said Gertrude, more bitterly still. 'It's true I haven't lost a husband—I have only lost the man who would have been my husband. I have lost no son—only the sons and daughters who might have been born to me—who will never be born to me now.'

"'It isn't ladylike to talk like that,' said Cousin Sophia in a shocked tone; and then Gertrude laughed right out, so wildly that Cousin Sophia was really frightened. And when poor tortured Gertrude, unable to endure it any longer, hurried out of the room, Cousin Sophia asked mother if the blow hadn't affected Miss Oliver's mind.

"'I suffered the loss of two good kind partners,' she said, 'but it did not affect me like that.'

"I should think it wouldn't! Those poor men must have been thankful to die.

"I heard Gertrude walking up and down her room most of the night. She walked like that every night. But never so long as that night. And once I heard her give a dreadful sudden little cry as if she had been stabbed. I couldn't sleep for suffering with her; and I couldn't help her. I thought the night would never end. But it did; and then 'joy came in the morning' as the Bible says. Only it didn't come exactly in the morning but well along in the afternoon. The telephone rang and I answered it. It was old Mrs. Grant speaking from Charlottetown, and her news was that it was all a mistake—Robert wasn't killed at all; he had only been slightly wounded in the arm and was safe in the hospital out of harm's way for a time anyhow. They hadn't learned yet how the mistake had happened but supposed there must have been another Robert Grant.

"I hung up the telephone and flew to Rainbow Valley. I'm sure I did fly—I can't remember my feet ever touching the ground. I met Gertrude on her way home from school in the glade of spruces where we used to play, and I just gasped out the news to her. I ought to have had more sense, of course. But I was so crazy with joy and excitement that I never stopped to think. Gertrude just dropped there among the golden young ferns as if she had been shot. The fright it gave me ought to make me sensible—in this respect at least—for the rest of my life. I thought I had killed her—I remembered that her mother had died very suddenly from heart failure when quite a young woman. It seemed years to me before I discovered that her heart was still beating. A pretty time I had! I never saw anybody faint before, and I knew there was nobody up at the house to help, because everybody else had gone to the station to meet Di and Nan coming home from Redmond. But I knew—theoretically—how people in a faint should be treated, and now I know it practically. Luckily the brook was handy, and after I had worked frantically over her for a while Gertrude came back to life. She never said one word about my news and I didn't dare to refer to it again. I helped her walk up through the maple grove and up to her room, and then she said, 'Rob—is—living,' as if the words were torn out of her, and flung herself on her bed and cried and cried and cried. I never saw anyone cry so before. All the tears that she hadn't shed all that week came then. She cried most of last night, I think, but her face this morning looked as if she had seen a vision of some kind, and we were all so happy that we were almost afraid.

"Di and Nan are home for a couple of weeks. Then they go back to Red Cross work in the training camp at Kingsport. I envy them. Father says I'm doing just as good work here, with Jims and my Junior Reds. But it lacks the romance theirs must have.

"Kut has fallen. It was almost a relief when it did fall, we had been dreading it so long. It crushed us flat for a day and then we picked up and put it behind us. Cousin Sophia was as gloomy as usual and came over and groaned that the British were losing everywhere.

"'They're good losers,' said Susan grimly. 'When they lose a thing they keep on looking till they find it again! Anyhow, my king and country need me now to cut potato sets for the back garden, so get you a knife and help me, Sophia Crawford. It will divert your thoughts and keep you from worrying over a campaign that you are not called upon to run.'

"Susan is an old brick, and the way she flattens out poor Cousin Sophia is beautiful to behold.

"As for Verdun, the battle goes on and on, and we see-saw between hope and fear. But I know that strange dream of Miss Oliver's foretold the victory of France. 'They shall not pass.'"

20. NORMAN DOUGLAS SPEAKS OUT IN MEETING

"Where are you wandering, Anne o' mine?" asked the doctor, who even yet, after twenty-four years of marriage, occasionally addressed his wife thus when nobody was about. Anne was sitting on the veranda steps, gazing absently over the wonderful bridal world of spring blossom, Beyond the white orchard was a copse of dark young firs and creamy wild cherries, where the robins were whistling madly; for it was evening and the fire of early stars was burning over the maple grove.

Anne came back with a little sigh.

"I was just taking relief from intolerable realities in a dream, Gilbert—a dream that all our children were home again—and all small again—playing in Rainbow Valley. It is always so silent now—but I was imagining I heard clear voices and gay, childish sounds coming up as I used to. I could hear Jem's whistle and Walter's yodel, and the twins' laughter, and for just a few blessed minutes I forgot about the guns on the Western front, and had a little false, sweet happiness."

The doctor did not answer. Sometimes his work tricked him into forgetting for a few moments the Western front, but not often. There was a good deal of grey now in his still thick curls that had not been there two years ago. Yet he smiled down into the starry eyes he loved—the eyes that had once been so full of laughter, and now seemed always full of unshed tears.

Susan wandered by with a hoe in her hand and her second best bonnet on her head.

"I have just finished reading a piece in the Enterprise which told of a couple being married in an aeroplane. Do you think it would be legal, doctor dear?" she inquired anxiously.

"I think so," said the doctor gravely.

"Well," said Susan dubiously, "it seems to me that a wedding is too solemn for anything so giddy as an aeroplane. But nothing is the same as it used to be. Well, it is half an hour yet before prayer-meeting time, so I am going around to the kitchen garden to have a little evening hate with the weeds. But all the time I am strafing them I will be thinking about this new worry in the Trentino. I do not like this Austrian caper, Mrs. Dr. dear."

"Nor I," said Mrs. Blythe ruefully. "All the forenoon I preserved rhubarb with my hands and waited for the war news with my soul. When it came I shrivelled. Well, I suppose I must go and get ready for the prayer-meeting, too."

Every village has its own little unwritten history, handed down from lip to lip through the generations, of tragic, comic, and dramatic events. They are told at weddings and festivals, and rehearsed around winter firesides. And in these oral annals of Glen St. Mary the tale of the union prayer-meeting held that night in the Methodist Church was destined to fill an imperishable place.

The union prayer-meeting was Mr. Arnold's idea. The county battalion, which had been training all winter in Charlottetown, was to leave shortly for overseas. The Four Winds Harbour boys belonging to it from the Glen and over-harbour and Harbour Head and Upper Glen were all home on their last leave, and Mr. Arnold thought, properly enough, that it would be a fitting thing to hold a union prayer-meeting for them before they went away. Mr. Meredith having agreed, the meeting was announced to be held in the Methodist Church. Glen prayer-meetings were not apt to be too well attended, but on this particular evening the Methodist Church was crowded. Everybody who could go was there. Even Miss Cornelia came—and it was the first time in her life that Miss Cornelia had ever set foot inside a Methodist Church. It took no less than a world conflict to bring that about.

"I used to hate Methodists," said Miss Cornelia calmly, when her husband expressed surprise over her going, "but I don't hate them now. There is no sense in hating Methodists when there is a Kaiser or a Hindenburg in the world."

So Miss Cornelia went. Norman Douglas and his wife went too. And Whiskers-on-the-moon strutted up the aisle to a front pew, as if he fully realized what a distinction he conferred upon the building. People were somewhat surprised that he should be there, since he usually avoided all assemblages connected in any way with the war. But Mr. Meredith had said that he hoped his session would be well represented, and Mr. Pryor had evidently taken the request to heart. He wore his best black suit and white tie, his thick, tight, iron-grey curls were neatly arranged, and his broad, red round face looked, as Susan most uncharitably thought, more "sanctimonious" than ever.

"The minute I saw that man coming into the Church, looking like that, I felt that mischief was brewing, Mrs. Dr. dear," she said afterwards. "What form it would take I could not tell, but I knew from face of him that he had come there for no good."

The prayer-meeting opened conventionally and continued quietly. Mr. Meredith spoke first with his usual eloquence and feeling. Mr. Arnold followed with an address which even Miss Cornelia had to confess was irreproachable in taste and subject-matter.

And then Mr. Arnold asked Mr. Pryor to lead in prayer.

Miss Cornelia had always averred that Mr. Arnold had no gumption. Miss Cornelia was not apt to err on the side of charity in her judgment of Methodist ministers, but in this case she did not greatly overshoot the mark. The Rev. Mr. Arnold certainly did not have much of that desirable, indefinable quality known as gumption, or he would never have asked Whiskers-on-the-moon to lead in prayer at a khaki prayer-meeting. He thought he was returning the compliment to Mr. Meredith, who, at the conclusion of his address, had asked a Methodist deacon to lead.

Some people expected Mr. Pryor to refuse grumpily—and that would have made enough scandal. But Mr. Pryor bounded briskly to his feet, unctuously said, "Let us pray," and forthwith prayed. In a sonorous voice which penetrated to every corner of the crowded building Mr. Pryor poured forth a flood of fluent words, and was well on in his prayer before his dazed and horrified audience awakened to the fact that they were listening to a pacifist appeal of the rankest sort. Mr. Pryor had at least the courage of his convictions; or perhaps, as people afterwards said, he thought he was safe in a church and that it was an excellent chance to air certain opinions he dared not voice elsewhere, for fear of being mobbed. He prayed that the unholy war might cease—that the deluded armies being driven to slaughter on the Western front might have their eyes opened to their iniquity and repent while yet there was time—that the poor young men present in khaki, who had been hounded into a path of murder and militarism, should yet be rescued—

Mr. Pryor had got this far without let or hindrance; and so paralysed were his hearers, and so deeply imbued with their born-and-bred conviction that no disturbance must ever be made in a church, no matter what the provocation, that it seemed likely that he would continue unchecked to the end. But one man at least in that audience was not hampered by inherited or acquired reverence for the sacred edifice. Norman Douglas was, as Susan had often vowed crisply, nothing more or less than a "pagan." But he was a rampantly patriotic pagan, and when the significance of what Mr. Pryor was saying fully dawned on him, Norman Douglas suddenly went berserk. With a positive roar he bounded to his feet in his side pew, facing the audience, and shouted in tones of thunder:

"Stop—stop—STOP that abominable prayer! What an abominable prayer!"

Every head in the church flew up. A boy in khaki at the back gave a faint cheer. Mr. Meredith raised a deprecating hand, but Norman was past caring for anything like that. Eluding his wife's restraining grasp, he gave one mad spring over the front of the pew and caught the unfortunate Whiskers-on-the-moon by his coat collar. Mr. Pryor had not "stopped" when so bidden, but he stopped now, perforce, for Norman, his long red beard literally bristling with fury, was shaking him until his bones fairly rattled, and punctuating his shakes with a lurid assortment of abusive epithets.

"You blatant beast!"—shake—"You malignant carrion"—shake—"You pig-headed varmint!"—shake—"you putrid pup"—shake—"you pestilential parasite"—shake—"you—Hunnish scum"—shake—"you indecent reptile—you—you—" Norman choked for a moment. Everybody believed that the next thing he would say, church or no church, would be something that would have to be spelt with asterisks; but at that moment Norman encountered his wife's eye and he fell back with a thud on Holy Writ. "You whited sepulchre!" he bellowed, with a final shake, and cast Whiskers-on-the-moon from him with a vigour which impelled that unhappy pacifist to the very verge of the choir entrance door. Mr. Pryor's once ruddy face was ashen. But he turned at bay. "I'll have the law on you for this," he gasped.

"Do—do," roared Norman, making another rush. But Mr. Pryor was gone. He had no desire to fall a second time into the hands of an avenging militarist. Norman turned to the platform for one graceless, triumphant moment.

"Don't look so flabbergasted, parsons," he boomed. "You couldn't do it—nobody would expect it of the cloth—but somebody had to do it. You know you're glad I threw him out—he couldn't be let go on yammering and yodelling and yawping sedition and treason. Sedition and treason—somebody had to deal with it. I was born for this hour—I've had my innings in church at last. I can sit quiet for another sixty years now! Go ahead with your meeting, parsons. I reckon you won't be troubled with any more pacifist prayers."

But the spirit of devotion and reverence had fled. Both ministers realized it and realized that the only thing to do was to close the meeting quietly and let the excited people go. Mr.

Meredith addressed a few earnest words to the boys in khaki—which probably saved Mr. Pryor's windows from a second onslaught—and Mr. Arnold pronounced an incongruous benediction, at least he felt it was incongruous, for he could not at once banish from his memory the sight of gigantic Norman Douglas shaking the fat, pompous little Whiskers-on-the-moon as a huge mastiff might shake an overgrown puppy. And he knew that the same picture was in everybody's mind. Altogether the union prayer-meeting could hardly be called an unqualified success. But it was remembered in Glen St. Mary when scores of orthodox and undisturbed assemblies were totally forgotten.

"You will never, no, never, Mrs. Dr. dear, hear me call Norman Douglas a pagan again," said Susan when she reached home. "If Ellen Douglas is not a proud woman this night she should be."

"Norman Douglas did a wholly indefensible thing," said the doctor. "Pryor should have been let severely alone until the meeting was over. Then later on, his own minister and session should deal with him. That would have been the proper procedure. Norman's performance was utterly improper and scandalous and outrageous; but, by George,"—the doctor threw back his head and chuckled, "by George, Anne-girl, it was satisfying."

21. "LOVE AFFAIRS ARE HORRIBLE"

Ingleside
20th June 1916

"We have been so busy, and day after day has brought such exciting news, good and bad, that I haven't had time and composure to write in my diary for weeks. I like to keep it up regularly, for father says a diary of the years of the war should be a very interesting thing to hand down to one's children. The trouble is, I like to write a few personal things in this blessed old book that might not be exactly what I'd want my children to read. I feel that I shall be a far greater stickler for propriety in regard to them than I am for myself!

"The first week in June was another dreadful one. The Austrians seemed just on the point of overrunning Italy: and then came the first awful news of the Battle of Jutland, which the Germans claimed as a great victory. Susan was the only one who carried on. 'You need never tell me that the Kaiser has defeated the British Navy,' she said, with a contemptuous sniff. 'It is all a German lie and that you may tie to.' And when a couple of days later we found out that she was right and that it had been a British victory instead of a British defeat, we had to put up with a great many 'I told you so's,' but we endured them very comfortably.

"It took Kitchener's death to finish Susan. For the first time I saw her down and out. We all felt the shock of it but Susan plumbed the depths of despair. The news came at night by 'phone but Susan wouldn't believe it until she saw the Enterprise headline the next day. She did not cry or faint or go into hysterics; but she forgot to put salt in the soup, and that is something Susan never did in my recollection. Mother and Miss Oliver and I cried but Susan looked at us in stony sarcasm and said, 'The Kaiser and his six sons are all alive and thriving. So the world is not left wholly desolate. Why cry, Mrs. Dr. dear?' Susan continued in this stony, hopeless condition for twenty-four hours, and then Cousin Sophia appeared and began to condole with her.

"'This is terrible news, ain't it, Susan? We might as well prepare for the worst for it is bound to come. You said once—and well do I remember the words, Susan Baker—that you had complete confidence in God and Kitchener. Ah well, Susan Baker, there is only God left now.'

"Whereat Cousin Sophia put her handkerchief to her eyes pathetically as if the world were indeed in terrible straits. As for Susan, Cousin Sophia was the salvation of her. She came to life with a jerk.

"'Sophia Crawford, hold your peace!' she said sternly. 'You may be an idiot but you need not be an irreverent idiot. It is no more than decent to be weeping and wailing because the Almighty is the sole stay of the Allies now. As for Kitchener, his death is a great loss and I do not dispute it. But the outcome of this war does not depend on one man's life and now that the Russians are coming on again you will soon see a change for the better.'

"Susan said this so energetically that she convinced herself and cheered up immediately. But Cousin Sophia shook her head.

"'Albert's wife wants to call the baby after Brusiloff,' she said, 'but I told her to wait and see what becomes of him first. Them Russians has such a habit of petering out.'

"The Russians are doing splendidly, however, and they have saved Italy. But even when the daily news of their sweeping advance comes we don't feel like running up the flag as we used to do. As Gertrude says, Verdun has slain all exultation. We would all feel more like rejoicing if the victories were on the western front. 'When will the British strike?' Gertrude sighed this morning. 'We have waited so long—so long.'

"Our greatest local event in recent weeks was the route march the county battalion made through the county before it left for overseas. They marched from Charlottetown to Lowbridge, then round the Harbour Head and through the Upper Glen and so down to the St. Mary station. Everybody turned out to see them, except old Aunt Fannie Clow, who is bedridden and Mr. Pryor, who hadn't been seen out even in church since the night of the Union Prayer Meeting the previous week.

"It was wonderful and heartbreaking to see that battalion marching past. There were young men and middle-aged men in it. There was Laurie McAllister from over-harbour who is only sixteen but swore he was eighteen, so that he could enlist; and there was Angus Mackenzie, from the Upper Glen who is fifty-five if he is a day and swore he was forty-four. There were two South African veterans from Lowbridge, and the three eighteen-year-old Baxter triplets from Harbour Head. Everybody cheered as they went by, and they cheered Foster Booth, who is forty, walking side by side with his son Charley who is twenty. Charley's mother died when he was born, and when Charley enlisted Foster said he'd never yet let Charley go anywhere he daren't go himself, and he didn't mean to begin with the Flanders trenches. At the station Dog Monday nearly went out of his head. He tore about and sent messages to Jem by them all. Mr. Meredith read an address and Reta Crawford recited 'The Piper.' The soldiers cheered her like mad and cried 'We'll follow—we'll follow—we won't break faith,' and I felt so proud to think that it was my dear brother who had written such a wonderful, heart-stirring thing. And then I looked at the khaki ranks and wondered if those tall fellows in uniform could be the boys I've laughed with and played with and danced with and teased all my life. Something seems to have touched them and set them apart. They have heard the Piper's call.

"Fred Arnold was in the battalion and I felt dreadfully about him, for I realized that it was because of me that he was going away with such a sorrowful expression. I couldn't help it but I felt as badly as if I could.

"The last evening of his leave Fred came up to Ingleside and told me he loved me and asked me if I would promise to marry him some day, if he ever came back. He was desperately in earnest and I felt more wretched than I ever did in my life. I couldn't promise him that—why, even if there was no question of Ken, I don't care for Fred that way and never could—but it seemed so cruel and heartless to send him away to the front without any hope of comfort. I cried like a baby; and yet—oh, I am afraid that there must be something incurably frivolous about me, because, right in the middle of it all, with me crying and Fred looking so wild and tragic, the thought popped into my head that it would be an unendurable thing to see that nose across from me at the breakfast table every morning of my life. There, that is one of the entries I wouldn't want my descendants to read in this journal. But it is the humiliating truth; and perhaps it's just as well that thought did come or I might have been tricked by pity and remorse into giving him some rash assurance. If Fred's nose were as handsome as his eyes and mouth some such thing might have happened. And then what an unthinkable predicament I should have been in!

"When poor Fred became convinced that I couldn't promise him, he behaved beautifully—though that rather made things worse. If he had been nasty about it I wouldn't have felt so heartbroken and remorseful—though why I should feel remorseful I don't know, for I never encouraged Fred to think I cared a bit about him. Yet feel remorseful I did—and do. If Fred Arnold never comes back from overseas, this will haunt me all my life.

"Then Fred said if he couldn't take my love with him to the trenches at least he wanted to feel that he had my friendship, and would I kiss him just once in good-bye before he went—perhaps for ever?

"I don't know how I could ever had imagined that love affairs were delightful, interesting things. They are horrible. I couldn't even give poor heartbroken Fred one little kiss, because of my promise to Ken. It seemed so brutal. I had to tell Fred that of course he would have my friendship, but that I couldn't kiss him because I had promised somebody else I wouldn't.

"He said, 'It is—is it—Ken Ford?'

"I nodded. It seemed dreadful to have to tell it—it was such a sacred little secret just between me and Ken.

"When Fred went away I came up here to my room and cried so long and so bitterly that mother came up and insisted on knowing what was the matter. I told her. She listened to my tale with an expression that clearly said, 'Can it be possible that anyone has been wanting to marry this baby?' But she was so nice and understanding and sympathetic, oh, just so race-of-Josephy—that I felt indescribably comforted. Mothers are the dearest things.

"'But oh, mother,' I sobbed, 'he wanted me to kiss him good-bye—and I couldn't—and that hurt me worse than all the rest.'

"'Well, why didn't you kiss him?' asked mother coolly. 'Considering the circumstances, I think you might have.'

"'But I couldn't, mother—I promised Ken when he went away that I wouldn't kiss anybody else until he came back.'

"This was another high explosive for poor mother. She exclaimed, with the queerest little catch in her voice, 'Rilla, are you engaged to Kenneth Ford?'

"'I—don't—know,' I sobbed.

"'You—don't—know?' repeated mother.

"Then I had to tell her the whole story, too; and every time I tell it it seems sillier and sillier to imagine that Ken meant anything serious. I felt idiotic and ashamed by the time I got through.

"Mother sat a little while in silence. Then she came over, sat down beside me, and took me in her arms.

"'Don't cry, dear little Rilla-my-Rilla. You have nothing to reproach yourself with in regard to Fred; and if Leslie West's son asked you to keep your lips for him, I think you may consider yourself engaged to him. But—oh, my baby—my last little baby—I have lost you—the war has made a woman of you too soon.'

"I shall never be too much of a woman to find comfort in mother's hugs. Nevertheless, when I saw Fred marching by two days later in the parade, my heart ached unbearably.

"But I'm glad mother thinks I'm really engaged to Ken!"

22. LITTLE DOG MONDAY KNOWS

"It is two years tonight since the dance at the light, when Jack Elliott brought us news of the war. Do you remember, Miss Oliver?"

Cousin Sophia answered for Miss Oliver. "Oh, indeed, Rilla, I remember that evening only too well, and you a-prancing down here to show off your party clothes. Didn't I warn you that we could not tell what was before us? Little did you think that night what was before you."

"Little did any of us think that," said Susan sharply, "not being gifted with the power of prophecy. It does not require any great foresight, Sophia Crawford, to tell a body that she will have some trouble before her life is over. I could do as much myself."

"We all thought the war would be over in a few months then," said Rilla wistfully. "When I look back it seems so ridiculous that we ever could have supposed it."

"And now, two years later, it is no nearer the end than it was then," said Miss Oliver gloomily.

Susan clicked her knitting-needles briskly.

"Now, Miss Oliver, dear, you know that is not a reasonable remark. You know we are just two years nearer the end, whenever the end is appointed to be."

"Albert read in a Montreal paper today that a war expert gives it as his opinion that it will last five years more," was Cousin Sophia's cheerful contribution.

"It can't," cried Rilla; then she added with a sigh, "Two years ago we would have said 'It can't last two years.' But five more years of this!"

"If Rumania comes in, as I have strong hopes now of her doing, you will see the end in five months instead of five years," said Susan.

"I've no faith in furriners," sighed Cousin Sophia.

"The French are foreigners," retorted Susan, "and look at Verdun. And think of all the Somme victories this blessed summer. The Big Push is on and the Russians are still going well. Why, General Haig says that the German officers he has captured admit that they have lost the war."

"You can't believe a word the Germans say," protested Cousin Sophia. "There is no sense in believing a thing just because you'd like to believe it, Susan Baker. The British have lost millions of men at the Somme and how far have they got? Look facts in the face, Susan Baker, look facts in the face."

"They are wearing the Germans out and so long as that happens it does not matter whether it is done a few miles east or a few miles west. I am not," admitted Susan in tremendous humility, "I am not a military expert, Sophia Crawford, but even I can see that, and so could you if you were not determined to take a gloomy view of everything. The Huns have not got all the cleverness in the world. Have you not heard the story of Alistair MacCallum's son Roderick, from the Upper Glen? He is a prisoner in Germany and his mother got a letter from him last week. He wrote that he was being very kindly treated and that all the prisoners had plenty of food and so on, till you would have supposed everything was lovely. But when he signed his name, right in between Roderick and MacCallum, he wrote two Gaelic words that meant 'all lies' and the German censor did not understand Gaelic and thought it was all part of Roddy's name. So he let it pass, never dreaming how he was diddled. Well, I am going to leave the war to Haig for the rest of the day and make a frosting for my chocolate cake. And when it is made I shall put it on the top shelf. The last one I made I left it on the lower shelf and little Kitchener sneaked in and clawed all the icing off and ate it. We had company for tea that night and when I went to get my cake what a sight did I behold!"

"Has that pore orphan's father never been heerd from yet?" asked Cousin Sophia.

"Yes, I had a letter from him in July," said Rilla. "He said that when he got word of his wife's death and of my taking the baby—Mr. Meredith wrote him, you know—he wrote right away, but as he never got any answer he had begun to think his letter must have been lost."

"It took him two years to begin to think it," said Susan scornfully. "Some people think very slow. Jim Anderson has not got a scratch, for all he has been two years in the trenches. A fool for luck, as the old proverb says."

"He wrote very nicely about Jims and said he'd like to see him," said Rilla. "So I wrote and told him all about the wee man, and sent him snapshots. Jims will be two years old next week and he is a perfect duck."

"You didn't used to be very fond of babies," said Cousin Sophia.

"I'm not a bit fonder of babies in the abstract than ever I was," said Rilla, frankly. "But I do love Jims, and I'm afraid I wasn't really half as glad as I should have been when Jim Anderson's letter proved that he was safe and sound."

"You wasn't hoping the man would be killed!" cried Cousin Sophia in horrified accents.

"No—no—no! I just hoped he would go on forgetting about Jims, Mrs. Crawford."

"And then your pa would have the expense of raising him," said Cousin Sophia reprovingly. "You young creeturs are terrible thoughtless."

Jims himself ran in at this juncture, so rosy and curly and kissable, that he extorted a qualified compliment even from Cousin Sophia.

"He's a reel healthy-looking child now, though mebbee his colour is a mite too high—sorter consumptive looking, as you might say. I never thought you'd raise him when I saw him the day after you brung him home. I reely did not think it was in you and I told Albert's wife so when I got home. Albert's wife says, says she, 'There's more in Rilla Blythe than you'd think for, Aunt Sophia.' Them was her very words. 'More in Rilla Blythe than you'd think for.' Albert's wife always had a good opinion of you."

Cousin Sophia sighed, as if to imply that Albert's wife stood alone in this against the world. But Cousin Sophia really did not mean that. She was quite fond of Rilla in her own melancholy way; but young creeturs had to be kept down. If they were not kept down society would be demoralized.

"Do you remember your walk home from the light two years ago tonight?" whispered Gertrude Oliver to Rilla, teasingly.

"I should think I do," smiled Rilla; and then her smile grew dreamy and absent; she was remembering something else—that hour with Kenneth on the sandshore. Where would Ken be tonight? And Jem and Jerry and Walter and all the other boys who had danced and moonlighted on the old Four Winds Point that evening of mirth and laughter—their last joyous unclouded evening. In the filthy trenches of the Somme front, with the roar of the guns and the groans of stricken men for the music of Ned Burr's violin, and the flash of star shells for the silver sparkles on the old blue gulf. Two of them were sleeping under the Flanders poppies—Alec Burr from the Upper Glen, and Clark Manley of Lowbridge. Others were wounded in the hospitals. But so far nothing had touched the manse and the Ingleside boys. They seemed to bear charmed lives. Yet the suspense never grew any easier to bear as the weeks and months of war went by.

"It isn't as if it were some sort of fever to which you might conclude they were immune when they hadn't taken it for two years," sighed Rilla. "The danger is just as great and just as real as it was the first day they went into the trenches. I know this, and it tortures me every day. And yet I can't help hoping that since they've come this far unhurt they'll come through. Oh, Miss Oliver, what would it be like not to wake up in the morning feeling afraid of the news the day would bring? I can't picture such a state of things somehow. And two years ago this morning I woke wondering what delightful gift the new day would give me. These are the two years I thought would be filled with fun."

"Would you exchange them—now—for two years filled with fun?"

"No," said Rilla slowly. "I wouldn't. It's strange—isn't it?—They have been two terrible years—and yet I have a queer feeling of thankfulness for them—as if they had brought me something very precious, with all their pain. I wouldn't want to go back and be the girl I was two years ago, not even if I could. Not that I think I've made any wonderful progress—but I'm not quite the selfish, frivolous little doll I was then. I suppose I had a soul then, Miss Oliver—but I didn't know it. I know it now—and that is worth a great deal—worth all the suffering of the past two years. And still"—Rilla gave a little apologetic laugh, "I don't want to suffer any more—not even for the sake of more soul growth. At the end of two more years I might look back and be thankful for the development they had brought me, too; but I don't want it now."

"We never do," said Miss Oliver. "That is why we are not left to choose our own means and measure of development, I suppose. No matter how much we value what our lessons have brought us we don't want to go on with the bitter schooling. Well, let us hope for the best, as Susan says; things are really going well now and if Rumania lines up, the end may come with a suddenness that will surprise us all."

Rumania did come in—and Susan remarked approvingly that its king and queen were the finest looking royal couple she had seen pictures of. So the summer passed away. Early in September word came that the Canadians had been shifted to the Somme front and anxiety grew tenser and deeper. For the first time Mrs. Blythe's spirit failed her a little, and as the days of suspense wore on the doctor began to look gravely at her, and veto this or that special effort in Red Cross work.

"Oh, let me work—let me work, Gilbert," she entreated feverishly. "While I'm working I don't think so much. If I'm idle I imagine everything—rest is only torture for me. My two boys are on the frightful Somme front—and Shirley pores day and night over aviation literature and says nothing. But I see the purpose growing in his eyes. No, I cannot rest—don't ask it of me, Gilbert."

But the doctor was inexorable.

"I can't let you kill yourself, Anne-girl," he said. "When the boys come back I want a mother here to welcome them. Why, you're getting transparent. It won't do—ask Susan there if it will do."

"Oh, if Susan and you are both banded together against me!" said Anne helplessly.

One day the glorious news came that the Canadians had taken Courcelette and Martenpuich, with many prisoners and guns. Susan ran up the flag and said it was plain to be seen that Haig knew what soldiers to pick for a hard job. The others dared not feel exultant. Who knew what price had been paid?

Rilla woke that morning when the dawn was beginning to break and went to her window to look out, her thick creamy eyelids heavy with sleep. Just at dawn the world looks as it never looks at any other time. The air was cold with dew and the orchard and grove and Rainbow Valley were full of mystery and wonder. Over the eastern hill were golden deeps and silvery-pink shallows. There was no wind, and Rilla heard distinctly a dog howling in a melancholy way down in the direction of the station. Was it Dog Monday? And if it were, why was he howling like that? Rilla shivered; the sound had something boding and grievous in it. She remembered that Miss Oliver said once, when they were coming home in the darkness and heard a dog howl, "When a dog cries like that the Angel of Death is passing." Rilla listened with a curdling fear at her heart. It was Dog Monday—she felt sure of it. Whose dirge was he howling—to whose spirit was he sending that anguished greeting and farewell?

Rilla went back to bed but she could not sleep. All day she watched and waited in a dread of which she did not speak to anyone. She went down to see Dog Monday and the station-master said, "That dog of yours howled from midnight to sunrise something weird. I dunno what got into him. I got up once and went out and hollered at him but he paid no 'tention to me. He was sitting all alone in the moonlight out there at the end of the platform, and every few minutes the poor lonely little beggar'd lift his nose and howl as if his heart was breaking. He never did it afore—always slept in his kennel real quiet and canny from train to train. But he sure had something on his mind last night."

Dog Monday was lying in his kennel. He wagged his tail and licked Rilla's hand. But he would not touch the food she brought for him.

"I'm afraid he's sick," she said anxiously. She hated to go away and leave him. But no bad news came that day—nor the next—nor the next. Rilla's fear lifted. Dog Monday howled no more and resumed his routine of train meeting and watching. When five days had passed the Ingleside people began to feel that they might be cheerful again. Rilla dashed about the kitchen helping Susan with the breakfast and singing so sweetly and clearly that Cousin Sophia across the road heard her and croaked out to Mrs. Albert,

"'Sing before eating, cry before sleeping,' I've always heard."

But Rilla Blythe shed no tears before the nightfall. When her father, his face grey and drawn and old, came to her that afternoon and told her that Walter had been killed in action at Courcelette she crumpled up in a pitiful little heap of merciful unconsciousness in his arms. Nor did she waken to her pain for many hours.

23. "AND SO, GOODNIGHT"

The fierce flame of agony had burned itself out and the grey dust of its ashes was over all the world. Rilla's younger life recovered physically sooner than her mother. For weeks Mrs. Blythe lay ill from grief and shock. Rilla found it was possible to go on with existence, since existence had still to be reckoned with. There was work to be done, for Susan could not do all. For her mother's sake she had to put on calmness and endurance as a garment in the day; but night after night she lay in her bed, weeping the bitter rebellious tears of youth until at last tears were all wept out and the little patient ache that was to be in her heart until she died took their place.

She clung to Miss Oliver, who knew what to say and what not to say. So few people did. Kind, well-meaning callers and comforters gave Rilla some terrible moments.

"You'll get over it in time," Mrs. William Reese said, cheerfully. Mrs. Reese had three stalwart sons, not one of whom had gone to the front.

"It's such a blessing it was Walter who was taken and not Jem," said Miss Sarah Clow. "Walter was a member of the church, and Jem wasn't. I've told Mr. Meredith many a time that he should have spoken seriously to Jem about it before he went away."

"Pore, pore Walter," sighed Mrs. Reese.

"Do not you come here calling him poor Walter," said Susan indignantly, appearing in the kitchen door, much to the relief of Rilla, who felt that she could endure no more just then. "He was not poor. He was richer than any of you. It is you who stay at home and will not let your sons go who are poor—poor and naked and mean and small—pisen poor, and so are your sons, with all their prosperous farms and fat cattle and their souls no bigger than a flea's—if as big."

"I came here to comfort the afflicted and not to be insulted," said Mrs. Reese, taking her departure, unregretted by anyone. Then the fire went out of Susan and she retreated to her kitchen, laid her faithful old head on the table and wept bitterly for a time. Then she went to work and ironed Jims's little rompers. Rilla scolded her gently for it when she herself came in to do it.

"I am not going to have you kill yourself working for any war-baby," Susan said obstinately.

"Oh, I wish I could just keep on working all the time, Susan," cried poor Rilla. "And I wish I didn't have to go to sleep. It is hideous to go to sleep and forget it for a little while, and wake up and have it all rush over me anew the next morning. Do people ever get used to things like this, Susan? And oh, Susan, I can't get away from what Mrs. Reese said. Did Walter suffer much —he was always so sensitive to pain. Oh, Susan, if I knew that he didn't I think I could gather up a little courage and strength."

This merciful knowledge was given to Rilla. A letter came from Walter's commanding officer, telling them that he had been killed instantly by a bullet during a charge at Courcelette. The same day there was a letter for Rilla from Walter himself.

Rilla carried it unopened to Rainbow Valley and read it there, in the spot where she had had her last talk with him. It is a strange thing to read a letter after the writer is dead—a bitter-sweet thing, in which pain and comfort are strangely mingled. For the first time since the blow had fallen Rilla felt—a different thing from tremulous hope and faith—that Walter, of the glorious gift and the splendid ideals, still lived, with just the same gift and just the same ideals. That could not be destroyed—these could suffer no eclipse. The personality that had expressed itself in that last letter, written on the eve of Courcelette, could not be snuffed out by a German bullet. It must carry on, though the earthly link with things of earth were broken.

"We're going over the top tomorrow, Rilla-my-Rilla," wrote Walter. "I wrote mother and Di yesterday, but somehow I feel as if I must write you tonight. I hadn't intended to do any writing tonight—but I've got to. Do you remember old Mrs. Tom Crawford over-harbour, who was always saying that it was 'laid on her' to do such and such a thing? Well, that is just how I feel. It's 'laid on me' to write you tonight—you, sister and chum of mine. There are some things I want to say before—well, before tomorrow.

"You and Ingleside seem strangely near me tonight. It's the first time I've felt this since I came. Always home has seemed so far away—so hopelessly far away from this hideous welter of filth and blood. But tonight it is quite close to me—it seems to me I can almost see you—hear you speak. And I can see the moonlight shining white and still on the old hills of home. It has seemed to me ever since I came here that it was impossible that there could be calm gentle nights and unshattered moonlight anywhere in the world. But tonight somehow, all the beautiful things I have always loved seem to have become possible again—and this is good, and makes me feel a deep, certain, exquisite happiness. It must be autumn at home now—the harbour is a-dream and the old Glen hills blue with haze, and Rainbow Valley a haunt of delight with wild asters blowing all over it—our old "farewell-summers." I always liked that name better than 'aster'—it was a poem in itself.

"Rilla, you know I've always had premonitions. You remember the Pied Piper—but no, of course you wouldn't—you were too young. One evening long ago when Nan and Di and Jem and the Merediths and I were together in Rainbow Valley I had a queer vision or presentiment —whatever you like to call it. Rilla, I saw the Piper coming down the Valley with a shadowy host behind him. The others thought I was only pretending—but I saw him for just one moment. And Rilla, last night I saw him again. I was doing sentry-go and I saw him marching across No-man's-land from our trenches to the German trenches—the same tall shadowy form, piping weirdly—and behind him followed boys in khaki. Rilla, I tell you I saw him—it was no fancy—no illusion. I heard his music, and then—he was gone. But I had seen him—and I knew what it meant—I knew that I was among those who followed him.

"Rilla, the Piper will pipe me 'west' tomorrow. I feel sure of this. And Rilla, I'm not afraid. When you hear the news, remember that. I've won my own freedom here—freedom from all fear. I shall never be afraid of anything again—not of death—nor of life, if after all, I am to go on living. And life, I think, would be the harder of the two to face—for it could never be beautiful for me again. There would always be such horrible things to remember—things that would make life ugly and painful always for me. I could never forget them. But whether it's life or death, I'm not afraid, Rilla-my-Rilla, and I am not sorry that I came. I'm satisfied. I'll never write the poems I once dreamed of writing—but I've helped to make Canada safe for the poets of the future—for the workers of the future—ay, and the dreamers, too—for if no man dreams, there will be nothing for the workers to fulfil—the future, not of Canada only but of the world —when the 'red rain' of Langemarck and Verdun shall have brought forth a golden harvest— not in a year or two, as some foolishly think, but a generation later, when the seed sown now shall have had time to germinate and grow. Yes, I'm glad I came, Rilla. It isn't only the fate of the little sea-born island I love that is in the balance—nor of Canada nor of England. It's the fate of mankind. That is what we're fighting for. And we shall win—never for a moment doubt that, Rilla. For it isn't only the living who are fighting—the dead are fighting too. Such an army cannot be defeated.

"Is there laughter in your face yet, Rilla? I hope so. The world will need laughter and courage more than ever in the years that will come next. I don't want to preach—this isn't any time for it. But I just want to say something that may help you over the worst when you hear that I've gone 'west.' I've a premonition about you, Rilla, as well as about myself. I think Ken will go back to you—and that there are long years of happiness for you by-and-by. And you will tell your children of the Idea we fought and died for—teach them it must be lived for as well as died for, else the price paid for it will have been given for nought. This will be part of your work, Rilla. And if you—all you girls back in the homeland—do it, then we who don't come back will know that you have not 'broken faith' with us.

"I meant to write to Una tonight, too, but I won't have time now. Read this letter to her and tell her it's really meant for you both—you two dear, fine loyal girls. Tomorrow, when we go over the top—I'll think of you both—of your laughter, Rilla-my-Rilla, and the steadfastness in Una's blue eyes—somehow I see those eyes very plainly tonight, too. Yes, you'll both keep faith —I'm sure of that—you and Una. And so—goodnight. We go over the top at dawn."

Rilla read her letter over many times. There was a new light on her pale young face when she finally stood up, amid the asters Walter had loved, with the sunshine of autumn around her. For the moment at least, she was lifted above pain and loneliness.

"I will keep faith, Walter," she said steadily. "I will work—and teach—and learn—and laugh, yes, I will even laugh—through all my years, because of you and because of what you gave when you followed the call."

Rilla meant to keep Walter's letter as a a sacred treasure. But, seeing the look on Una Meredith's face when Una had read it and held it back to her, she thought of something. Could she do it? Oh, no, she could not give up Walter's letter—his last letter. Surely it was not selfishness to keep it. A copy would be such a soulless thing. But Una—Una had so little—and her eyes were the eyes of a woman stricken to the heart, who yet must not cry out or ask for sympathy.

"Una, would you like to have this letter—to keep?" she asked slowly.

"Yes—if you can give it to me," Una said dully.

"Then—you may have it," said Rilla hurriedly.

"Thank you," said Una. It was all she said, but there was something in her voice which repaid Rilla for her bit of sacrifice.

Una took the letter and when Rilla had gone she pressed it against her lonely lips. Una knew that love would never come into her life now—it was buried for ever under the blood-stained soil "Somewhere in France." No one but herself—and perhaps Rilla—knew it—would ever know it. She had no right in the eyes of her world to grieve. She must hide and bear her long pain as best she could—alone. But she, too, would keep faith.

24. MARY IS JUST IN TIME

The autumn of 1916 was a bitter season for Ingleside. Mrs. Blythe's return to health was slow, and sorrow and loneliness were in all hearts. Every one tried to hide it from the others and "carry on" cheerfully. Rilla laughed a good deal. Nobody at Ingleside was deceived by her laughter; it came from her lips only, never from her heart. But outsiders said some people got over trouble very easily, and Irene Howard remarked that she was surprised to find how shallow Rilla Blythe really was. "Why, after all her pose of being so devoted to Walter, she doesn't seem to mind his death at all. Nobody has ever seen her shed a tear or heard her mention his name. She has evidently quite forgotten him. Poor fellow—you'd really think his family would feel it more. I spoke of him to Rilla at the last Junior Red meeting—of how fine and brave and splendid he was—and I said life could never be just the same to me again, now that Walter had gone—we were such friends, you know—why I was the very first person he told about having enlisted—and Rilla answered, as coolly and indifferently as if she were speaking of an entire stranger, 'He was just one of many fine and splendid boys who have given everything for their country.' Well, I wish I could take things as calmly—but I'm not made like that. I'm so sensitive—things hurt me terribly—I really never get over them. I asked Rilla right out why she didn't put on mourning for Walter. She said her mother didn't wish it. But every one is talking about it."

"Rilla doesn't wear colours—nothing but white," protested Betty Mead.

"White becomes her better than anything else," said Irene significantly. "And we all know black doesn't suit her complexion at all. But of course I'm not saying that is the reason she doesn't wear it. Only, it's funny. If my brother had died I'd have gone into deep mourning. I wouldn't have had the heart for anything else. I confess I'm disappointed in Rilla Blythe."

"I am not, then," cried Betty Meade, loyally, "I think Rilla is just a wonderful girl. A few years ago I admit I did think she was rather too vain and gigglesome; but now she is nothing of the sort. I don't think there is a girl in the Glen who is so unselfish and plucky as Rilla, or who has done her bit as thoroughly and patiently. Our Junior Red Cross would have gone on the rocks a dozen times if it hadn't been for her tact and perseverance and enthusiasm—you know that perfectly well, Irene."

"Why, I am not running Rilla down," said Irene, opening her eyes widely. "It was only her lack of feeling I was criticizing. I suppose she can't help it. Of course, she's a born manager—everyone knows that. She's very fond of managing, too—and people like that are very necessary I admit. So don't look at me as if I'd said something perfectly dreadful, Betty, please. I'm quite willing to agree that Rilla Blythe is the embodiment of all the virtues, if that will please you. And no doubt it is a virtue to be quite unmoved by things that would crush most people."

Some of Irene's remarks were reported to Rilla; but they did not hurt her as they would once have done. They didn't matter, that was all. Life was too big to leave room for pettiness. She had a pact to keep and a work to do; and through the long hard days and weeks of that disastrous autumn she was faithful to her task. The war news was consistently bad, for Germany marched from victory to victory over poor Rumania. "Foreigners—foreigners," Susan muttered dubiously. "Russians or Rumanians or whatever they may be, they are foreigners and you cannot tie to them. But after Verdun I shall not give up hope. And can you tell me, Mrs. Dr. dear, if the Dobruja is a river or a mountain range, or a condition of the atmosphere?"

The Presidential election in the United States came off in November, and Susan was red-hot over that—and quite apologetic for her excitement.

"I never thought I would live to see the day when I would be interested in a Yankee election, Mrs. Dr. dear. It only goes to show we can never know what we will come to in this world, and therefore we should not be proud."

Susan stayed up late on the evening of the eleventh, ostensibly to finish a pair of socks. But she 'phoned down to Carter Flagg's store at intervals, and when the first report came through that Hughes had been elected she stalked solemnly upstairs to Mrs. Blythe's room and announced it in a thrilling whisper from the foot of the bed.

"I thought if you were not asleep you would be interested in knowing it. I believe it is for the best. Perhaps he will just fall to writing notes, too, Mrs. Dr. dear, but I hope for better things. I never was very partial to whiskers, but one cannot have everything."

When news came in the morning that after all Wilson was re-elected, Susan tacked to catch another breeze of optimism.

"Well, better a fool you know than a fool you do not know, as the old proverb has it," she remarked cheerfully. "Not that I hold Woodrow to be a fool by any means, though by times you would not think he has the sense he was born with. But he is a good letter writer at least, and we do not know if the Hughes man is even that. All things being considered I commend the Yankees. They have shown good sense and I do not mind admitting it. Cousin Sophia wanted them to elect Roosevelt, and is much disgruntled because they would not give him a chance. I had a hankering for him myself, but we must believe that Providence over-rules these matters and be satisfied—though what the Almighty means in this affair of Rumania I cannot fathom—saying it with all reverence."

Susan fathomed it—or thought she did—when the Asquith ministry went down and Lloyd George became Premier.

"Mrs. Dr. dear, Lloyd George is at the helm at last. I have been praying for this for many a day. Now we shall soon see a blessed change. It took the Rumanian disaster to bring it about, no less, and that is the meaning of it, though I could not see it before. There will be no more shilly-shallying. I consider that the war is as good as won, and that I shall tie to, whether Bucharest falls or not."

Bucharest did fall—and Germany proposed peace negotiations. Whereat Susan scornfully turned a deaf ear and absolutely refused to listen to such proposals. When President Wilson sent his famous December peace note Susan waxed violently sarcastic.

"Woodrow Wilson is going to make peace, I understand. First Henry Ford had a try at it and now comes Wilson. But peace is not made with ink, Woodrow, and that you may tie to," said Susan, apostrophizing the unlucky President out of the kitchen window nearest the United States. "Lloyd George's speech will tell the Kaiser what is what, and you may keep your peace screeds at home and save postage."

"What a pity President Wilson can't hear you, Susan," said Rilla slyly.

"Indeed, Rilla dear, it is a pity that he has no one near him to give him good advice, as it is clear he has not, in all those Democrats and Republicans," retorted Susan. "I do not know the difference between them, for the politics of the Yankees is a puzzle I cannot solve, study it as I may. But as far as seeing through a grindstone goes, I am afraid—" Susan shook her head dubiously, "that they are all tarred with the same brush."

"I am thankful Christmas is over," Rilla wrote in her diary during the last week of a stormy December. "We had dreaded it so—the first Christmas since Courcelette. But we had all the Merediths down for dinner and nobody tried to be gay or cheerful. We were all just quiet and friendly, and that helped. Then, too, I was so thankful that Jims had got better—so thankful that I almost felt glad—almost but not quite. I wonder if I shall ever feel really glad over anything again. It seems as if gladness were killed in me—shot down by the same bullet that pierced Walter's heart. Perhaps some day a new kind of gladness will be born in my soul—but the old kind will never live again.

"Winter set in awfully early this year. Ten days before Christmas we had a big snowstorm—at least we thought it big at the time. As it happened, it was only a prelude to the real performance. It was fine the next day, and Ingleside and Rainbow Valley were wonderful, with the trees all covered with snow, and big drifts everywhere, carved into the most fantastic shapes by the chisel of the northeast wind. Father and mother went up to Avonlea. Father thought the change would do mother good, and they wanted to see poor Aunt Diana, whose son Jock had been seriously wounded a short time before. They left Susan and me to keep house, and father expected to be back the next day. But he never got back for a week. That night it began to storm again, and it stormed unbrokenly for four days. It was the worst and longest storm that Prince Edward Island has known for years. Everything was disorganized—the roads were completely choked up, the trains blockaded, and the telephone wires put entirely out of commission.

"And then Jims took ill.

"He had a little cold when father and mother went away, and he kept getting worse for a couple of days, but it didn't occur to me that there was danger of anything serious. I never even took his temperature, and I can't forgive myself, because it was sheer carelessness. The truth is I had slumped just then. Mother was away, so I let myself go. All at once I was tired of keeping up and pretending to be brave and cheerful, and I just gave up for a few days and spent most of the time lying on my face on my bed, crying. I neglected Jims—that is the hateful truth—I was cowardly and false to what I promised Walter—and if Jims had died I could never have forgiven myself.

"Then, the third night after father and mother went away, Jims suddenly got worse—oh, so much worse—all at once. Susan and I were all alone. Gertrude had been at Lowbridge when the storm began and had never got back. At first we were not much alarmed. Jims has had several bouts of croup and Susan and Morgan and I have always brought him through without much trouble. But it wasn't very long before we were dreadfully alarmed.

"'I never saw croup like this before,' said Susan.

"As for me, I knew, when it was too late, what kind of croup it was. I knew it was not the ordinary croup—'false croup' as doctors call it—but the 'true croup'—and I knew that it was a deadly and dangerous thing. And father was away and there was no doctor nearer than Lowbridge—and we could not 'phone and neither horse nor man could get through the drifts that night.

"Gallant little Jims put up a good fight for his life,—Susan and I tried every remedy we could think of or find in father's books, but he continued to grow worse. It was heart-rending to see and hear him. He gasped so horribly for breath—the poor little soul—and his face turned a dreadful bluish colour and had such an agonized expression, and he kept struggling with his little hands, as if he were appealing to us to help him somehow. I found myself thinking that the boys who had been gassed at the front must have looked like that, and the thought haunted me amid all my dread and misery over Jims. And all the time the fatal membrane in his wee throat grew and thickened and he couldn't get it up.

"Oh, I was just wild! I never realized how dear Jims was to me until that moment. And I felt so utterly helpless."

"And then Susan gave up. 'We cannot save him! Oh, if your father was here—look at him, the poor little fellow! I know not what to do.'

"I looked at Jims and I thought he was dying. Susan was holding him up in his crib to give him a better chance for breath, but it didn't seem as if he could breathe at all. My little war-baby, with his dear ways and sweet roguish face, was choking to death before my very eyes, and I couldn't help him. I threw down the hot poultice I had ready in despair. Of what use was it? Jims was dying, and it was my fault—I hadn't been careful enough!

"Just then—at eleven o'clock at night—the door bell rang. Such a ring—it pealed all over the house above the roar of the storm. Susan couldn't go—she dared not lay Jims down—so I rushed downstairs. In the hall I paused just a minute—I was suddenly overcome by an absurd dread. I thought of a weird story Gertrude had told me once. An aunt of hers was alone in a house one night with her sick husband. She heard a knock at the door. And when she went and opened it there was nothing there—nothing that could be seen, at least. But when she opened the door a deadly cold wind blew in and seemed to sweep past her right up the stairs, although it was a calm, warm summer night outside. Immediately she heard a cry. She ran upstairs—and her husband was dead. And she always believed, so Gertrude said, that when she opened that door she let Death in.

"It was so ridiculous of me to feel so frightened. But I was distracted and worn out, and I simply felt for a moment that I dared not open the door—that death was waiting outside. Then I remembered that I had no time to waste—must not be so foolish—I sprang forward and opened the door.

"Certainly a cold wind did blow in and filled the hall with a whirl of snow. But there on the threshold stood a form of flesh and blood—Mary Vance, coated from head to foot with snow—and she brought Life, not Death, with her, though I didn't know that then. I just stared at her.

"'I haven't been turned out,' grinned Mary, as she stepped in and shut the door. 'I came up to Carter Flagg's two days ago and I've been stormed-stayed there ever since. But old Abbie Flagg got on my nerves at last, and tonight I just made up my mind to come up here. I thought I could wade this far, but I can tell you it was as much as a bargain. Once I thought I was stuck for keeps. Ain't it an awful night?'

"I came to myself and knew I must hurry upstairs. I explained as quickly as I could to Mary, and left her trying to brush the snow off. Upstairs I found that Jims was over that paroxysm, but almost as soon as I got back to the room he was in the grip of another. I couldn't do anything but moan and cry—oh, how ashamed I am when I think of it; and yet what could I do—we had tried everything we knew—and then all at once I heard Mary Vance saying loudly behind me, 'Why, that child is dying!'

"I whirled around. Didn't I know he was dying—my little Jims! I could have thrown Mary Vance out of the door or the window—anywhere—at that moment. There she stood, cool and composed, looking down at my baby, with those, weird white eyes of hers, as she might look at a choking kitten. I had always disliked Mary Vance—and just then I hated her.

"'We have tried everything,' said poor Susan dully. 'It is not ordinary croup.'

"'No, it's the dipthery croup,' said Mary briskly, snatching up an apron. 'And there's mighty little time to lose—but I know what to do. When I lived over-harbour with Mrs. Wiley, years ago, Will Crawford's kid died of dipthery croup, in spite of two doctors. And when old Aunt Christina MacAllister heard of it—she was the one brought me round when I nearly died of pneumonia you know—she was a wonder—no doctor was a patch on her—they don't hatch her breed of cats nowadays, let me tell you—she said she could have saved him with her grandmother's remedy if she'd been there. She told Mrs. Wiley what it was and I've never forgot it. I've the greatest memory ever—a thing just lies in the back of my head till the time comes to use it. Got any sulphur in the house, Susan?'

"Yes, we had sulphur. Susan went down with Mary to get it, and I held Jims. I hadn't any hope—not the least. Mary Vance might brag as she liked—she was always bragging—but I didn't believe any grandmother's remedy could save Jims now. Presently Mary came back. She had tied a piece of thick flannel over her mouth and nose, and she carried Susan's old tin chip pan, half full of burning coals.

"'You watch me,' she said boastfully. 'I've never done this, but it's kill or cure that child is dying anyway.'

"She sprinkled a spoonful of sulphur over the coals; and then she picked up Jims, turned him over, and held him face downward, right over those choking, blinding fumes. I don't know why I didn't spring forward and snatch him away. Susan says it was because it was fore-ordained that I shouldn't, and I think she is right, because it did really seem that I was powerless to move. Susan herself seemed transfixed, watching Mary from the doorway. Jims writhed in those big, firm, capable hands of Mary—oh yes, she is capable all right—and choked and wheezed—and choked and wheezed—and I felt that he was being tortured to death—and then all at once, after what seemed to me an hour, though it really wasn't long, he coughed up the membrane that was killing him. Mary turned him over and laid him back on his bed. He was white as marble and the tears were pouring out of his brown eyes—but that awful livid look was gone from his face and he could breathe quite easily.

"'Wasn't that some trick?' said Mary gaily. 'I hadn't any idea how it would work, but I just took a chance. I'll smoke his throat out again once or twice before morning, just to kill all the germs, but you'll see he'll be all right now.'

"Jims went right to sleep—real sleep, not coma, as I feared at first. Mary 'smoked him,' as she called it, twice through the night, and at daylight his throat was perfectly clear and his temperature was almost normal. When I made sure of that I turned and looked at Mary Vance. She was sitting on the lounge laying down the law to Susan on some subject about which Susan must have known forty times as much as she did. But I didn't mind how much law she laid down or how much she bragged. She had a right to brag—she had dared to do what I would never have dared, and had saved Jims from a horrible death. It didn't matter any more that she had once chased me through the Glen with a codfish; it didn't matter that she had smeared goose-grease all over my dream of romance the night of the lighthouse dance; it didn't matter that she thought she knew more than anybody else and always rubbed it in—I would never dislike Mary Vance again. I went over to her and kissed her.

"'What's up now?' she said.

"'Nothing—only I'm so grateful to you, Mary.'

"'Well, I think you ought to be, that's a fact. You two would have let that baby die on your hands if I hadn't happened along,' said Mary, just beaming with complacency. She got Susan and me a tip-top breakfast and made us eat it, and 'bossed the life out of us,' as Susan says, for two days, until the roads were opened so that she could get home. Jims was almost well by that time, and father turned up. He heard our tale without saying much. Father is rather scornful generally about what he calls 'old wives' remedies.' He laughed a little and said, 'After this, Mary Vance will expect me to call her in for consultation in all my serious cases.'

"So Christmas was not so hard as I expected it to be; and now the New Year is coming—and we are still hoping for the 'Big Push' that will end the war—and Little Dog Monday is getting stiff and rheumatic from his cold vigils, but still he 'carries on,' and Shirley continues to read the exploits of the aces. Oh, nineteen-seventeen, what will you bring?"

25. SHIRLEY GOES

"No, Woodrow, there will be no peace without victory," said Susan, sticking her knitting needle viciously through President Wilson's name in the newspaper column. "We Canadians mean to have peace and victory, too. You, if it pleases you, Woodrow, can have the peace without the victory"—and Susan stalked off to bed with the comfortable consciousness of having got the better of the argument with the President. But a few days later she rushed to Mrs. Blythe in red-hot excitement.

"Mrs. Dr. dear, what do you think? A 'phone message has just come through from Charlottetown that Woodrow Wilson has sent that German ambassador man to the right about at last. They tell me that means war. So I begin to think that Woodrow's heart is in the right place after all, wherever his head may be, and I am going to commandeer a little sugar and celebrate the occasion with some fudge, despite the howls of the Food Board. I thought that submarine business would bring things to a crisis. I told Cousin Sophia so when she said it was the beginning of the end for the Allies."

"Don't let the doctor hear of the fudge, Susan," said Anne, with a smile. "You know he has laid down very strict rules for us along the lines of economy the government has asked for."

"Yes, Mrs. Dr. dear, and a man should be master in his own household, and his women folk should bow to his decrees. I flatter myself that I am becoming quite efficient in economizing"—Susan had taken to using certain German terms with killing effect—"but one can exercise a little gumption on the quiet now and then. Shirley was wishing for some of my fudge the other day—the Susan brand, as he called it—and I said 'The first victory there is to celebrate I shall make you some.' I consider this news quite equal to a victory, and what the doctor does not know will never grieve him. I take the whole responsibility, Mrs. Dr. dear, so do not you vex your conscience."

Susan spoiled Shirley shamelessly that winter. He came home from Queen's every week-end, and Susan had all his favourite dishes for him, in so far as she could evade or wheedle the doctor, and waited on him hand and foot. Though she talked war constantly to everyone else she never mentioned it to him or before him, but she watched him like a cat watching a mouse; and when the German retreat from the Bapaume salient began and continued, Susan's exultation was linked up with something deeper than anything she expressed. Surely the end was in sight—would come now before—anyone else—could go.

"Things are coming our way at last. We have got the Germans on the run," she boasted. "The United States has declared war at last, as I always believed they would, in spite of Woodrow's gift for letter writing, and you will see they will go into it with a vim since I understand that is their habit, when they do start. And we have got the Germans on the run, too."

"The States mean well," moaned Cousin Sophia, "but all the vim in the world cannot put them on the fighting line this spring, and the Allies will be finished before that. The Germans are just luring them on. That man Simonds says their retreat has put the Allies in a hole."

"That man Simonds has said more than he will ever live to make good," retorted Susan. "I do not worry myself about his opinion as long as Lloyd George is Premier of England. He will not be bamboozled and that you may tie to. Things look good to me. The U. S. is in the war, and we have got Kut and Bagdad back—and I would not be surprised to see the Allies in Berlin by

June—and the Russians, too, since they have got rid of the Czar. That, in my opinion was a good piece of work."

"Time will show if it is," said Cousin Sophia, who would have been very indignant if anyone had told her that she would rather see Susan put to shame as a seer, than a successful overthrow of tyranny, or even the march of the Allies down Unter den Linden. But then the woes of the Russian people were quite unknown to Cousin Sophia, while this aggravating, optimistic Susan was an ever-present thorn in her side.

Just at that moment Shirley was sitting on the edge of the table in the living-room, swinging his legs—a brown, ruddy, wholesome lad, from top to toe, every inch of him—and saying coolly, "Mother and dad, I was eighteen last Monday. Don't you think it's about time I joined up?"

The pale mother looked at him.

"Two of my sons have gone and one will never return. Must I give you too, Shirley?"

The age-old cry—"Joseph is not and Simeon is not; and ye will take Benjamin away." How the mothers of the Great War echoed the old Patriarch's moan of so many centuries agone!

"You wouldn't have me a slacker, mother? I can get into the flying-corps. What say, dad?"

The doctor's hands were not quite steady as he folded up the powders he was concocting for Abbie Flagg's rheumatism. He had known this moment was coming, yet he was not altogether prepared for it. He answered slowly, "I won't try to hold you back from what you believe to be your duty. But you must not go unless your mother says you may."

Shirley said nothing more. He was not a lad of many words. Anne did not say anything more just then, either. She was thinking of little Joyce's grave in the old burying-ground over-harbour—little Joyce who would have been a woman now, had she lived—of the white cross in France and the splendid grey eyes of the little boy who had been taught his first lessons of duty and loyalty at her knee—of Jem in the terrible trenches—of Nan and Di and Rilla, waiting—waiting—waiting, while the golden years of youth passed by—and she wondered if she could bear any more. She thought not; surely she had given enough.

Yet that night she told Shirley that he might go.

They did not tell Susan right away. She did not know it until, a few days later, Shirley presented himself in her kitchen in his aviation uniform. Susan didn't make half the fuss she had made when Jem and Walter had gone. She said stonily, "So they're going to take you, too."

"Take me? No. I'm going, Susan—got to."

Susan sat down by the table, folded her knotted old hands, that had grown warped and twisted working for the Ingleside children to still their shaking, and said:

"Yes, you must go. I did not see once why such things must be, but I can see now."

"You're a brick, Susan," said Shirley. He was relieved that she took it so coolly—he had been a little afraid, with a boy's horror of "a scene." He went out whistling gaily; but half an hour later, when pale Anne Blythe came in, Susan was still sitting there.

"Mrs. Dr. dear," said Susan, making an admission she would once have died rather than make, "I feel very old. Jem and Walter were yours but Shirley is mine. And I cannot bear to think of him flying—his machine crashing down—the life crushed out of his body—the dear little body I nursed and cuddled when he was a wee baby."

"Susan—don't," cried Anne.

"Oh, Mrs. Dr. dear, I beg your pardon. I ought not to have said anything like that out loud. I sometimes forget that I resolved to be a heroine. This—this has shaken me a little. But I will not forget myself again. Only if things do not go as smoothly in the kitchen for a few days I hope you will make due allowance for me. At least," said poor Susan, forcing a grim smile in a desperate effort to recover lost standing, "at least flying is a clean job. He will not get so dirty and messed up as he would in the trenches, and that is well, for he has always been a tidy child."

So Shirley went—not radiantly, as to a high adventure, like Jem, not in a white flame of sacrifice, like Walter, but in a cool, business-like mood, as of one doing something, rather dirty and disagreeable, that had just got to be done. He kissed Susan for the first time since he was five years old, and said, "Good-bye, Susan—mother Susan."

"My little brown boy—my little brown boy," said Susan. "I wonder," she thought bitterly, as she looked at the doctor's sorrowful face, "if you remember how you spanked him once when he was a baby. I am thankful I have nothing like that on my conscience now."

The doctor did not remember the old discipline. But before he put on his hat to go out on his round of calls he stood for a moment in the great silent living-room that had once been full of children's laughter.

"Our last son—our last son," he said aloud. "A good, sturdy, sensible lad, too. Always reminded me of my father. I suppose I ought to be proud that he wanted to go—I was proud when Jem went—even when Walter went—but 'our house is left us desolate.'"

"I have been thinking, doctor," old Sandy of the Upper Glen said to him that afternoon, "that your house will be seeming very big the day."

Highland Sandy's quaint phrase struck the doctor as perfectly expressive. Ingleside did seem very big and empty that night. Yet Shirley had been away all winter except for week-ends, and had always been a quiet fellow even when home. Was it because he had been the only one left that his going seemed to leave such a huge blank—that every room seemed vacant and deserted—that the very trees on the lawn seemed to be trying to comfort each other with caresses of freshly-budding boughs for the loss of the last of the little lads who had romped under them in childhood?

Susan worked very hard all day and late into the night. When she had wound the kitchen clock and put Dr. Jekyll out, none too gently, she stood for a little while on the doorstep, looking down the Glen, which lay tranced in faint, silvery light from a sinking young moon. But Susan did not see the familiar hills and harbour. She was looking at the aviation camp in Kingsport where Shirley was that night.

"He called me 'Mother Susan,'" she was thinking. "Well, all our men folk have gone now—Jem and Walter and Shirley and Jerry and Carl. And none of them had to be driven to it. So we have a right to be proud. But pride—" Susan sighed bitterly—"pride is cold company and that there is no gainsaying."

The moon sank lower into a black cloud in the west, the Glen went out in an eclipse of sudden shadow—and thousands of miles away the Canadian boys in khaki—the living and the dead—were in possession of Vimy Ridge.

Vimy Ridge is a name written in crimson and gold on the Canadian annals of the Great War. "The British couldn't take it and the French couldn't take it," said a German prisoner to his captors, "but you Canadians are such fools that you don't know when a place can't be taken!"

So the "fools" took it—and paid the price.

Jerry Meredith was seriously wounded at Vimy Ridge—shot in the back, the telegram said.

"Poor Nan," said Mrs. Blythe, when the news came. She thought of her own happy girlhood at old Green Gables. There had been no tragedy like this in it. How the girls of to-day had to suffer! When Nan came home from Redmond two weeks later her face showed what those weeks had meant to her. John Meredith, too, seemed to have grown old suddenly in them. Faith did not come home; she was on her way across the Atlantic as a V.A.D. Di had tried to wring from her father consent to her going also, but had been told that for her mother's sake it could not be given. So Di, after a flying visit home, went back to her Red Cross work in Kingsport.

The mayflowers bloomed in the secret nooks of Rainbow Valley. Rilla was watching for them. Jem had once taken his mother the earliest mayflowers; Walter brought them to her when Jem was gone; last spring Shirley had sought them out for her; now, Rilla thought she must take the boys' place in this. But before she had discovered any, Bruce Meredith came to Ingleside one twilight with his hands full of delicate pink sprays. He stalked up the steps of the veranda and laid them on Mrs. Blythe's lap.

"Because Shirley isn't here to bring them," he said in his funny, shy, blunt way.

"And you thought of this, you darling," said Anne, her lips quivering, as she looked at the stocky, black-browed little chap, standing before her, with his hands thrust into his pockets.

"I wrote Jem to-day and told him not to worry 'bout you not getting your mayflowers," said Bruce seriously, "'cause I'd see to that. And I told him I would be ten pretty soon now, so it won't be very long before I'll be eighteen, and then I'll go to help him fight, and maybe let him come home for a rest while I took his place. I wrote Jerry, too. Jerry's getting better, you know."

"Is he? Have you had any good news about him?"

"Yes. Mother had a letter to-day, and it said he was out of danger."

"Oh, thank God," murmured Mrs. Blythe, in a half-whisper.

Bruce looked at her curiously.

"That is what father said when mother told him. But when I said it the other day when I found out Mr. Mead's dog hadn't hurt my kitten—I thought he had shooken it to death, you know—father looked awful solemn and said I must never say that again about a kitten. But I couldn't understand why, Mrs. Blythe. I felt awful thankful, and it must have been God that saved Stripey, because that Mead dog had 'normous jaws, and oh, how it shook poor Stripey. And so why couldn't I thank Him? 'Course," added Bruce reminiscently, "maybe I said it too loud—'cause I was awful glad and excited when I found Stripey was all right. I 'most shouted it, Mrs. Blythe. Maybe if I'd said it sort of whispery like you and father it would have been all right. Do you know, Mrs. Blythe"—Bruce dropped to a "whispery" tone, edging a little nearer to Anne—"what I would like to do to the Kaiser if I could?"

"What would you like to do, laddie?"

"Norman Reese said in school to-day that he would like to tie the Kaiser to a tree and set cross dogs to worrying him," said Bruce gravely. "And Emily Flagg said she would like to put him in a cage and poke sharp things into him. And they all said things like that. But Mrs. Blythe"—Bruce took a little square paw out of his pocket and put it earnestly on Anne's knee—"I would like to turn the Kaiser into a good man—a very good man—all at once if I could. That is what I would do. Don't you think, Mrs. Blythe, that would be the very worstest punishment of all?"

"Bless the child," said Susan, "how do you make out that would be any kind of a punishment for that wicked fiend?"

"Don't you see," said Bruce, looking levelly at Susan, out of his blackly blue eyes, "if he was turned into a good man he would understand how dreadful the things he has done are, and he would feel so terrible about it that he would be more unhappy and miserable than he could ever be in any other way. He would feel just awful—and he would go on feeling like that forever. Yes"—Bruce clenched his hands and nodded his head emphatically, "yes, I would make the Kaiser a good man—that is what I would do—it would serve him 'zackly right."

26. SUSAN HAS A PROPOSAL OF MARRIAGE

An aeroplane was flying over Glen St. Mary, like a great bird poised against the western sky—a sky so clear and of such a pale, silvery yellow, that it gave an impression of a vast, wind-freshened space of freedom. The little group on the Ingleside lawn looked up at it with fascinated eyes, although it was by no means an unusual thing to see an occasional hovering plane that summer. Susan was always intensely excited. Who knew but that it might be Shirley away up there in the clouds, flying over to the Island from Kingsport? But Shirley had gone overseas now, so Susan was not so keenly interested in this particular aeroplane and its pilot. Nevertheless, she looked at it with awe.

"I wonder, Mrs. Dr. dear," she said solemnly, "what the old folks down there in the graveyard would think if they could rise out of their graves for one moment and behold that sight. I am sure my father would disapprove of it, for he was a man who did not believe in new-fangled ideas of any sort. He always cut his grain with a reaping hook to the day of his death. A mower he would not have. What was good enough for his father was good enough for him, he used to say. I hope it is not unfilial to say that I think he was wrong in that point of view, but I am not sure I go so far as to approve of aeroplanes, though they may be a military necessity. If the Almighty had meant us to fly he would have provided us with wings. Since He did not it is plain He meant us to stick to the solid earth. At any rate, you will never see me, Mrs. Dr. dear, cavorting through the sky in an aeroplane."

"But you won't refuse to cavort a bit in father's new automobile when it comes, will you, Susan?" teased Rilla.

"I do not expect to trust my old bones in automobiles, either," retorted Susan. "But I do not look upon them as some narrow-minded people do. Whiskers-on-the-moon says the Government should be turned out of office for permitting them to run on the Island at all. He foams at the mouth, they tell me, when he sees one. The other day he saw one coming along that narrow side-road by his wheatfield, and Whiskers bounded over the fence and stood right in the middle of the road, with his pitchfork. The man in the machine was an agent of some kind, and Whiskers hates agents as much as he hates automobiles. He made the car come to a halt, because there was not room to pass him on either side, and the agent could not actually run over him. Then he raised his pitchfork and shouted, 'Get out of this with your devil-machine or I will run this pitchfork clean through you.' And Mrs. Dr. dear, if you will believe me, that poor agent had to back his car clean out to the Lowbridge road, nearly a mile, Whiskers following him every step, shaking his pitchfork and bellowing insults. Now, Mrs. Dr. dear, I call such conduct unreasonable; but all the same," added Susan, with a sigh, "what with aeroplanes and automobiles and all the rest of it, this Island is not what it used to be."

The aeroplane soared and dipped and circled, and soared again, until it became a mere speck far over the sunset hills.

"'With the majesty of pinion Which the Theban eagles bear Sailing with supreme dominion Through the azure fields of air.'"

quoted Anne Blythe dreamily.

"I wonder," said Miss Oliver, "if humanity will be any happier because of aeroplanes. It seems to me that the sum of human happiness remains much the same from age to age, no matter how it may vary in distribution, and that all the 'many inventions' neither lessen nor increase it."

"After all, the 'kingdom of heaven is within you,'" said Mr. Meredith, gazing after the vanishing speck which symbolized man's latest victory in a world-old struggle. "It does not depend on material achievements and triumphs."

"Nevertheless, an aeroplane is a fascinating thing," said the doctor. "It has always been one of humanity's favourite dreams—the dream of flying. Dream after dream comes true—or rather is made true by persevering effort. I should like to have a flight in an aeroplane myself."

"Shirley wrote me that he was dreadfully disappointed in his first flight," said Rilla. "He had expected to experience the sensation of soaring up from the earth like a bird—and instead he just had the feeling that he wasn't moving at all, but that the earth was dropping away under him. And the first time he went up alone he suddenly felt terribly homesick. He had never felt like that before; but all at once, he said, he felt as if he were adrift in space—and he had a wild desire to get back home to the old planet and the companionship of fellow creatures. He soon got over that feeling, but he says his first flight alone was a nightmare to him because of that dreadful sensation of ghastly loneliness."

The aeroplane disappeared. The doctor threw back his head with a sigh.

"When I have watched one of those bird-men out of sight I come back to earth with an odd feeling of being merely a crawling insect. Anne," he said, turning to his wife, "do you remember the first time I took you for a buggy ride in Avonlea—that night we went to the Carmody concert, the first fall you taught in Avonlea? I had out little black mare with the white star on her forehead, and a shining brand-new buggy—and I was the proudest fellow in the world, barring none. I suppose our grandson will be taking his sweetheart out quite casually for an evening 'fly' in his aeroplane."

"An aeroplane won't be as nice as little Silverspot was," said Anne. "A machine is simply a machine—but Silverspot, why she was a personality, Gilbert. A drive behind her had something in it that not even a flight among sunset clouds could have. No, I don't envy my grandson's sweetheart, after all. Mr. Meredith is right. 'The kingdom of Heaven'—and of love—and of happiness—doesn't depend on externals."

"Besides," said the doctor gravely, "our said grandson will have to give most of his attention to the aeroplane—he won't be able to let the reins lie on its back while he gazes into his lady's eyes. And I have an awful suspicion that you can't run an aeroplane with one arm. No"—the doctor shook his head—"I believe I'd still prefer Silverspot after all."

The Russian line broke again that summer and Susan said bitterly that she had expected it ever since Kerensky had gone and got married.

"Far be it from me to decry the holy state of matrimony, Mrs. Dr. dear, but I felt that when a man was running a revolution he had his hands full and should have postponed marriage until a more fitting season. The Russians are done for this time and there would be no sense in shutting our eyes to the fact. But have you seen Woodrow Wilson's reply to the Pope's peace proposals? It is magnificent. I really could not have expressed the rights of the matter better myself. I feel that I can forgive Wilson everything for it. He knows the meaning of words and that you may tie to. Speaking of meanings, have you heard the latest story about Whiskers-on-the-moon, Mrs. Dr. dear? It seems he was over at the Lowbridge Road school the other day and took a notion to examine the fourth class in spelling. They have the summer term there yet, you know, with the spring and fall vacations, being rather backward people on that road. My niece, Ella Baker, goes to that school and she it was who told me the story. The teacher was not feeling well, having a dreadful headache, and she went out to get a little fresh air while Mr. Pryor was examining the class. The children got along all right with the spelling but when Whiskers began to question them about the meanings of the words they were all at sea, because they had not learned them. Ella and the other big scholars felt terrible over it. They love their teacher so, and it seems Mr. Pryor's brother, Abel Pryor, who is trustee of that school, is against her and has been trying to turn the other trustees over to his way of thinking. And Ella and the rest were afraid that if the fourth class couldn't tell Whiskers the meanings of the words he would think the teacher was no good and tell Abel so, and Abel would have a fine handle. But little Sandy Logan saved the situation. He is a Home boy, but he is as smart as a steel trap, and he sized up Whiskers-on-the-moon right off. 'What does "anatomy" mean?' Whiskers demanded. 'A pain in your stomach,' Sandy replied, quick as a flash and never batting an eyelid. Whiskers-on-the-moon is a very ignorant man, Mrs. Dr. dear; he didn't know the meaning of the words himself, and he said 'Very good—very good.' The class caught right on—at least three or four of the brighter ones did—and they kept up the fun. Jean Blane said that 'acoustic' meant 'a religious squabble,' and Muriel Baker said that an 'agnostic' was 'a man who had indigestion,' and Jim Carter said that 'acerbity' meant that 'you ate nothing but vegetable food,' and so on all down the list. Whiskers swallowed it all, and kept saying 'Very good—very good' until Ella thought that die she would trying to keep a straight face. When the teacher came in, Whiskers complimented her on the splendid understanding the children had of their lesson and said he meant to tell the trustees what a jewel they had. It was 'very unusual,' he said, to find a fourth class who could answer up so prompt when it came to explaining what words meant. He went off beaming. But Ella told me this as a great secret, Mrs. Dr. dear, and we must keep it as such, for the sake of the Lowbridge Road teacher. It would likely be the ruin of her chances of keeping the school if Whiskers should ever find out how he had been bamboozled."

Mary Vance came up to Ingleside that same afternoon to tell them that Miller Douglas, who had been wounded when the Canadians took Hill 70, had had to have his leg amputated. The Ingleside folk sympathized with Mary, whose zeal and patriotism had taken some time to kindle but now burned with a glow as steady and bright as any one's.

"Some folks have been twitting me about having a husband with only one leg. But," said Mary, rising to a lofty height, "I would rather Miller with only one leg than any other man in the world with a dozen—unless," she added as an after-thought, "unless it was Lloyd George. Well, I must be going. I thought you'd be interested in hearing about Miller so I ran up from the store, but I must hustle home for I promised Luke MacAllister I'd help him build his grain stack this evening. It's up to us girls to see that the harvest is got in, since the boys are so scarce. I've got overalls and I can tell you they're real becoming. Mrs. Alec Douglas says they're indecent and shouldn't be allowed, and even Mrs. Elliott kinder looks askance at them. But bless you, the world moves, and anyhow there's no fun for me like shocking Kitty Alec."

"By the way, father," said Rilla, "I'm going to take Jack Flagg's place in his father's store for a month. I promised him today that I would, if you didn't object. Then he can help the farmers get the harvest in. I don't think I'd be much use in a harvest myself—though lots of the girls are —but I can set Jack free while I do his work. Jims isn't much bother in the daytime now, and I'll always be home at night."

"Do you think you'll like weighing out sugar and beans, and trafficking in butter and eggs?" said the doctor, twinkling.

"Probably not. That isn't the question. It's just one way of doing my bit." So Rilla went behind Mr. Flagg's counter for a month; and Susan went into Albert Crawford's oat-fields.

"I am as good as any of them yet," she said proudly. "Not a man of them can beat me when it comes to building a stack. When I offered to help Albert looked doubtful. 'I am afraid the work will be too hard for you,' he said. 'Try me for a day and see,' said I. 'I will do my darnedest.'"

None of the Ingleside folks spoke for just a moment. Their silence meant that they thought Susan's pluck in "working out" quite wonderful. But Susan mistook their meaning and her sun-burned face grew red.

"This habit of swearing seems to be growing on me, Mrs. Dr. dear," she said apologetically. "To think that I should be acquiring it at my age! It is such a dreadful example to the young girls. I am of the opinion it comes of reading the newspapers so much. They are so full of profanity and they do not spell it with stars either, as used to be done in my young days. This war is demoralizing everybody."

Susan, standing on a load of grain, her grey hair whipping in the breeze and her skirt kilted up to her knees for safety and convenience—no overalls for Susan, if you please—neither a beautiful nor a romantic figure; but the spirit that animated her gaunt arms was the self-same one that captured Vimy Ridge and held the German legions back from Verdun.

It is not the least likely, however, that this consideration was the one which appealed most strongly to Mr. Pryor when he drove past one afternoon and saw Susan pitching sheaves gamely.

"Smart woman that," he reflected. "Worth two of many a younger one yet. I might do worse —I might do worse. If Milgrave comes home alive I'll lose Miranda and hired housekeepers cost more than a wife and are liable to leave a man in the lurch any time. I'll think it over."

A week later Mrs. Blythe, coming up from the village late in the afternoon, paused at the gate of Ingleside in an amazement which temporarily bereft her of the power of motion. An extraordinary sight met her eyes. Round the end of the kitchen burst Mr. Pryor, running as stout, pompous Mr. Pryor had not run in years, with terror imprinted on every lineament—a terror quite justifiable, for behind him, like an avenging fate, came Susan, with a huge, smoking iron pot grasped in her hands, and an expression in her eye that boded ill to the object of her indignation, if she should overtake him. Pursuer and pursued tore across the lawn. Mr. Pryor reached the gate a few feet ahead of Susan, wrenched it open, and fled down the road, without a glance at the transfixed lady of Ingleside.

"Susan," gasped Anne.

Susan halted in her mad career, set down her pot, and shook her fist after Mr. Pryor, who had not ceased to run, evidently believing that Susan was still full cry after him.

"Susan, what does this mean?" demanded Anne, a little severely.

"You may well ask that, Mrs. Dr. dear," Susan replied wrathfully. "I have not been so upset in years. That—that—that pacifist has actually had the audacity to come up here and, in my own kitchen, to ask me to marry him. HIM!"

Anne choked back a laugh.

"But—Susan! Couldn't you have found a—well, a less spectacular method of refusing him? Think what a gossip this would have made if anyone had been going past and had seen such a performance."

"Indeed, Mrs. Dr. dear, you are quite right. I did not think of it because I was quite past thinking rationally. I was just clean mad. Come in the house and I will tell you all about it."

Susan picked up her pot and marched into the kitchen, still trembling with wrathful excitement. She set her pot on the stove with a vicious thud. "Wait a moment until I open all the windows to air this kitchen well, Mrs. Dr. dear. There, that is better. And I must wash my hands, too, because I shook hands with Whiskers-on-the-moon when he came in—not that I wanted to, but when he stuck out his fat, oily hand I did not know just what else to do at the moment. I had just finished my afternoon cleaning and thanks be, everything was shining and spotless; and thought I 'now that dye is boiling and I will get my rug rags and have them nicely out of the way before supper.'

"Just then a shadow fell over the floor and looking up I saw Whiskers-on-the-moon, standing in the doorway, dressed up and looking as if he had just been starched and ironed. I shook hands with him, as aforesaid, Mrs. Dr. dear, and told him you and the doctor were both away. But he said,

"I have come to see you, Miss Baker.'

"I asked him to sit down, for the sake of my own manners, and then I stood there right in the middle of the floor and gazed at him as contemptuously as I could. In spite of his brazen assurance this seemed to rattle him a little; but he began trying to look sentimental at me out of his little piggy eyes, and all at once an awful suspicion flashed into my mind. Something told me, Mrs. Dr. dear, that I was about to receive my first proposal. I have always thought that I would like to have just one offer of marriage to reject, so that I might be able to look other women in the face, but you will not hear me bragging of this. I consider it an insult and if I could have thought of any way of preventing it I would. But just then, Mrs. Dr. dear, you will see I was at a disadvantage, being taken so completely by surprise. Some men, I am told, consider a little preliminary courting the proper thing before a proposal, if only to give fair warning of their intentions; but Whiskers-on-the-moon probably thought it was any port in a storm for me and that I would jump at him. Well, he is undeceived—yes, he is undeceived, Mrs. Dr. dear. I wonder if he has stopped running yet."

"I understand that you don't feel flattered, Susan. But couldn't you have refused him a little more delicately than by chasing him off the premises in such a fashion?"

"Well, maybe I might have, Mrs. Dr. dear, and I intended to, but one remark he made aggravated me beyond my powers of endurance. If it had not been for that I would not have chased him with my dye-pot. I will tell you the whole interview. Whiskers sat down, as I have said, and right beside him on another chair Doc was lying. The animal was pretending to be asleep but I knew very well he was not, for he has been Hyde all day and Hyde never sleeps. By the way, Mrs. Dr. dear, have you noticed that that cat is far oftener Hyde than Jekyll now? The more victories Germany wins the Hyder he becomes. I leave you to draw your own conclusions from that. I suppose Whiskers thought he might curry favour with me by praising the creature, little dreaming what my real sentiments towards it were, so he stuck out his pudgy hand and stroked Mr. Hyde's back. 'What a nice cat,' he said. The nice cat flew at him and bit him. Then it gave a fearful yowl, and bounded out of the door. Whiskers looked after it quite amazed. 'That is a queer kind of a varmint,' he said. I agreed with him on that point, but I was not going to let him see it. Besides, what business had he to call our cat a varmint? 'It may be a varmint or it may not,' I said, 'but it knows the difference between a Canadian and a Hun.' You would have thought, would you not, Mrs. Dr. dear, that a hint like that would have been enough for him! But it went no deeper than his skin. I saw him settling back quite comfortable, as if for a good talk, and thought I, 'If there is anything coming it may as well come soon and be done with, for with all these rags to dye before supper I have no time to waste in flirting,' so I spoke right out. 'If you have anything particular to discuss with me, Mr. Pryor, I would feel obliged if you would mention it without loss of time, because I am very busy this afternoon.' He fairly beamed at me out of that circle of red whisker, and said, 'You are a business-like woman and I agree with you. There is no use in wasting time beating around the bush. I came up here today to ask you to marry me.' So there it was, Mrs. Dr. dear. I had a proposal at last, after waiting sixty-four years for one.

"I just glared at that presumptuous creature and I said, 'I would not marry you if you were the last man on earth, Josiah Pryor. So there you have my answer and you can take it away forthwith.' You never saw a man so taken aback as he was, Mrs. Dr. dear. He was so flabbergasted that he just blurted out the truth. 'Why, I thought you'd be only too glad to get a chance to be married,' he said. That was when I lost my head, Mrs. Dr. dear. Do you think I had a good excuse, when a Hun and a pacifist made such an insulting remark to me? 'Go,' I thundered, and I just caught up that iron pot. I could see that he thought I had suddenly gone insane, and I suppose he considered an iron pot full of boiling dye was a dangerous weapon in the hands of a lunatic. At any rate he went, and stood not upon the order of his going, as you saw for yourself. And I do not think we will see him back here proposing to us again in a hurry. No, I think he has learned that there is at least one single woman in Glen St. Mary who has no hankering to become Mrs. Whiskers-on-the-moon."

27. WAITING

Ingleside,
1st November 1917

"It is November—and the Glen is all grey and brown, except where the Lombardy poplars stand up here and there like great golden torches in the sombre landscape, although every other tree has shed its leaves. It has been very hard to keep our courage alight of late. The Caporetto disaster is a dreadful thing and not even Susan can extract much consolation out of the present state of affairs. The rest of us don't try. Gertrude keeps saying desperately, 'They must not get Venice—they must not get Venice,' as if by saying it often enough she can prevent them. But what is to prevent them from getting Venice I cannot see. Yet, as Susan fails not to point out, there was seemingly nothing to prevent them from getting to Paris in 1914, yet they did not get it, and she affirms they shall not get Venice either. Oh, how I hope and pray they will not—Venice the beautiful Queen of the Adriatic. Although I've never seen it I feel about it just as Byron did—I've always loved it—it has always been to me 'a fairy city of the heart.' Perhaps I caught my love of it from Walter, who worshipped it. It was always one of his dreams to see Venice. I remember we planned once—down in Rainbow Valley one evening just before the war broke out—that some time we would go together to see it and float in a gondola through its moonlit streets.

"Every fall since the war began there has been some terrible blow to our troops—Antwerp in 1914, Serbia in 1915; last fall, Rumania, and now Italy, the worst of all. I think I would give up in despair if it were not for what Walter said in his dear last letter—that 'the dead as well as the living were fighting on our side and such an army cannot be defeated.' No it cannot. We will win in the end. I will not doubt it for one moment. To let myself doubt would be to 'break faith.'

"We have all been campaigning furiously of late for the new Victory Loan. We Junior Reds canvassed diligently and landed several tough old customers who had at first flatly refused to invest. I—even I—tackled Whiskers-on-the-moon. I expected a bad time and a refusal. But to my amazement he was quite agreeable and promised on the spot to take a thousand dollar bond. He may be a pacifist, but he knows a good investment when it is handed out to him. Five and a half per cent is five and a half per cent, even when a militaristic government pays it.

"Father, to tease Susan, says it was her speech at the Victory Loan Campaign meeting that converted Mr. Pryor. I don't think that at all likely, since Mr. Pryor has been publicly very bitter against Susan ever since her quite unmistakable rejection of his lover-like advances. But Susan did make a speech—and the best one made at the meeting, too. It was the first time she ever did such a thing and she vows it will be the last. Everybody in the Glen was at the meeting, and quite a number of speeches were made, but somehow things were a little flat and no especial enthusiasm could be worked up. Susan was quite dismayed at the lack of zeal, because she had been burningly anxious that the Island should go over the top in regard to its quota. She kept whispering viciously to Gertrude and me that there was 'no ginger' in the speeches; and when nobody went forward to subscribe to the loan at the close Susan 'lost her head.' At least, that is how she describes it herself. She bounded to her feet, her face grim and set under her bonnet—Susan is the only woman in Glen St. Mary who still wears a bonnet—and said sarcastically and loudly, 'No doubt it is much cheaper to talk patriotism than it is to pay for it. And we are asking charity, of course—we are asking you to lend us your money for nothing! No doubt the Kaiser will feel quite downcast when he hears of this meeting!"

"Susan has an unshaken belief that the Kaiser's spies—presumably represented by Mr. Pryor—promptly inform him of every happening in our Glen.

"Norman Douglas shouted out 'Hear! Hear!' and some boy at the back said, 'What about Lloyd George?' in a tone Susan didn't like. Lloyd George is her pet hero, now that Kitchener is gone.

"'I stand behind Lloyd George every time,' retorted Susan.

"'I suppose that will hearten him up greatly,' said Warren Mead, with one of his disagreeable 'haw-haws.'

"Warren's remark was spark to powder. Susan just 'sailed in' as she puts it, and 'said her say.' She said it remarkably well, too. There was no lack of 'ginger' in her speech, anyhow. When Susan is warmed up she has no mean powers of oratory, and the way she trimmed those men down was funny and wonderful and effective all at once. She said it was the likes of her, millions of her, that did stand behind Lloyd George, and did hearten him up. That was the key-note of her speech. Dear old Susan! She is a perfect dynamo of patriotism and loyalty and contempt for slackers of all kinds, and when she let it loose on that audience in her one grand outburst she electrified it. Susan always vows she is no suffragette, but she gave womanhood its due that night, and she literally made those men cringe. When she finished with them they were ready to eat out of her hand. She wound up by ordering them—yes, ordering them—to march up to the platform forthwith and subscribe for Victory Bonds. And after wild applause most of them did it, even Warren Mead. When the total amount subscribed came out in the Charlottetown dailies the next day we found that the Glen led every district on the Island—and certainly Susan has the credit for it. She, herself, after she came home that night was quite ashamed and evidently feared that she had been guilty of unbecoming conduct: she confessed to mother that she had been 'rather unladylike.'

"We were all—except Susan—out for a trial ride in father's new automobile tonight. A very good one we had, too, though we did get ingloriously ditched at the end, owing to a certain grim old dame—to wit, Miss Elizabeth Carr of the Upper Glen—who wouldn't rein her horse out to let us pass, honk as we might. Father was quite furious; but in my heart I believe I sympathized with Miss Elizabeth. If I had been a spinster lady, driving along behind my own old nag, in maiden meditation fancy free, I wouldn't have lifted a rein when an obstreperous car hooted blatantly behind me. I should just have sat up as dourly as she did and said 'Take the ditch if you are determined to pass.'

"We did take the ditch—and got up to our axles in sand—and sat foolishly there while Miss Elizabeth clucked up her horse and rattled victoriously away.

"Jem will have a laugh when I write him this. He knows Miss Elizabeth of old.

"But—will—Venice—be—saved?"

19th November 1917

"It is not saved yet—it is still in great danger. But the Italians are making a stand at last on the Piave line. To be sure military critics say they cannot possibly hold it and must retreat to the Adige. But Susan and Gertrude and I say they must hold it, because Venice must be saved, so what are the military critics to do?

"Oh, if I could only believe that they can hold it!

"Our Canadian troops have won another great victory—they have stormed the Passchendaele Ridge and held it in the face of all counter attacks. None of our boys were in the battle—but oh, the casualty list of other people's boys! Joe Milgrave was in it but came through safe. Miranda had some bad days until she got word from him. But it is wonderful how Miranda has bloomed out since her marriage. She isn't the same girl at all. Even her eyes seem to have darkened and deepened—though I suppose that is just because they glow with the greater intensity that has come to her. She makes her father stand round in a perfectly amazing fashion; she runs up the flag whenever a yard of trench on the western front is taken; and she comes up regularly to our Junior Red Cross; and she does—yes, she does—put on funny little 'married woman' airs that are quite killing. But she is the only war-bride in the Glen and surely nobody need grudge her the satisfaction she gets out of it.

"The Russian news is bad, too—Kerensky's government has fallen and Lenin is dictator of Russia. Somehow, it is very hard to keep up courage in the dull hopelessness of these grey autumn days of suspense and boding news. But we are beginning to 'get in a low,' as old Highland Sandy says, over the approaching election. Conscription is the real issue at stake and it will be the most exciting election we ever had. All the women 'who have got de age'—to quote Jo Poirier, and who have husbands, sons, and brothers at the front, can vote. Oh, if I were only twenty-one! Gertrude and Susan are both furious because they can't vote.

"'It is not fair,' Gertrude says passionately. 'There is Agnes Carr who can vote because her husband went. She did everything she could to prevent him from going, and now she is going to vote against the Union Government. Yet I have no vote, because my man at the front is only my sweetheart and not my husband!"

"As for Susan, when she reflects that she cannot vote, while a rank old pacifist like Mr. Pryor can—and will—her comments are sulphurous.

"I really feel sorry for the Elliotts and Crawfords and MacAllisters over-harbour. They have always lined up in clearly divided camps of Liberal and Conservative, and now they are torn from their moorings—I know I'm mixing my metaphors dreadfully—and set hopelessly adrift. It will kill some of those old Grits to vote for Sir Robert Borden's side—and yet they have to because they believe the time has come when we must have conscription. And some poor Conservatives who are against conscription must vote for Laurier, who always has been anathema to them. Some of them are taking it terribly hard. Others seem to be in much the same attitude as Mrs. Marshall Elliott has come to be regarding Church Union.

"She was up here last night. She doesn't come as often as she used to. She is growing too old to walk this far—dear old 'Miss Cornelia.' I hate to think of her growing old—we have always loved her so and she has always been so good to us Ingleside young fry.

"She used to be so bitterly opposed to Church Union. But last night, when father told her it was practically decided, she said in a resigned tone, 'Well, in a world where everything is being rent and torn what matters one more rending and tearing? Anyhow, compared with Germans even Methodists seem attractive to me.'

"Our Junior R.C. goes on quite smoothly, in spite of the fact that Irene has come back to it—having fallen out with the Lowbridge society, I understand. She gave me a sweet little jab last meeting—about knowing me across the square in Charlottetown 'by my green velvet hat.' Everybody knows me by that detestable and detested hat. This will be my fourth season for it. Even mother wanted me to get a new one this fall; but I said, 'No.' As long as the war lasts so long do I wear that velvet hat in winter."

23rd November 1917

"The Piave line still holds—and General Byng has won a splendid victory at Cambrai. I did run up the flag for that—but Susan only said 'I shall set a kettle of water on the kitchen range tonight. I notice little Kitchener always has an attack of croup after any British victory. I do hope he has no pro-German blood in his veins. Nobody knows much about his father's people.'

"Jims has had a few attacks of croup this fall—just the ordinary croup—not that terrible thing he had last year. But whatever blood runs in his little veins it is good, healthy blood. He is rosy and plump and curly and cute; and he says such funny things and asks such comical questions. He likes very much to sit in a special chair in the kitchen; but that is Susan's favourite chair, too, and when she wants it, out Jims must go. The last time she put him out of it he turned around and asked solemnly, 'When you are dead, Susan, can I sit in that chair?' Susan thought it quite dreadful, and I think that was when she began to feel anxiety about his possible ancestry. The other night I took Jims with me for a walk down to the store. It was the first time he had ever been out so late at night, and when he saw the stars he exclaimed, 'Oh, Willa, see the big moon and all the little moons!' And last Wednesday morning, when he woke up, my little alarm clock had stopped because I had forgotten to wind it up. Jims bounded out of his crib and ran across to me, his face quite aghast above his little blue flannel pyjamas. 'The clock is dead,' he gasped, 'oh Willa, the clock is dead.'

"One night he was quite angry with both Susan and me because we would not give him something he wanted very much. When he said his prayers he plumped down wrathfully, and when he came to the petition 'Make me a good boy' he tacked on emphatically, 'and please make Willa and Susan good, 'cause they're not.'

"I don't go about quoting Jims's speeches to all I meet. That always bores me when other people do it! I just enshrine them in this old hotch-potch of a journal!

"This very evening as I put Jims to bed he looked up and asked me gravely, 'Why can't yesterday come back, Willa?'

"Oh, why can't it, Jims? That beautiful 'yesterday' of dreams and laughter—when our boys were home—when Walter and I read and rambled and watched new moons and sunsets together in Rainbow Valley. If it could just come back! But yesterdays never come back, little Jims—and the todays are dark with clouds—and we dare not think about the tomorrows."

11th December 1917

"Wonderful news came today. The British troops captured Jerusalem yesterday. We ran up the flag and some of Gertrude's old sparkle came back to her for a moment.

"'After all,' she said, 'it is worth while to live in the days which see the object of the Crusades attained. The ghosts of all the Crusaders must have crowded the walls of Jerusalem last night, with Coeur-de-lion at their head.'

"Susan had cause for satisfaction also.

"'I am so thankful I can pronounce Jerusalem and Hebron,' she said. 'They give me a real comfortable feeling after Przemysl and Brest-Litovsk! Well, we have got the Turks on the run, at least, and Venice is safe and Lord Lansdowne is not to be taken seriously; and I see no reason why we should be downhearted.'

"Jerusalem! The 'meteor flag of England!' floats over you—the Crescent is gone. How Walter would have thrilled over that!"

18th December 1917

"Yesterday the election came off. In the evening mother and Susan and Gertrude and I forgathered in the living-room and waited in breathless suspense, father having gone down to the village. We had no way of hearing the news, for Carter Flagg's store is not on our line, and when we tried to get it Central always answered that the line 'was busy'—as no doubt it was, for everybody for miles around was trying to get Carter's store for the same reason we were.

"About ten o'clock Gertrude went to the 'phone and happened to catch someone from over-harbour talking to Carter Flagg. Gertrude shamelessly listened in and got for her comforting what eavesdroppers are proverbially supposed to get—to wit, unpleasant hearing; the Union Government had 'done nothing' in the West.

"We looked at each other in dismay. If the Government had failed to carry the West, it was defeated.

"'Canada is disgraced in the eyes of the world,' said Gertrude bitterly.

"'If everybody was like the Mark Crawfords over-harbour this would not have happened,' groaned Susan. 'They locked their Uncle up in the barn this morning and would not let him out until he promised to vote Union. That is what I call effective argument, Mrs. Dr. dear.'

"Gertrude and I couldn't rest after all that. We walked the floor until our legs gave out and we had to sit down perforce. Mother knitted away as steadily as clockwork and pretended to be calm and serene—pretended so well that we were all deceived and envious until the next day, when I caught her ravelling out four inches of her sock. She had knit that far past where the heel should have begun!

"It was twelve before father came home. He stood in the doorway and looked at us and we looked at him. We did not dare ask him what the news was. Then he said that it was Laurier who had 'done nothing' in the West, and that the Union Government was in with a big majority. Gertrude clapped her hands. I wanted to laugh and cry, mother's eyes flashed with their old-time starriness and Susan emitted a queer sound between a gasp and a whoop.

"This will not comfort the Kaiser much,' she said.

"Then we went to bed, but were too excited to sleep. Really, as Susan said solemnly this morning, 'Mrs. Dr. dear, I think politics are too strenuous for women.'"

31st December 1917

"Our fourth War Christmas is over. We are trying to gather up some courage wherewith to face another year of it. Germany has, for the most part, been victorious all summer. And now they say she has all her troops from the Russian front ready for a 'big push' in the spring. Sometimes it seems to me that we just cannot live through the winter waiting for that.

"I had a great batch of letters from overseas this week. Shirley is at the front now, too, and writes about it all as coolly and matter-of-factly as he used to write of football at Queen's. Carl wrote that it had been raining for weeks and that nights in the trenches always made him think of the night of long ago when he did penance in the graveyard for running away from Henry Warren's ghost. Carl's letters are always full of jokes and bits of fun. They had a great rat-hunt the night before he wrote—spearing rats with their bayonets—and he got the best bag and won the prize. He has a tame rat that knows him and sleeps in his pocket at night. Rats don't worry Carl as they do some people—he was always chummy with all little beasts. He says he is making a study of the habits of the trench rat and means to write a treatise on it some day that will make him famous.

"Ken wrote a short letter. His letters are all rather short now—and he doesn't often slip in those dear little sudden sentences I love so much. Sometimes I think he has forgotten all about the night he was here to say goodbye—and then there will be just a line or a word that makes me think he remembers and always will remember. For instance to-day's letter hadn't a thing in it that mightn't have been written to any girl, except that he signed himself 'Your Kenneth,' instead of 'Yours, Kenneth,' as he usually does. Now, did he leave that 's' off intentionally or was it only carelessness? I shall lie awake half the night wondering. He is a captain now. I am glad and proud—and yet Captain Ford sounds so horribly far away and high up. Ken and Captain Ford seem like two different persons. I may be practically engaged to Ken—mother's opinion on that point is my stay and bulwark—but I can't be to Captain Ford!

"And Jem is a lieutenant now—won his promotion on the field. He sent me a snap-shot, taken in his new uniform. He looked thin and old—old—my boy-brother Jem. I can't forget mother's face when I showed it to her. 'That—my little Jem—the baby of the old House of Dreams?' was all she said.

"There was a letter from Faith, too. She is doing V.A.D. work in England and writes hopefully and brightly. I think she is almost happy—she saw Jem on his last leave and she is so near him she could go to him, if he were wounded. That means so much to her. Oh, if I were only with her! But my work is here at home. I know Walter wouldn't have wanted me to leave mother and in everything I try to 'keep faith' with him, even to the little details of daily life. Walter died for Canada—I must live for her. That is what he asked me to do."

28th January 1918

"'I shall anchor my storm-tossed soul to the British fleet and make a batch of bran biscuits,' said Susan today to Cousin Sophia, who had come in with some weird tale of a new and all-conquering submarine, just launched by Germany. But Susan is a somewhat disgruntled woman at present, owing to the regulations regarding cookery. Her loyalty to the Union Government is being sorely tried. It surmounted the first strain gallantly. When the order about flour came Susan said, quite cheerfully, 'I am an old dog to be learning new tricks, but I shall learn to make war bread if it will help defeat the Huns.'

"But the later suggestions went against Susan's grain. Had it not been for father's decree I think she would have snapped her fingers at Sir Robert Borden.

"'Talk about trying to make bricks without straw, Mrs. Dr. dear! How am I to make a cake without butter or sugar? It cannot be done—not cake that is cake. Of course one can make a slab, Mrs. Dr. dear. And we cannot even camooflash it with a little icing! To think that I should have lived to see the day when a government at Ottawa should step into my kitchen and put me on rations!'

"Susan would give the last drop of her blood for her 'king and country,' but to surrender her beloved recipes is a very different and much more serious matter.

"I had letters from Nan and Di too—or rather notes. They are too busy to write letters, for exams are looming up. They will graduate in Arts this spring. I am evidently to be the dunce of the family. But somehow I never had any hankering for a college course, and even now it doesn't appeal to me. I'm afraid I'm rather devoid of ambition. There is only one thing I really want to be—and I don't know if I'll be it or not. If not—I don't want to be anything. But I shan't write it down. It is all right to think it; but, as Cousin Sophia would say, it might be brazen to write it down.

"I will write it down. I won't be cowed by the conventions and Cousin Sophia! I want to be Kenneth Ford's wife! There now!

"I've just looked in the glass, and I hadn't the sign of a blush on my face. I suppose I'm not a properly constructed damsel at all.

"I was down to see little Dog Monday today. He has grown quite stiff and rheumatic but there he sat, waiting for the train. He thumped his tail and looked pleadingly into my eyes. 'When will Jem come?' he seemed to say. Oh, Dog Monday, there is no answer to that question; and there is, as yet, no answer to the other which we are all constantly asking 'What will happen when Germany strikes again on the western front—her one great, last blow for victory!"

1st March 1918

"'What will spring bring?' Gertrude said today. 'I dread it as I never dreaded spring before. Do you suppose there will ever again come a time when life will be free from fear? For almost four years we have lain down with fear and risen up with it. It has been the unbidden guest at every meal, the unwelcome companion at every gathering.'

"'Hindenburg says he will be in Paris on 1st April,' sighed Cousin Sophia.

"'Hindenburg!' There is no power in pen and ink to express the contempt which Susan infused into that name. 'Has he forgotten what day the first of April is?'

"'Hindenburg has kept his word hitherto,' said Gertrude, as gloomily as Cousin Sophia herself could have said it.

"'Yes, fighting against the Russians and Rumanians,' retorted Susan. 'Wait you till he comes up against the British and French, not to speak of the Yankees, who are getting there as fast as they can and will no doubt give a good account of themselves.'

"'You said just the same thing before Mons, Susan,' I reminded her.

"'Hindenburg says he will spend a million lives to break the Allied front,' said Gertrude. 'At such a price he must purchase some successes and how can we live through them, even if he is baffled in the end. These past two months when we have been crouching and waiting for the blow to fall have seemed as long as all the preceding months of the war put together. I work all day feverishly and waken at three o'clock at night to wonder if the iron legions have struck at last. It is then I see Hindenburg in Paris and Germany triumphant. I never see her so at any other time than that accursed hour.'

"Susan looked dubious over Gertrude's adjective, but evidently concluded that the 'a' saved the situation.

"'I wish it were possible to take some magic draught and go to sleep for the next three months—and then waken to find Armageddon over,' said mother, almost impatiently.

"It is not often that mother slumps into a wish like that—or at least the verbal expression of it. Mother has changed a great deal since that terrible day in September when we knew that Walter would not come back; but she has always been brave and patient. Now it seemed as if even she had reached the limit of her endurance.

"Susan went over to mother and touched her shoulder.

"'Do not you be frightened or downhearted, Mrs. Dr. dear,' she said gently. 'I felt somewhat that way myself last night, and I rose from my bed and lighted my lamp and opened my Bible; and what do you think was the first verse my eyes lighted upon? It was 'And they shall fight against thee but they shall not prevail against thee, for I am with thee, saith the Lord of Hosts, to deliver thee.' I am not gifted in the way of dreaming, as Miss Oliver is, but I knew then and there, Mrs. Dr. dear, that it was a manifest leading, and that Hindenburg will never see Paris. So

I read no further but went back to my bed and I did not waken at three o'clock or at any other hour before morning.'

"I say that verse Susan read over and over again to myself. The Lord of Hosts is with us—and the spirits of all just men made perfect—and even the legions and guns that Germany is massing on the western front must break against such a barrier. This is in certain uplifted moments; but when other moments come I feel, like Gertrude, that I cannot endure any longer this awful and ominous hush before the coming storm."

23rd March 1918

"Armageddon has begun!—'the last great fight of all!' Is it, I wonder? Yesterday I went down to the post office for the mail. It was a dull, bitter day. The snow was gone but the grey, lifeless ground was frozen hard and a biting wind was blowing. The whole Glen landscape was ugly and hopeless.

"Then I got the paper with its big black headlines. Germany struck on the twenty-first. She makes big claims of guns and prisoners taken. General Haig reports that 'severe fighting continues.' I don't like the sound of that last expression.

"We all find we cannot do any work that requires concentration of thought. So we all knit furiously, because we can do that mechanically. At least the dreadful waiting is over—the horrible wondering where and when the blow will fall. It has fallen—but they shall not prevail against us!

"Oh, what is happening on the western front tonight as I write this, sitting here in my room with my journal before me? Jims is asleep in his crib and the wind is wailing around the window; over my desk hangs Walter's picture, looking at me with his beautiful deep eyes; the Mona Lisa he gave me the last Christmas he was home hangs on one side of it, and on the other a framed copy of "The Piper." It seems to me that I can hear Walter's voice repeating it—that little poem into which he put his soul, and which will therefore live for ever, carrying Walter's name on through the future of our land. Everything about me is calm and peaceful and 'homey.' Walter seems very near me—if I could just sweep aside the thin wavering little veil that hangs between, I could see him—just as he saw the Pied Piper the night before Courcelette.

"Over there in France tonight—does the line hold?"

28. BLACK SUNDAY

In March of the year of grace 1918 there was one week into which must have crowded more of searing human agony than any seven days had ever held before in the history of the world. And in that week there was one day when all humanity seemed nailed to the cross; on that day the whole planet must have been agroan with universal convulsion; everywhere the hearts of men were failing them for fear.

It dawned calmly and coldly and greyly at Ingleside. Mrs. Blythe and Rilla and Miss Oliver made ready for church in a suspense tempered by hope and confidence. The doctor was away, having been summoned during the wee sma's to the Marwood household in Upper Glen, where a little war-bride was fighting gallantly on her own battleground to give life, not death, to the world. Susan announced that she meant to stay home that morning—a rare decision for Susan.

"But I would rather not go to church this morning, Mrs. Dr. dear," she explained. "If Whiskers-on-the-moon were there and I saw him looking holy and pleased, as he always looks when he thinks the Huns are winning, I fear I would lose my patience and my sense of decorum and hurl a Bible or hymn-book at him, thereby disgracing myself and the sacred edifice. No, Mrs. Dr. dear, I shall stay home from church till the tide turns and pray hard here."

"I think I might as well stay home, too, for all the good church will do me today," Miss Oliver said to Rilla, as they walked down the hard-frozen red road to the church. "I can think of nothing but the question, 'Does the line still hold?'"

"Next Sunday will be Easter," said Rilla. "Will it herald death or life to our cause?"

Mr. Meredith preached that morning from the text, "He that endureth to the end shall be saved," and hope and confidence rang through his inspiring sentences. Rilla, looking up at the memorial tablet on the wall above their pew, "sacred to the memory of Walter Cuthbert Blythe," felt herself lifted out of her dread and filled anew with courage. Walter could not have laid down his life for naught. His had been the gift of prophetic vision and he had foreseen victory. She would cling to that belief—the line would hold.

In this renewed mood she walked home from church almost gaily. The others, too, were hopeful, and all went smiling into Ingleside. There was no one in the living-room, save Jims, who had fallen asleep on the sofa, and Doc, who sat "hushed in grim repose" on the hearth-rug, looking very Hydeish indeed. No one was in the dining-room either—and, stranger still, no dinner was on the table, which was not even set. Where was Susan?

"Can she have taken ill?" exclaimed Mrs. Blythe anxiously. "I thought it strange that she did not want to go to church this morning."

The kitchen door opened and Susan appeared on the threshold with such a ghastly face that Mrs. Blythe cried out in sudden panic.

"Susan, what is it?"

"The British line is broken and the German shells are falling on Paris," said Susan dully.

The three women stared at each other, stricken.

"It's not true—it's not," gasped Rilla.

"The thing would be—ridiculous," said Gertrude Oliver—and then she laughed horribly.

"Susan, who told you this—when did the news come?" asked Mrs. Blythe.

"I got it over the long-distance phone from Charlottetown half an hour ago," said Susan. "The news came to town late last night. It was Dr. Holland phoned it out and he said it was only too true. Since then I have done nothing, Mrs. Dr. dear. I am very sorry dinner is not ready. It is the first time I have been so remiss. If you will be patient I will soon have something for you to eat. But I am afraid I let the potatoes burn."

"Dinner! Nobody wants any dinner, Susan," said Mrs. Blythe wildly. "Oh, this thing is unbelievable—it must be a nightmare."

"Paris is lost—France is lost—the war is lost," gasped Rilla, amid the utter ruins of hope and confidence and belief.

"Oh God—Oh God," moaned Gertrude Oliver, walking about the room and wringing her hands, "Oh—God!"

Nothing else—no other words—nothing but that age old plea—the old, old cry of supreme agony and appeal, from the human heart whose every human staff has failed it.

"Is God dead?" asked a startled little voice from the doorway of the living-room. Jims stood there, flushed from sleep, his big brown eyes filled with dread, "Oh Willa—oh, Willa, is God dead?"

Miss Oliver stopped walking and exclaiming, and stared at Jims, in whose eyes tears of fright were beginning to gather. Rilla ran to his comforting, while Susan bounded up from the chair upon which she had dropped.

"No," she said briskly, with a sudden return of her real self. "No, God isn't dead—nor Lloyd

George either. We were forgetting that, Mrs. Dr. dear. Don't cry, little Kitchener. Bad as things are, they might be worse. The British line may be broken but the British navy is not. Let us tie to that. I will take a brace and get up a bite to eat, for strength we must have."

They made a pretence of eating Susan's "bite," but it was only a pretence. Nobody at Ingleside ever forgot that black afternoon. Gertrude Oliver walked the floor—they all walked the floor; except Susan, who got out her grey war sock.

"Mrs. Dr. dear, I must knit on Sunday at last. I have never dreamed of doing it before for, say what might be said, I have considered it was a violation of the third commandment. But whether it is or whether it is not I must knit today or I shall go mad."

"Knit if you can, Susan," said Mrs. Blythe restlessly. "I would knit if I could—but I cannot—I cannot."

"If we could only get fuller information," moaned Rilla. "There might be something to encourage us—if we knew all."

"We know that the Germans are shelling Paris," said Miss Oliver bitterly. "In that case they must have smashed through everywhere and be at the very gates. No, we have lost—let us face the fact as other peoples in the past have had to face it. Other nations, with right on their side, have given their best and bravest—and gone down to defeat in spite of it. Ours is 'but one more To baffled millions who have gone before.'"

"I won't give up like that," cried Rilla, her pale face suddenly flushing. "I won't despair. We are not conquered—no, if Germany overruns all France we are not conquered. I am ashamed of myself for this hour of despair. You won't see me slump again like that, I'm going to ring up town at once and ask for particulars."

But town could not be got. The long-distance operator there was submerged by similar calls from every part of the distracted country. Rilla finally gave up and slipped away to Rainbow Valley. There she knelt down on the withered grey grasses in the little nook where she and Walter had had their last talk together, with her head bowed against the mossy trunk of a fallen tree. The sun had broken through the black clouds and drenched the valley with a pale golden splendour. The bells on the Tree Lovers twinkled elfinly and fitfully in the gusty March wind.

"Oh God, give me strength," Rilla whispered. "Just strength—and courage." Then like a child she clasped her hands together and said, as simply as Jims could have done, "Please send us better news tomorrow."

She knelt there a long time, and when she went back to Ingleside she was calm and resolute. The doctor had arrived home, tired but triumphant, little Douglas Haig Marwood having made a safe landing on the shores of time. Gertrude was still pacing restlessly but Mrs. Blythe and Susan had reacted from the shock, and Susan was already planning a new line of defence for the channel ports.

"As long as we can hold them," she declared, "the situation is saved. Paris has really no military significance."

"Don't," said Gertrude sharply, as if Susan had run something into her. She thought the old worn phrase 'no military significance' nothing short of ghastly mockery under the circumstances, and more terrible to endure than the voice of despair would have been.

"I heard up at Marwood's of the line being broken," said the doctor, "but this story of the Germans shelling Paris seems to be rather incredible. Even if they broke through they were fifty miles from Paris at the nearest point and how could they get their artillery close enough to shell it in so short a time? Depend upon it, girls, that part of the message can't be true. I'm going to try to try a long-distance call to town myself."

The doctor was no more successful than Rilla had been, but his point of view cheered them all a little, and helped them through the evening. And at nine o'clock a long-distance message came through at last, that helped them through the night.

"The line broke only in one place, before St. Quentin," said the doctor, as he hung up the receiver, "and the British troops are retreating in good order. That's not so bad. As for the shells that are falling on Paris, they are coming from a distance of seventy miles—from some amazing long-range gun the Germans have invented and sprung with the opening offensive. That is all the news to date, and Dr. Holland says it is reliable."

"It would have been dreadful news yesterday," said Gertrude, "but compared to what we heard this morning it is almost like good news. But still," she added, trying to smile, "I am afraid I will not sleep much tonight."

"There is one thing to be thankful for at any rate, Miss Oliver, dear," said Susan, "and that is that Cousin Sophia did not come in today. I really could not have endured her on top of all the rest."

29. "WOUNDED AND MISSING"

"Battered but Not Broken" was the headline in Monday's paper, and Susan repeated it over and over to herself as she went about her work. The gap caused by the St. Quentin disaster had been patched up in time, but the Allied line was being pushed relentlessly back from the territory they had purchased in 1917 with half a million lives. On Wednesday the headline was "British and French Check Germans"; but still the retreat went on. Back—and back—and back! Where would it end? Would the line break again—this time disastrously?

On Saturday the headline was "Even Berlin Admits Offensive Checked," and for the first time in that terrible week the Ingleside folk dared to draw a long breath.

"Well, we have got one week over—now for the next," said Susan staunchly.

"I feel like a prisoner on the rack when they stopped turning it," Miss Oliver said to Rilla, as they went to church on Easter morning. "But I am not off the rack. The torture may begin again at any time."

"I doubted God last Sunday," said Rilla, "but I don't doubt him today. Evil cannot win. Spirit is on our side and it is bound to outlast flesh."

Nevertheless her faith was often tried in the dark spring that followed. Armageddon was not, as they had hoped, a matter of a few days. It stretched out into weeks and months. Again and again Hindenburg struck his savage, sudden blows, with alarming, though futile success. Again and again the military critics declared the situation extremely perilous. Again and again Cousin Sophia agreed with the military critics.

"If the Allies go back three miles more the war is lost," she wailed.

"Is the British navy anchored in those three miles?" demanded Susan scornfully.

"It is the opinion of a man who knows all about it," said Cousin Sophia solemnly.

"There is no such person," retorted Susan. "As for the military critics, they do not know one blessed thing about it, any more than you or I. They have been mistaken times out of number. Why do you always look on the dark side, Sophia Crawford?"

"Because there ain't any bright side, Susan Baker."

"Oh, is there not? It is the twentieth of April, and Hindy is not in Paris yet, although he said he would be there by April first. Is that not a bright spot at least?"

"It is my opinion that the Germans will be in Paris before very long and more than that, Susan Baker, they will be in Canada."

"Not in this part of it. The Huns shall never set foot in Prince Edward Island as long as I can handle a pitchfork," declared Susan, looking, and feeling quite equal to routing the entire

German army single-handed. "No, Sophia Crawford, to tell you the plain truth I am sick and tired of your gloomy predictions. I do not deny that some mistakes have been made. The Germans would never have got back Passchendaele if the Canadians had been left there; and it was bad business trusting to those Portuguese at the Lys River. But that is no reason why you or anyone should go about proclaiming the war is lost. I do not want to quarrel with you, least of all at such a time as this, but our morale must be kept up, and I am going to speak my mind out plainly and tell you that if you cannot keep from such croaking your room is better than your company."

Cousin Sophia marched home in high dudgeon to digest her affront, and did not reappear in Susan's kitchen for many weeks. Perhaps it was just as well, for they were hard weeks, when the Germans continued to strike, now here, now there, and seemingly vital points fell to them at every blow. And one day in early May, when wind and sunshine frolicked in Rainbow Valley and the maple grove was golden-green and the harbour all blue and dimpled and white-capped, the news came about Jem.

There had been a trench raid on the Canadian front—a little trench raid so insignificant that it was never even mentioned in the dispatches and when it was over Lieutenant James Blythe was reported "wounded and missing."

"I think this is even worse than the news of his death would have been," moaned Rilla through her white lips, that night.

"No—no—'missing' leaves a little hope, Rilla," urged Gertrude Oliver.

"Yes—torturing, agonized hope that keeps you from ever becoming quite resigned to the worst," said Rilla. "Oh, Miss Oliver—must we go for weeks and months—not knowing whether Jem is alive or dead? Perhaps we will never know. I—I cannot bear it—I cannot. Walter—and now Jem. This will kill mother—look at her face, Miss Oliver, and you will see that. And Faith—poor Faith—how can she bear it?"

Gertrude shivered with pain. She looked up at the pictures hanging over Rilla's desk and felt a sudden hatred of Mona Lisa's endless smile.

"Will not even this blot it off your face?" she thought savagely.

But she said gently, "No, it won't kill your mother. She's made of finer mettle than that. Besides, she refuses to believe Jem is dead; she will cling to hope and we must all do that. Faith, you may be sure, will do it."

"I cannot," moaned Rilla, "Jem was wounded—what chance would he have? Even if the Germans found him—we know how they have treated wounded prisoners. I wish I could hope, Miss Oliver—it would help, I suppose. But hope seems dead in me. I can't hope without some reason for it—and there is no reason."

When Miss Oliver had gone to her own room and Rilla was lying on her bed in the moonlight, praying desperately for a little strength, Susan stepped in like a gaunt shadow and sat down beside her.

"Rilla, dear, do not you worry. Little Jem is not dead."

"Oh, how can you believe that, Susan?"

"Because I know. Listen you to me. When that word came this morning the first thing I thought of was Dog Monday. And tonight, as soon as I got the supper dishes washed and the bread set, I went down to the station. There was Dog Monday, waiting for the train, just as patient as usual. Now, Rilla, dear, that trench raid was four days ago—last Monday—and I said to the station-agent, 'Can you tell me if that dog howled or made any kind of a fuss last Monday night?' He thought it over a bit, and then he said, 'No, he did not.' 'Are you sure?' I said. 'There's more depends on it than you think!' 'Dead sure,' he said. 'I was up all night last Monday night because my mare was sick, and there was never a sound out of him. I would have heard if there had been, for the stable door was open all the time and his kennel is right across from it!' Now Rilla dear, those were the man's very words. And you know how that poor little dog howled all night after the battle of Courcelette. Yet he did not love Walter as much as he loved Jem. If he mourned for Walter like that, do you suppose he would sleep sound in his kennel the night after Jem had been killed? No, Rilla dear, little Jem is not dead, and that you may tie to. If he were, Dog Monday would have known, just as he knew before, and he would not be still waiting for the trains."

It was absurd—and irrational—and impossible. But Rilla believed it, for all that; and Mrs. Blythe believed it; and the doctor, though he smiled faintly in pretended derision, felt an odd confidence replace his first despair; and foolish and absurd or not, they all plucked up heart and courage to carry on, just because a faithful little dog at the Glen station was still watching with unbroken faith for his master to come home. Common sense might scorn—incredulity might mutter "Mere superstition"—but in their hearts the folk of Ingleside stood by their belief that Dog Monday knew.

30. THE TURNING OF THE TIDE

Susan was very sorrowful when she saw the beautiful old lawn of Ingleside ploughed up that spring and planted with potatoes. Yet she made no protest, even when her beloved peony bed was sacrificed. But when the Government passed the Daylight Saving law Susan balked. There was a Higher Power than the Union Government, to which Susan owed allegiance.

"Do you think it right to meddle with the arrangements of the Almighty?" she demanded indignantly of the doctor. The doctor, quite unmoved, responded that the law must be observed, and the Ingleside clocks were moved on accordingly. But the doctor had no power over Susan's little alarm.

"I bought that with my own money, Mrs. Dr. dear," she said firmly, "and it shall go on God's time and not Borden's time."

Susan got up and went to bed by "God's time," and regulated her own goings and comings by it. She served the meals, under protest, by Borden's time, and she had to go to church by it, which was the crowning injury. But she said her prayers by her own clock, and fed the hens by it; so that there was always a furtive triumph in her eye when she looked at the doctor. She had got the better of him by so much at least.

"Whiskers-on-the-moon is very much delighted with this daylight saving business," she told him one evening. "Of course he naturally would be, since I understand that the Germans invented it. I hear he came near losing his entire wheat-crop lately. Warren Mead's cows broke into the field one day last week—it was the very day the Germans captured the Chemang-de-dam, which may have been a coincidence or may not—and were making fine havoc of it when Mrs. Dick Clow happened to see them from her attic window. At first she had no intention of letting Mr. Pryor know. She told me she had just gloated over the sight of those cows pasturing on his wheat. She felt it served him exactly right. But presently she reflected that the wheat-crop was a matter of great importance and that 'save and serve' meant that those cows must be routed out as much as it meant anything. So she went down and phoned over to Whiskers about the matter. All the thanks she got was that he said something queer right out to her. She is not prepared to state that it was actually swearing for you cannot be sure just what you hear over the phone; but she has her own opinion, and so have I, but I will not express it for here comes Mr. Meredith, and Whiskers is one of his elders, so we must be discreet."

"Are you looking for the new star?" asked Mr. Meredith, joining Miss Oliver and Rilla, who were standing among the blossoming potatoes gazing skyward.

"Yes—we have found it—see, it is just above the tip of the tallest old pine."

"It's wonderful to be looking at something that happened three thousand years ago, isn't it?" said Rilla. "That is when astronomers think the collision took place which produced this new star. It makes me feel horribly insignificant," she added under her breath.

"Even this event cannot dwarf into what may be the proper perspective in star systems the fact that the Germans are again only one leap from Paris," said Gertrude restlessly.

"I think I would like to have been an astronomer," said Mr. Meredith dreamily, gazing at the star.

"There must be a strange pleasure in it," agreed Miss Oliver, "an unearthly pleasure, in more senses than one. I would like to have a few astronomers for my friends."

"Fancy talking the gossip of the hosts of heaven," laughed Rilla.

"I wonder if astronomers feel a very deep interest in earthly affairs?" said the doctor. "Perhaps students of the canals of Mars would not be so keenly sensitive to the significance of a few yards of trenches lost or won on the western front."

"I have read somewhere," said Mr. Meredith, "that Ernest Renan wrote one of his books during the siege of Paris in 1870 and 'enjoyed the writing of it very much.' I suppose one would call him a philosopher."

"I have read also," said Miss Oliver, "that shortly before his death he said that his only regret in dying was that he must die before he had seen what that 'extremely interesting young man, the German Emperor,' would do in his life. If Ernest Renan 'walked' today and saw what that interesting young man had done to his beloved France, not to speak of the world, I wonder if his mental detachment would be as complete as it was in 1870."

"I wonder where Jem is tonight," thought Rilla, in a sudden bitter inrush of remembrance.

It was over a month since the news had come about Jem. Nothing had been discovered concerning him, in spite of all efforts. Two or three letters had come from him, written before the trench raid, and since then there had been only unbroken silence. Now the Germans were again at the Marne, pressing nearer and nearer Paris; now rumours were coming of another Austrian offensive against the Piave line. Rilla turned away from the new star, sick at heart. It was one of the moments when hope and courage failed her utterly—when it seemed impossible to go on even one more day. If only they knew what had happened to Jem—you can face anything you know. But a beleaguerment of fear and doubt and suspense is a hard thing for the morale. Surely, if Jem were alive, some word would have come through. He must be dead. Only—they would never know—they could never be quite sure; and Dog Monday would wait for the train until he died of old age. Monday was only a poor, faithful, rheumatic little dog, who knew nothing more of his master's fate than they did.

Rilla had a "white night" and did not fall asleep until late. When she wakened Gertrude Oliver was sitting at her window leaning out to meet the silver mystery of the dawn. Her clever, striking profile, with the masses of black hair behind it, came out clearly against the pallid gold of the eastern sky. Rilla remembered Jem's admiration of the curve of Miss Oliver's brow and chin, and she shuddered. Everything that reminded her of Jem was beginning to give intolerable pain. Walter's death had inflicted on her heart a terrible wound. But it had been a clean wound and had healed slowly, as such wounds do, though the scar must remain for ever. But the torture of Jem's disappearance was another thing: there was a poison in it that kept it from healing. The alternations of hope and despair, the endless watching each day for the letter that never came—that might never come—the newspaper tales of ill-usage of prisoners—the bitter wonder as to Jem's wound—all were increasingly hard to bear.

Gertrude Oliver turned her head. There was an odd brilliancy in her eyes.

"Rilla, I've had another dream."

"Oh, no—no," cried Rilla, shrinking. Miss Oliver's dreams had always foretold coming disaster.

"Rilla, it was a good dream. Listen—I dreamed just as I did four years ago, that I stood on the veranda steps and looked down the Glen. And it was still covered by waves that lapped about my feet. But as I looked the waves began to ebb—and they ebbed as swiftly as, four years ago, they rolled in—ebbed out and out, to the gulf; and the Glen lay before me, beautiful and green, with a rainbow spanning Rainbow Valley—a rainbow of such splendid colour that it dazzled me—and I woke. Rilla—Rilla Blythe—the tide has turned."

"I wish I could believe it," sighed Rilla.

"Sooth was my prophecy of fear
Believe it when it augurs cheer,"

quoted Gertrude, almost gaily. "I tell you I have no doubt."

Yet, in spite of the great Italian victory at the Piave that came a few days later, she had doubt many a time in the hard month that followed; and when in mid-July the Germans crossed the Marne again despair came sickeningly. It was idle, they all felt, to hope that the miracle of the Marne would be repeated. But it was: again, as in 1914, the tide turned at the Marne. The French and the American troops struck their sudden smashing blow on the exposed flank of the enemy and, with the almost inconceivable rapidity of a dream, the whole aspect of the war changed.

"The Allies have won two tremendous victories," said the doctor on 20th July.

"It is the beginning of the end—I feel it—I feel it," said Mrs. Blythe.

"Thank God," said Susan, folding her trembling old hands, Then she added, under her breath, "but it won't bring our boys back."

Nevertheless she went out and ran up the flag, for the first time since the fall of Jerusalem. As it caught the breeze and swelled gallantly out above her, Susan lifted her hand and saluted it, as she had seen Shirley do. "We've all given something to keep you flying," she said. "Four hundred thousand of our boys gone overseas—fifty thousand of them killed. But—you are worth it!" The wind whipped her grey hair about her face and the gingham apron that shrouded her from head to foot was cut on lines of economy, not of grace; yet, somehow, just then Susan made an imposing figure. She was one of the women—courageous, unquailing, patient, heroic—who had made victory possible. In her, they all saluted the symbol for which their dearest had fought. Something of this was in the doctor's mind as he watched her from the door.

"Susan," he said, when she turned to come in, "from first to last of this business you have been a brick!"

31. MRS. MATILDA PITTMAN

Rilla and Jims were standing on the rear platform of their car when the train stopped at the little Millward siding. The August evening was so hot and close that the crowded cars were stifling. Nobody ever knew just why trains stopped at Millward siding. Nobody was ever known to get off there or get on. There was only one house nearer to it than four miles, and it was surrounded by acres of blueberry barrens and scrub spruce-trees.

Rilla was on her way into Charlottetown to spend the night with a friend and the next day in Red Cross shopping; she had taken Jims with her, partly because she did not want Susan or her mother to be bothered with his care, partly because of a hungry desire in her heart to have as much of him as she could before she might have to give him up forever. James Anderson had written to her not long before this; he was wounded and in the hospital; he would not be able to go back to the front and as soon as he was able he would be coming home for Jims.

Rilla was heavy-hearted over this, and worried also. She loved Jims dearly and would feel deeply giving him up in any case; but if Jim Anderson were a different sort of a man, with a proper home for the child, it would not be so bad. But to give Jims up to a roving, shiftless, irresponsible father, however kind and good-hearted he might be—and she knew Jim Anderson was kind and good-hearted enough—was a bitter prospect to Rilla. It was not even likely Anderson would stay in the Glen; he had no ties there now; he might even go back to England. She might never see her dear, sunshiny, carefully brought-up little Jims again. With such a father what might his fate be? Rilla meant to beg Jim Anderson to leave him with her, but, from his letter, she had not much hope that he would.

"If he would only stay in the Glen, where I could keep an eye on Jims and have him often with me I wouldn't feel so worried over it," she reflected. "But I feel sure he won't—and Jims will never have any chance. And he is such a bright little chap—he has ambition, wherever he got it—and he isn't lazy. But his father will never have a cent to give him any education or start in life. Jims, my little war-baby, whatever is going to become of you?"

Jims was not in the least concerned over what was to become of him. He was gleefully watching the antics of a striped chipmunk that was frisking over the roof of the little siding. As the train pulled out Jims leaned eagerly forward for a last look at Chippy, pulling his hand from Rilla's. Rilla was so engrossed in wondering what was to become of Jims in the future that she forgot to take notice of what was happening to him in the present. What did happen was that Jims lost his balance, shot headlong down the steps, hurtled across the little siding platform, and landed in a clump of bracken fern on the other side.

Rilla shrieked and lost her head. She sprang down the steps and jumped off the train.

Fortunately, the train was still going at a comparatively slow speed; fortunately also, Rilla retained enough sense to jump the way it was going; nevertheless, she fell and sprawled helplessly down the embankment, landing in a ditch full of a rank growth of golden-rod and fireweed.

Nobody had seen what had happened and the train whisked briskly away round a curve in the barrens. Rilla picked herself up, dizzy but unhurt, scrambled out of the ditch, and flew wildly across the platform, expecting to find Jims dead or broken in pieces. But Jims, except for a few bruises, and a big fright, was quite uninjured. He was so badly scared that he didn't even cry, but Rilla, when she found that he was safe and sound, burst into tears and sobbed wildly.

"Nasty old twain," remarked Jims in disgust. "And nasty old God," he added, with a scowl at the heavens.

A laugh broke into Rilla's sobbing, producing something very like what her father would have called hysterics. But she caught herself up before the hysteria could conquer her.

"Rilla Blythe, I'm ashamed of you. Pull yourself together immediately. Jims, you shouldn't have said anything like that."

"God frew me off the twain," declared Jims defiantly. "Somebody frew me; you didn't frow me; so it was God."

"No, it wasn't. You fell because you let go of my hand and bent too far forward. I told you not to do that. So that it was your own fault."

Jims looked to see if she meant it; then glanced up at the sky again.

"Excuse me, then, God," he remarked airily.

Rilla scanned the sky also; she did not like its appearance; a heavy thundercloud was appearing in the northwest. What in the world was to be done? There was no other train that night, since the nine o'clock special ran only on Saturdays. Would it be possible for them to reach Hannah Brewster's house, two miles away, before the storm broke? Rilla thought she could do it alone easily enough, but with Jims it was another matter. Were his little legs good for it?

"We've got to try it," said Rilla desperately. "We might stay in the siding until the thunderstorm is over; but it may keep on raining all night and anyway it will be pitch dark. If we can get to Hannah's she will keep us all night."

Hannah Brewster, when she had been Hannah Crawford, had lived in the Glen and gone to school with Rilla. They had been good friends then, though Hannah had been three years the older. She had married very young and had gone to live in Millward. What with hard work and babies and a ne'er-do-well husband, her life had not been an easy one, and Hannah seldom revisited her old home. Rilla had visited her once soon after her marriage, but had not seen her or even heard of her for years; she knew, however, that she and Jims would find welcome and harbourage in any house where rosy-faced, open-hearted, generous Hannah lived.

For the first mile they got on very well but the second one was harder. The road, seldom used, was rough and deep-rutted. Jims grew so tired that Rilla had to carry him for the last quarter. She reached the Brewster house, almost exhausted, and dropped Jims on the walk with a sigh of thankfulness. The sky was black with clouds; the first heavy drops were beginning to fall; and the rumble of thunder was growing very loud. Then she made an unpleasant discovery. The blinds were all down and the doors locked. Evidently the Brewsters were not at home. Rilla ran to the little barn. It, too, was locked. No other refuge presented itself. The bare whitewashed little house had not even a veranda or porch.

It was almost dark now and her plight seemed desperate.

"I'm going to get in if I have to break a window," said Rilla resolutely. "Hannah would want me to do that. She'd never get over it if she heard I came to her house for refuge in a thunderstorm and couldn't get in."

Luckily she did not have to go to the length of actual housebreaking. The kitchen window went up quite easily. Rilla lifted Jims in and scrambled through herself, just as the storm broke in good earnest.

"Oh, see all the little pieces of thunder," cried Jims in delight, as the hail danced in after them. Rilla shut the window and with some difficulty found and lighted a lamp. They were in a very snug little kitchen. Opening off it on one side was a trim, nicely furnished parlour, and on the other a pantry, which proved to be well stocked.

"I'm going to make myself at home," said Rilla. "I know that is just what Hannah would want me to do. I'll get a little snack for Jims and me, and then if the rain continues and nobody comes home I'll just go upstairs to the spare room and go to bed. There is nothing like acting sensibly in an emergency. If I had not been a goose when I saw Jims fall off the train I'd have rushed back into the car and got some one to stop it. Then I wouldn't have been in this scrape. Since I am in it I'll make the best of it.

"This house," she added, looking around, "is fixed up much nicer than when I was here before. Of course Hannah and Ted were just beginning housekeeping then. But somehow I've had the idea that Ted hasn't been very prosperous. He must have done better than I've been led to believe, when they can afford furniture like this. I'm awfully glad for Hannah's sake."

The thunderstorm passed, but the rain continued to fall heavily. At eleven o'clock Rilla decided that nobody was coming home. Jims had fallen asleep on the sofa; she carried him up to the spare room and put him to bed. Then she undressed, put on a nightgown she found in the washstand drawer, and scrambled sleepily in between very nice lavender-scented sheets.

She was so tired, after her adventures and exertions, that not even the oddity of her situation could keep her awake; she was sound asleep in a few minutes.

Rilla slept until eight o'clock the next morning and then wakened with startling suddenness. Somebody was saying in a harsh, gruff voice, "Here, you two, wake up. I want to know what this means."

Rilla did wake up, promptly and effectually. She had never in all her life wakened up so thoroughly before. Standing in the room were three people, one of them a man, who were absolute strangers to her. The man was a big fellow with a bushy black beard and an angry scowl. Beside him was a woman—a tall, thin, angular person, with violently red hair and an indescribable hat. She looked even crosser and more amazed than the man, if that were possible. In the background was another woman—a tiny old lady who must have been at least eighty. She was, in spite of her tinyness, a very striking-looking personage; she was dressed in unrelieved black, had snow-white hair, a dead-white face, and snapping, vivid, coal-black eyes. She looked as amazed as the other two, but Rilla realized that she didn't look cross.

Rilla also was realizing that something was wrong—fearfully wrong. Then the man said, more gruffly than ever, "Come now. Who are you and what business have you here?"

Rilla raised herself on one elbow, looking and feeling hopelessly bewildered and foolish. She heard the old black-and-white lady in the background chuckle to herself. "She must be real," Rilla thought. "I can't be dreaming her." Aloud she gasped,

"Isn't this Theodore Brewster's place?"

"No," said the big woman, speaking for the first time, "this place belongs to us. We bought it from the Brewsters last fall. They moved to Greenvale. Our name is Chapley."

Poor Rilla fell back on her pillow, quite overcome.

"I beg your pardon," she said. "I—I—thought the Brewsters lived here. Mrs. Brewster is a friend of mine. I am Rilla Blythe—Dr. Blythe's daughter from Glen St. Mary. I—I was going to town with my—my—this little boy—and he fell off the train—and I jumped off after him—and nobody knew of it. I knew we couldn't get home last night and a storm was coming up—so we came here and when we found nobody at home—we—we—just got in through the window and—and—made ourselves at home."

"So it seems," said the woman sarcastically.

"A likely story," said the man.

"We weren't born yesterday," added the woman.

Madam Black-and-White didn't say anything; but when the other two made their pretty speeches she doubled up in a silent convulsion of mirth, shaking her head from side to side and beating the air with her hands.

Rilla, stung by the disagreeable attitude of the Chapleys, regained her self-possession and lost her temper. She sat up in bed and said in her haughtiest voice, "I do not know when you were born, or where, but it must have been somewhere where very peculiar manners were taught. If you will have the decency to leave my room—er—this room—until I can get up and dress I shall not transgress upon your hospitality"—Rilla was killingly sarcastic—"any longer. And I shall pay you amply for the food we have eaten and the night's lodging I have taken."

The black-and-white apparition went through the motion of clapping her hands, but not a sound did she make. Perhaps Mr. Chapley was cowed by Rilla's tone—or perhaps he was appeased at the prospect of payment; at all events, he spoke more civilly.

"Well, that's fair. If you pay up it's all right."

"She shall do no such thing as pay you," said Madam Black-and-White in a surprisingly clear, resolute, authoritative tone of voice. "If you haven't got any shame for yourself, Robert Chapley, you've got a mother-in-law who can be ashamed for you. No strangers shall be charged for room and lodging in any house where Mrs. Matilda Pitman lives. Remember that, though I may have come down in the world, I haven't quite forgot all decency for all that. I knew you was a skinflint when Amelia married you, and you've made her as bad as yourself. But Mrs. Matilda Pitman has been boss for a long time, and Mrs. Matilda Pitman will remain boss. Here you, Robert Chapley, take yourself out of here and let that girl get dressed. And you, Amelia, go downstairs and cook a breakfast for her."

Never, in all her life, had Rilla seen anything like the abject meekness with which those two big people obeyed that mite. They went without word or look of protest. As the door closed behind them Mrs. Matilda Pitman laughed silently, and rocked from side to side in her merriment.

"Ain't it funny?" she said. "I mostly lets them run the length of their tether, but sometimes I has to pull them up, and then I does it with a jerk. They don't dast aggravate me, because I've got considerable hard cash, and they're afraid I won't leave it all to them. Neither I will. I'll leave 'em some, but some I won't, just to vex 'em. I haven't made up my mind where I will leave it but I'll have to, soon, for at eighty a body is living on borrowed time. Now, you can take your time about dressing, my dear, and I'll go down and keep them mean scallawags in order. That's a handsome child you have there. Is he your brother?"

"No, he's a little war-baby I've been taking care of, because his mother died and his father was overseas," answered Rilla in a subdued tone.

"War-baby! Humph! Well, I'd better skin out before he wakes up or he'll likely start crying. Children don't like me—never did. I can't recollect any youngster ever coming near me of its own accord. Never had any of my own. Amelia was my step-daughter. Well, it's saved me a world of bother. If kids don't like me I don't like them, so that's an even score. But that certainly is a handsome child."

Jims chose this moment for waking up. He opened his big brown eyes and looked at Mrs. Matilda Pitman unblinkingly. Then he sat up, dimpled deliciously, pointed to her and said solemnly to Rilla, "Pwitty lady, Willa, pwitty lady."

Mrs. Matilda Pitman smiled. Even eighty-odd is sometimes vulnerable in vanity. "I've heard that children and fools tell the truth," she said. "I was used to compliments when I was young—but they're scarcer when you get as far along as I am. I haven't had one for years. It tastes good. I s'pose now, you monkey, you wouldn't give me a kiss."

Then Jims did a quite surprising thing. He was not a demonstrative youngster and was chary with kisses even to the Ingleside people. But without a word he stood up in bed, his plump little body encased only in his undershirt, ran to the footboard, flung his arms about Mrs. Matilda Pitman's neck, and gave her a bear hug, accompanied by three or four hearty, ungrudging smacks.

"Jims," protested Rilla, aghast at this liberty.

"You leave him be," ordered Mrs. Matilda Pitman, setting her bonnet straight.

"Laws I like to see some one that isn't skeered of me. Everybody is—you are, though you're trying to hide it. And why? Of course Robert and Amelia are because I make 'em skeered on purpose. But folks always are—no matter how civil I be to them. Are you going to keep this child?"

"I'm afraid not. His father is coming home before long."

"Is he any good—the father, I mean?"

"Well—he's kind and nice—but he's poor—and I'm afraid he always will be," faltered Rilla.

"I see—shiftless—can't make or keep. Well, I'll see—I'll see. I have an idea. It's a good idea, and besides it will make Robert and Amelia squirm. That's its main merit in my eyes, though I like that child, mind you, because he ain't skeered of me. He's worth some bother. Now, you get dressed, as I said before, and come down when you're good and ready."

Rilla was stiff and sore after her tumble and walk of the night before but she was not long in dressing herself and Jims. When she went down to the kitchen she found a smoking hot breakfast on the table. Mr. Chapley was nowhere in sight and Mrs. Chapley was cutting bread with a sulky air. Mrs. Matilda Pitman was sitting in an armchair, knitting a grey army sock. She still wore her bonnet and her triumphant expression.

"Set right in, dears, and make a good breakfast," she said.

"I am not hungry," said Rilla almost pleadingly. "I don't think I can eat anything. And it is time I was starting for the station. The morning train will soon be along. Please excuse me and let us go—I'll take a piece of bread and butter for Jims."

Mrs. Matilda Pitman shook a knitting-needle playfully at Rilla.

"Sit down and take your breakfast," she said. "Mrs. Matilda Pitman commands you. Everybody obeys Mrs. Matilda Pitman—even Robert and Amelia. You must obey her too."

Rilla did obey her. She sat down and, such was the influence of Mrs. Matilda Pitman's mesmeric eye, she ate a tolerable breakfast. The obedient Amelia never spoke; Mrs. Matilda Pitman did not speak either; but she knitted furiously and chuckled. When Rilla had finished, Mrs. Matilda Pitman rolled up her sock.

"Now you can go if you want to," she said, "but you don't have to go. You can stay here as long as you want to and I'll make Amelia cook your meals for you."

The independent Miss Blythe, whom a certain clique of Junior Red Cross girls accused of being domineering and "bossy," was thoroughly cowed.

"Thank you," she said meekly, "but we must really go."

"Well, then," said Mrs. Matilda Pitman, throwing open the door, "your conveyance is ready for you. I told Robert he must hitch up and drive you to the station. I enjoy making Robert do things. It's almost the only sport I have left. I'm over eighty and most things have lost their flavour except bossing Robert."

Robert sat before the door on the front seat of a trim, double-seated, rubber-tired buggy. He must have heard every word his mother-in-law said but he gave no sign.

"I do wish," said Rilla, plucking up what little spirit she had left, "that you would let me—oh—ah—" then she quailed again before Mrs. Matilda Pitman's eye—"recompense you for—for—"

"Mrs. Matilda Pitman said before—and meant it—that she doesn't take pay for entertaining strangers, nor let other people where she lives do it, much as their natural meanness would like to do it. You go along to town and don't forget to call the next time you come this way. Don't be scared. Not that you are scared of much, I reckon, considering the way you sassed Robert back this morning. I like your spunk. Most girls nowadays are such timid, skeery creeturs. When I was a girl I wasn't afraid of nothing nor nobody. Mind you take good care of that boy. He ain't any common child. And make Robert drive round all the puddles in the road. I won't have that new buggy splashed."

As they drove away Jims threw kisses at Mrs. Matilda Pitman as long as he could see her, and Mrs. Matilda Pitman waved her sock back at him. Robert spoke no word, either good or bad, all the way to the station, but he remembered the puddles. When Rilla got out at the siding she thanked him courteously. The only response she got was a grunt as Robert turned his horse and started for home.

"Well"—Rilla drew a long breath—"I must try to get back into Rilla Blythe again. I've been somebody else these past few hours—I don't know just who—some creation of that extraordinary old person's. I believe she hypnotized me. What an adventure this will be to write the boys."

And then she sighed. Bitter remembrance came that there were only Jerry, Ken, Carl and Shirley to write it to now. Jem—who would have appreciated Mrs. Matilda Pitman keenly—where was Jem?

32. WORD FROM JEM

4th August 1918

"It is four years tonight since the dance at the lighthouse—four years of war. It seems like three times four. I was fifteen then. I am nineteen now. I expected that these past four years would be the most delightful years of my life and they have been years of war—years of fear and grief and worry—but I humbly hope, of a little growth in strength and character as well.

"Today I was going through the hall and I heard mother saying something to father about me. I didn't mean to listen—I couldn't help hearing her as I went along the hall and upstairs—so perhaps that is why I heard what listeners are said never to hear—something good of myself. And because it was mother who said it I'm going to write it here in my journal, for my comforting when days of discouragement come upon me, in which I feel that I am vain and selfish and weak and that there is no good thing in me.

"'Rilla has developed in a wonderful fashion these past four years. She used to be such an irresponsible young creature. She has changed into a capable, womanly girl and she is such a comfort to me. Nan and Di have grown a little away from me—they have been so little at home—but Rilla has grown closer and closer to me. We are chums. I don't see how I could have got through these terrible years without her, Gilbert.'

"There, that is just what mother said—and I feel glad—and sorry—and proud—and humble! It's beautiful to have my mother think that about me—but I don't deserve it quite. I'm not as good and strong as all that. There are heaps of times when I have felt cross and impatient and woeful and despairing. It is mother and Susan who have been this family's backbone. But I have helped a little, I believe, and I am so glad and thankful.

"The war news has been good right along. The French and Americans are pushing the Germans back and back and back. Sometimes I am afraid it is too good to last—after nearly four years of disasters one has a feeling that this constant success is unbelievable. We don't rejoice noisily over it. Susan keeps the flag up but we go softly. The price paid has been too high for jubilation. We are just thankful that it has not been paid in vain.

"No word has come from Jem. We hope—because we dare not do anything else. But there are hours when we all feel—though we never say so—that such hoping is foolishness. These hours come more and more frequently as the weeks go by. And we may never know. That is the most terrible thought of all. I wonder how Faith is bearing it. To judge from her letters she has never for a moment given up hope, but she must have had her dark hours of doubt like the rest of us."

20th August 1918

"The Canadians have been in action again and Mr. Meredith had a cable today saying that Carl had been slightly wounded and is in the hospital. It did not say where the wound was, which is unusual, and we all feel worried. There is news of a fresh victory every day now."

30th August 1918

"The Merediths had a letter from Carl today. His wound was "only a slight one"—but it was in his right eye and the sight is gone for ever!

"'One eye is enough to watch bugs with,' Carl writes cheerfully. And we know it might have been oh so much worse! If it had been both eyes! But I cried all the afternoon after I saw Carl's letter. Those beautiful, fearless blue eyes of his!

"There is one comfort—he will not have to go back to the front. He is coming home as soon as he is out of the hospital—the first of our boys to return. When will the others come?

"And there is one who will never come. At least we will not see him if he does. But, oh, I think he will be there—when our Canadian soldiers return there will be a shadow army with them—the army of the fallen. We will not see them—but they will be there!"

1st September 1918

"Mother and I went into Charlottetown yesterday to see the moving picture, "Hearts of the World." I made an awful goose of myself—father will never stop teasing me about it for the rest of my life. But it all seemed so horribly real—and I was so intensely interested that I forgot everything but the scenes I saw enacted before my eyes. And then, quite near the last came a terribly exciting one. The heroine was struggling with a horrible German soldier who was trying to drag her away. I knew she had a knife—I had seen her hide it, to have it in readiness—and I couldn't understand why she didn't produce it and finish the brute. I thought she must have forgotten it, and just at the tensest moment of the scene I lost my head altogether. I just stood right up on my feet in that crowded house and shrieked at the top of my voice—'The knife is in your stocking—the knife is in your stocking!'

"I created a sensation!

"The funny part was, that just as I said it, the girl did snatch out the knife and stab the soldier with it!

"Everybody in the house laughed. I came to my senses and fell back in my seat, overcome with mortification. Mother was shaking with laughter. I could have shaken her. Why hadn't she pulled me down and choked me before I had made such an idiot of myself. She protests that there wasn't time.

"Fortunately the house was dark, and I don't believe there was anybody there who knew me. And I thought I was becoming sensible and self-controlled and womanly! It is plain I have some distance to go yet before I attain that devoutly desired consummation."

20th September 1918

"In the east Bulgaria has asked for peace, and in the west the British have smashed the Hindenburg line; and right here in Glen St. Mary little Bruce Meredith has done something that I think wonderful—wonderful because of the love behind it. Mrs. Meredith was here tonight and told us about it—and mother and I cried, and Susan got up and clattered the things about the stove.

"Bruce always loved Jem very devotedly, and the child has never forgotten him in all these years. He has been as faithful in his way as Dog Monday was in his. We have always told him that Jem would come back. But it seems that he was in Carter Flagg's store last night and he heard his Uncle Norman flatly declaring that Jem Blythe would never come back and that the Ingleside folk might as well give up hoping he would. Bruce went home and cried himself to sleep. This morning his mother saw him going out of the yard, with a very sorrowful and determined look, carrying his pet kitten. She didn't think much more about it until later on he came in, with the most tragic little face, and told her, his little body shaking with sobs, that he had drowned Stripey.

"'Why did you do that?' Mrs. Meredith exclaimed.

"'To bring Jem back,' sobbed Bruce. 'I thought if I sacrificed Stripey God would send Jem back. So I drownded him—and, oh mother, it was awful hard—but surely God will send Jem back now, 'cause Stripey was the dearest thing I had. I just told God I would give Him Stripey if He would send Jem back. And He will, won't He, mother?'

"Mrs. Meredith didn't know what to say to the poor child. She just could not tell him that perhaps his sacrifice wouldn't bring Jem back—that God didn't work that way. She told him that he mustn't expect it right away—that perhaps it would be quite a long time yet before Jem came back.

"But Bruce said, 'It oughtn't to take longer'n a week, mother. Oh, mother, Stripey was such a nice little cat. He purred so pretty. Don't you think God ought to like him enough to let us have Jem?"

"Mr. Meredith is worried about the effect on Bruce's faith in God, and Mrs. Meredith is worried about the effect on Bruce himself if his hope isn't fulfilled. And I feel as if I must cry every time I think of it. It was so splendid—and sad—and beautiful. The dear devoted little fellow! He worshipped that kitten. And if it all goes for nothing—as so many sacrifices seem to go for nothing—he will be brokenhearted, for he isn't old enough to understand that God doesn't answer our prayers just as we hope—and doesn't make bargains with us when we yield something we love up to Him."

24th September 1918

"I have been kneeling at my window in the moonshine for a long time, just thanking God over and over again. The joy of last night and today has been so great that it seemed half pain—as if our hearts weren't big enough to hold it.

"Last night I was sitting here in my room at eleven o'clock writing a letter to Shirley. Every one else was in bed, except father, who was out. I heard the telephone ring and I ran out to the hall to answer it, before it should waken mother. It was long-distance calling, and when I answered it said 'This is the telegraph Company's office in Charlottetown. There is an overseas cable for Dr. Blythe.'

"I thought of Shirley—my heart stood still—and then I heard him saying, 'It's from Holland.'

"The message was,

'Just arrived. Escaped from Germany. Quite well. Writing.
James Blythe.'

"I didn't faint or fall or scream. I didn't feel glad or surprised. I didn't feel anything. I felt numb, just as I did when I heard Walter had enlisted. I hung up the receiver and turned round. Mother was standing in her doorway. She wore her old rose kimono, and her hair was hanging down her back in a long thick braid, and her eyes were shining. She looked just like a young girl.

"'There is word from Jem?' she said.

"How did she know? I hadn't said a word at the phone except 'Yes—yes—yes.' She says she doesn't know how she knew, but she did know. She was awake and she heard the ring and she knew that there was word from Jem.

"'He's alive—he's well—he's in Holland,' I said.

"Mother came out into the hall and said, 'I must get your father on the 'phone and tell him. He is in the Upper Glen.'

"She was very calm and quiet—not a bit like I would have expected her to be. But then I wasn't either. I went and woke up Gertrude and Susan and told them. Susan said 'Thank God,' firstly, and secondly she said 'Did I not tell you Dog Monday knew?' and thirdly, 'I'll go down and make a cup of tea'—and she stalked down in her nightdress to make it. She did make it—and made mother and Gertrude drink it—but I went back to my room and shut my door and locked it, and I knelt by my window and cried—just as Gertrude did when her great news came.

"I think I know at last exactly what I shall feel like on the resurrection morning."

4th October 1918

"Today Jem's letter came. It has been in the house only six hours and it is almost read to pieces. The post-mistress told everybody in the Glen it had come, and everybody came up to hear the news.

"Jem was badly wounded in the thigh—and he was picked up and taken to prison, so delirious with fever that he didn't know what was happening to him or where he was. It was weeks before he came to his senses and was able to write. Then he did write—but it never came. He wasn't treated at all badly at his camp—only the food was poor. He had nothing to eat but a little black bread and boiled turnips and now and then a little soup with black peas in it. And we sat down every one of those days to three good square luxurious meals! He wrote us as often as he could but he was afraid we were not getting his letters because no reply came. As soon as he was strong enough he tried to escape, but was caught and brought back; a month later he and a comrade made another attempt and succeeded in reaching Holland.

"Jem can't come home right away. He isn't quite so well as his cable said, for his wound has not healed properly and he has to go into a hospital in England for further treatment. But he says he will be all right eventually, and we know he is safe and will be back home sometime, and oh, the difference it makes in everything!

"I had a letter from Jim Anderson today, too. He has married an English girl, got his discharge, and is coming right home to Canada with his bride. I don't know whether to be glad or sorry. It will depend on what kind of a woman she is. I had a second letter also of a somewhat mysterious tenor. It is from a Charlottetown lawyer, asking me to go in to see him at my earliest convenience in regard to a certain matter connected with the estate of the 'late Mrs. Matilda Pitman.'

"I read a notice of Mrs. Pitman's death—from heart failure—in the Enterprise a few weeks ago. I wonder if this summons has anything to do with Jims."

5th October 1918

"I went into town this morning and had an interview with Mrs. Pitman's lawyer—a little thin, wispy man, who spoke of his late client with such a profound respect that it is evident that he as was much under her thumb as Robert and Amelia were. He drew up a new will for her a short time before her death. She was worth thirty thousand dollars, the bulk of which was left to Amelia Chapley. But she left five thousand to me in trust for Jims. The interest is to be used as I see fit for his education, and the principal is to be paid over to him on his twentieth birthday. Certainly Jims was born lucky. I saved him from slow extinction at the hands of Mrs. Conover—Mary Vance saved him from death by diptheritic croup—his star saved him when he fell off the train. And he tumbled not only into a clump of bracken, but right into this nice little legacy.

"Evidently, as Mrs. Matilda Pitman said, and as I have always believed, he is no common child and he has no common destiny in store for him.

"At all events he is provided for, and in such a fashion that Jim Anderson can't squander his inheritance if he wanted to. Now, if the new English stepmother is only a good sort I shall feel quite easy about the future of my war-baby.

"I wonder what Robert and Amelia think of it. I fancy they will nail down their windows when they leave home after this!"

33. VICTORY!

"A day 'of chilling winds and gloomy skies,'" Rilla quoted one Sunday afternoon—the sixth of October to be exact. It was so cold that they had lighted a fire in the living-room and the merry little flames were doing their best to counteract the outside dourness. "It's more like November than October—November is such an ugly month."

Cousin Sophia was there, having again forgiven Susan, and Mrs. Martin Clow, who was not visiting on Sunday but had dropped in to borrow Susan's cure for rheumatism—that being cheaper than getting one from the doctor. "I'm afeared we're going to have an airly winter," foreboded Cousin Sophia. "The muskrats are building awful big houses round the pond, and that's a sign that never fails. Dear me, how that child has grown!" Cousin Sophia sighed again, as if it were an unhappy circumstance that a child should grow. "When do you expect his father?"

"Next week," said Rilla.

"Well, I hope the stepmother won't abuse the pore child," sighed Cousin Sophia, "but I have my doubts—I have my doubts. Anyhow, he'll be sure to feel the difference between his usage here and what he'll get anywhere else. You've spoiled him so, Rilla, waiting on him hand and foot the way you've always done."

Rilla smiled and pressed her cheek to Jims' curls. She knew sweet-tempered, sunny, little Jims was not spoiled. Nevertheless her heart was anxious behind her smile. She, too, thought much about the new Mrs. Anderson and wondered uneasily what she would be like.

"I can't give Jims up to a woman who won't love him," she thought rebelliously.

"I b'lieve it's going to rain," said Cousin Sophia. "We have had an awful lot of rain this fall already. It's going to make it awful hard for people to get their roots in. It wasn't so in my young days. We gin'rally had beautiful Octobers then. But the seasons is altogether different now from what they used to be." Clear across Cousin Sophia's doleful voice cut the telephone bell. Gertrude Oliver answered it. "Yes—what? What? Is it true—is it official? Thank you—thank you."

Gertrude turned and faced the room dramatically, her dark eyes flashing, her dark face flushed with feeling. All at once the sun broke through the thick clouds and poured through the big crimson maple outside the window. Its reflected glow enveloped her in a weird immaterial flame. She looked like a priestess performing some mystic, splendid rite.

"Germany and Austria are suing for peace," she said.

Rilla went crazy for a few minutes. She sprang up and danced around the room, clapping her hands, laughing, crying.

"Sit down, child," said Mrs. Clow, who never got excited over anything, and so had missed a tremendous amount of trouble and delight in her journey through life.

"Oh," cried Rilla, "I have walked the floor for hours in despair and anxiety in these past four years. Now let me walk in joy. It was worth living long dreary years for this minute, and it would be worth living them again just to look back to it. Susan, let's run up the flag—and we must phone the news to every one in the Glen."

"Can we have as much sugar as we want to now?" asked Jims eagerly.

It was a never-to-be-forgotten afternoon. As the news spread excited people ran about the village and dashed up to Ingleside. The Merediths came over and stayed to supper and everybody talked and nobody listened. Cousin Sophia tried to protest that Germany and Austria were not to be trusted and it was all part of a plot, but nobody paid the least attention to her.

"This Sunday makes up for that one in March," said Susan.

"I wonder," said Gertrude dreamily, apart to Rilla, "if things won't seem rather flat and insipid when peace really comes. After being fed for four years on horrors and fears, terrible reverses, amazing victories, won't anything less be tame and uninteresting? How strange—and blessed—and dull it will be not to dread the coming of the mail every day."

"We must dread it for a little while yet, I suppose," said Rilla. "Peace won't come—can't come—for some weeks yet. And in those weeks dreadful things may happen. My excitement is over. We have won the victory—but oh, what a price we have paid!"

"Not too high a price for freedom," said Gertrude softly. "Do you think it was, Rilla?"

"No," said Rilla, under her breath. She was seeing a little white cross on a battlefield of France. "No—not if those of us who live will show ourselves worthy of it—if we 'keep faith.'"

"We will keep faith," said Gertrude. She rose suddenly. A silence fell around the table, and in the silence Gertrude repeated Walter's famous poem "The Piper." When she finished Mr. Meredith stood up and held up his glass. "Let us drink," he said, "to the silent army—to the boys who followed when the Piper summoned. 'For our tomorrow they gave their today'—theirs is the victory!"

34. MR. HYDE GOES TO HIS OWN PLACE AND SUSAN TAKES A HONEYMOON

Early in November Jims left Ingleside. Rilla saw him go with many tears but a heart free from boding. Mrs. Jim Anderson, Number Two, was such a nice little woman that one was rather inclined to wonder at the luck which bestowed her on Jim. She was rosy-faced and blue-eyed and wholesome, with the roundness and trigness of a geranium leaf. Rilla saw at first glance that she was to be trusted with Jims.

"I'm fond of children, miss," she said heartily. "I'm used to them—I've left six little brothers and sisters behind me. Jims is a dear child and I must say you've done wonders in bringing him up so healthy and handsome. I'll be as good to him as if he was my own, miss. And I'll make

Jim toe the line all right. He's a good worker—all he needs is some one to keep him at it, and to take charge of his money. We've rented a little farm just out of the village, and we're going to settle down there. Jim wanted to stay in England but I says 'No.' I hankered to try a new country and I've always thought Canada would suit me."

"I'm so glad you are going to live near us. You'll let Jims come here often, won't you? I love him dearly."

"No doubt you do, miss, for a lovabler child I never did see. We understand, Jim and me, what you've done for him, and you won't find us ungrateful. He can come here whenever you want him and I'll always be glad of any advice from you about his bringing up. He is more your baby than anyone else's I should say, and I'll see that you get your fair share of him, miss."

So Jims went away—with the soup tureen, though not in it. Then the news of the Armistice came, and even Glen St. Mary went mad. That night the village had a bonfire, and burned the Kaiser in effigy. The fishing village boys turned out and burned all the sandhills off in one grand glorious conflagration that extended for seven miles. Up at Ingleside Rilla ran laughing to her room.

"Now I'm going to do a most unladylike and inexcusable thing," she said, as she pulled her green velvet hat out of its box. "I'm going to kick this hat about the room until it is without form and void; and I shall never as long as I live wear anything of that shade of green again."

"You've certainly kept your vow pluckily," laughed Miss Oliver.

"It wasn't pluck—it was sheer obstinacy—I'm rather ashamed of it," said Rilla, kicking joyously. "I wanted to show mother. It's mean to want to show your own mother—most unfilial conduct! But I have shown her. And I've shown myself a few things! Oh, Miss Oliver, just for one moment I'm really feeling quite young again—young and frivolous and silly. Did I ever say November was an ugly month? Why it's the most beautiful month in the whole year. Listen to the bells ringing in Rainbow Valley! I never heard them so clearly. They're ringing for peace—and new happiness—and all the dear, sweet, sane, homey things that we can have again now, Miss Oliver. Not that I am sane just now—I don't pretend to be. The whole world is having a little crazy spell today. Soon we'll sober down—and 'keep faith'—and begin to build up our new world. But just for today let's be mad and glad."

Susan came in from the outdoor sunlight looking supremely satisfied.

"Mr. Hyde is gone," she announced.

"Gone! Do you mean he is dead, Susan?"

"No, Mrs. Dr. dear, that beast is not dead. But you will never see him again. I feel sure of that."

"Don't be so mysterious, Susan. What has happened to him?"

"Well, Mrs. Dr. dear, he was sitting out on the back steps this afternoon. It was just after the news came that the Armistice had been signed and he was looking his Hydest. I can assure you he was an awesome looking beast. All at once, Mrs. Dr. dear, Bruce Meredith came around the corner of the kitchen walking on his stilts. He has been learning to walk on them lately and came over to show me how well he could do it. Mr. Hyde just took a look and one bound carried him over the yard fence. Then he went tearing through the maple grove in great leaps with his ears laid back. You never saw a creature so terrified, Mrs. Dr. dear. He has never returned."

"Oh, he'll come back, Susan, probably chastened in spirit by his fright."

"We will see, Mrs. Dr. dear—we will see. Remember, the Armistice has been signed. And that reminds me that Whiskers-on-the-moon had a paralytic stroke last night. I am not saying it is a judgment on him, because I am not in the counsels of the Almighty, but one can have one's own thoughts about it. Neither Whiskers-on-the-moon or Mr. Hyde will be much more heard of in Glen St. Mary, Mrs. Dr. dear, and that you may tie to."

Mr. Hyde certainly was heard of no more. As it could hardly have been his fright that kept him away the Ingleside folk decided that some dark fate of shot or poison had descended on him—except Susan, who believed and continued to affirm that he had merely "gone to his own place." Rilla lamented him, for she had been very fond of her stately golden pussy, and had liked him quite as well in his weird Hyde moods as in his tame Jekyll ones.

"And now, Mrs. Dr. dear," said Susan, "since the fall house-cleaning is over and the garden truck is all safe in cellar, I am going to take a honeymoon to celebrate the peace."

"A honeymoon, Susan?"

"Yes, Mrs. Dr. dear, a honeymoon," repeated Susan firmly. "I shall never be able to get a husband but I am not going to be cheated out of everything and a honeymoon I intend to have. I am going to Charlottetown to visit my married brother and his family. His wife has been ailing all the fall, but nobody knows whether she is going to die not. She never did tell anyone what she was going to do until she did it. That is the main reason why she was never liked in our family. But to be on the safe side I feel that I should visit her. I have not been in town for over a day for twenty years and I have a feeling that I might as well see one of those moving pictures there is so much talk of, so as not to be wholly out of the swim. But have no fear that I shall be carried away with them, Mrs. Dr. dear. I shall be away a fortnight if you can spare me so long."

"You certainly deserve a good holiday, Susan. Better take a month—that is the proper length for a honeymoon."

"No, Mrs. Dr. dear, a fortnight is all I require. Besides, I must be home for at least three weeks before Christmas to make the proper preparations. We will have a Christmas that is a Christmas this year, Mrs. Dr. dear. Do you think there is any chance of our boys being home for it?"

"No, I think not, Susan. Both Jem and Shirley write that they don't expect to be home before spring—it may be even midsummer before Shirley comes. But Carl Meredith will be home, and Nan and Di, and we will have a grand celebration once more. We'll set chairs for all, Susan, as you did our first war Christmas—yes, for all—for my dear lad whose chair must always be vacant, as well as for the others, Susan."

"It is not likely I would forget to set his place, Mrs. Dr. dear," said Susan, wiping her eyes as she departed to pack up for her "honeymoon."

35. "RILLA-MY-RILLA!"

Carl Meredith and Miller Douglas came home just before Christmas and Glen St. Mary met them at the station with a brass band borrowed from Lowbridge and speeches of home manufacture. Miller was brisk and beaming in spite of his wooden leg; he had developed into a broad-shouldered, imposing looking fellow and the D. C. Medal he wore reconciled Miss Cornelia to the shortcomings of his pedigree to such a degree that she tacitly recognized his engagement to Mary.

The latter put on a few airs—especially when Carter Flagg took Miller into his store as head clerk—but nobody grudged them to her.

"Of course farming's out of the question for us now," she told Rilla, "but Miller thinks he'll like storekeeping fine once he gets used to a quiet life again, and Carter Flagg will be a more agreeable boss than old Kitty. We're going to be married in the fall and live in the old Mead house with the bay windows and the mansard roof. I've always thought that the handsomest house in the Glen, but never did I dream I'd ever live there. We're only renting it, of course, but if things go as we expect and Carter Flagg takes Miller into partnership we'll own it some day. Say, I've got on some in society, haven't I, considering what I come from? I never aspired to being a storekeeper's wife. But Miller's real ambitious and he'll have a wife that'll back him up. He says he never saw a French girl worth looking at twice and that his heart beat true to me every moment he was away."

Jerry Meredith and Joe Milgrave came back in January, and all winter the boys from the Glen and its environs came home by twos and threes. None of them came back just as they went away, not even those who had been so fortunate as to escape injury.

One spring day, when the daffodils were blowing on the Ingleside lawn, and the banks of the brook in Rainbow Valley were sweet with white and purple violets, the little, lazy afternoon accommodation train pulled into the Glen station. It was very seldom that passengers for the Glen came by that train, so nobody was there to meet it except the new station agent and a small black-and-yellow dog, who for four and a half years had met every train that had steamed into Glen St. Mary. Thousands of trains had Dog Monday met and never had the boy he waited and watched for returned. Yet still Dog Monday watched on with eyes that never quite lost hope. Perhaps his dog-heart failed him at times; he was growing old and rheumatic; when he walked back to his kennel after each train had gone his gait was very sober now—he never trotted but went slowly with a drooping head and a depressed tail that had quite lost its old saucy uplift.

One passenger stepped off the train—a tall fellow in a faded lieutenant's uniform, who walked with a barely perceptible limp. He had a bronzed face and there were some grey hairs in the ruddy curls that clustered around his forehead. The new station agent looked at him anxiously. He was used to seeing the khaki-clad figures come off the train, some met by a tumultuous crowd, others, who had sent no word of their coming, stepping off quietly like this one. But there was a certain distinction of bearing and features in this soldier that caught his attention and made him wonder a little more interestedly who he was.

A black-and-yellow streak shot past the station agent. Dog Monday stiff? Dog Monday rheumatic? Dog Monday old? Never believe it. Dog Monday was a young pup, gone clean mad with rejuvenating joy.

He flung himself against the tall soldier, with a bark that choked in his throat from sheer rapture. He flung himself on the ground and writhed in a frenzy of welcome. He tried to climb the soldier's khaki legs and slipped down and groveled in an ecstasy that seemed as if it must tear his little body in pieces. He licked his boots and when the lieutenant had, with laughter on his lips and tears in his eyes, succeeded in gathering the little creature up in his arms Dog Monday laid his head on the khaki shoulder and licked the sunburned neck, making queer sounds between barks and sobs.

The station agent had heard the story of Dog Monday. He knew now who the returned soldier was. Dog Monday's long vigil was ended. Jem Blythe had come home.

"We are all very happy—and sad—and thankful," wrote Rilla in her diary a week later, "though Susan has not yet recovered—never will recover, I believe—from the shock of having Jem come home the very night she had, owing to a strenuous day, prepared a 'pick up' supper. I shall never forget the sight of her, tearing madly about from pantry to cellar, hunting out stored away goodies. Just as if anybody cared what was on the table—none of us could eat, anyway. It was meat and drink just to look at Jem. Mother seemed afraid to take her eyes off him lest he vanish out of her sight. It is wonderful to have Jem back—and little Dog Monday. Monday refuses to be separated from Jem for a moment. He sleeps on the foot of his bed and squats beside him at meal-times. And on Sunday he went to church with him and insisted on going right into our pew, where he went to sleep on Jem's feet. In the middle of the sermon he woke up and seemed to think he must welcome Jem all over again, for he bounded up with a series of barks and wouldn't quiet down until Jem took him up in his arms. But nobody seemed to mind, and Mr. Meredith came and patted his head after the service and said, "'Faith and affection and loyalty are precious things wherever they are found. That little dog's love is a treasure, Jem.'

"One night when Jem and I were talking things over in Rainbow Valley, I asked him if he had ever felt afraid at the front.

"Jem laughed.

"'Afraid! I was afraid scores of times—sick with fear—I who used to laugh at Walter when he was frightened. Do you know, Walter was never frightened after he got to the front. Realities never scared him—only his imagination could do that. His colonel told me that Walter was the bravest man in the regiment. Rilla, I never realized that Walter was dead till I came back home. You don't know how I miss him now—you folks here have got used to it in a sense—but it's all fresh to me. Walter and I grew up together—we were chums as well as brothers—and now here, in this old valley we loved when we were children, it has come home to me that I'm not to see him again.'

"Jem is going back to college in the fall and so are Jerry and Carl. I suppose Shirley will, too. He expects to be home in July. Nan and Di will go on teaching. Faith doesn't expect to be home before September. I suppose she will teach then too, for she and Jem can't be married until he gets through his course in medicine. Una Meredith has decided, I think, to take a course in Household Science at Kingsport—and Gertrude is to be married to her Major and is frankly happy about it—'shamelessly happy' she says; but I think her attitude is very beautiful. They are all talking of their plans and hopes—more soberly than they used to do long ago, but still with interest, and a determination to carry on and make good in spite of lost years.

"'We're in a new world,' Jem says, 'and we've got to make it a better one than the old. That isn't done yet, though some folks seem to think it ought to be. The job isn't finished—it isn't really begun. The old world is destroyed and we must build up the new one. It will be the task of years. I've seen enough of war to realize that we've got to make a world where wars can't happen. We've given Prussianism its mortal wound but it isn't dead yet and it isn't confined to Germany either. It isn't enough to drive out the old spirit—we've got to bring in the new.'

"I'm writing down those words of Jem's in my diary so that I can read them over occasionally and get courage from them, when moods come when I find it not so easy to 'keep faith.'"

Rilla closed her journal with a little sigh. Just then she was not finding it easy to keep faith. All the rest seemed to have some special aim or ambition about which to build up their lives—she had none. And she was very lonely, horribly lonely. Jem had come back—but he was not the laughing boy-brother who had gone away in 1914 and he belonged to Faith. Walter would never come back. She had not even Jims left. All at once her world seemed wide and empty—that is, it had seemed wide and empty from the moment yesterday when she had read in a Montreal paper a fortnight-old list of returned soldiers in which was the name of Captain Kenneth Ford.

So Ken was home—and he had not even written her that he was coming. He had been in Canada two weeks and she had not had a line from him. Of course he had forgotten—if there was ever anything to forget—a handclasp—a kiss—a look—a promise asked under the influence of a passing emotion. It was all absurd—she had been a silly, romantic, inexperienced goose. Well, she would be wiser in the future—very wise—and very discreet—and very contemptuous of men and their ways.

"I suppose I'd better go with Una and take up Household Science too," she thought, as she stood by her window and looked down through a delicate emerald tangle of young vines on Rainbow Valley, lying in a wonderful lilac light of sunset. There did not seem anything very attractive just then about Household Science, but, with a whole new world waiting to be built, a girl must do something.

The door bell rang, Rilla turned reluctantly stairwards. She must answer it—there was no one else in the house; but she hated the idea of callers just then. She went downstairs slowly, and opened the front door.

A man in khaki was standing on the steps—a tall fellow, with dark eyes and hair, and a narrow white scar running across his brown cheek. Rilla stared at him foolishly for a moment. Who was it?

She ought to know him—there was certainly something very familiar about him—"Rilla-my-Rilla," he said.

"Ken," gasped Rilla. Of course, it was Ken—but he looked so much older—he was so much changed—that scar—the lines about his eyes and lips—her thoughts went whirling helplessly.

Ken took the uncertain hand she held out, and looked at her. The slim Rilla of four years ago had rounded out into symmetry. He had left a school girl, and he found a woman—a woman with wonderful eyes and a dented lip, and rose-bloom cheek—a woman altogether beautiful and desirable—the woman of his dreams.

"Is it Rilla-my-Rilla?" he asked, meaningly.

Emotion shook Rilla from head to foot. Joy—happiness—sorrow—fear—every passion that had wrung her heart in those four long years seemed to surge up in her soul for a moment as the deeps of being were stirred. She had tried to speak; at first voice would not come. Then —"Yeth," said Rilla.

FURTHER CHRONICLES OF AVONLEA

FURTHER CHRONICLES OF AVONLEA

AUNT CYNTHIA'S PERSIAN CAT

MAX ALWAYS BLESSES the animal when it is referred to; and I don't deny that things have worked together for good after all. But when I think of the anguish of mind which Ismay and I underwent on account of that abominable cat, it is not a blessing that arises uppermost in my thoughts.

I never was fond of cats, although I admit they are well enough in their place, and I can worry along comfortably with a nice, matronly old tabby who can take care of herself and be of some use in the world. As for Ismay, she hates cats and always did.

But Aunt Cynthia, who adored them, never could bring herself to understand that any one could possibly dislike them. She firmly believed that Ismay and I really liked cats deep down in our hearts, but that, owing to some perverse twist in our moral natures, we would not own up to it, but willfully persisted in declaring we didn't.

Of all cats I loathed that white Persian cat of Aunt Cynthia's. And, indeed, as we always suspected and finally proved, Aunt herself looked upon the creature with more pride than affection. She would have taken ten times the comfort in a good, common puss that she did in that spoiled beauty. But a Persian cat with a recorded pedigree and a market value of one hundred dollars tickled Aunt Cynthia's pride of possession to such an extent that she deluded herself into believing that the animal was really the apple of her eye.

It had been presented to her when a kitten by a missionary nephew who had brought it all the way home from Persia; and for the next three years Aunt Cynthia's household existed to wait on that cat, hand and foot. It was snow-white, with a bluish-gray spot on the tip of its tail; and it was blue-eyed and deaf and delicate. Aunt Cynthia was always worrying lest it should take cold and die. Ismay and I used to wish that it would—we were so tired of hearing about it and its whims. But we did not say so to Aunt Cynthia. She would probably never have spoken to us again and there was no wisdom in offending Aunt Cynthia. When you have an unencumbered aunt, with a fat bank account, it is just as well to keep on good terms with her, if you can. Besides, we really liked Aunt Cynthia very much—at times. Aunt Cynthia was one of those rather exasperating people who nag at and find fault with you until you think you are justified in hating them, and who then turn round and do something so really nice and kind for you that you feel as if you were compelled to love them dutifully instead.

So we listened meekly when she discoursed on Fatima—the cat's name was Fatima—and, if it was wicked of us to wish for the latter's decease, we were well punished for it later on.

One day, in November, Aunt Cynthia came sailing out to Spencervale. She really came in a phaeton, drawn by a fat gray pony, but somehow Aunt Cynthia always gave you the impression of a full rigged ship coming gallantly on before a favorable wind.

That was a Jonah day for us all through. Everything had gone wrong. Ismay had spilled grease on her velvet coat, and the fit of the new blouse I was making was hopelessly askew, and the kitchen stove smoked and the bread was sour. Moreover, Huldah Jane Keyson, our tried and trusty old family nurse and cook and general "boss," had what she called the "realagy" in her shoulder; and, though Huldah Jane is as good an old creature as ever lived, when she has the "realagy" other people who are in the house want to get out of it and, if they can't, feel about as comfortable as St. Lawrence on his gridiron.

And on top of this came Aunt Cynthia's call and request.

"Dear me," said Aunt Cynthia, sniffing, "don't I smell smoke? You girls must manage your range very badly. Mine never smokes. But it is no more than one might expect when two girls try to keep house without a man about the place."

"We get along very well without a man about the place," I said loftily. Max hadn't been in for four whole days and, though nobody wanted to see him particularly, I couldn't help wondering why. "Men are nuisances."

"I dare say you would like to pretend you think so," said Aunt Cynthia, aggravatingly. "But no woman ever does really think so, you know. I imagine that pretty Anne Shirley, who is visiting Ella Kimball, doesn't. I saw her and Dr. Irving out walking this afternoon, looking very well satisfied with themselves. If you dilly-dally much longer, Sue, you will let Max slip through your fingers yet."

That was a tactful thing to say to ME, who had refused Max Irving so often that I had lost count. I was furious, and so I smiled most sweetly on my maddening aunt.

"Dear Aunt, how amusing of you," I said, smoothly. "You talk as if I wanted Max."

"So you do," said Aunt Cynthia.

"If so, why should I have refused him time and again?" I asked, smilingly. Right well Aunt Cynthia knew I had. Max always told her.

"Goodness alone knows why," said Aunt Cynthia, "but you may do it once too often and find yourself taken at your word. There is something very fascinating about this Anne Shirley."

"Indeed there is," I assented. "She has the loveliest eyes I ever saw. She would be just the wife for Max, and I hope he will marry her."

"Humph," said Aunt Cynthia. "Well, I won't entice you into telling any more fibs. And I didn't drive out here to-day in all this wind to talk sense into you concerning Max. I'm going to Halifax for two months and I want you to take charge of Fatima for me, while I am away."

"Fatima!" I exclaimed.

"Yes. I don't dare to trust her with the servants. Mind you always warm her milk before you give it to her, and don't on any account let her run out of doors."

I looked at Ismay and Ismay looked at me. We knew we were in for it. To refuse would mortally offend Aunt Cynthia. Besides, if I betrayed any unwillingness, Aunt Cynthia would be sure to put it down to grumpiness over what she had said about Max, and rub it in for years. But I ventured to ask, "What if anything happens to her while you are away?"

"It is to prevent that, I'm leaving her with you," said Aunt Cynthia. "You simply must not let anything happen to her. It will do you good to have a little responsibility. And you will have a chance to find out what an adorable creature Fatima really is. Well, that is all settled. I'll send Fatima out to-morrow."

"You can take care of that horrid Fatima beast yourself," said Ismay, when the door closed behind Aunt Cynthia. "I won't touch her with a yard-stick. You had no business to say we'd take her."

"Did I say we would take her?" I demanded, crossly. "Aunt Cynthia took our consent for granted. And you know, as well as I do, we couldn't have refused. So what is the use of being grouchy?"

"If anything happens to her Aunt Cynthia will hold us responsible," said Ismay darkly.

"Do you think Anne Shirley is really engaged to Gilbert Blythe?" I asked curiously.

"I've heard that she was," said Ismay, absently. "Does she eat anything but milk? Will it do to give her mice?"

"Oh, I guess so. But do you think Max has really fallen in love with her?"

"I dare say. What a relief it will be for you if he has."

"Oh, of course," I said, frostily. "Anne Shirley or Anne Anybody Else, is perfectly welcome to Max if she wants him. *I* certainly do not. Ismay Meade, if that stove doesn't stop smoking I shall fly into bits. This is a detestable day. I hate that creature!"

"Oh, you shouldn't talk like that, when you don't even know her," protested Ismay. "Every one says Anne Shirley is lovely—"

"I was talking about Fatima," I cried in a rage.

"Oh!" said Ismay.

Ismay is stupid at times. I thought the way she said "Oh" was inexcusably stupid.

Fatima arrived the next day. Max brought her out in a covered basket, lined with padded crimson satin. Max likes cats and Aunt Cynthia. He explained how we were to treat Fatima and when Ismay had gone out of the room—Ismay always went out of the room when she knew I particularly wanted her to remain—he proposed to me again. Of course I said no, as usual, but I was rather pleased. Max had been proposing to me about every two months for two years. Sometimes, as in this case, he went three months, and then I always wondered why. I concluded that he could not be really interested in Anne Shirley, and I was relieved. I didn't want to marry Max but it was pleasant and convenient to have him around, and we would miss him dreadfully if any other girl snapped him up. He was so useful and always willing to do anything for us—nail a shingle on the roof, drive us to town, put down carpets—in short, a very present help in all our troubles.

So I just beamed on him when I said no. Max began counting on his fingers. When he got as far as eight he shook his head and began over again.

"What is it?" I asked.

"I'm trying to count up how many times I have proposed to you," he said. "But I can't remember whether I asked you to marry me that day we dug up the garden or not. If I did it makes—"

"No, you didn't," I interrupted.

"Well, that makes it eleven," said Max reflectively. "Pretty near the limit, isn't it? My manly pride will not allow me to propose to the same girl more than twelve times. So the next time will be the last, Sue darling."

"Oh," I said, a trifle flatly. I forgot to resent his calling me darling. I wondered if things wouldn't be rather dull when Max gave up proposing to me. It was the only excitement I had. But of course it would be best—and he couldn't go on at it forever, so, by the way of gracefully dismissing the subject, I asked him what Miss Shirley was like.

"Very sweet girl," said Max. "You know I always admired those gray-eyed girls with that splendid Titian hair."

I am dark, with brown eyes. Just then I detested Max. I got up and said I was going to get some milk for Fatima.

I found Ismay in a rage in the kitchen. She had been up in the garret, and a mouse had run across her foot. Mice always get on Ismay's nerves.

"We need a cat badly enough," she fumed, "but not a useless, pampered thing, like Fatima. That garret is literally swarming with mice. You'll not catch me going up there again."

Fatima did not prove such a nuisance as we had feared. Huldah Jane liked her, and Ismay, in spite of her declaration that she would have nothing to do with her, looked after her comfort scrupulously. She even used to get up in the middle of the night and go out to see if Fatima was warm. Max came in every day and, being around, gave us good advice.

Then one day, about three weeks after Aunt Cynthia's departure, Fatima disappeared—just simply disappeared as if she had been dissolved into thin air. We left her one afternoon, curled up asleep in her basket by the fire, under Huldah Jane's eye, while we went out to make a call. When we came home Fatima was gone.

Huldah Jane wept and was as one whom the gods had made mad. She vowed that she had never let Fatima out of her sight the whole time, save once for three minutes when she ran up to the garret for some summer savory. When she came back the kitchen door had blown open and Fatima had vanished.

Ismay and I were frantic. We ran about the garden and through the out-houses, and the woods behind the house, like wild creatures, calling Fatima, but in vain. Then Ismay sat down on the front doorsteps and cried.

"She has got out and she'll catch her death of cold and Aunt Cynthia will never forgive us."

"I'm going for Max," I declared. So I did, through the spruce woods and over the field as fast as my feet could carry me, thanking my stars that there was a Max to go to in such a predicament.

Max came over and we had another search, but without result. Days passed, but we did not find Fatima. I would certainly have gone crazy had it not been for Max. He was worth his weight in gold during the awful week that followed. We did not dare advertise, lest Aunt Cynthia should see it; but we inquired far and wide for a white Persian cat with a blue spot on its tail, and offered a reward for it; but nobody had seen it, although people kept coming to the house, night and day, with every kind of a cat in baskets, wanting to know if it was the one we had lost.

"We shall never see Fatima again," I said hopelessly to Max and Ismay one afternoon. I had just turned away an old woman with a big, yellow tommy which she insisted must be ours—"cause it kem to our place, mem, a-yowling fearful, mem, and it don't belong to nobody not down Grafton way, mem."

"I'm afraid you won't," said Max. "She must have perished from exposure long ere this."

"Aunt Cynthia will never forgive us," said Ismay, dismally. "I had a presentiment of trouble the moment that cat came to this house."

We had never heard of this presentiment before, but Ismay is good at having presentiments—after things happen.

"What shall we do?" I demanded, helplessly. "Max, can't you find some way out of this scrape for us?"

"Advertise in the Charlottetown papers for a white Persian cat," suggested Max. "Some one may have one for sale. If so, you must buy it, and palm it off on your good Aunt as Fatima. She's very short-sighted, so it will be quite possible."

"But Fatima has a blue spot on her tail," I said.

"You must advertise for a cat with a blue spot on its tail," said Max.

"It will cost a pretty penny," said Ismay dolefully. "Fatima was valued at one hundred dollars."

"We must take the money we have been saving for our new furs," I said sorrowfully. "There is no other way out of it. It will cost us a good deal more if we lose Aunt Cynthia's favor. She is quite capable of believing that we have made away with Fatima deliberately and with malice aforethought."

So we advertised. Max went to town and had the notice inserted in the most important daily. We asked any one who had a white Persian cat, with a blue spot on the tip of its tail, to dispose of, to communicate with M. I., care of the *Enterprise*.

We really did not have much hope that anything would come of it, so we were surprised and delighted over the letter Max brought home from town four days later. It was a type-written screed from Halifax stating that the writer had for sale a white Persian cat answering to our description. The price was a hundred and ten dollars, and, if M. I. cared to go to Halifax and inspect the animal, it would be found at 110 Hollis Street, by inquiring for "Persian."

"Temper your joy, my friends," said Ismay, gloomily. "The cat may not suit. The blue spot may be too big or too small or not in the right place. I consistently refuse to believe that any good thing can come out of this deplorable affair."

Just at this moment there was a knock at the door and I hurried out. The postmaster's boy was there with a telegram. I tore it open, glanced at it, and dashed back into the room.

"What is it now?" cried Ismay, beholding my face.

I held out the telegram. It was from Aunt Cynthia. She had wired us to send Fatima to Halifax by express immediately.

For the first time Max did not seem ready to rush into the breach with a suggestion. It was I who spoke first.

"Max," I said, imploringly, "you'll see us through this, won't you? Neither Ismay nor I can rush off to Halifax at once. You must go to-morrow morning. Go right to 110 Hollis Street and ask for 'Persian.' If the cat looks enough like Fatima, buy it and take it to Aunt Cynthia. If it doesn't—but it must! You'll go, won't you?"

"That depends," said Max.

I stared at him. This was so unlike Max.

"You are sending me on a nasty errand," he said, coolly. "How do I know that Aunt Cynthia will be deceived after all, even if she be short-sighted. Buying a cat in a joke is a huge risk. And if she should see through the scheme I shall be in a pretty mess."

"Oh, Max," I said, on the verge of tears.

"Of course," said Max, looking meditatively into the fire, "if I were really one of the family, or had any reasonable prospect of being so, I would not mind so much. It would be all in the day's work then. But as it is—"

Ismay got up and went out of the room.

"Oh, Max, please," I said.

"Will you marry me, Sue?" demanded Max sternly. "If you will agree, I'll go to Halifax and beard the lion in his den unflinchingly. If necessary, I will take a black street cat to Aunt Cynthia, and swear that it is Fatima. I'll get you out of the scrape, if I have to prove that you never had Fatima, that she is safe in your possession at the present time, and that there never was such an animal as Fatima anyhow. I'll do anything, say anything—but it must be for my future wife."

"Will nothing else content you?" I said helplessly.

"Nothing."

I thought hard. Of course Max was acting abominably—but—but—he was really a dear fellow—and this was the twelfth time—and there was Anne Shirley! I knew in my secret soul that life would be a dreadfully dismal thing if Max were not around somewhere. Besides, I would have married him long ago had not Aunt Cynthia thrown us so pointedly at each other's heads ever since he came to Spencervale.

"Very well," I said crossly.

Max left for Halifax in the morning. Next day we got a wire saying it was all right. The evening of the following day he was back in Spencervale. Ismay and I put him in a chair and glared at him impatiently.

Max began to laugh and laughed until he turned blue.

"I am glad it is so amusing," said Ismay severely. "If Sue and I could see the joke it might be more so."

"Dear little girls, have patience with me," implored Max. "If you knew what it cost me to keep a straight face in Halifax you would forgive me for breaking out now."

"We forgive you—but for pity's sake tell us all about it," I cried.

"Well, as soon as I arrived in Halifax I hurried to 110 Hollis Street, but—see here! Didn't you tell me your Aunt's address was 10 Pleasant Street?"

"So it is."

"'T isn't. You look at the address on a telegram next time you get one. She went a week ago to visit another friend who lives at 110 Hollis."

"Max!"

"It's a fact. I rang the bell, and was just going to ask the maid for 'Persian' when your Aunt Cynthia herself came through the hall and pounced on me."

"'Max,' she said, 'have you brought Fatima?'

"'No,' I answered, trying to adjust my wits to this new development as she towed me into the library. 'No, I—I—just came to Halifax on a little matter of business.'

"'Dear me,' said Aunt Cynthia, crossly, 'I don't know what those girls mean. I wired them to send Fatima at once. And she has not come yet and I am expecting a call every minute from some one who wants to buy her.'

"'Oh!' I murmured, mining deeper every minute.

"'Yes,' went on your aunt, 'there is an advertisement in the Charlottetown *Enterprise* for a Persian cat, and I answered it. Fatima is really quite a charge, you know—and so apt to die and be a dead loss,'—did your aunt mean a pun, girls?—'and so, although I am considerably attached to her, I have decided to part with her.'

"By this time I had got my second wind, and I promptly decided that a judicious mixture of the truth was the thing required.

"'Well, of all the curious coincidences,' I exclaimed. 'Why, Miss Ridley, it was I who advertised for a Persian cat—on Sue's behalf. She and Ismay have decided that they want a cat like Fatima for themselves.'

"You should have seen how she beamed. She said she knew you always really liked cats, only you would never own up to it. We clinched the dicker then and there. I passed her over your hundred and ten dollars—she took the money without turning a hair—and now you are the joint owners of Fatima. Good luck to your bargain!"

"Mean old thing," sniffed Ismay. She meant Aunt Cynthia, and, remembering our shabby furs, I didn't disagree with her.

"But there is no Fatima," I said, dubiously. "How shall we account for her when Aunt Cynthia comes home?"

"Well, your aunt isn't coming home for a month yet. When she comes you will have to tell her that the cat—is lost—but you needn't say WHEN it happened. As for the rest, Fatima is your property now, so Aunt Cynthia can't grumble. But she will have a poorer opinion than ever of your fitness to run a house alone."

When Max left I went to the window to watch him down the path. He was really a handsome fellow, and I was proud of him. At the gate he turned to wave me good-by, and, as he did, he glanced upward. Even at that distance I saw the look of amazement on his face. Then he came bolting back.

"Ismay, the house is on fire!" I shrieked, as I flew to the door.

"Sue," cried Max, "I saw Fatima, or her ghost, at the garret window a moment ago!"

"Nonsense!" I cried. But Ismay was already half way up the stairs and we followed. Straight to the garret we rushed. There sat Fatima, sleek and complacent, sunning herself in the window.

Max laughed until the rafters rang.

"She can't have been up here all this time," I protested, half tearfully. "We would have heard her meowing."

"But you didn't," said Max.

"She would have died of the cold," declared Ismay.

"But she hasn't," said Max.

"Or starved," I cried.

"The place is alive with mice," said Max. "No, girls, there is no doubt the cat has been here the whole fortnight. She must have followed Huldah Jane up here, unobserved, that day. It's a wonder you didn't hear her crying—if she did cry. But perhaps she didn't, and, of course, you sleep downstairs. To think you never thought of looking here for her!"

"It has cost us over a hundred dollars," said Ismay, with a malevolent glance at the sleek Fatima.

"It has cost me more than that," I said, as I turned to the stairway.

Max held me back for an instant, while Ismay and Fatima pattered down.

"Do you think it has cost too much, Sue?" he whispered.

I looked at him sideways. He was really a dear. Niceness fairly exhaled from him.

"No-o-o," I said, "but when we are married you will have to take care of Fatima, *I* won't."

"Dear Fatima," said Max gratefully.

THE MATERIALIZING OF CECIL

It had never worried me in the least that I wasn't married, although everybody in Avonlea pitied old maids; but it DID worry me, and I frankly confess it, that I had never had a chance to be. Even Nancy, my old nurse and servant, knew that, and pitied me for it. Nancy is an old maid herself, but she has had two proposals. She did not accept either of them because one was a widower with seven children, and the other a very shiftless, good-for-nothing fellow; but, if anybody twitted Nancy on her single condition, she could point triumphantly to those two as evidence that "she could an she would." If I had not lived all my life in Avonlea I might have had the benefit of the doubt; but I had, and everybody knew everything about me—or thought they did.

I had really often wondered why nobody had ever fallen in love with me. I was not at all homely; indeed, years ago, George Adoniram Maybrick had written a poem addressed to me, in which he praised my beauty quite extravagantly; that didn't mean anything because George Adoniram wrote poetry to all the good-looking girls and never went with anybody but Flora

King, who was cross-eyed and red-haired, but it proves that it was not my appearance that put me out of the running. Neither was it the fact that I wrote poetry myself—although not of George Adoniram's kind—because nobody ever knew that. When I felt it coming on I shut myself up in my room and wrote it out in a little blank book I kept locked up. It is nearly full now, because I have been writing poetry all my life. It is the only thing I have ever been able to keep a secret from Nancy. Nancy, in any case, has not a very high opinion of my ability to take care of myself; but I tremble to imagine what she would think if she ever found out about that little book. I am convinced she would send for the doctor post-haste and insist on mustard plasters while waiting for him.

Nevertheless, I kept on at it, and what with my flowers and my cats and my magazines and my little book, I was really very happy and contented. But it DID sting that Adella Gilbert, across the road, who has a drunken husband, should pity "poor Charlotte" because nobody had ever wanted her. Poor Charlotte indeed! If I had thrown myself at a man's head the way Adella Gilbert did at—but there, there, I must refrain from such thoughts. I must not be uncharitable.

The Sewing Circle met at Mary Gillespie's on my fortieth birthday. I have given up talking about my birthdays, although that little scheme is not much good in Avonlea where everybody knows your age—or if they make a mistake it is never on the side of youth. But Nancy, who grew accustomed to celebrating my birthdays when I was a little girl, never gets over the habit, and I don't try to cure her, because, after all, it's nice to have some one make a fuss over you. She brought me up my breakfast before I got up out of bed—a concession to my laziness that Nancy would scorn to make on any other day of the year. She had cooked everything I like best, and had decorated the tray with roses from the garden and ferns from the woods behind the house. I enjoyed every bit of that breakfast, and then I got up and dressed, putting on my second best muslin gown. I would have put on my really best if I had not had the fear of Nancy before my eyes; but I knew she would never condone THAT, even on a birthday. I watered my flowers and fed my cats, and then I locked myself up and wrote a poem on June. I had given up writing birthday odes after I was thirty.

In the afternoon I went to the Sewing Circle. When I was ready for it I looked in my glass and wondered if I could really be forty. I was quite sure I didn't look it. My hair was brown and wavy, my cheeks were pink, and the lines could hardly be seen at all, though possibly that was because of the dim light. I always have my mirror hung in the darkest corner of my room. Nancy cannot imagine why. I know the lines are there, of course; but when they don't show very plain I forget that they are there.

We had a large Sewing Circle, young and old alike attending. I really cannot say I ever enjoyed the meetings—at least not up to that time—although I went religiously because I thought it my duty to go. The married women talked so much of their husbands and children, and of course I had to be quiet on those topics; and the young girls talked in corner groups about their beaux, and stopped it when I joined them, as if they felt sure that an old maid who had never had a beau couldn't understand at all. As for the other old maids, they talked gossip about every one, and I did not like that either. I knew the minute my back was turned they would fasten into me and hint that I used hair-dye and declare it was perfectly ridiculous for a woman of FIFTY to wear a pink muslin dress with lace-trimmed frills.

There was a full attendance that day, for we were getting ready for a sale of fancy work in aid of parsonage repairs. The young girls were merrier and noisier than usual. Wilhelmina Mercer was there, and she kept them going. The Mercers were quite new to Avonlea, having come here only two months previously.

I was sitting by the window and Wilhelmina Mercer, Maggie Henderson, Susette Cross and

Georgie Hall were in a little group just before me. I wasn't listening to their chatter at all, but presently Georgie exclaimed teasingly:

"Miss Charlotte is laughing at us. I suppose she thinks we are awfully silly to be talking about beaux."

The truth was that I was simply smiling over some very pretty thoughts that had come to me about the roses which were climbing over Mary Gillespie's sill. I meant to inscribe them in the little blank book when I went home. Georgie's speech brought me back to harsh realities with a jolt. It hurt me, as such speeches always did.

"Didn't you ever have a beau, Miss Holmes?" said Wilhelmina laughingly.

Just as it happened, a silence had fallen over the room for a moment, and everybody in it heard Wilhelmina's question.

I really do not know what got into me and possessed me. I have never been able to account for what I said and did, because I am naturally a truthful person and hate all deceit. It seemed to me that I simply could not say "No" to Wilhelmina before that whole roomful of women. It was TOO humiliating. I suppose all the prickles and stings and slurs I had endured for fifteen years on account of never having had a lover had what the new doctor calls "a cumulative effect" and came to a head then and there.

"Yes, I had one once, my dear," I said calmly.

For once in my life I made a sensation. Every woman in that room stopped sewing and stared at me. Most of them, I saw, didn't believe me, but Wilhelmina did. Her pretty face lighted up with interest.

"Oh, won't you tell us about him, Miss Holmes?" she coaxed, "and why didn't you marry him?"

"That is right, Miss Mercer," said Josephine Cameron, with a nasty little laugh. "Make her tell. We're all interested. It's news to us that Charlotte ever had a beau."

If Josephine had not said that, I might not have gone on. But she did say it, and, moreover, I caught Mary Gillespie and Adella Gilbert exchanging significant smiles. That settled it, and made me quite reckless. "In for a penny, in for a pound," thought I, and I said with a pensive smile:

"Nobody here knew anything about him, and it was all long, long ago."

"What was his name?" asked Wilhelmina.

"Cecil Fenwick," I answered promptly. Cecil had always been my favorite name for a man; it figured quite frequently in the blank book. As for the Fenwick part of it, I had a bit of newspaper in my hand, measuring a hem, with "Try Fenwick's Porous Plasters" printed across it, and I simply joined the two in sudden and irrevocable matrimony.

"Where did you meet him?" asked Georgie.

I hastily reviewed my past. There was only one place to locate Cecil Fenwick. The only time I had ever been far enough away from Avonlea in my life was when I was eighteen and had gone to visit an aunt in New Brunswick.

"In Blakely, New Brunswick," I said, almost believing that I had when I saw how they all took it in unsuspectingly. "I was just eighteen and he was twenty-three."

"What did he look like?" Susette wanted to know.

"Oh, he was very handsome." I proceeded glibly to sketch my ideal. To tell the dreadful truth, I was enjoying myself; I could see respect dawning in those girls' eyes, and I knew that I had forever thrown off my reproach. Henceforth I should be a woman with a romantic past, faithful to the one love of her life—a very, very different thing from an old maid who had never had a lover.

"He was tall and dark, with lovely, curly black hair and brilliant, piercing eyes. He had a splendid chin, and a fine nose, and the most fascinating smile!"

"What was he?" asked Maggie.

"A young lawyer," I said, my choice of profession decided by an enlarged crayon portrait of Mary Gillespie's deceased brother on an easel before me. He had been a lawyer.

"Why didn't you marry him?" demanded Susette.

"We quarreled," I answered sadly. "A terribly bitter quarrel. Oh, we were both so young and so foolish. It was my fault. I vexed Cecil by flirting with another man"—wasn't I coming on!—"and he was jealous and angry. He went out West and never came back. I have never seen him since, and I do not even know if he is alive. But—but—I could never care for any other man."

"Oh, how interesting!" sighed Wilhelmina. "I do so love sad love stories. But perhaps he will come back some day yet, Miss Holmes."

"Oh, no, never now," I said, shaking my head. "He has forgotten all about me, I dare say. Or if he hasn't, he has never forgiven me."

Mary Gillespie's Susan Jane announced tea at this moment, and I was thankful, for my imagination was giving out, and I didn't know what question those girls would ask next. But I felt already a change in the mental atmosphere surrounding me, and all through supper I was thrilled with a secret exultation. Repentant? Ashamed? Not a bit of it! I'd have done the same thing over again, and all I felt sorry for was that I hadn't done it long ago.

When I got home that night Nancy looked at me wonderingly, and said:

"You look like a girl to-night, Miss Charlotte."

"I feel like one," I said laughing; and I ran to my room and did what I had never done before—wrote a second poem in the same day. I had to have some outlet for my feelings. I called it "In Summer Days of Long Ago," and I worked Mary Gillespie's roses and Cecil Fenwick's eyes into it, and made it so sad and reminiscent and minor-musicky that I felt perfectly happy.

For the next two months all went well and merrily. Nobody ever said anything more to me about Cecil Fenwick, but the girls all chattered freely to me of their little love affairs, and I became a sort of general confidant for them. It just warmed up the cockles of my heart, and I began to enjoy the Sewing Circle famously. I got a lot of pretty new dresses and the dearest hat, and I went everywhere I was asked and had a good time.

But there is one thing you can be perfectly sure of. If you do wrong you are going to be punished for it sometime, somehow and somewhere. My punishment was delayed for two months, and then it descended on my head and I was crushed to the very dust.

Another new family besides the Mercers had come to Avonlea in the spring—the Maxwells. There were just Mr. and Mrs. Maxwell; they were a middle-aged couple and very well off. Mr. Maxwell had bought the lumber mills, and they lived up at the old Spencer place which had always been "the" place of Avonlea. They lived quietly, and Mrs. Maxwell hardly ever went anywhere because she was delicate. She was out when I called and I was out when she returned my call, so that I had never met her.

It was the Sewing Circle day again—at Sarah Gardiner's this time. I was late; everybody else was there when I arrived, and the minute I entered the room I knew something had happened, although I couldn't imagine what. Everybody looked at me in the strangest way. Of course, Wilhelmina Mercer was the first to set her tongue going.

"Oh, Miss Holmes, have you seen him yet?" she exclaimed.

"Seen whom?" I said non-excitedly, getting out my thimble and patterns.

"Why, Cecil Fenwick. He's here—in Avonlea—visiting his sister, Mrs. Maxwell."

I suppose I did what they expected me to do. I dropped everything I held, and Josephine Cameron said afterwards that Charlotte Holmes would never be paler when she was in her coffin. If they had just known why I turned so pale!

"It's impossible!" I said blankly.

"It's really true," said Wilhelmina, delighted at this development, as she supposed it, of my romance. "I was up to see Mrs. Maxwell last night, and I met him."

"It—can't be—the same—Cecil Fenwick," I said faintly, because I had to say something.

"Oh, yes, it is. He belongs in Blakely, New Brunswick, and he's a lawyer, and he's been out West twenty-two years. He's oh! so handsome, and just as you described him, except that his hair is quite gray. He has never married—I asked Mrs. Maxwell—so you see he has never forgotten you, Miss Holmes. And, oh, I believe everything is going to come out all right."

I couldn't exactly share her cheerful belief. Everything seemed to me to be coming out most horribly wrong. I was so mixed up I didn't know what to do or say. I felt as if I were in a bad dream—it MUST be a dream—there couldn't really be a Cecil Fenwick! My feelings were simply indescribable. Fortunately every one put my agitation down to quite a different cause, and they very kindly left me alone to recover myself. I shall never forget that awful afternoon. Right after tea I excused myself and went home as fast as I could go. There I shut myself up in my room, but NOT to write poetry in my blank book. No, indeed! I felt in no poetical mood.

I tried to look the facts squarely in the face. There was a Cecil Fenwick, extraordinary as the coincidence was, and he was here in Avonlea. All my friends—and foes—believed that he was the estranged lover of my youth. If he stayed long in Avonlea, one of two things was bound to happen. He would hear the story I had told about him and deny it, and I would be held up to shame and derision for the rest of my natural life; or else he would simply go away in ignorance, and everybody would suppose he had forgotten me and would pity me maddeningly. The latter possibility was bad enough, but it wasn't to be compared to the former; and oh, how I prayed—yes, I DID pray about it—that he would go right away. But Providence had other views for me.

Cecil Fenwick didn't go away. He stayed right on in Avonlea, and the Maxwells blossomed out socially in his honor and tried to give him a good time. Mrs. Maxwell gave a party for him. I got a card—but you may be very sure I didn't go, although Nancy thought I was crazy not to. Then every one else gave parties in honor of Mr. Fenwick and I was invited and never went. Wilhelmina Mercer came and pleaded and scolded and told me if I avoided Mr. Fenwick like that he would think I still cherished bitterness against him, and he wouldn't make any advances towards a reconciliation. Wilhelmina means well, but she hasn't a great deal of sense.

Cecil Fenwick seemed to be a great favorite with everybody, young and old. He was very rich, too, and Wilhelmina declared that half the girls were after him.

"If it wasn't for you, Miss Holmes, I believe I'd have a try for him myself, in spite of his gray hair and quick temper—for Mrs. Maxwell says he has a pretty quick temper, but it's all over in a minute," said Wilhelmina, half in jest and wholly in earnest.

As for me, I gave up going out at all, even to church. I fretted and pined and lost my appetite and never wrote a line in my blank book. Nancy was half frantic and insisted on dosing me with her favorite patent pills. I took them meekly, because it is a waste of time and energy to oppose Nancy, but, of course, they didn't do me any good. My trouble was too deep-seated for pills to cure. If ever a woman was punished for telling a lie I was that woman. I stopped my subscription to the *Weekly Advocate* because it still carried that wretched porous plaster advertisement, and I couldn't bear to see it. If it hadn't been for that I would never have thought of Fenwick for a name, and all this trouble would have been averted.

One evening, when I was moping in my room, Nancy came up.

"There's a gentleman in the parlor asking for you, Miss Charlotte."

My heart gave just one horrible bounce.

"What—sort of a gentleman, Nancy?" I faltered.

"I think it's that Fenwick man that there's been such a time about," said Nancy, who didn't know anything about my imaginary escapades, "and he looks to be mad clean through about something, for such a scowl I never seen."

"Tell him I'll be down directly, Nancy," I said quite calmly.

As soon as Nancy had clumped downstairs again I put on my lace fichu and put two hankies in my belt, for I thought I'd probably need more than one. Then I hunted up an old *Advocate* for proof, and down I went to the parlor. I know exactly how a criminal feels going to execution, and I've been opposed to capital punishment ever since.

I opened the parlor door and went in, carefully closing it behind me, for Nancy has a deplorable habit of listening in the hall. Then my legs gave out completely, and I couldn't have walked another step to save my life. I just stood there, my hand on the knob, trembling like a leaf.

A man was standing by the south window looking out; he wheeled around as I went in, and, as Nancy said, he had a scowl on and looked angry clear through. He was very handsome, and his gray hair gave him such a distinguished look. I recalled this afterward, but just at the moment you may be quite sure I wasn't thinking about it at all.

Then all at once a strange thing happened. The scowl went right off his face and the anger out of his eyes. He looked astonished, and then foolish. I saw the color creeping up into his cheeks. As for me, I still stood there staring at him, not able to say a single word.

"Miss Holmes, I presume," he said at last, in a deep, thrilling voice. "I—I—oh, confound it! I have called—I heard some foolish stories and I came here in a rage. I've been a fool—I know now they weren't true. Just excuse me and I'll go away and kick myself."

"No," I said, finding my voice with a gasp, "you mustn't go until you've heard the truth. It's dreadful enough, but not as dreadful as you might otherwise think. Those—those stories—I have a confession to make. I did tell them, but I didn't know there was such a person as Cecil Fenwick in existence."

He looked puzzled, as well he might. Then he smiled, took my hand and led me away from the door—to the knob of which I was still holding with all my might—to the sofa.

"Let's sit down and talk it over 'comfy,'" he said.

I just confessed the whole shameful business. It was terribly humiliating, but it served me right. I told him how people were always twitting me for never having had a beau, and how I had told them I had; and then I showed him the porous plaster advertisement.

He heard me right through without a word, and then he threw back his big, curly, gray head and laughed.

"This clears up a great many mysterious hints I've been receiving ever since I came to Avonlea," he said, "and finally a Mrs. Gilbert came to my sister this afternoon with a long farrago of nonsense about the love affair I had once had with some Charlotte Holmes here. She declared you had told her about it yourself. I confess I flamed up. I'm a peppery chap, and I thought—I thought—oh, confound it, it might as well out: I thought you were some lank old maid who was amusing herself telling ridiculous stories about me. When you came into the room I knew that, whoever was to blame, you were not."

"But I was," I said ruefully. "It wasn't right of me to tell such a story—and it was very silly, too. But who would ever have supposed that there could be a real Cecil Fenwick who had lived in Blakely? I never heard of such a coincidence."

"It's more than a coincidence," said Mr. Fenwick decidedly. "It's predestination; that is what it is. And now let's forget it and talk of something else."

We talked of something else—or at least Mr. Fenwick did, for I was too ashamed to say much—so long that Nancy got restive and clumped through the hall every five minutes; but Mr. Fenwick never took the hint. When he finally went away he asked if he might come again.

"It's time we made up that old quarrel, you know," he said, laughing.

And I, an old maid of forty, caught myself blushing like a girl. But I felt like a girl, for it was such a relief to have that explanation all over. I couldn't even feel angry with Adella Gilbert. She was always a mischief maker, and when a woman is born that way she is more to be pitied than blamed. I wrote a poem in the blank book before I went to sleep; I hadn't written anything for a month, and it was lovely to be at it once more.

Mr. Fenwick did come again—the very next evening, but one. And he came so often after that that even Nancy got resigned to him. One day I had to tell her something. I shrank from doing it, for I feared it would make her feel badly.

"Oh, I've been expecting to hear it," she said grimly. "I felt the minute that man came into the house he brought trouble with him. Well, Miss Charlotte, I wish you happiness. I don't know how the climate of California will agree with me, but I suppose I'll have to put up with it."

"But, Nancy," I said, "I can't expect you to go away out there with me. It's too much to ask of you."

"And where else would I be going?" demanded Nancy in genuine astonishment. "How under the canopy could you keep house without me? I'm not going to trust you to the mercies of a yellow Chinee with a pig-tail. Where you go I go, Miss Charlotte, and there's an end of it."

I was very glad, for I hated to think of parting with Nancy even to go with Cecil. As for the blank book, I haven't told my husband about it yet, but I mean to some day. And I've subscribed for the *Weekly Advocate* again.

HER FATHER'S DAUGHTER

"We must invite your Aunt Jane, of course," said Mrs. Spencer.

Rachel made a protesting movement with her large, white, shapely hands—hands which were so different from the thin, dark, twisted ones folded on the table opposite her. The difference was not caused by hard work or the lack of it; Rachel had worked hard all her life. It was a difference inherent in temperament. The Spencers, no matter what they did, or how hard they labored, all had plump, smooth, white hands, with firm, supple fingers; the Chiswicks, even those who toiled not, neither did they spin, had hard, knotted, twisted ones. Moreover, the contrast went deeper than externals, and twined itself with the innermost fibers of life, and thought, and action.

"I don't see why we must invite Aunt Jane," said Rachel, with as much impatience as her soft, throaty voice could express. "Aunt Jane doesn't like me, and I don't like Aunt Jane."

"I'm sure I don't see why you don't like her," said Mrs. Spencer. "It's ungrateful of you. She has always been very kind to you."

"She has always been very kind with one hand," smiled Rachel. "I remember the first time I ever saw Aunt Jane. I was six years old. She held out to me a small velvet pincushion with beads on it. And then, because I did not, in my shyness, thank her quite as promptly as I should have done, she rapped my head with her bethimbled finger to 'teach me better manners.' It hurt horribly—I've always had a tender head. And that has been Aunt Jane's way ever since. When I grew too big for the thimble treatment she used her tongue instead—and that hurt worse. And you know, mother, how she used to talk about my engagement. She is able to spoil the whole atmosphere if she happens to come in a bad humor. I don't want her."

"She must be invited. People would talk so if she wasn't."

"I don't see why they should. She's only my great-aunt by marriage. I wouldn't mind in the least if people did talk. They'll talk anyway—you know that, mother."

"Oh, we must have her," said Mrs. Spencer, with the indifferent finality that marked all her words and decisions—a finality against which it was seldom of any avail to struggle. People, who knew, rarely attempted it; strangers occasionally did, misled by the deceit of appearances.

Isabella Spencer was a wisp of a woman, with a pale, pretty face, uncertainly-colored, long-lashed grayish eyes, and great masses of dull, soft, silky brown hair. She had delicate aquiline features and a small, babyish red mouth. She looked as if a breath would sway her. The truth was that a tornado would hardly have caused her to swerve an inch from her chosen path.

For a moment Rachel looked rebellious; then she yielded, as she generally did in all differences of opinion with her mother. It was not worth while to quarrel over the comparatively unimportant matter of Aunt Jane's invitation. A quarrel might be inevitable later on; Rachel wanted to save all her resources for that. She gave her shoulders a shrug, and wrote Aunt Jane's name down on the wedding list in her large, somewhat untidy handwriting—a handwriting which always seemed to irritate her mother. Rachel never could understand this irritation. She could never guess that it was because her writing looked so much like that in a certain packet of faded letters which Mrs. Spencer kept at the bottom of an old horsehair trunk in her bedroom. They were postmarked from seaports all over the world. Mrs. Spencer never read them or looked at them; but she remembered every dash and curve of the handwriting.

Isabella Spencer had overcome many things in her life by the sheer force and persistency of her will. But she could not get the better of heredity. Rachel was her father's daughter at all points, and Isabella Spencer escaped hating her for it only by loving her the more fiercely because of it. Even so, there were many times when she had to avert her eyes from Rachel's face because of the pang of the more subtle remembrances; and never, since her child was born, could Isabella Spencer bear to gaze on that child's face in sleep.

Rachel was to be married to Frank Bell in a fortnight's time. Mrs. Spencer was pleased with the match. She was very fond of Frank, and his farm was so near to her own that she would not lose Rachel altogether. Rachel fondly believed that her mother would not lose her at all; but Isabella Spencer, wiser by olden experience, knew what her daughter's marriage must mean to her, and steeled her heart to bear it with what fortitude she might.

They were in the sitting-room, deciding on the wedding guests and other details. The September sunshine was coming in through the waving boughs of the apple tree that grew close up to the low window. The glints wavered over Rachel's face, as white as a wood lily, with only a faint dream of rose in the cheeks. She wore her sleek, golden hair in a quaint arch around it. Her forehead was very broad and white. She was fresh and young and hopeful. The mother's heart contracted in a spasm of pain as she looked at her. How like the girl was to—to—to the Spencers! Those easy, curving outlines, those large, mirthful blue eyes, that finely molded chin! Isabella Spencer shut her lips firmly and crushed down some unbidden, unwelcome memories.

"There will be about sixty guests, all told," she said, as if she were thinking of nothing else. "We must move the furniture out of this room and set the supper-table here. The dining-room is too small. We must borrow Mrs. Bell's forks and spoons. She offered to lend them. I'd never have been willing to ask her. The damask table cloths with the ribbon pattern must be bleached to-morrow. Nobody else in Avonlea has such tablecloths. And we'll put the little dining-room table on the hall landing, upstairs, for the presents."

Rachel was not thinking about the presents, or the housewifely details of the wedding. Her breath was coming quicker, and the faint blush on her smooth cheeks had deepened to crimson. She knew that a critical moment was approaching. With a steady hand she wrote the last name on her list and drew a line under it.

"Well, have you finished?" asked her mother impatiently. "Hand it here and let me look over it to make sure that you haven't left anybody out that should be in."

Rachel passed the paper across the table in silence. The room seemed to her to have grown very still. She could hear the flies buzzing on the panes, the soft purr of the wind about the low eaves and through the apple boughs, the jerky beating of her own heart. She felt frightened and nervous, but resolute.

Mrs. Spencer glanced down the list, murmuring the names aloud and nodding approval at each. But when she came to the last name, she did not utter it. She cast a black glance at Rachel, and a spark leaped up in the depths of the pale eyes. On her face were anger, amazement, incredulity, the last predominating.

The final name on the list of wedding guests was the name of David Spencer. David Spencer lived alone in a little cottage down at the Cove. He was a combination of sailor and fisherman. He was also Isabella Spencer's husband and Rachel's father.

"Rachel Spencer, have you taken leave of your senses? What do you mean by such nonsense as this?"

"I simply mean that I am going to invite my father to my wedding," answered Rachel quietly.

"Not in my house," cried Mrs. Spencer, her lips as white as if her fiery tone had scathed them.

Rachel leaned forward, folded her large, capable hands deliberately on the table, and gazed unflinchingly into her mother's bitter face. Her fright and nervousness were gone. Now that the conflict was actually on she found herself rather enjoying it. She wondered a little at herself, and thought that she must be wicked. She was not given to self-analysis, or she might have concluded that it was the sudden assertion of her own personality, so long dominated by her mother's, which she was finding so agreeable.

"Then there will be no wedding, mother," she said. "Frank and I will simply go to the manse, be married, and go home. If I cannot invite my father to see me married, no one else shall be invited."

Her lips narrowed tightly. For the first time in her life Isabella Spencer saw a reflection of herself looking back at her from her daughter's face—a strange, indefinable resemblance that was more of soul and spirit than of flesh and blood. In spite of her anger her heart thrilled to it. As never before, she realized that this girl was her own and her husband's child, a living bond between them wherein their conflicting natures mingled and were reconciled. She realized too, that Rachel, so long sweetly meek and obedient, meant to have her own way in this case—and would have it.

"I must say that I can't see why you are so set on having your father see you married," she said with a bitter sneer. "HE has never remembered that he is your father. He cares nothing about you—never did care."

Rachel took no notice of this taunt. It had no power to hurt her, its venom being neutralized by a secret knowledge of her own in which her mother had no share.

"Either I shall invite my father to my wedding, or I shall not have a wedding," she repeated steadily, adopting her mother's own effective tactics of repetition undistracted by argument.

"Invite him then," snapped Mrs. Spencer, with the ungraceful anger of a woman, long accustomed to having her own way, compelled for once to yield. "It'll be like chips in porridge anyhow—neither good nor harm. He won't come."

Rachel made no response. Now that the battle was over, and the victory won, she found herself tremulously on the verge of tears. She rose quickly and went upstairs to her own room, a dim little place shadowed by the white birches growing thickly outside—a virginal room, where everything bespoke the maiden. She lay down on the blue and white patchwork quilt on her bed, and cried softly and bitterly.

Her heart, at this crisis in her life, yearned for her father, who was almost a stranger to her. She knew that her mother had probably spoken the truth when she said that he would not come. Rachel felt that her marriage vows would be lacking in some indefinable sacredness if her father were not by to hear them spoken.

Twenty-five years before this, David Spencer and Isabella Chiswick had been married. Spiteful people said there could be no doubt that Isabella had married David for love, since he had neither lands nor money to tempt her into a match of bargain and sale. David was a handsome fellow, with the blood of a seafaring race in his veins.

He had been a sailor, like his father and grandfather before him; but, when he married Isabella, she induced him to give up the sea and settle down with her on a snug farm her father had left her. Isabella liked farming, and loved her fertile acres and opulent orchards. She abhorred the sea and all that pertained to it, less from any dread of its dangers than from an inbred conviction that sailors were "low" in the social scale—a species of necessary vagabonds. In her eyes there was a taint of disgrace in such a calling. David must be transformed into a respectable, home-abiding tiller of broad lands.

For five years all went well enough. If, at times, David's longing for the sea troubled him, he stifled it, and listened not to its luring voice. He and Isabella were very happy; the only drawback to their happiness lay in the regretted fact that they were childless.

Then, in the sixth year, came a crisis and a change. Captain Barrett, an old crony of David's, wanted him to go with him on a voyage as mate. At the suggestion all David's long-repressed craving for the wide blue wastes of the ocean, and the wind whistling through the spars with the salt foam in its breath, broke forth with a passion all the more intense for that very repression. He must go on that voyage with James Barrett—he MUST! That over, he would be contented again; but go he must. His soul struggled within him like a fettered thing.

Isabella opposed the scheme vehemently and unwisely, with mordant sarcasm and unjust reproaches. The latent obstinacy of David's character came to the support of his longing—a longing which Isabella, with five generations of land-loving ancestry behind her, could not understand at all.

He was determined to go, and he told Isabella so.

"I'm sick of plowing and milking cows," he said hotly.

"You mean that you are sick of a respectable life," sneered Isabella.

"Perhaps," said David, with a contemptuous shrug of his shoulders. "Anyway, I'm going."

"If you go on this voyage, David Spencer, you need never come back here," said Isabella resolutely.

David had gone; he did not believe that she meant it. Isabella believed that he did not care whether she meant it or not. David Spencer left behind him a woman, calm outwardly, inwardly a seething volcano of anger, wounded pride, and thwarted will.

He found precisely the same woman when he came home, tanned, joyous, tamed for a while of his *wanderlust*, ready, with something of real affection, to go back to the farm fields and the stock-yard.

Isabella met him at the door, smileless, cold-eyed, set-lipped.

"What do you want here?" she said, in the tone she was accustomed to use to tramps and Syrian peddlers.

"Want!" David's surprise left him at a loss for words. "Want! Why, I—I—want my wife. I've come home."

"This is not your home. I'm no wife of yours. You made your choice when you went away," Isabella had replied. Then she had gone in, shut the door, and locked it in his face.

David had stood there for a few minutes like a man stunned. Then he had turned and walked away up the lane under the birches. He said nothing—then or at any other time. From that day no reference to his wife or her concerns ever crossed his lips.

He went directly to the harbor, and shipped with Captain Barrett for another voyage. When he came back from that in a month's time, he bought a small house and had it hauled to the "Cove," a lonely inlet from which no other human habitation was visible. Between his sea voyages he lived there the life of a recluse; fishing and playing his violin were his only employments. He went nowhere and encouraged no visitors.

Isabella Spencer also had adopted the tactics of silence. When the scandalized Chiswicks, Aunt Jane at their head, tried to patch up the matter with argument and entreaty, Isabella met them stonily, seeming not to hear what they said, and making no response. She worsted them totally. As Aunt Jane said in disgust, "What can you do with a woman who won't even TALK?"

Five months after David Spencer had been turned from his wife's door, Rachel was born. Perhaps, if David had come to them then, with due penitence and humility, Isabella's heart, softened by the pain and joy of her long and ardently desired motherhood might have cast out the rankling venom of resentment that had poisoned it and taken him back into it. But David had not come; he gave no sign of knowing or caring that his once longed-for child had been born.

When Isabella was able to be about again, her pale face was harder than ever; and, had there been about her any one discerning enough to notice it, there was a subtle change in her bearing and manner. A certain nervous expectancy, a fluttering restlessness was gone. Isabella had ceased to hope secretly that her husband would yet come back. She had in her secret soul thought he would; and she had meant to forgive him when she had humbled him sufficiently, and when he had abased himself as she considered he should. But now she knew that he did not mean to sue for her forgiveness; and the hate that sprang out of her old love was a rank and speedy and persistent growth.

Rachel, from her earliest recollection, had been vaguely conscious of a difference between her own life and the lives of her playmates. For a long time it puzzled her childish brain. Finally, she reasoned it out that the difference consisted in the fact that they had fathers and she, Rachel Spencer, had none—not even in the graveyard, as Carrie Bell and Lilian Boulter had. Why was this? Rachel went straight to her mother, put one little dimpled hand on Isabella Spencer's knee, looked up with great searching blue eyes, and said gravely,

"Mother, why haven't I got a father like the other little girls?"

Isabella Spencer laid aside her work, took the seven year old child on her lap, and told her the whole story in a few direct and bitter words that imprinted themselves indelibly on Rachel's remembrance. She understood clearly and hopelessly that she could never have a father—that, in this respect, she must always be unlike other people.

"Your father cares nothing for you," said Isabella Spencer in conclusion. "He never did care. You must never speak of him to anybody again."

Rachel slipped silently from her mother's knee and ran out to the Springtime garden with a full heart. There she cried passionately over her mother's last words. It seemed to her a terrible thing that her father should not love her, and a cruel thing that she must never talk of him.

Oddly enough, Rachel's sympathies were all with her father, in as far as she could understand the old quarrel. She did not dream of disobeying her mother and she did not disobey her. Never again did the child speak of her father; but Isabella had not forbidden her to think of him, and thenceforth Rachel thought of him constantly—so constantly that, in some strange way, he seemed to become an unguessed-of part of her inner life—the unseen, ever-present companion in all her experiences.

She was an imaginative child, and in fancy she made the acquaintance of her father. She had never seen him, but he was more real to her than most of the people she had seen. He played and talked with her as her mother never did; he walked with her in the orchard and field and garden; he sat by her pillow in the twilight; to him she whispered secrets she told to none other.

Once her mother asked her impatiently why she talked so much to herself.

"I am not talking to myself. I am talking to a very dear friend of mine," Rachel answered gravely.

"Silly child," laughed her mother, half tolerantly, half disapprovingly.

Two years later something wonderful had happened to Rachel. One summer afternoon she had gone to the harbor with several of her little playmates. Such a jaunt was a rare treat to the child, for Isabella Spencer seldom allowed her to go from home with anybody but herself. And Isabella was not an entertaining companion. Rachel never particularly enjoyed an outing with her mother.

The children wandered far along the shore; at last they came to a place that Rachel had never seen before. It was a shallow cove where the waters purred on the yellow sands. Beyond it, the sea was laughing and flashing and preening and alluring, like a beautiful, coquettish woman. Outside, the wind was boisterous and rollicking; here, it was reverent and gentle. A white boat was hauled up on the skids, and there was a queer little house close down to the sands, like a big shell tossed up by the waves. Rachel looked on it all with secret delight; she, too, loved the lonely places of sea and shore, as her father had done. She wanted to linger awhile in this dear spot and revel in it.

"I'm tired, girls," she announced. "I'm going to stay here and rest for a spell. I don't want to go to Gull Point. You go on yourselves; I'll wait for you here."

"All alone?" asked Carrie Bell, wonderingly.

"I'm not so afraid of being alone as some people are," said Rachel, with dignity.

The other girls went on, leaving Rachel sitting on the skids, in the shadow of the big white boat. She sat there for a time dreaming happily, with her blue eyes on the far, pearly horizon, and her golden head leaning against the boat.

Suddenly she heard a step behind her. When she turned her head a man was standing beside her, looking down at her with big, merry, blue eyes. Rachel was quite sure that she had never seen him before; yet those eyes seemed to her to have a strangely familiar look. She liked him. She felt no shyness nor timidity, such as usually afflicted her in the presence of strangers.

He was a tall, stout man, dressed in a rough fishing suit, and wearing an oilskin cap on his head. His hair was very thick and curly and fair; his cheeks were tanned and red; his teeth, when he smiled, were very even and white. Rachel thought he must be quite old, because there was a good deal of gray mixed with his fair hair.

"Are you watching for the mermaids?" he said.

Rachel nodded gravely. From any one else she would have scrupulously hidden such a thought.

"Yes, I am," she said. "Mother says there is no such thing as a mermaid, but I like to think there is. Have you ever seen one?"

The big man sat down on a bleached log of driftwood and smiled at her.

"No, I'm sorry to say that I haven't. But I have seen many other very wonderful things. I might tell you about some of them, if you would come over here and sit by me."

Rachel went unhesitatingly. When she reached him he pulled her down on his knee, and she liked it.

"What a nice little craft you are," he said. "Do you suppose, now, that you could give me a kiss?"

As a rule, Rachel hated kissing. She could seldom be prevailed upon to kiss even her uncles—who knew it and liked to tease her for kisses until they aggravated her so terribly that she told them she couldn't bear men. But now she promptly put her arms about this strange man's neck and gave him a hearty smack.

"I like you," she said frankly.

She felt his arms tighten suddenly about her. The blue eyes looking into hers grew misty and very tender. Then, all at once, Rachel knew who he was. He was her father. She did not say anything, but she laid her curly head down on his shoulder and felt a great happiness, as of one who had come into some longed-for haven.

If David Spencer realized that she understood he said nothing. Instead, he began to tell her fascinating stories of far lands he had visited, and strange things he had seen. Rachel listened entranced, as if she were hearkening to a fairy tale. Yes, he was just as she had dreamed him. She had always been sure he could tell beautiful stories.

"Come up to the house and I'll show you some pretty things," he said finally.

Then followed a wonderful hour. The little low-ceilinged room, with its square window, into which he took her, was filled with the flotsam and jetsam of his roving life—things beautiful and odd and strange beyond all telling. The things that pleased Rachel most were two huge shells on the chimney piece—pale pink shells with big crimson and purple spots.

"Oh, I didn't know there could be such pretty things in the world," she exclaimed.

"If you would like," began the big man; then he paused for a moment. "I'll show you something prettier still."

Rachel felt vaguely that he meant to say something else when he began; but she forgot to wonder what it was when she saw what he brought out of a little corner cupboard. It was a teapot of some fine, glistening purple ware, coiled over by golden dragons with gilded claws and scales. The lid looked like a beautiful golden flower and the handle was a coil of a dragon's tail. Rachel sat and looked at it rapt-eyed.

"That's the only thing of any value I have in the world—now," he said.

Rachel knew there was something very sad in his eyes and voice. She longed to kiss him again and comfort him. But suddenly he began to laugh, and then he rummaged out some goodies for her to eat, sweetmeats more delicious than she had ever imagined. While she nibbled them he took down an old violin and played music that made her want to dance and sing. Rachel was perfectly happy. She wished she might stay forever in that low, dim room with all its treasures.

"I see your little friends coming around the point," he said, finally. "I suppose you must go. Put the rest of the goodies in your pocket."

He took her up in his arms and held her tightly against his breast for a single moment. She felt him kissing her hair.

"There, run along, little girl. Good-by," he said gently.

"Why don't you ask me to come and see you again?" cried Rachel, half in tears. "I'm coming ANYHOW."

"If you can come, COME," he said. "If you don't come, I shall know it is because you can't—and that is much to know. I'm very, very, VERY glad, little woman, that you have come once."

Rachel was sitting demurely on the skids when her companions came back. They had not seen her leaving the house, and she said not a word to them of her experiences. She only smiled mysteriously when they asked her if she had been lonesome.

That night, for the first time, she mentioned her father's name in her prayers. She never forgot to do so afterwards. She always said, "bless mother—and father," with an instinctive pause between the two names—a pause which indicated new realization of the tragedy which had sundered them. And the tone in which she said "father" was softer and more tender than the one which voiced "mother."

Rachel never visited the Cove again. Isabella Spencer discovered that the children had been there, and, although she knew nothing of Rachel's interview with her father, she told the child that she must never again go to that part of the shore.

Rachel shed many a bitter tear in secret over this command; but she obeyed it. Thenceforth there had been no communication between her and her father, save the unworded messages of soul to soul across whatever may divide them.

David Spencer's invitation to his daughter's wedding was sent with the others, and the remaining days of Rachel's maidenhood slipped away in a whirl of preparation and excitement in which her mother reveled, but which was distasteful to the girl.

The wedding day came at last, breaking softly and fairly over the great sea in a sheen of silver and pearl and rose, a September day, as mild and beautiful as June.

The ceremony was to be performed at eight o'clock in the evening. At seven Rachel stood in her room, fully dressed and alone. She had no bridesmaid, and she had asked her cousins to leave her to herself in this last solemn hour of girlhood. She looked very fair and sweet in the sunset-light that showered through the birches. Her wedding gown was a fine, sheer organdie, simply and daintily made. In the loose waves of her bright hair she wore her bridegroom's flowers, roses as white as a virgin's dream. She was very happy; but her happiness was faintly threaded with the sorrow inseparable from all change.

Presently her mother came in, carrying a small basket.

"Here is something for you, Rachel. One of the boys from the harbor brought it up. He was bound to give it into your own hands—said that was his orders. I just took it and sent him to the right-about—told him I'd give it to you at once, and that that was all that was necessary."

She spoke coldly. She knew quite well who had sent the basket, and she resented it; but her resentment was not quite strong enough to overcome her curiosity. She stood silently by while Rachel unpacked the basket.

Rachel's hands trembled as she took off the cover. Two huge pink-spotted shells came first. How well she remembered them! Beneath them, carefully wrapped up in a square of foreign-looking, strangely scented silk, was the dragon teapot. She held it in her hands and gazed at it with tears gathering thickly in her eyes.

"Your father sent that," said Isabella Spencer with an odd sound in her voice. "I remember it well. It was among the things I packed up and sent after him. His father had brought it home from China fifty years ago, and he prized it beyond anything. They used to say it was worth a lot of money."

"Mother, please leave me alone for a little while," said Rachel, imploringly. She had caught sight of a little note at the bottom of the basket, and she felt that she could not read it under her mother's eyes.

Mrs. Spencer went out with unaccustomed acquiescence, and Rachel went quickly to the window, where she read her letter by the fading gleams of twilight. It was very brief, and the writing was that of a man who holds a pen but seldom.

"My dear little girl," it ran, "I'm sorry I can't go to your wedding. It was like you to ask me—for I know it was your doing. I wish I could see you married, but I can't go to the house I was turned out of. I hope you will be very happy. I am sending you the shells and teapot you liked so much. Do you remember that day we had such a good time? I would liked to have seen you again before you were married, but it can't be.

"Your loving father,

"DAVID SPENCER."

Rachel resolutely blinked away the tears that filled her eyes. A fierce desire for her father sprang up in her heart—an insistent hunger that would not be denied. She MUST see her father; she MUST have his blessing on her new life. A sudden determination took possession of her whole being—a determination to sweep aside all conventionalities and objections as if they had not been.

It was now almost dark. The guests would not be coming for half an hour yet. It was only fifteen minutes' walk over the hill to the Cove. Hastily Rachel shrouded herself in her new raincoat, and drew a dark, protecting hood over her gay head. She opened the door and slipped noiselessly downstairs. Mrs. Spencer and her assistants were all busy in the back part of the house. In a moment Rachel was out in the dewy garden. She would go straight over the fields. Nobody would see her.

It was quite dark when she reached the Cove. In the crystal cup of the sky over her the stars were blinking. Flying flakes of foam were scurrying over the sand like elfin things. A soft little wind was crooning about the eaves of the little gray house where David Spencer was sitting, alone in the twilight, his violin on his knee. He had been trying to play, but could not. His heart yearned after his daughter—yes, and after a long-estranged bride of his youth. His love of the sea was sated forever; his love for wife and child still cried for its own under all his old anger and stubbornness.

The door opened suddenly and the very Rachel of whom he was dreaming came suddenly in, flinging off her wraps and standing forth in her young beauty and bridal adornments, a splendid creature, almost lighting up the gloom with her radiance.

"Father," she cried, brokenly, and her father's eager arms closed around her.

Back in the house she had left, the guests were coming to the wedding. There were jests and laughter and friendly greeting. The bridegroom came, too, a slim, dark-eyed lad who tiptoed bashfully upstairs to the spare room, from which he presently emerged to confront Mrs. Spencer on the landing.

"I want to see Rachel before we go down," he said, blushing.

Mrs. Spencer deposited a wedding present of linen on the table which was already laden with gifts, opening the door of Rachel's room, and called her. There was no reply; the room was dark and still. In sudden alarm, Isabella Spencer snatched the lamp from the hall table and held it up. The little white room was empty. No blushing, white-clad bride tenanted it. But David Spencer's letter was lying on the stand. She caught it up and read it.

"Rachel is gone," she gasped. A flash of intuition had revealed to her where and why the girl had gone.

"Gone!" echoed Frank, his face blanching. His pallid dismay recalled Mrs. Spencer to herself. She gave a bitter, ugly little laugh.

"Oh, you needn't look so scared, Frank. She hasn't run away from you. Hush; come in here —shut the door. Nobody must know of this. Nice gossip it would make! That little fool has gone to the Cove to see her—her father. I know she has. It's just like what she would do. He sent her those presents—look—and this letter. Read it. She has gone to coax him to come and see her married. She was crazy about it. And the minister is here and it is half-past seven. She'll ruin her dress and shoes in the dust and dew. And what if some one has seen her! Was there ever such a little fool?"

Frank's presence of mind had returned to him. He knew all about Rachel and her father. She had told him everything.

"I'll go after her," he said gently. "Get me my hat and coat. I'll slip down the back stairs and over to the Cove."

"You must get out of the pantry window, then," said Mrs. Spencer firmly, mingling comedy and tragedy after her characteristic fashion. "The kitchen is full of women. I won't have this known and talked about if it can possibly be helped."

The bridegroom, wise beyond his years in the knowledge that it was well to yield to women in little things, crawled obediently out of the pantry window and darted through the birch wood. Mrs. Spencer had stood quakingly on guard until he had disappeared.

So Rachel had gone to her father! Like had broken the fetters of years and fled to like.

"It isn't much use fighting against nature, I guess," she thought grimly. "I'm beat. He must have thought something of her, after all, when he sent her that teapot and letter. And what does he mean about the 'day they had such a good time'? Well, it just means that she's been to see him before, sometime, I suppose, and kept me in ignorance of it all."

Mrs. Spencer shut down the pantry window with a vicious thud.

"If only she'll come quietly back with Frank in time to prevent gossip I'll forgive her," she said, as she turned to the kitchen.

Rachel was sitting on her father's knee, with both her white arms around his neck, when Frank came in. She sprang up, her face flushed and appealing, her eyes bright and dewy with tears. Frank thought he had never seen her look so lovely.

"Oh, Frank, is it very late? Oh, are you angry?" she exclaimed timidly.

"No, no, dear. Of course I'm not angry. But don't you think you'd better come back now? It's nearly eight and everybody is waiting."

"I've been trying to coax father to come up and see me married," said Rachel. "Help me, Frank."

"You'd better come, sir," said Frank, heartily, "I'd like it as much as Rachel would."

David Spencer shook his head stubbornly.

"No, I can't go to that house. I was locked out of it. Never mind me. I've had my happiness in this half hour with my little girl. I'd like to see her married, but it isn't to be."

"Yes, it is to be—it shall be," said Rachel resolutely. "You SHALL see me married. Frank, I'm going to be married here in my father's house! That is the right place for a girl to be married. Go back and tell the guests so, and bring them all down."

Frank looked rather dismayed. David Spencer said deprecatingly: "Little girl, don't you think it would be—"

"I'm going to have my own way in this," said Rachel, with a sort of tender finality. "Go, Frank. I'll obey you all my life after, but you must do this for me. Try to understand," she added beseechingly.

"Oh, I understand," Frank reassured her. "Besides, I think you are right. But I was thinking of your mother. She won't come."

"Then you tell her that if she doesn't come I shan't be married at all," said Rachel. She was betraying unsuspected ability to manage people. She knew that ultimatum would urge Frank to his best endeavors.

Frank, much to Mrs. Spencer's dismay, marched boldly in at the front door upon his return. She pounced on him and whisked him out of sight into the supper room.

"Where's Rachel? What made you come that way? Everybody saw you!"

"It makes no difference. They will all have to know, anyway. Rachel says she is going to be married from her father's house, or not at all. I've come back to tell you so."

Isabella's face turned crimson.

"Rachel has gone crazy. I wash my hands of this affair. Do as you please. Take the guests—the supper, too, if you can carry it."

"We'll all come back here for supper," said Frank, ignoring the sarcasm. "Come, Mrs. Spencer, let's make the best of it."

"Do you suppose that *I* am going to David Spencer's house?" said Isabella Spencer violently.

"Oh you MUST come, Mrs. Spencer," cried poor Frank desperately. He began to fear that he would lose his bride past all finding in this maze of triple stubbornness. "Rachel says she won't be married at all if you don't go, too. Think what a talk it will make. You know she will keep her word."

Isabella Spencer knew it. Amid all the conflict of anger and revolt in her soul was a strong desire not to make a worse scandal than must of necessity be made. The desire subdued and tamed her, as nothing else could have done.

"I will go, since I have to," she said icily. "What can't be cured must be endured. Go and tell them."

Five minutes later the sixty wedding guests were all walking over the fields to the Cove, with the minister and the bridegroom in the front of the procession. They were too amazed even to talk about the strange happening. Isabella Spencer walked behind, fiercely alone.

They all crowded into the little room of the house at the Cove, and a solemn hush fell over it, broken only by the purr of the sea-wind around it and the croon of the waves on the shore. David Spencer gave his daughter away; but, when the ceremony was concluded, Isabella was the first to take the girl in her arms. She clasped her and kissed her, with tears streaming down her pale face, all her nature melted in a mother's tenderness.

"Rachel! Rachel! My child, I hope and pray that you may be happy," she said brokenly.

In the surge of the suddenly merry crowd of well-wishers around the bride and groom, Isabella was pushed back into a shadowy corner behind a heap of sails and ropes. Looking up, she found herself crushed against David Spencer. For the first time in twenty years the eyes of husband and wife met. A strange thrill shot to Isabella's heart; she felt herself trembling.

"Isabella." It was David's voice in her ear—a voice full of tenderness and pleading—the voice of the young wooer of her girlhood—"Is it too late to ask you to forgive me? I've been a stubborn fool—but there hasn't been an hour in all these years that I haven't thought about you and our baby and longed for you."

Isabella Spencer had hated this man; yet her hate had been but a parasite growth on a nobler stem, with no abiding roots of its own. It withered under his words, and lo, there was the old love, fair and strong and beautiful as ever.

"Oh—David—I—was—all—to—blame," she murmured brokenly.

Further words were lost on her husband's lips.

When the hubbub of handshaking and congratulating had subsided, Isabella Spencer stepped out before the company. She looked almost girlish and bridal herself, with her flushed cheeks and bright eyes.

"Let's go back now and have supper, and be sensible," she said crisply. "Rachel, your father is coming, too. He is coming to STAY,"—with a defiant glance around the circle. "Come, everybody."

They went back with laughter and raillery over the quiet autumn fields, faintly silvered now by the moon that was rising over the hills. The young bride and groom lagged behind; they were very happy, but they were not so happy, after all, as the old bride and groom who walked swiftly in front. Isabella's hand was in her husband's and sometimes she could not see the moonlit hills for a mist of glorified tears.

"David," she whispered, as he helped her over the fence, "how can you ever forgive me?"

"There's nothing to forgive," he said. "We're only just married. Who ever heard of a bridegroom talking of forgiveness? Everything is beginning over new for us, my girl."

JANE'S BABY

Miss Rosetta Ellis, with her front hair in curl-papers, and her back hair bound with a checked apron, was out in her breezy side yard under the firs, shaking her parlor rugs, when Mr. Nathan Patterson drove in. Miss Rosetta had seen him coming down the long red hill, but she had not supposed he would be calling at that time of the morning. So she had not run. Miss Rosetta always ran if anybody called and her front hair was in curl-papers; and, though the errand of the said caller might be life or death, he or she had to wait until Miss Rosetta had taken her hair out. Everybody in Avonlea knew this, because everybody in Avonlea knew everything about everybody else.

But Mr. Patterson had wheeled into the lane so quickly and unexpectedly that Miss Rosetta had had no time to run; so, twitching off the checked apron, she stood her ground as calmly as might be under the disagreeable consciousness of curl-papers.

"Good morning, Miss Ellis," said Mr. Patterson, so somberly that Miss Rosetta instantly felt that he was the bearer of bad news. Usually Mr. Patterson's face was as broad and beaming as a harvest moon. Now his expression was very melancholy and his voice positively sepulchral.

"Good morning," returned Miss Rosetta, crisply and cheerfully. She, at any rate, would not go into eclipse until she knew the reason therefor. "It is a fine day."

"A very fine day," assented Mr. Patterson, solemnly. "I have just come from the Wheeler place, Miss Ellis, and I regret to say—"

"Charlotte is sick!" cried Miss Rosetta, rapidly. "Charlotte has got another spell with her heart! I knew it! I've been expecting to hear it! Any woman that drives about the country as much as she does is liable to heart disease at any moment. *I* never go outside of my gate but I meet her gadding off somewhere. Goodness knows who looks after her place. I shouldn't like to trust as much to a hired man as she does. Well, it is very kind of you, Mr. Patterson, to put yourself out to the extent of calling to tell me that Charlotte is sick, but I don't really see why you should take so much trouble—I really don't. It doesn't matter to me whether Charlotte is sick or whether she isn't. YOU know that perfectly well, Mr. Patterson, if anybody does. When Charlotte went and got married, on the sly, to that good-for-nothing Jacob Wheeler—"

"Mrs. Wheeler is quite well," interrupted Mr. Patterson desperately. "Quite well. Nothing at all the matter with her, in fact. I only—"

"Then what do you mean by coming here and telling me she wasn't, and frightening me half to death?" demanded Miss Rosetta, indignantly. "My own heart isn't very strong—it runs in our family—and my doctor warned me to avoid all shocks and excitement. I don't want to be excited, Mr. Patterson. I won't be excited, not even if Charlotte has another spell. It's perfectly useless for you to try to excite me, Mr. Patterson."

"Bless the woman, I'm not trying to excite anybody!" declared Mr. Patterson in exasperation. "I merely called to tell you—"

"To tell me WHAT?" said Miss Rosetta. "How much longer do you mean to keep me in suspense, Mr. Patterson. No doubt you have abundance of spare time, but—I—have NOT."

"—that your sister, Mrs. Wheeler, has had a letter from a cousin of yours, and she's in Charlottetown. Mrs. Roberts, I think her name is—"

"Jane Roberts," broke in Miss Rosetta. "Jane Ellis she was, before she was married. What was she writing to Charlotte about? Not that I want to know, of course. I'm not interested in Charlotte's correspondence, goodness knows. But if Jane had anything in particular to write about she should have written to ME. I am the oldest. Charlotte had no business to get a letter from Jane Roberts without consulting me. It's just like her underhanded ways. She got married the same way. Never said a word to me about it, but just sneaked off with that unprincipled Jacob Wheeler—"

"Mrs. Roberts is very ill. I understand," persisted Mr. Patterson, nobly resolved to do what he had come to do, "dying, in fact, and—"

"Jane ill! Jane dying!" exclaimed Miss Rosetta. "Why, she was the healthiest girl I ever knew! But then I've never seen her, nor heard from her, since she got married fifteen years ago. I dare say her husband was a brute and neglected her, and she's pined away by slow degrees. I've no faith in husbands. Look at Charlotte! Everybody knows how Jacob Wheeler used her. To be sure, she deserved it, but—"

"Mrs. Roberts' husband is dead," said Mr. Patterson. "Died about two months ago, I understand, and she has a little baby six months old, and she thought perhaps Mrs. Wheeler would take it for old times' sake—"

"Did Charlotte ask you to call and tell me this?" demanded Miss Rosetta eagerly.

"No; she just told me what was in the letter. She didn't mention you; but I thought, perhaps, you ought to be told—"

"I knew it," said Miss Rosetta in a tone of bitter assurance. "I could have told you so. Charlotte wouldn't even let me know that Jane was ill. Charlotte would be afraid I would want to get the baby, seeing that Jane and I were such intimate friends long ago. And who has a better right to it than me, I should like to know? Ain't I the oldest? And haven't I had experience in bringing up babies? Charlotte needn't think she is going to run the affairs of our family just because she happened to get married. Jacob Wheeler—"

"I must be going," said Mr. Patterson, gathering up his reins thankfully.

"I am much obliged to you for coming to tell me about Jane," said Miss Rosetta, "even though you have wasted a lot of precious time getting it out. If it hadn't been for you I suppose I should never have known it at all. As it is, I shall start for town just as soon as I can get ready."

"You'll have to hurry if you want to get ahead of Mrs. Wheeler," advised Mr. Patterson. "She's packing her trunk and going on the morning train."

"I'll pack a valise and go on the afternoon train," retorted Miss Rosetta triumphantly. "I'll show Charlotte she isn't running the Ellis affairs. She married out of them into the Wheelers. She can attend to them. Jacob Wheeler was the most—"

But Mr. Patterson had driven away. He felt that he had done his duty in the face of fearful odds, and he did not want to hear anything more about Jacob Wheeler.

Rosetta Ellis and Charlotte Wheeler had not exchanged a word for ten years. Before that time they had been devoted to each other, living together in the little Ellis cottage on the White Sands road, as they had done ever since their parents' death. The trouble began when Jacob Wheeler had commenced to pay attention to Charlotte, the younger and prettier of two women who had both ceased to be either very young or very pretty. Rosetta had been bitterly opposed to the match from the first. She vowed she had no use for Jacob Wheeler. There were not lacking malicious people to hint that this was because the aforesaid Jacob Wheeler had selected the wrong sister upon whom to bestow his affections. Be that as it might, Miss Rosetta certainly continued to render the course of Jacob Wheeler's true love exceedingly rough and tumultuous. The end of it was that Charlotte had gone quietly away one morning and married Jacob Wheeler without Miss Rosetta's knowing anything about it. Miss Rosetta had never forgiven her for it, and Charlotte had never forgiven the things Rosetta had said to her when she and Jacob returned to the Ellis cottage. Since then the sisters had been avowed and open foes, the only difference being that Miss Rosetta aired her grievances publicly, in season and out of season, while Charlotte was never heard to mention Rosetta's name. Even the death of Jacob Wheeler, five years after the marriage, had not healed the breach.

Miss Rosetta took out her curl-papers, packed her valise, and caught the late afternoon train for Charlottetown, as she had threatened. All the way there she sat rigidly upright in her seat and held imaginary dialogues with Charlotte in her mind, running something like this on her part:—

"No, Charlotte Wheeler, you are not going to have Jane's baby, and you're very much mistaken if you think so. Oh, all right—we'll see! You don't know anything about babies, even if you are married. I do. Didn't I take William Ellis's baby, when his wife died? Tell me that, Charlotte Wheeler! And didn't the little thing thrive with me, and grow strong and healthy? Yes, even you have to admit that it did, Charlotte Wheeler. And yet you have the presumption to think that you ought to have Jane's baby! Yes, it is presumption, Charlotte Wheeler. And when William Ellis got married again, and took the baby, didn't the child cling to me and cry as if I was its real mother? You know it did, Charlotte Wheeler. I'm going to get and keep Jane's baby in spite of you, Charlotte Wheeler, and I'd like to see you try to prevent me—you that went and got married and never so much as let your own sister know of it! If I had got married in such a fashion, Charlotte Wheeler, I'd be ashamed to look anybody in the face for the rest of my natural life!"

Miss Rosetta was so interested in thus laying down the law to Charlotte, and in planning out the future life of Jane's baby, that she didn't find the journey to Charlottetown so long or tedious as might have been expected, considering her haste. She soon found her way to the house where her cousin lived. There, to her dismay and real sorrow, she learned that Mrs. Roberts had died at four o'clock that afternoon.

"She seemed dreadful anxious to live until she heard from some of her folks out in Avonlea," said the woman who gave Miss Rosetta the information. "She had written to them about her little girl. She was my sister-in-law, and she lived with me ever since her husband died. I've done my best for her; but I've a big family of my own and I can't see how I'm to keep the child. Poor Jane looked and longed for some one to come from Avonlea, but she couldn't hold out. A patient, suffering creature she was!"

"I'm her cousin," said Miss Rosetta, wiping her eyes, "and I have come for the baby. I'll take it home with me after the funeral; and, if you please, Mrs. Gordon, let me see it right away, so it can get accustomed to me. Poor Jane! I wish I could have got here in time to see her, she and I were such friends long ago. We were far more intimate and confidential than ever her and Charlotte was. Charlotte knows that, too!"

The vim with which Miss Rosetta snapped this out rather amazed Mrs. Gordon, who couldn't understand it at all. But she took Miss Rosetta upstairs to the room where the baby was sleeping.

"Oh, the little darling," cried Miss Rosetta, all her old maidishness and oddity falling away from her like a garment, and all her innate and denied motherhood shining out in her face like a transforming illumination. "Oh, the sweet, dear, pretty little thing!"

The baby was a darling—a six-months' old beauty with little golden ringlets curling and glistening all over its tiny head. As Miss Rosetta hung over it, it opened its eyes and then held out its tiny hands to her with a gurgle of confidence.

"Oh, you sweetest!" said Miss Rosetta rapturously, gathering it up in her arms. "You belong to me, darling—never, never, to that under-handed Charlotte! What is its name, Mrs. Gordon?"

"It wasn't named," said Mrs. Gordon. "Guess you'll have to name it yourself, Miss Ellis."

"Camilla Jane," said Miss Rosetta without a moment's hesitation. "Jane after its mother, of course; and I have always thought Camilla the prettiest name in the world. Charlotte would be sure to give it some perfectly heathenish name. I wouldn't put it past her calling the poor innocent Mehitable."

Miss Rosetta decided to stay in Charlottetown until after the funeral. That night she lay with the baby on her arm, listening with joy to its soft little breathing. She did not sleep or wish to sleep. Her waking fancies were more alluring than any visions of dreamland. Moreover, she gave a spice to them by occasionally snapping some vicious sentences out loud at Charlotte.

Miss Rosetta fully expected Charlotte along on the following morning and girded herself for the fray; but no Charlotte appeared. Night came; no Charlotte. Another morning and no Charlotte. Miss Rosetta was hopelessly puzzled. What had happened? Dear, dear, had Charlotte taken a bad heart spell, on hearing that she, Rosetta, had stolen a march on her to Charlottetown? It was quite likely. You never knew what to expect of a woman who had married Jacob Wheeler!

The truth was, that the very evening Miss Rosetta had left Avonlea Mrs. Jacob Wheeler's hired man had broken his leg and had had to be conveyed to his distant home on a feather bed in an express wagon. Mrs. Wheeler could not leave home until she had obtained another hired man. Consequently, it was the evening after the funeral when Mrs. Wheeler whisked up the steps of the Gordon house and met Miss Rosetta coming out with a big white bundle in her arms.

The eyes of the two women met defiantly. Miss Rosetta's face wore an air of triumph, chastened by a remembrance of the funeral that afternoon. Mrs. Wheeler's face, except for eyes, was as expressionless as it usually was. Unlike the tall, fair, fat Miss Rosetta, Mrs. Wheeler was small and dark and thin, with an eager, careworn face.

"How is Jane?" she said abruptly, breaking the silence of ten years in saying it.

"Jane is dead and buried, poor thing," said Miss Rosetta calmly. "I am taking her baby, little Camilla Jane, home with me."

"The baby belongs to me," cried Mrs. Wheeler passionately. "Jane wrote to me about her. Jane meant that I should have her. I've come for her."

"You'll go back without her then," said Miss Rosetta, serene in the possession that is nine points of the law. "The child is mine, and she is going to stay mine. You can make up your mind to that, Charlotte Wheeler. A woman who eloped to get married isn't fit to be trusted with a baby, anyhow. Jacob Wheeler—"

But Mrs. Wheeler had rushed past into the house. Miss Rosetta composedly stepped into the cab and drove to the station. She fairly bridled with triumph; and underneath the triumph ran a queer undercurrent of satisfaction over the fact that Charlotte had spoken to her at last. Miss Rosetta would not look at this satisfaction, or give it a name, but it was there.

Miss Rosetta arrived safely back in Avonlea with Camilla Jane and within ten hours everybody in the settlement knew the whole story, and every woman who could stand on her feet had been up to the Ellis cottage to see the baby. Mrs. Wheeler arrived home twenty-four hours later, and silently betook herself to her farm. When her Avonlea neighbors sympathized with her in her disappointment, she said nothing, but looked all the more darkly determined. Also, a week later, Mr. William J. Blair, the Carmody storekeeper, had an odd tale to tell. Mrs. Wheeler had come to the store and bought a lot of fine flannel and muslin and valenciennes. Now, what in the name of time, did Mrs. Wheeler want with such stuff? Mr. William J. Blair couldn't make head or tail of it, and it worried him. Mr. Blair was so accustomed to know what everybody bought anything for that such a mystery quite upset him.

Miss Rosetta had exulted in the possession of little Camilla Jane for a month, and had been so happy that she had almost given up inveighing against Charlotte. Her conversations, instead of tending always to Jacob Wheeler, now ran Camilla Janeward; and this, folks thought, was an improvement.

One afternoon, Miss Rosetta, leaving Camilla Jane snugly sleeping in her cradle in the kitchen, had slipped down to the bottom of the garden to pick her currants. The house was hidden from her sight by the copse of cherry trees, but she had left the kitchen window open, so that she could hear the baby if it awakened and cried. Miss Rosetta sang happily as she picked her currants. For the first time since Charlotte had married Jacob Wheeler Miss Rosetta felt really happy—so happy that there was no room in her heart for bitterness. In fancy she looked forward to the coming years, and saw Camilla Jane growing up into girlhood, fair and lovable.

"She'll be a beauty," reflected Miss Rosetta complacently. "Jane was a handsome girl. She shall always be dressed as nice as I can manage it, and I'll get her an organ, and have her take painting and music lessons. Parties, too! I'll give her a real coming-out party when she's eighteen and the very prettiest dress that's to be had. Dear me, I can hardly wait for her to grow up, though she's sweet enough now to make one wish she could stay a baby forever."

When Miss Rosetta returned to the kitchen, her eyes fell on an empty cradle. Camilla Jane was gone!

Miss Rosetta promptly screamed. She understood at a glance what had happened. Six months' old babies do not get out of their cradles and disappear through closed doors without any assistance.

"Charlotte has been here," gasped Miss Rosetta. "Charlotte has stolen Camilla Jane! I might have expected it. I might have known when I heard that story about her buying muslin and flannel. It's just like Charlotte to do such an underhand trick. But I'll go after her! I'll show her! She'll find out she has got Rosetta Ellis to deal with and no Wheeler!"

Like a frantic creature and wholly forgetting that her hair was in curl-papers, Miss Rosetta hurried up the hill and down the shore road to the Wheeler Farm—a place she had never visited in her life before.

The wind was off-shore and only broke the bay's surface into long silvery ripples, and sent sheeny shadows flying out across it from every point and headland, like transparent wings.

The little gray house, so close to the purring waves that in storms their spray splashed over its very doorstep, seemed deserted. Miss Rosetta pounded lustily on the front door. This producing no result, she marched around to the back door and knocked. No answer. Miss Rosetta tried the door. It was locked.

"Guilty conscience," sniffed Miss Rosetta. "Well, I shall stay here until I see that perfidious Charlotte, if I have to camp in the yard all night."

Miss Rosetta was quite capable of doing this, but she was spared the necessity; walking boldly up to the kitchen window, and peering through it, she felt her heart swell with anger as she beheld Charlotte sitting calmly by the table with Camilla Jane on her knee. Beside her was a befrilled and bemuslined cradle, and on a chair lay the garments in which Miss Rosetta had dressed the baby. It was clad in an entirely new outfit, and seemed quite at home with its new possessor. It was laughing and cooing, and making little dabs at her with its dimpled hands.

"Charlotte Wheeler," cried Miss Rosetta, rapping sharply on the window-pane. "I've come for that child! Bring her out to me at once—at once, I say! How dare you come to my house and steal a baby? You're no better than a common burglar. Give me Camilla Jane, I say!"

Charlotte came over to the window with the baby in her arms and triumph glittering in her eyes.

"There is no such child as Camilla Jane here," she said. "This is Barbara Jane. She belongs to me."

With that Mrs. Wheeler pulled down the shade.

Miss Rosetta had to go home. There was nothing else for her to do. On her way she met Mr. Patterson and told him in full the story of her wrongs. It was all over Avonlea by night, and created quite a sensation. Avonlea had not had such a toothsome bit of gossip for a long time.

Mrs. Wheeler exulted in the possession of Barbara Jane for six weeks, during which Miss Rosetta broke her heart with loneliness and longing, and meditated futile plots for the recovery of the baby. It was hopeless to think of stealing it back or she would have tried to. The hired man at the Wheeler place reported that Mrs. Wheeler never left it night or day for a single moment. She even carried it with her when she went to milk the cows.

"But my turn will come," said Miss Rosetta grimly. "Camilla Jane is mine, and if she was called Barbara for a century it wouldn't alter that fact! Barbara, indeed! Why not have called her Methusaleh and have done with it?"

One afternoon in October, when Miss Rosetta was picking her apples and thinking drearily about lost Camilla Jane, a woman came running breathlessly down the hill and into the yard. Miss Rosetta gave an exclamation of amazement and dropped her basket of apples. Of all incredible things! The woman was Charlotte—Charlotte who had never set foot on the grounds of the Ellis cottage since her marriage ten years ago, Charlotte, bare-headed, wild-eyed, distraught, wringing her hands and sobbing.

Miss Rosetta flew to meet her.

"You've scalded Camilla Jane to death!" she exclaimed. "I always knew you would—always expected it!"

"Oh, for heaven's sake, come quick, Rosetta!" gasped Charlotte. "Barbara Jane is in convulsions and I don't know what to do. The hired man has gone for the doctor. You were the nearest, so I came to you. Jenny White was there when they came on, so I left her and ran. Oh, Rosetta, come, come, if you have a spark of humanity in you! You know what to do for convulsions—you saved the Ellis baby when it had them. Oh, come and save Barbara Jane!"

"You mean Camilla Jane, I presume?" said Miss Rosetta firmly, in spite of her agitation.

For a second Charlotte Wheeler hesitated. Then she said passionately: "Yes, yes, Camilla Jane—any name you like! Only come."

Miss Rosetta went, and not a moment too soon, either. The doctor lived eight miles away and the baby was very bad. The two women and Jenny White worked over her for hours. It was not until dark, when the baby was sleeping soundly and the doctor had gone, after telling Miss Rosetta that she had saved the child's life, that a realization of the situation came home to them.

"Well," said Miss Rosetta, dropping into an armchair with a long sigh of weariness, "I guess you'll admit now, Charlotte Wheeler, that you are hardly a fit person to have charge of a baby, even if you had to go and steal it from me. I should think your conscience would reproach you—that is, if any woman who would marry Jacob Wheeler in such an underhanded fashion has a—"

"I—I wanted the baby," sobbed Charlotte, tremulously. "I was so lonely here. I didn't think it was any harm to take her, because Jane gave her to me in her letter. But you have saved her life, Rosetta, and you—you can have her back, although it will break my heart to give her up.

But, oh, Rosetta, won't you let me come and see her sometimes? I love her so I can't bear to give her up entirely."

"Charlotte," said Miss Rosetta firmly, "the most sensible thing for you to do is just to come back with the baby. You are worried to death trying to run this farm with the debt Jacob Wheeler left on it for you. Sell it, and come home with me. And we'll both have the baby then."

"Oh, Rosetta, I'd love to," faltered Charlotte. "I've—I've wanted to be good friends with you again so much. But I thought you were so hard and bitter you'd never make up."

"Maybe I've talked too much," conceded Miss Rosetta, "but you ought to know me well enough to know I didn't mean a word of it. It was your never saying anything, no matter what I said, that riled me up so bad. Let bygones be bygones, and come home, Charlotte."

"I will," said Charlotte resolutely, wiping away her tears. "I'm sick of living here and putting up with hired men. I'll be real glad to go home, Rosetta, and that's the truth. I've had a hard enough time. I s'pose you'll say I deserved it; but I was fond of Jacob, and—"

"Of course, of course. Why shouldn't you be?" said Miss Rosetta briskly. "I'm sure Jacob Wheeler was a good enough soul, if he was a little slack-twisted. I'd like to hear anybody say a word against him in my presence. Look at that blessed child, Charlotte. Isn't she the sweetest thing? I'm desperate glad you are coming back home, Charlotte. I've never been able to put up a decent mess of mustard pickles since you went away, and you were always such a hand with them! We'll be real snug and cozy again—you and me and little Camilla Barbara Jane."

THE DREAM-CHILD

A man's heart—aye, and a woman's, too—should be light in the spring. The spirit of resurrection is abroad, calling the life of the world out of its wintry grave, knocking with radiant fingers at the gates of its tomb. It stirs in human hearts, and makes them glad with the old primal gladness they felt in childhood. It quickens human souls, and brings them, if so they will, so close to God that they may clasp hands with Him. It is a time of wonder and renewed life, and a great outward and inward rapture, as of a young angel softly clapping his hands for creation's joy. At least, so it should be; and so it always had been with me until the spring when the dream-child first came into our lives.

That year I hated the spring—I, who had always loved it so. As boy I had loved it, and as man. All the happiness that had ever been mine, and it was much, had come to blossom in the springtime. It was in the spring that Josephine and I had first loved each other, or, at least, had first come into the full knowledge that we loved. I think that we must have loved each other all our lives, and that each succeeding spring was a word in the revelation of that love, not to be understood until, in the fullness of time, the whole sentence was written out in that most beautiful of all beautiful springs.

How beautiful it was! And how beautiful she was! I suppose every lover thinks that of his lass; otherwise he is a poor sort of lover. But it was not only my eyes of love that made my dear lovely. She was slim and lithe as a young, white-stemmed birch tree; her hair was like a soft, dusky cloud; and her eyes were as blue as Avonlea harbor on a fair twilight, when all the sky is abloom over it. She had dark lashes, and a little red mouth that quivered when she was very sad or very happy, or when she loved very much—quivered like a crimson rose too rudely shaken by the wind. At such times what was a man to do save kiss it?

The next spring we were married, and I brought her home to my gray old homestead on the gray old harbor shore. A lonely place for a young bride, said Avonlea people. Nay, it was not so. She was happy here, even in my absences. She loved the great, restless harbor and the vast, misty sea beyond; she loved the tides, keeping their world-old tryst with the shore, and the gulls, and the croon of the waves, and the call of the winds in the fir woods at noon and even; she loved the moonrises and the sunsets, and the clear, calm nights when the stars seemed to have fallen into the water and to be a little dizzy from such a fall. She loved these things, even as I did. No, she was never lonely here then.

The third spring came, and our boy was born. We thought we had been happy before; now we knew that we had only dreamed a pleasant dream of happiness, and had awakened to this exquisite reality. We thought we had loved each other before; now, as I looked into my wife's pale face, blanched with its baptism of pain, and met the uplifted gaze of her blue eyes, aglow with the holy passion of motherhood, I knew we had only imagined what love might be. The imagination had been sweet, as the thought of the rose is sweet before the bud is open; but as the rose to the thought, so was love to the imagination of it.

"All my thoughts are poetry since baby came," my wife said once, rapturously.

Our boy lived for twenty months. He was a sturdy, toddling rogue, so full of life and laughter and mischief that, when he died, one day, after the illness of an hour, it seemed a most absurd thing that he should be dead—a thing I could have laughed at, until belief forced itself into my soul like a burning, searing iron.

I think I grieved over my little son's death as deeply and sincerely as ever man did, or could. But the heart of the father is not as the heart of the mother. Time brought no healing to Josephine; she fretted and pined; her cheeks lost their pretty oval, and her red mouth grew pale and drooping.

I hoped that spring might work its miracle upon her. When the buds swelled, and the old earth grew green in the sun, and the gulls came back to the gray harbor, whose very grayness grew golden and mellow, I thought I should see her smile again. But, when the spring came, came the dream-child, and the fear that was to be my companion, at bed and board, from sunsetting to sunsetting.

One night I awakened from sleep, realizing in the moment of awakening that I was alone. I listened to hear whether my wife were moving about the house. I heard nothing but the little splash of waves on the shore below and the low moan of the distant ocean.

I rose and searched the house. She was not in it. I did not know where to seek her; but, at a venture, I started along the shore.

It was pale, fainting moonlight. The harbor looked like a phantom harbor, and the night was as still and cold and calm as the face of a dead man. At last I saw my wife coming to me along the shore. When I saw her, I knew what I had feared and how great my fear had been.

As she drew near, I saw that she had been crying; her face was stained with tears, and her dark hair hung loose over her shoulders in little, glossy ringlets like a child's. She seemed to be very tired, and at intervals she wrung her small hands together.

She showed no surprise when she met me, but only held out her hands to me as if glad to see me.

"I followed him—but I could not overtake him," she said with a sob. "I did my best—I hurried so; but he was always a little way ahead. And then I lost him—and so I came back. But I did my best—indeed I did. And oh, I am so tired!"

"Josie, dearest, what do you mean, and where have you been?" I said, drawing her close to me. "Why did you go out so—alone in the night?"

She looked at me wonderingly.

"How could I help it, David? He called me. I had to go."

"WHO called you?"

"The child," she answered in a whisper. "Our child, David—our pretty boy. I awakened in the darkness and heard him calling to me down on the shore. Such a sad, little wailing cry,

David, as if he were cold and lonely and wanted his mother. I hurried out to him, but I could not find him. I could only hear the call, and I followed it on and on, far down the shore. Oh, I tried so hard to overtake it, but I could not. Once I saw a little white hand beckoning to me far ahead in the moonlight. But still I could not go fast enough. And then the cry ceased, and I was there all alone on that terrible, cold, gray shore. I was so tired and I came home. But I wish I could have found him. Perhaps he does not know that I tried to. Perhaps he thinks his mother never listened to his call. Oh, I would not have him think that."

"You have had a bad dream, dear," I said. I tried to say it naturally; but it is hard for a man to speak naturally when he feels a mortal dread striking into his very vitals with its deadly chill.

"It was no dream," she answered reproachfully. "I tell you I heard him calling me—me, his mother. What could I do but go to him? You cannot understand—you are only his father. It was not you who gave him birth. It was not you who paid the price of his dear life in pain. He would not call to you—he wanted his mother."

I got her back to the house and to her bed, whither she went obediently enough, and soon fell into the sleep of exhaustion. But there was no more sleep for me that night. I kept a grim vigil with dread.

When I had married Josephine, one of those officious relatives that are apt to buzz about a man's marriage told me that her grandmother had been insane all the latter part of her life. She had grieved over the death of a favorite child until she lost her mind, and, as the first indication of it, she had sought by nights a white dream-child which always called her, so she said, and led her afar with a little, pale, beckoning hand.

I had smiled at the story then. What had that grim old bygone to do with springtime and love and Josephine? But it came back to me now, hand in hand with my fear. Was this fate coming on my dear wife? It was too horrible for belief. She was so young, so fair, so sweet, this girl-wife of mine. It had been only a bad dream, with a frightened, bewildered waking. So I tried to comfort myself.

When she awakened in the morning she did not speak of what had happened and I did not dare to. She seemed more cheerful that day than she had been, and went about her household duties briskly and skillfully. My fear lifted. I was sure now that she had only dreamed. And I was confirmed in my hopeful belief when two nights had passed away uneventfully.

Then, on the third night, the dream-child called to her again. I wakened from a troubled doze to find her dressing herself with feverish haste.

"He is calling me," she cried. "Oh, don't you hear him? Can't you hear him? Listen—listen—the little, lonely cry! Yes, yes, my precious, mother is coming. Wait for me. Mother is coming to her pretty boy!"

I caught her hand and let her lead me where she would. Hand in hand we followed the dream-child down the harbor shore in that ghostly, clouded moonlight. Ever, she said, the little cry sounded before her. She entreated the dream-child to wait for her; she cried and implored and uttered tender mother-talk. But, at last, she ceased to hear the cry; and then, weeping, wearied, she let me lead her home again.

What a horror brooded over that spring—that so beautiful spring! It was a time of wonder and marvel; of the soft touch of silver rain on greening fields; of the incredible delicacy of young leaves; of blossom on the land and blossom in the sunset. The whole world bloomed in a flush and tremor of maiden loveliness, instinct with all the evasive, fleeting charm of spring and girlhood and young morning. And almost every night of this wonderful time the dream-child called his mother, and we roved the gray shore in quest of him.

In the day she was herself; but, when the night fell, she was restless and uneasy until she heard the call. Then follow it she would, even through storm and darkness. It was then, she said, that the cry sounded loudest and nearest, as if her pretty boy were frightened by the tempest. What wild, terrible rovings we had, she straining forward, eager to overtake the dream-child; I, sick at heart, following, guiding, protecting, as best I could; then afterwards leading her gently home, heart-broken because she could not reach the child.

I bore my burden in secret, determining that gossip should not busy itself with my wife's condition so long as I could keep it from becoming known. We had no near relatives—none with any right to share any trouble—and whoso accepteth human love must bind it to his soul with pain.

I thought, however, that I should have medical advice, and I took our old doctor into my confidence. He looked grave when he heard my story. I did not like his expression nor his few guarded remarks. He said he thought human aid would avail little; she might come all right in time; humor her, as far as possible, watch over her, protect her. He needed not to tell me THAT.

The spring went out and summer came in—and the horror deepened and darkened. I knew that suspicions were being whispered from lip to lip. We had been seen on our nightly quests. Men and women began to look at us pityingly when we went abroad.

One day, on a dull, drowsy afternoon, the dream-child called. I knew then that the end was near; the end had been near in the old grandmother's case sixty years before when the dream-child called in the day. The doctor looked graver than ever when I told him, and said that the time had come when I must have help in my task. I could not watch by day and night. Unless I had assistance I would break down.

I did not think that I should. Love is stronger than that. And on one thing I was determined —they should never take my wife from me. No restraint sterner than a husband's loving hand should ever be put upon her, my pretty, piteous darling.

I never spoke of the dream-child to her. The doctor advised against it. It would, he said, only serve to deepen the delusion. When he hinted at an asylum I gave him a look that would have been a fierce word for another man. He never spoke of it again.

One night in August there was a dull, murky sunset after a dead, breathless day of heat, with not a wind stirring. The sea was not blue as a sea should be, but pink—all pink—a ghastly, staring, painted pink. I lingered on the harbor shore below the house until dark. The evening bells were ringing faintly and mournfully in a church across the harbor. Behind me, in the kitchen, I heard my wife singing. Sometimes now her spirits were fitfully high, and then she would sing the old songs of her girlhood. But even in her singing was something strange, as if a wailing, unearthly cry rang through it. Nothing about her was sadder than that strange singing.

When I went back to the house the rain was beginning to fall; but there was no wind or sound in the air—only that dismal stillness, as if the world were holding its breath in expectation of a calamity.

Josie was standing by the window, looking out and listening. I tried to induce her to go to bed, but she only shook her head.

"I might fall asleep and not hear him when he called," she said. "I am always afraid to sleep now, for fear he should call and his mother fail to hear him."

Knowing it was of no use to entreat, I sat down by the table and tried to read. Three hours passed on. When the clock struck midnight she started up, with the wild light in her sunken blue eyes.

"He is calling," she cried, "calling out there in the storm. Yes, yes, sweet, I am coming!"

She opened the door and fled down the path to the shore. I snatched a lantern from the wall, lighted it, and followed. It was the blackest night I was ever out in, dark with the very darkness of death. The rain fell thickly and heavily. I overtook Josie, caught her hand, and stumbled along in her wake, for she went with the speed and recklessness of a distraught woman. We moved in the little flitting circle of light shed by the lantern. All around us and above us was a horrible, voiceless darkness, held, as it were, at bay by the friendly light.

"If I could only overtake him once," moaned Josie. "If I could just kiss him once, and hold him close against my aching heart. This pain, that never leaves me, would leave me than. Oh, my pretty boy, wait for mother! I am coming to you. Listen, David; he cries—he cries so pitifully; listen! Can't you hear it?"

I DID hear it! Clear and distinct, out of the deadly still darkness before us, came a faint, wailing cry. What was it? Was I, too, going mad, or WAS there something out there—something that cried and moaned—longing for human love, yet ever retreating from human footsteps? I am not a superstitious man; but my nerve had been shaken by my long trial, and I was weaker than I thought. Terror took possession of me—terror unnameable. I trembled in every limb; clammy perspiration oozed from my forehead; I was possessed by a wild impulse to turn and flee—anywhere, away from that unearthly cry. But Josephine's cold hand gripped mine firmly, and led me on. That strange cry still rang in my ears. But it did not recede; it sounded clearer and stronger; it was a wail; but a loud, insistent wail; it was nearer—nearer; it was in the darkness just beyond us.

Then we came to it; a little dory had been beached on the pebbles and left there by the receding tide. There was a child in it—a boy, of perhaps two years old, who crouched in the bottom of the dory in water to his waist, his big, blue eyes wild and wide with terror, his face white and tear-stained. He wailed again when he saw us, and held out his little hands.

My horror fell away from me like a discarded garment. THIS child was living. How he had come there, whence and why, I did not know and, in my state of mind, did not question. It was no cry of parted spirit I had heard—that was enough for me.

"Oh, the poor darling!" cried my wife.

She stooped over the dory and lifted the baby in her arms. His long, fair curls fell on her shoulder; she laid her face against his and wrapped her shawl around him.

"Let me carry him, dear," I said. "He is very wet, and too heavy for you."

"No, no, I must carry him. My arms have been so empty—they are full now. Oh, David, the pain at my heart has gone. He has come to me to take the place of my own. God has sent him to me out of the sea. He is wet and cold and tired. Hush, sweet one, we will go home."

Silently I followed her home. The wind was rising, coming in sudden, angry gusts; the storm was at hand, but we reached shelter before it broke. Just as I shut our door behind us it smote the house with the roar of a baffled beast. I thanked God that we were not out in it, following the dream-child.

"You are very wet, Josie," I said. "Go and put on dry clothes at once."

"The child must be looked to first," she said firmly. "See how chilled and exhausted he is, the pretty dear. Light a fire quickly, David, while I get dry things for him."

I let her have her way. She brought out the clothes our own child had worn and dressed the waif in them, rubbing his chilled limbs, brushing his wet hair, laughing over him, mothering him. She seemed like her old self.

For my own part, I was bewildered. All the questions I had not asked before came crowding to my mind how. Whose child was this? Whence had he come? What was the meaning of it all?

He was a pretty baby, fair and plump and rosy. When he was dried and fed, he fell asleep in Josie's arms. She hung over him in a passion of delight. It was with difficulty I persuaded her to leave him long enough to change her wet clothes. She never asked whose he might be or from where he might have come. He had been sent to her from the sea; the dream-child had led her to him; that was what she believed, and I dared not throw any doubt on that belief. She slept that night with the baby on her arm, and in her sleep her face was the face of a girl in her youth, untroubled and unworn.

I expected that the morrow would bring some one seeking the baby. I had come to the conclusion that he must belong to the "Cove" across the harbor, where the fishing hamlet was; and all day, while Josie laughed and played with him, I waited and listened for the footsteps of those who would come seeking him. But they did not come. Day after day passed, and still they did not come.

I was in a maze of perplexity. What should I do? I shrank from the thought of the boy being taken away from us. Since we had found him the dream-child had never called. My wife seemed to have turned back from the dark borderland, where her feet had strayed to walk again with me in our own homely paths. Day and night she was her old, bright self, happy and serene in the new motherhood that had come to her. The only thing strange in her was her calm acceptance of the event. She never wondered who or whose the child might be—never seemed to fear that he would be taken from her; and she gave him our dream-child's name.

At last, when a full week had passed, I went, in my bewilderment, to our old doctor.

"A most extraordinary thing," he said thoughtfully. "The child, as you say, must belong to the Spruce Cove people. Yet it is an almost unbelievable thing that there has been no search or inquiry after him. Probably there is some simple explanation of the mystery, however. I advise you to go over to the Cove and inquire. When you find the parents or guardians of the child, ask them to allow you to keep it for a time. It may prove your wife's salvation. I have known such cases. Evidently on that night the crisis of her mental disorder was reached. A little thing might have sufficed to turn her feet either way—back to reason and sanity, or into deeper darkness. It is my belief that the former has occurred, and that, if she is left in undisturbed possession of this child for a time, she will recover completely."

I drove around the harbor that day with a lighter heart than I had hoped ever to possess again. When I reached Spruce Cove the first person I met was old Abel Blair. I asked him if any child were missing from the Cove or along shore. He looked at me in surprise, shook his head, and said he had not heard of any. I told him as much of the tale as was necessary, leaving him to think that my wife and I had found the dory and its small passenger during an ordinary walk along the shore.

"A green dory!" he exclaimed. "Ben Forbes' old green dory has been missing for a week, but it was so rotten and leaky he didn't bother looking for it. But this child, sir—it beats me. What might he be like?"

I described the child as closely as possible.

"That fits little Harry Martin to a hair," said old Abel, perplexedly, "but, sir, it can't be. Or, if it is, there's been foul work somewhere. James Martin's wife died last winter, sir, and he died the next month. They left a baby and not much else. There weren't nobody to take the child but Jim's half-sister, Maggie Fleming. She lived here at the Cove, and, I'm sorry to say, sir, she hadn't too good a name. She didn't want to be bothered with the baby, and folks say she neglected him scandalous. Well, last spring she begun talking of going away to the States. She said a friend of hers had got her a good place in Boston, and she was going to go and take little Harry. We supposed it was all right. Last Saturday she went, sir. She was going to walk to the station, and the last seen of her she was trudging along the road, carrying the baby. It hasn't been thought of since. But, sir, d'ye suppose she set that innocent child adrift in that old leaky dory to send him to his death? I knew Maggie was no better than she should be, but I can't believe she was as bad as that."

"You must come over with me and see if you can identify the child," I said. "If he is Harry

Martin I shall keep him. My wife has been very lonely since our baby died, and she has taken a fancy to this little chap."

When we reached my home old Abel recognized the child as Harry Martin.

He is with us still. His baby hands led my dear wife back to health and happiness. Other children have come to us, she loves them all dearly; but the boy who bears her dead son's name is to her—aye, and to me—as dear as if she had given him birth. He came from the sea, and at his coming the ghostly dream-child fled, nevermore to lure my wife away from me with its exciting cry. Therefore I look upon him and love him as my first-born.

THE BROTHER WHO FAILED

The Monroe family were holding a Christmas reunion at the old Prince Edward Island homestead at White Sands. It was the first time they had all been together under one roof since the death of their mother, thirty years before. The idea of this Christmas reunion had originated with Edith Monroe the preceding spring, during her tedious convalescence from a bad attack of pneumonia among strangers in an American city, where she had not been able to fill her concert engagements, and had more spare time in which to feel the tug of old ties and the homesick longing for her own people than she had had for years. As a result, when she recovered, she wrote to her second brother, James Monroe, who lived on the homestead; and the consequence was this gathering of the Monroes under the old roof-tree. Ralph Monroe for once laid aside the cares of his railroads, and the deceitfulness of his millions, in Toronto and took the long-promised, long-deferred trip to the homeland. Malcolm Monroe journeyed from the far western university of which he was president. Edith came, flushed with the triumph of her latest and most successful concert tour. Mrs. Woodburn, who had been Margaret Monroe, came from the Nova Scotia town where she lived a busy, happy life as the wife of a rising young lawyer. James, prosperous and hearty, greeted them warmly at the old homestead whose fertile acres had well repaid his skillful management.

They were a merry party, casting aside their cares and years, and harking back to joyous boyhood and girlhood once more. James had a family of rosy lads and lasses; Margaret brought her two blue-eyed little girls; Ralph's dark, clever-looking son accompanied him, and Malcolm brought his, a young man with a resolute face, in which there was less of boyishness than in his father's, and the eyes of a keen, perhaps a hard bargainer. The two cousins were the same age to a day, and it was a family joke among the Monroes that the stork must have mixed the babies, since Ralph's son was like Malcolm in face and brain, while Malcolm's boy was a second edition of his uncle Ralph.

To crown all, Aunt Isabel came, too—a talkative, clever, shrewd old lady, as young at eighty-five as she had been at thirty, thinking the Monroe stock the best in the world, and beamingly proud of her nephews and nieces, who had gone out from this humble, little farm to destinies of such brilliance and influence in the world beyond.

I have forgotten Robert. Robert Monroe was apt to be forgotten. Although he was the oldest of the family, White Sands people, in naming over the various members of the Monroe family, would add, "and Robert," in a tone of surprise over the remembrance of his existence.

He lived on a poor, sandy little farm down by the shore, but he had come up to James' place on the evening when the guests arrived; they had all greeted him warmly and joyously, and then did not think about him again in their laughter and conversation. Robert sat back in a corner and listened with a smile, but he never spoke. Afterwards he had slipped noiselessly away and gone home, and nobody noticed his going. They were all gayly busy recalling what had happened in the old times and telling what had happened in the new.

Edith recounted the successes of her concert tours; Malcolm expatiated proudly on his plans for developing his beloved college; Ralph described the country through which his new railroad ran, and the difficulties he had had to overcome in connection with it. James, aside, discussed his orchard and his crops with Margaret, who had not been long enough away from the farm to lose touch with its interests. Aunt Isabel knitted and smiled complacently on all, talking now with one, now with the other, secretly quite proud of herself that she, an old woman of eighty-five, who had seldom been out of White Sands in her life, could discuss high finance with Ralph, and higher education with Malcolm, and hold her own with James in an argument on drainage.

The White Sands school teacher, an arch-eyed, red-mouthed bit a girl—a Bell from Avonlea —who boarded with the James Monroes, amused herself with the boys. All were enjoying themselves hugely, so it is not to be wondered at that they did not miss Robert, who had gone home early because his old housekeeper was nervous if left alone at night.

He came again the next afternoon. From James, in the barnyard, he learned that Malcolm and Ralph had driven to the harbor, that Margaret and Mrs. James had gone to call on friends in Avonlea, and that Edith was walking somewhere in the woods on the hill. There was nobody in the house except Aunt Isabel and the teacher.

"You'd better wait and stay the evening," said James, indifferently. "They'll all be back soon."

Robert went across the yard and sat down on the rustic bench in the angle of the front porch. It was a fine December evening, as mild as autumn; there had been no snow, and the long fields, sloping down from the homestead, were brown and mellow. A weird, dreamy stillness had fallen upon the purple earth, the windless woods, the rain of the valleys, the sere meadows. Nature seemed to have folded satisfied hands to rest, knowing that her long, wintry slumber was coming upon her. Out to sea, a dull, red sunset faded out into somber clouds, and the ceaseless voice of many waters came up from the tawny shore.

Robert rested his chin on his hand and looked across the vales and hills, where the feathery gray of leafless hardwoods was mingled with the sturdy, unfailing green of the conebearers. He was a tall, bent man, with thin, gray hair, a lined face, and deeply-set, gentle brown eyes—the eyes of one who, looking through pain, sees rapture beyond.

He felt very happy. He loved his family clannishly, and he was rejoiced that they were all again near to him. He was proud of their success and fame. He was glad that James had prospered so well of late years. There was no canker of envy or discontent in his soul.

He heard absently indistinct voices at the open hall window above the porch, where Aunt Isabel was talking to Kathleen Bell. Presently Aunt Isabel moved nearer to the window, and her words came down to Robert with startling clearness.

"Yes, I can assure you, Miss Bell, that I'm real proud of my nephews and nieces. They're a smart family. They've almost all done well, and they hadn't any of them much to begin with. Ralph had absolutely nothing and to-day he is a millionaire. Their father met with so many losses, what with his ill-health and the bank failing, that he couldn't help them any. But they've all succeeded, except poor Robert—and I must admit that he's a total failure."

"Oh, no, no," said the little teacher deprecatingly.

"A total failure!" Aunt Isabel repeated her words emphatically. She was not going to be contradicted by anybody, least of all a Bell from Avonlea. "He has been a failure since the time he was born. He is the first Monroe to disgrace the old stock that way. I'm sure his brothers and sisters must be dreadfully ashamed of him. He has lived sixty years and he hasn't done a thing worth while. He can't even make his farm pay. If he's kept out of debt it's as much as he's ever managed to do."

"Some men can't even do that," murmured the little school teacher. She was really so much in awe of this imperious, clever old Aunt Isabel that it was positive heroism on her part to venture even this faint protest.

"More is expected of a Monroe," said Aunt Isabel majestically. "Robert Monroe is a failure, and that is the only name for him."

Robert Monroe stood up below the window in a dizzy, uncertain fashion. Aunt Isabel had been speaking of him! He, Robert, was a failure, a disgrace to his blood, of whom his nearest and dearest were ashamed! Yes, it was true; he had never realized it before; he had known that he could never win power or accumulate riches, but he had not thought that mattered much. Now, through Aunt Isabel's scornful eyes, he saw himself as the world saw him—as his brothers and sisters must see him. THERE lay the sting. What the world thought of him did not matter; but that his own should think him a failure and disgrace was agony. He moaned as he started to walk across the yard, only anxious to hide his pain and shame away from all human sight, and in his eyes was the look of a gentle animal which had been stricken by a cruel and unexpected blow.

Edith Monroe, who, unaware of Robert's proximity, had been standing on the other side of the porch, saw that look, as he hurried past her, unseeing. A moment before her dark eyes had been flashing with anger at Aunt Isabel's words; now the anger was drowned in a sudden rush of tears.

She took a quick step after Robert, but checked the impulse. Not then—and not by her alone—could that deadly hurt be healed. Nay, more, Robert must never suspect that she knew of any hurt. She stood and watched him through her tears as he went away across the low-lying shore fields to hide his broken heart under his own humble roof. She yearned to hurry after him and comfort him, but she knew that comfort was not what Robert needed now. Justice, and justice only, could pluck out the sting, which otherwise must rankle to the death.

Ralph and Malcolm were driving into the yard. Edith went over to them.

"Boys," she said resolutely, "I want to have a talk with you."

The Christmas dinner at the old homestead was a merry one. Mrs. James spread a feast that was fit for the halls of Lucullus. Laughter, jest, and repartee flew from lip to lip. Nobody appeared to notice that Robert ate little, said nothing, and sat with his form shrinking in his shabby "best" suit, his gray head bent even lower than usual, as if desirous of avoiding all observation. When the others spoke to him he answered deprecatingly, and shrank still further into himself.

Finally all had eaten all they could, and the remainder of the plum pudding was carried out. Robert gave a low sigh of relief. It was almost over. Soon he would be able to escape and hide himself and his shame away from the mirthful eyes of these men and women who had earned the right to laugh at the world in which their success gave them power and influence. He—he—only—was a failure.

He wondered impatiently why Mrs. James did not rise. Mrs. James merely leaned comfortably back in her chair, with the righteous expression of one who has done her duty by her fellow creatures' palates, and looked at Malcolm.

Malcolm rose in his place. Silence fell on the company; everybody looked suddenly alert and expectant, except Robert. He still sat with bowed head, wrapped in his own bitterness.

"I have been told that I must lead off," said Malcolm, "because I am supposed to possess the gift of gab. But, if I do, I am not going to use it for any rhetorical effect to-day. Simple, earnest words must express the deepest feelings of the heart in doing justice to its own. Brothers and sisters, we meet to-day under our own roof-tree, surrounded by the benedictions of the past years. Perhaps invisible guests are here—the spirits of those who founded this home and whose work on earth has long been finished. It is not amiss to hope that this is so and our family circle made indeed complete. To each one of us who are here in visible bodily presence some measure of success has fallen; but only one of us has been supremely successful in the only things that really count—the things that count for eternity as well as time—sympathy and unselfishness and self-sacrifice.

"I shall tell you my own story for the benefit of those who have not heard it. When I was a lad of sixteen I started to work out my own education. Some of you will remember that old Mr. Blair of Avonlea offered me a place in his store for the summer, at wages which would go far towards paying my expenses at the country academy the next winter. I went to work, eager and hopeful. All summer I tried to do my faithful best for my employer. In September the blow fell. A sum of money was missing from Mr. Blair's till. I was suspected and discharged in disgrace. All my neighbors believed me guilty; even some of my own family looked upon me with suspicion—nor could I blame them, for the circumstantial evidence was strongly against me."

Ralph and James looked ashamed; Edith and Margaret, who had not been born at the time referred to, lifted their faces innocently. Robert did not move or glance up. He hardly seemed to be listening.

"I was crushed in an agony of shame and despair," continued Malcolm. "I believed my career was ruined. I was bent on casting all my ambitions behind me, and going west to some place where nobody knew me or my disgrace. But there was one person who believed in my innocence, who said to me, 'You shall not give up—you shall not behave as if you were guilty. You are innocent, and in time your innocence will be proved. Meanwhile show yourself a man. You have nearly enough to pay your way next winter at the Academy. I have a little I can give to help you out. Don't give in—never give in when you have done no wrong.'

"I listened and took his advice. I went to the Academy. My story was there as soon as I was, and I found myself sneered at and shunned. Many a time I would have given up in despair, had it not been for the encouragement of my counselor. He furnished the backbone for me. I was determined that his belief in me should be justified. I studied hard and came out at the head of my class. Then there seemed to be no chance of my earning any more money that summer. But a farmer at Newbridge, who cared nothing about the character of his help, if he could get the work out of them, offered to hire me. The prospect was distasteful but, urged by the man who believed in me, I took the place and endured the hardships. Another winter of lonely work passed at the Academy. I won the Farrell Scholarship the last year it was offered, and that meant an Arts course for me. I went to Redmond College. My story was not openly known there, but something of it got abroad, enough to taint my life there also with its suspicion. But the year I graduated, Mr. Blair's nephew, who, as you know, was the real culprit, confessed his guilt, and I was cleared before the world. Since then my career has been what is called a brilliant one. But"—Malcolm turned and laid his hand on Robert's thin shoulder—"all of my success I owe to my brother Robert. It is his success—not mine—and here to-day, since we have agreed to say what is too often left to be said over a coffin lid, I thank him for all he did for me, and tell him that there is nothing I am more proud of and thankful for than such a brother."

Robert had looked up at last, amazed, bewildered, incredulous. His face crimsoned as Malcolm sat down. But now Ralph was getting up.

"I am no orator as Malcolm is," he quoted gayly, "but I've got a story to tell, too, which only one of you knows. Forty years ago, when I started in life as a business man, money wasn't so plentiful with me as it may be to-day. And I needed it badly. A chance came my way to make a pile of it. It wasn't a clean chance. It was a dirty chance. It looked square on the surface; but, underneath, it meant trickery and roguery. I hadn't enough perception to see that, though—I was fool enough to think it was all right. I told Robert what I meant to do. And Robert saw clear through the outward sham to the real, hideous thing underneath. He showed me what it meant and he gave me a preachment about a few Monroe Traditions of truth and honor. I saw what I had been about to do as he saw it—as all good men and true must see it. And I vowed then and there that I'd never go into anything that I wasn't sure was fair and square and clean through and through. I've kept that vow. I am a rich man, and not a dollar of my money is 'tainted' money. But I didn't make it. Robert really made every cent of my money. If it hadn't been for him I'd have been a poor man to-day, or behind prison bars, as are the other men who went into that deal when I backed out. I've got a son here. I hope he'll be as clever as his Uncle Malcolm; but I hope, still more earnestly, that he'll be as good and honorable a man as his Uncle Robert."

By this time Robert's head was bent again, and his face buried in his hands.

"My turn next," said James. "I haven't much to say—only this. After mother died I took typhoid fever. Here I was with no one to wait on me. Robert came and nursed me. He was the most faithful, tender, gentle nurse ever a man had. The doctor said Robert saved my life. I don't suppose any of the rest of us here can say we have saved a life."

Edith wiped away her tears and sprang up impulsively.

"Years ago," she said, "there was a poor, ambitious girl who had a voice. She wanted a musical education and her only apparent chance of obtaining it was to get a teacher's certificate and earn money enough to have her voice trained. She studied hard, but her brains, in mathematics at least, weren't as good as her voice, and the time was short. She failed. She was lost in disappointment and despair, for that was the last year in which it was possible to obtain a teacher's certificate without attending Queen's Academy, and she could not afford that. Then her oldest brother came to her and told her he could spare enough money to send her to the conservatory of music in Halifax for a year. He made her take it. She never knew till long afterwards that he had sold the beautiful horse which he loved like a human creature, to get the money. She went to the Halifax conservatory. She won a musical scholarship. She has had a happy life and a successful career. And she owes it all to her brother Robert—"

But Edith could go no further. Her voice failed her and she sat down in tears. Margaret did not try to stand up.

"I was only five when my mother died," she sobbed. "Robert was both father and mother to me. Never had child or girl so wise and loving a guardian as he was to me. I have never forgotten the lessons he taught me. Whatever there is of good in my life or character I owe to him. I was often headstrong and willful, but he never lost patience with me. I owe everything to Robert."

Suddenly the little teacher rose with wet eyes and crimson cheeks.

"I have something to say, too," she said resolutely. "You have spoken for yourselves. I speak for the people of White Sands. There is a man in this settlement whom everybody loves. I shall tell you some of the things he has done."

"Last fall, in an October storm, the harbor lighthouse flew a flag of distress. Only one man was brave enough to face the danger of sailing to the lighthouse to find out what the trouble was. That was Robert Monroe. He found the keeper alone with a broken leg; and he sailed back and made—yes, MADE the unwilling and terrified doctor go with him to the lighthouse. I saw him when he told the doctor he must go; and I tell you that no man living could have set his will against Robert Monroe's at that moment.

"Four years ago old Sarah Cooper was to be taken to the poorhouse. She was broken-hearted. One man took the poor, bed-ridden, fretful old creature into his home, paid for medical attendance, and waited on her himself, when his housekeeper couldn't endure her tantrums and temper. Sarah Cooper died two years afterwards, and her latest breath was a benediction on Robert Monroe—the best man God ever made.

"Eight years ago Jack Blewitt wanted a place. Nobody would hire him, because his father was in the penitentiary, and some people thought Jack ought to be there, too. Robert Monroe hired him—and helped him, and kept him straight, and got him started right—and Jack Blewitt is a hard-working, respected young man to-day, with every prospect of a useful and honorable life. There is hardly a man, woman, or child in White Sands who doesn't owe something to Robert Monroe!"

As Kathleen Bell sat down, Malcolm sprang up and held out his hands.

"Every one of us stand up and sing Auld Lang Syne," he cried.

Everybody stood up and joined hands, but one did not sing. Robert Monroe stood erect, with a great radiance on his face and in his eyes. His reproach had been taken away; he was crowned among his kindred with the beauty and blessing of sacred yesterdays.

When the singing ceased Malcolm's stern-faced son reached over and shook Robert's hands.

"Uncle Rob," he said heartily, "I hope that when I'm sixty I'll be as successful a man as you."

"I guess," said Aunt Isabel, aside to the little school teacher, as she wiped the tears from her keen old eyes, "that there's a kind of failure that's the best success."

THE RETURN OF HESTER

Just at dusk, that evening, I had gone upstairs and put on my muslin gown. I had been busy all day attending to the strawberry preserving—for Mary Sloane could not be trusted with that—and I was a little tired, and thought it was hardly worth while to change my dress, especially since there was nobody to see or care, since Hester was gone. Mary Sloane did not count.

But I did it because Hester would have cared if she had been here. She always liked to see me neat and dainty. So, although I was tired and sick at heart, I put on my pale blue muslin and dressed my hair.

At first I did my hair up in a way I had always liked; but had seldom worn, because Hester had disapproved of it. It became me; but I suddenly felt as if it were disloyal to her, so I took the puffs down again and arranged my hair in the plain, old-fashioned way she had liked. My hair, though it had a good many gray threads in it, was thick and long and brown still; but that did not matter—nothing mattered since Hester was dead and I had sent Hugh Blair away for the second time.

The Newbridge people all wondered why I had not put on mourning for Hester. I did not tell them it was because Hester had asked me not to. Hester had never approved of mourning; she said that if the heart did not mourn crape would not mend matters; and if it did there was no need of the external trappings of woe. She told me calmly, the night before she died, to go on wearing my pretty dresses just as I had always worn them, and to make no difference in my outward life because of her going.

"I know there will be a difference in your inward life," she said wistfully.

And oh, there was! But sometimes I wondered uneasily, feeling almost conscience-stricken, whether it were wholly because Hester had left me—whether it were not partly because, for a second time, I had shut the door of my heart in the face of love at her bidding.

When I had dressed I went downstairs to the front door, and sat on the sandstone steps under the arch of the Virginia creeper. I was all alone, for Mary Sloane had gone to Avonlea.

It was a beautiful night; the full moon was just rising over the wooded hills, and her light fell through the poplars into the garden before me. Through an open corner on the western side

I saw the sky all silvery blue in the afterlight. The garden was very beautiful just then, for it was the time of the roses, and ours were all out—so many of them—great pink, and red, and white, and yellow roses.

Hester had loved roses and could never have enough of them. Her favorite bush was growing by the steps, all gloried over with blossoms—white, with pale pink hearts. I gathered a cluster and pinned it loosely on my breast. But my eyes filled as I did so—I felt so very, very desolate.

I was all alone, and it was bitter. The roses, much as I loved them, could not give me sufficient companionship. I wanted the clasp of a human hand, and the love-light in human eyes. And then I fell to thinking of Hugh, though I tried not to.

I had always lived alone with Hester. I did not remember our parents, who had died in my babyhood. Hester was fifteen years older than I, and she had always seemed more like a mother than a sister. She had been very good to me and had never denied me anything I wanted, save the one thing that mattered.

I was twenty-five before I ever had a lover. This was not, I think, because I was more unattractive than other women. The Merediths had always been the "big" family of Newbridge. The rest of the people looked up to us, because we were the granddaughters of old Squire Meredith. The Newbridge young men would have thought it no use to try to woo a Meredith.

I had not a great deal of family pride, as perhaps I should be ashamed to confess. I found our exalted position very lonely, and cared more for the simple joys of friendship and companionship which other girls had. But Hester possessed it in a double measure; she never allowed me to associate on a level of equality with the young people of Newbridge. We must be very nice and kind and affable to them—*noblesse oblige*, as it were—but we must never forget that we were Merediths.

When I was twenty-five, Hugh Blair came to Newbridge, having bought a farm near the village. He was a stranger, from Lower Carmody, and so was not imbued with any preconceptions of Meredith superiority. In his eyes I was just a girl like others—a girl to be wooed and won by any man of clean life and honest heart. I met him at a little Sunday-School picnic over at Avonlea, which I attended because of my class. I thought him very handsome and manly. He talked to me a great deal, and at last he drove me home. The next Sunday evening he walked up from church with me.

Hester was away, or, of course, this would never have happened. She had gone for a month's visit to distant friends.

In that month I lived a lifetime. Hugh Blair courted me as the other girls in Newbridge were courted. He took me out driving and came to see me in the evenings, which we spent for the most part in the garden. I did not like the stately gloom and formality of our old Meredith parlor, and Hugh never seemed to feel at ease there. His broad shoulders and hearty laughter were oddly out of place among our faded, old-maidish furnishings.

Mary Sloane was very much pleased at Hugh's visit. She had always resented the fact that I had never had a "beau," seeming to think it reflected some slight or disparagement upon me. She did all she could to encourage him.

But when Hester returned and found out about Hugh she was very angry—and grieved, which hurt me far more. She told me that I had forgotten myself and that Hugh's visits must cease.

I had never been afraid of Hester before, but I was afraid of her then. I yielded. Perhaps it was very weak of me, but then I was always weak. I think that was why Hugh's strength had appealed so to me. I needed love and protection. Hester, strong and self-sufficient, had never felt such a need. She could not understand. Oh, how contemptuous she was.

I told Hugh timidly that Hester did not approve of our friendship and that it must end. He took it quietly enough, and went away. I thought he did not care much, and the thought selfishly made my own heartache worse. I was very unhappy for a long time, but I tried not to let Hester see it, and I don't think she did. She was not very discerning in some things.

After a time I got over it; that is, the heartache ceased to ache all the time. But things were never quite the same again. Life always seemed rather dreary and empty, in spite of Hester and my roses and my Sunday-School.

I supposed that Hugh Blair would find him a wife elsewhere, but he did not. The years went by and we never met, although I saw him often at church. At such times Hester always watched me very closely, but there was no need of her to do so. Hugh made no attempt to meet me, or speak with me, and I would not have permitted it if he had. But my heart always yearned after him. I was selfishly glad he had not married, because if he had I could not have thought and dreamed of him—it would have been wrong. Perhaps, as it was, it was foolish; but it seemed to me that I must have something, if only foolish dreams, to fill my life.

At first there was only pain in the thought of him, but afterwards a faint, misty little pleasure crept in, like a mirage from a land of lost delight.

Ten years slipped away thus. And then Hester died. Her illness was sudden and short; but, before she died, she asked me to promise that I would never marry Hugh Blair.

She had not mentioned his name for years. I thought she had forgotten all about him.

"Oh, dear sister, is there any need of such a promise?" I asked, weeping. "Hugh Blair does not want to marry me now. He never will again."

"He has never married—he has not forgotten you," she said fiercely. "I could not rest in my grave if I thought you would disgrace your family by marrying beneath you. Promise me, Margaret."

I promised. I would have promised anything in my power to make her dying pillow easier. Besides, what did it matter? I was sure that Hugh would never think of me again.

She smiled when she heard me, and pressed my hand.

"Good little sister—that is right. You were always a good girl, Margaret—good and obedient, though a little sentimental and foolish in some ways. You are like our mother—she was always weak and loving. I took after the Merediths."

She did, indeed. Even in her coffin her dark, handsome features preserved their expression of pride and determination. Somehow, that last look of her dead face remained in my memory, blotting out the real affection and gentleness which her living face had almost always shown me. This distressed me, but I could not help it. I wished to think of her as kind and loving, but I could remember only the pride and coldness with which she had crushed out my new-born happiness. Yet I felt no anger or resentment towards her for what she had done. I knew she had meant it for the best—my best. It was only that she was mistaken.

And then, a month after she had died, Hugh Blair came to me and asked me to be his wife. He said he had always loved me, and could never love any other woman.

All my old love for him reawakened. I wanted to say yes—to feel his strong arms about me, and the warmth of his love enfolding and guarding me. In my weakness I yearned for his strength.

But there was my promise to Hester—that promise give by her deathbed. I could not break it, and I told him so. It was the hardest thing I had ever done.

He did not go away quietly this time. He pleaded and reasoned and reproached. Every word of his hurt me like a knife-thrust. But I could not break my promise to the dead. If Hester had been living I would have braved her wrath and her estrangement and gone to him. But she was dead and I could not do it.

Finally he went away in grief and anger. That was three weeks ago—and now I sat alone in the moonlit rose-garden and wept for him. But after a time my tears dried and a very strange feeling came over me. I felt calm and happy, as if some wonderful love and tenderness were very near me.

And now comes the strange part of my story—the part which will not, I suppose, be believed. If it were not for one thing I think I should hardly believe it myself. I should feel tempted to think I had dreamed it. But because of that one thing I know it was real. The night was very calm and still. Not a breath of wind stirred. The moonshine was the brightest I had ever seen. In the middle of the garden, where the shadow of the poplars did not fall, it was almost as bright as day. One could have read fine print. There was still a little rose glow in the west, and over the airy boughs of the tall poplars one or two large, bright stars were shining. The air was sweet with a hush of dreams, and the world was so lovely that I held my breath over its beauty.

Then, all at once, down at the far end of the garden, I saw a woman walking. I thought at first that it must be Mary Sloane; but, as she crossed a moonlit path, I saw it was not our old servant's stout, homely figure. This woman was tall and erect.

Although no suspicion of the truth came to me, something about her reminded me of Hester. Even so had Hester liked to wander about the garden in the twilight. I had seen her thus a thousand times.

I wondered who the woman could be. Some neighbor, of course. But what a strange way for her to come! She walked up the garden slowly in the poplar shade. Now and then she stooped, as if to caress a flower, but she plucked none. Half way up she out in to the moonlight and walked across the plot of grass in the center of the garden. My heart gave a great throb and I stood up. She was quite near to me now—and I saw that it was Hester.

I can hardly say just what my feelings were at this moment. I know that I was not surprised. I was frightened and yet I was not frightened. Something in me shrank back in a sickening terror; but *I*, the real I, was not frightened. I knew that this was my sister, and that there could be no reason why I should be frightened of her, because she loved me still, as she had always done. Further than this I was not conscious of any coherent thought, either of wonder or attempt at reasoning.

Hester paused when she came to within a few steps of me. In the moonlight I saw her face quite plainly. It wore an expression I had never before seen on it—a humble, wistful, tender look. Often in life Hester had looked lovingly, even tenderly, upon me; but always, as it were, through a mask of pride and sternness. This was gone now, and I felt nearer to her than ever before. I knew suddenly that she understood me. And then the half-conscious awe and terror some part of me had felt vanished, and I only realized that Hester was here, and that there was no terrible gulf of change between us.

Hester beckoned to me and said,

"Come."

I stood up and followed her out of the garden. We walked side by side down our lane, under the willows and out to the road, which lay long and still in that bright, calm moonshine. I felt as if I were in a dream, moving at the bidding of a will not my own, which I could not have disputed even if I had wished to do so. But I did not wish it; I had only the feeling of a strange, boundless content.

We went down the road between the growths of young fir that bordered it. I smelled their balsam as we passed, and noticed how clearly and darkly their pointed tops came out against the sky. I heard the tread of my own feet on little twigs and plants in our way, and the trail of my dress over the grass; but Hester moved noiselessly.

Then we went through the Avenue—that stretch of road under the apple trees that Anne Shirley, over at Avonlea, calls "The White Way of Delight." It was almost dark here; and yet I could see Hester's face just as plainly as if the moon were shining on it; and whenever I looked at her she was always looking at me with that strangely gentle smile on her lips.

Just as we passed out of the Avenue, James Trent overtook us, driving. It seems to me that our feelings at a given moment are seldom what we would expect them to be. I simply felt annoyed that James Trent, the most notorious gossip in Newbridge, should have seen me walking with Hester. In a flash I anticipated all the annoyance of it; he would talk of the matter far and wide.

But James Trent merely nodded and called out,

"Howdy, Miss Margaret. Taking a moonlight stroll by yourself? Lovely night, ain't it?"

Just then his horse suddenly swerved, as if startled, and broke into a gallop. They whirled around the curve of the road in an instant. I felt relieved, but puzzled. JAMES TRENT HAD NOT SEEN HESTER.

Down over the hill was Hugh Blair's place. When we came to it, Hester turned in at the gate. Then, for the first time, I understood why she had come back, and a blinding flash of joy broke over my soul. I stopped and looked at her. Her deep eyes gazed into mine, but she did not speak.

We went on. Hugh's house lay before us in the moonlight, grown over by a tangle of vines. His garden was on our right, a quaint spot, full of old-fashioned flowers growing in a sort of disorderly sweetness. I trod on a bed of mint, and the spice of it floated up to me like the incense of some strange, sacred, solemn ceremonial. I felt unspeakably happy and blessed.

When we came to the door Hester said,

"Knock, Margaret."

I rapped gently. In a moment, Hugh opened it. Then that happened by which, in after days, I was to know that this strange thing was no dream or fancy of mine. Hugh looked not at me, but past me.

"Hester!" he exclaimed, with human fear and horror in his voice.

He leaned against the door-post, the big, strong fellow, trembling from head to foot.

"I have learned," said Hester, "that nothing matters in all God's universe, except love. There is no pride where I have been, and no false ideals."

Hugh and I looked into each other's eyes, wondering, and then we knew that we were alone.

THE LITTLE BROWN BOOK OF MISS EMILY

The first summer Mr. Irving and Miss Lavendar—Diana and I could never call her anything else, even after she was married—were at Echo Lodge after their marriage, both Diana and I spent a great deal of time with them. We became acquainted with many of the Grafton people whom we had not known before, and among others, the family of Mr. Mack Leith. We often went up to the Leiths in the evening to play croquet. Millie and Margaret Leith were very nice girls, and the boys were nice, too. Indeed, we liked every one in the family, except poor old Miss Emily Leith. We tried hard enough to like her, because she seemed to like Diana and me very much, and always wanted to sit with us and talk to us, when we would much rather have been somewhere else. We often felt a good deal of impatience at these times, but I am very glad to think now that we never showed it.

In a way, we felt sorry for Miss Emily. She was Mr. Leith's old-maid sister and she was not of much importance in the household. But, though we felt sorry for her, we couldn't like her. She really was fussy and meddlesome; she liked to poke a finger into every one's pie, and she was not at all tactful. Then, too, she had a sarcastic tongue, and seemed to feel bitter towards all the young folks and their love affairs. Diana and I thought this was because she had never had a lover of her own.

Somehow, it seemed impossible to think of lovers in connection with Miss Emily. She was short and stout and pudgy, with a face so round and fat and red that it seemed quite featureless; and her hair was scanty and gray. She walked with a waddle, just like Mrs. Rachel Lynde, and she was always rather short of breath. It was hard to believe Miss Emily had ever been young; yet old Mr. Murray, who lived next door to the Leiths, not only expected us to believe it, but assured us that she had been very pretty.

"THAT, at least, is impossible," said Diana to me.

And then, one day, Miss Emily died. I'm afraid no one was very sorry. It seems to me a most dreadful thing to go out of the world and leave not one person behind to be sorry because you have gone. Miss Emily was dead and buried before Diana and I heard of it at all. The first I knew of it was when I came home from Orchard Slope one day and found a queer, shabby little black horsehair trunk, all studded with brass nails, on the floor of my room at Green Gables. Marilla told me that Jack Leith had brought it over, and said that it had belonged to Miss Emily and that, when she was dying, she asked them to send it to me.

"But what is in it? And what am I to do with it?" I asked in bewilderment.

"There was nothing said about what you were to do with it. Jack said they didn't know what was in it, and hadn't looked into it, seeing that it was your property. It seems a rather queer proceeding—but you're always getting mixed up in queer proceedings, Anne. As for what is in it, the easiest way to find out, I reckon, is to open it and see. The key is tied to it. Jack said Miss Emily said she wanted you to have it because she loved you and saw her lost youth in you. I guess she was a bit delirious at the last and wandered a good deal. She said she wanted you 'to understand her.'"

I ran over to Orchard Slope and asked Diana to come over and examine the trunk with me. I hadn't received any instructions about keeping its contents secret and I knew Miss Emily wouldn't mind Diana knowing about them, whatever they were.

It was a cool, gray afternoon and we got back to Green Gables just as the rain was beginning to fall. When we went up to my room the wind was rising and whistling through the boughs of the big old Snow Queen outside of my window. Diana was excited, and, I really believe, a little bit frightened.

We opened the old trunk. It was very small, and there was nothing in it but a big cardboard box. The box was tied up and the knots sealed with wax. We lifted it out and untied it. I touched Diana's fingers as we did it, and both of us exclaimed at once, "How cold your hand is!"

In the box was a quaint, pretty, old-fashioned gown, not at all faded, made of blue muslin, with a little darker blue flower in it. Under it we found a sash, a yellowed feather fan, and an envelope full of withered flowers. At the bottom of the box was a little brown book.

It was small and thin, like a girl's exercise book, with leaves that had once been blue and pink, but were now quite faded, and stained in places. On the fly leaf was written, in a very delicate hand, "Emily Margaret Leith," and the same writing covered the first few pages of the book. The rest were not written on at all. We sat there on the floor, Diana and I, and read the little book together, while the rain thudded against the window panes.

June 19, 18—

I came to-day to spend a while with Aunt Margaret in Charlottetown. It is so pretty here, where she lives—and ever so much nicer than on the farm at home. I have no cows to milk here or pigs to feed. Aunt Margaret has given me such a lovely blue muslin dress, and I am to have it made to wear at a garden party out at Brighton next week. I never had a muslin dress before—nothing but ugly prints and dark woolens. I wish we were rich, like Aunt Margaret. Aunt Margaret laughed when I said this, and declared she would give all her wealth for my youth and beauty and ight-heartedness. I am only eighteen and I know I am very merry but I wonder if I am really pretty. It seems to me that I am when I look in Aunt Margaret's beautiful mirrors. They make me look very different from the old cracked one in my room at home which always twisted my face and turned me green. But Aunt Margaret spoiled her compliment by telling me I look exactly as she did at my age. If I thought I'd ever look as Aunt Margaret does now, I don't know what I'd do. She is so fat and red.

June 29.

Last week I went to the garden party and I met a young man called Paul Osborne. He is a young artist from Montreal who is boarding over at Heppoch. He is the handsomest man I have ever seen—very tall and slender, with dreamy, dark eyes and a pale, clever face. I have not been able to keep from thinking about him ever since, and to-day he came over here and asked if he could paint me. I felt very much flattered and so pleased when Aunt Margaret gave him permission. He says he wants to paint me as "Spring," standing under the poplars where a fine rain of sunshine falls through. I am to wear my blue muslin gown and a wreath of flowers on my hair. He says I have such beautiful hair. He has never seen any of such a real pale gold. Somehow it seems even prettier than ever to me since he praised it.

I had a letter from home to-day. Ma says the blue hen stole her nest and came off with fourteen chickens, and that pa has sold the little spotted calf. Somehow those things don't interest me like they once did.

July 9.

The picture is coming on very well, Mr. Osborne says. I know he is making me look far too pretty in it, although he persists in saying he can't do me justice. He is going to send it to some great exhibition when finished, but he says he will make a little water-color copy for me.

He comes every day to paint and we talk a great deal and he reads me lovely things out of his books. I don't understand them all, but I try to, and he explains them so nicely and is so patient with my stupidity. And he says any one with my eyes and hair and coloring does not need to be clever. He says I have the sweetest, merriest laugh in the world. But I will not write down all the compliments he has paid me. I dare say he does not mean them at all.

In the evening we stroll among the spruces or sit on the bench under the acacia tree. Sometimes we don't talk at all, but I never find the time long. Indeed, the minutes just seem to fly—and then the moon will come up, round and red, over the harbor and Mr. Osborne will sigh and say he supposes it is time for him to go.

July 24.

I am so happy. I am frightened at my happiness. Oh, I didn't think life could ever be so beautiful for me as it is! Paul loves me! He told me so to-night as we walked by the harbor and watched the sunset, and he asked me to be his wife. I have cared for him ever since I met him, but I am afraid I am not clever and well-educated enough for a wife for Paul. Because, of course, I'm only an ignorant little country girl and have lived all my life on a farm. Why, my hands are quite rough yet from the work I've done. But Paul just laughed when I said so, and took my hands and kissed them. Then he looked into my eyes and laughed again, because I couldn't hide from him how much I loved him.

We are to be married next spring and Paul says he will take me to Europe. That will be very nice, but nothing matters so long as I am with him.

Paul's people are very wealthy and his mother and sisters are very fashionable. I am frightened of them, but I did not tell Paul so because I think it would hurt him and oh, I wouldn't do that for the world.

There is nothing I wouldn't suffer if it would do him any good. I never thought any one could feel so. I used to think if I loved anybody I would want him to do everything for me and wait on me as if I were a princess. But that is not the way at all. Love makes you very humble and you want to do everything yourself for the one you love.

August 10.

Paul went home to-day. Oh, it is so terrible! I don't know how I can bear to live even for a little while without him. But this is silly of me, because I know he has to go and he will write often and come to me often. But, still, it is so lonesome. I didn't cry when he left me because I wanted him to remember me smiling in the way he liked best, but I have been crying ever since and I can't stop, no matter how hard I try. We have had such a beautiful fortnight. Every day seemed dearer and happier than the last, and now it is ended and I feel as if it could never be the same again. Oh, I am very foolish—but I love him so dearly and if I were to lose his love I know I would die.

August 17.

I think my heart is dead. But no, it can't be, for it aches too much.

Paul's mother came here to see me to-day. She was not angry or disagreeable. I wouldn't have been so frightened of her if she had been. As it was, I felt that I couldn't say a word. She is very beautiful and stately and wonderful, with a low, cold voice and proud, dark eyes. Her face is like Paul's but without the loveableness of his.

She talked to me for a long time and she said terrible things—terrible, because I knew they were all true. I seemed to see everything through her eyes. She said that Paul was infatuated with my youth and beauty but that it would not last and what else had I to give him? She said Paul must marry a woman of his own class, who could do honor to his fame and position. She said that he was very talented and had a great career before him, but that if he married me it would ruin his life.

I saw it all, just as she explained it out, and I told her at last that I would not marry Paul, and she might tell him so. But she smiled and said I must tell him myself, because he would not believe any one else. I could have begged her to spare me that, but I knew it would be of no use. I do not think she has any pity or mercy for any one. Besides, what she said was quite true.

When she thanked me for being so REASONABLE I told her I was not doing it to please her, but for Paul's sake, because I would not spoil his life, and that I would always hate her. She smiled again and went away.

Oh, how can I bear it? I did not know any one could suffer like this!

August 18.

I have done it. I wrote to Paul to-day. I knew I must tell him by letter, because I could never make him believe it face to face. I was afraid I could not even do it by letter. I suppose a clever woman easily could, but I am so stupid. I wrote a great many letters and tore them up, because I felt sure they wouldn't convince Paul. At last I got one that I thought would do. I knew I must make it seem as if I were very frivolous and heartless, or he would never believe. I spelled some words wrong and put in some mistakes of grammar on purpose. I told him I had just been flirting with him, and that I had another fellow at home I liked better. I said FELLOW because I knew it would disgust him. I said that it was only because he was rich that I was tempted to marry him.

I thought my heart would break while I was writing those dreadful falsehoods. But it was for his sake, because I must not spoil his life. His mother told me I would be a millstone around his neck. I love Paul so much that I would do anything rather than be that. It would be easy to die for him, but I don't see how I can go on living. I think my letter will convince Paul.

I suppose it convinced Paul, because there was no further entry in the little brown book. When we had finished it the tears were running down both our faces.

"Oh, poor, dear Miss Emily," sobbed Diana. "I'm so sorry I ever thought her funny and meddlesome."

"She was good and strong and brave," I said. "I could never have been as unselfish as she was."

I thought of Whittier's lines,

"The outward, wayward life we see
The hidden springs we may not know."

At the back of the little brown book we found a faded water-color sketch of a young girl—such a slim, pretty little thing, with big blue eyes and lovely, long, rippling golden hair. Paul Osborne's name was written in faded ink across the corner.

We put everything back in the box. Then we sat for a long time by my window in silence and thought of many things, until the rainy twilight came down and blotted out the world.

SARA'S WAY

The warm June sunshine was coming down through the trees, white with the virginal bloom of apple-blossoms, and through the shining panes, making a tremulous mosaic upon Mrs. Eben Andrews' spotless kitchen floor. Through the open door, a wind, fragrant from long wanderings over orchards and clover meadows, drifted in, and, from the window, Mrs. Eben and her guest could look down over a long, misty valley sloping to a sparkling sea.

Mrs. Jonas Andrews was spending the afternoon with her sister-in-law. She was a big, sonsy woman, with full-blown peony cheeks and large, dreamy, brown eyes. When she had been a slim, pink-and-white girl those eyes had been very romantic. Now they were so out of keeping with the rest of her appearance as to be ludicrous.

Mrs. Eben, sitting at the other end of the small tea-table that was drawn up against the window, was a thin little woman, with a very sharp nose and light, faded blue eyes. She looked like a woman whose opinions were always very decided and warranted to wear.

"How does Sara like teaching at Newbridge?" asked Mrs. Jonas, helping herself a second time to Mrs. Eben's matchless black fruit cake, and thereby bestowing a subtle compliment which Mrs. Eben did not fail to appreciate.

"Well, I guess she likes it pretty well—better than down at White Sands, anyway," answered Mrs. Eben. "Yes, I may say it suits her. Of course it's a long walk there and back. I think it would have been wiser for her to keep on boarding at Morrison's, as she did all winter, but Sara is bound to be home all she can. And I must say the walk seems to agree with her."

"I was down to see Jonas' aunt at Newbridge last night," said Mrs. Jonas, "and she said she'd heard that Sara had made up her mind to take Lige Baxter at last, and that they were to be married in the fall. She asked me if it was true. I said I didn't know, but I hoped to mercy it was. Now, is it, Louisa?"

"Not a word of it," said Mrs. Eben sorrowfully. "Sara hasn't any more notion of taking Lige than ever she had. I'm sure it's not MY fault. I've talked and argued till I'm tired. I declare to you, Amelia, I am terribly disappointed. I'd set my heart on Sara's marrying Lige—and now to think she won't!"

"She is a very foolish girl," said Mrs. Jonas, judicially. "If Lige Baxter isn't good enough for her, who is?"

"And he's so well off," said Mrs. Eben, "and does such a good business, and is well spoken of by every one. And that lovely new house of his at Newbridge, with bay windows and hardwood floors! I've dreamed and dreamed of seeing Sara there as mistress."

"Maybe you'll see her there yet," said Mrs. Jonas, who always took a hopeful view of everything, even of Sara's contrariness. But she felt discouraged, too. Well, she had done her best.

If Lige Baxter's broth was spoiled it was not for lack of cooks. Every Andrews in Avonlea had been trying for two years to bring about a match between him and Sara, and Mrs. Jonas had borne her part valiantly.

Mrs. Eben's despondent reply was cut short by the appearance of Sara herself. The girl stood for a moment in the doorway and looked with a faintly amused air at her aunts. She knew quite well that they had been discussing her, for Mrs. Jonas, who carried her conscience in her face, looked guilty, and Mrs. Eben had not been able wholly to banish her aggrieved expression.

Sara put away her books, kissed Mrs. Jonas' rosy cheek, and sat down at the table. Mrs. Eben brought her some fresh tea, some hot rolls, and a little jelly-pot of the apricot preserves Sara liked, and she cut some more fruit cake for her in moist plummy slices. She might be out of patience with Sara's "contrariness," but she spoiled and petted her for all that, for the girl was the very core of her childless heart.

Sara Andrews was not, strictly speaking, pretty; but there was that about her which made people look at her twice. She was very dark, with a rich, dusky sort of darkness, her deep eyes were velvety brown, and her lips and cheeks were crimson.

She ate her rolls and preserves with a healthy appetite, sharpened by her long walk from Newbridge, and told amusing little stories of her day's work that made the two older women shake with laughter, and exchange shy glances of pride over her cleverness.

When tea was over she poured the remaining contents of the cream jug into a saucer.

"I must feed my pussy," she said as she left the room.

"That girl beats me," said Mrs. Eben with a sigh of perplexity. "You know that black cat we've had for two years? Eben and I have always made a lot of him, but Sara seemed to have a dislike to him. Never a peaceful nap under the stove could he have when Sara was home—out he must go. Well, a little spell ago he got his leg broke accidentally and we thought he'd have to be killed. But Sara wouldn't hear of it. She got splints and set his leg just as knacky, and bandaged it up, and she has tended him like a sick baby ever since. He's just about well now, and he lives in clover, that cat does. It's just her way. There's them sick chickens she's been doctoring for a week, giving them pills and things!

"And she thinks more of that wretched-looking calf that got poisoned with paris green than of all the other stock on the place."

As the summer wore away, Mrs. Eben tried to reconcile herself to the destruction of her air castles. But she scolded Sara considerably.

"Sara, why don't you like Lige? I'm sure he is a model young man."

"I don't like model young men," answered Sara impatiently. "And I really think I hate Lige Baxter. He has always been held up to me as such a paragon. I'm tired of hearing about all his perfections. I know them all off by heart. He doesn't drink, he doesn't smoke, he doesn't steal, he doesn't tell fibs, he never loses his temper, he doesn't swear, and he goes to church regularly. Such a faultless creature as that would certainly get on my nerves. No, no, you'll have to pick out another mistress for your new house at the Bridge, Aunt Louisa."

When the apple trees, that had been pink and white in June, were russet and bronze in October, Mrs. Eben had a quilting. The quilt was of the "Rising Star" pattern, which was considered in Avonlea to be very handsome. Mrs. Eben had intended it for part of Sara's "setting out," and, while she sewed the red-and-white diamonds together, she had regaled her fancy by imagining she saw it spread out on the spare-room bed of the house at Newbridge, with herself laying her bonnet and shawl on it when she went to see Sara. Those bright visions had faded with the apple blossoms, and Mrs. Eben hardly had the heart to finish the quilt at all.

The quilting came off on Saturday afternoon, when Sara could be home from school. All Mrs. Eben's particular friends were ranged around the quilt, and tongues and fingers flew. Sara flitted about, helping her aunt with the supper preparations. She was in the room, getting the custard dishes out of the cupboard, when Mrs. George Pye arrived.

Mrs. George had a genius for being late. She was later than usual to-day, and she looked excited. Every woman around the "Rising Star" felt that Mrs. George had some news worth listening to, and there was an expectant silence while she pulled out her chair and settled herself at the quilt.

She was a tall, thin woman with a long pale face and liquid green eyes. As she looked around the circle she had the air of a cat daintily licking its chops over some titbit.

"I suppose," she said, "that you have heard the news?"

She knew perfectly well that they had not. Every other woman at the frame stopped quilting. Mrs. Eben came to the door with a pan of puffy, smoking-hot soda biscuits in her hand. Sara stopped counting the custard dishes, and turned her ripely-colored face over her shoulder. Even the black cat, at her feet, ceased preening his fur. Mrs. George felt that the undivided attention of her audience was hers.

"Baxter Brothers have failed," she said, her green eyes shooting out flashes of light. "Failed DISGRACEFULLY!"

She paused for a moment; but, since her hearers were as yet speechless from surprise, she went on.

"George came home from Newbridge, just before I left, with the news. You could have knocked me down with a feather. I should have thought that firm was as steady as the Rock of Gibraltar! But they're ruined—absolutely ruined. Louisa, dear, can you find me a good needle?"

"Louisa, dear," had set her biscuits down with a sharp thud, reckless of results. A sharp, metallic tinkle sounded at the closet where Sara had struck the edge of her tray against a shelf. The sound seemed to loosen the paralyzed tongues, and everybody began talking and exclaiming at once. Clear and shrill above the confusion rose Mrs. George Pye's voice.

"Yes, indeed, you may well say so. It IS disgraceful. And to think how everybody trusted them! George will lose considerable by the crash, and so will a good many folks. Everything will have to go—Peter Baxter's farm and Lige's grand new house. Mrs. Peter won't carry her head so high after this, I'll be bound. George saw Lige at the Bridge, and he said he looked dreadful cut up and ashamed."

"Who, or what's to blame for the failure?" asked Mrs. Rachel Lynde sharply. She did not like Mrs. George Pye.

"There are a dozen different stories on the go," was the reply. "As far as George could make out, Peter Baxter has been speculating with other folks' money, and this is the result. Everybody always suspected that Peter was crooked; but you'd have thought that Lige would have kept him straight. HE had always such a reputation for saintliness."

"I don't suppose Lige knew anything about it," said Mrs. Rachel indignantly.

"Well, he'd ought to, then. If he isn't a knave he's a fool," said Mrs. Harmon Andrews, who had formerly been among his warmest partisans. "He should have kept watch on Peter and found out how the business was being run. Well, Sara, you were the level-headest of us all—I'll admit that now. A nice mess it would be if you were married or engaged to Lige, and him left without a cent—even if he can clear his character!"

"There is a good deal of talk about Peter, and swindling, and a lawsuit," said Mrs. George Pye, quilting industriously. "Most of the Newbridge folks think it's all Peter's fault, and that Lige isn't to blame. But you can't tell. I dare say Lige is as deep in the mire as Peter. He was always a little too good to be wholesome, *I* thought."

There was a clink of glass at the cupboard, as Sara set the tray down. She came forward and stood behind Mrs. Rachel Lynde's chair, resting her shapely hands on that lady's broad shoulders. Her face was very pale, but her flashing eyes sought and faced defiantly Mrs. George Pye's cat-like orbs. Her voice quivered with passion and contempt.

"You'll all have a fling at Lige Baxter, now that he's down. You couldn't say enough in his praise, once. I'll not stand by and hear it hinted that Lige Baxter is a swindler. You all know perfectly well that Lige is as honest as the day, if he IS so unfortunate as to have an unprincipled brother. You, Mrs. Pye, know it better than any one, yet you come here and run him down the minute he's in trouble. If there's another word said here against Lige Baxter I'll leave the room and the house till you're gone, every one of you."

She flashed a glance around the quilt that cowed the gossips. Even Mrs. George Pye's eyes flickered and waned and quailed. Nothing more was said until Sara had picked up her glasses and marched from the room. Even then they dared not speak above a whisper. Mrs. Pye, alone, smarting from the snub, ventured to ejaculate, "Pity save us!" as Sara slammed the door.

For the next fortnight gossip and rumor held high carnival in Avonlea and Newbridge, and Mrs. Eben grew to dread the sight of a visitor.

"They're bound to talk about the Baxter failure and criticize Lige," she deplored to Mrs. Jonas. "And it riles Sara up so terrible. She used to declare that she hated Lige, and now she won't listen to a word against him. Not that I say any, myself. I'm sorry for him, and I believe he's done his best. But I can't stop other people from talking."

One evening Harmon Andrews came in with a fresh budget of news.

"The Baxter business is pretty near wound up at last," he said, as he lighted his pipe. "Peter has got his lawsuits settled and has hushed up the talk about swindling, somehow. Trust him for slipping out of a scrape clean and clever. He don't seem to worry any, but Lige looks like a walking skeleton. Some folks pity him, but I say he should have kept the run of things better and not have trusted everything to Peter. I hear he's going out West in the Spring, to take up land in Alberta and try his hand at farming. Best thing he can do, I guess. Folks hereabouts have had enough of the Baxter breed. Newbridge will be well rid of them."

Sara, who had been sitting in the dark corner by the stove, suddenly stood up, letting the black cat slip from her lap to the floor. Mrs. Eben glanced at her apprehensively, for she was afraid the girl was going to break out in a tirade against the complacent Harmon.

But Sara only walked fiercely out of the kitchen, with a sound as if she were struggling for breath. In the hall she snatched a scarf from the wall, flung open the front door, and rushed down the lane in the chill, pure air of the autumn twilight. Her heart was throbbing with the pity she always felt for bruised and baited creatures.

On and on she went heedlessly, intent only on walking away her pain, over gray, brooding fields and winding slopes, and along the skirts of ruinous, dusky pine woods, curtained with fine spun purple gloom. Her dress brushed against the brittle grasses and sere ferns, and the moist night wind, loosed from wild places far away, blew her hair about her face.

At last she came to a little rustic gate, leading into a shadowy wood-lane. The gate was bound with willow withes, and, as Sara fumbled vainly at them with her chilled hands, a man's firm step came up behind her, and Lige Baxter's hand closed over her's.

"Oh, Lige!" she said, with something like a sob.

He opened the gate and drew her through. She left her hand in his, as they walked through the lane where lissome boughs of young saplings flicked against their heads, and the air was wildly sweet with the woodsy odors.

"It's a long while since I've seen you, Lige," Sara said at last.

Lige looked wistfully down at her through the gloom.

"Yes, it seems very long to me, Sara. But I didn't think you'd care to see me, after what you said last spring. And you know things have been going against me. People have said hard things. I've been unfortunate, Sara, and may be too easy-going, but I've been honest. Don't believe folks if they tell you I wasn't."

"Indeed, I never did—not for a minute!" fired Sara.

"I'm glad of that. I'm going away, later on. I felt bad enough when you refused to marry me, Sara; but it's well that you didn't. I'm man enough to be thankful my troubles don't fall on you."

Sara stopped and turned to him. Beyond them the lane opened into a field and a clear lake of crocus sky cast a dim light into the shadow where they stood. Above it was a new moon, like a gleaming silver scimitar. Sara saw it was over her left shoulder, and she saw Lige's face above her, tender and troubled.

"Lige," she said softly, "do you love me still?"

"You know I do," said Lige sadly.

That was all Sara wanted. With a quick movement she nestled into his arms, and laid her warm, tear-wet cheek against his cold one.

When the amazing rumor that Sara was going to marry Lige Baxter, and go out West with him, circulated through the Andrews clan, hands were lifted and heads were shaken. Mrs. Jonas puffed and panted up the hill to learn if it were true. She found Mrs. Eben stitching for dear life on an "Irish Chain" quilt, while Sara was sewing the diamonds on another "Rising Star" with a martyr-like expression on her face. Sara hated patchwork above everything else, but Mrs. Eben was mistress up to a certain point.

"You'll have to make that quilt, Sara Andrews. If you're going to live out on those prairies, you'll need piles of quilts, and you shall have them if I sew my fingers to the bone. But you'll have to help make them."

And Sara had to.

When Mrs. Jonas came, Mrs. Eben sent Sara off to the post-office to get her out of the way.

"I suppose it's true, this time?" said Mrs. Jonas.

"Yes, indeed," said Mrs. Eben briskly. "Sara is set on it. There is no use trying to move her—you know that—so I've just concluded to make the best of it. I'm no turn-coat. Lige Baxter is Lige Baxter still, neither more nor less. I've always said he's a fine young man, and I say so still. After all, he and Sara won't be any poorer than Eben and I were when we started out."

Mrs. Jonas heaved a sigh of relief.

"I'm real glad you take that view of it, Louisa. I'm not displeased, either, although Mrs. Harmon would take my head off if she heard me say so. I always liked Lige. But I must say I'm amazed, too, after the way Sara used to rail at him."

"Well, we might have expected it," said Mrs. Eben sagely. "It was always Sara's way. When any creature got sick or unfortunate she seemed to take it right into her heart. So you may say Lige Baxter's failure was a success after all."

THE SON OF HIS MOTHER

Thyra Carewe was waiting for Chester to come home. She sat by the west window of the kitchen, looking out into the gathering of the shadows with the expectant immovability that characterized her. She never twitched or fidgeted. Into whatever she did she put the whole force of her nature. If it was sitting still, she sat still.

"A stone image would be twitchedly beside Thyra," said Mrs. Cynthia White, her neighbor across the lane. "It gets on my nerves, the way she sits at that window sometimes, with no more motion than a statue and her great eyes burning down the lane. When I read the commandment, 'Thou shalt have no other gods before me,' I declare I always think of Thyra. She worships that son of hers far ahead of her Creator. She'll be punished for it yet."

Mrs. White was watching Thyra now, knitting furiously, as she watched, in order to lose no time. Thyra's hands were folded idly in her lap. She had not moved a muscle since she sat down. Mrs. White complained it gave her the weeps.

"It doesn't seem natural to see a woman sit so still," she said. "Sometimes the thought comes to me, 'what if she's had a stroke, like her old Uncle Horatio, and is sitting there stone dead!'"

The evening was cold and autumnal. There was a fiery red spot out at sea, where the sun had set, and, above it, over a chill, clear, saffron sky, were reefs of purple-black clouds. The river, below the Carewe homestead, was livid. Beyond it, the sea was dark and brooding. It was an evening to make most people shiver and forebode an early winter; but Thyra loved it, as she loved all stern, harshly beautiful things. She would not light a lamp because it would blot out the savage grandeur of sea and sky. It was better to wait in the darkness until Chester came home.

He was late to-night. She thought he had been detained over-time at the harbor, but she was not anxious. He would come straight home to her as soon as his business was completed—of that she felt sure. Her thoughts went out along the bleak harbor road to meet him. She could see him plainly, coming with his free stride through the sandy hollows and over the windy hills, in the harsh, cold light of that forbidding sunset, strong and handsome in his comely youth, with her own deeply cleft chin and his father's dark gray, straightforward eyes. No other woman in Avonlea had a son like hers—her only one. In his brief absences she yearned after him with a maternal passion that had in it something of physical pain, so intense was it. She thought of Cynthia White, knitting across the road, with contemptuous pity. That woman had no son—nothing but pale-faced girls. Thyra had never wanted a daughter, but she pitied and despised all sonless women.

Chester's dog whined suddenly and piercingly on the doorstep outside. He was tired of the cold stone and wanted his warm corner behind the stove. Thyra smiled grimly when she heard him. She had no intention of letting him in. She said she had always disliked dogs, but the truth, although she would not glance at it, was that she hated the animal because Chester loved him. She could not share his love with even a dumb brute. She loved no living creature in the world but her son, and fiercely demanded a like concentrated affection from him. Hence it pleased her to hear his dog whine.

It was now quite dark; the stars had begun to shine out over the shorn harvest fields, and Chester had not come. Across the lane Cynthia White had pulled down her blind, in despair of out-watching Thyra, and had lighted a lamp. Lively shadows of little girl-shapes passed and repassed on the pale oblong of light. They made Thyra conscious of her exceeding loneliness. She had just decided that she would walk down the lane and wait for Chester on the bridge, when a thunderous knock came at the east kitchen door.

She recognized August Vorst's knock and lighted a lamp in no great haste, for she did not like him. He was a gossip and Thyra hated gossip, in man or woman. But August was privileged.

She carried the lamp in her hand, when she went to the door, and its upward-striking light gave her face a ghastly appearance. She did not mean to ask August in, but he pushed past her cheerfully, not waiting to be invited. He was a midget of a man, lame of foot and hunched of back, with a white, boyish face, despite his middle age and deep-set, malicious black eyes.

He pulled a crumpled newspaper from his pocket and handed it to Thyra. He was the unofficial mail-carrier of Avonlea. Most of the people gave him a trifle for bringing their letters and papers from the office. He earned small sums in various other ways, and so contrived to keep the life in his stunted body. There was always venom in August's gossip. It was said that he made more mischief in Avonlea in a day than was made otherwise in a year, but people tolerated him by reason of his infirmity. To be sure, it was the tolerance they gave to inferior creatures, and August felt this. Perhaps it accounted for a good deal of his malignity. He hated most those who were kindest to him, and, of these, Thyra Carewe above all. He hated Chester, too, as he hated strong, shapely creatures. His time had come at last to wound them both, and his exultation shone through his crooked body and pinched features like an illuminating lamp. Thyra perceived it and vaguely felt something antagonistic in it. She pointed to the rocking-chair, as she might have pointed out a mat to a dog.

August crawled into it and smiled. He was going to make her writhe presently, this woman who looked down upon him as some venomous creeping thing she disdained to crush with her foot.

"Did you see anything of Chester on the road?" asked Thyra, giving August the very opening he desired. "He went to the harbor after tea to see Joe Raymond about the loan of his boat, but it's the time he should be back. I can't think what keeps the boy."

"Just what keeps most men—leaving out creatures like me—at some time or other in their lives. A girl—a pretty girl, Thyra. It pleases me to look at her. Even a hunchback can use his eyes, eh? Oh, she's a rare one!"

"What is the man talking about?" said Thyra wonderingly.

"Damaris Garland, to be sure. Chester's down at Tom Blair's now, talking to her—and looking more than his tongue says, too, of that you may be sure. Well, well, we were all young once, Thyra—all young once, even crooked little August Vorst. Eh, now?"

"What do you mean?" said Thyra.

She had sat down in a chair before him, with her hands folded in her lap. Her face, always pale, had not changed; but her lips were curiously white. August Vorst saw this and it pleased him. Also, her eyes were worth looking at, if you liked to hurt people—and that was the only pleasure August took in life. He would drink this delightful cup of revenge for her long years of disdainful kindness—ah, he would drink it slowly to prolong its sweetness. Sip by sip—he rubbed his long, thin, white hands together—sip by sip, tasting each mouthful.

"Eh, now? You know well enough, Thyra."

"I know nothing of what you would be at, August Vorst. You speak of my son and Damaris—was that the name?—Damaris Garland as if they were something to each other. I ask you what you mean by it?"

"Tut, tut, Thyra, nothing very terrible. There's no need to look like that about it. Young men will be young men to the end of time, and there's no harm in Chester's liking to look at a lass, eh, now? Or in talking to her either? The little baggage, with the red lips of her! She and Chester will make a pretty pair. He's not so ill-looking for a man, Thyra."

"I am not a very patient woman, August," said Thyra coldly. "I have asked you what you mean, and I want a straight answer. Is Chester down at Tom Blair's while I have been sitting here, alone, waiting for him?"

August nodded. He saw that it would not be wise to trifle longer with Thyra.

"That he is. I was there before I came here. He and Damaris were sitting in a corner by themselves, and very well-satisfied they seemed to be with each other. Tut, tut, Thyra, don't take the news so. I thought you knew. It's no secret that Chester has been going after Damaris ever since she came here. But what then? You can't tie him to your apron strings forever, woman. He'll be finding a mate for himself, as he should. Seeing that he's straight and well-shaped, no doubt Damaris will look with favor on him. Old Martha Blair declares the girl loves him better than her eyes."

Thyra made a sound like a strangled moan in the middle of August's speech. She heard the rest of it immovably. When it came to an end she stood and looked down upon him in a way that silenced him.

"You've told the news you came to tell, and gloated over it, and now get you gone," she said slowly.

"Now, Thyra," he began, but she interrupted him threateningly.

"Get you gone, I say! And you need not bring my mail here any longer. I want no more of your misshapen body and lying tongue!"

August went, but at the door he turned for a parting stab.

"My tongue is not a lying one, Mrs. Carewe. I've told you the truth, as all Avonlea knows it. Chester is mad about Damaris Garland. It's no wonder I thought you knew what all the settlement can see. But you're such a jealous, odd body, I suppose the boy hid it from you for fear you'd go into a tantrum. As for me, I'll not forget that you've turned me from your door because I chanced to bring you news you'd no fancy for."

Thyra did not answer him. When the door closed behind him she locked it and blew out the light. Then she threw herself face downward on the sofa and burst into wild tears. Her very soul ached. She wept as tempestuously and unreasoningly as youth weeps, although she was not young. It seemed as if she was afraid to stop weeping lest she should go mad thinking. But, after a time, tears failed her, and she began bitterly to go over, word by word, what August Vorst had said.

That her son should ever cast eyes of love on any girl was something Thyra had never thought about. She would not believe it possible that he should love any one but herself, who loved him so much. And now the possibility invaded her mind as subtly and coldly and remorselessly as a sea-fog stealing landward.

Chester had been born to her at an age when most women are letting their children slip from them into the world, with some natural tears and heartaches, but content to let them go, after enjoying their sweetest years. Thyra's late-come motherhood was all the more intense and passionate because of its very lateness. She had been very ill when her son was born, and had lain helpless for long weeks, during which other women had tended her baby for her. She had never been able to forgive them for this.

Her husband had died before Chester was a year old. She had laid their son in his dying arms and received him back again with a last benediction. To Thyra that moment had something of a sacrament in it. It was as if the child had been doubly given to her, with a right to him solely that nothing could take away or transcend.

Marrying! She had never thought of it in connection with him. He did not come of a marrying race. His father had been sixty when he had married her, Thyra Lincoln, likewise well on in life. Few of the Lincolns or Carewes had married young, many not at all. And, to her, Chester was her baby still. He belonged solely to her.

And now another woman had dared to look upon him with eyes of love. Damaris Garland! Thyra now remembered seeing her. She was a new-comer in Avonlea, having come to live with her uncle and aunt after the death of her mother. Thyra had met her on the bridge one day a month previously. Yes, a man might think she was pretty—a low-browed girl, with a wave of reddish-gold hair, and crimson lips blossoming out against the strange, milk-whiteness of her skin. Her eyes, too—Thyra recalled them—hazel in tint, deep, and laughter-brimmed.

The girl had gone past her with a smile that brought out many dimples. There was a certain insolent quality in her beauty, as if it flaunted itself somewhat too defiantly in the beholder's eye. Thyra had turned and looked after the lithe, young creature, wondering who she might be.

And to-night, while she, his mother, waited for him in darkness and loneliness, he was down at Blair's, talking to this girl! He loved her; and it was past doubt that she loved him. The thought was more bitter than death to Thyra. That she should dare! Her anger was all against the girl. She had laid a snare to get Chester and he, like a fool, was entangled in it, thinking, man-fashion, only of her great eyes and red lips. Thyra thought savagely of Damaris' beauty.

"She shall not have him," she said, with slow emphasis. "I will never give him up to any other woman, and, least of all, to her. She would leave me no place in his heart at all—me, his mother, who almost died to give him life. He belongs to me! Let her look for the son of some other woman—some woman who has many sons. She shall not have my only one!"

She got up, wrapped a shawl about her head, and went out into the darkly golden evening. The clouds had cleared away, and the moon was shining. The air was chill, with a bell-like clearness. The alders by the river rustled eerily as she walked by them and out upon the bridge. Here she paced up and down, peering with troubled eyes along the road beyond, or leaning over the rail, looking at the sparkling silver ribbon of moonlight that garlanded the waters. Late travelers passed her, and wondered at her presence and mien. Carl White saw her, and told his wife about her when he got home.

"Striding to and fro over the bridge like mad! At first I thought it was old, crazy May Blair. What do you suppose she was doing down there at this hour of the night?"

"Watching for Ches, no doubt," said Cynthia. "He ain't home yet. Likely he's snug at Blairs'. I do wonder if Thyra suspicions that he goes after Damaris. I've never dared to hint it to her. She'd be as liable to fly at me, tooth and claw, as not."

"Well, she picks out a precious queer night for moon-gazing," said Carl, who was a jolly soul and took life as he found it. "It's bitter cold—there'll be a hard frost. It's a pity she can't get it grained into her that the boy is grown up and must have his fling like the other lads. She'll go out of her mind yet, like her old grandmother Lincoln, if she doesn't ease up. I've a notion to go down to the bridge and reason a bit with her."

"Indeed, and you'll do no such thing!" cried Cynthia. "Thyra Carewe is best left alone, if she is in a tantrum. She's like no other woman in Avonlea—or out of it. I'd as soon meddle with a tiger as her, if she's rampaging about Chester. I don't envy Damaris Garland her life if she goes in there. Thyra'd sooner strangle her than not, I guess."

"You women are all terrible hard on Thyra," said Carl, good-naturedly. He had been in love with Thyra, himself, long ago, and he still liked her in a friendly fashion. He always stood up for her when the Avonlea women ran her down. He felt troubled about her all night, recalling her as she paced the bridge. He wished he had gone back, in spite of Cynthia.

When Chester came home he met his mother on the bridge. In the faint, yet penetrating, moonlight they looked curiously alike, but Chester had the milder face. He was very handsome. Even in the seething of her pain and jealousy Thyra yearned over his beauty. She would have liked to put up her hands and caress his face, but her voice was very hard when she asked him where he had been so late.

"I called in at Tom Blair's on my way home from the harbor," he answered, trying to walk on. But she held him back by his arm.

"Did you go there to see Damaris?" she demanded fiercely.

Chester was uncomfortable. Much as he loved his mother, he felt, and always had felt, an awe of her and an impatient dislike of her dramatic ways of speaking and acting. He reflected, resentfully, that no other young man in Avonlea, who had been paying a friendly call, would be met by his mother at midnight and held up in such tragic fashion to account for himself. He tried vainly to loosen her hold upon his arm, but he understood quite well that he must give her an answer. Being strictly straight-forward by nature and upbringing, he told the truth, albeit with more anger in his tone than he had ever shown to his mother before.

"Yes," he said shortly.

Thyra released his arm, and struck her hands together with a sharp cry. There was a savage note in it. She could have slain Damaris Garland at that moment.

"Don't go on so, mother," said Chester, impatiently. "Come in out of the cold. It isn't fit for you to be here. Who has been tampering with you? What if I did go to see Damaris?"

"Oh—oh—oh!" cried Thyra. "I was waiting for you—alone—and you were thinking only of her! Chester, answer me—do you love her?"

The blood rolled rapidly over the boy's face. He muttered something and tried to pass on, but she caught him again. He forced himself to speak gently.

"What if I do, mother? It wouldn't be such a dreadful thing, would it?"

"And me? And me?" cried Thyra. "What am I to you, then?"

"You are my mother. I wouldn't love you any the less because I cared for another, too."

"I won't have you love another," she cried. "I want all your love—all! What's that baby-face to you, compared to your mother? I have the best right to you. I won't give you up."

Chester realized that there was no arguing with such a mood. He walked on, resolved to set the matter aside until she might be more reasonable. But Thyra would not have it so. She followed on after him, under the alders that crowded over the lane.

"Promise me that you'll not go there again," she entreated. "Promise me that you'll give her up."

"I can't promise such a thing," he cried angrily.

His anger hurt her worse than a blow, but she did not flinch.

"You're not engaged to her?" she cried out.

"Now, mother, be quiet. All the settlement will hear you. Why do you object to Damaris? You don't know how sweet she is. When you know her—"

"I will never know her!" cried Thyra furiously. "And she shall not have you! She shall not, Chester!"

He made no answer. She suddenly broke into tears and loud sobs. Touched with remorse, he stopped and put his arms about her.

"Mother, mother, don't! I can't bear to see you cry so. But, indeed, you are unreasonable. Didn't you ever think the time would come when I would want to marry, like other men?"

"No, no! And I will not have it—I cannot bear it, Chester. You must promise not to go to see her again. I won't go into the house this night until you do. I'll stay out here in the bitter cold until you promise to put her out of your thoughts."

"That's beyond my power, mother. Oh, mother, you're making it hard for me. Come in, come in! You're shivering with cold now. You'll be sick."

"Not a step will I stir till you promise. Say you won't go to see that girl any more, and there's nothing I won't do for you. But if you put her before me, I'll not go in—I never will go in."

With most women this would have been an empty threat; but it was not so with Thyra, and Chester knew it. He knew she would keep her word. And he feared more than that. In this frenzy of hers what might she not do? She came of a strange breed, as had been said disapprovingly when Luke Carewe married her. There was a strain of insanity in the Lincolns. A Lincoln woman had drowned herself once. Chester thought of the river, and grew sick with fright. For a moment even his passion for Damaris weakened before the older tie.

"Mother, calm yourself. Oh, surely there's no need of all this! Let us wait until to-morrow, and talk it over then. I'll hear all you have to say. Come in, dear."

Thyra loosened her arms from about him, and stepped back into a moon-lit space. Looking at him tragically, she extended her arms and spoke slowly and solemnly.

"Chester, choose between us. If you choose her, I shall go from you to-night, and you will never see me again!"

"Mother!"

"Choose!" she reiterated, fiercely.

He felt her long ascendancy. Its influence was not to be shaken off in a moment. In all his life he had never disobeyed her. Besides, with it all, he loved her more deeply and understandingly than most sons love their mothers. He realized that, since she would have it so, his choice was already made—or, rather that he had no choice.

"Have your way," he said sullenly.

She ran to him and caught him to her heart. In the reaction of her feeling she was half laughing, half crying. All was well again—all would be well; she never doubted this, for she knew he would keep his ungracious promise sacredly.

"Oh, my son, my son," she murmured, "you'd have sent me to my death if you had chosen otherwise. But now you are mine again!"

She did not heed that he was sullen—that he resented her unjustice with all her own intensity. She did not heed his silence as they went into the house together. Strangely enough, she slept well and soundly that night. Not until many days had passed did she understand that, though Chester might keep his promise in the letter, it was beyond his power to keep it in the spirit. She had taken him from Damaris Garland; but she had not won him back to herself. He could never be wholly her son again. There was a barrier between them which not all her passionate love could break down. Chester was gravely kind to her, for it was not in his nature to remain sullen long, or visit his own unhappiness upon another's head; besides, he understood her exacting affection, even in its injustice, and it has been well-said that to understand is to forgive. But he avoided her, and she knew it. The flame of her anger burned bitterly towards Damaris.

"He thinks of her all the time," she moaned to herself. "He'll come to hate me yet, I fear, because it's I who made him give her up. But I'd rather even that than share him with another woman. Oh, my son, my son!"

She knew that Damaris was suffering, too. The girl's wan face told that when she met her. But this pleased Thyra. It eased the ache in her bitter heart to know that pain was gnawing at Damaris' also.

Chester was absent from home very often now. He spent much of his spare time at the harbor, consorting with Joe Raymond and others of that ilk, who were but sorry associates for him, Avonlea people thought.

In late November he and Joe started for a trip down the coast in the latter's boat. Thyra protested against it, but Chester laughed at her alarm.

Thyra saw him go with a heart sick from fear. She hated the sea, and was afraid of it at any time; but, most of all, in this treacherous month, with its sudden, wild gales.

Chester had been fond of the sea from boyhood. She had always tried to stifle this fondness and break off his associations with the harbor fishermen, who liked to lure the high-spirited boy out with them on fishing expeditions. But her power over him was gone now.

After Chester's departure she was restless and miserable, wandering from window to window to scan the dour, unsmiling sky. Carl White, dropping in to pay a call, was alarmed when he heard that Chester had gone with Joe, and had not tact enough to conceal his alarm from Thyra.

"'T isn't safe this time of year," he said. "Folks expect no better from that reckless, harum-scarum Joe Raymond. He'll drown himself some day, there's nothing surer. This mad freak of starting off down the shore in November is just of a piece with his usual performances. But you shouldn't have let Chester go, Thyra."

"I couldn't prevent him. Say what I could, he would go. He laughed when I spoke of danger. Oh, he's changed from what he was! I know who has wrought the change, and I hate her for it!"

Carl shrugged his fat shoulders. He knew quite well that Thyra was at the bottom of the sudden coldness between Chester Carewe and Damaris Garland, about which Avonlea gossip was busying itself. He pitied Thyra, too. She had aged rapidly the past month.

"You're too hard on Chester, Thyra. He's out of leading-strings now, or should be. You must just let me take an old friend's privilege, and tell you that you're taking the wrong way with him. You're too jealous and exacting, Thyra."

"You don't know anything about it. You have never had a son," said Thyra, cruelly enough, for she knew that Carl's sonlessness was a rankling thorn in his mind. "You don't know what it is to pour out your love on one human being, and have it flung back in your face!"

Carl could not cope with Thyra's moods. He had never understood her, even in his youth. Now he went home, still shrugging his shoulders, and thinking that it was a good thing Thyra had not looked on him with favor in the old days. Cynthia was much easier to get along with.

More than Thyra looked anxiously to sea and sky that night in Avonlea. Damaris Garland listened to the smothered roar of the Atlantic in the murky northeast with a prescience of coming disaster. Friendly longshoremen shook their heads and said that Ches and Joe would better have kept to good, dry land.

"It's sorry work joking with a November gale," said Abel Blair. He was an old man and, in his life, had seen some sad things along the shore.

Thyra could not sleep that night. When the gale came shrieking up the river, and struck the house, she got out of bed and dressed herself. The wind screamed like a ravening beast at her window. All night she wandered to and fro in the house, going from room to room, now wringing her hands with loud outcries, now praying below her breath with white lips, now listening in dumb misery to the fury of the storm.

The wind raged all the next day; but spent itself in the following night, and the second morning was calm and fair. The eastern sky was a great arc of crystal, smitten through with auroral crimsonings. Thyra, looking from her kitchen window, saw a group of men on the bridge. They were talking to Carl White, with looks and gestures directed towards the Carewe house.

She went out and down to them. None of these who saw her white, rigid face that day ever forgot the sight.

"You have news for me," she said.

They looked at each other, each man mutely imploring his neighbor to speak.

"You need not fear to tell me," said Thyra calmly. "I know what you have come to say. My son is drowned."

"We don't know THAT, Mrs. Carewe," said Abel Blair quickly. "We haven't got the worst to tell you—there's hope yet. But Joe Raymond's boat was found last night, stranded bottom up, on the Blue Point sand shore, forty miles down the coast."

"Don't look like that, Thyra," said Carl White pityingly. "They may have escaped—they may have been picked up."

Thyra looked at him with dull eyes.

"You know they have not. Not one of you has any hope. I have no son. The sea has taken him from me—my bonny baby!"

She turned and went back to her desolate home. None dared to follow her. Carl White went home and sent his wife over to her.

Cynthia found Thyra sitting in her accustomed chair. Her hands lay, palms upward, on her lap. Her eyes were dry and burning. She met Cynthia's compassionate look with a fearful smile.

"Long ago, Cynthia White," she said slowly, "you were vexed with me one day, and you told me that God would punish me yet, because I made an idol of my son, and set it up in His place. Do you remember? Your word was a true one. God saw that I loved Chester too much, and He meant to take him from me. I thwarted one way when I made him give up Damaris. But one can't fight against the Almighty. It was decreed that I must lose him—if not in one way, then in another. He has been taken from me utterly. I shall not even have his grave to tend, Cynthia."

"As near to a mad woman as anything you ever saw, with her awful eyes," Cynthia told Carl, afterwards. But she did not say so there. Although she was a shallow, commonplace soul, she had her share of womanly sympathy, and her own life had not been free from suffering. It taught her the right thing to do now. She sat down by the stricken creature and put her arms about her, while she gathered the cold hands in her own warm clasp. The tears filled her big, blue eyes and her voice trembled as she said:

"Thyra, I'm sorry for you. I—I—lost a child once—my little first-born. And Chester was a dear, good lad."

For a moment Thyra strained her small, tense body away from Cynthia's embrace. Then she shuddered and cried out. The tears came, and she wept her agony out on the other woman's breast.

As the ill news spread, other Avonlea women kept dropping in all through the day to condole with Thyra. Many of them came in real sympathy, but some out of mere curiosity to see how she took it. Thyra knew this, but she did not resent it, as she would once have done. She listened very quietly to all the halting efforts at consolation, and the little platitudes with which they strove to cover the nakedness of bereavement.

When darkness came Cynthia said she must go home, but would send one of her girls over for the night.

"You won't feel like staying alone," she said.

Thyra looked up steadily.

"No. But I want you to send for Damaris Garland."

"Damaris Garland!" Cynthia repeated the name as if disbelieving her own ears. There was never any knowing what whim Thyra might take, but Cynthia had not expected this.

"Yes. Tell her I want her—tell her she must come. She must hate me bitterly; but I am punished enough to satisfy even her hate. Tell her to come to me for Chester's sake."

Cynthia did as she was bid, she sent her daughter, Jeanette, for Damaris. Then she waited. No matter what duties were calling for her at home she must see the interview between Thyra and Damaris. Her curiosity would be the last thing to fail Cynthia White. She had done very well all day; but it would be asking too much of her to expect that she would consider the meeting of these two women sacred from her eyes.

She half believed that Damaris would refuse to come. But Damaris came. Jeanette brought her in amid the fiery glow of a November sunset. Thyra stood up, and for a moment they looked at each other.

The insolence of Damaris' beauty was gone. Her eyes were dull and heavy with weeping, her lips were pale, and her face had lost its laughter and dimples. Only her hair, escaping from the shawl she had cast around it, gushed forth in warm splendor in the sunset light, and framed her wan face like the aureole of a Madonna. Thyra looked upon her with a shock of remorse. This was not the radiant creature she had met on the bridge that summer afternoon. This—this—was HER work. She held out her arms.

"Oh, Damaris, forgive me. We both loved him—that must be a bond between us for life."

Damaris came forward and threw her arms about the older woman, lifting her face. As their lips met even Cynthia White realized that she had no business there. She vented the irritation of her embarrassment on the innocent Jeanette.

"Come away," she whispered crossly. "Can't you see we're not wanted here?"

She drew Jeanette out, leaving Thyra rocking Damaris in her arms, and crooning over her like a mother over her child.

When December had grown old Damaris was still with Thyra. It was understood that she was to remain there for the winter, at least. Thyra could not bear her to be out of her sight. They talked constantly about Chester; Thyra confessed all her anger and hatred. Damaris had forgiven her; but Thyra could never forgive herself. She was greatly changed, and had grown very gentle and tender. She even sent for August Vorst and begged him to pardon her for the way she had spoken to him.

Winter came late that year, and the season was a very open one. There was no snow on the ground and, a month after Joe Raymond's boat had been cast up on the Blue Point sand shore, Thyra, wandering about in her garden, found some pansies blooming under their tangled leaves. She was picking them for Damaris when she heard a buggy rumble over the bridge and drive up the White lane, hidden from her sight by the alders and firs. A few minutes later Carl and Cynthia came hastily across their yard under the huge balm-of-gileads. Carl's face was flushed, and his big body quivered with excitement. Cynthia ran behind him, with tears rolling down her face.

Thyra felt herself growing sick with fear. Had anything happened to Damaris? A glimpse of the girl, sewing by an upper window of the house, reassured her.

"Oh, Thyra, Thyra!" gasped Cynthia.

"Can you stand some good news, Thyra?" asked Carl, in a trembling voice. "Very, very good news!"

Thyra looked wildly from one to the other.

"There's but one thing you would dare to call good news to me," she cried. "Is it about —about—"

"Chester! Yes, it's about Chester! Thyra, he is alive—he's safe—he and Joe, both of them, thank God! Cynthia, catch her!"

"No, I am not going to faint," said Thyra, steadying herself by Cynthia's shoulder. "My son alive! How did you hear? How did it happen? Where has he been?"

"I heard it down at the harbor, Thyra. Mike McCready's vessel, the *Nora Lee*, was just in from the Magdalens. Ches and Joe got capsized the night of the storm, but they hung on to their boat somehow, and at daybreak they were picked up by the *Nora Lee*, bound for Quebec. But she was damaged by the storm and blown clear out of her course. Had to put into the

Magdalens for repairs, and has been there ever since. The cable to the islands was out of order, and no vessels call there this time of year for mails. If it hadn't been an extra open season the *Nora Lee* wouldn't have got away, but would have had to stay there till spring. You never saw such rejoicing as there was this morning at the harbor, when the *Nora Lee* came in, flying flags at the mast head."

"And Chester—where is he?" demanded Thyra.

Carl and Cynthia looked at each other.

"Well, Thyra," said the latter, "the fact is, he's over there in our yard this blessed minute. Carl brought him home from the harbor, but I wouldn't let him come over until we had prepared you for it. He's waiting for you there."

Thyra made a quick step in the direction of the gate. Then she turned, with a little of the glow dying out of her face.

"No, there's one has a better right to go to him first. I can atone to him—thank God, I can atone to him!"

She went into the house and called Damaris. As the girl came down the stairs Thyra held out her hands with a wonderful light of joy and renunciation on her face.

"Damaris," she said, "Chester has come back to us—the sea has given him back to us. He is over at Carl White's house. Go to him, my daughter, and bring him to me!"

THE EDUCATION OF BETTY

When Sara Currie married Jack Churchill I was broken-hearted...or believed myself to be so, which, in a boy of twenty-two, amounts to pretty much the same thing. Not that I took the world into my confidence; that was never the Douglas way, and I held myself in honor bound to live up to the family traditions. I thought, then, that nobody but Sara knew; but I dare say, now, that Jack knew it also, for I don't think Sara could have helped telling him. If he did know, however, he did not let me see that he did, and never insulted me by any implied sympathy; on the contrary, he asked me to be his best man. Jack was always a thoroughbred.

I was best man. Jack and I had always been bosom friends, and, although I had lost my sweetheart, I did not intend to lose my friend into the bargain. Sara had made a wise choice, for Jack was twice the man I was; he had had to work for his living, which perhaps accounts for it.

So I danced at Sara's wedding as if my heart were as light as my heels; but, after she and Jack had settled down at Glenby I closed The Maples and went abroad...being, as I have hinted, one of those unfortunate mortals who need consult nothing but their own whims in the matter of time and money. I stayed away for ten years, during which The Maples was given over to moths and rust, while I enjoyed life elsewhere. I did enjoy it hugely, but always under protest, for I felt that a broken-hearted man ought not to enjoy himself as I did. It jarred on my sense of fitness, and I tried to moderate my zest, and think more of the past than I did. It was no use; the present insisted on being intrusive and pleasant; as for the future...well, there was no future.

Then Jack Churchill, poor fellow, died. A year after his death, I went home and again asked Sara to marry me, as in duty bound. Sara again declined, alleging that her heart was buried in Jack's grave, or words to that effect. I found that it did not much matter...of course, at thirty-two one does not take these things to heart as at twenty-two. I had enough to occupy me in getting The Maples into working order, and beginning to educate Betty.

Betty was Sara's ten year-old daughter, and she had been thoroughly spoiled. That is to say, she had been allowed her own way in everything and, having inherited her father's outdoor tastes, had simply run wild. She was a thorough tomboy, a thin, scrawny little thing with a trace of Sara's beauty. Betty took after her father's dark, tall race and, on the occasion of my first introduction to her, seemed to be all legs and neck. There were points about her, though, which I considered promising. She had fine, almond-shaped, hazel eyes, the smallest and most shapely hands and feet I ever saw, and two enormous braids of thick, nut-brown hair.

For Jack's sake I decided to bring his daughter up properly. Sara couldn't do it, and didn't try. I saw that, if somebody didn't take Betty in hand, wisely and firmly, she would certainly be ruined. There seemed to be nobody except myself at all interested in the matter, so I determined to see what an old bachelor could do as regards bringing up a girl in the way she should go. I might have been her father; as it was, her father had been my best friend. Who had a better right to watch over his daughter? I determined to be a father to Betty, and do all for her that the most devoted parent could do. It was, self-evidently, my duty.

I told Sara I was going to take Betty in hand. Sara sighed one of the plaintive little sighs which I had once thought so charming, but now, to my surprise, found faintly irritating, and said that she would be very much obliged if I would.

"I feel that I am not able to cope with the problem of Betty's education, Stephen," she admitted, "Betty is a strange child...all Churchill. Her poor father indulged her in everything, and she has a will of her own, I assure you. I have really no control over her, whatever. She does as she pleases, and is ruining her complexion by running and galloping out of doors the whole time. Not that she had much complexion to start with. The Churchills never had, you know."...Sara cast a complacent glance at her delicately tinted reflection in the mirror.... "I tried to make Betty wear a sunbonnet this summer, but I might as well have talked to the wind."

A vision of Betty in a sunbonnet presented itself to my mind, and afforded me so much amusement that I was grateful to Sara for having furnished it. I rewarded her with a compliment.

"It is to be regretted that Betty has not inherited her mother's charming color," I said, "but we must do the best we can for her under her limitations. She may have improved vastly by the time she has grown up. And, at least, we must make a lady of her; she is a most alarming tomboy at present, but there is good material to work upon...there must be, in the Churchill and Currie blend. But even the best material may be spoiled by unwise handling. I think I can promise you that I will not spoil it. I feel that Betty is my vocation; and I shall set myself up as a rival of Wordsworth's 'nature,' of whose methods I have always had a decided distrust, in spite of his insidious verses."

Sara did not understand me in the least; but, then, she did not pretend to.

"I confide Betty's education entirely to you, Stephen," she said, with another plaintive sigh. "I feel sure I could not put it into better hands. You have always been a person who could be thoroughly depended on."

Well, that was something by way of reward for a life-long devotion. I felt that I was satisfied with my position as unofficial advisor-in-chief to Sara and self-appointed guardian of Betty. I also felt that, for the furtherance of the cause I had taken to heart, it was a good thing that Sara had again refused to marry me. I had a sixth sense which informed me that a staid old family friend might succeed with Betty where a stepfather would have signally failed. Betty's loyalty to her father's memory was passionate, and vehement; she would view his supplanter with resentment and distrust; but his old familiar comrade was a person to be taken to her heart.

Fortunately for the success of my enterprise, Betty liked me. She told me this with the same engaging candor she would have used in informing me that she hated me, if she had happened to take a bias in that direction, saying frankly:

"You are one of the very nicest old folks I know, Stephen. Yes, you are a ripping good fellow!"

This made my task a comparatively easy one; I sometimes shudder to think what it might have been if Betty had not thought I was a "ripping good fellow." I should have stuck to it, because that is my way; but Betty would have made my life a misery to me. She had startling capacities for tormenting people when she chose to exert them; I certainly should not have liked to be numbered among Betty's foes.

I rode over to Glenby the next morning after my paternal interview with Sara, intending to have a frank talk with Betty and lay the foundations of a good understanding on both sides. Betty was a sharp child, with a disconcerting knack of seeing straight through grindstones; she would certainly perceive and probably resent any underhanded management. I thought it best to tell her plainly that I was going to look after her.

When, however, I encountered Betty, tearing madly down the beech avenue with a couple of dogs, her loosened hair streaming behind her like a banner of independence, and had lifted her, hatless and breathless, up before me on my mare, I found that Sara had saved me the trouble of an explanation.

"Mother says you are going to take charge of my education, Stephen," said Betty, as soon as she could speak. "I'm glad, because I think that, for an old person, you have a good deal of sense. I suppose my education has to be seen to, some time or other, and I'd rather you'd do it than anybody else I know."

"Thank you, Betty," I said gravely. "I hope I shall deserve your good opinion of my sense. I shall expect you to do as I tell you, and be guided by my advice in everything."

"Yes, I will," said Betty, "because I'm sure you won't tell me to do anything I'd really hate to do. You won't shut me up in a room and make me sew, will you? Because I won't do it."

I assured her I would not.

"Nor send me to a boarding-school," pursued Betty. "Mother's always threatening to send me to one. I suppose she would have done it before this, only she knew I'd run away. You won't send me to a boarding-school, will you, Stephen? Because I won't go."

"No," I said obligingly. "I won't. I should never dream of cooping a wild little thing, like you, up in a boarding-school. You'd fret your heart out like a caged skylark."

"I know you and I are going to get along together splendidly, Stephen," said Betty, rubbing her brown cheek chummily against my shoulder. "You are so good at understanding. Very few people are. Even dad darling didn't understand. He let me do just as I wanted to, just because I wanted to, not because he really understood that I couldn't be tame and play with dolls. I hate dolls! Real live babies are jolly; but dogs and horses are ever so much nicer than dolls."

"But you must have lessons, Betty. I shall select your teachers and superintend your studies, and I shall expect you to do me credit along that line, as well as along all others."

"I'll try, honest and true, Stephen," declared Betty. And she kept her word.

At first I looked upon Betty's education as a duty; in a very short time it had become a pleasure...the deepest and most abiding interest of my life. As I had premised, Betty was good material, and responded to my training with gratifying plasticity. Day by day, week by week, month by month, her character and temperament unfolded naturally under my watchful eye. It was like beholding the gradual development of some rare flower in one's garden. A little checking and pruning here, a careful training of shoot and tendril there, and, lo, the reward of grace and symmetry!

Betty grew up as I would have wished Jack Churchill's girl to grow—spirited and proud, with the fine spirit and gracious pride of pure womanhood, loyal and loving, with the loyalty and love of a frank and unspoiled nature; true to her heart's core, hating falsehood and sham—as crystal-clear a mirror of maidenhood as ever man looked into and saw himself reflected back in such a halo as made him ashamed of not being more worthy of it. Betty was kind enough to say that I had taught her everything she knew. But what had she not taught me? If there were a debt between us, it was on my side.

Sara was fairly well satisfied. It was not my fault that Betty was not better looking, she said. I had certainly done everything for her mind and character that could be done. Sara's manner implied that these unimportant details did not count for much, balanced against the lack of a pink-and-white skin and dimpled elbows; but she was generous enough not to blame me.

"When Betty is twenty-five," I said patiently—I had grown used to speaking patiently to Sara—"she will be a magnificent woman—far handsomer than you ever were, Sara, in your pinkest and whitest prime. Where are your eyes, my dear lady, that you can't see the promise of loveliness in Betty?"

"Betty is seventeen, and she is as lanky and brown as ever she was," sighed Sara. "When I was seventeen I was the belle of the county and had had five proposals. I don't believe the thought of a lover has ever entered Betty's head."

"I hope not," I said shortly. Somehow, I did not like the suggestion. "Betty is a child yet. For pity's sake, Sara, don't go putting nonsensical ideas into her head."

"I'm afraid I can't," mourned Sara, as if it were something to be regretted. "You have filled it too full of books and things like that. I've every confidence in your judgment, Stephen—and really you've done wonders with Betty. But don't you think you've made her rather too clever? Men don't like women who are too clever. Her poor father, now—he always said that a woman who liked books better than beaux was an unnatural creature."

I didn't believe Jack had ever said anything so foolish. Sara imagined things. But I resented the aspersion of blue-stockingness cast on Betty.

"When the time comes for Betty to be interested in beaux," I said severely, "she will probably give them all due attention. Just at present her head is a great deal better filled with books than with silly premature fancies and sentimentalities. I'm a critical old fellow—but I'm satisfied with Betty, Sara—perfectly satisfied."

Sara sighed.

"Oh, I dare say she is all right, Stephen. And I'm really grateful to you. I'm sure I could have done nothing at all with her. It's not your fault, of course,—but I can't help wishing she were a little more like other girls."

I galloped away from Glenby in a rage. What a blessing Sara had not married me in my absurd youth! She would have driven me wild with her sighs and her obtuseness and her everlasting pink-and-whiteness. But there—there—there—gently! She was a sweet, good-hearted little woman; she had made Jack happy; and she had contrived, heaven only knew how, to bring a rare creature like Betty into the world. For that, much might be forgiven her. By the time I reached The Maples and had flung myself down in an old, kinky, comfortable chair in my library I had forgiven her and was even paying her the compliment of thinking seriously over what she had said.

Was Betty really unlike other girls? That is to say, unlike them in any respect wherein she should resemble them? I did not wish this; although I was a crusty old bachelor I approved of girls, holding them the sweetest things the good God has made. I wanted Betty to have her full complement of girlhood in all its best and highest manifestation. Was there anything lacking?

I observed Betty very closely during the next week or so, riding over to Glenby every day and riding back at night, meditating upon my observations. Eventually I concluded to do what I had never thought myself in the least likely to do. I would send Betty to a boarding-school for a year. It was necessary that she should learn how to live with other girls.

I went over to Glenby the next day and found Betty under the beeches on the lawn, just back from a canter. She was sitting on the dappled mare I had given her on her last birthday, and was laughing at the antics of her rejoicing dogs around her. I looked at her with much pleasure; it gladdened me to see how much, nay, how totally a child she still was, despite her Churchill height. Her hair, under her velvet cap, still hung over her shoulders in the same thick plaits; her face had the firm leanness of early youth, but its curves were very fine and delicate. The brown skin, that worried Sara so, was flushed through with dusky color from her gallop; her long, dark eyes were filled with the beautiful unconsciousness of childhood. More than all, the soul in her was still the soul of a child. I found myself wishing that it could always remain so. But I knew it could not; the woman must blossom out some day; it was my duty to see that the flower fulfilled the promise of the bud.

When I told Betty that she must go away to a school for a year, she shrugged, frowned and consented. Betty had learned that she must consent to what I decreed, even when my decrees were opposed to her likings, as she had once fondly believed they never would be. But Betty had acquired confidence in me to the beautiful extent of acquiescing in everything I commanded.

"I'll go, of course, since you wish it, Stephen," she said. "But why do you want me to go? You must have a reason—you always have a reason for anything you do. What is it?"

"That is for you to find out, Betty," I said. "By the time you come back you will have discovered it, I think. If not, it will not have proved itself a good reason and shall be forgotten."

When Betty went away I bade her good-by without burdening her with any useless words of advice.

"Write to me every week, and remember that you are Betty Churchill," I said.

Betty was standing on the steps above, among her dogs. She came down a step and put her arms about my neck.

"I'll remember that you are my friend and that I must live up to you," she said. "Good-by, Stephen."

She kissed me two or three times—good, hearty smacks! did I not say she was still a child? —and stood waving her hand to me as I rode away. I looked back at the end of the avenue and saw her standing there, short-skirted and hatless, fronting the lowering sun with those fearless eyes of hers. So I looked my last on the child Betty.

That was a lonely year. My occupation was gone and I began to fear that I had outlived my usefulness. Life seemed flat, stale, and unprofitable. Betty's weekly letters were all that lent it any savor. They were spicy and piquant enough. Betty was discovered to have unsuspected talents in the epistolary line. At first she was dolefully homesick, and begged me to let her come home. When I refused—it was amazingly hard to refuse—she sulked through three letters, then cheered up and began to enjoy herself. But it was nearly the end of the year when she wrote:

"I've found out why you sent me here, Stephen—and I'm glad you did."

I had to be away from home on unavoidable business the day Betty returned to Glenby. But the next afternoon I went over. I found Betty out and Sara in. The latter was beaming. Betty was so much improved, she declared delightedly. I would hardly know "the dear child."

This alarmed me terribly. What on earth had they done to Betty? I found that she had gone up to the pineland for a walk, and thither I betook myself speedily. When I saw her coming down a long, golden-brown alley I stepped behind a tree to watch her—I wished to see her, myself unseen. As she drew near I gazed at her with pride, and admiration and amazement—and, under it all, a strange, dreadful, heart-sinking, which I could not understand and which I had never in all my life experienced before—no, not even when Sara had refused me.

Betty was a woman! Not by virtue of the simple white dress that clung to her tall, slender figure, revealing lines of exquisite grace and litheness; not by virtue of the glossy masses of dark brown hair heaped high on her head and held there in wonderful shining coils; not by virtue of added softness of curve and daintiness of outline; not because of all these, but because of the dream and wonder and seeking in her eyes. She was a woman, looking, all unconscious of her quest, for love.

The understanding of the change in her came home to me with a shock that must have left me, I think, something white about the lips. I was glad. She was what I had wished her to become. But I wanted the child Betty back; this womanly Betty seemed far away from me.

I stepped out into the path and she saw me, with a brightening of her whole face. She did not rush forward and fling herself into my arms as she would have done a year ago; but she came towards me swiftly, holding out her hand. I had thought her slightly pale when I had first seen her; but now I concluded I had been mistaken, for there was a wonderful sunrise of color in her face. I took her hand—there were no kisses this time.

"Welcome home, Betty," I said.

"Oh, Stephen, it is so good to be back," she breathed, her eyes shining.

She did not say it was good to see me again, as I had hoped she would do. Indeed, after the first minute of greeting, she seemed a trifle cool and distant. We walked for an hour in the pine wood and talked. Betty was brilliant, witty, self-possessed, altogether charming. I thought her perfect and yet my heart ached. What a glorious young thing she was, in that splendid youth of hers! What a prize for some lucky man—confound the obtrusive thought! No doubt we should soon be overrun at Glenby with lovers. I should stumble over some forlorn youth at every step! Well, what of it? Betty would marry, of course. It would be my duty to see that she got a good husband, worthy of her as men go. I thought I preferred the old duty of superintending her studies. But there, it was all the same thing—merely a post-graduate course in applied knowledge. When she began to learn life's greatest lesson of love, I, the tried and true old family friend and mentor, must be on hand to see that the teacher was what I would have him be, even as I had formerly selected her instructor in French and botany. Then, and not until then, would Betty's education be complete.

I rode home very soberly. When I reached The Maples I did what I had not done for years...looked critically at myself in the mirror. The realization that I had grown older came home to me with a new and unpleasant force. There were marked lines on my lean face, and silver glints in the dark hair over my temples. When Betty was ten she had thought me "an old person." Now, at eighteen, she probably thought me a veritable ancient of days. Pshaw, what did it matter? And yet...I thought of her as I had seen her, standing under the pines, and something cold and painful laid its hand on my heart.

My premonitions as to lovers proved correct. Glenby was soon infested with them. Heaven knows where they all came from. I had not supposed there was a quarter as many young men in the whole county; but there they were. Sara was in the seventh heaven of delight. Was not Betty at last a belle? As for the proposals...well, Betty never counted her scalps in public; but every once in a while a visiting youth dropped out and was seen no more at Glenby. One could guess what that meant.

Betty apparently enjoyed all this. I grieve to say that she was a bit of a coquette. I tried to cure her of this serious defect, but for once I found that I had undertaken something I could not accomplish. In vain I lectured, Betty only laughed; in vain I gravely rebuked, Betty only flirted more vivaciously than before. Men might come and men might go, but Betty went on forever. I endured this sort of thing for a year and then I decided that it was time to interfere seriously. I must find a husband for Betty...my fatherly duty would not be fulfilled until I had...nor, indeed, my duty to society. She was not a safe person to have running at large.

None of the men who haunted Glenby was good enough for her. I decided that my nephew,

Frank, would do very well. He was a capital young fellow, handsome, clean-souled, and whole-hearted. From a worldly point of view he was what Sara would have termed an excellent match; he had money, social standing and a rising reputation as a clever young lawyer. Yes, he should have Betty, confound him!

They had never met. I set the wheels going at once. The sooner all the fuss was over the better. I hated fuss and there was bound to be a good deal of it. But I went about the business like an accomplished matchmaker. I invited Frank to visit The Maples and, before he came, I talked much...but not too much...of him to Betty, mingling judicious praise and still more judicious blame together. Women never like a paragon. Betty heard me with more gravity than she usually accorded to my dissertations on young men. She even condescended to ask several questions about him. This I thought a good sign.

To Frank I had said not a word about Betty; when he came to The Maples I took him over to Glenby and, coming upon Betty wandering about among the beeches in the sunset, I introduced him without any warning.

He would have been more than mortal if he had not fallen in love with her upon the spot. It was not in the heart of man to resist her...that dainty, alluring bit of womanhood. She was all in white, with flowers in her hair, and, for a moment, I could have murdered Frank or any other man who dared to commit the sacrilege of loving her.

Then I pulled myself together and left them alone. I might have gone in and talked to Sara...two old folks gently reviewing their youth while the young folks courted outside...but I did not. I prowled about the pine wood, and tried to forget how blithe and handsome that curly-headed boy, Frank, was, and what a flash had sprung into his eyes when he had seen Betty. Well, what of it? Was not that what I had brought him there for? And was I not pleased at the success of my scheme? Certainly I was! Delighted!

Next day Frank went to Glenby without even making the poor pretense of asking me to accompany him. I spent the time of his absence overseeing the construction of a new greenhouse I was having built. I was conscientious in my supervision; but I felt no interest in it. The place was intended for roses, and roses made me think of the pale yellow ones Betty had worn at her breast one evening the week before, when, all lovers being unaccountably absent, we had wandered together under the pines and talked as in the old days before her young womanhood and my gray hairs had risen up to divide us. She had dropped a rose on the brown floor, and I had sneaked back, after I had left her the house, to get it, before I went home. I had it now in my pocket-book. Confound it, mightn't a future uncle cherish a family affection for his prospective niece?

Frank's wooing seemed to prosper. The other young sparks, who had haunted Glenby, faded away after his advent. Betty treated him with most encouraging sweetness; Sara smiled on him; I stood in the background, like a benevolent god of the machine, and flattered myself that I pulled the strings.

At the end of a month something went wrong. Frank came home from Glenby one day in the dumps, and moped for two whole days. I rode down myself on the third. I had not gone much to Glenby that month; but, if there were trouble Bettyward, it was my duty to make smooth the rough places.

As usual, I found Betty in the pineland. I thought she looked rather pale and dull...fretting about Frank no doubt. She brightened up when she saw me, evidently expecting that I had come to straighten matters out; but she pretended to be haughty and indifferent.

"I am glad you haven't forgotten us altogether, Stephen," she said coolly. "You haven't been down for a week."

"I'm flattered that you noticed it," I said, sitting down on a fallen tree and looking up at her as she stood, tall and lithe, against an old pine, with her eyes averted. "I shouldn't have supposed you'd want an old fogy like myself poking about and spoiling the idyllic moments of love's young dream."

"Why do you always speak of yourself as old?" said Betty, crossly, ignoring my reference to Frank.

"Because I am old, my dear. Witness these gray hairs."

I pushed up my hat to show them the more recklessly.

Betty barely glanced at them.

"You have just enough to give you a distinguished look," she said, "and you are only forty. A man is in his prime at forty. He never has any sense until he is forty—and sometimes he doesn't seem to have any even then," she concluded impertinently.

My heart beat. Did Betty suspect? Was that last sentence meant to inform me that she was aware of my secret folly, and laughed at it?

"I came over to see what has gone wrong between you and Frank," I said gravely.

Betty bit her lips.

"Nothing," she said.

"Betty," I said reproachfully, "I brought you up...or endeavored to bring you up...to speak the truth, the whole truth, and nothing but the truth. Don't tell me I have failed. I'll give you another chance. Have you quarreled with Frank?"

"No," said the maddening Betty, "HE quarreled with me. He went away in a temper and I do not care if he never comes back!"

I shook my head.

"This won't do, Betty. As your old family friend I still claim the right to scold you until you have a husband to do the scolding. You mustn't torment Frank. He is too fine a fellow. You must marry him, Betty."

"Must I?" said Betty, a dusky red flaming out on her cheek. She turned her eyes on me in a most disconcerting fashion. "Do YOU wish me to marry Frank, Stephen?"

Betty had a wretched habit of emphasizing pronouns in a fashion calculated to rattle anybody.

"Yes, I do wish it, because I think it will be best for you," I replied, without looking at her. "You must marry some time, Betty, and Frank is the only man I know to whom I could trust you. As your guardian, I have an interest in seeing you well and wisely settled for life. You have always taken my advice and obeyed my wishes; and you've always found my way the best, in the long run, haven't you, Betty? You won't prove rebellious now, I'm sure. You know quite well that I am advising you for your own good. Frank is a splendid young fellow, who loves you with all his heart. Marry him, Betty. Mind, I don't COMMAND. I have no right to do that, and you are too old to be ordered about, if I had. But I wish and advise it. Isn't that enough, Betty?"

I had been looking away from her all the time I was talking, gazing determinedly down a sunlit vista of pines. Every word I said seemed to tear my heart, and come from my lips stained with life-blood. Yes, Betty should marry Frank! But, good God, what would become of me!

Betty left her station under the pine tree, and walked around me until she got right in front of my face. I couldn't help looking at her, for if I moved my eyes she moved too. There was nothing meek or submissive about her; her head was held high, her eyes were blazing, and her cheeks were crimson. But her words were meek enough.

"I will marry Frank if you wish it, Stephen," she said. "You are my friend. I have never crossed your wishes, and, as you say, I have never regretted being guided by them. I will do exactly as you wish in this case also, I promise you that. But, in so solemn a question, I must be very certain what you DO wish. There must be no doubt in my mind or heart. Look me squarely in the eyes, Stephen—as you haven't done once to-day, no, nor once since I came home from school—and, so looking, tell me that you wish me to marry Frank Douglas and I will do it! DO you, Stephen?"

I had to look her in the eyes, since nothing else would do her; and, as I did so, all the might of manhood in me rose up in hot revolt against the lie I would have told her. That unfaltering, impelling gaze of hers drew the truth from my lips in spite of myself.

"No, I don't wish you to marry Frank Douglas, a thousand times no!" I said passionately. "I don't wish you to marry any man on earth but myself. I love you—I love you, Betty. You are dearer to me than life—dearer to me than my own happiness. It was your happiness I thought of—and so I asked you to marry Frank because I believed he would make you a happy woman. That is all!"

Betty's defiance went from her like a flame blown out. She turned away and drooped her proud head.

"It could not have made me a happy woman to marry one man, loving another," she said, in a whisper.

I got up and went over to her.

"Betty, whom do you love?" I asked, also in a whisper.

"You," she murmured meekly—oh, so meekly, my proud little girl!

"Betty," I said brokenly, "I'm old—too old for you—I'm more than twenty years your senior —I'm—"

"Oh!" Betty wheeled around on me and stamped her foot. "Don't mention your age to me again. I don't care if you're as old as Methuselah. But I'm not going to coax you to marry me, sir! If you won't, I'll never marry anybody—I'll live and die an old maid. You can please yourself, of course!"

She turned away, half-laughing, half-crying; but I caught her in my arms and crushed her sweet lips against mine.

"Betty, I'm the happiest man in the world—and I was the most miserable when I came here."

"You deserved to be," said Betty cruelly. "I'm glad you were. Any man as stupid as you deserves to be unhappy. What do you think I felt like, loving you with all my heart, and seeing you simply throwing me at another man's head. Why, I've always loved you, Stephen; but I didn't know it until I went to that detestable school. Then I found out—and I thought that was why you had sent me. But, when I came home, you almost broke my heart. That was why I flirted so with all those poor, nice boys—I wanted to hurt you but I never thought I succeeded. You just went on being FATHERLY. Then, when you brought Frank here, I almost gave up hope; and I tried to make up my mind to marry him; I should have done it if you had insisted. But I had to have one more try for happiness first. I had just one little hope to inspire me with sufficient boldness. I saw you, that night, when you came back here and picked up my rose! I had come back, myself, to be alone and unhappy."

"It is the most wonderful thing that ever happened—that you should love me," I said.

"It's not—I couldn't help it," said Betty, nestling her brown head on my shoulder. "You taught me everything else, Stephen, so nobody but you could teach me how to love. You've made a thorough thing of educating me."

"When will you marry me, Betty?" I asked.

"As soon as I can fully forgive you for trying to make me marry somebody else," said Betty.

It was rather hard lines on Frank, when you come to think of it. But, such is the selfishness of human nature that we didn't think much about Frank. The young fellow behaved like the

Douglas he was. Went a little white about the lips when I told him, wished me all happiness, and went quietly away, "gentleman unafraid."

He has since married and is, I understand, very happy. Not as happy as I am, of course; that is impossible, because there is only one Betty in the world, and she is my wife.

IN HER SELFLESS MOOD

The raw wind of an early May evening was puffing in and out the curtains of the room where Naomi Holland lay dying. The air was moist and chill, but the sick woman would not have the window closed.

"I can't get my breath if you shut everything up so tight," she said. "Whatever comes, I ain't going to be smothered to death, Car'line Holland."

Outside of the window grew a cherry tree, powdered with moist buds with the promise of blossoms she would not live to see. Between its boughs she saw a crystal cup of sky over hills that were growing dim and purple. The outside air was full of sweet, wholesome springtime sounds that drifted in fitfully. There were voices and whistles in the barnyard, and now and then faint laughter. A bird alighted for a moment on a cherry bough, and twittered restlessly. Naomi knew that white mists were hovering in the silent hollows, that the maple at the gate wore a misty blossom red, and that violet stars were shining bluely on the brooklands.

The room was a small, plain one. The floor was bare, save for a couple of braided rugs, the plaster discolored, the walls dingy and glaring. There had never been much beauty in Naomi Holland's environment, and, now that she was dying, there was even less.

At the open window a boy of about ten years was leaning out over the sill and whistling. He was tall for his age, and beautiful—the hair a rich auburn with a glistening curl in it, skin very white and warm-tinted, eyes small and of a greenish blue, with dilated pupils and long lashes. He had a weak chin, and a full, sullen mouth.

The bed was in the corner farthest from the window; on it the sick woman, in spite of the pain that was her portion continually, was lying as quiet and motionless as she had done ever since she had lain down upon it for the last time. Naomi Holland never complained; when the agony was at its worst, she shut her teeth more firmly over her bloodless lip, and her great black eyes glared at the blank wall before in a way that gave her attendants what they called "the creeps," but no word or moan escaped her.

Between the paroxysms she kept up her keen interest in the life that went on about her. Nothing escaped her sharp, alert eyes and ears. This evening she lay spent on the crumpled pillows; she had had a bad spell in the afternoon and it had left her very weak. In the dim light her extremely long face looked corpse-like already. Her black hair lay in a heavy braid over the pillow and down the counterpane. It was all that was left of her beauty, and she took a fierce joy in it. Those long, glistening, sinuous tresses must be combed and braided every day, no matter what came.

A girl of fourteen was curled up on a chair at the head of the bed, with her head resting on the pillow. The boy at the window was her half-brother; but, between Christopher Holland and Eunice Carr, not the slightest resemblance existed.

Presently the sibilant silence was broken by a low, half-strangled sob. The sick woman, who had been watching a white evening star through the cherry boughs, turned impatiently at the sound.

"I wish you'd get over that, Eunice," she said sharply. "I don't want any one crying over me until I'm dead; and then you'll have plenty else to do, most likely. If it wasn't for Christopher I wouldn't be anyways unwilling to die. When one has had such a life as I've had, there isn't much in death to be afraid of. Only, a body would like to go right off, and not die by inches, like this. 'Tain't fair!"

She snapped out the last sentence as if addressing some unseen, tyrannical presence; her voice, at least, had not weakened, but was as clear and incisive as ever. The boy at the window stopped whistling, and the girl silently wiped her eyes on her faded gingham apron.

Naomi drew her own hair over her lips, and kissed it.

"You'll never have hair like that, Eunice," she said. "It does seem most too pretty to bury, doesn't it? Mind you see that it is fixed nice when I'm laid out. Comb it right up on my head and braid it there."

A sound, such as might be wrung from a suffering animal, came from the girl, but at the same moment the door opened and a woman entered.

"Chris," she said sharply, "you get right off for the cows, you lazy little scamp! You knew right well you had to go for them, and here you've been idling, and me looking high and low for you. Make haste now; it's ridiculous late."

The boy pulled in his head and scowled at his aunt, but he dared not disobey, and went out slowly with a sulky mutter.

His aunt subdued a movement, that might have developed into a sound box on his ears, with a rather frightened glance at the bed. Naomi Holland was spent and dying, but her temper was still a thing to hold in dread, and her sister-in-law did not choose to rouse it by slapping Christopher. To her and her co-nurse the spasms of rage, which the sick woman sometimes had, seemed to partake of the nature of devil possession. The last one, only three days before, had been provoked by Christopher's complaint of some real or fancied ill-treatment from his aunt, and the latter had no mind to bring on another. She went over to the bed, and straightened the clothes.

"Sarah and I are going out to milk, Naomi, Eunice will stay with you. She can run for us if you feel another spell coming on."

Naomi Holland looked up at her sister-in-law with something like malicious enjoyment.

"I ain't going to have any more spells, Car'line Anne. I'm going to die to-night. But you needn't hurry milking for that, at all. I'll take my time."

She liked to see the alarm that came over the other woman's face. It was richly worth while to scare Caroline Holland like that.

"Are you feeling worse, Naomi?" asked the latter shakily. "If you are I'll send for Charles to go for the doctor."

"No, you won't. What good can the doctor do me? I don't want either his or Charles' permission to die. You can go and milk at your ease. I won't die till you're done—I won't deprive you of the pleasure of seeing me."

Mrs. Holland shut her lips and went out of the room with a martyr-like expression. In some ways Naomi Holland was not an exacting patient, but she took her satisfaction out in the biting, malicious speeches she never failed to make. Even on her death-bed her hostility to her sister-in-law had to find vent.

Outside, at the steps, Sarah Spencer was waiting, with the milk pails over her arm. Sarah Spencer had no fixed abiding place, but was always to be found where there was illness. Her experience, and an utter lack of nerves, made her a good nurse. She was a tall, homely woman with iron gray hair and a lined face. Beside her, the trim little Caroline Anne, with her light step and round, apple-red face, looked almost girlish.

The two women walked to the barnyard, discussing Naomi in undertones as they went. The house they had left behind grew very still.

In Naomi Holland's room the shadows were gathering. Eunice timidly bent over her mother.

"Ma, do you want the light lit?"

"No, I'm watching that star just below the big cherry bough. I'll see it set behind the hill. I've seen it there, off and on, for twelve years, and now I'm taking a good-by look at it. I want you to keep still, too. I've got a few things to think over, and I don't want to be disturbed."

The girl lifted herself about noiselessly and locked her hands over the bed-post. Then she laid her face down on them, biting at them silently until the marks of her teeth showed white against their red roughness.

Naomi Holland did not notice her. She was looking steadfastly at the great, pearl-like sparkle in the faint-hued sky. When it finally disappeared from her vision she struck her long, thin hands together twice, and a terrible expression came over her face for a moment. But, when she spoke, her voice was quite calm.

"You can light the candle now, Eunice. Put it up on the shelf here, where it won't shine in my eyes. And then sit down on the foot of the bed where I can see you. I've got something to say to you."

Eunice obeyed her noiselessly. As the pallid light shot up, it revealed the child plainly. She was thin and ill-formed—one shoulder being slightly higher than the other. She was dark, like her mother, but her features were irregular, and her hair fell in straggling, dim locks about her face. Her eyes were a dark brown, and over one was the slanting red scar of a birth mark.

Naomi Holland looked at her with the contempt she had never made any pretense of concealing. The girl was bone of her bone and flesh of her flesh, but she had never loved her; all the mother love in her had been lavished on her son.

When Eunice had placed the candle on the shelf and drawn down the ugly blue paper blinds, shutting out the strips of violet sky where a score of glimmering points were now visible, she sat down on the foot of the bed, facing her mother.

"The door is shut, is it, Eunice?"

Eunice nodded.

"Because I don't want Car'line or any one else peeking and harking to what I've got to say. She's out milking now, and I must make the most of the chance. Eunice, I'm going to die, and..."

"Ma!"

"There now, no taking on! You knew it had to come sometime soon. I haven't the strength to talk much, so I want you just to be quiet and listen. I ain't feeling any pain now, so I can think and talk pretty clear. Are you listening, Eunice?"

"Yes, ma."

"Mind you are. It's about Christopher. It hasn't been out of my mind since I laid down here. I've fought for a year to live, on his account, and it ain't any use. I must just die and leave him, and I don't know what he'll do. It's dreadful to think of."

She paused, and struck her shrunken hand sharply against the table.

"If he was bigger and could look out for himself it wouldn't be so bad. But he is only a little fellow, and Car'line hates him. You'll both have to live with her until you're grown up. She'll put on him and abuse him. He's like his father in some ways; he's got a temper and he is stubborn. He'll never get on with Car'line. Now, Eunice, I'm going to get you to promise to take my place with Christopher when I'm dead, as far as you can. You've got to; it's your duty. But I want you to promise."

"I will, ma," whispered the girl solemnly.

"You haven't much force—you never had. If you was smart, you could do a lot for him. But you'll have to do your best. I want you to promise me faithfully that you'll stand by him and protect him—that you won't let people impose on him; that you'll never desert him as long as he needs you, no matter what comes. Eunice, promise me this!"

In her excitement the sick woman raised herself up in the bed, and clutched the girl's thin arm. Her eyes were blazing and two scarlet spots glowed in her thin cheeks.

Eunice's face was white and tense. She clasped her hands as one in prayer.

"Mother, I promise it!"

Naomi relaxed her grip on the girl's arm and sank back exhausted on the pillow. A death-like look came over her face as the excitement faded.

"My mind is easier now. But if I could only have lived another year or two! And I hate Car'line—hate her! Eunice, don't you ever let her abuse my boy! If she did, or if you neglected him, I'd come back from my grave to you! As for the property, things will be pretty straight. I've seen to that. There'll be no squabbling and doing Christopher out of his rights. He's to have the farm as soon as he's old enough to work it, and he's to provide for you. And, Eunice, remember what you've promised!"

Outside, in the thickly gathering dusk, Caroline Holland and Sarah Spencer were at the dairy, straining the milk into creamers, for which Christopher was sullenly pumping water. The house was far from the road, up to which a long red lane led; across the field was the old Holland homestead where Caroline lived; her unmarried sister-in-law, Electa Holland, kept house for her while she waited on Naomi.

It was her night to go home and sleep, but Naomi's words haunted her, although she believed they were born of pure "cantankerousness."

"You'd better go in and look at her, Sarah," she said, as she rinsed out the pails. "If you think I'd better stay here to-night, I will. If the woman was like anybody else a body would know what to do; but, if she thought she could scare us by saying she was going to die, she'd say it."

When Sarah went in, the sick room was very quiet. In her opinion, Naomi was no worse than usual, and she told Caroline so; but the latter felt vaguely uneasy and concluded to stay.

Naomi was as cool and defiant as customary. She made them bring Christopher in to say good-night and had him lifted up on the bed to kiss her. Then she held him back and looked at him admiringly—at the bright curls and rosy cheeks and round, firm limbs. The boy was uncomfortable under her gaze and squirmed hastily down. Her eyes followed him greedily, as he went out. When the door closed behind him, she groaned. Sarah Spencer was startled. She had never heard Naomi Holland groan since she had come to wait on her.

"Are you feeling any worse, Naomi? Is the pain coming back?"

"No. Go and tell Car'line to give Christopher some of that grape jelly on his bread before he goes to bed. She'll find it in the cupboard under the stairs."

Presently the house grew very still. Caroline had dropped asleep on the sitting-room lounge, across the hall. Sarah Spencer nodded over her knitting by the table in the sick room. She had told Eunice to go to bed, but the child refused. She still sat huddled up on the foot of the bed, watching her mother's face intently. Naomi appeared to sleep. The candle burned long, and the wick was crowned by a little cap of fiery red that seemed to watch Eunice like some impish goblin. The wavering light cast grotesque shadows of Sarah Spencer's head on the wall. The thin curtains at the window wavered to and fro, as if shaken by ghostly hands.

At midnight Naomi Holland opened her eyes. The child she had never loved was the only one to go with her to the brink of the Unseen.

"Eunice—remember!"

It was the faintest whisper. The soul, passing over the threshold of another life, strained back to its only earthly tie. A quiver passed over the long, pallid face.

A horrible scream rang through the silent house. Sarah Spencer sprang out of her doze in consternation, and gazed blankly at the shrieking child. Caroline came hurrying in with distended eyes. On the bed Naomi Holland lay dead.

In the room where she had died Naomi Holland lay in her coffin. It was dim and hushed; but, in the rest of the house, the preparations for the funeral were being hurried on. Through it all Eunice moved, calm and silent. Since her one wild spasm of screaming by her mother's death-bed she had shed no tear, given no sign of grief. Perhaps, as her mother had said, she had no time. There was Christopher to be looked after. The boy's grief was stormy and uncontrolled. He had cried until he was utterly exhausted. It was Eunice who soothed him, coaxed him to eat, kept him constantly by her. At night she took him to her own room and watched over him while he slept.

When the funeral was over the household furniture was packed away or sold. The house was locked up and the farm rented. There was nowhere for the children to go, save to their uncle's. Caroline Holland did not want them, but, having to take them, she grimly made up her mind to do what she considered her duty by them. She had five children of her own and between them and Christopher a standing feud had existed from the time he could walk.

She had never liked Naomi. Few people did. Benjamin Holland had not married until late in life, and his wife had declared war on his family at sight. She was a stranger in Avonlea,—a widow, with a three year-old child. She made few friends, as some people always asserted that she was not in her right mind.

Within a year of her second marriage Christopher was born, and from the hour of his birth his mother had worshiped him blindly. He was her only solace. For him she toiled and pinched and saved. Benjamin Holland had not been "fore-handed" when she married him; but, when he died, six years after his marriage, he was a well-to-do man.

Naomi made no pretense of mourning for him. It was an open secret that they had quarreled like the proverbial cat and dog. Charles Holland and his wife had naturally sided with Benjamin, and Naomi fought her battles single-handed. After her husband's death, she managed to farm alone, and made it pay. When the mysterious malady which was to end her life first seized on her she fought against it with all the strength and stubbornness of her strong and stubborn nature. Her will won for her an added year of life, and then she had to yield. She tasted all the bitterness of death the day on which she lay down on her bed, and saw her enemy come in to rule her house.

But Caroline Holland was not a bad or unkind woman. True, she did not love Naomi or her children; but the woman was dying and must be looked after for the sake of common humanity. Caroline thought she had done well by her sister-in-law.

When the red clay was heaped over Naomi's grave in the Avonlea burying ground, Caroline took Eunice and Christopher home with her. Christopher did not want to go; it was Eunice who reconciled him. He clung to her with an exacting affection born of loneliness and grief.

In the days that followed Caroline Holland was obliged to confess to herself that there would have been no doing anything with Christopher had it not been for Eunice. The boy was sullen and obstinate, but his sister had an unfailing influence over him.

In Charles Holland's household no one was allowed to eat the bread of idleness. His own children were all girls, and Christopher came in handy as a chore boy. He was made to work—perhaps too hard. But Eunice helped him, and did half his work for him when nobody knew. When he quarreled with his cousins, she took his part; whenever possible she took on herself the blame and punishment of his misdeeds.

Electa Holland was Charles' unmarried sister. She had kept house for Benjamin until he married; then Naomi had bundled her out. Electa had never forgiven her for it. Her hatred passed on to Naomi's children. In a hundred petty ways she revenged herself on them. For herself, Eunice bore it patiently; but it was a different matter when it touched Christopher.

Once Electa boxed Christopher's ears. Eunice, who was knitting by the table, stood up. A resemblance to her mother, never before visible, came out in her face like a brand. She lifted her hand and slapped Electa's cheek deliberately twice, leaving a dull red mark where she struck.

"If you ever strike my brother again," she said, slowly and vindictively, "I will slap your face every time you do. You have no right to touch him."

"My patience, what a fury!" said Electa. "Naomi Holland'll never be dead as long as you're alive!"

She told Charles of the affair and Eunice was severely punished. But Electa never interfered with Christopher again.

All the discordant elements in the Holland household could not prevent the children from growing up. It was a consummation which the harrassed Caroline devoutly wished. When Christopher Holland was seventeen he was a man grown—a big, strapping fellow. His childish beauty had coarsened, but he was thought handsome by many.

He took charge of his mother's farm then, and the brother and sister began their new life together in the long-unoccupied house. There were few regrets on either side when they left Charles Holland's roof. In her secret heart Eunice felt an unspeakable relief.

Christopher had been "hard to manage," as his uncle said, in the last year. He was getting into the habit of keeping late hours and doubtful company. This always provoked an explosion of wrath from Charles Holland, and the conflicts between him and his nephew were frequent and bitter.

For four years after their return home Eunice had a hard and anxious life. Christopher was idle and dissipated. Most people regarded him as a worthless fellow, and his uncle washed his hands of him utterly. Only Eunice never failed him; she never reproached or railed; she worked like a slave to keep things together. Eventually her patience prevailed. Christopher, to a great extent, reformed and worked harder. He was never unkind to Eunice, even in his rages. It was not in him to appreciate or return her devotion; but his tolerant acceptance of it was her solace.

When Eunice was twenty-eight, Edward Bell wanted to marry her. He was a plain, middle-aged widower with four children; but, as Caroline did not fail to remind her, Eunice herself was not for every market, and the former did her best to make the match. She might have succeeded had it not been for Christopher. When he, in spite of Caroline's skillful management, got an inkling of what was going on, he flew into a true Holland rage. If Eunice married and left him—he would sell the farm and go to the Devil by way of the Klondike. He could not, and would not, do without her. No arrangement suggested by Caroline availed to pacify him, and, in the end, Eunice refused to marry Edward Bell. She could not leave Christopher, she said simply, and in this she stood rock-firm. Caroline could not budge her an inch.

"You're a fool, Eunice," she said, when she was obliged to give up in despair. "It's not likely you'll ever have another chance. As for Chris, in a year or two he'll be marrying himself, and where will you be then? You'll find your nose nicely out of joint when he brings a wife in here."

The shaft went home. Eunice's lips turned white. But she said, faintly, "The house is big enough for us both, if he does."

Caroline sniffed.

"Maybe so. You'll find out. However, there's no use talking. You're as set as your mother was, and nothing would ever budge her an inch. I only hope you won't be sorry for it."

When three more years had passed Christopher began to court Victoria Pye. The affair went on for some time before either Eunice or the Hollands go wind of it. When they did there was an explosion. Between the Hollands and the Pyes, root and branch, existed a feud that dated back for three generations. That the original cause of the quarrel was totally forgotten did not matter; it was matter of family pride that a Holland should have no dealings with a Pye.

When Christopher flew so openly in the face of this cherished hatred, there could be nothing less than consternation. Charles Holland broke through his determination to have nothing to do with Christopher, to remonstrate. Caroline went to Eunice in as much of a splutter as if Christopher had been her own brother.

Eunice did not care a row of pins for the Holland-Pye feud. Victoria was to her what any other girl, upon whom Christopher cast eyes of love, would have been—a supplanter. For the first time in her life she was torn with passionate jealousy; existence became a nightmare to her. Urged on by Caroline, and her own pain, she ventured to remonstrate with Christopher, also. She had expected a burst of rage, but he was surprisingly good-natured. He seemed even amused.

"What have you got against Victoria?" he asked, tolerantly.

Eunice had no answer ready. It was true that nothing could be said against the girl. She felt helpless and baffled. Christopher laughed at her silence.

"I guess you're a little jealous," he said. "You must have expected I would get married some time. This house is big enough for us all. You'd better look at the matter sensibly, Eunice. Don't let Charles and Caroline put nonsense into your head. A man must marry to please himself."

Christopher was out late that night. Eunice waited up for him, as she always did. It was a chilly spring evening, reminding her of the night her mother had died. The kitchen was in spotless order, and she sat down on a stiff-backed chair by the window to wait for her brother.

She did not want a light. The moonlight fell in with faint illumination. Outside, the wind was blowing over a bed of new-sprung mint in the garden, and was suggestively fragrant. It was a very old-fashioned garden, full of perennials Naomi Holland had planted long ago. Eunice always kept it primly neat. She had been working in it that day, and felt tired.

She was all alone in the house and the loneliness filled her with a faint dread. She had tried all that day to reconcile herself to Christopher's marriage, and had partially succeeded. She told herself that she could still watch over him and care for his comfort. She would even try to love Victoria; after all, it might be pleasant to have another woman in the house. So, sitting there, she fed her hungry soul with these husks of comfort.

When she heard Christopher's step she moved about quickly to get a light. He frowned when he saw her; he had always resented her sitting up for him. He sat down by the stove and took off his boots, while Eunice got a lunch for him. After he had eaten it in silence he made no move to go to bed. A chill, premonitory fear crept over Eunice. It did not surprise her at all when Christopher finally said, abruptly, "Eunice, I've a notion to get married this spring."

Eunice clasped her hands together under the table. It was what she had been expecting. She said so, in a monotonous voice.

"We must make some arrangement for—for you, Eunice," Christopher went on, in a hurried, hesitant way, keeping his eyes riveted doggedly on his plate. "Victoria doesn't exactly like—well, she thinks it's better for young married folks to begin life by themselves, and I guess she's about right. You wouldn't find it comfortable, anyhow, having to step back to second place after being mistress here so long."

Eunice tried to speak, but only an indistinct murmur came from her bloodless lips. The sound made Christopher look up. Something in her face irritated him. He pushed back his chair impatiently.

"Now, Eunice, don't go taking on. It won't be any use. Look at this business in a sensible way. I'm fond of you, and all that, but a man is bound to consider his wife first. I'll provide for you comfortably."

"Do you mean to say that your wife is going to turn me out?" Eunice gasped, rather than spoke, the words.

Christopher drew his reddish brows together.

"I just mean that Victoria says she won't marry me if she has to live with you. She's afraid of you. I told her you wouldn't interfere with her, but she wasn't satisfied. It's your own fault, Eunice. You've always been so queer and close that people think you're an awful crank. Victoria's young and lively, and you and she wouldn't get on at all. There isn't any question of turning you out. I'll build a little house for you somewhere, and you'll be a great deal better off there than you would be here. So don't make a fuss."

Eunice did not look as if she were going to make a fuss. She sat as if turned to stone, her hands lying palm upward in her lap. Christopher got up, hugely relieved that the dreaded explanation was over.

"Guess I'll go to bed. You'd better have gone long ago. It's all nonsense, this waiting up for me."

When he had gone Eunice drew a long, sobbing breath and looked about her like a dazed soul. All the sorrow of her life was as nothing to the desolation that assailed her now.

She rose and, with uncertain footsteps, passed out through the hall and into the room where her mother died. She had always kept it locked and undisturbed; it was arranged just as Naomi Holland had left it. Eunice tottered to the bed and sat down on it.

She recalled the promise she had made to her mother in that very room. Was the power to keep it to be wrested from her? Was she to be driven from her home and parted from the only creature she had on earth to love? And would Christopher allow it, after all her sacrifices for him? Aye, that he would! He cared more for that black-eyed, waxen-faced girl at the old Pye place than for his own kin. Eunice put her hands over her dry, burning eyes and groaned aloud.

Caroline Holland had her hour of triumph over Eunice when she heard it all. To one of her nature there was no pleasure so sweet as that of saying, "I told you so." Having said it, however, she offered Eunice a home. Electa Holland was dead, and Eunice might fill her place very acceptably, if she would.

"You can't go off and live by yourself," Caroline told her. "It's all nonsense to talk of such a thing. We will give you a home, if Christopher is going to turn you out. You were always a fool, Eunice, to pet and pamper him as you've done. This is the thanks you get for it—turned out like a dog for his fine wife's whim! I only wish your mother was alive!"

It was probably the first time Caroline had ever wished this. She had flown at Christopher like a fury about the matter, and had been rudely insulted for her pains. Christopher had told her to mind her own business.

When Caroline cooled down she made some arrangements with him, to all of which Eunice listlessly assented. She did not care what became of her. When Christopher Holland brought Victoria as mistress to the house where his mother had toiled, and suffered, and ruled with her rod of iron, Eunice was gone. In Charles Holland's household she took Electa's place—an unpaid upper servant.

Charles and Caroline were kind enough to her, and there was plenty to do. For five years her dull, colorless life went on, during which time she never crossed the threshold of the house where Victoria Holland ruled with a sway as absolute as Naomi's had been. Caroline's curiosity led her, after her first anger had cooled, to make occasional calls, the observations of which she faithfully reported to Eunice. The latter never betrayed any interest in them, save once. This was when Caroline came home full of the news that Victoria had had the room where Naomi died opened up, and showily furnished as a parlor. Then Eunice's sallow face crimsoned, and her eyes flashed, over the desecration. But no word of comment or complaint ever crossed her lips.

She knew, as every one else knew, that the glamor soon went from Christopher Holland's married life. The marriage proved an unhappy one. Not unnaturally, although unjustly, Eunice blamed Victoria for this, and hated her more than ever for it.

Christopher seldom came to Charles' house. Possibly he felt ashamed. He had grown into a morose, silent man, at home and abroad. It was said he had gone back to his old drinking habits.

One fall Victoria Holland went to town to visit her married sister. She took their only child with her. In her absence Christopher kept house for himself.

It was a fall long remembered in Avonlea. With the dropping of the leaves, and the shortening of the dreary days, the shadow of a fear fell over the land. Charles Holland brought the fateful news home one night.

"There's smallpox in Charlottetown—five or six cases. Came in one of the vessels. There was a concert, and a sailor from one of the ships was there, and took sick the next day."

This was alarming enough. Charlottetown was not so very far away and considerable traffic went on between it and the north shore districts.

When Caroline recounted the concert story to Christopher the next morning his ruddy face turned quite pale. He opened his lips as if to speak, then closed them again. They were sitting in the kitchen; Caroline had run over to return some tea she had borrowed, and, incidentally, to see what she could of Victoria's housekeeping in her absence. Her eyes had been busy while her tongue ran on, so she did not notice the man's pallor and silence.

"How long does it take for smallpox to develop after one has been exposed to it?" he asked abruptly, when Caroline rose to go.

"Ten to fourteen days, I calc'late," was her answer. "I must see about having the girls vaccinated right off. It'll likely spread. When do you expect Victoria home?"

"When she's ready to come, whenever that will be," was the gruff response.

A week later Caroline said to Eunice, "Whatever's got Christopher? He hasn't been out anywhere for ages—just hangs round home the whole time. It's something new for him. I s'pose the place is so quiet, now Madam Victoria's away, that he can find some rest for his soul. I believe I'll run over after milking and see how he's getting on. You might as well come, too, Eunice."

Eunice shook her head. She had all her mother's obstinacy, and darken Victoria's door she would not. She went on patiently darning socks, sitting at the west window, which was her favorite position—perhaps because she could look from it across the sloping field and past the crescent curve of maple grove to her lost home.

After milking, Caroline threw a shawl over her head and ran across the field. The house looked lonely and deserted. As she fumbled at the latch of the gate the kitchen door opened, and Christopher Holland appeared on the threshold.

"Don't come any farther," he called.

Caroline fell back in blank astonishment. Was this some more of Victoria's work?

"I ain't an agent for the smallpox," she called back viciously.

Christopher did not heed her.

"Will you go home and ask uncle if he'll go, or send for Doctor Spencer? He's the smallpox doctor. I'm sick."

Caroline felt a thrill of dismay and fear. She faltered a few steps backward.

"Sick? What's the matter with you?"

"I was in Charlottetown that night, and went to the concert. That sailor sat right beside me. I thought at the time he looked sick. It was just twelve days ago. I've felt bad all day yesterday and to-day. Send for the doctor. Don't come near the house, or let any one else come near."

He went in and shut the door. Caroline stood for a few moments in an almost ludicrous panic. Then she turned and ran, as if for her life, across the field. Eunice saw her coming and met her at the door.

"Mercy on us!" gasped Caroline. "Christopher's sick and he thinks he's got the smallpox. Where's Charles?"

Eunice tottered back against the door. Her hand went up to her side in a way that had been getting very common with her of late. Even in the midst of her excitement Caroline noticed it.

"Eunice, what makes you do that every time anything startles you?" she asked sharply. "Is it anything about your heart?"

"I don't—know. A little pain—it's gone now. Did you say that Christopher has—the smallpox?"

"Well, he says so himself, and it's more than likely, considering the circumstances. I declare, I never got such a turn in my life. It's a dreadful thing. I must find Charles at once—there'll be a hundred things to do."

Eunice hardly heard her. Her mind was centered upon one idea. Christopher was ill—alone—she must go to him. It did not matter what his disease was. When Caroline came in from her breathless expedition to the barn, she found Eunice standing by the table, with her hat and shawl on, tying up a parcel.

"Eunice! Where on earth are you going?"

"Over home," said Eunice. "If Christopher is going to be ill he must be nursed, and I'm the one to do it. He ought to be seen to right away."

"Eunice Carr! Have you gone clean out of your senses? It's the smallpox—the smallpox! If he's got it he'll have to be taken to the smallpox hospital in town. You shan't stir a step to go to that house!"

"I will." Eunice faced her excited aunt quietly. The odd resemblance to her mother, which only came out in moments of great tension, was plainly visible. "He shan't go to the hospital—they never get proper attention there. You needn't try to stop me. It won't put you or your family in any danger."

Caroline fell helplessly into a chair. She felt that it would be of no use to argue with a woman so determined. She wished Charles was there. But Charles had already gone, post-haste, for the doctor.

With a firm step, Eunice went across the field foot-path she had not trodden for so long. She felt no fear—rather a sort of elation. Christopher needed her once more; the interloper who had come between them was not there. As she walked through the frosty twilight she thought of the promise made to Naomi Holland, years ago.

Christopher saw her coming and waved her back.

"Don't come any nearer, Eunice. Didn't Caroline tell you? I'm taking smallpox."

Eunice did not pause. She went boldly through the yard and up the porch steps. He retreated before her and held the door.

"Eunice, you're crazy, girl! Go home, before it's too late."

Eunice pushed open the door resolutely and went in.

"It's too late now. I'm here, and I mean to stay and nurse you, if it's the smallpox you've got. Maybe it's not. Just now, when a person has a finger-ache, he thinks it's smallpox. Anyhow, whatever it is, you ought to be in bed and looked after. You'll catch cold. Let me get a light and have a look at you."

Christopher had sunk into a chair. His natural selfishness reasserted itself, and he made no further effort to dissuade Eunice. She got a lamp and set it on the table by him, while she scrutinized his face closely.

"You look feverish. What do you feel like? When did you take sick?"

"Yesterday afternoon. I have chills and hot spells and pains in my back. Eunice, do you think it's really smallpox? And will I die?"

He caught her hands, and looked imploringly up at her, as a child might have done. Eunice felt a wave of love and tenderness sweep warmly over her starved heart.

"Don't worry. Lots of people recover from smallpox if they're properly nursed, and you'll be that, for I'll see to it. Charles has gone for the doctor, and we'll know when he comes. You must go straight to bed."

She took off her hat and shawl, and hung them up. She felt as much at home as if she had never been away. She had got back to her kingdom, and there was none to dispute it with her. When Dr. Spencer and old Giles Blewett, who had had smallpox in his youth, came, two hours later, they found Eunice in serene charge. The house was in order and reeking of disinfectants. Victoria's fine furniture and fixings were being bundled out of the parlor. There was no bedroom downstairs, and, if Christopher was going to be ill, he must be installed there.

The doctor looked grave.

"I don't like it," he said, "but I'm not quite sure yet. If it is smallpox the eruption will probably be out by morning. I must admit he has most of the symptoms. Will you have him taken to the hospital?"

"No," said Eunice, decisively. "I'll nurse him myself. I'm not afraid and I'm well and strong."

"Very well. You've been vaccinated lately?"

"Yes."

"Well, nothing more can be done at present. You may as well lie down for a while and save your strength."

But Eunice could not do that. There was too much to attend to. She went out to the hall and threw up the window. Down below, at a safe distance, Charles Holland was waiting. The cold wind blew up to Eunice the odor of the disinfectants with which he had steeped himself.

"What does the doctor say?" he shouted.

"He thinks it's the smallpox. Have you sent word to Victoria?"

"Yes, Jim Blewett drove into town and told her. She'll stay with her sister till it is over. Of course it's the best thing for her to do. She's terribly frightened."

Eunice's lip curled contemptuously. To her, a wife who could desert her husband, no matter what disease he had, was an incomprehensible creature. But it was better so; she would have Christopher all to herself.

The night was long and wearisome, but the morning came all too soon for the dread certainty it brought. The doctor pronounced the case smallpox. Eunice had hoped against hope, but now, knowing the worst, she was very calm and resolute.

By noon the fateful yellow flag was flying over the house, and all arrangements had been made. Caroline was to do the necessary cooking, and Charles was to bring the food and leave it in the yard. Old Giles Blewett was to come every day and attend to the stock, as well as help Eunice with the sick man; and the long, hard fight with death began.

It was a hard fight, indeed. Christopher Holland, in the clutches of the loathsome disease, was an object from which his nearest and dearest might have been pardoned for shrinking. But Eunice never faltered; she never left her post. Sometimes she dozed in a chair by the bed, but she never lay down. Her endurance was something wonderful, her patience and tenderness almost superhuman. To and fro she went, in noiseless ministry, as the long, dreadful days wore away, with a quiet smile on her lips, and in her dark, sorrowful eyes the rapt look of a pictured saint in some dim cathedral niche. For her there was no world outside the bare room where lay the repulsive object she loved.

One day the doctor looked very grave. He had grown well-hardened to pitiful scenes in his life-time; but he shrunk from telling Eunice that her brother could not live. He had never seen such devotion as hers. It seemed brutal to tell her that it had been in vain.

But Eunice had seen it for herself. She took it very calmly, the doctor thought. And she had her reward at last—such as it was. She thought it amply sufficient.

One night Christopher Holland opened his swollen eyes as she bent over him. They were alone in the old house. It was raining outside, and the drops rattled noisily on the panes.

Christopher smiled at his sister with parched lips, and put out a feeble hand toward her.

"Eunice," he said faintly, "you've been the best sister ever a man had. I haven't treated you right; but you've stood by me to the last. Tell Victoria—tell her—to be good to you—"

His voice died away into an inarticulate murmur. Eunice Carr was alone with her dead.

They buried Christopher Holland in haste and privacy the next day. The doctor disinfected the house, and Eunice was to stay there alone until it might be safe to make other arrangements. She had not shed a tear; the doctor thought she was a rather odd person, but he had a great admiration for her. He told her she was the best nurse he had ever seen. To Eunice, praise or blame mattered nothing. Something in her life had snapped—some vital interest had departed. She wondered how she could live through the dreary, coming years.

Late that night she went into the room where her mother and brother had died. The window was open and the cold, pure air was grateful to her after the drug-laden atmosphere she had breathed so long. She knelt down by the stripped bed.

"Mother," she said aloud, "I have kept my promise."

When she tried to rise, long after, she staggered and fell across the bed, with her hand pressed on her heart. Old Giles Blewett found her there in the morning. There was a smile on her face.

THE CONSCIENCE CASE OF DAVID BELL

Eben Bell came in with an armful of wood and banged it cheerfully down in the box behind the glowing Waterloo stove, which was coloring the heart of the little kitchen's gloom with tremulous, rose-red whirls of light.

"There, sis, that's the last chore on my list. Bob's milking. Nothing more for me to do but put on my white collar for meeting. Avonlea is more than lively since the evangelist came, ain't it, though!"

Mollie Bell nodded. She was curling her hair before the tiny mirror that hung on the whitewashed wall and distorted her round, pink-and-white face into a grotesque caricature.

"Wonder who'll stand up to-night," said Eben reflectively, sitting down on the edge of the wood-box. "There ain't many sinners left in Avonlea—only a few hardened chaps like myself."

"You shouldn't talk like that," said Mollie rebukingly. "What if father heard you?"

"Father wouldn't hear me if I shouted it in his ear," returned Eben. "He goes around, these days, like a man in a dream and a mighty bad dream at that. Father has always been a good man. What's the matter with him?"

"I don't know," said Mollie, dropping her voice. "Mother is dreadfully worried over him. And everybody is talking, Eb. It just makes me squirm. Flora Jane Fletcher asked me last night why father never testified, and him one of the elders. She said the minister was perplexed about it. I felt my face getting red."

"Why didn't you tell her it was no business of hers?" said Eben angrily. "Old Flora Jane had better mind her own business."

"But all the folks are talking about it, Eb. And mother is fretting her heart out over it. Father has never acted like himself since these meetings began. He just goes there night after night, and sits like a mummy, with his head down. And almost everybody else in Avonlea has testified."

"Oh, no, there's lots haven't," said Eben. "Matthew Cuthbert never has, nor Uncle Elisha, nor any of the Whites."

"But everybody knows they don't believe in getting up and testifying, so nobody wonders when they don't. Besides," Mollie laughed—"Matthew could never get a word out in public, if he did believe in it. He'd be too shy. But," she added with a sigh, "it isn't that way with father. He believes in testimony, so people wonder why he doesn't get up. Why, even old Josiah Sloane gets up every night."

"With his whiskers sticking out every which way, and his hair ditto," interjected the graceless Eben.

"When the minister calls for testimonials and all the folks look at our pew, I feel ready to sink through the floor for shame," sighed Mollie. "If father would get up just once!"

Miriam Bell entered the kitchen. She was ready for the meeting, to which Major Spencer was to take her. She was a tall, pale girl, with a serious face, and dark, thoughtful eyes, totally unlike Mollie. She had "come under conviction" during the meetings, and had stood up for prayer and testimony several times. The evangelist thought her very spiritual. She heard Mollie's concluding sentence and spoke reprovingly.

"You shouldn't criticize your father, Mollie. It isn't for you to judge him."

Eben had hastily slipped out. He was afraid Miriam would begin talking religion to him if he stayed. He had with difficulty escaped from an exhortation by Robert in the cow-stable. There was no peace in Avonlea for the unregenerate, he reflected. Robert and Miriam had both "come out," and Mollie was hovering on the brink.

"Dad and I are the black sheep of the family," he said, with a laugh, for which he at once felt guilty. Eben had been brought up with a strict reverence for all religious matters. On the surface he might sometimes laugh at them, but the deeps troubled him whenever he did so.

Indoors, Miriam touched her younger sister's shoulder and looked at her affectionately.

"Won't you decide to-night, Mollie?" she asked, in a voice tremulous with emotion.

Mollie crimsoned and turned her face away uncomfortably. She did not know what answer to make, and was glad that a jingle of bells outside saved her the necessity of replying.

"There's your beau, Miriam," she said, as she darted into the sitting room.

Soon after, Eben brought the family pung and his chubby red mare to the door for Mollie. He had not as yet attained to the dignity of a cutter of his own. That was for his elder brother, Robert, who presently came out in his new fur coat and drove dashingly away with bells and glitter.

"Thinks he's the people," remarked Eben, with a fraternal grin.

The rich winter twilight was purpling over the white world as they drove down the lane under the over-arching wild cherry trees that glittered with gemmy hoar-frost. The snow creaked and crisped under the runners. A shrill wind was keening in the leafless dogwoods. Over the trees the sky was a dome of silver, with a lucent star or two on the slope of the west. Earth-stars gleamed warmly out here and there, where homesteads were tucked snugly away in their orchards or groves of birch.

"The church will be jammed to-night," said Eben. "It's so fine that folks will come from near and far. Guess it'll be exciting."

"If only father would testify!" sighed Mollie, from the bottom of the pung, where she was snuggled amid furs and straw. "Miriam can say what she likes, but I do feel as if we were all disgraced. It sends a creep all over me to hear Mr. Bentley say, 'Now, isn't there one more to say a word for Jesus?' and look right over at father."

Eben flicked his mare with his whip, and she broke into a trot. The silence was filled with a faint, fairy-like melody from afar down the road where a pungful of young folks from White Sands were singing hymns on their way to meeting.

"Look here, Mollie," said Eben awkwardly at last, "are you going to stand up for prayers to-night?"

"I—I can't as long as father acts this way," answered Mollie, in a choked voice. "I—I want to, Eb, and Mirry and Bob want me to, but I can't. I do hope that the evangelist won't come and talk to me special to-night. I always feels as if I was being pulled two different ways, when he does."

Back in the kitchen at home Mrs. Bell was waiting for her husband to bring the horse to the door. She was a slight, dark-eyed little woman, with thin, vivid-red cheeks. From out of the swathings in which she had wrapped her bonnet, her face gleamed sad and troubled. Now and then she sighed heavily.

The cat came to her from under the stove, languidly stretching himself, and yawning until all the red cavern of his mouth and throat was revealed. At the moment he had an uncanny resemblance to Elder Joseph Blewett of White Sands—Roaring Joe, the irreverent boys called him—when he grew excited and shouted. Mrs. Bell saw it—and then reproached herself for the sacrilege.

"But it's no wonder I've wicked thoughts," she said, wearily. "I'm that worried I ain't rightly myself. If he would only tell me what the trouble is, maybe I could help him. At any rate, I'd KNOW. It hurts me so to see him going about, day after day, with his head hanging and that look on his face, as if he had something fearful on his conscience—him that never harmed a living soul. And then the way he groans and mutters in his sleep! He has always lived a just, upright life. He hasn't no right to go on like this, disgracing his family."

Mrs. Bell's angry sob was cut short by the sleigh at the door. Her husband poked in his busy, iron-gray head and said, "Now, mother." He helped her into the sleigh, tucked the rugs warmly around her, and put a hot brick at her feet. His solicitude hurt her. It was all for her material comfort. It did not matter to him what mental agony she might suffer over his strange attitude. For the first time in their married life Mary Bell felt resentment against her husband.

They drove along in silence, past the snow-powdered hedges of spruce, and under the arches of the forest roadways. They were late, and a great stillness was over all the land. David Bell never spoke. All his usual cheerful talkativeness had disappeared since the revival meetings had begun in Avonlea. From the first he had gone about as a man over whom some strange doom is impending, seemingly oblivious to all that might be said or thought of him in his own family or in the church. Mary Bell thought she would go out of her mind if her husband continued to act in this way. Her reflections were bitter and rebellious as they sped along through the glittering night of the winter's prime.

"I don't get one bit of good out of the meetings," she thought resentfully. "There ain't any peace or joy for me, not even in testifying myself, when David sits there like a stick or stone. If he'd been opposed to the revivalist coming here, like old Uncle Jerry, or if he didn't believe in public testimony, I wouldn't mind. I'd understand. But, as it is, I feel dreadful humiliated."

Revival meetings had never been held in Avonlea before. "Uncle" Jerry MacPherson, who was the supreme local authority in church matters, taking precedence of even the minister, had been uncompromisingly opposed to them. He was a stern, deeply religious Scotchman, with a horror of the emotional form of religion. As long as Uncle Jerry's spare, ascetic form and deeply-graved square-jawed face filled his accustomed corner by the northwest window of Avonlea church no revivalist might venture therein, although the majority of the congregation, including the minister, would have welcomed one warmly.

But now Uncle Jerry was sleeping peacefully under the tangled grasses and white snows of the burying ground, and, if dead people ever do turn in their graves, Uncle Jerry might well have turned in his when the revivalist came to Avonlea church, and there followed the emotional services, public testimonies, and religious excitement which the old man's sturdy soul had always abhorred.

Avonlea was a good field for an evangelist. The Rev. Geoffrey Mountain, who came to assist the Avonlea minister in revivifying the dry bones thereof, knew this and reveled in the knowledge. It was not often that such a virgin parish could be found nowadays, with scores of impressionable, unspoiled souls on which fervid oratory could play skillfully, as a master on a mighty organ, until every note in them thrilled to life and utterance. The Rev. Geoffrey Mountain was a good man; of the earth, earthy, to be sure, but with an unquestionable sincerity of belief and purpose which went far to counterbalance the sensationalism of some of his methods.

He was large and handsome, with a marvelously sweet and winning voice—a voice that could melt into irresistible tenderness, or swell into sonorous appeal and condemnation, or ring like a trumpet calling to battle.

His frequent grammatical errors, and lapses into vulgarity, counted for nothing against its charm, and the most commonplace words in the world would have borrowed much of the power of real oratory from its magic. He knew its value and used it effectively—perhaps even ostentatiously.

Geoffrey Mountain's religion and methods, like the man himself, were showy, but, of their kind, sincere, and, though the good he accomplished might not be unmixed, it was a quantity to be reckoned with.

So the Rev. Geoffrey Mountain came to Avonlea, conquering and to conquer. Night after night the church was crowded with eager listeners, who hung breathlessly on his words and wept and thrilled and exulted as he willed. Into many young souls his appeals and warnings burned their way, and each night they rose for prayer in response to his invitation. Older Christians, too, took on a new lease of intensity, and even the unregenerate and the scoffers found a certain fascination in the meetings. Threading through it all, for old and young, converted and unconverted, was an unacknowledged feeling for religious dissipation. Avonlea was a quiet place,—and the revival meetings were lively.

When David and Mary Bell reached the church the services had begun, and they heard the refrain of a hallelujah hymn as they were crossing Harmon Andrews' field. David Bell left his wife at the platform and drove to the horse-shed.

Mrs. Bell unwound the scarf from her bonnet and shook the frost crystals from it. In the porch Flora Jane Fletcher and her sister, Mrs. Harmon Andrews, were talking in low whispers. Presently Flora Jane put out her lank, cashmere-gloved hand and plucked Mrs. Bell's shawl.

"Mary, is the elder going to testify to-night?" she asked, in a shrill whisper.

Mrs. Bell winced. She would have given much to be able to answer "Yes," but she had to say stiffly,

"I don't know."

Flora Jane lifted her chin.

"Well, Mrs. Bell, I only asked because every one thinks it is strange he doesn't—and an elder, of all people. It looks as if he didn't think himself a Christian, you know. Of course, we all know better, but it LOOKS that way. If I was you, I'd tell him folks was talking about it. Mr. Bentley says it is hindering the full success of the meetings."

Mrs. Bell turned on her tormentor in swift anger. She might resent her husband's strange behavior herself, but nobody else should dare to criticize him to her.

"I don't think you need to worry yourself about the elder, Flora Jane," she said bitingly. "Maybe 'tisn't the best Christians that do the most talking about it always. I guess, as far as living up to his profession goes, the elder will compare pretty favorably with Levi Boulter, who gets up and testifies every night, and cheats the very eye-teeth out of people in the daytime."

Levi Boulter was a middle-aged widower, with a large family, who was supposed to have cast a matrimonial eye Flora Janeward. The use of his name was an effective thrust on Mrs. Bell's part, and silenced Flora Jane. Too angry for speech she seized her sister's arm and hurried her into church.

But her victory could not remove from Mary Bell's soul the sting implanted there by Flora Jane's words. When her husband came up to the platform she put her hand on his snowy arm appealingly.

"Oh, David, won't you get up to-night? I do feel so dreadful bad—folks are talking so—I just feel humiliated."

David Bell hung his head like a shamed schoolboy.

"I can't, Mary," he said huskily. "'Tain't no use to pester me."

"You don't care for my feelings," said his wife bitterly. "And Mollie won't come out because you're acting so. You're keeping her back from salvation. And you're hindering the success of the revival—Mr. Bentley says so."

David Bell groaned. This sign of suffering wrung his wife's heart. With quick contrition she whispered,

"There, never mind, David. I oughtn't to have spoken to you so. You know your duty best. Let's go in."

"Wait." His voice was imploring.

"Mary, is it true that Mollie won't come out because of me? Am I standing in my child's light?"

"I—don't—know. I guess not. Mollie's just a foolish young girl yet. Never mind—come in."

He followed her dejectedly in, and up the aisle to their pew in the center of the church. The building was warm and crowded. The pastor was reading the Bible lesson for the evening. In the choir, behind him, David Bell saw Mollie's girlish face, tinged with a troubled seriousness. His own wind-ruddy face and bushy gray eyebrows worked convulsively with his inward throes. A sigh that was almost a groan burst from him.

"I'll have to do it," he said to himself in agony.

When several more hymns had been sung, and late arrivals began to pack the aisles, the evangelist arose. His style for the evening was the tender, the pleading, the solemn. He modulated his tones to marvelous sweetness, and sent them thrillingly over the breathless pews, entangling the hearts and souls of his listeners in a mesh of subtle emotion. Many of the women began to cry softly. Fervent amens broke from some of the members. When the evangelist sat down, after a closing appeal which, in its way, was a masterpiece, an audible sigh of relieved tension passed like a wave over the audience.

After prayer the pastor made the usual request that, if any of those present wished to come out on the side of Christ, they would signify the wish by rising for a moment in their places. After a brief interval, a pale boy under the gallery rose, followed by an old man at the top of the church. A frightened, sweet-faced child of twelve got tremblingly upon her feet, and a dramatic thrill passed over the congregation when her mother suddenly stood up beside her. The evangelist's "Thank God" was hearty and insistent.

David Bell looked almost imploringly at Mollie; but she kept her seat, with downcast eyes. Over in the big square "stone pew" he saw Eben bending forward, with his elbows on his knees, gazing frowningly at the floor.

"I'm a stumbling block to them both," he thought bitterly.

A hymn was sung and prayer offered for those under conviction. Then testimonies were called for. The evangelist asked for them in tones which made it seem a personal request to every one in that building.

Many testimonies followed, each infused with the personality of the giver. Most of them were brief and stereotyped. Finally a pause ensued. The evangelist swept the pews with his kindling eyes and exclaimed, appealingly,

"Has EVERY Christian in this church to-night spoken a word for his Master?"

There were many who had not testified, but every eye in the building followed the pastor's accusing glance to the Bell pew. Mollie crimsoned with shame. Mrs. Bell cowered visibly.

Although everybody looked thus at David Bell, nobody now expected him to testify. When he rose to his feet, a murmur of surprise passed over the audience, followed by a silence so complete as to be terrible. To David Bell it seemed to possess the awe of final judgment.

Twice he opened his lips, and tried vainly to speak. The third time he succeeded; but his voice sounded strangely in his own ears. He gripped the back of the pew before him with his knotty hands, and fixed his eyes unseeingly on the Christian Endeavor pledge that hung over the heads of the choir.

"Brethren and sisters," he said hoarsely, "before I can say a word of Christian testimony here to-night I've got something to confess. It's been lying hard and heavy on my conscience ever since these meetings begun. As long as I kept silence about it I couldn't get up and bear witness for Christ. Many of you have expected me to do it. Maybe I've been a stumbling block to some of you. This season of revival has brought no blessing to me because of my sin, which I repented of, but tried to conceal. There has been a spiritual darkness over me.

"Friends and neighbors, I have always been held by you as an honest man. It was the shame of having you know I was not which has kept me back from open confession and testimony. Just afore these meetings commenced I come home from town one night and found that somebody had passed a counterfeit ten-dollar bill on me. Then Satan entered into me and possessed me. When Mrs. Rachel Lynde come next day, collecting for foreign missions, I give her that ten dollar bill. She never knowed the difference, and sent it away with the rest. But I knew I'd done a mean and sinful thing. I couldn't drive it out of my thoughts. A few days afterwards I went down to Mrs. Rachel's and give her ten good dollars for the fund. I told her I had come to the conclusion I ought to give more than ten dollars, out of my abundance, to the Lord. That was a lie. Mrs. Lynde thought I was a generous man, and I felt ashamed to look her in the face. But I'd done what I could to right the wrong, and I thought it would be all right. But it wasn't. I've never known a minute's peace of mind or conscience since. I tried to cheat the Lord, and then tried to patch it up by doing something that redounded to my worldly credit. When these meetings begun, and everybody expected me to testify, I couldn't do it. It would have seemed like blasphemy. And I couldn't endure the thought of telling what I'd done, either. I argued it all out a thousand times that I hadn't done any real harm after all, but it was no use. I've been so wrapped up in my own brooding and misery that I didn't realize I was inflicting suffering on those dear to me by my conduct, and, maybe, holding some of them back from the paths of salvation. But my eyes have been opened to this to-night, and the Lord has given me strength to confess my sin and glorify His holy name."

The broken tones ceased, and David Bell sat down, wiping the great drops of perspiration from his brow. To a man of his training, and cast of thought, no ordeal could be more terrible than that through which he had just passed. But underneath the turmoil of his emotion he felt a great calm and peace, threaded with the exultation of a hard-won spiritual victory.

Over the church was a solemn hush. The evangelist's "amen" was not spoken with his usual unctuous fervor, but very gently and reverently. In spite of his coarse fiber, he could appreciate the nobility behind such a confession as this, and the deeps of stern suffering it sounded.

Before the last prayer the pastor paused and looked around.

"Is there yet one," he asked gently, "who wishes to be especially remembered in our concluding prayer?"

For a moment nobody moved. Then Mollie Bell stood up in the choir seat, and, down by the stove, Eben, his flushed, boyish face held high, rose sturdily to his feet in the midst of his companions.

"Thank God," whispered Mary Bell.

"Amen," said her husband huskily.

"Let us pray," said Mr. Bentley.

ONLY A COMMON FELLOW

On my dearie's wedding morning I wakened early and went to her room. Long and long ago she had made me promise that I would be the one to wake her on the morning of her wedding day.

"You were the first to take me in your arms when I came into the world, Aunt Rachel," she had said, "and I want you to be the first to greet me on that wonderful day."

But that was long ago, and now my heart foreboded that there would be no need of wakening her. And there was not. She was lying there awake, very quiet, with her hand under her cheek, and her big blue eyes fixed on the window, through which a pale, dull light was creeping in—a joyless light it was, and enough to make a body shiver. I felt more like weeping than rejoicing, and my heart took to aching when I saw her there so white and patient, more like a girl who was waiting for a winding-sheet than for a bridal veil. But she smiled brave-like, when I sat down on her bed and took her hand.

"You look as if you haven't slept all night, dearie," I said.

"I didn't—not a great deal," she answered me. "But the night didn't seem long; no, it seemed too short. I was thinking of a great many things. What time is it, Aunt Rachel?"

"Five o'clock."

"Then in six hours more—"

She suddenly sat up in her bed, her great, thick rope of brown hair falling over her white shoulders, and flung her arms about me, and burst into tears on my old breast. I petted and soothed her, and said not a word; and, after a while, she stopped crying; but she still sat with her head so that I couldn't see her face.

"We didn't think it would be like this once, did we, Aunt Rachel?" she said, very softly.

"It shouldn't be like this, now," I said. I had to say it. I never could hide the thought of that marriage, and I couldn't pretend to. It was all her stepmother's doings—right well I knew that. My dearie would never have taken Mark Foster else.

"Don't let us talk of that," she said, soft and beseeching, just the same way she used to speak when she was a baby-child and wanted to coax me into something. "Let us talk about the old days—and HIM."

"I don't see much use in talking of HIM, when you're going to marry Mark Foster to-day," I said.

But she put her hand on my mouth.

"It's for the last time, Aunt Rachel. After to-day I can never talk of him, or even think of him. It's four years since he went away. Do you remember how he looked, Aunt Rachel?"

"I mind well enough, I reckon," I said, kind of curt-like. And I did. Owen Blair hadn't a face a body could forget—that long face of his with its clean color and its eyes made to look love into a woman's. When I thought of Mark Foster's sallow skin and lank jaws I felt sick-like. Not that Mark was ugly—he was just a common-looking fellow.

"He was so handsome, wasn't he, Aunt Rachel?" my dearie went on, in that patient voice of hers. "So tall and strong and handsome. I wish we hadn't parted in anger. It was so foolish of us to quarrel. But it would have been all right if he had lived to come back. I know it would have been all right. I know he didn't carry any bitterness against me to his death. I thought once, Aunt Rachel, that I would go through life true to him, and then, over on the other side, I'd meet him just as before, all his and his only. But it isn't to be."

"Thanks to your stepma's wheedling and Mark Foster's scheming," said I.

"No, Mark didn't scheme," she said patiently. "Don't be unjust to Mark, Aunt Rachel. He has been very good and kind."

"He's as stupid as an owlet and as stubborn as Solomon's mule," I said, for I WOULD say it. "He's just a common fellow, and yet he thinks he's good enough for my beauty."

"Don't talk about Mark," she pleaded again. "I mean to be a good, faithful wife to him. But I'm my own woman yet—YET—for just a few more sweet hours, and I want to give them to HIM. The last hours of my maidenhood—they must belong to HIM."

So she talked of him, me sitting there and holding her, with her lovely hair hanging down over my arm, and my heart aching so for her that it hurt bitter. She didn't feel as bad as I did, because she'd made up her mind what to do and was resigned. She was going to marry Mark Foster, but her heart was in France, in that grave nobody knew of, where the Huns had buried Owen Blair—if they had buried him at all. And she went over all they had been to each other, since they were mites of babies, going to school together and meaning, even then, to be married when they grew up; and the first words of love he'd said to her, and what she'd dreamed and hoped for. The only thing she didn't bring up was the time he thrashed Mark Foster for bringing her apples. She never mentioned Mark's name; it was all Owen—Owen—and how he looked, and what might have been, if he hadn't gone off to the awful war and got shot. And there was me, holding her and listening to it all, and her stepma sleeping sound and triumphant in the next room.

When she had talked it all out she lay down on her pillow again. I got up and went downstairs to light the fire. I felt terrible old and tired. My feet seemed to drag, and the tears kept coming to my eyes, though I tried to keep them away, for well I knew it was a bad omen to be weeping on a wedding day.

Before long Isabella Clark came down; bright and pleased-looking enough, SHE was. I'd never liked Isabella, from the day Phillippa's father brought her here; and I liked her less than ever this morning. She was one of your sly, deep women, always smiling smooth, and scheming underneath it. I'll say it for her, though, she had been good to Phillippa; but it was her doings that my dearie was to marry Mark Foster that day.

"Up betimes, Rachel," she said, smiling and speaking me fair, as she always did, and hating me in her heart, as I well knew. "That is right, for we'll have plenty to do to-day. A wedding makes lots of work."

"Not this sort of a wedding," I said, sour-like. "I don't call it a wedding when two people get married and sneak off as if they were ashamed of it—as well they might be in this case."

"It was Phillippa's own wish that all should be very quiet," said Isabella, as smooth as cream. "You know I'd have given her a big wedding, if she'd wanted it."

"Oh, it's better quiet," I said. "The fewer to see Phillippa marry a man like Mark Foster the better."

"Mark Foster is a good man, Rachel."

"No good man would be content to buy a girl as he's bought Phillippa," I said, determined to give it in to her. "He's a common fellow, not fit for my dearie to wipe her feet on. It's well that her mother didn't live to see this day; but this day would never have come, if she'd lived."

"I dare say Phillippa's mother would have remembered that Mark Foster is very well off, quite as readily as worse people," said Isabella, a little spitefully.

I liked her better when she was spiteful than when she was smooth. I didn't feel so scared of her then.

The marriage was to be at eleven o'clock, and, at nine, I went up to help Phillippa dress. She was no fussy bride, caring much what she looked like. If Owen had been the bridegroom it would have been different. Nothing would have pleased her then; but now it was only just "That will do very well, Aunt Rachel," without even glancing at it.

Still, nothing could prevent her from looking lovely when she was dressed. My dearie would have been a beauty in a beggarmaid's rags. In her white dress and veil she was as fair as a queen. And she was as good as she was pretty. It was the right sort of goodness, too, with just enough spice of original sin in it to keep it from spoiling by reason of over-sweetness.

Then she sent me out.

"I want to be alone my last hour," she said. "Kiss me, Aunt Rachel—MOTHER Rachel."

When I'd gone down, crying like the old fool I was, I heard a rap at the door. My first thought was to go out and send Isabella to it, for I supposed it was Mark Foster, come ahead of time, and small stomach I had for seeing him. I fall trembling, even yet, when I think, "What if I had sent Isabella to that door?"

But go I did, and opened it, defiant-like, kind of hoping it was Mark Foster to see the tears on my face. I opened it—and staggered back like I'd got a blow.

"Owen! Lord ha' mercy on us! Owen!" I said, just like that, going cold all over, for it's the truth that I thought it was his spirit come back to forbid that unholy marriage.

But he sprang right in, and caught my wrinkled old hands in a grasp that was of flesh and blood.

"Aunt Rachel, I'm not too late?" he said, savage-like. "Tell me I'm in time."

I looked up at him, standing over me there, tall and handsome, no change in him except he was so brown and had a little white scar on his forehead; and, though I couldn't understand at all, being all bewildered-like, I felt a great deep thankfulness.

"No, you're not too late," I said.

"Thank God," said he, under his breath. And then he pulled me into the parlor and shut the door.

"They told me at the station that Phillippa was to be married to Mark Foster to-day. I couldn't believe it, but I came here as fast as horse-flesh could bring me. Aunt Rachel, it can't be true! She can't care for Mark Foster, even if she had forgotten me!"

"It's true enough that she is to marry Mark," I said, half-laughing, half-crying, "but she doesn't care for him. Every beat of her heart is for you. It's all her stepma's doings. Mark has got a mortgage on the place, and he told Isabella Clark that, if Phillippa would marry him, he'd burn the mortgage, and, if she wouldn't, he'd foreclose. Phillippa is sacrificing herself to save her stepma for her dead father's sake. It's all your fault," I cried, getting over my bewilderment. "We thought you were dead. Why didn't you come home when you were alive? Why didn't you write?"

"I DID write, after I got out of the hospital, several times," he said, "and never a word in answer, Aunt Rachel. What was I to think when Phillippa wouldn't answer my letters?"

"She never got one," I cried. "She wept her sweet eyes out over you. SOMEBODY must have got those letters."

And I knew then, and I know now, though never a shadow of proof have I, that Isabella Clark had got them—and kept them. That woman would stick at nothing.

"Well, we'll sift that matter some other time," said Owen impatiently. "There are other things to think of now. I must see Phillippa."

"I'll manage it for you," I said eagerly; but, just as I spoke, the door opened and Isabella and Mark came in. Never shall I forget the look on Isabella's face. I almost felt sorry for her. She turned sickly yellow and her eyes went wild; they were looking at the downfall of all her schemes and hopes. I didn't look at Mark Foster, at first, and, when I did, there wasn't anything to see. His face was just as sallow and wooden as ever; he looked undersized and common beside Owen. Nobody'd ever have picked him out for a bridegroom.

Owen spoke first.

"I want to see Phillippa," he said, as if it were but yesterday that he had gone away.

All Isabella's smoothness and policy had dropped away from her, and the real woman stood there, plotting and unscrupulous, as I'd always know her.

"You can't see her," she said desperate-like. "She doesn't want to see you. You went and left her and never wrote, and she knew you weren't worth fretting over, and she has learned to care for a better man."

"I DID write and I think you know that better than most folks," said Owen, trying hard to speak quiet. "As for the rest, I'm not going to discuss it with you. When I hear from Phillippa's own lips that she cares for another man I'll believe it—and not before."

"You'll never hear it from her lips," said I.

Isabella gave me a venomous look.

"You'll not see Phillippa until she is a better man's wife," she said stubbornly, "and I order you to leave my house, Owen Blair!"

"No!"

It was Mark Foster who spoke. He hadn't said a word; but he came forward now, and stood before Owen. Such a difference as there was between them! But he looked Owen right in the face, quiet-like, and Owen glared back in fury.

"Will it satisfy you, Owen, if Phillippa comes down here and chooses between us?"

"Yes, it will," said Owen.

Mark Foster turned to me.

"Go and bring her down," said he.

Isabella, judging Phillippa by herself, gave a little moan of despair, and Owen, blinded by love and hope, thought his cause was won. But I knew my dearie too well to be glad, and Mark Foster did, too, and I hated him for it.

I went up to my dearie's room, all pale and shaking. When I went in she came to meet me, like a girl going to meet death.

"Is—it—time?" she said, with her hands locked tight together.

I said not a word, hoping that the unlooked-for sight of Owen would break down her resolution. I just held out my hand to her, and led her downstairs. She clung to me and her hands were as cold as snow. When I opened the parlor door I stood back, and pushed her in before me.

She just cried, "Owen!" and shook so that I put my arms about her to steady her.

Owen made a step towards her, his face and eyes all aflame with his love and longing, but Mark barred his way.

"Wait till she has made her choice," he said, and then he turned to Phillippa. I couldn't see my dearie's face, but I could see Mark's, and there wasn't a spark of feeling in it. Behind it was Isabella's, all pinched and gray.

"Phillippa," said Mark, "Owen Blair has come back. He says he has never forgotten you, and that he wrote to you several times. I have told him that you have promised me, but I leave you freedom of choice. Which of us will you marry, Phillippa?"

My dearie stood straight up and the trembling left her. She stepped back, and I could see her face, white as the dead, but calm and resolved.

"I have promised to marry you, Mark, and I will keep my word," she said.

The color came back to Isabella Clark's face; but Mark's did not change.

"Phillippa," said Owen, and the pain in his voice made my old heart ache bitterer than ever, "have you ceased to love me?"

My dearie would have been more than human, if she could have resisted the pleading in his tone. She said no word, but just looked at him for a moment. We all saw the look; her whole soul, full of love for Owen, showed out in it. Then she turned and stood by Mark.

Owen never said a word. He went as white as death, and started for the door. But again Mark Foster put himself in the way.

"Wait," he said. "She has made her choice, as I knew she would; but I have yet to make mine. And I choose to marry no woman whose love belongs to another living man. Phillippa, I thought Owen Blair was dead, and I believed that, when you were my wife, I could win your love. But I love you too well to make you miserable. Go to the man you love—you are free!"

"And what is to become of me?" wailed Isabella.

"Oh, you!—I had forgotten about you," said Mark, kind of weary-like. He took a paper from his pocket, and dropped it in the grate. "There is the mortgage. That is all you care about, I think. Good-morning."

He went out. He was only a common fellow, but, somehow, just then he looked every inch the gentleman. I would have gone after him and said something but—the look on his face—no, it was no time for my foolish old words!

Phillippa was crying, with her head on Owen's shoulder. Isabella Clark waited to see the mortgage burned up, and then she came to me in the hall, all smooth and smiling again.

"Really, it's all very romantic, isn't it? I suppose it's better as it is, all things considered. Mark behaved splendidly, didn't he? Not many men would have done as he did."

For once in my life I agreed with Isabella. But I felt like having a good cry over it all—and I had it. I was glad for my dearie's sake and Owen's; but Mark Foster had paid the price of their joy, and I knew it had beggared him of happiness for life.

TANNIS OF THE FLATS

Few people in Avonlea could understand why Elinor Blair had never married. She had been one of the most beautiful girls in our part of the Island and, as a woman of fifty, she was still very attractive. In her youth she had had ever so many beaux, as we of our generation well remembered; but, after her return from visiting her brother Tom in the Canadian Northwest, more than twenty-five years ago, she had seemed to withdraw within herself, keeping all men at a safe, though friendly, distance. She had been a gay, laughing girl when she went West; she came back quiet and serious, with a shadowed look in her eyes which time could not quite succeed in blotting out.

Elinor had never talked much about her visit, except to describe the scenery and the life, which in that day was rough indeed. Not even to me, who had grown up next door to her and who had always seemed more a sister than a friend, did she speak of other than the merest commonplaces. But when Tom Blair made a flying trip back home, some ten years later, there were one or two of us to whom he related the story of Jerome Carey,—a story revealing only too well the reason for Elinor's sad eyes and utter indifference to masculine attentions. I can recall almost his exact words and the inflections of his voice, and I remember, too, that it seemed to me a far cry from the tranquil, pleasant scene before us, on that lovely summer day, to the elemental life of the Flats.

The Flats was a forlorn little trading station fifteen miles up the river from Prince Albert, with a scanty population of half-breeds and three white men. When Jerome Carey was sent to take charge of the telegraph office there, he cursed his fate in the picturesque language permissible in the far Northwest.

Not that Carey was a profane man, even as men go in the West. He was an English gentleman, and he kept both his life and his vocabulary pretty clean. But—the Flats!

Outside of the ragged cluster of log shacks, which comprised the settlement, there was always a shifting fringe of teepees where the Indians, who drifted down from the Reservation, camped with their dogs and squaws and papooses. There are standpoints from which Indians are interesting, but they cannot be said to offer congenial social attractions. For three weeks after Carey went to the Flats he was lonelier than he had ever imagined it possible to be, even in the Great Lone Land. If it had not been for teaching Paul Dumont the telegraphic code, Carey believed he would have been driven to suicide in self-defense.

The telegraphic importance of the Flats consisted in the fact that it was the starting point of three telegraph lines to remote trading posts up North. Not many messages came therefrom, but the few that did come generally amounted to something worth while. Days and even weeks would pass without a single one being clicked to the Flats. Carey was debarred from talking over the wires to the Prince Albert man for the reason that they were on officially bad terms. He blamed the latter for his transfer to the Flats.

Carey slept in a loft over the office, and got his meals at Joe Esquint's, across the "street." Joe Esquint's wife was a good cook, as cooks go among the breeds, and Carey soon became a great pet of hers. Carey had a habit of becoming a pet with women. He had the "way" that has to be born in a man and can never be acquired. Besides, he was as handsome as clean-cut features, deep-set, dark-blue eyes, fair curls and six feet of muscle could make him. Mrs. Joe Esquint thought that his mustache was the most wonderfully beautiful thing, in its line, that she had ever seen.

Fortunately, Mrs. Joe was so old and fat and ugly that even the malicious and inveterate gossip of skulking breeds and Indians, squatting over teepee fires, could not hint at anything questionable in the relations between her and Carey. But it was a different matter with Tannis Dumont.

Tannis came home from the academy at Prince Albert early in July, when Carey had been at the Flats a month and had exhausted all the few novelties of his position. Paul Dumont had already become so expert at the code that his mistakes no longer afforded Carey any fun, and the latter was getting desperate. He had serious intentions of throwing up the business altogether, and betaking himself to an Alberta ranch, where at least one would have the excitement of roping horses. When he saw Tannis Dumont he thought he would hang on awhile longer, anyway.

Tannis was the daughter of old Auguste Dumont, who kept the one small store at the Flats, lived in the one frame house that the place boasted, and was reputed to be worth an amount of money which, in half-breed eyes, was a colossal fortune. Old Auguste was black and ugly and notoriously bad-tempered. But Tannis was a beauty.

Tannis' great-grandmother had been a Cree squaw who married a French trapper. The son of this union became in due time the father of Auguste Dumont. Auguste married a woman whose mother was a French half-breed and whose father was a pure-bred Highland Scotchman. The result of this atrocious mixture was its justification—Tannis of the Flats—who looked as if all the blood of all the Howards might be running in her veins.

But, after all, the dominant current in those same veins was from the race of plain and prairie. The practiced eye detected it in the slender stateliness of carriage, in the graceful, yet voluptuous, curves of the lithe body, in the smallness and delicacy of hand and foot, in the purple sheen on straight-falling masses of blue-black hair, and, more than all else, in the long, dark eye, full and soft, yet alight with a slumbering fire. France, too, was responsible for somewhat in Tannis. It gave her a light step in place of the stealthy half-breed shuffle, it arched her red upper lip into a more tremulous bow, it lent a note of laughter to her voice and a sprightlier wit to her tongue. As for her red-headed Scotch grandfather, he had bequeathed her a somewhat whiter skin and ruddier bloom than is usually found in the breeds.

Old Auguste was mightily proud of Tannis. He sent her to school for four years in Prince Albert, bound that his girl should have the best. A High School course and considerable mingling in the social life of the town—for old Auguste was a man to be conciliated by astute politicians, since he controlled some two or three hundred half-breed votes—sent Tannis home to the Flats with a very thin, but very deceptive, veneer of culture and civilization overlying the primitive passions and ideas of her nature.

Carey saw only the beauty and the veneer. He made the mistake of thinking that Tannis was what she seemed to be—a fairly well-educated, up-to-date young woman with whom a friendly flirtation was just what it was with white womankind—the pleasant amusement of an hour or season. It was a mistake—a very big mistake. Tannis understood something of piano playing, something less of grammar and Latin, and something less still of social prevarications. But she understood absolutely nothing of flirtation. You can never get an Indian to see the sense of Platonics.

Carey found the Flats quite tolerable after the homecoming of Tannis. He soon fell into the habit of dropping into the Dumont house to spend the evening, talking with Tannis in the parlor—which apartment was amazingly well done for a place like the Flats—Tannis had not studied Prince Albert parlors four years for nothing—or playing violin and piano duets with her. When music and conversation palled, they went for long gallops over the prairies together. Tannis rode to perfection, and managed her bad-tempered brute of a pony with a skill and grace that made Carey applaud her. She was glorious on horseback.

Sometimes he grew tired of the prairies and then he and Tannis paddled themselves over the river in Nitchie Joe's dug-out, and landed on the old trail that struck straight into the wooded belt of the Saskatchewan valley, leading north to trading posts on the frontier of civilization. There they rambled under huge pines, hoary with the age of centuries, and Carey talked to Tannis about England and quoted poetry to her. Tannis liked poetry; she had studied it at school, and understood it fairly well. But once she told Carey that she thought it a long, round-about way of saying what you could say just as well in about a dozen plain words.

Carey laughed. He liked to evoke those little speeches of hers. They sounded very clever, dropping from such arched, ripely-tinted lips.

If you had told Carey that he was playing with fire he would have laughed at you. In the first place he was not in the slightest degree in love with Tannis—he merely admired and liked her. In the second place, it never occurred to him that Tannis might be in love with him. Why, he had never attempted any love-making with her! And, above all, he was obsessed with that aforesaid fatal idea that Tannis was like the women he had associated with all his life, in reality as well as in appearance. He did not know enough of the racial characteristics to understand.

But, if Carey thought his relationship with Tannis was that of friendship merely, he was the only one at the Flats who did think so. All the half-breeds and quarter-breeds and any-fractional breeds there believed that he meant to marry Tannis. There would have been nothing surprising to them in that. They did not know that Carey's second cousin was a baronet, and they would not have understood that it need make any difference, if they had. They thought that rich old Auguste's heiress, who had been to school for four years in Prince Albert, was a catch for anybody.

Old Auguste himself shrugged his shoulders over it and was well-pleased enough. An Englishman was a prize by way of a husband for a half-breed girl, even if he were only a telegraph operator. Young Paul Dumont worshipped Carey, and the half-Scotch mother, who might have understood, was dead. In all the Flats there were but two people who disapproved of the match they thought an assured thing. One of these was the little priest, Father Gabriel. He liked Tannis, and he liked Carey; but he shook his head dubiously when he heard the gossip of the shacks and teepees. Religions might mingle, but the different bloods—ah, it was not the right thing! Tannis was a good girl, and a beautiful one; but she was no fit mate for the fair, thorough-bred Englishman. Father Gabriel wished fervently that Jerome Carey might soon be transferred elsewhere. He even went to Prince Albert and did a little wire-pulling on his own account, but nothing came of it. He was on the wrong side of politics.

The other malcontent was Lazarre Mérimée, a lazy, besotted French half-breed, who was, after his fashion, in love with Tannis. He could never have got her, and he knew it—old Auguste and young Paul would have incontinently riddled him with bullets had he ventured near the house as a suitor,—but he hated Carey none the less, and watched for a chance to do him an ill-turn. There is no worse enemy in all the world than a half-breed. Your true Indian is bad enough, but his diluted descendant is ten times worse.

As for Tannis, she loved Carey with all her heart, and that was all there was about it.

If Elinor Blair had never gone to Prince Albert there is no knowing what might have happened, after all. Carey, so powerful in propinquity, might even have ended by learning to love Tannis and marrying her, to his own worldly undoing. But Elinor did go to Prince Albert, and her going ended all things for Tannis of the Flats.

Carey met her one evening in September, when he had ridden into town to attend a dance, leaving Paul Dumont in charge of the telegraph office. Elinor had just arrived in Prince Albert on a visit to Tom, to which she had been looking forward during the five years since he had married and moved out West from Avonlea. As I have already said, she was very beautiful at that time, and Carey fell in love with her at the first moment of their meeting.

During the next three weeks he went to town nine times and called at the Dumonts' only once. There were no more rides and walks with Tannis. This was not intentional neglect on his part. He had simply forgotten all about her. The breeds surmised a lover's quarrel, but Tannis understood. There was another woman back there in town.

It would be quite impossible to put on paper any adequate idea of her emotions at this stage. One night, she followed Carey when he went to Prince Albert, riding out of earshot, behind him on her plains pony, but keeping him in sight. Lazarre, in a fit of jealousy, had followed Tannis, spying on her until she started back to the Flats. After that he watched both Carey and Tannis incessantly, and months later had told Tom all he had learned through his low sneaking.

Tannis trailed Carey to the Blair house, on the bluffs above the town, and saw him tie his horse at the gate and enter. She, too, tied her pony to a poplar, lower down, and then crept stealthily through the willows at the side of the house until she was close to the windows. Through one of them she could see Carey and Elinor. The half-breed girl crouched down in the shadow and glared at her rival. She saw the pretty, fair-tinted face, the fluffy coronal of golden hair, the blue, laughing eyes of the woman whom Jerome Carey loved, and she realized very plainly that there was nothing left to hope for. She, Tannis of the Flats, could never compete with that other. It was well to know so much, at least.

After a time, she crept softly away, loosed her pony, and lashed him mercilessly with her whip through the streets of the town and out the long, dusty river trail. A man turned and looked after her as she tore past a brightly lighted store on Water Street.

"That was Tannis of the Flats," he said to a companion. "She was in town last winter, going to school—a beauty and a bit of the devil, like all those breed girls. What in thunder is she riding like that for?"

One day, a fortnight later, Carey went over the river alone for a ramble up the northern trail, and an undisturbed dream of Elinor. When he came back Tannis was standing at the canoe landing, under a pine tree, in a rain of finely sifted sunlight. She was waiting for him and she said, without any preface:

"Mr. Carey, why do you never come to see me, now?"

Carey flushed like any girl. Her tone and look made him feel very uncomfortable. He remembered, self-reproachfully, that he must have seemed very neglectful, and he stammered something about having been busy.

"Not very busy," said Tannis, with her terrible directness. "It is not that. It is because you are going to Prince Albert to see a white woman!"

Even in his embarrassment Carey noted that this was the first time he had ever heard Tannis use the expression, "a white woman," or any other that would indicate her sense of a difference between herself and the dominant race. He understood, at the same moment, that this girl was not to be trifled with—that she would have the truth out of him, first or last. But he felt indescribably foolish.

"I suppose so," he answered lamely.

"And what about me?" asked Tannis.

When you come to think of it, this was an embarrassing question, especially for Carey, who had believed that Tannis understood the game, and played it for its own sake, as he did.

"I don't understand you, Tannis," he said hurriedly.

"You have made me love you," said Tannis.

The words sound flat enough on paper. They did not sound flat to Tom, as repeated by Lazarre, and they sounded anything but flat to Carey, hurled at him as they were by a woman trembling with all the passions of her savage ancestry. Tannis had justified her criticism of poetry. She had said her half-dozen words, instinct with all the despair and pain and wild appeal that all the poetry in the world had ever expressed.

They made Carey feel like a scoundrel. All at once he realized how impossible it would be to explain matters to Tannis, and that he would make a still bigger fool of himself, if he tried.

"I am very sorry," he stammered, like a whipped schoolboy.

"It is no matter," interrupted Tannis violently. "What difference does it make about me—a half-breed girl? We breed girls are only born to amuse the white men. That is so—is it not? Then, when they are tired of us, they push us aside and go back to their own kind. Oh, it is very well. But I will not forget—my father and brother will not forget. They will make you sorry to some purpose!"

She turned, and stalked away to her canoe. He waited under the pines until she crossed the river; then he, too, went miserably home. What a mess he had contrived to make of things! Poor Tannis! How handsome she had looked in her fury—and how much like a squaw! The racial marks always come out plainly under the stress of emotion, as Tom noted later.

Her threat did not disturb him. If young Paul and old Auguste made things unpleasant for him, he thought himself more than a match for them. It was the thought of the suffering he had brought upon Tannis that worried him. He had not, to be sure, been a villain; but he had been a fool, and that is almost as bad, under some circumstances.

The Dumonts, however, did not trouble him. After all, Tannis' four years in Prince Albert had not been altogether wasted. She knew that white girls did not mix their male relatives up in a vendetta when a man ceased calling on them—and she had nothing else to complain of that could be put in words. After some reflection she concluded to hold her tongue. She even laughed when old Auguste asked her what was up between her and her fellow, and said she had grown tired of him. Old Auguste shrugged his shoulders resignedly. It was just as well, maybe. Those English sons-in-law sometimes gave themselves too many airs.

So Carey rode often to town and Tannis bided her time, and plotted futile schemes of revenge, and Lazarre Mérimée scowled and got drunk—and life went on at the Flats as usual, until the last week in October, when a big wind and rainstorm swept over the northland.

It was a bad night. The wires were down between the Flats and Prince Albert and all communication with the outside world was cut off. Over at Joe Esquint's the breeds were having a carouse in honor of Joe's birthday. Paul Dumont had gone over, and Carey was alone in the office, smoking lazily and dreaming of Elinor.

Suddenly, above the plash of rain and whistle of wind, he heard outcries in the street. Running to the door he was met by Mrs. Joe Esquint, who grasped him breathlessly.

"Meestair Carey—come quick! Lazarre, he kill Paul—they fight!"

Carey, with a smothered oath, rushed across the street. He had been afraid of something of the sort, and had advised Paul not to go, for those half-breed carouses almost always ended in a free fight. He burst into the kitchen at Joe Esquint's, to find a circle of mute spectators ranged around the room and Paul and Lazarre in a clinch in the center. Carey was relieved to find it was only an affair of fists. He promptly hurled himself at the combatants and dragged Paul away, while Mrs. Joe Esquint—Joe himself being dead-drunk in a corner—flung her fat arms about Lazarre and held him back.

"Stop this," said Carey sternly.

"Let me get at him," foamed Paul. "He insulted my sister. He said that you—let me get at him!"

He could not writhe free from Carey's iron grip. Lazarre, with a snarl like a wolf, sent Mrs. Joe spinning, and rushed at Paul. Carey struck out as best he could, and Lazarre went reeling back against the table. It went over with a crash and the light went out!

Mrs. Joe's shrieks might have brought the roof down. In the confusion that ensued, two pistol shots rang out sharply. There was a cry, a groan, a fall—then a rush for the door. When Mrs. Joe Esquint's sister-in-law, Marie, dashed in with another lamp, Mrs. Joe was still shrieking, Paul Dumont was leaning sickly against the wall with a dangling arm, and Carey lay face downward on the floor, with blood trickling from under him.

Marie Esquint was a woman of nerve. She told Mrs. Joe to shut up, and she turned Carey over. He was conscious, but seemed dazed and could not help himself. Marie put a coat under his head, told Paul to lie down on the bench, ordered Mrs. Joe to get a bed ready, and went for the doctor. It happened that there was a doctor at the Flats that night—a Prince Albert man who had been up at the Reservation, fixing up some sick Indians, and had been stormstaid at old Auguste's on his way back.

Marie soon returned with the doctor, old Auguste, and Tannis. Carey was carried in and laid on Mrs. Esquint's bed. The doctor made a brief examination, while Mrs. Joe sat on the floor and howled at the top of her lungs. Then he shook his head.

"Shot in the back," he said briefly.

"How long?" asked Carey, understanding.

"Perhaps till morning," answered the doctor. Mrs. Joe gave a louder howl than ever at this, and Tannis came and stood by the bed. The doctor, knowing that he could do nothing for Carey, hurried into the kitchen to attend to Paul, who had a badly shattered arm, and Marie went with him.

Carey looked stupidly at Tannis.

"Send for her," he said.

Tannis smiled cruelly.

"There is no way. The wires are down, and there is no man at the Flats who will go to town to-night," she answered.

"My God, I MUST see her before I die," burst out Carey pleadingly. "Where is Father Gabriel? HE will go."

"The priest went to town last night and has not come back," said Tannis.

Carey groaned and shut his eyes. If Father Gabriel was away, there was indeed no one to go. Old Auguste and the doctor could not leave Paul and he knew well that no breed of them all at the Flats would turn out on such a night, even if they were not, one and all, mortally scared of being mixed up in the law and justice that would be sure to follow the affair. He must die without seeing Elinor.

Tannis looked inscrutably down on the pale face on Mrs. Joe Esquint's dirty pillows. Her immobile features gave no sign of the conflict raging within her. After a short space she turned and went out, shutting the door softly on the wounded man and Mrs. Joe, whose howls had now simmered down to whines. In the next room, Paul was crying out with pain as the doctor worked on his arm, but Tannis did not go to him. Instead, she slipped out and hurried down the stormy street to old Auguste's stable. Five minutes later she was galloping down the black, wind-lashed river trail, on her way to town, to bring Elinor Blair to her lover's deathbed.

I hold that no woman ever did anything more unselfish than this deed of Tannis! For the sake of love she put under her feet the jealousy and hatred that had clamored at her heart. She held, not only revenge, but the dearer joy of watching by Carey to the last, in the hollow of her hand, and she cast both away that the man she loved might draw his dying breath somewhat easier. In a white woman the deed would have been merely commendable. In Tannis of the Flats, with her ancestry and tradition, it was lofty self-sacrifice.

It was eight o'clock when Tannis left the Flats; it was ten when she drew bridle before the house on the bluff. Elinor was regaling Tom and his wife with Avonlea gossip when the maid came to the door.

"Pleas'm, there's a breed girl out on the verandah and she's asking for Miss Blair."

Elinor went out wonderingly, followed by Tom. Tannis, whip in hand, stood by the open door, with the stormy night behind her, and the warm ruby light of the hall lamp showering over her white face and the long rope of drenched hair that fell from her bare head. She looked wild enough.

"Jerome Carey was shot in a quarrel at Joe Esquint's to-night," she said. "He is dying—he wants you—I have come for you."

Elinor gave a little cry, and steadied herself on Tom's shoulder. Tom said he knew he made some exclamation of horror. He had never approved of Carey's attentions to Elinor, but such news was enough to shock anybody. He was determined, however, that Elinor should not go out in such a night and to such a scene, and told Tannis so in no uncertain terms.

"I came through the storm," said Tannis, contemptuously. "Cannot she do as much for him as I can?"

The good, old Island blood in Elinor's veins showed to some purpose. "Yes," she answered firmly. "No, Tom, don't object—I must go. Get my horse—and your own."

Ten minutes later three riders galloped down the bluff road and took the river trail. Fortunately the wind was at their backs and the worst of the storm was over. Still, it was a wild, black ride enough. Tom rode, cursing softly under his breath. He did not like the whole thing—Carey done to death in some low half-breed shack, this handsome, sullen girl coming as his messenger, this nightmare ride, through wind and rain. It all savored too much of melodrama, even for the Northland, where people still did things in a primitive way. He heartily wished Elinor had never left Avonlea.

It was past twelve when they reached the Flats. Tannis was the only one who seemed to be able to think coherently. It was she who told Tom where to take the horses and then led Elinor to the room where Carey was dying. The doctor was sitting by the bedside and Mrs. Joe was curled up in a corner, sniffling to herself. Tannis took her by the shoulder and turned her, none too gently, out of the room. The doctor, understanding, left at once. As Tannis shut the door she saw Elinor sink on her knees by the bed, and Carey's trembling hand go out to her head.

Tannis sat down on the floor outside of the door and wrapped herself up in a shawl Marie Esquint had dropped. In that attitude she looked exactly like a squaw, and all comers and goers, even old Auguste, who was hunting for her, thought she was one, and left her undisturbed. She watched there until dawn came whitely up over the prairies and Jerome Carey died. She knew when it happened by Elinor's cry.

Tannis sprang up and rushed in. She was too late for even a parting look.

The girl took Carey's hand in hers, and turned to the weeping Elinor with a cold dignity.

"Now go," she said. "You had him in life to the very last. He is mine now."

"There must be some arrangements made," faltered Elinor.

"My father and brother will make all arrangements, as you call them," said Tannis steadily. "He had no near relatives in the world—none at all in Canada—he told me so. You may send out a Protestant minister from town, if you like; but he will be buried here at the Flats and his grave will be mine—all mine! Go!"

And Elinor, reluctant, sorrowful, yet swayed by a will and an emotion stronger than her own, went slowly out, leaving Tannis of the Flats alone with her dead.

Made in the USA
Columbia, SC
09 July 2023